D1488657

PHILOSOPHY IN PROCESS

PHILOSOPHY

By PAUL WEISS

IN PROCESS

VOL. 2: 1960-1964

Southern Illinois University Press
Carbondale and Edwardsville

Feffer & Simons, Inc.
London and Amsterdam

To Edward Poznanski

PREFACE

THE FIRST VOLUME of this work was originally published at intervals in twelve fascicles. I have been most agreeably surprised at the favorable comments these elicited both from philosophers and non-philosophers. It has been said that the medium of a journal, such as this, is peculiarly congenial to my thought, and that it has an immediacy and vitality not to be found elsewhere. Encouraged by these observations, I have for the time being given up the writing of books and the incidental writing of this journal to make the latter my major concern. In the latter part of this work one will therefore find sustained discussions carried out almost daily. As a consequence the volume is, I think, stronger and more tightly knit than the previous one. It is to be followed by a third and perhaps still others.

New Haven, Conn.   P. W.
December 9, 1964

PHILOSOPHY IN PROCESS

1960

December 26

It is not altogether false to say that science distorts common-sense facts, philosophy ignores them, and theology invents them. Nor is it altogether wrong to say that philosophy is a sane man who sounds mad, and science a madman who has persuaded all to believe he is sane.

We can dissect the common-sense world in two ways. 1] We can take out strands which are ontological slices, i.e., are forms of the modes of being in a delimited area, and are oriented toward a cosmology where they have their proper being. Common sense is a cosmological product, an intensification of the togetherness of the modes with an orientation toward individuals and Existence. 2] The other way is to accept the cosmological character of the common-sense world and redefine it. This we do in history, politics, religion, and individual action. Strands can be taken out of the refinements; here the analysis of the history, etc., is direct and simple, in contrast with the analysis of the common-sense world. Thus to get science or perception, etc., from common sense we must subject common sense to certain conditions; if we get science or perception from history, e.g., we get it from a refined form of common sense and thus do not have to add further conditions. A science which is built up as the articulation in formal terms of what is happening in history, is thus an analytic element in the history and expresses the structure of that history and thus of the cosmic interplay of the modes (though one which stresses Existence and individuals more than it does the other components). The cosmology portrayed in a science then is not a neutral cosmology, not a perfect portrayal of the togetherness of the modes. This it would be only if it were derived not from history, but from history as unified with politics, religion, and action.

A cosmological science, whether biased or neutral, is an inductive product until it has been rectified by being subjugated to the control and demands of three modes of being—Ideality for its rationality, Existence for its extension, and Actuality for its relevance. It is itself a cosmological derivative representing God, and needs no rectification from Him. (Similarly, perception needs no rectification from Actuality, events from Existence, or importance from the Ideal.)

We have then at least the following sciences: A] *crude* science which is a simple formalization of common sense, B] *empirical* science which is a strand derived from common sense, or which is an analytic component in history, politics, action, or religion, C] *cosmological neutral* science which is a rectified form of the empirical science. Cosmological neutral science is a solidification of the rectified forms of the biased cosmological science. Since the latter can be rectified in three ways, the neutral cosmological science must have three forms— one in which the rectification is accomplished by the Ideal, another by Actuality, and a third by Existence. D] Since one can combine a science rectified by the Ideal, issuing from history, say, with a science which is derived from politics and which is rectified by Actuality, there can be a number of combinations of the sciences. The result is neutral in the sense that it solidifies the abstractions derived from different disciplines, such as history and politics. It subjects the results to one rectification or another and does not rectify any one abstraction in all three possible ways.

The above is clarified, extended and improved in the following table:

1] The common-sense world yields ontologically representative strands —empirical science, daily perception, encountered events, and acknowledged importance.

2] The common-sense world also yields cosmological refinement— action, politics, history, and religion.

3] Each strand can be rectified in one of three ways:
    A. science is rectified by the Ideal and becomes mathematical
    B. science is rectified by Existence and becomes pragmatic
    C. science is rectified by Actuality and becomes localizable

D. perception is rectified by the Ideal and becomes intelligible
E. perception is rectified by Existence and becomes adumbrative
F. perception is rectified by God and becomes systematically unified

G. events are rectified by the Ideal and achieve a futurity
H. events are rectified by Actuality and become focused areas
I. events are rectified by God and become interrelated and unified

J. importance is rectified by Actuality and yields an existential component
K. importance is rectified by Existence and yields purpose
L. importance is rectified by God and yields comparability

4] Each refinement is rectified in three ways:

A. history is rectified by Actuality to acquire causes
history is rectified by Ideality to acquire rationality
history is rectified by God to acquire objectivity

B. politics is rectified by Ideality to acquire natural law
politics is rectified by Actuality to acquire justice
politics is rectified by God to acquire requirements

C. action is rectified by Ideality to acquire goodness
action is rectified by Existence to acquire beauty
action is rectified by God to acquire worthiness

D. religion is rectified by Ideality to acquire providential value
religion is rectified by Existence to acquire effectiveness
religion is rectified by Actuality to acquire power

5] Each strand can be derived from each refinement:

A. science can be derived from history
B. science can be derived from politics
C. science can be derived from religion
D. science can be derived from action

E. perception can be derived from history
F. perception can be derived from politics
G. perception can be derived from religion
H. perception can be derived from action

I. events can be derived from history
J. events can be derived from politics
K. events can be derived from religion
L. events can be derived from action

M. importance can be derived from history
N. importance can be derived from politics
O. importance can be derived from religion
P. importance can be derived from action

6] Each strand can be derived from rectified forms of refinements—
see 4 above. This means we can get 12 forms of science, 12 forms of
perception, 12 forms of events, and 12 forms of importance. There is,
for example, a science of historic causes, rational order, and objective
history; a science of natural law, justice, and political requirements; a
science of goodness, beauty, worthiness; a science of providential values,
effectiveness, and power. All of these are inductive generalized forms
of the rectifications of refinements of common sense; I call them *Codifi-*
cations.

7] Each of the 48 codifications is subject to three rectifications. Thus
the science of historic causes can be rectified by making it mathematical,
pragmatic, or localizable (see 3 above).

8] Combinations of 4A, 4B, 4C, 4D give partial cosmologies, humanly
oriented, and a complete cosmology by combining all kinds of rectifications with all refinements. A complete cosmology has history, politics,
action, religion, all rectified in three ways and then combined. This is
Philosophical Cosmology. It is to be contrasted with a *Speculative*
Cosmology which involves the basic permanent interplay of the four
modes.

9] Strands can be derived from the cosmologies in *8*. A scientific cosmology may be partial in two ways—it may not encompass the cosmological import of, say, history or some other refinement, or it may not encompass all the rectifications of a given refinement. As the first it neglects a dimension of the world, as the second it is not sufficiently basic, being too humanly oriented. We can also get a scientific strand, etc., from Philosophical Cosmology.

10] Strands in *9* can be rectified (see *3*). An Ideally formal complete cosmology is obtained by rectifying a scientific cosmology *9* by the Ideal to get a mathematical scheme. (see *7*).

Putting aside all other disciplines but science, then we have:

1] empirical science, a strand

*3*A–G] a rectified strand—mathematical, pragmatic, and localizable science

*5*A–D] a strand derived from history, politics, religion, action

6] a strand derived from rectified forms of the above, to give codifications for history, politics, action, and religion

7] rectified forms of the strand in *6*

9] a strand derived from combinations in *4*A–D

10] a rectified form of the strand in *9*

1, 5, 6, 9 give us an inductive generalization, a kind of "nominalistic" universal, whereas *3, 7,* and *10* give mathematical science, pragmatic science, and localizable science, *3* relating to a science oriented in experience, *7* to a science for the humanistic disciplines, and *10* relating to cosmology, dealt with mathematically. A genuinely neutral cosmology would look for data in politics, religion, and action, as well as in history, or in the combination of these in common sense—and this is what I think Whitehead tried to do.

January 3

When Collingwood speaks of re-enacting history, he first converts the occurrences in history into mental content (despite his own statement that anything whatsoever can serve as evidence for anything whatsoever), and then supposes that the expression or fact "Euclid knew of the equality of triangles," or even "Euclid knew that the base angles of an isoceles triangle are equal" is identical with the component in "Collingwood knows that 'Euclid knew that the base angles of an isosceles triangle are equal.'" But in the former case Euclid stands out as a man thinking over against a content, whereas in the latter case Collingwood stands out as a thinker against a content which is that former case. In other words, Euclid functions one way in the former and in another way in the latter—unless one identifies Euclid with mere thinking, as apparently Collingwood intends to do. His whole discussion of the identity of his mind with Euclid's is unwarranted, for in his own case his thinking is distinct from the thinking of Euclid; they have distinct subject matters. And if he and Euclid had the same subject matters to think about, in what sense would there be a re-enactment, in what sense would history have passed away?

Collingwood is struggling with the basic question of how I here and now can know what is not here any longer. He thinks he must identify his own thinking with the thinking which he believes is at the root of the past happening. Such identification presupposes an awareness of the difference between past and present. He is on stronger grounds when he speaks of the historian making use of all the evidence he can find and then reconstructing the nature of the past. Such a reconstructed past is an hypothesis serving to explain the evidence, by showing that through the normal process of causation we will arrive at that evidence. The evidence used in history is thus a product of a definite sort; it is a derivative from that which we are trying to construct on the basis of it. What we are seeking in history is that state of affairs from which, in the normal course of events, the evidence would necessarily follow as a matter of fact.

Collingwood acutely observes that the "scissors and paste" historians who do nothing but select and order written statements (and thus are essentially academic historians usually copying out of one another's books), cannot see the issue of using evidences rather than sources, because they think that the only reputable items for an historian to study are just those which were amenable to their method. He remarks that this is what landscape painters in the last century did when they concentrated on "painterly" subjects, and thereby avoided the items which would have challenged their mistaken view of painting. The observation applies to all fields. Had the positivists for example not concentrated on the kind of items which were amenable to mathematical treatment, they would have seen that their view was not adequate to ethics, metaphysics, politics, etc. Of course one might say that this is but a tautological observation: any view defines a certain area of permissible material. The judgment that the view is too narrow in range depends on the recognition that there is content outside the areas of the discipline, which everyone knows. Can one define or describe this? It should be the least common denominator of all disciplines—matters such as life and death, being and becoming, responsibility, self-identity, power, possibility, unity, creativity. Perhaps we can get a list of these only in a metaphysical system, or by facing up a given view with the content of experience and allowing experience to force into focus the items the view cannot handle. The latter depends on an acceptance of the experience, and then a use of theory as a focus on that which is outside it.

Must there always be something outside? Yes, but the fact of its being outside and the manner of its functioning should, in an adequate system, be stated within that system. In short, a philosophy of being must account for the brutal fact of becoming, and if it cannot have a category inside its system which tells about this, the philosophy of being must be said to ignore a root reality.

January 5

Experience can be said to have four stresses—interplay, stability, immensity, and futurity, answering to the fact that man is involved in Existence, has steady habits, is part of a larger scheme of things, and is directed toward ideals. When the interplay is sharpened we get a grasp of Existence; when stability becomes prominent we get the daily world of common sense; when immensity comes into focus we get a religious attitude, and when futurity, we get concern, anxiety, involvement. All these stresses occur at the same time; they blend into one another, and one sometimes comes to the fore while the others move into the background. Normally we identify the whole of experience as though it were concentrated in one of them and accrete to that one the virtues of the other stresses. If we start with an awareness of the immensity, we readily suppose that it contains the components of interplay, stability, and futurity within it, and call all of them together by the name of "God." But strictly speaking God should be that component which has been separated out of the fourfold stress by speculation as an objective being. We do not initially experience Him in isolation but only as involved with these others.

Experience is a muddle; the various elements we focus and name as God, Common Sense, Existence, and Ideal, are muddled precisely because they are not altogether separated from one another, and because they are approached with stresses which do not allow us to recognize them for what they are. We bring in ourselves as individuals or social beings rather than as representative ones, and therefore have even the distinguished God, common-sense object, etc., infected with improper accretions. We recover the pure object, the true substance, by abstracting strands and engaging in a synthesis.

Experience is a kind of togetherness which results from the way in which the items in a cosmological whole interplay with respect to man as a focal object. It is therefore, strictly speaking, neutral with respect to all the stresses; or better, we would have an ideal experience if we could have the four stresses in equipoise.

January 6

If the various modes of togetherness be interpreted as cosmological for the comma, ontological for the period, experiential for the therefore, and systematically abstract for the implication, we can say that all four occur together, and that we can, when concentrating on one, eventually find a need to move to the others. Therefore the argument in *Modes of Being,* in effect is one which dissolves the comma for the dot, or better, moves from the comma to the dot as that which is its correlative. But the argument in the book actually moves from the termini of the comma rather than from the nature of the comma, though this is surely an alternative way of doing it (and is incidentally done in doing the other). There should also be ways of moving from experience to philosophy, philosophy to ontology, etc., etc. The procedure in each case will evidently be one which is mediated by the other two types of togetherness, or by two modes of being.

Can we move from a system of philosophy to experience, cosmology, and ontology, and conversely? Is it not the case that the system presents these, so that if it is a system of philosophy it must be something other than these three in content—perhaps epistemology? If it is, then we must move to experience, cosmology, and ontology by different routes. We get to ontology by a movement from implication to a dot, for example. If this be the case we dissolve an internal relation to get a freedom for the terms which they did not have before, to allow them to be merely the many of the universe. To get to experience from the epistemology is to move from the implication to the therefore. This is of course the movement to the act of inference; and this means that in effect the movement from a philosophic theory regarding the nature of the universe to an experience of this, as a thick interpenetration of items, involves the risk which all inference entrains. To get from the theory to cosmology is to move to the comma and thus to have the items in the epistemology blend with and make a difference to one another.

We could, though, in theory begin with an item in the epistemology and show that it requires not merely the other items in the implicative set but that it rests upon entities having a different career from what they have in the implicative set. Just as the movement from an item in the cosmology to the ontology is the achievement of it as by itself, and thus as related to the initial item in a new way, so the realization that, say, an idea of judgment claims truth will throw us into another domain where the relation to the other items will be different from those which their counterparts may have in the epistemology.

Starting now with experience we ought to be able to move in any one of three directions—toward epistemology, cosmology, or ontology. We get the first as a movement from therefore to implication, by focussing on the termini of the therefore and finding a formal relation amongst the termini. This is the way in which we in fact analyze. It is analysis then that enables us to get to an epistemology which issues out of a pre-reflective experience having a cosmic reach. We get to cosmology either by moving from the epistemology or directly from the experience. If we do the latter we are moving to the comma (and thus keeping the initial blur), but are seeing how each part interplays with the others. If instead, we move from experience to ontology, we isolate, as in analysis, the various elements and see how they dissolve the to-getherness of experience to give a mere dot.

In each of these cases all four modes of togetherness are to be found, but in each, three of them have a somewhat subordinate role. This means that in ontology we do give the position of God a somewhat superior role, though it is one which is qualified by the fact that the individual philosopher himself never gets his mind entirely free from his own body. Accordingly, the four kinds of togetherness given in the *Modes of Being* are not only biased by being known by an individual man (and thus biased in terms of an epistemology which is occupied primarily with God in the role of a togetherness), but all are subject to a kind of divinizing. If we, e.g, have the modes merged together, we have them understood as merged together in a togetherness which stands apart from the items as something intelligible.

Put another way: the epistemological approach of the individual, which is partly biased because of the individual's body, has three possible topics—ontology (dealt with in the *Modes* in chapter 11), cosmology (assumed in the *Modes of Being*), and experience (more or less neglected in *Modes of Being*). But then there should also be a way in which the three alternatives to ontology are subordinated by it; ditto for cosmology, and ditto for experience. Thus in experience we should be able to find stresses on ontology, cosmology, and epistemology—i.e., the ultimate substantival, the interplaying, and the abstractable and cognitional. At the same time we should find it a locus of four modes of togetherness, in each of which presumably there is a focus for one of the four dimensions—ontology, cosmology, epistemology, and experience. In experience then we should find a particular experiential locus, and other experienced items which dissect out as ontology, cosmology, and epistemology. And of course there should be similar things in the other dimensions. But what is the experientially stressed element in experience? It should be that part of it which is exclusively or primarily a therefore, a vital, existential stress, and thus the item which is the primary concern of art, and which is also acknowledged in history.

January 7

If we start with experience we find we have it in two ways: 1] as encompassing us and the entire world, all somehow muddled together;   2] as a focal point in a larger domain which stands over against us in our privacies. In both we have a vital ongoing, a kind of therefore expressed as the insistence on each distinctive area, but with a primary emphasis on the process by which these are being separated from one another. The second form of experience is one in which we can distinguish subordinated notes of cosmology, etc. This is encountered primarily as a vital form of ongoing, one of the dimensions of the universe, a kind of togetherness within which we can discern at a distance, as it were, other forms of togetherness. But alongside the focal experience there are other types of togetherness. These like the focal experience are found within the all-encompassing experience. They come into focus because the all-encompassing experience allows one to concentrate in an appropriate way on the other focal points. Until this all-encompassing experience is so subdivided, the cosmological, ontological, and epistemological forms of togetherness (which are encountered) are acknowledged only in their dynamic capacities, and thus in terms of what should be subordinated and controlled aspects of themselves. The recognition of substantial interplay, ontological independence, and epistemological systematization requires a separation out of distinctive powers in man and a consequent insistence on noting a certain kind of togetherness in the content we confront.

Ontology can be said to be a component inside both the all-encompassing experience and the focal experience. In the latter it appears only as a subordinated note; in the former it appears as a focal item, but one in which its mode of presentation is distorted. To get to the latter we have to engage in philosophic speculation; we then find that it is primarily characterized by a static comma, and that this has over against it (and thus in some sense as subordinated modes) the other forms of togetherness. Here we have the justification for the theological insistence on the primacy of the One. However, it is to be noted that A] this grasp of the ontological is not perfect since it is affected by the individual's incapacity to be a perfect neutral mind, and B] the grasp of the ontological as primary involves a neglect of the other forms of togetherness.

A genuinely neutral position would have to give all the forms of togetherness their own weight. To see, for example, that the comma is necessary is not the same thing as to participate in it. An ontological approach to the modes thus in a way does full justice to the comma, but deals with the other modes of togetherness as though they were subordinated, or reflected by, or in the comma. If this be the case, can we be said to know all four modes? In the *Modes* mind is made a function of

Actuality; if that position be accepted, the basic cognitional approach to ontology is via Actuality. But whether this be accepted or not, and perhaps it ought not to be, ontology or any other basic discipline should be seen to favor one of the forms of togetherness even when acknowledging the presence, interplay, and distinctive roles of the others.

January 8

I think I interchanged the role of the dot and the comma in the last few days. This is what happens when I do not check against the *Modes*. (Some of these have been caught in the rereading, 3/9/61.)

If the all-encompassing approach to the content of the world be termed "intuited," one can speak of the focal points as being A] intuited experience, B] intuited cosmology, C] intuited ontology D] intuited epistemology. Each of these intuited areas has subordinate notes reflecting three other modes of being; each also is related to the other intuited areas to constitute a single undivided whole of intuited content. But we can concentrate on any one of the intuited areas, and can also attend to fragmented forms of them. Thus history is a fragment of cosmology; it deals primarily with the interplay of Actuality and Existence. Such history can be experienced, i.e., intuited, possessed without reflection. When this occurs we get a grasp of two modes of being in a vital interplay, as having some character of their own but as essentially governed by the fact that they are termini of a new kind of dot. Similarly, the realm of politics, religion, and action, because also concerned with limited interplays of the modes in a cosmological setting, should offer us unique intuited contents.

We ought to be able to go further: all kinds of combinations of the factors which make up a cosmology, ontology, epistemology, or an experience, should be intuited, and there should be intuitions in which there is a bias toward one of the factors rather than the other.

January 12

A man may be said to be faced with annihilation in four ways: by losing his status with respect to other actualities, by failing to live up to the Ideal, by failing to find his place with respect to ultimate excellence, and by being ignored by the power of Existence. He will then die, be guilty, be worthless, or be futile. He enters into the realms of action, politics, religion, and history, to overcome these failures. When he enters any one realm he assumes a particular role; he is, say, religious or historical. He must then tackle the very problems that the other realms provide, but in a transformed shape. He must in each realm face a distinctive extension, Ideal, excellence, or power. In each realm, too, he must make himself into a being with a definite function to perform, for he is in that realm as a being facing a peculiar kind of universe. In each realm, too, he will get a satisfaction by offering a replacement for what he had not done. If he is purely religious, he must deal with other men as part of a religious community, must have a distinctive Ideal, be subject to providence, and must see his work as carrying out God's work on Existence. By functioning as a kind of representative of God, he gets a kind of life, forgiveness, and effectiveness, despite the fact that he will still die in the realm of Actualities, will be guilty in the realm of the Ideal, will be futile in the realm of Existence. His satisfactions are then not ultimate but only ideational. (A satisfaction but shows that a realm is autonomous, a kind of cosmos in miniature, oriented toward man.) Full and proper satisfaction for man requires that he be part of every realm equally and find in each the satisfaction that it provides him as concerned with its reality.

This is essentially the view, in history, of the modern with respect to men of service or "heroes." The Greek hero represented Existence itself, and came in when he willed; the modern hero represents mankind or his society and enters history by acting on Existence. The two kinds of heroes are in opposition. A saint is one who has oriented himself with respect to God; so is a prophet, but the prophet, like the classical hero, represents God rather than acts with respect to Him, even in submission. There should also be men who have tasks with respect to Actuality, and others who have to do with the Ideal. Do we have here a contrast of explorers, adventurers over against the practical, and a contrast between the reformer and the man who does his duty?

In Russia we have, under the influence of Marx, historical men who find their satisfaction in history; history for them is also the place where their dignity, virtue, and worth is incidentally achieved. In contrast with them, we in America stress the achievement of dignity, the overcoming of the power of the other actualities. We find our virtue in this conquest, our worth by identifying ourselves with mankind as engaged in this activity, and avoid futility by accepting the destiny of our people or mankind as sufficient. Both they and we contrast with the Orient where the stress is on the acceptance of the status of excellence defined by an ultimate excellence. Consequently there, there is no history, no mastery of nature, no ethics in our western sense. There should be a fourth type of man, one who finds his completion by living in the realm of politics or ethics. Would this be the Confucian view? Or is it not essentially the European outlook? If so, we have Russia, America, the Orient, and Europe exploiting four basic ways of being satisfied. The final answer must be that we should live in all four ways.

January 13

From childhood on we are trained and educated to fit inside the conventional common-sense world. The only men who really master that world are the lawyers; their mastery is a clear holding of it over against the rest of the world. This in fact is experienced with the common-sense world, and encountered in an inchoate fashion. Through emotions we are constantly directing ourselves beyond the common-sense world to the realm beyond; and even our common-sense judgments, since they have an adumbrated component, make reference to it.

We treat the rest of the world, encountered in emotional experience, primarily as natural or Existential, divine or awesome, inspiring or Ideal. It takes analysis to separate these out, and speculation to understand them. When we engage in art, ethics, religion, we try to forge judgments which, without destroying the adumbrated, actually absorbs its meaning within its being. Art work has Existence within it; ethical activity exhibits the Good; the religious man has the divine within him.

In an ordinary judgment a proper name has a double function; it refers to a denoted aspect and it refers to the being of the external object, as bounded and substantial. A transcendental such as beauty has the double function of being a predicate and of spreading through, characterizing the whole object. When, then, we say that such and such a painting is beautiful, what we are evidently doing is having a double encompassment of the object as a bounded being which has a feature permeating it—the Good as throughout the sensuous material. But it is to be noted that the beautiful, which is functioning inside the judgment, unlike the proper name, has actually brought within the judgment (and of course within the art object) the object which is permeated. In the judgment the object is enjoyed; in the art object it is exhibited. Or is it the case that the judgment of a work of art or any other form of beauty is an ordinary judgment, and that the functioning of beauty as a predicate and an adumbrating copula occurs only in the work of art itself?

The answer would seem to be both, for we can make detached and also involved judgments of beauty.

In connection with religion, ethics, and categorial knowing, there must be a similar absorption within the discourse or the object—sacramental, virtuous, or speculative—of the adumbrated element. All the basic approaches to reality provide opaque contents which are translucent in the sense that they have taken into themselves an item which "imitates" the very adumbrated content that makes the judgment or object true.

January 14

The different modes require different "judgments." The proper judgment for Existence is to be found in the work of art itself; if we are to make a judgment of Existence in a conceptual way, we must introduce the emotions. Only thus does the transcendental function not only as a predicate but as a subject matter iconizing the subject matter, Existence, which is outside it. The cognized judgment thus does essentially what the art work does. When then we judge an art work, a mere reinstatement of it intellectually should enable us to use the transcendental term properly. In this area we have the derivative transcendentals of beauty (answering to the Ideal), harmony (answering to the divine), and the enjoyed (answering to the Actual).

In connection with God we have the proper judgment made in worship; the judgment which is conceptual is derivative and must be sustained by reverence. If it is to be a report of the worship itself it must reinstate in reverence what was actually practiced in fact with respect to the divine. There should be derivative transcendentals here, too, answering to the Ideal, Actual, and Existence—the providential, the pious, and required works.

In connection with the Ideal we have the proper judgment made in obligation; the judgment that is conceptual is derivative and must be sustained by a sense of obligation, of being "practical." If the conceptual judgment is to be a report of the obligation actually accepted, it must be sustained by a sense of obligation. There should be derivative transcendentals here, answering to the Actual, the Divine, and Existence— virtue, the united kingdom of ends, and proper action of an ethical sort.

In connection with the Actual the true judgment is an intellectual one. If we judge it, it must be in terms of the same or other categories used in the initial judgment. There should be derivative transcendentals here, too. These should answer to the Ideal, the divine, and Existence. They are the predicates which are conceived in the course of a philosophic speculation.

In dealing with such fragmentary and humanly oriented disciplines as history (and politics, institutional religion, and social action) we find various components which are transformed in it and there have special roles and distinctive functions. We also find each component getting a direct derivative satisfaction. (Religion, e.g., is to be found in a muted form inside history; it there provides satisfaction to a representative of mankind or to one's own society.) The disciplines must be sustained by the remaining modes and thereby give still another satisfaction to their constituents.

There are then seven satisfactions which a man can get for his need to be worthy, for his need to have dignity, for his need to be guiltless, and for his need to be significant. He can, for example, acquire a worthiness inside the realm of social action, politics, and history; he can also acquire a worthiness three times from a divine sustaining of the realm of social action, politics, and history; and he obtains an additional worthiness through his direct relationship to God. Other kinds of worthiness can also be obtained since there are other fragmentary cosmological schemes besides those of social action, politics, and history. There is, e.g., the combination of Existence and the Ideal, which defines teleological nature. Such a combination should find a place for a worthiness inside it, and should be sustained by the divine as well.

Hegel speaks of history as God's work. But one can say of it just as well that it is the displaying of the mode of Actuality as a power, of Existence as that which alters over the course of time inside the frame of mankind, that it is displaying the Ideal as that which provides it with a rationality and in terms of which alone it is intelligible, as well as that it is God displaying himself by sustaining history as an objective reality. In every one of these cases something is taken as fixed, as the field in which the power is to be displayed.

Actually, history is constituted by Actuality and Existence; the objective role which God provides, and the rationality which the Ideal provides for history do not (except for one who leaves history and looks at it from the standpoint of God or the Ideal and thus outside history itself) come into history. History should be seen in and of itself; the lessons it teaches are ingredient in it. If we wish to say it is God's work, it must be only so far as history is treated as an objective reality and the capacities which history has, when made objective—the accumulation of the past, the unifying role of the present, the comparability of past and future, etc.—are taken to be of its essence. In short, if we were to say that we do not have history until we accumulate the past, etc., we should speak of it as the displaying of God. But we also have a warrant for speaking of it as the displaying of the Ideal, for the Ideal transforms the dark content of the historical into a rational movement toward the final intelligible end.

If history, as I have supposed, can be properly said to involve nothing more than the interplay of mankind and Existence, then a reference to God and to the Ideal will be not to what makes history possible, but to what makes history the reference of historiography, and to what makes it intelligible. This means that history might conceivably not be open to historiography, and may not be intelligible. In the former case we would accumulate the past in the present and live entirely in the present without attempting to know what had been; in the latter case we would recognize no laws of history and no principles in terms of which one epoch could be compared with another. This is but to say that the roles of God and the Ideal are to make historiography, not history, possible.

Taking the above as a clue, one can say that the role of the excluded modes in any fragmentary cosmology is epistemological. In the realm of politics, for example, God would provide a basic unity, so that the political whole represents mankind, and Existence would provide a basic dynamics so that the political whole can persist. The provided unity and persistence will not make the political whole possible. This possibility is assured by the interplay of mankind and the Ideal. Unity and persistence here make such an interplay, have a meaning and a career which can be studied in political theory. Without them the political world would be a fragmentary occurrence which was self-contained and existed in and of itself, so that only he who lived inside it would know it—and this is to say that it would be an anthropological-sociological unit having no meaning for one who stands outside. To put it all another way, we can give history, e.g., a genuine cosmological setting, in which case the cosmological resultant, if called history, will be the locus of the display of all the four modes. If this is not to be confounded with cosmology itself, there would have to be an orientation toward man. So, if one were to say with Hegel that history is the locus of God's work, it is work done, as it were, at a distance from God, and is no simple display of His being.

Whether, then, one speaks of the role of God and the Ideal as essentially epistemological, or views them as completing the cosmological totality, it is a fact that, even for the Hegelian, there is a bias toward the combination of mankind and Existence. This, even if viewed as only a nuclear constituent in a wider cosmology, incapable of existing by itself, has a nature over against God and the Ideal.

Not only then, when living in a common-sense conventional world, but also when living in history, politics, etc., we have an adumbration of a reality beyond. Growing up is the learning of the conventions of the common-sense world; being academic is the subjugation of the exterior reality to the conventions of that world. When we move from common sense to the realms of history, etc., we have analogous problems. The "professional" is one who subjugates the exterior reality to the conditions of expression of the humanized realm; apprenticeship is learning to master those conditions. There are, then, the professional men of religion, politics, history, and social action, whose object it is to take the adumbrated modes of being which lie outside (and which either constitute new realms or serve to sustain one's own), and make these take the shape of one's own realm, as merely subordinated elements. This is in effect to deny the supportive role of these elements, and to be content with having them function inside the realm (as answers to oneself), exercising some specialized role or function.

In Hegel the adumbrated is the immediate, and the conventional or professional is the negative. Strictly speaking the negative negatives itself, that is, it is self-negating, pulverized. He missed seeing this in the beginning of his *Logic,* for he there thought that Nothing was identical with Being, when what he should have said (since he wanted Nothing to be an antithesis too) is that a plurality of Nothings is identical with Being, that Being is analyzable into an endless plurality of Nothings, each of which is, only as negating and being negated by the others. The whole is in one continual transition, not merely to Being (for it is this only as the totality of Nothings), but from one Nothing to another. There is, in short, no single Nothing with which one can rest. To have a Nothing is to move on to other Nothings and thus to have a kind of becoming from one Nothing to another; it is also to move on to Being as that which is to unite or terminate all the Nothings. There is a radical kind of becoming produced by the movement to the unity of the plurality of Nothings. There is another kind of becoming which is merely a transition from Nothing to Nothing. This in the end negates itself to be that which is to be unified in a radical becoming. A superficial becoming thus gives way to a genuine becoming. (Could it be said of every triad, that the second member has the third in an explicit form, just as the second has the first in an articulate form?)

On the side of the conventional there are beings who are more apt than others to show the effectiveness of the adumbrated side. In religion it is of course the virtuous man and in the exemplary case, Christ; in history it is the hero and in the exemplary case, the great leader; in politics it is the man of service and in the exemplary case, the authority or king; in social action it is the healthy man and in the exemplary case, the reasonable man. Each one of these is in the end destroyed. Christ's death is essential to his role. The historical men have, as Hegel remarked, only labor and trouble. In politics the great man is the one who is assassinated or overthrown. And the reasonable man assumes the burden of being the conservative, and is overthrown by the next generation. These men in effect are on the other side, where the adumbrated is, and it is their task to do justice to it and to the other, the conventional as well. (The conventional man neglects and even denies the adumbrated. In the end his punishment is that the lower half, the conventional side which he is willing to adopt, is the part where he is undone. If he left the conventional altogether he would be mad or criminal; indeed his taking account of that adumbrated side is precisely the charge which is brought against him inside the conventional world. This is surely clear regarding the religious man, the prophet particularly; it is true too of the political man, such as Socrates as he in effect was standing before his judges; it is not so evident in connection with the hero unless he be seen to be a man of destiny or mankind epitomized; and it is not so evident in the case of the reasonable man except so far as he clings to values that ought to be preserved in the face of a change in conventional standards.)

The pragmatist attempts to civilize the adumbrated by making it part of the problem of reconstituting the "conventional" or "professional." His answer is thus somewhat different from the ordinary conventional or professional one; he recognizes that the realm of the commonsensical or the special discipline is not adequate to the adumbrated, but instead A] of denying the adumbrated, B] subjugating and transforming it, he C] tries instead to reorganize the commonsensical and professional until it has room for that adumbrated. But this he finds is an endless, an infinite, process, and in effect presupposes that there is something he must transmute—the adumbrated side which is his raw material, and his immediacy which is to be translated into a plurality of negatives or particulars.

The prophet, etc., reveal that the adumbrated component is too large; it shatters the conventional world, and is known to be capable of doing this. The pragmatic answer in effect is: keep on trying, never admit that the task has been done. Indeed, the pragmatist sets himself to shatter the conventional world in order to accommodate the adumbrated side, and as a consequence he may be said to anticipate the destruction which would have been his had he remained conventional and tried to accommodate the adumbrated side without altering either it or the conventional.

The Hegelian answer in root is like that of the pragmatist. He wants to bring the infinite within the pattern of the totality of negations. But is it possible for him to have a totality of negations? Is there an end to the set of finite categories, so that they contain the whole "substance"? Does the absolute ever get to the stage where it can articulate itself fully? Must not each of his categories be broken up into an infinite set of them? Kant's position is stronger in the sense that he preserves the rights of what lies "beyond," and does not try to bring it inside the confines of the "here." But Kant, unfortunately, allows it to be too beyond. The "beyond" should be seen to be experiencable, known through speculation, interacting with what is here and now, and allowing its presence to be felt here and now. It must not be absorbed in the here and now and must not be cut off from it. Hegel tends to have it absorbed and Kant to have it cut off; we must therefore not stay with either. Kant also makes the mistake of staying on this side, and trying to define the "beyond" as merely "beyond this side." But if he is really caught on this side he cannot speak of the beyond at all; this is something open to him only so far as he makes contact with it. The contrast between the beyond and here is to be made within the common area of both, and not from one side or the other.

Experience encompasses both the common-sense dimension with its conventionalities and the beyond in which the Ideal, divine, and Existence are all merged, and has all these dimensions not altogether distinguished. A focussing on the common-sense dimension merely throws the other into contrast.

Why is it that one of these dimensions comes out into focus at one time and another at another? Is there something in the movement of the dimensions inter se, or is it due to what we here and now concentrate on? In terror, we seem to be conditioned from without, but in our experiences, with our concentration on this or that item, we seem to dictate where we shall look. Perhaps then the answer is twofold; we concentrate on the here and now and at the same time open ourselves up to whatever in the beyond contrasts with it. When there is no emphasized element in the beyond we tend to neglect the beyond; when there is, we become aware of the limitations of our conventional life.

January 15

Intellection is most appropriate to the mode of Actuality. But the best way of using the mind in connection with the other modes is mathematics for the Ideal, rhythmics for Existence, and reverence for God. The latter two are undeveloped intellectual disciplines; the first has to do with the kind of divisions which Existence allows and produces, the second has to do with the grasp of the nature of unity in depth. When we speculate in philosophy and deal with the different modes, we have a bias toward Actuality, not only in the sense that we are engaged in intellection, but in the sense that the form of our intellection is that which is appropriate to Actualities. When we engage in mathematics, e.g., on the other hand, we are still using our minds, but are allowing them to be contoured by the Ideal.

Each of these modes of intellection divides into two arenas, in which there is an orientation with respect to man; one arena is personal, the other objective. Speculation divides into categorial knowledge and social action; mathematics into ethics and politics (Plato's insight); rhythmics into art and history; reverence into adoration or worship and creedal religion or good works. Each of these subdivisions involves two modes and is sustained by two others. The personalized forms involve a kind of creativity and thus the production of a substitute for the cosmos, with a stress though on the exhibition of one mode. Categorial knowledge reveals the substantial nature of Actuality; ethics, the omnipresent insistence of the Ideal; art, the nature of Existence; and worship the glory of God. The objectified forms keep to two modes, using the other two to sustain them and make them have an objective being, a reality of their own.

Every one of these enterprises can be conventionalized; strictly speaking though, each is the result of a breakaway from the earlier forms of conventionalism characteristic of a member of the society in which we live. Minority people—Jews, Negroes, women, and the disenfranchised —never fit completely into the larger society; they are therefore more able to deal with the world beyond common sense. Women seem to experience the world beyond, out of which the speculatively known modes are to be analyzed; Negroes seem to have mastered rhythmics in the form of art and sport; the disenfranchised seem to be concerned with politics as an object of reform, or the ethical as demanding, but not with the pure cognitional mathematics which underlie both; Jews seem to be concerned either with categorial knowledge or with a social adjustment to other Actualities—i.e., they are naturalists, this-worldly. If these are not merely contingent outcomes there should, strictly speaking, be parallels in minorities interested in mathematics, speculation, and reverence.

More likely the issue is dependent on the degree of exclusion from a society. In America we have excluded only the Negroes effectively. In other societies where the Jews were excluded, they either became masters of the world of common sense, in the guise of lawyers and doctors, or took the basic actuality to be Jewry and made it their business to adjust to it, and to adjust it to the rest of the world. (But explorers and adventurers would seem to have a somewhat analogous concern with respect to Actuality, and these come from a different kind of people. Minority? I don't know.) The proletariat or the disenfranchised do promote the revolutionary side of politics, but do not seem to move to the study of mathematics. (Who are the minority people who study mathematics, if any?) And worship seems to catch men in all walks, though there is no doubt that in time of great trial, it is the disenfranchised who turn to religion and adopt the new or promising forms of it, and give themselves over to worship. Perhaps mathematics is too austere and distant for most, and one must look to song or mythology to find the topic which would alert the minority—but which minority, if any, responds by song or myth to what lies beyond common sense?

Each of the dimensions of the beyond has its effect on the common-sensical world. The Incarnation expresses this vividly for the divine; but the substantial Actuality is manifest in the brutality of things, the Ideal in the dedicated man, and Existence in the sublime and awesome.

Hegel's assumption that knowledge can not finally have something alien as its content, requires the consciousness in the end to become self-conscious. His view can and ought to be carried over into the other modes of apprehension—the obligation to the Good, the struggle with Existence, the submission to the divine. A genuine obligation to the Good must involve an interiorization of it in intent; a proper struggle with Existence must involve the having of Existence within oneself, which is meeting the onslaught of the Existence outside; the submission to the divine must involve the repetition in oneself of the divine so that one becomes an image of the divine.

Just as knowledge is, strictly speaking, fully appropriate to only one mode, so are the other forms of apprehension. "Self-consciousness" or "self-reinstatement" is always fragmentary and partial, since consciousness never can get the rest of the universe into full focus only by means of one mode of apprehension. A fully self-conscious being would be one who had four modes of apprehension at the same time, and focussed on the appropriate mode in each one; he would then be in effect "a self-conscious, virtuous, adjusted image of the divine." The consciousness is always passionate, since it penetrates to another realm; it is also overwhelmed since it faces a greater reality than the individual. In self-consciousness there is a re-establishment of oneself, a recovery of sobriety in the face of or with a moment of passion—consciousness here being used as the generic name for the different forms of apprehension of the various modes.

When it is said that there is a dependence on God to make historiography possible, we make evident that history exists apart from the writing about it. On the other hand, unless the support of God had nothing to do with the historical world which is being supported and made objective for the historian, we must say with Hegel that the subjective sides are one, and that God's role is vital. The reconciliation of the two positions (i.e., one which holds historiography to exist in and of itself, and the other which says that history does), is in the affirmation that the final historiography, the complete and total story, is to be seen as from God's perspective. This requires the translation of the actual dynamics of the world into a systematic, organized, articulated account. Accordingly, in and of itself there is a history. God enables that history to be spread out as a totality of facts, which is but the restatement of the history in another form, as knowledge rather than as occurrences.

What is said of God has an analogue in relation to the Ideal. This gives value, direction, purpose, rationality to the historic occurrences and provides them with an order which they otherwise would not have. In connection with all other enterprises, from the ontological to the cosmological, to the fragments of cosmology such as politics, we have a similar re-articulation or re-presentation of the objective facts, though in different cases there are different roles which the modes perform. In politics, e.g., the union of Actuality and Ideality is sustained not only by God, who gives it objectivity, but by Existence, which gives it power, energy, being. The political world must re-present the Existence outside it in a limited form. In connection with worship, the religious world is sustained by Existence and Ideality; these relate the religious community to its final aim.

If it be a fact that consciousness becomes self-conscious by taking the other to be itself, and this by virtue of making itself be that other, art can be said to be an achievement or a self-conscious exterior to the individual. It is the exposition of one's self-consciousness since it takes existence into itself to enable us to portray the Existence outside. It is not self-conscious of course except so far as the outside is known to be consciousness itself. There is an analogous situation in connection with knowledge, virtue, and worship.

The public form of knowledge is language; of virtue, improving acts; and of worship, charity. Each of these should, by making itself contain the other, become the self-conscious public reality so far as it refers to the other as itself. A language, which is holy or sacramental, has this role; so have acts which are responsibly undertaken; so does charity done in the name of the divine.

In taking this approach the position of Hegel is reversed. He takes the modes or his one mode, the Absolute, to spend itself in a series of negativities so as to have itself articulated, whereas here it is being held that man provides an articulation which answers only in a partial way to the full being of the reality beyond. Only when functioning representatively does man articulate Actuality and become identical with it. In this case alone do we have a perfect self-consciousness.

Is pragmatism the first step in the American ethos, a one-dimensional attempt to become self-conscious with respect to the Actual? If so, it must be supplemented by comparable attempts at achieving virtue and charity and art, or (more externally) by engaging in social action, good deeds, communal religion, and history. These are all forms of a self-consciousness produced by recovering on this side the nature of what lies beyond—Actuality, Ideal, God, and Existence. The case of history is peculiar, for it is matched by an historiography in a sense in which social action is not matched by self-knowledge, deeds by reflection, and communal religion by adequate expressions. This would seem to show that the self-conscious status of history requires supplementation by another self-consciousness achieved in historiography. We would then have history absorbing Existence in itself, and then historiography absorbing history in itself. But why this doubling?

Hegel makes a mistake in thinking that the antithesis to Being is Nothing. Not only should he have made it an infinite plurality of Nothings, each determinate, and determinately as a whole standing over against Being and thereby making Being itself become determinate, but he should have viewed the progress of the dialectic as the solidification of this realm of Nothings into areas or categories. The negative in short negates itself as sheer negativity, to become more and more solid and therefore immediate, saving itself from final immediacy and thus duplication of being by remaining with a few categorial divisions. We can then say at every moment that the plurality or the limited finite stage is real and exhibits the ultimate Absolute, at the same time that it fails to do so completely because it has not been solidified enough. One might also add that in the progression from a plurality of negatives to a more solid set of negatives, there is an increase in the degree of negativity between the immediate being and the negative dimension. The progress then might also be viewed as a progress in the way in which the subject is related to the substance. In the beginning it is related in an immediate, hardly determinate way; in the end the relation is multiplied, intensified. In other words, the negativity that in the beginning was all on the side of the subject, becomes more and more the negativity between the subject and the substance, so that in the end we have (when we come to the Absolute Idea) the repetition of the substance in the subject, with an endless number of negations between them. The articulation thus collapses into a single unit which is multiply related to the original unity of being. The next stage of the history of the Ultimate would involve the reconversion of the negative relation into a unity, having itself a negative relation of a plural sort to the Ultimate, and so on, and so on.

January 16

An alternative interpretation of Hegel, and one which is perhaps in closer keeping with the text, is to view the first antithesis to be Being. As a single item it is immediate, achieving distinction from Being only because it is negated. There would then be a negation in operation between Being and Being, the latter being termed Nothing because exteriorized. The progression of the dialectic would then consist in the fractionating of the Nothing, with a solidification of the gain, thereby enabling it to negate the Being from which it had issued.

Nothing initially negates Being only so far as it is being negated in turn; that is why one has a persistent movement back and forth, or Becoming. Later the Nothing acquires more power to negate on its own, but it never succeeds in having all it needs until the entire dialectic is completed. That dialectic is completed by means of a negative, which is the concept of the Ultimate Being, as united with all the previous moments. These previous moments are all solidified in the successive ones and thus in the final Idea. What we have then, is a succession of negative moments each of which has an interiority and thus a kind of negation within it, made up of the preceding moments.

The final stage is a Being which negates the idea of itself, inside of which are all the fragmentary ideas needed in order to reach the idea of Being. The idea of Being is positive by virtue of its possession of all the preceding ideas or moments within it, and as such it effectively negates what negates it—or what now is the same thing, is identical with itself as in itself. The substance has become subject in the sense that the subject is substantial, having interior content, and the initial substance sinks back into just being an Other. Having fulfilled itself in a totality of negations, it is possible to continue in the dialectic by taking the achieved idea, and having this exteriorize itself so as to come to know its own interiority. This would mean in the end that the achieved idea would function as a kind of base or ultimate, and would face a dialectic of ideas which would be like those that it had itself assimilated. The dialectic of ideas on this new level would be over against an idea and not over against Being as such. At the end of this second movement of the dialectic we would have an idea with an interior set of ideas, over against an idea with an interior set of ideas, and thus have a genuine self-consciousness. There could then be a third movement, though there would be nothing new learned; all one would have then is a base in an idea which rested on an idea and not, as in the second movement, which rested on Being. Or, if there were a gain here, there would not be a similar gain in the fourth movement.

If we are to think of the dialectic going on forever, we ought to say that on the second round the division of the categories is different from what it was on the first—the fact that it is a dialectic with respect to an idea having an interior set of ideas, requires that its exteriorization be expressed in a new set of ideas. At the end, then, the initial idea will face itself, but itself as having traversed a different route from that traversed by the initial idea. It will face itself, be self-conscious of itself as having been articulated differently on the second round. One can then move on to a third round to find another kind of articulation, and so on. We will then always have the idea of Being having within it the plurality of moments which preceded it, but the plurality will be distinct, making the idea in its details different from the immediate Being, and from any previous fulfilled idea which had assimilated all its previous moments.

The churches institutionalize the divine, the state institutionalizes the Ideal, society the Actual, and industry Existence. All conventionalize a mode of Being and all of them are constantly faced with the fact that the Being continues to be outside them, and that they fail to live up to its measure. The Christ of the Grand Inquisitor has a counterpart in the state in the shape of one who founded it, or who produced a revolution to get it; in society he has one in the shape of the reformer who wants to cut through established practices in order to produce health and happiness; and in the guise of the innovator and inventor he has one with respect to Existence (one thinks here of the attempt to introduce coal or the airplane).

Freud's *Totem and Taboo* suggests that there are special areas or modes in which the beyond may not be interiorized, brought into play here and now. There are profane objects, foods, acts, and words in religion; incestuous, disloyal, improper words, acts, relations in Actuality; the hated, despised, alien, barbaric in politics; improper topics, forbidden works, low-grade jobs in Existence. Yet for each mode, nothing should be alien, though some things are better, more open, than others. This would suggest that all these rejections turn the relatively undesirable into an absolutely undesirable. Freud, though, is suggesting that there is in the taboo an inhibition against a strong desire. Might not one say that we have a strong desire to make a relative into an absolute in one way, but that it is turned into an absolute in another way? Thus, the forceful, this-worldly man is a poor vehicle through which to get to the divine, but one might erect him into a semi-god or make him into a leader. In response to this one might turn around and deny such a being any right or dignity altogether, take him to be an "anti-Christ."

The incest taboo, on such an account, would be the result first of an effort to act sexually, and thus assertively and definitively, with respect to those with whom it is not for the society's peace very desirable to so act. Such acts are not in themselves entirely undesirable; but the taboo defines them to be entirely undesirable. The fighting against the taboo is in effect a violent reassertion of the right of the act to a proper status, to be, e.g., a genuine sexual act having the same ultimate intent as any other—the penetration to the Actual.

It is harder to reach the same goal in the tabooed form than in others. This does not mean that a taboo is actually a poor symbol in and of itself, but only that it has proved to be so for the people in some historic setting. Therefore the incest taboo will vary in content from place to place.

There seems to be a constant taboo against mother-son relations. Is this not due to the fact that the mother is a minority person? The minority person, though freer to see the ultimate than others, insists on bringing the children up more strictly, so as to make them conform to the conventions that prevail. The mother wants the child to belong to a world outside her, even while she clings to him, and it is she who insists on the taboo, rather than her husband—for he might no longer be alive, or not know—and rather than the son, who has to be disciplined.

Hegel criticizes mathematics for having an external way of proving; it does not have a self-development as (so he thinks) philosophy has. He rightly objects to using mathematics as a model for philosophy, but the reason he is right is different from the reason he assumes. It is not that philosophy is self-developing and mathematics is not, but that the procedure of mathematics is appropriate to the mode of the Ideal, and philosophy is appropriate primarily to the Actual. The knowledge of philosophy is categorial; the knowledge of mathematics is of a different sort, involving as it does the dissection of the Ideal. Mathematics is analysis, the providing of determinations in an initial possibility, the filling out of it, the very thing that Hegel thinks is characteristic of the expression of Being. It is mind coming out of itself, the general making itself particularized by a plurality of items, proof being but the external re-presentation of the initial adventure freed from the act of particularization. (A proof stays with the exteriorized items and gives them a kind of unity; it reintroduces the original general, but as made subservient to the items which it is uniting and justifying, in the sense that it allows them to remain what they had been exteriorized to be. This of course is proof after the fact, the proof for communication.) Philosophy lives with the external items, particularly the modes, and sees them in their proper relationship to one another. Neither way of proceeding is to give way to the other; each has its own proper province, and should remain in it.

Hegel becomes intoxicated with philosophy, and thus is strong in his rejection of substitutes. He is weak in not seeing the strength of other methods for other purposes. His method is in fact mathematical, for having achieved the Nothing he then proceeds to find determinations within it. He fractionates it to make it more and more articulate; the Nothing is for him what the Ideal is for the mathematician. A self-enclosed philosophic method would have proceeded from the Actual or the knowledge of it. If the Absolute were an Actuality and we accepted the Hegelian idea of self-consciousness, we would have to say that the knowledge is an attenuated form of the Actual and was known only because knowledge is a form of being. Since Hegel is an Idealist, he necessarily deals with the real as though it were only the Ideal. He does this most evidently when he leaves the positive or immediate behind, to deal with expressions of it. It is as if one said there was the Ideal simply, then recognized that this Ideal had to be divisible, and then proceeded with the division as a continuation of the process of recognizing the divisible. To see that it is divisible is to have divided it off from itself as possible, and to have begun to divide it within itself.

How do the divisions begin? The answer would seem to have been given by Plotinus, and should proceed somewhat along the lines of Plato's definition by division. We ought to begin with the One and then have this subdivide into a pair, and each of these into pairs and so on until we come to a domain where all of them are pulverized. This is raw nature, having over against it the limits of thought. Or better, the end should come when the subdivisions are A] irreducible because infinitesimal, as in Existence; B] irreducible because individual, as in Actuality; C] irreducible because simple unity, as in God; and D] irreducible because they are ultimate species, as in the Ideal.

D is already reached in A, B, and C, and further dialectical activity must either deal with A, B, C in their own realms, or must concern itself with D, breaking this up once more into an A, B, C, and D. In the last case, A, B, C will have the irreducibility, not of the basic modes of being, but of specialized forms of these. Once we have the idea of Existence, for example, the divisions of the Ideal which we can then institute will relate not to the mere having of Existence as a domain with infinitesimals, but to categorial features of that Existence, such as space, time, dynamics. And once we have divided these off, the remaining D will be subdivided into subdivisions of space, time, dynamics, and so on and on, until we do in fact come to an ultimate species. This is perhaps man and correlative realities—animal and thing, society and state, individuals and representatives.

Hegel misconstrued the nature of mathematics, identifying it with the textbook methods by which it is communicated, and because he muddled together two ideas of negation—a vertical one going from substance to subject, and a horizontal one going from subject to subject. Strictly speaking, the second is not possible for him. All negation must be a moving away, a speciation, and thus requires a continual process of movement from substance until we come to an ultimate set of species. The pluralization is the result of a falling or moving away. Nature or Existence is at the furthest remove.

If one takes the four modes as basic, one can nevertheless look at the Ideal as something to be dealt with "mathematically" in an ultimate sense and thereupon can engage in this Hegelian process. This would seem to allow somewhat analogous activities with respect to the other modes, for they all answer to one another's distinctions. This means that when one (for example) considers seriously the nature of Existence he will have to solidify the ultimate divisions of it in such a way as to mount the steps of the dialectic to recover the Ideal. He will also have to engage in somewhat analogous feats for Existence, to enable it to match the other modes.

January 23

Memory involves a reference to the past; recollection involves a reconstituting of the past on the basis of present evidence. Memory need not actually terminate in an object; still it can be said to be reliable or true if the reference it makes is one which allows determinate content to have objective status. Recollection need not actually reach an object; still it can be said to be accurate or true if what it abstracts from the present or reconstructs from evidence in the present can provide an antecedent from which the present can be obtained by following the paths of natural and historical processes. Why not say the same thing about history; why not view it as a kind of scientifically produced recollection or "memory"? Is it because one wants to be able to have a base for comparing the past and the present in terms of value?

Memory, recollection, and comparison all involve the subjectification of present content; they are able to content themselves with what may be only a mental construction because the material with which they begin in the present is already subjective. The remembered or recollected event is not treated as on a par with something we confront, but with something as known, despite the fact that the known and the remembered are oriented outside themselves in a determinate sphere. In history, though, we are concerned with what occurs apart from our own experience. We may experience and know this material; our knowledge here is not about the content we have, but about the reality in which that content is ingredient.

A reference to an objective past can be avoided only if we deny the need to make comparisons, the need to have both past and present on a level, and the need to deal with the present as an objective, de-personalized reality. But to get objectivity for the past we will need something which will hold the past over against the present. This can apparently be either the future, or some being outside present, past, and future. But it cannot be the future, for this serves to give rationality, a goal, an end to history.

God is the being who gives an objective de-personalized reality to the past, so that all of it is in or for Him. We presuppose God when we speak of truth in history; if we know that He exists we have a warrant for saying that historical assertions can be true; if we do not know that He exists, we make a "practical" rather than a theoretical judgment—a practical judgment being one which serves to organize and in general alter a given content. (A theoretical judgment provides the categories in terms of which we may know it.) So far as a theoretical judgment alters the content of knowledge, it is in fact a practical judgment, restricted merely in the content to which it applies and the nature of its result. But also if it be the case that the organization of knowledge is a theoretical act on the part of reason, the supposed practical reason is also theoretical, having as its content the reality in an ontological rather than an epistemological or phenomenological role. Consequently, we have a theoretical use of God in history as giving an ontological grounding to it; if we had just wanted to have God function as a cognitive principle we would have used Him "theoretically" in a narrow way. But from the standpoint of an ontology, a theoretical use of anything in this narrow way is in fact a practical use of reason.

If it be said that we cannot know God as a consequence of the dialectic of the *Modes* or in any other way, the use of God in history would still be significant as a "theoretical" principle for organizing the past and giving it objectivity. But here we would have no warrant that God existed outside the use here made of Him. And this perhaps is what Kant had in mind: we call those principles or ideas practical for which we have no other warrant except that they organize a particular material. But what organizes a particular material may have another role to play with respect to other material. When having such another role to play, the principle which is used as practical in one sphere would be theoretical in another. If, in short, God is "practical" for history he is "theoretical" for knowledge; if "practical" for knowledge, he is "theoretical" for history. (Here we use "practical" and "theoretical" in a somewhat different sense than before, for we now use them to mean merely that which is meaningful with respect to a given subject matter. In this sense, reason is theoretical in knowledge if practical in ethics, and practical in knowledge if theoretical in ethics.)

Another way of approaching this matter is to say that both "theoretical" and "practical" reason can be viewed as theoretical, or as practical. They are the first in the sense that they are transcendental organizing principles for what we know; they are the second in the sense that they are realized in their activity of organization and are dealt with as though they had no application elsewhere.

January 24

Kenneth M. Stampp's *The Causes of the Civil War* has the following suggested causes strewn through the book: economic (tariffs, subsidies, appropriations); states' rights; slavery; expansion; abolitionism and other moral reforms; fear of slave rebellion; desire for internal union; agricultural culture and economy; desire for independence; slave power; violation of southern rights; fear of destruction of liberty; control of policies of the Federal Government; formation of aristocracy; minority control; loss of traditional controls over liberty; capitalism; fear of miscegenation and social order; refusal to compromise; the cause of freedom; democratic theory; conspiracy; lust of power; wickedness and foolishness of men; pride; class distinctions; conflict of different ideas of good (i.e., slavery good, not evil); constitutional interpretations; necessary expansion of established power; intelligence versus ignorance; history of wrongs (imprisonment of Negro seamen, burning of mails, etc); institution of slavery; sectionalism; different economies; different ideology and language, etc.; mutual contempt; political ambition; unjust and unequal laws, felt and real; need to escape from injury and strife; disequilibrium between otherwise equal sides; denial of property and property rights; states' rights and nationalism; the preservation of the union; the ascendancy of a sectional party; natural versus positive law; aggrandisement; southern wealth and northern profits; different systems of production; slave versus free farming; debtor versus dear money class; monopoly versus free enterprise; selfishness versus altruism; grievances; events at Sumter; desire for redress; emotion; overbold leadership; idea of sin; defense of status quo; basic conflicts on all sides; ill will; deliberate wrong doing; fear; class distinctions versus equality;

servile versus voluntary labor; divine justice; expansion versus restriction or confinement; tryanny versus democracy; majority rule and minority rights; geography; rivalry; personality and psychological factors; right and rights; romanticism and realism; culture and industry; racial differences; feudalism and modernism; different kinds of masses.

These evidently overlap in many ways. Is it possible to make a single systematic map which will include them all and perhaps make evident the causes of war and eventually the causes of history? Here is a tentative beginning: Each mode can be differently understood or it can be differently divided in intent or fact amongst the factions; it can also be specified in divergent and even opposing ways; and it can save the common specifications divided differently in intent or fact.

1] Existence can be interpreted as a source of destruction, and there is a fear of disequilibrium and failure from it. It can be divided into different kinds of institutions, modes of expressing and using power, ways of increasing power, controlling and using power. It can be interpreted as political power of diverse kinds such as wealth versus profits, minority and majority. It can be distributed in economic ways by virtue of tariffs, subsidies, appropriations.

2] Actuality as individualized or in groups can be interpreted as essentially equal or caste, aristocracy or democracy, psychologically and personally diverse. The Actuality may be diversely distributed in population, geography, intelligence. It can be specified as a kind of freedom for some or all; fear of miscegenation; feudalism versus modernism; and the specifications can be diversely distributed under pride, foolishness, lust for power; wickedness, intransigence, refusal to compromise; emotionalism; contempt; conspiracy.

3] The Ideal can be interpreted as a present or future good pursued selfishly or altruistically; different meanings of freedom; evil and worth of slavery. There can be different distributions, so that we have a defense of the part and of the whole; rights and right; property rights versus human rights; tyranny versus democracy; status quo. It can be specified as an ideology, expressed in language, culture, romanticism versus realism, constitutional interpretations, natural and positive law. And the specifications can be distributed into states' and national rights; right of self-determination and freedom; majority and minority.

4] God can be subject to different interpretations, such as mercy and justice; He can be distributed in different ways, expressing His justice, and understanding of sin; He can be quoted differently and thus differently specified, and there can be a different distribution of the specifications in the shape of slogans.

The above must still be reduced to a simpler set; also some of the items must be shifted from one class to another. The classifications too are not altogether satisfactory.

Men or groups can be said to diverge with respect to the four modes in   A] attitude,   B] specification,   C] use. The first gives us an evaluation, the second a plan of action, and the third an actual course of action. In addition, they can relate themselves to the diverse attitudes, specifications and use of others   A] as competitors,   B] as in conflict, C] as coordinate,   D] as dominant and recessive,   E] as rejective. A allows for a continuation without end; B requires a terminus but not necessarily in something else; C allows for peace; D may be stable, and E, unless it be a way of expressing satisfaction with one's own status and is reciprocated (thus allowing it to fall under the previous cases), is a basic source of radical oppositionality.

Consequently, we should deal with attitudes and specifications; and we should use those which others reject because they feel they are wrong, or (if they involve actions on the part of others) which are felt as rejections—and thus if there be attitudes, specifications, and uses which are felt by one or both sides to be rejective by the other.

1] Existence: Rejective attitudes: threat of power as is and as promised. Specifications in the form of wealth or profits, majority or minority, tariffs, subsidies, appropriations. Rejective uses: actual abuses suffered, denial of rights, freedom, the power of government, conspiracies.
2] Actuality: Rejective attitudes: superiority in race, background, personality, ancestry, mode of life. Specifications: intelligence, degree of freedom, purity. Rejective uses: distribution in population, geography, pride, foolishness, lust for power, wickedness, emotionalism.
3] Ideal: Rejective attitudes: selfishness, meanings of freedom, attitude toward enslavement. Specifications: right of part and whole (rights and right), property and human rights, tyranny and democracy, ancient and modern ways, ideology. Rejective uses: language, culture, romanticism, realism, natural and positive law, self-determination and freedom, majority and minority.
4] God: Rejective attitudes: atheism and belief; mercy and justice. Specifications: rituals, virtues, and sins. Rejective uses: raids, movements, fanaticism, reform.
These are better than the previous listings, but still fall short. Rejective

attitudes are not causes until accepted as such, which is to say it must be the felt rejection in the attitudes, the specifications, and the uses of others, which make one antagonistic. This does not take care of the cases where there is a desire for war on the part of a rejecting group, which feels no resentment at being rejected. Here war is thought to be a good for one who is superior and thinks he ought to rule. (This case though could be brought under that of a rejection of what is felt to be an acceptance of what ought not to be.)

We have wars then which are the outcome of a response to a felt rejection, and wars which are the outcome of an implied rejection (by an acceptance of a false status). Both can be said to be the outcome of a supposition that others are opposed to and would unnecessarily limit (either by continuing the status quo, reducing the present position, or restricting the advance) the position or role of oneself with respect to *power* (physical, political, economic), *status* (native, social, freedom, virtue); an *objective* (ethical, political method, social rights, culture); a *commitment* (belief, mercy, justice, ritual, duty). Where these fail to explain, recourse is had to the irrationality of man, the defect of a system, the will of God, or the irrationality of history and the universe —i.e., defects in Actuality, Ideal, God, and Existence.

We have then an unnecessary limitation being imposed in fact or supposition by others (deliberately or even accidentally) on the proper achievement of power, status, objective, or obligation. More briefly: a felt need to overcome an unnecessary limitation on one's supposed proper power, status, objective, or commitment. In the end, power, objective, and commitment are for status. We have then the conflict arising because there is a felt need on the part of one or both to overcome an unnecessary limitation of a supposed proper status. The others may merely be in the way, or they may offer a threat by their existence, practices, tendency, or ideology, etc. The felt need may be self-originating or a reflex to a threat. The very desire for war may be thought of as showing the right to wage it. The status is not necessarily relative to other groups but may be absolute with respect to what man is.

Status is defined by the objective, promoted by power, and justified by the commitment. It tells us what Actuality is supposed to be. The war then is a struggle to be what one thinks one (one's group) ought to be, i.e., what it *in principle* is, and eventually what mankind in principle is.

War to the death is not so much then a destruction of others, but an effort to overcome the obstacles which prevent oneself and thus the best in mankind from being what it ought to be, has a right to be, is justified in being, and should have the power to continue to be. No matter how unprovoked or how concerned with expansion and selfish ends, it is always for the sake of one's rights; it is an act of self-defense even when self-initiated. One's need to expand makes a right to expand, and this in turn makes the act of expansion accompanied by war a defense, in fact or in promise, on behalf of one's population (thought to have a right to be in the face of all obstacles).

If we can make this reduction in history, with respect to Actuality, can we not do the same for the other modes? The ultimate rationale must be given by the Ideal as encompassing all mankind as the epitomization of all Actuality, and then derivatively as encompassing this or that subdivision of mankind as representative of mankind. It is an Ideal which encompasses peace, health, prosperity, the arts and the sciences —in short, civilization. The ultimate *objectivity* is to be defined by God as concerned with all history; as *encompassing,* it is coordinated and interrelated by the Ideal; the ultimate *vitality* of history is defined by Existence as the extension of mankind.

January 25

The Kantian schematism exhibits a formal structure on the one side and an applicable one on the other. This is analogous to Mc-Taggart's (*a*) and (*b*) series. If the two are thought to be entirely alien we will have to relate them arbitrarily—and from a third position which we have not acknowledged. If the two are thought to be pertinent then a schematism has in principle been accepted for them. McTaggart overlooks the fact that the (*a*) series is in fact the (*b*) series transposed, or the (*b*) series is oriented toward a world, in contrast with the (*a*) series which is held apart from it. His (*c*) series, and the schematism of Kant, are but new ways of presenting the problem of essence and existence which has been exploited by Aquinas: the difference between the idea of a sphere and the idea of a balloon is that the idea of a sphere is purely formal, whereas the balloon, though merely conceptual, has an orientating factor, the "material" of the balloon as part of its meaning.

The other side of the schematism, the "balloon" or the applicable mathematics itself, can be viewed as having a schematism, for the balloon as idea is distinct from the balloon in fact. When the balloon as idea is thought of as true it is part of a referential act of knowledge, which is a schema in a sense analogous to Kant's.

Northrop in his doctrine of correlation and Tillich in his acceptance of any entity as a possible symbol for God suppose that the world of the senses or of nature is entirely sundered from that of the conceptual. They deny the reality of a "schema" which has an intrinsic correlation built in the very nature of concepts, God, senses, experience, and objects. They supposed that all things are equally indifferent. For Northrop, one sense datum should be as good as another as a correlative for his constructs; for Tillich, Christ should be an arbitrarily chosen object (like a Hebrew prophet) having no nature making him worthy of selection. But Catholicism, with its doctrine of the Virgin Birth, knows that the humanity of Christ must be different from any other in the sense that it is a specially chosen receptacle. Or more generally, the symbols which are appropriate for reaching God are schematically related to Him. There is no need of course for the two sides of a schema to be alike in quality or even relationship; all one needs to recognize is that they are the extremes of a basic kind of reality, terminal points of a "space" capable of having an existence apart from the "space." Also, when one starts with one side of the "space," uses one of the factors, the formal or the applicable as primary, the other must be a locus for or an abstraction from it.

In history there is a juncture of the formal and the dynamic in the present. The present can be viewed as a kind of schema for both. The passage of time is the becoming past of the formal and the moving forward to the future of the dynamic. From the perspective of God the entire past formal reality is spread out; He sees time as "spatialized" in Bergson's sense, but we live through it as pure durée. But the present itself is the juncture of these two, not as though they were prior to it, but as consequences of it, as results of the dissolution of the present. The very being of the present is expressible as the entire formality of the past oriented in this zero moment, or as the entire dynamics of the oncoming future beginning in this zero moment. Or conversely, the present is the entire formal past correlative with the dynamics; it is the juncture of a cosmic formality with a cosmic dynamics which dissolves as soon as achieved.

If we start with experience we move to ontology by analyzing out the ultimate units which made for the experiential totality. But we could have gone to cosmology instead; when we do, instead of analyzing out, holding the ultimate elements apart, we merely terminate in them, see them as the bearers of relations in interplay, and then move from this to ontology by recognizing the internally determined qualities of the termini and the properties they possess in and of themselves. We can do the same thing for the derivative cosmological enterprises, such as history, by recognizing the terminal elements (which are its constituents and have a shape which is other than what they have as independent entities), and then going on to see what they are as apart from the history.

Further analogues are that art as the unity of Actuality and Existence in experience requires the unifying work of an actual maker. He must be replaced by God or the Ideal to enable the art to have a permanence greater than what he can give it, and to enable it to *be* a work of art, and thus comparable with others.

Politics, actions, and churches are like history. This means that the combinations of Actuality and Ideal, Actuality and God, must have Actuality or some other mode as a unifying power. Thus the political whole may be said to be the result of Actuality, as organization unifying individuals, and the Ideal; or individuals unifying organizations and the Ideal; or God or the Ideal, or Existence unifying either individuals or organizations with the Ideal. Different theories of politics will follow from different acceptances; it has been my position that the unity of Ideal with Actuality is social. Consequently, I ought also to hold that God or the Ideal replaces the social power of unification, so as to enable individuals with rights (divinely or rationally warranted), and the Ideal, to have pertinence in a natural mythos or outcome (rationally or divinely warranted).

The churches are the product of a unification of Actuality and God by means of men (religious leaders), or God (the invisible church). These unifications are replaced by either the Ideal or Existence so as to enable the church to be valuable to men (as something rational and powerful) or to be the tabernacle of God (as something appropriate or factual).

The unity of Actuality with Actuality through action, is evidently Existence. It can be replaced by either the Ideal or God so as to enable the action to be intelligible or ultimately warranted.

One can say that in Hegel the thesis and antithesis are, from the start, already related in a tenuous way, and that the progress of the dialectic is the intensification of the relation until it precipitates out as the synthetic unity of these components—itself but a term in a wider whole. On this view the progress of the dialectic is the gradual discovery of the largest medium in which terms are to be found. It would mean that the movement from thesis to antithesis is in fact but the discovery of the other component which reveals that we live in the medium between them. The dialectic would then come to an end when we had embraced the entire cosmos.

January 26

Cosmology, strictly speaking, involves all the modes and in a neutral way. This involves the use of all four constants; the dot, comma, therefore, and implication, answering to the activity characteristic of God, Actuality, Existence, and Ideality. When we isolate two of the modes in history, politics, religion (in each case one of these is Actuality), we make use of only two constants. History requires the use of the dot and the therefore; it is the domain in which contingent occurrences are joined with a progressive production of occurrences. Politics requires the use of the dot and the implication; it is the domain in which contingent occurrences are joined with the demands of an ultimate ideology and final value for society. Institutionalized religion requires the use of the comma and the dot; there is a juncture here of the contingent and the necessary or prescriptive. The remaining combinations of comma and therefore, comma and implication, therefore and ideality, relate evidently to combinations of God and Existence, God and Ideality, and Existence and Ideality. The first two relate to theocentric views of the cosmos and ideals—i.e. to a divinely governed world and to providence; the third relates to a teleological view of the course of the world as exploited by Kant in the *Critique of Judgment*.

The combinations produced by the interplay of modes in cosmology are evidently derivative. The cosmological universe seems to have no intrinsic power of its own; it is a screen thrown across the emptiness between the modes to constitute a complex product. It would seem not to be a subject for study except in a descriptive way, though the elements which compose it and the way in which they interplay can be analyzed. This would seem to be in consonance with Whitehead's insight in *Process and Reality*. When we take this approach, the modes as altered in their interrelationship are but appearances of themselves as they truly are—distinct modes having beings of their own. But since the modes do need one another in order to truly be, and this need requires that they be in interplay, there should be a minimal cosmological status which each one has, and this should be as real as the ontological status. The cos-

mology will have a kind of substantiality, a kind of being which requires
one to take the constants of interplay as having being together, and
thereby requiring that the terminal items in the ontology be not as
neatly unified as a pure ontology would seem to require. They would be
basic and unified and concrete, in a process of recovering themselves as
unities at every moment, at the same time that the different constants are
spreading out and merging into one another. So far as the constants
function separately, the modes themselves become interfused. The
process of cosmology would seem to be the vibrating interchange of
focus and merging on the part of the modes and on the part of the
constants of togetherness, in reciprocal relation.

When we turn to particular disciplines such as history, it would
seem even more evident that there must be some kind of substantiality
provided by the constants. Though one can say that history is a contingent outcome, one must also recognize that it has its own causality,
or productivity. If we go this far we must recognize that the constants
themselves are not contingent products, but are essential to the being
of the modes. Consequently, the being of history, taken merely as the
locus of the constants, will have a kind of substantiality. Combining
this consideration with that which recognizes that   A] the characteristics of the components of history are different from what they were
apart from it, and   B] that these characteristics are real, it follows that
the juncture of the two constants permits of the distinction of the
constituents of history, and that the merging of those constituents to
constitute a content of history requires that they be governed both by a
contingent and a productive mode of being together. The contingent
will be integral to the content obtained by merging the modes of Actuality and Existence in history, but the productive will have a kind of
prescriptive function for that contingency. It will function as the demand
that there be occurrences in history. The merging of the modes in history
will occur as a contingency having various degrees and involving them
in one another with new features, and will be related by the therefore
as merely two coordinated items which define a productivity (and conversely by a productivity which requires that the two be coordinate).

The dot for history is a merging of two items with respect to a
single prescriptive therefore; but the modes which are in history merge
in different ways with respect to all three constants together, partly
because in history we do not have pure modes or sheer neutrality, but
only limited and specialized forms of the modes biased toward mankind;
partly because the modes do not act in cosmology whereas there is real

interplay in history; and partly because each of the ways in which the items are together in cosmology is on a footing with the others, whereas in history we have the two modes in interplay thereby stressing the dot, a genuine merging. The dot is real. The merging is genuine and transformative of the modes which are merged, but only for that moment where they are interplaying. Consequently the nature of the result, rooted as it is in something like the power of an Actuality (for this has a contingent unity), will be lost unless it be recovered by some other power.

Actualities remember, Existence is coherent, Ideality is law-imposing, but God has the unified power to take the dismembered components of the historical occurrence and spread them over one another. It takes God to see the Existence, which has escaped from history, to be an historically pertinent existence; He does this by making Actuality serve as the unifying essence for that Existence. He also sees that the factualities of the past are historically pertinent; He does this by making Existence serve as the field in which those Actualities are displayed. The factualities, though they are less than the Actual, and are indeed possibility made determinate, are characterizable as derivatives from Actuality rather than as ideal entities, by virtue of the fact that they do demand and through God do get an appropriate Existence enabling them to be related to one another as the actualities in fact are. They are, though, in a static temporal order rather than in a moving one, due to the fact that the Existence given them is a God-derived one and thus not a genuine Existence as a vital element. The Existence of the past is in fact nothing more than that modicum of Existence which was in the present historic moment, spread out over the entire past, just as the historical meaning of Existence is acquired from the meaning of Actuality here and now in the present.

The content of history, both past and future, must change at every moment. But since mankind is more or less constant in range and power as well as meaning, this has little effect. The Existence which is made use of today is somewhat like that used yesterday; the mankind which today defines the future of history is somewhat like that of yesterday. If there be signal crises they are more evident in the use of mankind to define the historically relevant existent, telling it where and how it should go. This historically relevant Existence is not controlled, however, and the next moment of history involves the interplay of Actuality as a self-constituted reality (or as ontologically grounded) with its modicum of Existence newly united with Existence itself. But the interplay must work through the barrier of the meaning of Actuality imposed by God on Existence. In short, ontological Actuality interplays with ontological Existence at the next moment, but only across the barrier of a prior determination of Existence by God as being historically relevant. God therefore makes it possible for history to be something more than a freshly derived product from ontological beings; he forces the Actuality to act with respect to a tinged Existence, and Existence to be ordered with respect to the Actuality of the moment before. His "foresight" and "precognition" is but the knowledge of the conditions to which Existence and Actuality are subject. But each of these has the power to act in ways which neither He nor they can prescribe.

If we keep mankind steady in meaning or nature, then the changes which result in history must be attributed to Existence as outside the control of God; if we keep Existence steady in meaning or nature, then the changes in history must be attributed to mankind as irrational and thus as outside the control by God. If we think of history as predictive, then we see the God-determined future to be one which is prescriptive of both the actualities and Existence. If we look at the present as that which had been previsioned, we can see history to be autonomous (for the previsioning depends on Existence having an historically relevant nature), and to be the realization of the previsioned future, demarcated, divided, and specialized.

God gives objectivity to the past, makes the future historically relevant, and makes the present historical occurrence autonomous. It is He who guarantees that there is no need for the constituents to spring out from their ontological base and make a new moment of history; they do work as ontological beings, but within a frame which defines their work to be historical; they work over against the imposed meaning of mankind which God derived from the present moment, and which He extended to the escaped Existence (thereby providing it with an "historic" essence).

If we look at the other disciplines in a similar way, we must say that it is the function of God to make politics substantival by imposing a meaning on the Ideal as reflecting the achievements of the present. (This is partly done by the planning and ideology of the political organization; God carries this out further.) And when we come to religion, it will be necessary to invoke not God but Existence to do for dissolved components what He did for Actuality and Existence. However, there is also another mode which is in operation in these enterprises. History, e.g., makes use not only of God but of the Ideal; this means that the divinely sustained past, made up of factuality and a modicum of Existence, is given a law-abiding nature by Ideality, and that the future is given a rationale, a meaning in terms of which occurrences-to-be are to be understood.

January 28

Why must Existence be qualified by God? This question breaks up into a number of queries. A] Is it so qualified? B] Must it be so qualified? c] Can it be qualified by something other than God? D] If God qualifies Existence must there not be analogous acts with respect to Existence (for the past and art), with respect to the Ideal (for politics and ethics), and with respect to God (for religion)?

A and B. Were Existence not qualified so as to become historically pertinent, men would have to struggle with raw Existence at every moment. But the beings with which men struggle are limited objects in the immediate environment, serving as primary loci for part of Existence. These objects are outside the governance of the political system or of mankind as an integrated whole; they are either commonsensical or natural, but in all cases are potentially part of the whole of mankind. The question then is whether what is potentially part of mankind need be historically pertinent. The potential would not be historically pertinent if it had no other role but that of being integrated into mankind; but Existence serves to display it, make mankind have an extension. Because the potential is integral to a larger Existence, one must take it to be historical rather than merely social or political.

c. Would it be possible to make Existence historically potential by viewing it as the projection of mankind? After all, men do expect, anticipate, and plan; their institutions and habits guarantee that they will continue to work on Existence in the ways they did before. Once upon a time men were not historical, not merely in the sense that they stood outside the realm of Existence (as they do at every moment in fact), but in the sense that they faced an Existence which was raw and unqualified. The unqualified Existence which they once faced was slowly, over the years, qualified in a limited way. When they first entered into history men consequently could forge something like an historic moment out of Existence by dealing with only a restricted environmental portion of it —say that of surrounding nature—and then only as quite clearly demarcated. Did men do this today, they would not have a history of mankind in a cosmos, but only mankind in nature, and then only so far as men were occupied with the achievement of a certain outcome. But is there not a history of mankind's neglect of its opportunities? Must we not say that even when men were at their most primitive they were historic beings who somewhat adventitiously interplayed with Existence? That Existence had to be qualified as historically pertinent if men were to make it part of history in the course of their daily lives (and thus without retreating back into their ontological selves). There is a history of mankind even for the most primitive and indolent, due to the fact that they face and must interplay with a qualified portion of Existence, an Existence whose nature is affected by the nature of mankind at a previous moment, whether or not men pay attention to this fact, and whether or not they have institutions which allow them to utilize it effectively.

But then must not one make reference to the Ideal as that which also qualifies Existence? After all, a nature is a specialized form of an Ideal. The meaning which God imposes could be conceived of as being imposed by the Ideal itself, and as being qualified by Existence when thus imposed. This would require one to take a teleological rationalistic view of history. There is some truth in this position, as is evident from the fact that the Ideal does have a role to play in history alongside of God. But it cannot provide a power of union. Its imposition of the specialized form of the present meaning on Existence does not mean that Existence will be receptive to it, and therefore it cannot be said to be the meaning which Existence will have for mankind at the next moment.

Might not men, facing their own ideals, specialize them in the shape of particular limited objectives, the meanings of which are germane at the next moment, and act on Existence in the light of these conditions? If we take this position we in effect deny that men are historical every moment. Let this be assumed. Historically pertinent men will then be faced with a raw Existence, and there would have to be a radical transformation of the latter. But it would be better to recognize that both men and Existence are potentially historical.

D. If God qualifies Existence in such a way as to make the meaning integral to the portion of it that is ready for history, must He not do a similar thing for the past, endowing the facts with historical pertinence at the same time that He gives Existence an historical use there? This would seem to be the case. Must He do a similar thing in art? No, for here man is the being who qualifies what is to be used by history the next moment.

There should be something analogous in connection with politics, and with institutionalized religion. There should be a "rationalizing" of Actualities and an "actualizing" of political ideals performed by God and Existence; also there should be a "divinizing of actualities and an "actualizing" of the divine performed by Existence and the Ideal. This is true only on the supposition that there is a dissolution of the juncture of actualities and Ideal in politics, and of actualities and God in religion. This need not be the case. The imposition of the Ideal on actualities, if met by actualities with a reciprocal adoption, can persist. Similarly the imposition of God on religious institutions may be met by those institutions in a way which will not require dissolution from moment to moment. There is no similar power on the part of actualities to make their being felt on Existence and no reciprocal reception of Existence by them, which guarantees that the two will remain together in history. Put another way, while there is a contingent juncture in all three cases, in the case of politics and religion there is also a juncture which is prescriptively rational in the first case and prescriptively identifying in the second.

Is it necessary that what a speculative reason discovers be real? If not, the speculative outcome would be irrelevant. But it still might be practically relevant, something one ought to take as a regulative principle, a guide, an indication of what one ought to accept in order to live a coherent life, etc.—so a Kantian argument might run. But this view supposes that reason in its speculative or theoretical employment is not practical, that it is not another way in which one is engaged in making what is outside and Ideal relevant to what is here and now.

The issue turns about the questions 1] as to whether this or that specialized version of the application of Ideals or reasons holds, 2] and whether the specialization does not qualify and alter the meaning. To the first question the answer must be that we do reason and thus do entertain the Ideal in another way than that in which we practically make use of it, even though the entertainment is a way of making use. To the second question a double answer can be given. Ideals are altered in all cases—that is what it means to have them be applicable. We also attend to them speculatively, and when we so master them, we know the real, though only in a highly speculative abstract form. They are so far unaltered. The more we interrelate them with one another, the more we bring them to bear on the content of daily experience, the more we make them fit one another and thereby alter both. But then can we say that the object of speculative reason is real? We can, provided that we see that an altered object, when brought into relation with experience or objects which we in fact encounter, adds details, determinateness. Need this be true? Might not what we have speculatively reached, though necessarily relevant to what is here and now, be not as we think it to be?

God does not appear in *propria persona,* but in the shape of sacramentals; the Ideal is faced as the Good or as Myth; Actuality appears in the guise of particular things; we see but aspects of Existence. Why believe that these, in and of themselves, have a being grasped through speculation? Is it not that we can sheer off the adventitious features and have a residuum left; is it not that we can analyze our experience and find termini; is it not that we men can identify ourselves as actualities and thus can find what else there is as Actuality's necessary correlate—and that these different methods all concur? We are still left with the question as to whether or not there are residua, termini, and correlates.

There must be a residuum if the encountered object is to be all that it is encountered to be, for we have sheared away only part. There must be termini to analysis, for we are ourselves precipitated out, and this involves a precipitation of the termini. There must be correlates to ourselves, for otherwise we would be complete, perfect, containing all within us. Our ontological demand for others must be met if we are to be. And we are.

January 31

If we begin with experience we occasionally find ourselves in focus as common-sense men involved with a segment of that experience in the shape of familiar objects. We then face a muddled counterpart of dynamic, valued ultimacy. If we isolate ourselves as mere actualities we subdivide that counterpart into three modes. If we hold on to a fragment of the muddle, stressing the dynamic interplay with common sense, we get history; if we insist on the value we get politics. The latter can be placed in history, just as the historic experience with Existence can be made part of the political whole determined by the interplay of actuality with value.

There is then a justification of history in experience, as well as in the need for man and Existence to achieve a satisfaction in a new way, particularly for man as a being who in fact is experiencing.

Man has ontological needs, but these satisfy him only as a mere representative of Actuality; as a concrete, substantial individual, he must achieve that satisfaction in his own name, and this requires him to find it in new types of situations, of which history offers one. History provides him with an opportunity to be satisfied, to achieve a satisfaction as a man who is both individual and commonsensical. History provides the individual with an Existence which allows him to be coordinate with his fellow man, and to have a new kind of efficacy and duration; Existence in turn acquires from man new termini, agencies, and causes.

For the individual, history is mankind epitomized. We can learn from history what man will do in response to an interplay with Existence, provided that   A] there are no accidents,   B] he remains somewhat as before,   C] Existence acts as it did before, and   D] we take account of the differences between ourselves now and before, to make possible an understanding of a transformation of the past into the future. From the standpoint of the Ideal it tells us what reason allows, or what is rational in the course of time; from the standpoint of God it tells us what the unity of man and Existence is like. When we see a man acting on a people, or two people in conflict, one of these must be viewed as the localization or transformation of Existence, acting on a representative of mankind.

We can take the hero to be Existence incarnate, or we can take him to be a representative of a people. He is the latter only if he succeeds in expressing the people or in making the people take the shape which he is assigning to it, by bringing into focus the myths, art, science, culture, and the like.

The question of the reality of experience is one with the question of the reality of appearances, and the reality of a cosmology, or of a history. We can say: A] that the appearances are unreal, in which case we deny all evidences,   B] that they are articulations of the real, in which case we have no primary concern for them in and of themselves, C] that they are the real in another guise, in which case we do not see how they really add anything to the nature of a being,   D] that they are expressions of the real, and once again we will have no basic philosophy for them,   E] that they are the real, and the substantial is a derivative from it, in any of the above four senses, but then we will have no right to say it is an appearance, for this presupposes the substantial, the persistent, the powerful, the terminal,   F] that they are realities in and of themselves, yet reducible to the ultimately real—a view I held in the past (but what then sustains them as realities in and of themselves?), G] that they have a being of their own which is correlate with the being of themselves as in and of themselves, so that the career of an entity will then consist in the adjustment of these two dimensions of itself. Only by keeping them in equilibrium will it then be able to be a unity.

The last position enables us to do justice to history, common sense, cosmology, as domains which have an integrity of their own. This they can have because there are not only the four modes, but a plurality in each of them. It is because men must satisfy themselves as individuals and as representatives of mankind, as well as in the form of representatives of Actuality as such, that these realms provide a content not to be found in sheer ontology or a purely neutral cosmology. Man brings into play his emotions and individual stresses, forcing the modes with which he interplays to be tainted by and biased toward man. Consequently, history and common sense reveal that the individual, as a representative of mankind, must adjust himself to his status as a representative of Actuality, and that only in this adjustment is he fully a man.

When we turn to perception, science, etc., ought we then to say that these constitute domains of their own, and that the basic fact is the adjustment of them and beings in and of themselves? We could. Ordinary experience is the outcome of that adjustment. This does not make experience a greater reality than the objects in and of themselves, or even greater than the objects of perception, science, etc. The adjustment of the two sides is one in which experience is dissolved just so far as we are in the realm of the modes; it is one in which the experience becomes the *tertium quid* only so far as there is, while we have both sides, a stress on man and his activities. If we want to make an adjustment of science, perception, etc., with what is in and of itself—and this apparently would be Actualities in their substantiality as constituting a single domain of interlocked beings, perhaps within the adopted field of space, time, and dynamics—we must recognize that science, perception, etc., have no power of their own. Once we recognize that actualities in their plurality have a degenerate way of being together inside the mode of Actuality, we are able to look at science, perception, etc., as also degenerate ways of having actualities together, in a way which is correlative with the mode of togetherness offered by common sense. But then the power of their unification must lie outside both of them in a being capable of having a stronger mode of togetherness—e.g., a man in his role of a representative of Actuality. The union of the derivatives from common sense is then to be achieved by recognizing the being in which they are unified to be a representative, and thus to be Actuality as such rather than this or that actuality or set of them.

Common sense is the togetherness of all the modes as sheerly contingently there, and as biased toward man. It can be expanded to give us experience in its broadest and most inclusive sense as involving all the modes, and then freed from the bias toward man, to yield a cosmology. The cosmology is an existential kind of a togetherness of the modes—it is compulsive. Nature would seem to be the togetherness which is merely contingent; system would seem to be that which is implicative; the ontological would seem to be that which is purely prescriptive. Cosmology must be reconciled with the other three ways of being together.

Each mode is a solidification which allows all four ways of being together to have a minimal being, each with its own rationale. The more solidity the togethernesses acquire the more do the modes themselves become attenuated. We can then speak of the rhythm of the modes, as they internally move toward being fully solidified, to being wholly attenuated, and back again (cf. Empedocles).

If God be thought to be essentially the being who provides the comma, we can speak of Him as providing a way in which the other three kinds of togetherness (dot, implication, therefore) are adjusted to one another in each mode. Each mode offers a peculiar unity of four ways of reconciling nature, cosmology, etc. In the realm of Actuality, which would be primarily the locus of a dot, we would have all four ways in which nature, cosmology, etc., interplay, interrelated by virtue of a dot, which is to say contingently. Each kind of interplay forces Actuality to do what it can to make a unity of that interplay with the others.

In history we have a similar situation, except that we here are primarily concerned with only two modes. These two modes are together in a double way, and they are reconcilable in a number of places. If reconciled in the realm of Actuality they are so contingently. If reconciled in Existence, they are so over the course of a new kind of time and compulsion in which the contingent actualities and the dynamic extension of Existence in history are dynamically connected. If reconciled in God, they are made subject to a prescribing unity in which each part is modified in accordance with the demand, by that unity, that each have an equal value; if in the Ideal, they will be reconciled as elements making a rational whole—causes and causation ending in intelligible processes productive of a desirable end.

The problem then of the reality of history comes down to the recognition that it has the being of a fragment of experience or of a cosmology, and that this, when dealt with by itself or as made to include the rest of experience or cosmology, can be said to require its components to be reconciled in other ways as well. (It is not, then, that history must be shown to be reconciled with the real, but that history is but one mode of uniting components.) The merely ontological is either each mode taken severally or is the modes as merely separated by a comma, i.e., from the standpoint of God. Consequently, there is no need to reduce history, or other divisions of cosmology, or cosmology itself (or nature or system) to the ontological. The ontological is but one facet itself, and the final reconciliation is the having of the ontological on a footing with the cosmological, etc., in each of the modes. So far as our concern is with the mode of Actuality, primarily, we would have to say that we here have a contingent juncture of cosmology, etc., with ontology, or in the more limited case of history, of representative man with representatives of Actuality and Existence. We tend to take the ontological as basic, for we treat the comma as though it were not possessed of any nature of its own. But it has a minimal being. So far as this is true, what it presents—beings as separate—needs to be interrelated with those very beings in other kinds of togetherness.

We can ask whether history's components are also reconciled in other ways. Or we can treat history as a single enterprise constituted by the double togetherness of dot and therefore, and look to the other two kinds of togetherness to supplement them. Or we can look to other ways in which the dot and therefore are together. If we look for supplements, we view history in terms of God and the Ideal, or we bring history together with God and the Ideal to make something else. If we look to other ways in which the dot and therefore can be together—compulsively, implicatively, or merely as separate—we can see history as having different thicknesses, of which the kind with which we are familiar—dot and therefore together in a dot—would be but one aspect. The other ways of having them together need not be called history. But whether they are together or not, history will not be a mere appearance, nor an ultimate reality. It will be one of a number of component items which is being constantly adjusted to other items, to constitute what can be best described as a cosmological-ontological-systematic-unitary pulsative whole.

History reconciles Existence and Actuality in only one way—contingently. There are three other ways. And the four must be united in four ways. Only a contingent unity of the four ways tells us how history is to fit together with a systematic, a prescriptive and a compulsive juncture of Existence and man, inside the field of the Actual. All four ways of combining Existence and man demand of man a representative role. He is a representative of mankind when he is part of history; representative of Actuality when he is seen to have a prescriptive relation to Existence; representative of all the modes when he is seen to have a systematic rational relation to Existence; and representative of God and the Ideal when he is seen to be part of a cosmology. We must interconnect these various representative capacities in four ways. But a man does it in only one way: contingently. When he is a representative of all other men (e.g., when he thinks) he contingently unites his result with other ways of being representative, thereby revealing himself in root to be a representative of mankind. Put the other way: as a representative of mankind he contingently unites four ways of being a representative, including that of being a representative of mankind.

February 1

There are four ways of apprehending—knowledge, action, sympathy, and system. There are four ways in which items can be conjoined: contingently, i.e., cosmologically; prescriptively, i.e., ontologically; compulsively, i.e., in nature; and rationally, i.e., abstractly. In history we have a conjunction which is cosmological in that it is contingent, and "natural" in that it is compulsive. This history can not be integrated with other ways in which Actuality and Existence are conjoined, the abstract and the ontological. Such a conjunction is a kind of systematic formulation regarding Actuality and Existence as having natures in and of themselves. A combining of these two in a man can be achieved in knowledge. We will then know how history and system make a unity in a man.

If history is to be an object of experience a man must recognize himself to be conjoined with Experience. An individual representative of man or Actuality, in other words, must see himself to be a representative of particular men and thus of mankind. History here is a domain. We can also view man as interplaying with Existence to constitute a cosmic experience or a fragment of this; this experience is to be reconciled with other ways of dealing with the world.

Can we say that perception and science are reconciled in the adjustment of man, or in the object? But the object has no power to so reconcile them; and man faces them not as governed by basic forms of togetherness but only as abstractions. We can say that perceiving and cognizing man must be united, so as to give us a single man who is able to face the world. They do not constitute him; he remains one who knows in two ways. The perceptual and scientific worlds have no being of their own, and do not conjoin elements in such a way as to allow of their own conjunction in turn. They are togethernesses whose union would depend on the reorganization of the perceiver and the object, without regard for what the togethernesses themselves are expressing. They are reconciled to be made part of a single common-sense experience, but this is the locus from which they were derived, or a purged version of this. In the case of history, e.g. when it is reconciled with some other way of dealing with Existence, we do not get back to where we started, but instead preserve the history and the other in ourselves, as complex beings with a plurality of powers; we modify ourselves in such a way as to accommodate both as distinct.

History provides an opportunity to get a satisfaction in the experiencing of Existence which one did not get in the cognizing, etc., of it. This opportunity, when accepted, gives us history at its best.

Another way of saying all this is to recognize that man can be a representative of Actuality in ontology, of mankind in cosmology, of all the modes in a system, and of God, Ideal, and Existence in nature. What he seeks to do is to be complete, by finding himself in the cosmology. But this completion involves him in a contingent union of the cosmological elements. As a consequence he becomes contingently a representative of mankind, Actuality, the remainder of the modes, and all the modes at the same time. He allows all of these to be alongside one another, and himself to have the role of a mere contingent union of them all.

February 3

The various disciplines—history, politics, institutionalized religion, and social action—are all ways of giving body to the primary constants of togetherness in restricted areas (where one component always is man). If we move out to the cosmos and seek neutrality, we get nature (therefore), system (implies), ontology (comma), and cosmology (period). A philosophic system is a reiteration of the modes of being as together, by means of an implicative relation. It takes as subsidiary subjects the realms of ontology and cosmology, and faces nature as something over against it. A philosophic system thus takes the position of the Ideal and then moves on to subordinate, rationalized versions of God and Actuality. Existent nature is a locus of encounters which provide a counteracting therefore.

A cosmology merges the modes and does it contingently; history as a sub-branch of cosmology contingently merges Actuality and Existence. Could one say that it involves a union of cosmology and nature since it unites actualities and Existence? No, cosmology already has Existence and Actuality merged and nature has them connected by a therefore. To bring cosmology and nature together would be to bring together two different ways in which Existence and Actuality were related. It would not be a way of expressing history, but a way of expressing how the interaction (technology, economics, use of materials, etc.) of man with Existence makes a single "sociological" discipline. It is also questionable whether such a union is concrete or abstract.

In the case of history we have a concrete union, for we make use of a basic constant, that of mere contingency, or period, involving actualities and Existence. The latter must be preserved in any solidification of history with other parts of cosmology, or with technology, etc. We have a right to say that the union with technology is concrete so far as we can find a man or other being which will, by virtue of the unity of it, allow history and technology to be diverse lines, and ultimately relations connecting the union with Existence. If we merge history and technology, we make two unities of their diverse kinds of togetherness, and in effect make man and Existence each lose its unity as a being. They will become relations between the two forms of togetherness.

A man who served as a relation between the two forms of togetherness of cosmology and nature, and history and technology, would be an adjusting being, a blurred one, an emotional one, or a prescribing one. He would face one sociological unit in which there was a stress on history, and another in which there was a stress on technology, and would relate them as separate and as merged. As a consequence he would see himself as having an obligation to deal with them together, and find that he was fulfilling the obligation more or less.

The merging marked by a dot, which is characteristic of experience, and of cosmology, and of history, is not one which involves a loss of the unity of man or of Existence. And since man and Existence are primary realities, we must say that history remains a separate domain, never to be identified with other domains. It is a dependent reality with its own rationale, but it requires for its being that it remain constituted by its own constant of togetherness over against other ways of being together. The reconciliation of it with other domains is a reconciliation which keeps them apace, correlated, in gear; it is not one which makes them part of a more solid reality, except in the sense that man, as a

u⟍   ⟍domains, is more solid than any of them. We can
ma   ⟍ther with other domains in a unity; we can, in
sho⟍   ⟍ into a relation, but then he becomes the living
emb⟍   ⟍nt types of togetherness, such as mind as an im-
plicat⟍   ⟍herefore, emotion or experience as a dot, and self
or priv⟍   ⟍.

If h⟍   ⟍ational subject, there must be a radical distinction
between ⟍.. space, time, etc., characteristic of it and the space, time,
etc., which is a dimension of Existence. The former must be closer to
what in the *Modes* was called a field. In any case the space and time
and becoming of history will be a joint product of Existence and
Actuality.

History's extension is to be reconciled, not with other extensions,
but with other ways in which Existence and man are together. The
space, etc., of history can be said to overlay that of Existence only in
the sense that it is a barrier constituted by man, which he has placed
between himself and Existence, through the help of Existence itself. It
is such a barrier, though, only for man as ontological, looking as it were,
through cosmology, at Existence. Ontologically viewed, man has a
minimal togetherness with Existence. If there were a need to say that
only one kind of space, time, etc., was real, there would be more justification in claiming it was history's, or some cosmological enterprise's, or
some other realm's than Existence's; history's space, etc., are observable,
used, and measurable. And yet if Existence were not extended, we could
not account for the historic products achieved by the interlocking of
actualities with Existence.

One might interrelate history's extensions with a "theological" resulting from the interplay of God and Existence (an aeon might be a
temporal extension, and theological space a spatial extension while
fulgurations and creations might be becomings), and a "political" interplay of Ideal and Existence. But staying only with Actuality and Existence, the problem of the reality of the extensions of history should be
one of reconciling extension with other ways of being together—
compulsively, ontologically, and systematically.

February 1

What is the relation of the extensions which characterize history to those of common sense, and therefore derivatively to those of
science, etc? The question is a difficult one, because history is the to-

getherness of a number of modes, whereas common sense, though it is a blurred domain, bearing the marks of other domains, is primarily a realm of Actuality, while science, etc., are ways of articulating and clarifying this.

The extension of Actuality is due to the presence of Existence, but it is an Existence which is ingredient and sustaining, and not one which is newly made by virtue of the interplay of Existence with man. Consequently, we are faced with a comparison of an Existence which is a used or an auxiliary realm, with an Existence which is a product. The product is evidently the outcome of using common-sense Existence (or purged versions of this) together with Existence itself, or with Existence as qualified by what had been done. The issue, then, is that of relating a product to its components, themselves having some kind of extensionality. It thus turns out to be a question of relating a togetherness to its components as they stand apart from it, and thus as together in another way—or, strictly speaking, in three other ways. Recognizing that the historic togetherness is a contingent one, united with compulsion, we see that there must also be a prescriptive and a systematic way of relating Existence and Actuality. If we ask what must Existence and Actuality be like as separate, or as making an intelligible unity, we ask what kind of extensions they have in and of themselves. We do not then reduce the extension of history to anything else, but see that there are other ways of having Existence and man together.

The common-sense world is one of the terms to be approached from a minimal togetherness. The science which it allows one to abstract is oriented there too, and its extensions are first to be rooted in common sense, then to be placed over against those of mere Existence, and then allowed to ground a new kind of extension.

Ontology, to put the matter more broadly, does not precede cosmology; the two are correlatives. But if we start with beings in a cosmological setting and then analyze them out, we find that they have essential and nonessential features. We can distinguish those features and thus see what each one is in and of itself, or we can use the nonessential features to ground inferences to the presence of other beings, and then try to get to the essential features of those beings. The arguments for God in the *Modes* are, in effect, ways of recovering an alternative to a cosmological form of togetherness, by recognizing that the termini of the cosmology have a being together as in and of themselves, as well as a being with others in a thicker togetherness.

There is nothing like a correlation of history with man or Existence, or more generally of cosmology with ontology. But the abstractions of science, and the common-sense world from which they were derived, must be brought together. This is properly done, as the pragmatists see, by action, or more accurately by engineering. Engineering is the adventure of reconstructing common-sense objects so as to utilize abstract science. We look at the results in terms of practical efficacy. Treated in this way, engineering becomes a kind of togetherness, which relates an abstraction to something from which it was derived. The engineering object is a togetherness of the Ideal, or formal, with the Actual, and is thus either a compulsive forging of the scientific and the commonsensical together, or a prescriptive togetherness, a way of recognizing that the scientific and commonsensical have an integrity of their own and must be treated as distinct with their own natures. If we take the latter approach we get an alternative to engineering. This is speculation, the adoption of the position of God, and the recognition of the rights and natures of the elements which are minimally together.

Since the various forms of togetherness are inseparable, and since the other two forms of togetherness which are to be found in Actuality and formal science are also capable of subsidiary roles relating them both, we must say that the relating of science to common sense always has them together in practical objects, as purely speculative termini, in a systematic connection, and in a contingent merging. The mistake of men such as Northrop is to first treat the two sides as distinct and then to be content with merely saying that they belong together. But they are had as distinct only as belonging together, and the belonging together is had in four ways, of which the being distinct is but one.

However, there are individual items in both science and the commonsensical world; what one wants is not merely a recognition that the two sides are together in four ways, but that the items in each actually make a togetherness in such a way that by following out the clues of one side, we can keep abreast of the other. Putting aside the fact that we can abstract one side from the other and follow out the implications of the abstracted item to see if our logic is in accord with what the world is in fact bringing about, we can relate the two in an adventure. Engineering will be one adventure in which there is no guarantee of success, and in which sometimes one side will give way to the other and then conversely. Engineering has a counterpart in another adventure which keeps the two sides in consonance, precisely by insisting on their radical separateness. Only, as it were, by going to the extreme of science on the one side and by immersing oneself in daily common sense on the other, can one have a position in which the items in the one are answered by the other. (We must say similar things with reference to perception, events, and values.) By taking this position we are also enabled to bracket the other side.

Those pure scientists who concentrate on pure formality tend with Descartes to neglect the counterpart which common sense provides, and as a consequence tend to speak as though the pure science was the world in fact. A converse error is performed by those radical existentialists and empiricists who put the realm of science to one side to concentrate on the common-sense reality.

The schematism of Kant is the realm of extension, which is the concern of the engineer; the "intellectual" pragmatism of Peirce provides the rational domain in which common sense and science are together minimally.

February 5

There are at least two meanings of "schematism" and a number of varieties of each. There is the schematism which relates abstractions to one another, and there is the schematism which relates an abstraction to (or by) something more concrete. The latter is the one Kant considers, the former is relevant to what Northrop is concerned with when he speaks of the correlating of the postulational world of science with that of perception.

Each pair of items can be schematized in two ways. Accordingly we have the following:

1] science and perception   schematized by events and by values
2] science and values   schematized by perception and events
3] science and events   schematized by perception and values
4] perception and values   schematized by science and events
5] perception and events   schematized by science and values
6] values and events   schematized by science and perception
7] science and common sense schematized by events and values
8] science and values   schematized by common sense and events
9] science and events   schematized by common sense and values
10] common sense and values schematized by science and events
11] common sense and events schematized by science and values
12] values and events   schematized by science and common sense

1] The schematism must be two-faced and must be more substantial than at least one of the items it interrelates. This means that it is not as abstractions that events, etc., function as schemata, but as integral to something more substantial. This is something like Whitehead's view; his schemes of science and perception (particularly in his 1920 books) are mediated by events which look both ways. A judgment of importance would seem to do the same thing for values.

2] Science and values could be interrelated by events. In *Process and Reality* this is apparently what Whitehead does when speaking of the objective and subjective poles. If interrelated by perception, we would see the perceptual content as allowing for an abstraction in the shape of science, and some selective power as allowing for the determination of what was real outside perception.

3] Another early view of Whitehead's seems to involve a schematism relating the realm of science with events, mediated by a perception which was free of subjective taints. But there could also be a schematism which took account of the way in which science and events could make a single satisfying whole. This seems to be the view of the later Dewey, and could be traced back to Peirce. Perhaps the pragmatic position actually intends the combination of the two mediations, the two schemata as interrelated.

4] There are times when Northrop speaks as though science yielded basic truths rectifying and interrelating perceptions with entertained values. But one can also have a schematism in which events carried both perceptions and values, and this is the way Whitehead sometimes speaks in *Process and Reality*.

5] Russell seems to hold the view at times that perception and events could be interrelated by scientific constructions; Bradley seems to hold that they are mediated by an absolute value which lies before them both as a common goal.

6] Northrop seems to hold the view, too, that science interrelates values and events. Hartshorne seems to hold something like the view that perception is a rich schematism out of which one can extract values and events.

7] Events as schematisms have the form of time; values have the form of plans and programs vitally pursued; common sense has the form of engineering or useful objects, and science has the form of disciplined inquiry. Kant uses time to schematize science and common sense, where science here has the form of mathematically expressed realities, and common sense the substantial being of Newtonian entities. Dewey's program is primarily the use of plans, etc., to unite science and common sense.

8] Science and values can be united by engineering; this is in fact done in all politically and socially oriented schemes. Time can relate them, as in a Marxian scheme.

9] Science and events can be united by engineering or practical objects —apparently the view of the *Timaeus,* and held by all those who with Russell think of science as over against a process world. But plans and programs can perform this function too, as Dewey seems to hold in his *Logic.*

10] Common sense and values can be related in a disciplined inquiry, which is what Peirce seems to intend; they can also be interrelated by time as at once a locus of eternal values and a transient common-sense realm. This is perhaps the essence of the Christian outlook; it makes time the instrument through which God's purpose is worked out.

11] Common sense and events can be related by a disciplined inquiry, which is apparently another position taken by Dewey; they can also be schematized by plans or programs, and this Dewey rightly takes to be the supplement of the other way of schematizing them.

12] Values and events can be schematized by disciplined inquiry and by engineering. The first seems to be the concern of Plato's dialectic, and the second seems to be the concern of social planning.

What is evident from the foregoing is that the question of the relation of science to perception is but one of a number of questions and that it has not one, but two answers, and that neither offers "correspondences" or "correlations," but rather a basic occurrence which has two sides to it. One side answers to one of the relata, the other to the other. The sides are not functions of the relata; rather they are presupposed as the ground and source of the relata.

If we are interested in seeing how the objects we confront in science and in perception are related, we must make use of either of the schemata offered in *1.* But the question is perhaps a misconstrued one; it is not perception but common sense which is the item with which we would like to connect with our science, and this, as is evident in *7,* requires the use of time, or plans and programs. Time, however, need not be viewed, as it is in Kant, as merely lying between them; it can be viewed as a perpetual reconstruction, a way of having the two of them together, and which, when the two are separated one from the other is a power for altering and interrelating them—and similarly the function of plans from the standpoint of the separated science and common sense, will be to provide constant reconstructions enabling them to be significantly together. Time and plans in this sense are like becoming, and not like mere structural sequences.

If time and becoming can both serve as schemata, why not space? Should we say that events are time, science is becoming, and values are space? If so, then common sense would represent a transportation of Existence into the realm of the items it relates. If so, we will not get becoming in No. 7, but only time and space. Becoming would enter as a kind of schematism only to reconcile common sense and values, common sense and events, and values and events. Still all four—science, common sense, events, and values—have a time side, a space side, a becoming side, and a rootage in Existence.

If we are interested in time, it is the time of events which should be of primary concern. If one wanted to interrelate these events to science, say (which has its own kind of time), one would have to look to common sense or to practical objects, or to the space of values, and not to a time. We cannot know what the nature of union of two items is by attending to some phase of them, such as time, and expecting to find them related in a more basic time. The times of science and common sense, say, are incidentally connected when one connects them either in the time of events, or in the space of values (though the primary task of the events and values would be to relate a becoming and an Existence).

If then we intend to reconcile the worlds of science and common sense we ought first to see what they are essentially—becoming and a kind of existence—and then find the space and time to relate them, incidentally, thereby relating the times involved in the becoming and Existence. This way of dealing with the matter though makes science represent a genuine dynamic nature, even though it itself is formal and abstract.

Metaphysical and theological discussions are suspect because they seem to claim to have proved the existence of something. To the answer that they prove no better or worse than anything else, it is countered that they are worse. But this I think cannot be shown. A better answer would be to say that we can encounter empirical things, but that the metaphysical and theological "realities" cannot be encountered and perhaps may not have any being at all. To be sure, we never get ourselves clearly in an ontological condition and therefore do not clearly have the other realities over against us as they are in and of themselves. However, this is like the situation which history presents. We do not encounter Washington in *propria persona*. But we can encounter the past as a kind of differential power in the present. To make out a similar case for metaphysics and theology we must show that experienced common-sense objects have features which require the differential activity of an ontological reality.

We must make out that there is a factor of unity, dynamism, and value in the world of common sense; also that we can isolate by analysis the three modes of being over against Actuality, reproduce them in art, or see that they enable us to be substantial and ontological. We must also show that the unit, etc., are independent elements, and that they twist the content before us in a way revelatory of their power and being.

The independence can be shown by the occurrence of one without the other as focal points or independently operating elements in experience. Though they then could be said to be the possession of some single underlying power, they are so far independent. The twist is more important. We must experience a final substantiality, an insistent dynamism, and a luring and demanding Ideality in the body of the counterpart of ourselves, making a difference to the way in which this is presented to us. Each must pull on the experienced content in its own way, so that we face the counterpart of ourselves as rooted away from us, in the form of unity, dynamism, and value. We do not encounter these three themselves, but only as different types of pull. The unity is not the unity of experience but of a finality; the dynamism stands over against the finality; and the value, luring and demanding, is distinct from the other two.

February 6

It is possible to come close to a more traditional view of art than I have, and yet not lose all the values of the alternative I have offered in *The World of Art*. If it is the task of the work of art to encourage the union of oneself with it, beauty would be a prospective capacity of the object to be assimilated. The emotions would be affected by the object and would determine in turn how the object was to be adopted. As a consequence of the adoption one would find over against oneself the realm of Existence, and particularly that portion or aspect of it which was spatial, temporal, or dynamic. The difference between this alternative and the one I explored in *The World of Art* is that there is no claim A] that there is beauty in the object and B] that there is no iconizing of Existence by the art object. Yet we seem able to contemplate works of art, hold them at a distance, see them from afar, and also recognize signs and symbols in them.

We can make the position of *The World of Art* the ground for the alternative view. Accepting the alternative offered, it is possible to treat the art object as a satisfying complement by which, when identified with oneself (and this happens most frequently in the performing arts), one is opened up into a realm beyond. In the case of architecture, painting, and sculpture, the distance between art work and spectator seems to remain, making evident that there is something not altogether adequate in the view alternative to *The World of Art*. The temporal arts seem in-between extremes represented by the spatial and dynamic arts.

The view that the work of art is a complement to be assimilated to the individual to constitute a satisfying or pleasurable experience is really the other side of the doctrine that the work of art is only a device for communicating some idea in the artist's mind, for neither allows the work of art an integrity or rationale of its own. Both also make art essentially a subjective affair, though the complement theory does allow it to have some kind of status and being apart from the individual spectator, and does recognize that the work of art is something made.

February 7

The ontological argument could be looked at as exhibiting in a heightened form the point made by Thomas Aquinas in his little book on *Essence and Existence*—despite the fact that Aquinas rejects the ontological argument. He distinguishes between a sphere and a balloon (to use the illustration of *The World of Art*) by recognizing that the material of the balloon underlies the sphere and makes it something more than a geometrical entity in the mind. The balloon is a sphere in matter, a matter to be sure which is conceived, but yet one which functions as a base or support of the sphere. The ontological argument in effect says that Existence has this role for the absolutely perfect being, since that is a being who is more than an idea. It apparently supposes too that Existence, as supporting the concept of the perfect, cannot be sundered from the Existence outside the conceiver. There is no attempt here to produce a being out of thought, or to make Existence into a predicate alongside other predicates. However, it is questionable whether what is proved is God, and not some reality, which may have many subordinate parts, of which God is but one. Also the problem is to get an adequate idea of that reality, or of the God part of it. Only such an adequate idea has Existence inseparable from it. And if the reality or God is expressed in a transcendental concept with an existential import, the Existence, inseparable from it, will itself be inseparable from an Existence outside. We will know there is an Existence outside, but we will not thereby be in the presence of it. This would require the Existence outside, not merely to be the continuation of the Existence which supports our concept, but to act on it and us.

If we can prove the existence of God, as one subordinate but basic reality, we can prove the existence of the other three modes—and conversely, if we can prove the existence of any we can prove that of God. The ground would have to be that each has existential import. And if it be the case that "Being altogether is not" as is claimed in the *Modes,* there can be no proof of the reality of the four modes as together, but only as four modes distributed, which is to say as together in only a minimal way, as separate, as they are from the perspective of a "divine comma." In the latter proof of the necessary being of a fourfold reality, we would be faced with the idea of a reality which must be split fourfold if it is to be a reality that necessarily exists. To make an ontological argument we must divide Existence (and other modes) in four distinct ways, with four distinct modes of functioning. One of the four kinds of Existence would be appropriate to God. This God is not a creator, nor a theologian's God; He is the God of the philosophers.

There are in effect two ontological arguments: one is programmatic, and the other is effective. The programmatic one starts with the idea of being, and seeks to find out if being is. In the attempt to give being (the concept of it, that is) an objective role, it finds itself forced to divide the being (or what is usually called Existence) into four parts, each of which attaches itself to a concrete, specialized division of the initial being. The traditional ontological argument goes wrong A] because it supposes that its argument will work for a mere being, as alone existing;   B] because it forgets that the God that it proves is a "philosopher's" God, a being not yet identifiable with the Gods of the religions;   C] because it forgets that the argument will hold of Actuality, Existence, and Ideality with equal force; and   D] because it does not underscore the fact that the beings whose existence is proved must be encountered. Without an encounter there is no satisfaction of the desire to know if the beings in fact exist.

It has been said that the ontological argument will prove the reality of the devil: if there be something thought of as having maximal evil, it would be still more evil if it existed than if it did not. Such an argument rightly admits that Existence adds power, meaning, content to what is supposed. But though it is a fact that an existing evil is a greater evil than one which is merely conceived, the Existence adds a *positive* feature to what was thought to be negative. This positive feature, precisely because it allows the evil to be operative, makes the whole more evil. In short, the addition of Existence to a conceived evil is not the addition of something which is even more evil, but the addition of something which is less evil, but which operates to make more evil—not conceptually, but in the realm where there are other Existences.

The addition of Existence to the idea of evil (granted that it is one which relates the evil to what lies outside the mind) is the production of a greater evil in the sense that something merely conceptual has been granted further power. In this sense the "ontological" argument works for every concept, good, bad, or indifferent, if the argument be understood to argue that what exists outside the mind is greater than what exists inside it. But an "ontological" argument to an evil being first must show that there is a necessary Existence which clings to the idea of evil, in order to make it be an idea of that which is "perfectly evil."

To this it is proper to counter with the observation that both the good and the evil are maximum when expressed as the unity of the idea of good, or the idea of evil, with Existence. Existence, by allowing each to be displayed in the world, makes each be part of a real excellence. Taken in this light evil would seem to be a proper object of an ontological argument. But if evil means the denial of Existence, the destruction of value, its Existence would require that it not be an absolute evil. A maximal evil, which involves Existence, is a subordinated being, since it will require the continuance of its own existence and whatever is needed to support this; it can be an evil only within the frame of a good.

If each mode be treated as excellent so far as it is a unity, and if plurality be thought of as in conflict with it, then we could say that there is an ontological argument of a subordinate kind which requires that if there be four modes of being, all excellent, there must be four subordinated pluralities—which are so far evil. The subordinated pluralities would be powers, which as existent, would be in conflict with the whole and occupied with the destruction of it. The destruction could not be carried out, because the existence of the destroyer would be dependent on the existence of that with which it was in conflict. Evil, then, is made possible by the good, since it borrows Existence from the good so that it can act against that good. And we must also say that it seeks to become good, to become consistent with its Existence by becoming the representative of its parts (in Ideality and God), or representative of the whole (in Actuality and Existence).

February 8

The greatest hindrance in the way of assuming that the artist makes something which is identified with himself, or which is embraced by his self in such a way as to enable him to face a world beyond (and thus in the way of assuming that the art object has no content or beauty of its own, but serves as an item which is to elicit one's emotions and eventually one's acceptance of it in the sense of identification or assimilation), is the fact that it does not allow one to make much sense of the artist's own work or of his criticism of what he is doing. He would have to become a master craftsman concerned with finding the right kind of object with which a spectator could identify himself, rather than be one who was willing to give up aesthetic experience and pleasures in order to be able to spend his time making his work of art.

We are warranted in looking to the work of art as an object having highly desirable features in itself, not because the spectator looks at it in these terms, but because the creator's energies and intent would make no sense if he did not give himself to the making of something other than himself, something having an excellence of its own and which, instead of allowing him to see what lies beyond in fact, serves to capture in itself what he in fact had seen beyond. And if he captures it, it is there. Consequently, we must see the creative process as one in which something is really created.

The artist is already beyond the work he makes. He makes the work in order to recover this beyond in another and better form. The spectator starts with the work; if he identifies himself with it he treats it as iconic, and therefore as testifying to the nature of what is beyond. The artist is of course a spectator in the course of his creating and thus is also occupied with re-presenting the beyond in his work. The spectator in turn, in reconstituting the work, engages in art in a derivative or secondary way. But this is only to say that he is learning how to read it;

his creative work is that of a "performer," one who remakes the work in a new way. As so making it, he has a vague apprehension of the world beyond which his reconstruction enables him to see better. But he reconstructs it, not to see the world beyond better, but to have something excellent.

February 9

The reconciliation of an individual and a role, of man by himself with man as together in society with others, is achieved by internally accepting the position of a representative of society when and as he does what he should as an individual. The reconciliation then in effect is the replication of the status of being together in society, inside a man who stands apart. What is done here should have its counterpart in man in society.

The reconciliation of man as an individual and as merged with others should also be expressible in some form where he brings out what he is, as an individual, inside the frame of the society. This involves the recognition of purpose or intent, the taking of another as an individual (and incidentally oneself), so that which is to be accepted as the exteriorly related, and thus as the substantial ground for the societal whole. It is to say that the societal whole is to be grounded in individuals; it is to see society, and one's activity and life within it, as also instrumental and dissolvable into separated beings.

We have then the individual as absorbing the totality in himself as a representative, and the role-bearing being acknowledging the reality of individuals as the ultimate purposed end of the activity of the social whole. One could speak of the latter as also involving a kind of representativeness. We would then have a representative *claim* made by an individual for the merged totality, and a representative *aim* made by part of the social whole on behalf of individuals.

If the above can serve as a model for all forms of reconciliation, then a reconciliation of two elements would consist in a being looking at each element from the perspective of the other, either as a claim or an aim, i.e., as standing in the place of or trying to get to the place of. In connection with man the reconciliation will evidently be in history and institutional religion, as well as in politics. The historical man will be reconciled with man as outside history (either in society or out of it) by a man representing the whole of historical mankind in his individual acts, and by him, as part of history, carrying out the intent of man to be a full individual. If, then, there is a purpose to history, it will be found in the fact that the individual as a substantial and reconciling being enters into history as a part of it with the intent to make it fulfill the individual as a separated being. The individual as substantial and reconciling will of course not be identical with the individual as separated; he is the unity of the separated with himself as a part of history. As reconciling, he is in a perpetual process of adjusting his inside and outside, his being as merged with his being as separated, holding the two apart while and in order to make possible the unity of himself.

In connection with religion the institutional role of the religious man must be used representatively when he is acting as an individual, and his being, as an individual religious man, will have to be aimed at (together with other individual religious men) when he takes on an institutional role in religion.

The unity of a man as a double representative would seem here to be a derivative fact, but it ought also to be thought of as primary. The individual as a unity must then have two sides. On the one side he must be an original unity expressing himself in four ways (or in our restricted cases, in two), and on the other side he must readopt these ways to make himself a representative in four ways. In addition to being a claimant and having an aim, he must be a representative actor, and a representative kind of unity. As a representative unity he will adopt the prescriptive unity of God, or absolute reason, as his own; as an original unity he will express himself as a contributor and term for that prescriptive unity.

If we have four representative roles, then the assumption of one of them will involve a carrying out in three other capacities and not (as was the case when only two tasks were considered) with one other capacity. The being a representative of the societal merging of men, or their historical unity as mankind, or their merged position inside a church, will then have to be carried out with respect to themselves as individuals who are wholes, separate and substantial, to themselves as individuals who are carriers of responsibility, and to themselves as sources of action.

Coming back to history then, we must find that   A] the historical status of a man as one with mankind must be infected by his three other functions if he is to achieve a reconciliating unity, and   B] the historical status must itself be used representatively in his three other functions. A] An individual component of history must aim at   1] the fulfillment of man as a separate substantial being;   2] the achievement of virtue on the part of each; 3] the recovery of himself as a basic and primal source of action. The aim of history would then be the withering away of history itself for the sake of the attainment of a threefold reconciled unity of individual man.

B] The individual who is the unity of history and other ways of being together with other individuals, acts representatively when he makes a claim for what he then knows and does, 1] as one who is unique, 2] as one who is ethical, and 3] as one who is engaged in a course of action.

If we ask for the purpose of history it is to (A) that we must attend. We then find that the purpose of history, as carried by man, is the fulfillment of man as a unified substance, as ethically perfect (the kingdom of ends), and as free. Briefly: to be self-sufficient, good, and free should be man's objectives when he enters into history, if he is to be a true unitary being. History can then be examined to see if these aims are fulfilled. To do this is to look at history from the standpoint of some rationally understood end. If we look for causes, we will then look to man (B3) as a representative actor. If we look for some objective import we will see him as a representative unique (B1) being. If we look for some significance (B2) we will see him as ethical. The causes, objective import, and significance require one to tear him out of the historic context; we use the aim to see him in the historic context.

February 11

We should be able to learn a number of correlative truths from history. Taking every actor and condition to be constant, we can look at it as mankind displayed, mankind as made manifest in a plurality of local circumstances, each of which adds up to the same truth regarding the nature of mankind, Existence, Ideal, and God. Keeping all things but man fixed, we can see history as the activity of man, man as a free or constructive cause. Keeping all but Existence fixed, we can see history as the dynamic force of the world filtered through or expressed within the human realm, in part perhaps as law-abiding and in part perhaps as spontaneous. Keeping all but God fixed, we can see history as the unfolding of a plan, the re-establishment of values or tonalities at different periods, the totality adding up to the maximal value possible in this world. Keeping all but the Ideal fixed, we can see history as the insistence or expression of a purpose, such as the achievement of rationality, justice, civilization.

Each epoch should be dealt with in these five ways, and the five should be integrated to constitute a domain of history. In this domain there were novelties due to the uncontrolled activities of four modes of Being and the occurrence of circumstances which are adventitious and yet which, when added to mankind, make for variation in what man is like publicly. Since the substance of history is constituted by man and Existence primarily, and only secondarily by God and the Ideal, there ought to be a concentration on three approaches—one in which man is displayed in adventitious circumstances, a second in which he is a free cause, and a third in which he is controlled and conditioned by powers rooted in Existence. In the first there will be a constant law-abidingness to Existence and a constant nature to man and his causal activity; in the second the circumstances will be minor or irrelevant and the Existence will be law-abiding; in the third the circumstances will be minor or irrelevant and man will be a constant cause.

A so-called historic cause is sometimes just a reason, a condition, a structure, etc. Any signal occurrence could be viewed in fact in five ways—1] as a circumstance which when added to the nature of man tells us how he is to be displayed so as to reveal his constant nature; 2] as that which elicits his action as man; 3] as a force altering the way in which he is to be in space, time, or a process of becoming; 4] as one of the devices by means of which man is moving to some end, rationally defined; 5] as a way of exhausting the unitary totality of history itself. Slavery has all five functions: man can be said to exhibit himself as ready for war when living with slavery; the slavery can be said to provoke him to war; the slavery could be a localization of Existence's terrible power; the slavery is one step on the way to achieving civilization; the nature of mankind is such that it must have a moment of subjugation and revulsion.

Since man is a complex being, and since everything which comes to public expression and qualifies his public life can be thought of as having a causal value in history, the problem of a cause of, say, the Civil War, is not the problem of isolating one factor, but of seeing which one is dominant, primary, controlling, while the others are also operative. States' rights, Lincoln, economic differences, cultural differences, fanaticism, geography, the development of America, the struggle for power, the need for independence, the expansion of the majority, all have some role. An adequate account of the war will have to bring in all of them, each in the five ways.

To decide which of the factors is to be treated as primary we can look to ourselves and see what it is that is relevant to what we are or what we would like to emphasize. In this sense history will always be rewritten. But there is no warrant for a relativism here, since the factors isolated are there to be known. Still, we would like to have an objective determinant of the basic causes. An understanding of what we are, and what is odd about what we are, will give us the cause. It is a fact that the Negro has a certain status in the United States which we would like to understand. He defines slavery as the issue which is mediated for today by the Civil War.

It is what we are today in its full concreteness which tells us the full range of the causes of the Civil War, the war being here treated as the mediator and transformer of those causes into the peace that followed. But we do have various ways of interpreting ourselves; so far as this is the case there is a plurality and perhaps even a kind of relativism in historical writing, even though the historical facts are there to be discovered, and are not created by the historian. The question then shifts to determining whether or not we can have an objective determination of what we are like today. The answer is given by sociology and political theory. These subjects define the problem for history and indicate what should be treated as primary in the past.

Are these truly objective disciplines? What is their check on having found the right basic controlling elements? This is another subject. The historian must start with sociology in the rough, or as professionally known. In the past it has been the first, in the future it should be the second.

February 18

An extreme scepticism is actually identifiable with an absolutism of an idealistic sort. The sceptic approaches every item of experience as a kind of "appearance" and applies the category of "non-being," or "error," or "unreality" to it, thereby reducing it to nought. His own mind is a blank or has in it the category of negation. He of course, like every idealistic absolutist, has to assume that there is a being to the items he negates; he in short presupposes the reality of his "appearances" in order to have content on which to operate. He therefore in the end is passive, and allows for an independent world beyond him, which in fact he claims to know as possessing a feature shared by every part—of being an appearance, of being negatable, of being external or given.

If every relation is internal, in the sense that it terminates in what are terms for it, it must have a counterpart in an external relation in which the terms can have the being of entities standing apart from the relation; otherwise they would not be able to enter into the relation. But when we turn to the items which are supposed to be in the external relation, we find them to be in fact internally related by the minimal relation of togetherness or otherness.

We can say that each relation is external from the standpoint of a given internal relation. If we take this view we will have to say that the closest possible merging of items is actually an external relation with respect to the items as being together in a minimal way. This sounds odd—and also mistaken. A man and a woman are externally related as male and female, but internally as husband and wife. To say that the mere being of man and woman is an internal relation for an external relation of husband and wife, is to refer to the kind of marriage some couples have, but it is not to express what is an intrinsic feature of the two kinds of relation. The biological relation seems to be steady and allows for independent movements in the way in which the other does not; the other depends on the biological and not conversely. We presuppose the separateness to have them together.

Another alternative is to recognize that the relation of separateness, which is internal, is one which merely allows the terms to be; the internality would be their common being, and they would stand outside that common being as external to one another by virtue of their interior nature. They would, as such interior beings, also merge with one another. Left over would be the beings as sustaining their merged togetherness. From the standpoint of the relation of separateness, what would be left over as external for the relation of merging would be the items as sheer, bare separates. The husband and wife would be internally related and so would the male and female, the one through a merging, the other as separates. The husband and wife would be sustained by the male and female beings; the male and female as separately together would be sustained by husband and wife. If we did not take this view, we would have to content ourselves with saying that the relation of mere separateness is that kind of internal relation which allows its terms to be substantial, so that male and female would, while being internally related, rest upon their several natures as having nothing to do with one another. In either way we get paradox, and the latter seems to leave over something unintelligible.

The view which alone seems tenable is that all the basic relations are internal, and are sustained by the beings which are, in that guise, internally related by a relation of a counter sort, connecting individual, separated substances. Is it paradoxical to say that A and B, who are male and female and are married, are able to be male and female with reference to one another only so far as they are in and of themselves repectively husband and wife? To be sure, the various terms used are relative terms, requiring one another, but this difficulty can be obviated by speaking of the husband and wife severally as responsible, as legal beings, etc. If the marriage is dissolved and they move into different relations, they would of course still be internally related as male and female, but they would then be sustained by different natures than before. There would then be a question as to whether or not the sustaining beings of an internal relation make the terms and eventually the relation be different from case to case, when those sustaining beings change in nature. We should, I think, say that it may make a difference in some cases, but that it may not in others. In principle it need not make a difference, for though an internal relation does demand certain kinds of terms, different beings might be able to provide those terms. But will they not provide them in different ways? If so, a change in the marriage-relation should demand that the male and female thereafter act upon a new internally related set of the same terms in a new way.

Does it not seem odd that a biological fact should be forced to behave differently because it is confronted with a legal or social one? In the first place, it is obvious that this does happen, and in the second place it is odd only from the position of one who assumes that the biological is more real than the social, that the social is not as demanding as the biological, or that the biological is not as efficacious, as effective substantially as the social. It would in short force the paradox that the biological, though thought to be basic, would in fact be unable to meet the demands of the social in such a way as to sustain it, without losing its own integrity, and that the social would not demand that the biological be sustained by its social terms, taken severally.

February 20

Keeping the problem of relations down to two relations, we can distinguish the object as related in a merged way, as "involved," and the object as separate, "by itself." Each side offers the substantial ground for the other. The being by itself sustains itself as involved, and the being as involved sustains itself as by itself. Each of these sustainings makes up the being of the object in and of itself. If we want to isolate the object in and of itself, look at it as over against the two terms of the relations (as involved and by itself), we must take it to be a complex, derivative product. This does not mean that there is nothing concrete uniting the two sides; it means that the concreteness is achieved from each side, and that the neutral position, where neither is functioning for the other, is an abstraction. That is, the concreteness of the object is in the sustaining role of the by-itself for the involved side of itself, and is in the sustaining role of the involved for the by-itself side. This sustaining activity is its substantiality or concreteness, in itself.

If we could make the in-itself substantial as a neutral entity, it would have the by-itself nature and the involved nature as derivative expressions. To have the object merely separate would still be to have it only as an abstraction. This does not seem to be in consonance with the outlook of the *Modes* in that it supposes the togethernesses of things are always secondary.

A] Does each mode make reference to the others, and   B] is separateness a way of having the modes in a neutral position?

A] The in-itself requires references to the others; the only question is whether the togetherness of the ways in which each relational side is sustained is substantial, concrete, or merely derivative. The former evidently. And it could be concrete and still require the two relational components to sustain relations of togetherness with other beings.

B] If separateness is neutral it still does not give us the objects *in* themselves; it gives them only as they are *by* themselves. It reaches to them but does not have them as they enjoy themselves, and does not even know them in this guise. Consequently, it would be better to say that the ultimate reality of a mode is in-itself and that this is concrete, unitary. Each terminal state, such as the by-itself or the involved, could be said to be it all over again as affected by and needing the presence of the others. But we are still left with the question of the nature of the in-itself unity of the two sides.

If a mode of being is truly in-itself, how can it be said to need the others, to be incomplete as a reality, particularly if the two sides are derivative? Shall we say that if we had it in-self completely we would have it indistinguishable from all the other modes? It is only because and so far as the in-itself is operative as a dynamics of sustaining, and thus as inseparable from itself as a term in internal relations, that it can be the in-itself of this mode rather than that.

We cannot isolate the substantial concrete being in-itself in a perfectly neutral way; it is such a being only so far as it exercises two different roles which exhaust its being. As merely in-itself, it is the terminus of the different terms of the togethernesses and thus is not ultimate and concrete.

In-itself, it exercises oppositional roles. Its unity is the achievement of the consonance of the two uses of its relational terms. It offers a unity for each side, and also a unitary nature for those unities. Apart from these sides it is concrete but blurred, one with the being of all the modes. Only when it expresses its unity in two ways does it have the distinctness of a substantial reality.

When a being is blurred it becomes the being of all the modes, transformed into one of the togethernesses—the involved. This means that we will be able to find termini for that togetherness, and then also a correlative togetherness, and thereupon will be able to locate the modes of being outside the in-itself we have fastened on. The in-itself is then, once again, found to be a being which is sustaining this supposed isolated in-itself. That sustaining is of course being performed by a by-itself. In short, we cannot ever get to the in-itself as a distinct mode of being, but only as the togetherness of all the modes as involved with one another.

The in-itself of a distinct being is the togetherness of all the distinct beings as involved with one another. But we had sought to have an in-itself for the being which is involved with others. Such an in-itself is a biased one; it is not to be found apart from its activity of sustaining the separateness of itself and the involvement of itself. The pure in-itself is all the modes as involved with one another; the in-itself of a given mode is only when it, as involved, sustains itself in a state of separateness. The beings as all together can thus be said to achieve distinctness, only so far as the involved togetherness precipitates out as sustaining termini for those beings as separate. The beings as separate can be said to be all in one universe so far as their separateness is made to carry them all, as involved with one another. It is, then, because there is a cosmology that we can have the beings as ontological; it is because there is an ontological status for each that there can be a cosmology for all.

The in-itself is not then A] derivative, nor B] a mere togetherness of the by-itself and the involved sides of itself. As A it would lose the beings themselves; as B it would also lose the beings, and in addition would raise the question as to what had been made to be together, and would lead to the substantialization of the terms in the relations rather than in the being which provides the terms. But though it is not derivative, and not a togetherness, it functions only by utilizing the different sides of itself as groundings for the other sides. Since there are four sides it has a fourfold grounding operation which we can abstractly add up, but which we cannot recognize to be rooted in a single neutral state, in an in- and of-itself regardless and apart from all these four operations. It is a unity operative in biased ways; not a unity which is derived from the biased ways. Only because it is a single unity can it have the four ways of operating at the same time.

The man as male and husband is together with the woman as female and wife. There is a man and there is a woman (keeping to these features alone) but the being of the man consists in making the male sustain the husband, and the husband sustain the male—and similarly for the woman. There is a way of understanding what a man is by saying that it is the union of these two roles, but when we say this we do not have the male or husband actually sustaining the other. To get them to sustain one another we must have the man; being a man is the playing of this double role. If we wanted to see what the man was in-himself apart from these roles, we would get mere humanity, and could not differentiate the man from the woman. His differentiation lies in the fact that he exercises his being by making terms sustain one another. As a sheer unity a man is a product; that is, as a sustaining power, he is irreducible.

It is true then that a substance is sustained, is carried by the appearances—where substance is understood to mean "by-itself." When substance means "in-itself," then substance does not underlie but exhausts its being by making the "accident" of separateness sustain that of involvement, and conversely. It then serves as the tie, the way in which the roles of the terms in separateness are made symmetrical to the terms in involvement, and conversely. Taken in this latter sense, a substance is that multiple exercise of power by virtue of which terms serve as sustaining grounds for one another. A man is a substance because and so far as he makes the male sustain husband, and conversely; a state such as New York, is a substance because and so far as it makes itself, as part of the United States, sustain itself as a separate state, and conversely.

Whitehead rightly says that the actual occasion perishes when it attains unity; to have attained unity as a genuine in-itself is to perish in its singularity and to become merged with the totality, and this in turn must be dissolved into its components, and so on and on. But have we a right to say that there ever is a genuine unity attained by a given being, in such a way that it is purely and sheerly in-itself? Whitehead supposes that we must say this; he draws the inevitable consequence that no being persists and none therefore acts. We ought not to suppose that each being is struggling to become such a unity; it already is a unity, diversified in its operations. In Whitehead's language, each is using its physical prehensions to sustain its conceptual, and conversely. Whitehead also attends to particular actualities and misses therefore the fact that his analysis applies to modes of being (with the above qualifications) and not necessarily to particular beings, except so far as they are representative of the modes—which is the case only with man.

From the standpoint of knowledge, the analytic components which are united in judgment are sustained by the adumbrated object. That adumbrated object is the object as physically separate from us, used as a sustaining being. Conversely, we should say that the physically separate being is sustained by the distinct components of knowledge, not as they are in judgment, but precisely as they are in the object. In this sense the distinctions made in knowledge are actually present in the thing.

Analysis does give us the real components. It does seem odd though to say that what we know, the "perceived" or the "appearances," sustain the "physical." But this is not so paradoxical once it is recognized that it is not percepta with power which sustain, and that the "physical" is just as "abstract" or in need of support as the "perceived."

Can we carry this over to the relation, say of science and perception, and claim that the real object is one in which the scientifically known aspect sustains the perceptual, and conversely? This could be, were it not for the fact that there are other sides to be taken into consideration, and that these sides are not sufficiently basic to give us the real entity. All of them together constitute as it were one side of the object, and require support from the object as "existential." They are all the products of knowledge, and thus need the support of the existential being, but this, if the above is right, also needs their support, as dynamic, as actually operative in the thing. If this is correct, then the world revealed in art and history can be said to tell us what Existence is as making science, perception, etc., possible, and that these when they together tell us the nature of real space, time, and becoming, tell us what Existence is as making art and history possible—as occurrences, not as knowledge. The common-sense object and the common-sense domain of Existence can be viewed as the perpetual muddle of these two sides, sometimes emphasizing the side which is being sustained in the form of, say perception, and sometimes emphasizing art as that which is being sustained by the world revealed in science and perception, etc. But then common sense goes on to suppose that the muddle is more concrete than either of these sides and underlies them both. It does serve as their origin for knowledge, and as their locus when we daily live, but it is not more basic than either, nor is it the power by means of which they severally sustain one another.

If we want to reconcile science with something else it ought not to be with perception or common sense, but either with art or history. When we do this we have them as correlatives in which each grounds the other. But we can say that the scientific world grounds the art world only so far as we see that scientific world as more than a reification of formulae, and take it to be a representative formulation of all that can be abstractly known and that is capable of sustaining the enjoyed. We cannot know Existence in itself without muddling it with all the modes of being, or without having the space, e.g., of science, merged with art and requiring a separate being and a new form of togetherness, etc., for cognition and enjoyment.

If an Hegelian perspective is assumed, each side, the involved and the by-itself (which for him are the mediated and the immediate—though perhaps the reversal of these expressions is also appropriate) can be said to take the other to be itself; its sustaining work is the acceptance of the other as the way it itself is involved; its identification with the other is the making itself concrete, the functioning as more than an abstraction. The dialectic of Hegel could be said to be the endeavor to make the abstract assume its role as fully concrete. When it is fully concrete it has its other as its expression, to be expressed in and by its other. Now if we have only one being, the Absolute, this other will not be an involvement (as it is in the *Modes*) with other beings, but will merely be itself as diversified. Taking it in this sense, we ought to say, for Hegel, that the diversified form sustains the unitary, and conversely. This is what it is to be Absolute: at once sustaining itself as unitary and diversified.

Hegel ought to say that we get further activity when one of the items of the diversified portion sets itself up as absolute—indeed that this is inevitable, and that it must therefore go through the process of attaining the position of seeing itself as one of the many in a sustained and sustaining role. No matter how often this is attained there will always be a member of the diversified asserting itself. History could then be said to begin when one member of the diversified insists on itself. The course of history would then be the inevitable development which this insistence sets off. Why this member rather than that? In one

sense we can say nothing but accident, and in another we can say it makes
no difference, for whatever the course of history be, it will always come
to the same outcome, both in the sense of a passage and in the sense of
a terminus.

Hegel says that the end of history is the attainment of freedom for
all. Putting aside the fact that freedom is not a basic or final value (for
it may be in a wilderness or with ignorance) as is civilization, where
science and the arts flourish and man prospers, he seems unable to say
where he can go from there in history. When we attain civilization each
being will once again fall away as an absolute, and require the re-
identification of itself in a new way with the others, and a union of all
of them, as together, with themselves as undiversified. This I think is the
answer Hegel should have given.

A man who comes to know the Absolute today as himself, and conversely (where himself is himself scientifically knowing), will at some
later stage know the Absolute as having other knowers too, which are
like himself. And when all are knowers in the same sense, the diversity
will have a new content and being, demanding that the sustaining part
have another nature.

Hegel seems to speak as if the in-itself came to expression; but it is
perhaps better to say (and even more accurate for him, and not alien to
some of his expressions) that the in-itself of the Absolute is really a
by-itself and that this changes when and as the involved or diversified
side changes. Only the sustaining power remains the same. The Absolute then as an in-itself awaits the development of the involved or diversified side of itself; until then it is a by-itself, in unstable equilibrium;
indeed it expresses itself as diversified so as to be able to remain by
itself. Since at the end of the dialectic we have not merely a set of di-
versities but a new by-itself which is enriched and ennobled by the set,
we need a new movement. The by-itself is not yet stable, since not every
member of the set is identical with it. Once all the items of the diversified set were representative of the by-itself, and in this sense identical
with it, we would have a perpetual history of their mutual sustaining,
and the abstract product they thereby produce. We would then have the
adventure of trying to make concrete the in-itself as neutral. The history
of the Absolute would then be the displaying of all possible biases, or all
possible abstract neutralities, in the hope that they will in the end add
up to the meaning and being of the in-itself. Because they cannot so add
up, we would have a perpetual but also a kind of futile activity, except
from the standpoint of the two sides of the Absolute, for each would

see in the perpetual display what it, as completely fulfilled, would be like, and could therefore (while remaining on one side or being a member of a plurality) be able to understand itself better or act better. But I think this cannot be the entire story, nor a satisfactory solution.

When we say that each being is the other of the rest we are dealing with them all as separate, by themselves, and not as they are in-themselves. In-themselves they are unrelated except as beings which are relating themselves, giving themselves the position of terms. They are then others related by a relation of otherness.

Different modes of beings in themselves are to be understood in the light of the kinds of terms they provide. The term for a relation of otherness has a nature like that of its correlate term, for otherness is a symmetrical relation. Each entity sustains itself as a term in a different way. An Actuality sustains its otherness to God in a different way from that by which God sustains His otherness.

February 22

If the thing-in-itself is the reconciliation of the thing by-itself and the thing as for-another, and if the thing by-itself is actually a thing for-another in a minimal way, then it is correct to say that Kant never had a thing-in-itself. His unity of apperception would be a thing by-itself facing his so-called "thing-in-itself," which is in fact another thing by-itself. His phenomenal world should be his thing-in-itself, since it is the union of the two things by-themselves. This world, as Kant deals with it, however, never reaches to and sustains the terminal points, the unity of apperception and his "thing-in-itself," and thus never becomes a true union of them. Had he made it reach, the phenomenal world would have been given a power and an ultimacy which is greater than that which he was able to provide. The categories would then be categories of the real, and the "thing-in-itself" and the unity of apperception would be as much constituted by the phenomenal world as constituting it. They would be constituted as products, or final termini; they would also constitute it by sustaining one another. This would mean that the phenomenal world would be bifocal; it would have one look as sustained by the object, and another look as sustained by the individual. We who were living in the midst of it would have the two sustainings not altogether distinguished, and so for us as living, the phenomenal world would be somewhat confused. If we took the object to be the sustainer we would see the phenomenal world as an appearance; if ourselves, we would see the phenomenal world as an expression or construct.

When Russell assumes the doctrine of perspectives he rightly draws the conclusion that at the center of a series of converging perspectives there is nothing (where nothing is understood to be "not a perspectival object"), since we would then have no perspective on it. But Hegel's analysis of a thing and its properties makes evident that such a nothing is a determinate nothing, a nothing which is A] conceptual, and B] related to the perspectives as a thing-by-itself to the thing-in-relation-to-others. The real object is the law of power or thinghood which relates the nothing to the perspectives. But this law of power itself, as Hegel says, has its own dialectical development. In any case, the doctrine of the perspectives is abandoned once one takes the real object to be a law for the relating of and producing of perspectives from a rational center. Also, if the law and the rational center are rational, the perspectives as their product will be rationally produced perspectives, and not encountered ones, and we would be back into something like a rationalism of a Cartesian type.

When Whitehead speaks of all the prehensions coming together in an actual occasion, he too draws the right conclusion: the dialectic is at an end, the object can no longer be. It must perish. (Here the prehensions of the eternal objects can be thought of as giving us the thing-by-itself, and the prehensions of physical objects the thing-for-another, or as issuing from another.) But the answer to him should then be: why suppose that the prehensions are ever so perfectly unified? Why not see the thing as the persistent struggle to unify them? An object persists so long as it has the two sides and tries to deal with them as a unity; but it never gets to be that unity; its being is a struggle to have the two sides unified perfectly. A struggling being has power left over by means of which it can act and interplay with others; as so struggling, it can be said to be a substance, which is no less real because it has not brought about the final synthesis.

Since there are four ways of being together, in addition to the by-itself (which is the ontological way of being together through the comma), and the being-with-others (which is the cosmological way through the use of the dot), there must be a formal togetherness (expressed by the horseshoe) and a dynamic togetherness (expressed by the therefore). Hegel seems to take it for granted that the first two are formal, and is inclined to define the dynamic as the in-itself. But there is a distinct way of being which involves others by virtue of their formality, and tells us what the being is *of*-itself (the horseshoe). And there is another distinct way of being which involves others through compulsions, and this tells us what the being is *from*-itself (the therefore).

We have then: being *by*- (,) itself, being *with*- (.) others, being *of*- (⊃) itself, and being *from*- (∴) itself. These sides are all used substantially to constitute the fourfold vitality of the *in*-itself. Each side can be thought of as sustained by the other three; by its appropriate correlative, with incidental support of the other two; or with two more, by some fourth. Since there is no reason why anyone should be functioning substantially alone, we can eliminate the last alternative. Since there is no necessary appropriate correlative for any one, we can eliminate the second alternative. There is, therefore, only the alternative: each side (the being-by-itself, with-others, of-itself, and from-itself) has a distinctive role and has this by virtue of the sustaining force of the other three sides, which as so sustaining it are the in-itself of the being, biased as it were toward the one expression. There is no simple in-itself which allows one to have all the expressions neutrally. It could be argued that this is a limitation of knowledge and not of being; that the in-itself is neutral to all. This is not here denied; it is neutral to all as the conjoint product of the plurality of biases; it is not neutral in the sense of being outside all bias and subtending all the biases. If it were neutral in the latter sense it would be an undifferentiated one, and in the end would be identical with nothing.

February 23

The by-itself is expressed by the comma; the being-with is expressed by the dot; the for-another is expressed by the horseshoe, and the from-itself is expressed by the therefore.

The proofs in the fourth chapter of the *Modes*, to begin with, neglect the "being-with"; yet this is the very way in which the modes are experienced, i.e., first encountered. We start with experience, the modes as merged, and then must get to them in other positions. If we are to start with one mode, say, Actuality, we must start with it as having a locus in experience. Testimony here would be the recognition that as having a locus in experience there are other modes with which it is involved, to constitute the nature it has as part of that experience. In Chapter 4 in the *Modes* though, I start with modes as by-themselves, and we then see how each as being for another is referential with respect to God. But we could have made a beginning with beings for-one-another and from-themselves. If we had tried starting with them as for-one-another we would have treated them in their idealized roles—actualities as essentially representative, Ideality as subdivided into representatives, God as completely articulate, and Existence as all-inclusive. We would then have had to find the other modes implied. If we had tried to start with the modes as from-themselves, we would find them exercising powers, and would look for that which elicited that exercise.

We have then four ways in which each mode is involved with other modes. Each one of these four ways provides testimony. To have any one of those modes providing testimony, however, it is necessary for the other three ways to substantialize the mode in that guise. The *Modes* considers only the by-itself, and more or less takes it for granted that we are left with the in-itself, the essential as the ground which sustains the by-itself. But in fact it is the other sides, not the in-itself, which sustain the by-itself. Also, the features of the by-itself are "essential" not unessential, and the features on the other sides are "descriptive," providing the evidence for a proof.

In the *Modes* there was a recognition that the structure of Actuality could mediate the testimony with the conclusion, God. But it was not there seen that the Actuality could relate experientially, effectively, and self-containedly (being-with, from-, and by-). Only the being-for-another of the Actuality was considered. Similar observations must be made with respect to Ideality and Existence. Not only then are there four direct testimonies to the mode of God, offered by each of the Modes, but the relationship which the testimony has to God has four aspects with respect to the three modes which carry the relationship.

The detachments of the conclusion offered in the *Modes* are also incomplete. Here the stress is on the form-itself side of each of the modes. But detachments are possible by an actuality, e.g., when it stands by-itself, when it is with-others, and when it is for-others. When it is by-itself it makes a decision, when it is with-the-others it is experiencing, and when it is for-others it brings its essence into play. Similar observations must be made of the other modes.

Consequently we must say that there are 4×3 direct testimonies, 4×3 primary relations, and 4×3 pure detachments, to give a total of $12 \times 12 \times 12$ direct proofs of God, or 1728. But the other three modes can be proved in similar ways; substituting God for them in the proof and them for God in the terminus, we get a total of 1728×4 proofs.

In none of the foregoing, does one reach the beings as they are in-themselves. They cannot be reached in-themselves in an encounter, except so far as we are entirely passive, or are wholly receptive to them in that encounter. But we can reach them speculatively by recognizing that the in-itself of each expresses itself in four ways, each expression being sustained by the remaining three ways. In-itself it will be the crisscrossing of the forms of expression and sustaining.

It is not clear in the *Modes* that the by-itself when used to sustain is not yet the in-itself. I seem to speak there sometimes as though the shearing off of cosmological features would leave us with a residuum of the ontological, where the ontological was identified with the in-itself. But A] the ontological is found not by shearing off the cosmological but by recognizing what sustains the cosmological, and   B] the ontological is sustained by the cosmological, as surely as the converse is true.

The recognition that a being in its essentiality is abstract is the recognition that the by-itself is only a side of the being. What is wrong, is saying that when we consider it in this way we do not consider it as part of this cosmos. It is part of the cosmos as surely as it is from the other sides. Being involved with others is not the only way in which it can be with-them.

One can reserve the term *cosmology* for the involved state with-others; *ontology* for the by-itself; *epistemology* for for-the-others; and *nature* for the from-each. No one of these must be thought to be more concrete than the others; if any one of them is abstract, so are the others. All will be "accidents" and all will sustain one another as "accidents." The beings *in*-themselves will be none of these, but only all of them, as sustaining one another in biased ways. Each of these ways will be irreducible, ultimate, genuine, and the life of the being will consist in keeping them in balance, coming close to the point where it has them in equilibrium only to move back to where they are maximally discrepant —the Empedoclean cycle of love and hate.

Women seem to gravitate toward the position of being "*by*-themselves." And they look at others as "by-themselves." This does not mean being alone, but being ontological, together as apart. Men on the other hand gravitate toward being *from*-themselves, and thus to being active. The two can be said to be related best by a *for*-one-another, and thus by regulative principles, and *with*-one-another, and thus as involved. Or one can say that each abandons his distinctive nature when he makes himself a part of a publicly organized domain, and when he involves himself with others. The nature of man is to lose himself in the structured whole, whereas that of woman is to lose herself in the social whole. What would a being be like which was primarily for-another, or primarily in-volved-with? The former would have a "human" nature, definitely over-against all other natures, and the latter would have an "animal" nature interplaying with all others.

If the different strands abstracted from common-sense objects be identified as "scientific," if *for*-another; "events," if *from*-each; "percep-tual," if *with*-others; then "importance" would be what the strand is as expressing the *by*-itself. But it would be more correct to say that each strand can be treated as though it represented the *by*-itself (which is done in *The World of Art* in reference to constructed substances), and in each of these representative cases each of the other strands will be capable of having any of the other three roles.

Better: the scientific strand can function, as can the other strands, in all four ways. If it is by-itself it is the ground for the others; if it is for-another, it is thought of mathematically and formally not only in-itself but as bearing on all else; if it is thought of as from-each, it will be the epitomization of what is going on in the world, the static result of their interplay, the structural aspect of them as effective in the shape of laws; and if it is thought of as with-others it will be one of a number of specializations to be derived through analysis. The common-sense ob-ject in fact presents itself as with-all-the-others; the known substance, gained by thought, shows it to be for-others; in abstraction it is by-itself; and it is from-itself when used as a guide or control, definitive of what is real or true.

If the in-itself is the dynamic interplay of the various sides, is there an in-itself of every human being which makes use of the different sides to substantialize, and as expressions? If so, the in-itself of man and woman would be the same, except that the bias of the one would be such that there would be an emphasis on the expression from-itself, whereas in the other it would be on the by-itself, at least so far as they were to-gether in the world of organization and living. But the essence of each, as the unity of all expressions, would be the same. And thus we would have the nature of man in both male and female being expressed as male and female with diverse stresses. The individuality of each, of course, would lie in the actual exercise of the stresses.

It seems to be a position assumed by some anthropologists today that the way to determine whether a remains is of a man, is to see if the arti-facts which environ it are made by means of some tool. This in effect says that we have human artifacts when we have a rationale connecting them, the tool in this case being their source or meaning. A tool could of course be used indifferently on a multiplicity of things; the presence of it is no indication then of the existence of a rationale. There must, in short, be a rationale present in the artifacts apart from the tool but which the presence of the tool will make evident and conspicuous. If we had the tool without such a rationale we would merely have one object used senselessly on others; if we had the rationale without the tool, we read into the situation what is true of our own. What we must do is to find a rationale and then apply it to the world of the objects as made by tool.

February 24

The ontological argument works for whatever necessarily exists, and this, as was argued in *Reality,* is nothing less than all that is. In the *Modes* this would be all the modes of being together. But there is another ontological argument which results when one moves through a theological testimony and a cosmological structure to get a transcendental concept with existential import. This would yield the philosopher's God. Here we prove one of the modes of being. A similar proof can be provided for the other modes of being. Consequently we can say that there are five ontological arguments: one for each of the modes and a fifth for all of the modes together.

Neither the God of Abraham, Isaac, and Jacob nor the God who is all-perfect is provable by the ontological argument. The latter in fact does not exist at all, and the former may not exist. The only objects which can be proved by means of the ontological argument are an impersonal reality in which God is one of the irreducible elements, and the four distinct modes, of which only one is God. Strictly speaking, then, of the five ontological arguments only one of them is applicable to God. Such an ontological argument is of course to be distinguished from the ontological detachments spoken of in the *Modes,* though to be sure there is a moment of detachment that it, too, requires. It is a proof which could however be identified with the termini of all the proofs of God offered in the *Modes.* Taken in this sense we have twenty-seven ontological proofs of God resulting from the ontological detachment of an adequate concept; to these we can add 27×3 ontological proofs of the other modes, and four proofs of all the modes as being together in four ways.

The unification which is the in-itself, strictly speaking, is to be understood from four perspectives. It is the act of one being; as self-contained it is a process of sustaining, of being from-each-side; it is a structural unity, with the sides for-one-another; and it is the sides involved-with-one-another. In short it is a One, a Uniting, a Unit, and a Unified.

If a mode of being in-and-of-itself is apart from the other modes (that is without anything of-them), Actuality must be without Existence in it. But Actuality is defined as being existent, and a fact is an actuality de-existentialized. This means that particular actualities are not identifiable with Actuality as such as such, and that the definition of Actuality should be a present inseparable from a past and future, thereby revealing the particular actuality to be one of the moments within Actuality as such. That moment represents the whole, and it has existence in it, enabling one to distinguish that moment from other equally genuine moments of Actuality as such.

February 25

We would be able to maintain that there is a rationality to a sequence or set of artifacts if we could show that the objects were not random, i.e., that there was some common intent or meaning which they expressed; that they were not independent, i.e., that there was some single focal point toward which they were oriented; and that they were not brute, i.e., that there was some kind of meaning that was being expressed. An animal might make use of some tool but it would presumably not use it to express a meaning, but only as a way of brutally making some random result. An animal might work dependently, being taught by another, but its own acts and work would start independently and would exhibit its own activity, but not an appreciation of the other activity. There would in short be no *acceptance* of another's work and a subsequent production of an imitation or modification of it, but only a resonance in the animal to make a work which was like the other. The resonating being would act independently by virtue of the nature of its body or its "instincts." An animal might express its anger and in this sense its meaning, but the anger would be discoverable not by what was in fact exhibited in the works, but by the distribution of irrelevancies throughout the works. There would be an exhibition of a rationale which was irrelevant to the being or nature of the works. All this comes down to saying that a realm which is essentially human is one in which a relevant meaning was exhibited in a number of works, and that this served to connect them. That meaning might be embodied in the use of a tool, entertained in some intent, or be in some connection apart from men.

If logic be defined as the study and presentation of those routes which warrant the transfer of some feature from a beginning to some desired terminus, then it is evident that we need not restrict the beginning to judgments or propositions, that we need not restrict our features to truth or modalities, that we need not follow a merely formal route, and that we need not terminate in something abstract. We can look at work, for example, as the way in which a purpose is being carried from the mind into the world; a logic of work would then consist in the understanding of those works which most completely and unfailingly do carry out the purpose. We can also look at such features as interesting, beautiful, valuable, and see how we might in attitude, act, concerted action, and the like, carry them, or something which they permit, into some desired outcome.

One can not only transfer but can transform a feature. In ordinary logic one moves from the *falsehood* of x to the *truth* of *non-x,* from the *contingent* truth of x to the *necessary* truth of x or *non-x.* The recognition that such transformations are possible depends apparently on the recognition that the objects to be characterized have a certain relation to one another. But it is possible to stay with an object as having one feature and infer to that very object as having another feature; thus from the truth of x we can infer to the truth-value (*i.e.,* that it is either true or false) of x; from the truth of x we can infer the assertibility of x, and so on.

In general what can be said is that the task of logic is the study of warranted transferrable and transformable features over any kind of route, and from any kind of beginning to any kind of end. The generality of logic has not been recognized sufficiently, largely because logic has been dealt with as essentially an instrumental agent—for rhetoric, law courts, mathematics, science, and the like—and not studied in its own terms, as having a plurality of guises, depending on the nature and powers of various structures and routes.

An ur-logic, a logic which was pertinent to all possible structures and routes, would be expressed in a metalogical fashion. It might have very few, perhaps only one, proposition, such as "if x has a feature alpha, then y will have a feature beta." But just what x and y must be like in relation to one another, and when and to what degree alpha is transformed into beta, would require an examination of features, the ways in which they were pertinent to different x's and y's, and how they were related to other features, justifying a movement from one to the other.

February 27

A single feature of an actuality has four roles. It is proper to give it four different names, providing only that it is not thought that there are four distinct features each enjoying a distinctive role. It is the very same item which sustains and which is expressed in three different ways. Red in-itself is expressed as red *from*-this-object, red *for*-others, red *with*-others, red *by*-itself. The first is the datum, the second is a quality (in relation to other qualities), the third is the confronted, and the fourth is a character. Red in-itself is the datum as expressed in the form of quality, confronted, and as a character; red in-itself is also a quality expressed as datum, confronted, character—and so on. Each facet is one expression alongside two others in three different ways.

The issue becomes clearer when we give new names to the different expressions and the in-itself. Thus man is man in-himself. From-himself, he is a biological being; for-others, he is a male; with-others he is masculine or husband, etc., and by-himself he is human, a rational animal, *homo sapiens*. The biological man is manifest as a male, husband, and human; the male is manifest as a biological being, husband, and human; the husband is manifest as a biological being, male, and human; the human is manifest as husband, biological being, and male.

The different ways in which the various facets are manifest depends on the presence of different ways of being together. Each one of these is, in the case of particular actualities, sustained by some mode of being. To be for-another is to be mediated by a togetherness which is oriented in the Ideal; to be with-another is to be related through Existence; to be from-itself is to be mediated by-itself as actuality; to be by-itself is to be mediated by the divine. Because of these orientations and because the four are never in perfect equilibrium, the being is able to, and is required to, act, move, change, etc. When we come to the four modes of being, however, there is no orientation of the modes of togetherness in one another; there is consequently no action or motion which they exhibit with respect to one another.

February 28

There are at least five approaches one can take toward God: There is first, and perhaps most often, *use*, through magic, prayer, supplication. Following this is *acknowledgment*, acceptance, the altering of one's attitude in the light of the fact that He is. This can take place in the individual—Whitehead speaks of what the individual does with his own solitariness. Or it can take place in some church or other organization, or be part of the very structure of a society or state. The third approach is that of *submission.* Here one acknowledges the awesome power of God and perhaps His mercy and wisdom, and accepts it as the basic norm and final truth of what one is and ought to be. A fourth approach is that of *adoration,* the joyous worship and acceptance of God for being what He is; one admires Him for His excellence. The final approach is that of *knowledge,* where there is an endeavor through theology and speculation, or the study of His works, revelations, books, messengers, and prophets to grasp what it is that He is, wants, intends, imports. When the Oriental retreats from-himself as immersed in-himself as here and now or in the world about, he is trying to take the second position, altering his own nature so as to make himself more accommodating to the divine reality, which may in fact be at the very core of his own being.

We approach history first in the spirit of judgment. We look at it, primarily under the influence of an absolute judge, or God, and see some occurrence in the past as deserving condemnation or praise. We move from this to consider it as subject to a standard reflecting the very nature of a pertinent Ideal, which is to be exhibited over the course of time. We then see that this is one way in which history takes place, but we see it as not necessarily on a level with the others, but perhaps better or worse comparatively. From here we move on to consider (under the aegis of Existence) the historic situation as a locus of causes or powers which have been made manifest at a given time. Only after we have done this do we (starting from something like the Actual) consider history as the display of various realities, and particularly Actuality.

We can also view history from the standpoint of God; this gives us a theocratic history of which we have little knowledge until we are sure we have stabilized all the other factors. A theocratic history supposes we really know man, the laws of nature, and the historic Ideal. A rationalistic history takes the position of the Ideal; but it too supposes we really know man, God's purpose, and the laws of nature. It is better, and perhaps of the essence of history as we know it today, secular history, to consider only man and Existence as the primary components; God and the Ideal will merely provide for the objectivity and rationality of the history.

When we are confronted with some signal event, say the Civil War (which we know by acknowledging the various documents and testimonies of today), and face it as something which we are going to view not as a topic of condemnation or praise, or as better or worse than some other occurrence at some other time, but merely as that which we want to account for, and which will enable us to know what it means for man to be in history, we put aside the supposition that God is expressing Himself in constant or in deliberate ways, and that the ultimate Ideal is being exhibited. Instead we concentrate on the fact that man or Existence, or both, are acting in ways they had not before. This forces us eventually to recognize that they make use of powers which they had not used before. This gives us a new insight into the nature or being of either or both. Attending to man for the moment, what this means is that we look for a power in man which he is then manifesting. That power tells us something about man, which he may never have revealed before. Whether it does or not, we can then look upon man as before or after that date as one who is manifesting himself in the absence or denial of this express power. Both the times earlier and later than the given date would be understood to be ways of exhibiting the selfsame man in different contexts, the man, however, now being known to be one who can exercise a power of a certain sort. In this sense history must always be rewritten, not merely from the standpoint of the present, but from the standpoint of discovered truth about the nature of man. If we conclude that the Civil War was the outcome of an expression of man's Christianization, man's indignation, man's awareness of the evil of slavery, we can say that what man did in the time of the Greeks was an expression of man as not yet Christianized, not sufficiently indignant, not sufficiently aware. Man would be as fully manifest at that time as he is at the time of the Civil War; he would, however, be fully manifest only as one for whom the Christianization, indignation, etc., were not essential, but external. If we take indignation, etc., as characteristic of him, then we must characterize him in the time of the Greeks to be potential, incomplete, unfulfilled; in terms of this we can see what he did at a different period as but a variation of what he is doing at a later one. As a consequence we can add the two periods together, to find man displayed. The display tells us something new about man in the sense that we see different powers elicited in different situations; in the sense that we see him as more or less complete at different times; and in the sense that we see him as one who measures up to standards imposed by the ideal man, by absolute values, by the nature of Existence, or nature as such, and by an eternal judge.

We can also view each historic epoch as being exactly of the same valuational order as any other when we attend to the fact that, given man as revealed by the history of a given period, we see him as at other periods expressing himself to the same degree via new circumstances or conditions. The Christianization which is characteristic of him at the time of the Civil War is an expression of one selfsame nature in new circumstances, but with or in certain conditions. The fact that he is a Christian is now a condition through which his selfsame nature will be manifested in the new circumstances presented by existence.

We can view each historic situation as revealing a new expression; every period gives us the nature of man as newly manifest. In the end this should add up to a single picture of man, the being who is displaying himself over the course of time. Having exhibited himself as a Greek (who is man no more and no less than he is man today), and taking into account all the circumstances, we can see him as having a constant power of rationality which we can say was suppressed, perverted, or expressed in the Greek and other periods.

March 1

The problem of knowing what we seek to know in history can be focussed on by considering an individual as representing mankind. We can see him behave in various ways. Let us say that he walks slowly across the street, and runs on the sidewalk. If we know what his nature is, say that he is perverse, we account for his behavior by showing that one power is being diversely exhibited in different circumstances. If instead the circumstances are unchanged, his behavior must be due to the fact that he exerted different powers at different times. If we start with the circumstances and maintain that these are effective—say that the street is clear and that he is being jostled by a passerby—we can refer his behavior to the expression of some single power, e.g., that of being reasonable; if we take him to be exhibiting different powers, say, wanting to walk and wanting to run, we can find the circumstances to be the same, e.g., that there is a roadbed, and he is expressing different desires.

We begin initially by seeing mankind displayed, we then move back to look for a power in either man or in Existence to account for the diverse ways in which the display occurs, and finally move down to use these diverse ways as contrary-to-fact conditionals which will tell us another truth about the nature of man.

If we turn to history, we can say that we identify a people or a period by acknowledging that so and so is a steady characteristic of it, and see Existence providing an occasion to display the nature of that people or period through different circumstances, and enabling one to use a contrary-to-fact procedure in order to be able to isolate a power which is being expressed in these different ways. (We suppose that we have a new people or period when we approach the matter as involving a different kind of man and see Existence itself as being displayed, and having something of its basic nature revealed.)

When do we know that a people exists or a period has come to an end? Is it not that we compare each with some other, recognizing that the circumstance is indifferent? To say, if it is normal to walk across the street, that I would run were there a great deal of traffic, is to speak about my constant sanity. To say I would walk slower were there traffic, reveals something new about me. It is the seeing that in the new situation I act in disproportionate ways that makes me refer to myself.

Suppose I were king. If I acted as kings usually do, we would say that the circumstances made the difference in the way I did and now act; if I did not act as kings usually do (and yet were king), we would say that I made the difference. In history if we find that men, confronted with similar situations as those that prevailed in the past, act in new ways, we refer to them for explanation. If we find new circumstances coming into being and the men remaining steadfast or acting in disproportionate ways, we refer to the men again. If we find that with new circumstances there is a new way of acting, and this is not deliberate, we refer to Existence for explanation.

Why did the industrial revolution occur? Is it that man was always on the alert for new opportunities? Was there a change in economy? Were some new things discovered, and new needs dominant? If the first, the circumstances are incidental and we reveal another side of man; if the second, it is something external to his nature perhaps which is making him act in new ways; and if the third, it is something outside him which is being revealed, he merely illustrating the diversity of outcome which the new powers produce.

We can look inside any given period and break this up into subordinate ones, requiring different types of man. To know whether it is the same type of man, or a single epoch or period and thus man as in principle using a single type of power or virtue at the root of all his expressions, we must know the import of the difference. We can always find differences in man from year to year; but we start in history with the supposition that a nation, a culture, an economy, and a language (with perhaps a given political structure) is basic, and that if there are no changes in these, there are no real reasons for attributing differences in cause to anything other than external circumstances, provided by an uncontrolled Existence (either as something public, or as something irrational, or unconscious in man)—putting aside the possible reference to the unfolding of some purpose or the will of a God.

One epoch can be said to be better than another, in the light of the measure which we ourselves today provide; in terms of some other epoch before or after the given one; in terms of ideal men, religions, ethical achievements, social goals; in terms of some external norm such as the Actual, the Ideal, Existence, or God; and finally in terms of the intrinsic nature of man and the different forms in which he expresses himself. We say that one epoch fails to give him in his full value, because the external world holds him down or does not stimulate him enough, because he fails to live up to the intrinsic nature of man, or is a primitive or incompleted being.

A man suddenly acts excessively though the circumstances are unchanged or slightly changed; or, despite the fact that they change radically, he remains proportionately unmoved. We then compare the epoch with other epochs where similar changes had different outcomes. Thus we hear the announcement of war and it leaves the people indifferent, rather than arouses them. We say this is the end of an epoch, not merely because they are then defeated—for they can be defeated if completely immersed in the war—but because this is a momentous occurrence and they do not treat it as such (unless perchance they deal with all similar occurrences in a similar way, in which case they will be defined as to be without sensitivity, or lassitudinous).

It is possible for a people to concentrate on some set of values and neglect only one of them, thereby remaining as it were in one epoch with respect to one set of features and in another with respect to another. Perhaps we must therefore say that no epoch changes completely, so that we can rightly subdivide history into many different places, depending on what we take to be constant. But there will be a predominant set of features expressive of the way man is in public, which will tell us that though there are continuities with the preceding period, the periods are distinct since there are so many independent and interlocked features which have altered. The explanation of the alteration we might try to find in the geographical, the social, the natural conditions, or in the coming to be of a side of man which had been suppressed, or which had never before existed.

The Civil War was prepared for; one was on the edge of it for a while. It thus is an occurrence which the Americans, even when viewed as divided into antagonistic groups and with opposite cultures, backgrounds, economies, etc., produced "naturally" through an interplay of their constant natures with an Existence expressed in the peculiar circumstances of the day. We can go back further in time to define the epoch, but the occurrence takes place on a certain day. That occurrence must be explained not as an irrational outburst of some segment, but as the spearhead and representative act of the American people when confronted with the election of Lincoln and the supplying of Fort Sumter. Suppose there had been no such election and no such supplying; the war could have taken place in other circumstances which enabled men, constituted the way the Americans were, to be faced with crucial issues which accentuated the differences between them. Was the war then inevitable? It was not inevitable in the shape of a shooting war; other circumstances could have been present which would have enabled the Americans to express their antagonism in another, perhaps even equally, destructive way. If one could find a circumstance which would enable the antagonism to be carried out without destruction, one would have learned how war might be avoided. And by a parity of reasoning, we could discover how the learning of Greece or the grandeur of Rome could be possessed by any men who were in principle like the Greeks or Romans.

March 2

A period or epoch is at an end when we have a change in A] depth, B] breadth, or C] value. By a change in depth is meant one which requires all or most of the powers of the beings to be reorganized to make a new unity; by breadth is meant the extent of involvement in or with others; by value, the kind of excellence that has been accepted, or abandoned, or neglected. Thus a war involves many people and also affects them deeply; it may not alter values. An industrial revolution may affect the breadth and the values, but not the depth. A history of philosophy, art, or culture, may deal only with value, or perhaps also with depth, but rarely touches breadth.

What we find in looking about in the present is some significant item. We then try to move back to a period where the antecedents of the item occur, and then try to understand those antecedents as themselves the outcome of a development from some preceding antecedents.

The initial antecedents, and those which are subsequently acknowledged to be prior to these, constitute the stretch of a single historic period. We begin thus with something having a distinctive depth, breadth, and value, and we move on from there to a subsequent occurrence with a new depth, breadth, or value. To understand how this new occurrence takes place we analyze the historic stretch into man and Existence, and see if we can accredit the change to one or the other. We look to Existence when we can distinguish at the beginning and end of the period a change in the depth, breadth, or value of Existence; i.e., when we see it (perhaps exhibited in the shape of raw nature, force, economics, movement of peoples, etc.) as having a new kind of unity with distinctive ways of being expressed; a new reach, including peoples and objects never before dealt with, or excluding those which had been; or a new excellence, in the shape of new virtues, efficiency, or productivity. We look to man for our explanation when we find that he has a new center of gravity, that mankind is now contracted or expanded, or that there has been a shift in interest from or toward some locus of excellence.

If we attribute the change to man, we look upon the change as essentially an expression of the nature of man coming to expression within one epoch, where that nature is constant (in that epoch and perhaps outside it too), the Existence offering nothing but a localization. If we attribute the change to Existence, we look upon it as having a steady nature, being law-abiding and steady from beginning to end of the epoch (and, of course, perhaps beyond), and coming to expression in these pivotal occurrences, with man providing the occasion.

The records show that there was a Civil War. Why did it occur? It is a question of importance because a war involves men in their breadth and maybe in their depth (in this case it does both), and also involves a change in value. But this we know only so far as we see history over a stretch which begins at some time before that war. If we keep both man and Existence together as historic, we of course see the war as involving both, and having its own consequences, defining a new period. In order to account for the war, we must know what man we are speaking of—man as living just then, Americans, Anglo-Saxons, Western Man, etc. We normally take it for granted that we have the same man at the end as at some more distant beginning—we want to deal with the war as the outcome of an American history, and perhaps as having an origin no earlier than the preceding war. In the case of the United States it would be the Revolutionary War, and not the preceding period. Having acknowledged that this is the beginning of a new epoch, because new values, depths, and breadths now constitute a new man, the American, we see the various episodes of the subsequent time of the period as so many different ways in which the American is displayed, and—so far as the activities are all significant—as so many different ways in which the nature of the American is exhibited. (The illustration of yesterday, about walking, is eliminated once it is seen that it does not touch some basic power as manifest in a capacity to alter the value, breadth, or depth.)

We look to Existence to provide localizations, opportunities, and occasions enabling that American nature to be exhibited in particular ways. The war is the outcome of the American, having had such and such a beginning, and being forced to go through such and such steps (by virtue of the changes in circumstance provided by the steady but variegated nature of Existence) until he is faced with a situation in which the war becomes a closure for that epoch. From this perspective the war becomes inevitable, even though it has its origin in man as the agent and uses Existence only as an occasion given by the very nature of things.

If instead one looked at Existence as having undergone a new kind of change, say the opening up of a new frontier, then one would take man to offer it an occasion to be manifest, now in this form and then in that. The war would be one of the ways in which Existence would press itself in on man, but it would do this only when he provided a particular kind of occasion, such as the grouping together in such and such places, etc.

The choice between these two ways of analyzing the single fact of a historic period beginning with (the end of) the Revolutionary War and ending with (the beginning of) the Civil War, would depend on our awareness of signal changes in one or the other of these two components. There is nothing to preclude both being used, and in the case of the United States it seems the best way of proceeding. We ought to say that the United States as a single country provides diverse occasions for the new man (American) to be exhibited, and with man (perhaps white, or Anglo-Saxon, or Western) providing diverse occasions for a new kind of Existence to be manifest, one in which a new world is being used.

If we turn to the individual we have a similar situation. A man behaves oddly. We can see this is the end of a period for him. We go back to some earlier stage. In both cases we can attribute the activity to him as having a single nature which is manifest in diverse ways on diverse occasions, or we can attribute the activity to the world beyond as having a single nature (say society's constant norm of decency and sanity), with the individual providing diverse occasions for this to be manifest. A paranoiac misconstrues his own activity; he gives too much credit to himself. A schizophrenic misconstrues the way in which the activity is to be divided between himself and others. A negative personality, a rejective one, misconstrues, minimizes what he in fact contributes.

A cure for the individual consists in showing him that what he took upon himself, say in guilt, is to be understood as the outcome of his treating the nature beyond as though it were only an occasion for himself (instead of as having a power and a nature of its own), thereby enabling him to keep as of himself only part of what he had accredited to himself. If the antecedent be properly understood, then his own nature, having now a new kind of antecedent, will be able to develop and function toward a new kind of consequent. The old history of the individual would not be undone, but a new epoch would be started with the same kind of antecedent now divided in a new way. Such a new start supposes of course that the antecedent is still present. The past serves then as a ground in the present as well as the antecedent of what is to be; it is in fact the antecedent functioning as a ground.

Going back to history we can then say that we can learn something from what had been (and change our ways) by recognizing that man can look at himself as an historic creature and take on himself some of the powers which Existence originally had. When he finds that Existence is not merely an occasion but a single power which uses him as an occasion —say with new economics, or a new source of raw materials, or new geography—he can adopt this as his own. Defining himself to be one whose being is integral to these new aspects of Existence, he can act on Existence as denuded of these, and as so far serving only as an occasion for him. The war that had been was inevitable, but he, as now on the brink of a war can alter his nature by adopting in himself a new value, breadth, or depth.

Where the ill man discovers an error to be rectified, the historic man discovers what the truth now is and alters it. The individual man could, of course, see a truth and alter it by changing his values, altering his way of life, or his contact with others. Conversely, the historic epoch could be viewed as an illness, and men as a consequence might readdress the entire situation, allocating different portions of the world to themselves and to Existence. In any case, the fact that a man alters the truth is also an historic change, and the cause of this might be asked, particularly if it is mankind which does this. In the case of man we rest with him as exercising some freedom, but in the case of mankind we once again ask for a cause. If men change their natures in the light of what they see has happened in history, this change is to be explained not as the outcome of some private reflection (for this is beyond the reach of history), but as the outcome either of a self-development of man himself in response to the existent world and the brutal fact of history, which he with the Existence helped constitute, or of the compulsions of Existence on him as one who is about to constitute a history with that Existence.

What can we learn from history? More particularly, what do we learn when we study the causes of the Civil War, i.e., when we study the antecedents of it and the way these are related in time to the Civil War as the terminus of an epoch? We learn what an American is like, and thus what his nature is and thus what he can be expected to do when confronted with another variation in Existence which gives him another occasion to be himself in public. That he should be a being who, when confronted with such and such conditions, responds in such and such a way, enables us to say that with such and such a change in conditions there will be a proportionate response by him—taking him as one who has not learned from history, but merely lived through it. We will not here be able to predict what he will do, unless we can predict the course of Existence.

We can also learn from history what a peculiar segment of Existence is like as manifesting itself in confrontation with different demands by man. The United States could be said to be the same geographic and existent unit, but having one import when empty and another when crowded, one import when occupied by farmers and another when occupied by industry, the different occupants enabling the very nature of that Existence to be manifested. This way of looking at history is not yet geographic determinism, for the Existence is a humanized Existence, or at least an Existence which is made relevant to man, and thus is more than geography as a physical phenomenon. Still, it does take for granted that history in one part of the world is being subject to the expression of Existence under diverse and in a sense exterior and irrelevant conditions.

We learn from history what Existence is like. If comparatively empty, the geography, and climate, and resources, etc., as germane to men will have one contribution to make to history. Knowing that contribution, we can say what will occur when men offer Existence such and such occasions. The knowledge of how these latter occasions differ from the former, together with a knowledge of the difference in the historic contribution made by Existence, tells us what Existence's nature is like. A knowledge of what Existence is like, gathered from a previous understanding of Existence as, e.g., comparatively empty, enables us to know what kind of a difference we will find when there is no more room, etc.

If we insist though in staying with history, and not dissecting it into components which maintain themselves as beings from which expressions are to be elicited, or which serve as occasions for such elicitations, we will find that we must say that both man and Existence have changed. We are now men who have had a Civil War and live in a world without geographic opportunities. This is what we have come to be in history. We can content ourselves with tracing the story of it and thereby learning not what man is or what Existence is, but simply what the historic world is. We can then go on and speak of that historic world as though it had a single nature, and used adventitious circumstances to express itself. We will then find that history is to be understood by finding the difference which something outside history makes to its expression, and that this difference at any one time gives a change in the nature of history proportionate to the way in which some other exterior occasion affects history. We will then learn how history maintains itself in reaction to the world beyond it. We will then learn from history what it means to have a temporal human realm: a human realm is a self-contained whole whose nature is manifest in equivalent ways by proportionate human responses to diverse occasions exterior to it.

To know that such and such is the historic fact today in such and such exterior circumstances, and to know what is the historic fact at some other time in other circumstances, and then to know how these circumstances differ, and that they are to be correlated with the historic facts (so that their difference matches the difference in those historic facts), is to know the nature of history. Or more simply and directly, if we know what history is in response to some exterior fact then, on the supposition that the fact is only an occasion, we can imagine any other fact and make a proportionate change in the exhibited history, knowing that all the while history is selfsame as a domain in which mankind lives through time, in an historic space, with a characteristic mode of becoming.

March 3

We look for the cause of an occurrence in history by first going back to some pivotal occurrence in which a new value, depth, or breadth was reached. We then seek a proximate cause of the occurrence—that which actually produced it. The process of production can, however, be attributed to either Existence or to man. When we subdivide history into these components we find that they stretch over different pasts. Though the crucial historical situation which defines the beginning of a period involves both man and Existence, it may be the case that one or the other of these had its crucial nature determined some time earlier or later. Though we may go back to the Revolutionary War for the beginning of the period ending with the Civil War, when we analyze the situation we find that the "American man" was perhaps a later product, and that he comes together with Existence to make possible a new American (who will be active in the Civil War).

We learn from history what man might do, by keeping the Existence as a domain of occasions, and then seeing how he might exteriorize his own nature in Existence to make it something with which he can freely interact. Or we can view man as offering a set of occasions to a manifested Existence; or we can view the entire historic situation as something which a man might attribute to Existence or to man. In all these cases we will have learned what man has been in history, and by analysis what he and Existence are like within a limited span, and eventually over all time.

History, then, teaches us   A] what man or Existence is like and   B] what man might do to make history different. His making history different would in effect be the outcome of his making himself or Existence change in value, depth, or breadth by an adoption or release of some feature (the one from Existence, the other from himself). To know the Civil War as an expression of a puritan man faced with a frontier, and undergoing a change from an agricultural to an industrial economy, let us say, is to see the Civil War being brought about by an occasion in which that man manifests himself as the selfsame being who had manifested himself proportionately in other circumstances before, or who is being used by Existence at the same time as an occasion for it to manifest its selfsame relentless nature.

Men could have taken upon themselves something of the relentlessness of Existence and thereby looked at the Existence beyond as something with which they could interplay; or they could endow Existence with the puritan strain, make it a kind of public morality, and thereupon face it as men who could act as though they were without that strain themselves. They could in the first case see the need to seek new resources and worlds to conquer; in the second case they could see themselves faced with a moral situation in which high ideals were dominant, and find that they were being challenged to interplay with this as free beings, to constitute a new historic situation.

We today, faced with a similar situation, can avoid the inevitable outcome which we at this moment are facing (as beings caught within an historic situation, with such and such a nature over against the occasions of Existence, or conversely) by shifting the balance between ourselves and

Existence. We can either adopt Existence and thereby interplay with a further Existence beyond, or release features, obligations, tasks from ourselves, and thereby enable ourselves to act untrammelled by the nature we had had before. We can avoid the outcome, in short, by changing the value, depth, breadth of either Existence or ourselves.

On the whole though, we take it for granted that we know what Existence is and that it is to serve only as an occasion; we settle for learning the nature of man as at this time or epoch, and therefore understand ourselves, as well as our forbears, to be acting proportionately in different situations.

March 5

As a consequence of conversations with Ellen Haring, I see that the discussion of history in the last weeks should be revised and expanded.

A being, or a set of beings, begins a period by virtue of a change in A] an Ideal value, B] an Actual outlook, C] Existential breadth, or D] divine unity in its depth. It then can continue in one of two ways: it can function as a link from case to case, utilizing the data of Existence as a source of content, thereby making its nature one which develops (or at least is temporal) and is to exhibit itself in diverse ways at the diverse times more or less proportionately to the kind of conditioning that is faced. Or it can function as something which stands outside time and merely comes to expression in it, thereby utilizing the realm of Existence as a mere locality and thereby transforming or moving beyond it to some more appropriate content. Only the latter way of functioning permits of the exteriorization of man in particular acts, in such a way that each case is but a way of having him or mankind completely.

Neither of these two ways is superior in value or importance. Each needs the other. A mere life of linkages would be all-determined; a mere life of expression would have no bearing on what was happening and have no temporal continuity. We live with links in order to prepare for a time when we are confronted with crises, where we can express our natures in an appropriate given setting, without having to redefine the Existence or having to look beyond it to something else. We express our natures discontinuously in order to provide pivotal points for our links.

If we have too many pivotal points we will preclude development and lose an opportunity to express ourselves as beings who are living in and with a world. Too long a linkage means we have allowed our natures to remain latent. Ideally our entire career in a linkage situation (which could be a linkage of a conventional sort in a society or institution, or could occur in the privacy of our beings, or even as plans in our minds) would be adequate to express the meaning of our natures. But since we individually do not live long enough, our natures must come to expression again and again. We would like our natures to be expressed adequately, but since each occasion is finite and since we cannot express our natures all the time, we must be satisfied with using links as a way of expressing ourselves. The art of life is the union of these two methods so as to achieve a maximum expression of what we are—beings in a world with natures which deserve to be expressed.

When we look at the Civil War we can say: A] we men who began in the Revolutionary War as Americans, let us say, functioned as links until we came to some link which brought in other parts of Existence and thereupon provoked us to express ourselves fully as Americans. The Civil War would then be Americans forced to express their full natures (thereby making a period come to an end) as a result of the work of Existence.   B] We can deal with the Civil War by deliberately flooding the particular occurrence with ourselves, thereby transforming it into an expression of our natures; the consequence would be that a new situation would be produced having its effect on our natures; once the transformation of the expression overflowed into other portions of Existence.   C] We can look at the Civil War as that which started with a link and which combined the above two additions—provoked us on the one side and brought in new portions of Existence on the other.

Faced with the Civil War, what tests have we to determine how it arose? If we find that the linked item was met with spontaneity and activity not proportionate to its nature, we look to man, as deliberately or at least as insistently giving expression to his nature; if we find that the linked item, when met in the ordinary way, was followed by the intrusion of other reaches of Existence, that, e.g., it opened the gates to the operation of some remorseless process in nature of society, we attribute the coming to be of the signal event, with its eventual change in us, to forces beyond ourselves. But in the latter case we cannot deny that it is possible for us to have met that linked item, or some previous one, with our own natures, and thereby either prevented the bringing in of the rest of Existence, or met it appropriately to constitute a new kind of consequence.

We ought to remain as links in minor situations and come to expression only in major ones, in crises. We ought to allow ourselves to be determined in minor matters and to freely express our natures in major ones (and in those minor ones which are pivotal or will entrain further wide reaches of Existence). We must get to the latter via the former, as a way of enabling the latter to be relevant to the course of the world.

Kant has a somewhat similar view in his solution to the third antinomy and in his *Ethics*. The noumenal self truly comes to expression in a phenomenal world which is a locus of determinacy. But when or how often? Does Kant not in the end leave this question unanswered, and substitute for it another: when and how can a linked item be made compatible with what a noumenal nature would want? His answer is that the linked (maxim) item should be viewed as itself a representative of the nature (as universalized). In this way he makes a realm of necessity into a structure of the noumenal being. But it is not only questionable whether this can be done, it is also questionable whether it is desirable. The realm of the phenomena should be allowed to be ruled by hypotheticals, and the nature of the individual should be expressed only in crises (provoked by conditions which are more inclusive than the linked world then encompasses), or in the preventing of such crises.

A] Hegel's answer is that the entire course of the world is but another way of expressing the nature of noumenal reality, and that this is due to the fact that the world itself is but another way in which the reality is being manifest. In the end this means that the reality abandons itself to the role of substantializing the linked world, thereby giving it a power and a force. B] There are times, though, when Hegel speaks as though he held that there was a constant interplay between the world of the linkages and reality in- or by-itself, and that the answer to the problem of how and when to combine the linked side with reality was to be found, not by an expression of reality in the realm of the linked, but in a world constituted by both. A linkage would, as it were, belong to the domain of reality; it would be exterior to us (presumably even when the linkage was a subjective one) and we in responding to it would proceed by vitalizing and punctuating it in a dialectical way. History would then be the domain of the interplay between the linked elements and the dialectically defined ones. C] Or one could view Hegel as saying that dialectic is precisely the way in which we have both the linkage and the expressions of reality, and that the separation of them would give us a dialectic without terms, or points without dialectic relationship. This interpretation is apparently what the Marxists have in mind. The first of these alternative interpretations takes dialectic without the pivotal points which it needs. The second views linkage and nature as others of one another, and yields something like the depth and richness of the

Phenomenology of Mind. The third gives the Hegel only of the philosophy of history. The second is more in consonance with my present view.

A better way of stating the second view is to say that the determined world of phenomena is constituted by two ordered schemes making one single domain—Existence and reality both functioning as links—and that over against this is the free world of noumenal nature and the compulsive world of Existence. If we find an excess flooding of ourselves in a situation so that more and more content is demanded, we refer to the expression of the nature; if instead we find more and more occasions in which we are required to act, or a pressure precluding the ordinary course of activity, we refer to the intrusion of Existence.

Every person must deal with the course of his life in a way analogous to that characteristic of a people. He must live a linked life in a linked world, and yet must every once in a while come to expression as a being who is free, and also find himself provoked to express more of his nature every once in a while by virtue of the compulsions imposed by the world beyond.

Historically-minded men, men who look for causes in the past for all acts, deal with all creative expression as a provoked response to conditioned occurrences; those who stress individuality and responsibility, look instead at all acts as the free expression of the individual. But individuals do freely express themselves and Existence does compel. The linked world is freely charged and brutally altered at every moment— here we have something like the third of the previous alternatives. But the independent expression of men and Existence constitute new turning points.

There is spontaneity at every moment, and the intrusion of a world beyond, but this is only to say that simple mechanism and determinism do not prevail (even apart from all expressions and all keeping to a human realm) in our reflections and technologies. In addition there are occasions when men need to express themselves as more than merely spontaneous; they must redress the entire situation, flood it with their natures, give it a new import, thereby altering the course of the world; and there are times when exterior Existence intrudes on them, provoking them to express themselves more fully.

Faced with Fort Sumter, or with Lincoln's election, we can say A] the Southern spirit which lay dormant came to its characteristic expression on this new occasion;   B] a whole series of energies and causes was unleashed which eventually provoked the expression of the Southern spirit;   c] the energies and causes which were unleashed altered the

Southern way of acting, so that, as a consequence, a new world of linkages was provided and the Southerner had to express a more basic human
nature;   D] the new linkages produced by the above, separately or together, redefined the nature of man or the extent and power of Existence
which will thereafter be able to be expressed as the spontaneities and
brutalities of the linked items (or as the freedom and ultimate natural
reality which help define the new pivotal points, as in A and B above).
(11:15 A.M.) It would be more accurate and complete to speak of the
individual, and derivatively of a people, as having an essential nature
(which is what they are by themselves), and an acquired nature (which
is what they constitute through a union of the essential nature with themselves as linkages). When they express themselves spontaneously, they
express their acquired nature either by itself or as mediating the essential
nature. Man in the world is one who has an acquired nature; it is the
interplay of this with the linked world (constituting steady man and
steady Existence interlocked) which gives us a history in which man is
the primary producer. On the side of Existence we have an essential
nature (sheer existence), and a linked status as a law-abiding realm.
These together make up the acquired nature of Existence which serves as
the base or ground on which man is exhibited, or better, which with
man interplays to constitute history. History is then a domain in which a
double-linkage is constantly affected by two acquired natures which
manifest themselves in minor ways most of the time, but occasionally
with violence.

The activity of the being as involving the acquired nature is it as
from-itself; the reference that its essential nature makes to Existence is
the being as for-another. So far as we are concerned only with the side
of the for-another as actually expressed, the being must be thought of as
having an essential nature inseparable from an acquired one, and a status
of a linkage with which it interplays to constitute the base for the for-
another—and so on for the other sides. The acquired nature in its full

complexity is the product not merely of an essential nature and a linkage in interplay, but of all four sides: it is the unity which allows the being to express itself as a mere linkage, together with another linkage coming from Existence; as a by-itself which is what it is in its immediacy and essential nature; as the import of itself for-another, Existence; and as the import of its from-itself, reality. In history, then, we not only have the crisscrossing of an essential nature and a linkage, each substantializing the other (though only the acquired nature which has the essential nature as a base comes to expression in history), but we have a crisscrossing which allows for the substantialization and expression of the for-another and from-itself sides of the being. These give its import in the universe, its rational role as, say, a geometric localization in Existence, and its dynamic existing side, where it makes itself felt in a brute way.

The theory of the Incarnation brings out some of these points in a rather vivid way. For some Protestants the Incarnation is the production of a being worthy of exemplifying God in this world. The Hindus see that no one incarnation is adequate, and that there must be an infinite number if there is to be justice done to the being and nature of God. The Catholics see that the Incarnation is not sufficient and that there must be a continued expression of God in a linked world of actions starting with the Incarnation and ending at the day of Last Judgment. The Catholic doctrine is most in accord with the view above. God can make a plurality of incarnations (in the form of miracles) which might be equal to the Incarnation of Christ; the linkage which God provides for the Church is inseparable from its temporal linkage, as an institution in the world, constituting with the latter the acquired nature of a Church. The Church in itself would be the crisscrossed outcome of the way in which the essential spirit, the temporal Existence, the formal reference to a world outside, and the effective expression of itself are each made into the expressed exteriorization of the other three.

The acquired nature can be urged upon the essential nature and the linkages, and upon what lies beyond itself. The substantializing components, the components which serve as grounds, thus do not merely express themselves as the other sides, but do it through the acquired nature they help constitute. The acquired nature which the American people now have is not only the product of the way in which man by himself made himself manifest as a linkage, or conversely, but one which man by himself, or man as a linkage, can urge on the other.

History itself, which has a kind of acquired nature, could be imposed on Existence, or on mankind; each could affect or implicate the other by means of history. History works through both man and Existence to help sustain them in their roles as elements in ontology, system, and nature. History in turn is the crisscrossed product of these three—ontology, system, and nature.

March 6

Further qualifications: The acquired nature is the linked reality of men. The American is the being or group of beings who link the various occasions in a certain way, bringing to bear something of their inward nature. The acquired unity never comes to expression as such; the being an American in a linked way is one way of expressing that unity as having its base in man as by-himself, for-another and from-himself. When we come to a crucial situation where a man decides to give himself fully, where a crisis is met by a full participation, the entire situation is reversed, and the American is now expressed in the form of a "from-itself," which is the American as having his base in a linked reality. The American, as it were, withdraws his linked being to make himself function as the power behind what he is as from-himself. (Man by-himself is a topic for ontology; men *for*-another is the way he is to be envisaged within a systematic account.) Consequently, he always expresses himself, the American, in the sense that each of the sides is the American as coming out in that particular way; but he never exhibits his unitary being as it is in- and of-itself.

The nature of a being as *with*-another and *from*-itself allows it to have its nature modified by the contribution made by other beings, and particularly Existence. We can no longer call the *in-itself* "American," after it expresses its *for*-another in such a way as to require it thereafter to forge a link with a new form of Existence. The unity of the American remains as it was, but its meaning, as that which does have being in a linked world and does show itself as a power acting on an Existence outside it, does alter in the light of the radical change which is produced in the value, depth, and breadth of-itself, in-itself, and as involved with-others.

March 7

Those who look to a Golden Age, the Founding Fathers, etc., for the explanation and pivot of all they do, are like the Protestants in their views of the Incarnation, and Kant in his *Ethics*. They exaggerate the meaning of some finite event, so as to make it an adequate expression of what is infinite, or so as to require an entire historic process to embody it, or so as to require multiple expressions. Their view is ahistorical and defeatist; the former because there is no provision for linkages, the latter because there is no demand for further expressions of the ultimate reality. Kant escapes in part by having a multiplicity of maxims which need universalization, and Protestants sometimes do by allowing for miracles.

Traditionalists insist more on the linkage nature of a people, a people having little development. Strictly speaking this view is the continued repetition of the former; it makes the initial event, recognized or not, be present at every moment, not by virtue of any activity on the part of the being from which it issued, but by virtue of a retention and a deliberate insertion of the past in the present. A developmental idea of tradition would insist that men merely provide links in the way they had before. The strict position might be termed antiquarianism or reactionaryism, while the other is historicism.

One can take the tack indicated by the Roman Catholics and view an historical development as a continued expression of some achieved position. There must be a constant but mitigated form of the Incarnation in every Church council and in every mass. Here we have an historicism quickened by some degree of fresh inspiration, but one which is subjugated to the initial inspiration, and the linkage this requires.

A more radical attitude toward inspiration is that of the Hindus, in which there is a need for a plurality of detached expressions of the ultimate, no one of which is superior to all the others, though there are gradations among them. But this, like the Protestant view, is non-historical in attitude, and does not make evident when the incarnations are to occur and what role they are to play with respect to them.

We should learn from history that there are times when we ought to take one rather than the other of these five attitudes—protestantism, reactionaryism, historicism, catholicism, hinduism—or a stress on the unique beginning, the repetition of a pivotal item, the transformation through linkage over time, the vivification of a linkage in a subordinate way, and a plurality of (secular) incarnations without linkages, i.e., mere expressions. Such a list of five leads one to consider a sixth in which there is a balance produced between the incarnations and the linkages (where each leads to the other, and is also being quickened by the other) so that we never have the one without any trace, or control, or qualification of the other.

We learn from history when we might have engaged A] in an

incarnation or B] linkage. A] We see the Civil War as that occurrence which could have had us express ourselves more fully at some preceding event, thereby changing our natures, or we could have dealt with the Civil War in such a way as to retain our natures or to change them in ways in which the war did not. B] We can also see it as allowing us to make linkages with new parts of Existence, so that we can turn our attention away from the development of some political organization, for example, and try to develop our natural resources, etc.

March 8

The Protestant view of the Incarnation requires that Jesus Christ be taken as symbolic. The Catholic view that there was an actual Incarnation is inseparable from the awareness that this Incarnation must be repeated, if only in a minor form, over the course of time in the shape of the presence of the Holy Ghost in the invisible church. The Kantian ethics, which ask us to universalize our maxims, must in the end treat the universalized maxim as representative, and not as equivalent with what the categorical imperative in itself requires. The Catholic analogue in ethics would involve the sustaining of acts by intents, even though there might be a first and primary intent which defined one to be responsible.

The best view would seem to be one which allows for pivotal incarnations at various times, each being prepared for by a series of linked activities (John the Baptist, etc.), and which understands the linked activities to be infected by the divine beyond (prophesies of the past, etc.). We must in the end have the Incarnation continuing all the time, but as coming to sharp focus at certain times, and as being caught up and subdued by a linkage of things at other times.

If we think of the Incarnation as making manifest the power of Being in the shape of a "*from-itself*," and if we think of the linkage as making manifest the power of the Being in the shape of a merging, of a *with*-others, then we would have to say that the Being, as being at once manifest from-itself and with-others, must have as its root (and be exhibiting) what it is *for-another* and what it is *by-itself*. The entity will, in itself, be thus the place where the theoretical (or intelligible) meaning and the separated being of an entity come to expression in the shape of a forceful action and a merging with Existence beyond, stressing one expression at one time, and the other at another.

The merged state is the cosmologic; the from-itself stage is the natural; cosmological nature will therefore be the manifested form of what the being is as an ontologic-rational entity. History, a merged state, would be inseparable from the vital interplay of its components when outside the historic frame. The components, man and Existence, both have a being by themselves and a rational import for one another which they insist upon through the body of themselves and in the shape of themselves, as cosmological and natural.

March 10

Freud observed that the realm of the linked is constantly affected by the private; for him a cure, in effect, consists in going back into the private realm and coming out again in another way so as to be involved in a different kind of linkage. When Eastern thinkers speak of engaging in what is required, while separating themselves from the fruits, they are, in effect, telling us to disconnect ourselves entirely from the world of linkages except so far as a linkage is required from beyond. They are asking for a minimum involvement in the realm of the linkage; indeed they want the linkage to be done by the world and to have the individual come down into it episodically, somewhat the way the Gods are incarnated in a series of distinct episodic realizations.

Faced with a linkage one can also attempt to modify it, to work over it, to make it embody a kind of excellence. In politics we try to make it embody justice; in ethical behavior, the Good; in art we try to make it embody beauty; in history, peace and prosperity. Knowledge is a way of exhibiting truth (when we work over the material to give us controlled content), and action is a way of exhibiting effectiveness. In religion, on the subjective side, the excellence is holiness, and on the objective side, sanctification. In all these cases we attend to the realm of the linked but work over it in the light of the respective excellencies. The excellencies are not objects of thought, but of schemata, in the light of which we reorganize the realm of the linked.

The linked can also be the locus of the expression of the other side of the world. In ethics and politics it exhibits the Ideal; in the fields of art and history, Existence; in religion, God; and in knowledge and action, Actuality. One of the things we learn from history, and in general from experience, is which of the items in the linked are the primary sources, the best symbols, the easiest avenues for the Ideal, Existence, God, and Actuality. In history, for example, we learn how we might today change our ways, not merely by coming down into the world in a new way, but by attending to those links which are most open to the activity of Existence. And therefore, more sharply, we learn from history to come down in a new way, in the light of our discovery of the openness to Existence of some elements in the linked.

When we ask why we are as we now are, we are in effect trying to find out how the combination of ourselves and Existence came about in the shape of this linked item; when we ask why things are so and so in the past, we take ourselves here and now to be models of normalcy, so as to discover what is aberrant about the past cause. When we are asking why we are as we now are, we evidently cannot have this recourse; but we then know what the ideal state should be. If we want to avoid all evaluative judgments, and merely find out why we are doing what we are, we go back into the past for causes. What we find are three-ply causes—ourselves as private, Existence itself, and the linked world which is constituted by both in part and governed by preceding law-abiding items.

The practical man contents himself with working over the linked world; the contemplative or religious man contents himself with freeing himself from the linked world (detaching himself, if not from linked items, at least from the fruits and thus from the system of linkages); the mystic contents himself with seeing what lies on the other side of the linked world. Buber would like to combine the first and the third; all creativity is primarily occupied with the first and the second; the second and the third is the concern of those who seek symbols and evidences of beings other than ourselves. Those who look at the linkage as a realm to be reorganized in the light of some schematism of excellence are innovators, creators, reformers, etc.

If account be taken of the two modes which sustain or ennoble the linked world (constituted by two interplaying modes), we can acknowledge the linked world to have a kind of substantiality, or at least to provide a kind of inescapable condition for the interplaying modes. Only because the linked world does provide such a condition are realms of action, politics, history, and church possible. Each of these has a reality, and constitutes a domain with its own rationale.

March 12

A controlled way of dealing with the world of the linked is to alter the nature of a proper consequence, either by adding value to it or giving it extra impetus; one can also provide an alternative outcome. In any of these ways there is an expression of a being in a controlled situation. All strategies, all activities which involve alteration in the light of what has been or has been done, all creative work in the arts, are in this situation. So is the Hebraic God; He allows the Hebrews to act, but He then imposes values on the consequences. The Jews are God's chosen people in the sense that they take the consequences of their acts to exhibit God's power and justice; other nations win and lose, enjoy and suffer, but the nature of the winning and losing, the kind of value then exhibited is of a lesser order. The values which accrue could be wholly accounted for by the nature of the antecedents and the ordinary course of development, or by the way a steady God expresses Himself. The Hebrews think that God expresses himself as a controlling force, altering the nature and value of the consequences which are linked to the antecedents.

The Hebrews live out a history of their own; they are an historical people. So are other nations. But in the case of the Hebrews there is supposed to be a controlled expression of the divine. The Hebrews think that one who reads their history properly can see that God is forever just—not loving and not particularly merciful, though sometimes forgiving.

We can say that a work of art, since it involves a constant reassessment of each step in the light of the previous ones, reveals the nature of the artist as a controlling being in a sense similar to that of the Hebrew's God. The Hebraic God, to put the matter the other way, is an artist making use of recalcitrant Hebrews. He contrasts with the Catholic Holy Ghost, for the latter comes in only episodically (or regularly, only to sustain a special subdivision of the Christians, those who make up the Catholic Church) and then in order to inspire and lift men up. But the Hebraic God perpetually takes account of what had been done, in order to see to it that the consequences have some moral bearing on what had been.

When men change their ways in the light of what they had done, they also act in a controlled way and thereby reveal what their characters and their natures are. They are so far deliberate, intending, thoughtful, responsible beings. The consequences they bring about are different from those brought about by others. There is no violation of the linked world in either case, but in the former there are additions in value. We learn what their purpose or intent is, but not what they are in themselves, just as in studying Hebraic history we see what God's purpose is, but not what God is, apart from that purpose. He does not express Himself in the sense of making evident who He is, but only what kind of intent He has, what His justice is like.

A history, which acknowledged that men or God altered consequences, would be oriented toward men and God, even though the consequences were part of a linked world. The linked world could not be properly understood without reference to the controlled activity they exhibit. Since Existence has no intent or power of control, it can come into the world of history only in a regular or in an episodic way, but not from any decision, or will, or purpose.

A history of philosophy could be viewed as one in which a controlled thought is being exercised, for a philosopher writes at later periods in the light of earlier periods. The history of philosophy would then reveal the nature of man as a controlling thinker, and we would learn from that history what an effective thought, as expressing mankind, is like.

Turning to the international field, it seems as if the Russians were more in line with the Hebraic, or artistic view. They take a controlling approach to the world of events. Americans instead content themselves with "ingenuity," the making over what does come about in the best possible way at the time. The Americans are more like the Hindus in relation to the incarnations of the ultimate, except that the Americans do go along with the linked world and thus have a way of connecting the places where the "incarnations," the ingenious expressions and usages, take place.

March 13

Were an animal or a machine to produce a poem, or a painting, or any other "work of art," we would have three alternatives to consider: 1] What it has done is not a work of art, but the surface, the residue of one. A work of art on this view is something controlled, made by a man. We might not know, confronted with a man-made work, whether it was made by a man or not, but this would not affect the fact that the object was made under the dominance of a controlled interest in bringing about a beautiful creation. The work of the machine or animal could have beauty, but it would be a "natural" beauty and not a created one, even though no one could see any difference between them. The controlled intent would be present to be discerned only by an "insight." 2] Both men and animals, or living beings and machines, are mere agents, mere instruments which do certain kinds of things. One of the things one or the other might do is to make what we call a poem. The making would be distinctive but it would not require any supposition of a power or an intent. What we have here is a view which takes the position accredited to the animal or machine in the first alternative, and extends it to man as well—a radical behaviorism or "higher criticism." It grants though that there is something peculiar in this making; what it denies is that it involves any demarcation of man from the rest of the world, and the supposition of any hidden power or psyche. 3] The third position shares with the second the view that man and the rest of the world should be treated in similar ways. It then goes on to take the position of man in the first alternative and supposes that when we have a poem or other work of art made by an animal or machine the animal or machine is inspired, made to do something it otherwise would not do. The work is thought to reflect the presence and control of some being, not necessarily resident in but governing the activities of the machine or animal. They would be said to be "inspired," or under special conditions to be enabled to make the unique object.

The first alternative, as was indicated, has the disadvantage of making us suppose that A] the intent of the artist is present in the work, and B] of seeming to divide off man from the rest of nature. But it has the advantage of keeping clearly in mind that a work of art is a created, man-made object, and that there is a difference between a poem and words strung together. The second alternative has the disadvantage of denying that there is intent, control, despite the fact that we seem to exercise it; it does not know how to bring in assessment, re-evaluation, purpose, and the like. It has the advantage of being cautious, of not making up hypotheses or supposing the existence of entities for which we have no other evidence but brute facts which could conceivably be accepted as they are. The third alternative has the disadvantage of making one suppose not only that there are psyches and the like in other men (even though we have at best only a tenuous grasp of the psyche in ourselves), but that something analogous is present in other things too. It has the advantage of taking the beauty of the made object seriously, and of recognizing that this involves more than a mere mechanical, indifferent, uninterested adding of piece after piece. It sees that the occurrence of this type of beauty in nature is so rare as to allow for the consideration of a divine or similar control in those special cases when a beauty is produced by an animal or machine which is indistinguishable from what a man might bring about.

In view of the fact that men produce their works partly in a mechanical, uncontrolled, or "accidental" way, the second alternative surely has something to say for itself. In view of the fact that men live in an artifactual world, and that the things they do are caught within a social web and meaning involving the produced work in multiple situations of which they perhaps are not aware, but which are nevertheless effective in the sense of involving implications beyond the capacity of an animal or machine to produce, the first alternative is plausible.

In light of the fact that beauty is an excellence which does involve the reassessment of every part, often unconsciously but nevertheless persistently on the part of an artist, it would seem plausible that in those few cases where we have a production of a beautiful object by a subhuman being that we ought to say it is being used or manipulated by a higher power. Consequently, it makes sense to say that all three hypotheses are plausible. Perhaps we ought to begin with the second, and when we find it difficult to continue to accept an odd way of behaving for which we have no antecedent conditioning so far as we can see, to move over to the first hypothesis and recognize that in those cases where we do find men involved in making beautiful objects, we will ascribe to them the artistic power of controlling their productions. Should we find an unusual case of a beauty produced by a machine or an animal, we can move to the third hypothesis and say that in just this case there seems to have been an intrusion by an external power.

We can look at the Bible in this threefold way. We can start with it as a written work having an unusual quality to it. When we cannot account for this quality except by saying "inspired," we ought to remark that it is the product of some power beyond the men, marking the work off from all others. Should we subsequently find in a secular context works of the same magnitude—say Shakespeare and the like—we can then go on and say that in these cases too the divine inspiration is present. The last position is evidently one we do, and ought to, adopt reluctantly, since it does lead us to "metaphysical" suppositions beyond necessity, except where a parity of reasoning forces us to acknowledge what we otherwise would not.

In the first and third alternatives beauty is recognized to be a distinctive, controlled product; in the second and third, it is recognized to be produced by either men or other beings. In the first and second alternatives it is denied that animals and machines exercise an artistic intent or are subject to a power which uses them to express such an intent or power. All three, though, do recognize the presence of the beauty as something distinctive. Similarly in the case of the Bible, the first and third alternatives allow us to recognize the inspired nature of the work; the second and third, that inspiration is exhibited both by religious and nonreligious men (so that God has a cosmic import); the first and second, that there is a difference between a religious and a secular work. In all three cases the Bible is taken to have a special quality, but until we select amongst the three hypotheses, we must say that we do not know if that inspired feature is religious or secular, whether it is the outcome of mere human activity, or whether the fact of its inspiration means that it must be the product of some power beyond (whether the work be thought of as religious or secular).

The third alternative makes too much to be "religious," "artistic," and the like; the second alternative makes too much to be a distinctive kind of behavior for which it has no explanation but the fact that it did occur, and thus that somehow at that time behavior was just that way and not otherwise; the first alternative insists too much on the distinctiveness of a human work even in the face of our inability at times to tell the difference between this and some other kind of work. The first alternative is, I think, the right one, but we ought to come to it only after we have tried to stay with the second, and thus have come to see that we do most justice to distinctive behavior by looking outside the realm of behavior for its explanation. But we ought not to close our minds to the possibility that in some special cases there could be a merely "mechanical" production on the part of men, that it does in fact occur to some degree, and that in other special cases entities which are not men are in fact controlled so as to produce works on a par with man's. We ought, then, not only move to the third via the second and the first under an intellectual compulsion—and only then—but we ought to recognize that at every moment each hypothesis does explain something about an actual creation by a man.

A man creates a work of art partly as a distinctive being exercising a special control or intent, partly as a mechanical, or habituated, or accidentally functioning being, and partly as one who is the creature of some other power, say, his unconscious, society, or some higher or distinctive force outside the natural or the human realm. The first alternative isolates the first, the second alternative, the second, and the third alternative, the third of these elements. The isolation of the elements is justified so far as they in effect are nothing more than insistencies on one over the others, but not as excluding them.

Consequently, we ought to say in the case of an animal making a poem that, though a man and an animal might have acted in different ways, or in similar ways (mechanically, or under some control outside them), the animal may or may not have had as a dominant element the inspiration or the mechanical aspect of its working; and that when a man makes a work of art he may or may not have had as dominant the peculiar power which is man, the mechanical facets he can share with animals, or the inspiration which he might obtain from nature or some other power. It is to be noted that we do not accredit the animal or machine with a "poetic" nature, and thus have only two cases to consider when we confront it, over against the three cases we must consider in connection with man. Given a work of art we take the first alternative of considering the special nature of man only when we can attribute it to a man; otherwise we would, when confronted with a work of art, have to move from the second alternative directly to the third and remark that we cannot stay with a simple behaviorism because of the unusual character of the work, but have no way of knowing whether what produced it is an individual or some power beyond it. From this perspective, the movement should be from the second to the third alternative, and then, when we have found warrant for relating the work to something which we know that we have deliberately produced, moving on to the first.

Another significant alternative is provided by supposing that in the particular case of an animal or other subhuman being, which produces what is indistinguishable from a human work of art, that at that moment there is localized in it (whether by accidental conformations or by the inspiration of some exterior power) a soul or psyche like the artist's. We could say that this lasts in the being only so long as it is evidently producing such a work, and that in the case of man alone (in part because of his organism, in part because of the society in which he belongs, and in part because of his other activities) we should say that he continues to possess the psyche which he occasionally exhibits in making the work of art. Similarly, in connection with secular literature of great magnitude we can say that it for the moment exhibits a religious dimension, whereas in the case of the Bible this is but one of a number of cases, all connected, where the divine power or inspiration is being made manifest through certain individuals who belong to a certain kind of enterprise. The divine or other transcendent or non-animal power would be said to operate in the particular cases in distinctive ways answering to the nature of those cases, but would do so episodically in the case of the subhuman or secular, and constantly in the case of the human or religious. Oddly enough, the common way of speaking of the artist as inspired in an unusual way at certain times, as being in the grip of some unusual force, is a way of speaking of him in terms of an episodically appearing power; this allows one to say that both men and animals, when they produce a work of art, are to be said to be momentarily in the grip of a power, which they may or may not have localized as their own psyches. Taking this as a distinctive alternative we then have:

1] Men are distinctive beings and may express this in the making of works of art.

2] Men and other beings all behave phenomenally; the work of art is but a distinctive natural product.

3] Men and other beings are agents for the expression of some outside power, particularly when they produce works of art.

4] Men and other beings, when they produce works of art, are momentarily functioning as instruments for some power, and will fall back into a natural or nonartistic state when the particular production is completed.

The fourth alternative is a cautious one; it is almost a "safe and stupid" one since it seems to repeat the facts in another form and on another level. It says in effect that a work of art is produced by a being who is then and there an artist, as testified by the fact that it has produced a work of art. It will lead one to say that the writers of the Bible and other classical works are then and there inspired religiously just so far and just so long as they in fact produce the works which we recognize to be beyond ordinary human power.

The fourth alternative can also be reconciled somewhat with the second. The behavioral pattern which eventuates in a work of art could be said to be a localization of some power, as is evident from the fact that it now produces what otherwise would not be produced. But instead of saying with the third or fourth view that such a power lives outside the activity, we content ourselves with remarking that it is present in the activity. It is as if we abandoned the view of a transcendent but interested God, for one who was episodically immanent, immanent only at those times when in fact the great works are produced—but immanent not because it had transformed itself, but because it had come to be as such an immanent force then and there, perhaps because of what had gone before. There would then be a kind of inheritance which would be acknowledged even inside a strict behavioristic account; to avoid mere blankness and failure of explanation one would say that the immanent power, the bringing about of the unusual result was no mere adventitious, inexplicable accident, but the consequence of a congealing of natural forces and the manifestation of them in an ordinary way, but under the influence of what had gone before. Consequently, we would be faced with the question of how the past could be effective in the present in those cases where we have no system of tradition or inheritance.

If we view history as an autonomous realm, we take something like this last stated position. We then suppose its changes are due not to powers outside it, but in fact to itself as effectively governed by what had been past. We would of course always have to wait to see what had happened, to see how the past had operated. The advantages of the other alternatives is to allow one to say that something could be done if it were desired by some power. In any case, to have an explanation we cannot content ourselves with the second alternative, but must go on to affirm as a fifth alternative:

5] The behavior which produces a work of art, whether it is exhibited by a man or a subhuman being, is the outcome of an operation of the past on the present, (allowing the behavior to be understood without recourse to a transcendent realm).

We then have a choice between looking for a human power, a transcendent power which uses men and other beings, a localization of a transcendent power, or a transmutation of occurrences in the present through the operation of the past. In all the cases we look to something outside the present activity to explain it, and are always confronted with the fact that it might be the product of chance or adventitious occurrences.

March 14

A sixth alternative can be added to the ones listed yesterday:

6] Nature can be thought of as congealing itself at a given moment in the shape of an animal or a man to produce a work of art.

Where the fifth alternative envisaged a temporal congealing of the past in the present, the sixth takes nature as at a given time. Also, it does not make the power of nature a "transcendent" one, except in the sense of being outside the given individual. This is perhaps a better way of speaking of the fifth and sixth—the occurrence of a work of art is to be viewed as one which is merely mediated by the individual being, it being left somewhat undetermined just what kind of being is using it or mediating by means of it. It could be a being which was deliberate or it could be one which worked blindly. In any case, we can here clearly distinguish machines which produce works of art, from animals or other subhumans which do. The machines could be said to have been perhaps unconsciously designed so that they are extensions of the intent or meaning of man. But when we come to the animal kingdom and nature as a whole and take account of them working, or living, or moving in their apparently habitual ways, without being affected by man, we are driven to affirm either that they do not produce works of art but only objects of beauty (the position taken in the first and second alternative, of which the first is in *The World of Art*), or that if they produce works of art it is as a result of both man and subhuman beings functioning as agents, instruments, accumulations, or localizations (the alternatives 3–6).

Confronted with a work of excellence by a subhuman being, we could say that this is one of the incidental productions of the whole of nature either in sense 5 and 6, and yet could be on a par with what men deliberately produce. But men, either because they have a power inside themselves, or because they belong to a society or to humanity, or because they are singularly sustained by some power outside themselves, natural or divine, will be recognized to be beings who could produce such works again and again. Should it turn out that a subhuman being again and again produces works which are indistinguishable from those made by men, we will have to revise our hypothesis about the nature of the works of art. We will have to say either A] that men once could produce them in the way I have said but animals could not (or nature as a whole could not), or could do so only occasionally at rare intervals, but now the situations have changed and men no longer are able to produce them; or B] that now animals can produce them and the power of artistic creativity has been extended to animalkind or nature as a whole. If we wish to distinguish men from animals or nature as a whole, on the second supposition we must say that men can engage in creative acts in other areas, or that they have created a society with traditions, which the animals or nature as a whole have not.

We can take advantage of the fact that excellent works which are presumably made by nature as a whole, or in or by some localized being, and which might even be thought to be the outcome of sheer chance concatenations, are infrequent. We could take the difference between man and animal to lie in mankind's being able to produce many artists, and in mankind's ability to exercise the same power in other areas. We could see the difference between a human artist and an animal to be in the capacity of the artist to continue to produce works of art and to be able to exhibit that power in other directions as well. If animals persisted in making works of art, we would have to say that man had lost his grip or that the animals had, so far, caught up with man.

The attempt to make an "epistemic correlation" between the formalities of science and the commonsensical or sensible elements exterior to it involves a bare external connection, and is bound to fail if there is no mid-point, no schematism in which both sides can be imbedded. There are, in fact, two such schematisms. One is in the shape of the common-sense objects and the world from which both sides were initially derived; another is in the shape of the engineering object (which is common sense refined under the supervision of scientific ideas). The engineering object does not involve a correlation with scientific ones; it is a common-sense object remade with the scientific formulae as guides, rules, principles, to be modified, qualified, added to, and ignored according to the demands of common-sense needs.

We could have gone the other way; we could make a schematism by altering the common-sense object in the light of a perceptual, valuational, sensible, or eventful, and perhaps even aesthetic demand. We would then be able to speak of those acceptable or permissible areas, or objects of common sense in which we find the kind of structures acknowledged by science, more or less altered. The aesthetic, perceptual, etc. (perhaps even the political and religious), could then serve as guides, and rules, and indices telling us what to do with, and how to classify, the various common-sense items, and in this sense alter them somewhat as engineering does from the other side. (The perceptual, etc., could tell us what are verifiable, useful, identifiable objects and thus those which are proper termini for scientific investigations and formulae.)

If we combine both devices—the engineering and the perceptual, etc.—we refine common sense in a double way and then have an engineering selected world in which we find loci for scientific formulae, and paradigmatic cases of the perceptual, etc. Such a result is however a constructed one; the solution of the problem of the relation of science, etc., to perceptual data, etc., would then be the making of an object (out of common sense) which will do most justice to both of these abstractions. The correlation is already accomplished in common-sense and needs only refinement, as should be obvious since the items were derived from common sense in the first place, and refine it in the second.

The realm of nature, of animals, etc., is itself something conceived— this would apparently be the way in which Hegel would confront the problem with which I have been struggling yesterday and today. He would try to show that the proper way to grasp what is other than the artist (to stay with this limited form of his approach) is to be seen as the artist from another side. Consequently, the approach from the standpoint of man, the being who can create, must take the entire world which he confronts, not to express some power beyond it, but only itself. Art, on this account, faces the subhuman as itself in another guise. In the end the production of a work of art from something in or by that realm is what is to be expected; but it should be attributed not to the subhuman or to man, but to both together. A world in which men create works of art is one in which, strictly speaking, works of art are neutral items, the very substance of the extremes, one side of which is artists or men and the other side of which is the rest of the universe. The work of art is not to be attributed to a man, or perhaps to anyone; it just occurs as the outcome of the action of men on the world, and conversely. That the production should be seen to issue out of this or that cranny is no indication, on this view, of its having originated there, nor does it warrant the attribution of it to this or that component of the production.

Man, though limited, and here treated as something "inner" over against works of art, would be faced with himself in the guise of known nature (where nature is being understood as short for the rest of the cosmos), and would interplay with this. When he makes a work of art, nature is contributing something, but the bias is toward him. If we say that nature is producing it, he will be viewed as making his contribution in a product having a bias toward nature. Nature in the first case contributes by virtue of its resistance and its conceptual status as a "thing" or nonhuman domain; man in the second case contributes by virtue of his acknowledgment of nature, and his placing of it inside the frame of aesthetic objects, and perhaps also by his resistance, his holding of his society over against nature.

We have then a seventh alternative:

7] Works of art are the joint products of man and the world beyond, and are, strictly speaking, to be attributed to neither.

If an animal or a machine produced a work, the adoption of it as excellent by us would bring it into the human realm. The fact that it came out of the animal or through the supposed contingent operations of nature would not indicate the basic source of the work of art, which in the end would be a synthesis of man and the world beyond.

It could be argued that the work was what it was when it came out of nature apart from man, that it had its beauty in and of itself. In what sense then could man be said to contribute to it? By his classifying it? We seem then to lose the integrity or dignity of individual artists and eventually of mankind as somehow superior, and as capable of producing things which others do not usually produce. Would it not be better then to move to:

8] Works of art are the joint products of man and non-man and are to   be attributed to man as a primary agent except in exceptional cases. The exceptional cases here are evident, controlled unique activities. Deliberation, control, possession, and expression will no longer be primary categories for the understanding of art. We will instead start with a kind of cosmic working, with an incidental election of primary agents through which the cosmic working becomes manifest. A work of art would then testify to something in the way in which the human and subhuman came together in certain primary ways, to produce excellence. When we attribute the main share to randomness, etc., we point up something of the way nature in and of itself is in operation; if randomness can produce this, nature is as magnificent and mysterious as the creative power of the artist.

This last alternative allows us to get back to the first, for we can say that though the work produced conjointly is beautiful, when attributed to man (even as only an agent) it is a work of art, and when attributed to animals it is not. So once again we would have the problem of knowing where to attribute a beautiful object whose origin we do not know. Our question is then whether the beauty came out deliberately (or at least humanly) or cosmically (or at least subhumanly) and if the latter, what it tells us about the nonhuman. Whichever way the first question is answered, we would have to say that the production of it involved the same principles. (An animal could be for the whole non-human realm, roughly what our hands, and feet, and our random movements are for ourselves. Since we do not attribute the work to those movements, but to ourselves—even when we are not aware of ourselves operating—we could similarly attribute the work to the world beyond the animal or beyond the randomness and not to them.)

We look at the subhuman as instruments and at ourselves as agents. Confronted with a work which might have been produced by an animal, we face the question as to whether the primary actor was an instrument (of the world beyond) or an agent (of himself in his recesses or of the world beyond). Since an agent makes use of instruments—his body—the question comes down to: Is there an agent or not? In either case the work is the product of instruments but we do not know whether there is or is not an agent which makes use of those instruments.

If we take into account the fact that every artistic production involves some criticism of the work, we can forge a ninth alternative:

9] All beautiful works are the product of nature, directly or indirectly.
   A work of art involves criticism. If made while the work is produced, it is a human work of art; if later, it is an appreciated work of art.

All spectators make appreciated works of art, if they appreciate works which are works of art. (If they appreciate as a work of art what does not have beauty, they are in error.) The question then remains as to whether the work was one which had been appreciated in the making. (Since it is appreciated later we can of course say that all works of art are the joint products of man and the world beyond.) To ascertain whether it was appreciated while being made, we would have to know if a man made it deliberately. This we do not surely know, even if we know that a man made it. Consequently, we are often in no better position, with respect to a human work, to know whether it was a work of art apart from an independent spectator or not, than we are with respect to a subhuman being. We now have another alternative:

10] Works of art are the joint products of appreciation and natural (or supernatural) forces. Only in special cases are the two forces operative in the same being; only in those cases do we have "created" works of art.

If we know a beautiful work to be the product of a random activity or of some subhuman being, we know that it is not created. But if we know that it is the product of a man working over material, we still do not know if it is a created work. Only in rare cases, perhaps only where we ourselves are self-consciously making a work, can we be sure. Of course, nature and animals are without much nuance, and as a rule we can readily distinguish those works which are made by constant reassessment through appreciation and those which are not. But the question concerns those cases where the latter looks like and can in fact be confounded with the former.

We should accept a monkey's work as a work of art once we appreciate it to be a work like those which men create, just as we accept men's works as works of art if they are like those which other men are known, self-consciously or appreciatively, to have made. If we hesitate with the monkey or the random movement, we should also hesitate with the men (unless we see men as standing outside nature and thus necessarily, by that fact, making a kind of work that no other beings can).

March 15

The question of subhumans making art boils down in the end to the fact that we think that a man exercises control at least some of the time; we suppose that he does some things in the light of what he did elsewhere. If we could find a model object of which various works are variations either by being adjusted to circumstance, need, or the conditions of the making, we would say that it had been controlled. But if we have no such model and confront the object as such, can we tell whether it has been occasionally organized in the light of what had been done, or not?

Hegel's answer, or better an answer which could be derived from Hegel, is that art is the product of a being who looks with his reassessments at a world which is the inverse of himself. When an animal produces the work of art it is the focal point of an act on the part of the Ideal, God, and Existence together working out their nature in a nonassessing way. A work of art indifferently expresses the nature of a reassessing man in a domain outside himself, and expresses the nature of a domain outside him as that which has him as the ultimate appreciator. In *The World of Art* it is said that art iconizes Existence; on this present view it would *exhibit* Existence, and *iconize* it only if it is integrated with Ideality and God. This present view is perhaps better than the other.

(When we apply this answer to the current question of the use of language for philosophy, we see that the English school in some blind way recognizes that common usage can answer only to the kind of problems which a common society faces, and that the man it expresses cannot be a speculative, but must in fact be a commonplace or "common-sensical" man. If we are to have a language adequate to the cosmos, we must ourselves have a "philosophic mind" and express ourselves in such a way that what we are reporting is the cosmos. The language will itself equally reveal what it is to think philosophically and what it is to be a cosmos; it will expose the categories of the one and the structures of the other.)

The knowledge that there have been reassessments in the course of the production of a work of art does not enable us to define a work of art but to classify it. If an animal can produce it, it is still a work of art—and more than a thing of beauty—so far as   A] it is made in humanized form—on canvas, with a typewriter, in words, etc.,   B] is inside the humanized tradition of painting, etc. These are the features which show that the work, though issuing from nature or a larger cosmos, is part of the background of man, even apart from his appreciation.

This type of solution, which seems to me so far to be the best, is in effect a further alternative to those considered on previous days. It also allows one to deal with the knowledge of other minds in a twofold way. We can say of other men that they constitute a single domain with us; so far as they do, to have a mind is nothing else but to belong to this domain over against the rest of the universe. The evidence of the existence of a mind is given by standing with other men to be over against all else.

We can also view other beings as part of and expressions of a universe over against us. Those which are like us in appearance are to be thought of as being, like us, focal points of something beyond them. But this beyond is actually larger than the individual; there need be no inference that other beings have minds like ours severally, but only as together, constituting a world to which we perhaps might want to belong.

When we ask about the minds of others we are perhaps asking how we can know how they feel, or whether they have minds like our own. The first question we cannot answer, but the second follows from our identification of our lot with theirs, for they must then, with us, be equally representative of all of us together.

A work of art is only one expression of man's creativity. An animal which could produce such a work could not be brought into the human orbit by that fact alone. Not even if it did nothing more than produce works of art. A man always belongs to a community of men and the work of art which he produces is inescapably an expression of that community as well as of himself. So we come back in the end to some modification of the first of the alternatives. But while recognizing that man alone produces art, it is now being allowed that animals might be said to do so too; also it is being said that the art work is the joint product of two dimensions, a human and a nonhuman, and that the "creative" reassessments characteristic of man are to be found to have their equivalents in the focalization of the world beyond man. A work becomes more and more an art work depending on what role it plays in the human realm. Having been accepted as a work of art, even though produced by an animal, a work becomes a significant part of the human realm and is part of the history of art.

A consequence of the foregoing view is that if an object is produced through random activity and is recognized to be on a par with what is produced deliberately, it can be taken to be the expression of a focalization having reference to the being of man. In short, we can say of an unusual concatenation, which could have been treated as a mere contingent occurrence in a random activity, that it is a focal, special way of exhibiting the randomness. Instead of following the cue, then, of social scientists and other statisticians and maintaining that when something of low probability occurs we have a causal situation, we can maintain that instead we have the inverse of what a man might deliberately do. In short, instead of treating it as an effect of an efficient cause, one can treat it as the product of an exteriorization of a "material" cause or "formal" cause, of the interior as such—an interior though which is not to be thought of as being deliberate, nor rational, but merely as that which is coming to expression.

A work of art, like a perfect language, would be the expression of an unusual power, carried out by men in part as individuals, and completely as parts of a human domain, and occasionally illustrated by subhuman beings as focalizations of whatever reality lies outside the human domain. Each domain, the human and the nonhuman, would be able to express itself in a language or a work of art against the background of the other. The language or the art taken neutrally will be equally attributable to one or the other.

Confronted with a beautiful work we ought to attribute it to men, for beautiful works are normally made by men. If we know it to be made by a subhuman we ought to see just how far it falls short of what men can do. If it is the very duplicate of a work of man, then we must see it as the expression of a power outside it which is the counterpart of human, individual, or community power. On the one side we have the free individual or the individual in a community (whose nature he expresses with more or less freedom, and which he helps constitute with his free act), and on the other we have the exteriorization of another world (which need not be viewed as a mechanical, or irrational, or inexplicable exteriorization, since we can find, in the constancy of the laws which the phenomena exhibit, a kind of rational being made manifest). The being of the other world over against man is one which requires constant focalization, constant expression in the phenomena in accord with the laws of probability. The occurrence of a probable event (whether of high or low probability is of no consequence), is never itself merely probable. It is a singular event, to be accounted for only as coming from the interior. The exterior world is governed by laws and probabilities and does not account for localizations and instantiations.

Architecture, as the discipline which combines both "artistic" and "engineering" elements, sees itself most clearly to be the juncture of the two worlds. More than the other arts, it looks to philosophers to tell it what the nature of the basic outlook on things is. It sees that a reference to mere art appreciation is insufficient to take care of the engineering side, and that a reference to utility and practical considerations is insufficient to take care of the aesthetic side. It sees itself as an art having both sides, and must therefore look for guidance from that discipline which alone is alert to the reality of both sides as belonging together.

One might go on to affirm that religious ritual or prayer, ethico-political activity, and pragmatic knowledge are also intermediary "languages" which reflect the coming together of the domain of man with whatever lies beyond, but within which the texture of one of the modes of being is caught. Perhaps it is best to say that developed art, religion, etc., reflect only the mode whose texture they catch, and that artistic experience, religious experience, etc., reflect all the modes at once. Also one can look at some intermediary as being the focal point of one mode standing over against man as together with the remaining modes. Thus God might be said to have a "language" (prophesy, miracle) expressing Himself as a counterweight of all else. The Ideal might be said to have a "language" (value, purpose, obligation) expressing itself and man as the counterweight of all else. Actuality might be said to have a language (personality, concern, love) expressing itself as the counterweight of the other modes and man as well (?). Existence might be said to have a language (force, brutality) expressing itself as the counterweight of all else. In these cases the language is actually a kind of experience or imposition of data. A language, strictly speaking, would require that it give itself to only one mode, whose texture it incorporates.

Every language seems to be a kind of togetherness, and so does every type of experience. These togethernesses function fully only when they do justice to both sides. The merging represented by the dot is specialized in the different languages and types of experiencing, so far as we begin from Actuality. To exhibit the type of togetherness represented by the comma, etc., recourse must be had to what is not a language or an experience. Perhaps what is needed A] is a name for the comma; B] a formula for the "if then"; and C] instruments for the "therefore."

If we take the position of language or experience, and thus if we take the position of a history (understood to be the juncture of two dimensions which reflect one another's nature, the one by virtue of its intent and career, the other by virtue of its law-abidingness and magnitude), we can read the outcome indifferently in one of two ways. We can say with equal justice and illumination that history reveals the American people's response to changes in the realm of Existence, or that it reveals how Existence elicited from men, at various points in their being, certain responses to it. In the one case Existence is taken to be routine and the men active; in the other Existence is probing and the men merely reactive or responsive. Men as active should make history revelatory of probing nature, clarifying it and in a sense possessing it. Existence as probing should be revelatory of the nature of man as capable of being active, controlling, decisive.

A proper awareness of the fact that a man produced a work of art should involve the awareness that nature could have done it herself by a focalization in an animal against the background of man. Conversely, the acknowledgment of the work as an animal's product, is the awareness of it as something which a man might have freely made.

March 16

Using a and b to represent man and the world beyond, either in the shape of one mode or a combination of them, we find each can act on the other to constitute a biased domain in between. The outcome, x, can be viewed by the producer—let this be a—as an externalization of itself in the passive being of b, in which case it has expressed a truth, or it can adopt this x and having then viewed it as nothing more than a continuation of itself, as itself self-expressed, can gaze into the being of the other. The b is then an object of intent.

When either a or b acts, it acts from within; but when either functions as a base for the other it acts as a linear structure. We can use x as a neutral reality if it can be seen to state the nature of the linear structure as well as of the producer. X is what b, as a domain of laws, is like at this moment; it is the epitomization of b in the sense of being a resting point and a convergent point in the whole realm of b, and is thus offered by a as the summary meaning of the whole of b. B could have produced x as that which is to fit inside the realm of a, taken linearly. If x be a work of art, then the mechanical products of man, even his "natural" behavior, is a variant of art, when all of nature is treated as the background against which man can display himself. This is of course true only so far as the work is treated as that which uses *b* passively.

Man is able to express what *b* is, by acting in any way whatsoever in the passive body of *b,* for *b* is for him precisely that domain which is 1] acceptive of these various products, and   2] that which is being funneled through him. The converse is equally true. From the standpoint of *b,* the product *x,* say a work of art, could be produced by it, against the background of mankind. The *x* is then a natural product.

Both artifactual and natural products are revelatory of the nature of mankind in the sense that   1] mankind is receptive to the production of these, and appreciates them as "works of art," as "mechanical," etc., and   2] that the depth of *b* is but a way in which the kind of creative power which we know in *a* is to be understood. Put still another way: to understand what man's power (*a*) is like, we look at what nature (*b*) can do. It (*b*) indifferently produces a work of art (*x*) or some miscellaneous grouping (x^1) in accordance with its own laws. It (*b*) then tells us what it means to be the truth of *a* (i.e. what *a* is as receptive), and what it means to be part of the linear order or domain of *a* (when we view the outcome of *b* as a classified object, whether this be art or anything else).

If we want to view the product *x* neutrally, we must see it as that which, though produced by *a* or by *b,* could have been produced by *b* or *a.* The full appreciation of *x* by *a* is to see it as that which expresses the meaning of the whole linear realm of *b.* To fully appreciate the work of art as a neutral product is to see it as that which could have been produced by nature itself within the context of nature's laws. To fully appreciate the work of art is to see that, if it were produced by an animal, it would be produced as a product of nature in and of itself working according to its own laws, and thus that it would be the full and concentrated expression of nature as an integral domain. But we can say this too of the work of art which a man has produced. Conversely, we can look at any chance happening, which occurs apart from man, as being, like a work of art, that which could have been made by man.

The chance happening, precisely by its defiance and exteriority to what is normally produced by man deliberately, is recognized to have a singular position in the human domain, exciting wonder there and perhaps forcing the use of words in a new way. This fact embodies the meaning of man as expressing himself within the human realm as surely as the created product *x* does (though the *x* is a better expression since, in a more direct and complete way, it is a product of control, a localization of excellence, and an exhibition of man as he is within).

Conversely, if a subhuman being turns out a portrait or a poem on a footing with a human creation, anything that a man might do (and thus all his created works) can be viewed as instantiations of nature herself, revealing her as a juncture of an internal power and a linear order. The absorption of all mankind inside her domain is but a recognition that the powers which man exhibits are natural powers— or even more sharply, are the expression of alien modes of being, using him as a vehicle. They would be no more significant than the ordinary things which come about daily in nature.

A work of art or a purely natural outcome are possible from both sides. If both *a* and *b* produced a work of art at the same time, if they cooperated, we would have a foolish duplication, for the work could have been achieved by *a* working on *b*. Conversely, for a mechanical act. It is for that reason unnecessary and even undesirable for man to engage in mechanical acts, for nature can do this perfectly well without his aid. In order to have a neutral content, a realm which could be read off as that which reveals what man and nature are inwardly and linearly, we must intersperse the one with the other, each working in its own way and producing its characteristic products. Sometimes the outcome might be mechanical and sometimes artistic. By referring the products of one to that one alone (whether beautiful or not, an art object or not), we learn only the nature of its working in its own peculiar way. What we want is the joint product of it and the other, viewed indifferently, and read off as expressive of both of them in different ways. We want to take a dialogue and, instead of ascribing the different components to different men, or viewing it indifferently as somehow bigger than either, we want it to tell us about each. In the extreme case the words uttered by *m* could be said to reveal *n*, and those uttered by *n* to reveal *m*—being addressed to him they are his, and are also descriptive of him. "I love you" means you are lovable, and "You are a liar" means that you have at least provoked me to speak in this fashion. The dissolution of the joint product is the recognition that there are other joint products constituted from other sides, making other kinds of togethernesses.

A and *b* are interspersed, pace one another. Can we not say the same thing for a production of a work of art, speak of it as an interspersing of, say, form and matter? If so, could we say that the matter is active or produced, and that the form or meaning receives the matter from us? Could we say that we make the grain, and that the meaning or the emotion is there? This surely can be said in the sense that the grain is used and the meaning or emotion is what we intend to have there.

Is the Civil War then the joint product of the American people and the realm of Existence? Can we divide it into different components, attributing this or that, as we like, to the American people? Do we not then have a radical relativity of interpretation? Is it not wrong to say that when men speak to one another one can break up the dialogue in any way he likes, attributing this to *a* and that to *b* indifferently? If the division is not arbitrary, if it is done on some principle, it should not be indifferent. The principle should be that which enables us to understand one side as expressing what the other is—i.e., to understand the combination of both as that which could have been produced by the other. My part in the dialogue is mine only so far as I see it as that which he understands and makes his own, and therefore does say what he does, as his part of the dialogue. I am him *sotto voce*. And conversely.

We attribute to one side (*a*) in the neutral language (which is between us both and constituted by both those elements—originating with (*a*) or not, and whether we know that it originated with it or not—what would, if accredited to the other, (*b*), act as that which demands, conditions, elicits, explains *a*. What then has nature done? She has done whatever in our joint work makes possible what I create. Conversely, what have I done? I have done whatever makes it possible for her to be a domain of intelligible laws which allow art, for example, to be produced. Could I say that she is fertile and I stagnant? No, for I cannot show how my stagnant being makes it possible for her to be fertile, or how her fertility explains my being stagnant.

Could we say that the Civil War is the result of geography? No, because we cannot see how this could cause the tension or hatred. Could we take the different tempers expressed by the North and South to define the cause? Yes, if we can then show how this might make for the working of physical geography on us, and reciprocally; if we can show how the different tempers affected that geography in the sense of making it an area in which men were to live with their diverse tempers.

Moving now over to the *Modes*, we must say that a full togetherness of the modes means that we can so dissect it that the contribution of one triggers those of the others. There will be four components in each, and there will be four kinds of togetherness. To understand how the modes can be neutrally merged we would have to see how each offers its kind of contribution to constitute the single whole in which each component serves to space the others. We will explain the presence of each in another as allowing for the understanding of the resulting togetherness.

But if a togetherness could be attributed to one mode, why do we need the others? If all that men do could be seen as the product of nature why do we have to suppose that men do anything? There is always a passive field on which to work. To attribute this, too, to the worker is to accept something like a Fichtean non-ego as postulated by the ego, and is to have the duality all over again, any way.

We cannot attribute the entire togetherness to a mode because there are resistances for it on which its own components are imposed. But it was just said that the entire business could have been viewed as the product of one of the modes. Yes, but only so far as a part of that product is held apart from that mode. The part held apart enters into the realm of the mode as a triggering for it, a condition for it. This does not mean that it produces the mode or owns the mode, but only that it operates there.

But might we not then turn the matter around and view the part as our own product, so that it is we who belong to that mode? No, for we are active. If we are to suppose that we are actively making a supposition that there is something which will be passive for us, we once again take a Fichtean position. What we have a right to say is that the part is a trigger in ourselves, forcing us to produce the contribution that we in fact make.

This means that a work produced by an animal is, as a work of art, part of our appreciated world, but can be given a place inside the more monotonous totality of nature. Our appreciation, together with the work, will be a focalized area in nature which then and there shows why nature does this next rather than that. In short, man must be understood to start over against nature (when nature produces things which have human import) just as surely as (when he works in characteristic ways) he is explicable by natural principles. Society should be understood as a moment in the entire realm of nature—as Spinoza indicated. But society also has a being apart; indeed, the whole of nature has a being inside it as a moment, as some modern sociologists such as Merton, have been contending.

A neutral togetherness is "organic" in time rather than a sequence of triggers; or better, perhaps—since every item is a trigger for the one that succeeds it, so far as this is understood to have originated elsewhere—every item has the potential role of being a trigger or being triggered when and as it constitutes a single, structured, vital ongoing with others. That ongoing has its own rationale; every item in it has the double import of being part of a linear order and being a member of some transcendent realm. The exact locus and nature of the latter, one does not know, but an item will be assigned to it in the attempt to understand how it comes about from sources outside itself. The realm of history on this view is a sequence of interrelated items which, though the product in fact of both, can be attributed to either mankind or Existence for origin. It is to be so attributed only so far as they can be understood as triggers. In history they have an affiliation for one another, stand on a footing with one another to constitute a new kind of interpenetrative, interdependent set of items.

Though each side can be said to be the locus or origin of the entire joint product, it must be emphasized that each side makes a distinctive contribution. It is not that man is natural or that nature is intelligent that allows for the attribution of their joint product to either, but the fact that they are one another's other. More completely, each mode has the other three modes as its other, and what the mode does with their aid, as passive, but expresses what they could have passively done with its aid.

A world of art made by nature is still not a world of art made by man; a mechanical world of men is not yet the mechanical world of nature. Where man knows and creates, Existence divides and terminates. The division and the termination, though they may end with the very same products as the creation, are nevertheless different modes of exteriorization and linearization. It is precisely in seeing how what is other than it triggers it (in contrast with the way in which its items can trigger that other) that one discovers their distinctive natures and roles.

Existence (and the other modes) interspersed between the activities of Actuality, function as divisive (and valuational and unifying) powers which enable the different activities of Actuality to constitute a single domain. (We could say that the four modes are equally paced and pacing, in all four ways of togetherness, but I think it more correct to say that there is God for the comma, Existence for the therefore, Ideal for the if-then, and Actuality for the dot as offering the elements to be triggered. If we want to see how, say, God functions as a trigger, we must turn from the togetherness of the comma to that of, say, a dot, etc.)

March 17

The two sides of an enterprise, *a* and *b,* might express themselves insufficiently, with the result that the product exhibits only a part of the meaning of both. Or one of them might express itself insufficiently and the other sufficiently. In that case the joint product is constituted of two types of item, and one would, in breaking up that product, have to do it in such a way that it becomes the evidence of the inward nature of one and of the superficial nature of the other. And if each side expresses itself fully it makes a proper response to the other side only if it adopts the contribution made by that other, as being as deeply grounded as its own.

Given two nations, say Russia and the United States, we have first to see if they express their "spirits" to the same degree, or if one (or perhaps both) has identified itself with one of its expressions or with the very conditions which enable it to operate. Let us suppose that the United States has identified itself with the land of the United States and the Russians are expressing themselves as a people. In that case their joint product will be the defense measures of the United States for the land and the spirit of ambition, or whatever, that might be characteristic of the Russian people, as manifested in, e.g., flexible policies of taking advantage of situations wherever they occur. This joint product will be defense measures interspersed with tactical maneuvers, and this will be the world they together constitute. We could not understand the Russians or they us until they recognized where we expressed our respective natures, and to what degree. If we on our side took the joint product to be the common language or world, we would have to take the tactics of the other as expressive—not, as with us, of a nature integrated with a land—of a free nature. We would in effect equate their free nature with ourselves-as-integrated-with-our-land, adopting their free expression in ourselves only in a restricted form, i.e., as effective only with respect to ourselves as involved in the land. They on their side would have to adopt our nature as involved in land as expressive of a power as basic, inward and ultimate as their own freedom. In effect this would mean that they would see us expressing some power which is not ourselves. And this they do when they see us as capitalists and themselves as a Russian people. We in dealing with them as willful or malicious, and ourselves as demanding no territory, take the other position. To understand ourselves and them fully it is desirable that both sides detach themselves to the degree of enabling themselves to be free, and that they then adopt the free expression of the other as on a footing in themselves with their own free expression. Only in this way will they see one another as on a footing with themselves, and the joint product as the expression of their coordinated togetherness.

If we think of the North in the Civil War as expressing itself in a new economy, and the South as involved in an economy which was part of its very meaning and being, we have the analogue of what was just taken to be the difference between Russia and the United States. Whatever the North and South did with reference to one another constituted the history of the United States. That history was not one which expressed the natures of both sides equally, since it was the product of the life of the South and the nature only of the North. (The product, let us say, was a semi-cultural Southern totality interspersed with an economic one on the part of the North.) If either side understood the other in the sense of adopting fully the expressions of the other as on a footing with its own, we would have a mutual understanding which might continue even while the product of the two sides issued in a war. To avoid the war it would have been necessary for each side to be free, to see the other as free in itself, to see the expression which resulted, and then to adopt it as equal to its own. The South should have separated itself off from its "way of life" as involving economics, to get back into itself as a free Southern spirit (which is of course not to be divorced from the way in which it is expressed in customs, laws, etc.). The North should have then treated the economics of the South as something which was to be interspersed with that of the North, and on a footing with it. It could then have seen that the United States economics was the joint product of both sides, and that either side could have expressed itself in such a joint product, the contribution of the other side functioning then as a recessive triggering of a tensional component for its own contribution. The recognition of the fact that one could have produced the triggering element oneself shows that one has the other nature in oneself, as one's counterpart. Consequently there could be a constant interplay of the two economies with a correlative free being of the diverse natures.

The immorality of slavery must be distinguished from the economics of it, from it as a publicly expressed institution. For the South it is immoral so far as it has identified its nature with slavery; the removal of slavery is one with the recognition that the Southern way is distinguishable from the practice of slavery, and the awareness that the institution of slavery must take its place within the totality of institutions which make up the American people. The South should not have identified its way of life with slavery, the North should not have identified the meaning of the spirit of the South as slave-holding.

A husband and wife make a marriage. The one comes home and says "I am hungry." He is met with silence, and then responds in anger. This marriage might end in divorce. To avoid that outcome it would be necessary for each to see the speech and silence as expressions of natures on a footing with its own.

Each must see that the speech produced the silence, that the silence produced the anger, that the silence is the creature of the speech, and that the anger is the creature of the silence. Each erred in identifying the other with the speech or silence, instead of seeing these as expressions of a being coordinate with itself and as capable as itself is of the sequence of speech, silence, and anger. Each might have identified itself with its own expression, in which case the center of gravity of the marriage would not have been in the speech, silence, and anger, but in the discrepant behavior which they together constituted outside those expressions. Their solution lies in seeing the other as itself (not as being identical in nature, but in freedom and value) and as doing from the other side what it itself is doing.

The victim does not commit the crime, of course, except in the sense that he too is humanity. The evildoer identifies the victim with a public expression, and works on that expression so as to preclude the victim from continuing to express himself in that way. The result is that the center between them is not between free men but between a man and a being (the victim) who is defined to be a condition for the other.

March 29

The so-called problem of other minds breaks down into the following problems:

1] Does something which I know have to be something for another? The answer is in the affirmative. And the other for which it must be is the correlative of myself. To be a conscious being, I must be othered by and must other another consciousness. If that which I know did not have a being for another, it would be entirely private and I could not know that I was substantial. My substantiality is one with the recognition that some content which I confront is content for some other being, who is conscious if I am conscious.

2] What is the other being like? It might conceivably be myself if I

could be my own other, say in the past or the future. It might be
nothing more or less than the entire cosmos. It could be God.

3] Must the object, which I know, be sustained by something else in
the same way that I am? This is what idealists and panpsychists suppose, but there is no warrant for the supposition. The content might be
sustained by an active God; and in any case it need not be in another
in the same way it is for me.

4] If it is not for another in the same way it is for me, it is so far not
the object of another consciousness. This is correct. But this means only
that, even if it be sustained by what is not a consciousness, it must still
be sustained by a consciousness.

5] Where is that consciousness? It could conceivably be at the place
where the item is known by me, or it might be outside this, or at a distance from it.

6] How can we locate that consciousness? We can see if the item is
part of a rational or purposive order. If it be a "secondary" quality or a
quantity, we can find no such order at the place where it is manifest,
but only in the cosmos or society. A convenient localization is in an
independently acting being, if its activities can be made rational by
having the given item as a focus or referent. In this case we have a
rationality, and thus an assumed consciousness in or sustaining or knowing the system in which the item is made rational.

7] When do we determine that the independent being is a conscious
being which has the given item as part of a rational order?   A] If the
item is neutral to the rest of the activities of that independent being, as
it is for us, and   B] if the item as a kind of guide or focal point makes
intelligible the diverse activities of the independent being.

8] Must not the items which we accredit to the conscious being be sustained by it? As consciously entertained by us they may not be consciously entertained by the conscious being. We who see the red, and
note that another delights in it (to judge from his smile, movement
toward it, etc.), acknowledge both the red and the smile to be objects
for another consciousness. The red here is recognized to be neutral to us
both, and as such to be rooted in a substantial being which is not necessarily conscious. The smile must be acknowledged to be either enjoyed
on the side of the other consciousness when and as it is used referentially
as part of the system of which the red is the focal point, and then in a
different shape from what it has for us (since it is not used referentially
by us in the same way), or it is open to some third consciousness, which
may be ourselves or the other at some subsequent time.

9] Might not the acts of the independent being and the neutral focal object be parts of a larger consciousness? They may. But if the independent being's acts do form a rational system, they are parts of a subsystem which is a consciousness. The object I consciously acknowledge is the principle of the rationality of the being to whom I attribute consciousness, and thereby recognize to be an other for myself.

10] But then are the acts of that conscious being different from those of the object of its consciousness? Yes, since the latter need not be conscious. And different from properties of that conscious being? Yes. When I see another person smile, the smile must be something other than the color which he has.

Smiling is only the visible form of the consciousness; we have to look through it either to some other act or to the consciousness. The smile, then, is not the object of my consciousness as a seen red is; it is the meaning of the otherness of the other as momentarily localized and being made rational by some common object.

11] The other is known to be conscious by a threefold act. 1] By virtue of the denial of his smile as having the role of a neutral content for him and me. 2] By the recognition of the smile's rationality as governed by the object of which we both are conscious. 3] By the acknowledgment that some other object of consciousness is rooted in a substantial being other than either of us.

12] But might there not be consciously known things which give a rational ground for the behavior of a nonconscious being? Iron filings explain the behavior of the magnet; they become part of a conscious system explaining the magnet's behavior only so far as they are reconstructed and thus made part of the consciousness of a scientific world. It is the objects as apprehended by daily consciousness which must serve as explanations. Can we not say that the filings as perceived by us are wanted by the magnet? We could, and we would, were it not for the fact that the magnet seems to be the only center of rationality of the filings.

13] What follows from the foregoing is that we need a plurality of objects of consciousness, each of which provides a rational account of part of the behavior of another being, and all of which add up to the meaning of a single consciousness, thereby making a rational whole out of the rational principle which we face in the guise of objects of our consciousness. We know another is conscious because we find features of him which we make into his substantial otherness, at the same time that we see them ordered in subsets by means of content which we consciously entertain, and which may itself not be consciously entertained by the beings in which the content may be resident.

14] The supposition that red is sustained by a substance is a more daring supposition than that it is the terminus of another consciousness, for it implies that we are more than consciousness, that we are realities which sustain our own consciousness. We then, in effect, take our consciousness and our behavior to be on a footing with the red. (We cannot suppose the red itself is substantial since it has no power to act, though we could think of it as an objective ideal serving to make a rational whole out of our multiple activities.) If the red be viewed as an expression of another being which is a substance, we can then treat it as that which can be explained by some isolated feature of ourselves. Such an explanation would require that it be connected with other features.

Our rational apprehension of another substance is the use of ourselves as expressed in the shape of this or that focused trait. The trait serves as the rational principle for organizing the encountered features of another. (The substance of that other is only the unity of those features, the power by virtue of which they are localized.) Similarly, I can view the smiles, frowns, movements of another man as being explicable by virtue of this or that feature of myself—and conversely, I can take any feature which he has and view it as the rational principle governing the interrelation of the various features ingredient in me. The explaining feature is an isolated one, a dislocated quality, and that which it is to explain is a set of ingredient features which, though they may have a common origin and internal explanation, are otherwise unintelligible as they present themselves to observation.

A feature can be treated as an object of consciousness, in which case I make reference to another consciousness, or as an ingredient expression of another being, in which case I make reference to some feature of myself as the rational principle (and thus expect that feature to be an objective for others as well). As an object of consciousness for another as well, it is a principle of explanation; as a referent of some feature of my own (or of someone else) it is something to be explained relative to other features (localized there where it is, or which are dependent on it).

March 30

In order to have the object of consciousness be objective and neutral it must be sustained outside myself. It can be ingredient in some other being, or it may testify to the presence of some being independent of it, by virtue of the way in which it explains that being's behavior. If it were ingredient in some other being which was without consciousness, it would be possessed by that being in a different sense than that in which it is acknowledged in my consciousness. And though consciousness is possessed by only some beings (and to that extent the supposition of it is more hazardous than the supposition of a substance), the supposition that there is a substance in which the known object is ingredient does demand that there be a being more ultimate than consciousness. Such a supposition thus goes further beyond the evidence than a supposition about consciousness would. Moreover, the supposition that what is the object of my consciousness is the object of some other as well, allows the object to be outside myself in the very guise in which I acknowledge it, whereas the supposition of an unthinking substance forces me to suppose that the object of my consciousness is conceivably transformed by the unthinking substance in a way I do not altogether understand.

The object of consciousness, even if ingredient in some substance, is capable of being exterior to me in the shape in which it is apprehended by me, if it is the object of some other consciousness. This other consciousness is either indefinite in its location or localized in some particular being. If indefinite in its location the object as known must explicate a variety of dispersed occurrences; if localized, the other being is known to be a consciousness like my own, only if other objects to which I attend serve to explicate other activities on the part of the other being. I call another "conscious" when a number of the objects of my consciousness serve to explicate by rationally connecting items in sets of behavior of that other.

The items in the sets, which are explicated by the objects of my consciousness, are themselves ingredient in the other being which has before its consciousness the very same objects that I do. The status of those items is then like the status of the qualities which I apprehend as ingredient in something outside me and which I do not suppose are sustained by a localized conscious being (but which I do suppose are sustained by a cosmic consciousness or at least one of indefinite range). We have then (*a*) items which explicate other items, and (*b*) items which are explicated as accompanying a consciousness, either in the sense that they accompany the act of a consciousness with respect to some other item (such as *a*), or in the sense that they merely make public one facet, a moment within the systematic rationale of another consciousness. The second of these alternatives makes the other mind, in effect, not a conscious one, but rather an unconscious totality which allows items to be visible in the very same shape in which I am con-

scious of them. If we wish to avoid the supposition that a rational order
has the items in the shape in which I consciously apprehended them in
their severalty, we must take the first of these alternatives and hold that
the items of which we are conscious are always explicated by some item
which is the object of another consciousness on a footing with our own,
or that the items explicate other items which accompany some consciousness that manifests itself in those items.

If the red of which I am conscious must explicate or be explicated by
a reference to consciousness, it must testify to either a local conscious
being, to some unlocalized conscious being (such as a society, or God,
which it helps us understand), or to the presence of some item which is
the common object of my, and some other, consciousness. But since
there may not be such a common object, I must take every item of
which I am conscious to be a source of explications. When, then, we
turn back to the items which are ingredient in the being who is conscious, say his frown or smile, we must, since we do acknowledge it in
our consciousness, take it to be an object of some other consciousness as
well. If there be only myself and another, then must he not only make
his consciousness manifest in the items which I note, but be conscious of
them in the way I am conscious of them? This surely is not the case; we
betray ourselves, expose ourselves, behave in ways we do not understand.
This means that we either have a direct apprehension of another consciousness by the very acknowledgment of these items, so that we are
conscious of them in a way we are not conscious of what explicates them,
or that what we apprehend must be apprehended by a third being. But
need there be a third being? If there need not, as seems to be the case,
we must say:

1] Whatever we apprehend explicates certain occurrences by making
   their public presence have a rationality, justifying the following of
   items on one another.

2] Or it is itself a way of encountering another consciousness, allowing
   us to pass from the object to its "meaning."

What is taken to be a meaning may also be explicated by an object
of our consciousness. Consequently, what we have are   A] meanings
which enable us to encounter another consciousness, and   B] meanings
explicated by some of the items of which we are conscious and which,
if external to both us and the other consciousness, must be ingredient in
and thereby enable us both to encounter a third consciousness. Whatever
we confront then, as external to us, is something which allows us to
encounter a consciousness in which what we confront is a meaning, and

which may allow us to know of the presence of another consciousness that, like us, has the item as an object. We either are acquainted with another consciousness (which may be located where the item is, and which may be amorphous and spread out as a kind of natural or supernatural consciousness), or we have the item in a neutral way and thus use it to explicate a consciousness with which we are then acquainted. The explicated items have the double role of being part of a single system of explained items and of being the manifested but otherwise inexplicable fragments of an encountered consciousness.

The red we confront is either a meaning in another consciousness (and is in that consciousness in a more meaningful and transformed manner than it is for us), or it is for another consciousness what it is for us (and then has the power to make the manifestations of that consciousness have a rationality they otherwise would not have). Consequently, what we confront is either more meaningful than it is as confronted, or it is more explanatory. As more meaningful, it is ingredient in a consciousness; as explanatory, it is at once more powerful than it is as confronted and is the object of a consciousness. The words I use have both roles, revealing what my consciousness is like and explaining some of the things I or another might do.

To know that there are other minds, I must take the items I confront to be more than they are in fact for me, since I must take them to be either the appearance of another consciousness or the explanation of the behavior of items (themselves having the role of appearances of some consciousness, local or diffuse). I cannot be a phenomenologist; for I always take some items to be appearances, manifestations of another consciousness. An Aristotelian might allow that this other consciousness is cosmic or divine, an active reason, but still maintain that the appearance might be those of "unthinking" substances. Consequently, he would allow one to take such a quality as red to be something explicated by the object of that consciousness (and our own), but to have a meaning unlike that which is possessed by a frown or a smile.

We could conceivably treat a nonconscious substance as involving a variation in the kind of translation which an item receives, from that which a consciousness would impose. If we take this view we can say that whatever we confront is a transformed form of something, with which we are acquainted by the very fact that we orient the confronted item outside ourselves, and that when the item serves, with a number of other items (which may operate in independence of it), to explicate behavior, we treat that behavior as a transformed form of a consciousness.

We have then: 1] the acknowledgment of something exterior to the apprehending consciousness,   2] the explication of other items by means of the acknowledged,   3] the acceptance of the explicating entity as one of a set of explicating entities which together account for the behavior of some being, and   4] the acknowledgment of the exterior item, and the items which it explicates, as being transformations of some more basic reality. If that more basic reality is one which is the object of the explications mentioned in 3 we acknowledge it to be a consciousness.

I have moved in the course of today's discussion to the position that what we confront in consciousness is both something exterior to us and a transformation of something. If the item, as exterior (together with other items), serves to provide a rational focus, an explanation, for the behavior of some being, that being is said to have a consciousness of the exterior item. The being's behavior can be read off as a transformation of its consciousness. I know that another is conscious, then, so far as I have a number of explications of its behavior and see that behavior as a transformation of an "intent," or "meaning," or "purpose," or "character."

In knowing that another is conscious, I know why he frowns now and smiles later, and also something about his private nature. But what is the latter kind of knowledge? Why and how do I understand the frown to mean "displeasure"? The child seems to so understand it without being taught, and there seem to be many evidences which we are able to read off well without previous knowledge or acquaintance— though, to be sure, accompanying behavior is often a guide to what we mean, or better perhaps, what the focalized item explicating the behavior means to the being which is behaving in this explained way.

If "red" explains that I will look and then move toward, the look and the movement are myself as "red-responsive." If "square" explains that I look and then move away, it is evidence of myself as "square-responsive." But the first is favorable and the second is not; the one can be said to reveal me as desiring and the other as avoiding. Then I am a being who is red-desiring and square-avoiding. If it is always so, I am persistent, otherwise I am vacillating, changeable, transformed, etc., and therefore capable of alteration in attitude.

We make reference to the character of a being when we find that we must not only explain behavior in terms of some object of consciousness (and derivatively other forms of being in focus), but must explain the fact that the behavior varies in ways which the object of consciousness does not explain. The "red" which now related "looking and movement toward" in a rational way, cannot also relate "looking and movement away." Either, then, the manner of explication will have to change from case to case or we must attribute the change to the behaving being. We can take the first behavior-group to be normative and account for the second by a change in nature, or we can go behind both and see both groups as expressions of the same character—a vacillating being. And this is apparently what we do. Consequently, what we do when we confront an item, is not only to look for a being for which it also might be conscious, but acknowledge that being (whose behavior is being explained by that item) as having a dimension beyond that and any other behavior, explained by that or other items.

When we find that many different objects of consciousness provoke the same kind of behavior we take the behavior to be transformative of some basic meaning, which accounts for the fact that the different items can serve to explicate the behavior. If I am not only red-responsive in a favorable way, but fat and tall and so on (arbitrarily supposing for the moment that we attend to such isolated qualities rather than to substantial or common-sense objects), then I am a desirous being, one who, say, "desires to come nearer to qualities than sight permits." My looking and moving toward are then explained by the objects of which I am conscious; my behavior is an expression of my consciousness, or even more substantially, of my character as one who is desirous.

What we have, then, is a confrontation of items which may serve to explicate others, but which are transformations of some deeper reality. And that deeper reality is said to be another "mind" A] when there are many kinds of behavior, B] when the explicated items are explicated by a miscellaneous set of other objects of my consciousness (or when the same explication accounts for diverse behaviors), and C] the being is thought to persist. The persistent nature of the being is the terminus of my translations of the explicated items which warranted my thinking that another was conscious. When we turn to such explicated items as the movement of iron filings toward the magnet, we are warranted in thinking, not that the filings are conscious—for we have only this one explicated behavior—but that their movement is to be translated into power, capacity, potentialities, "magnetic," particularly if the movement can be elicited by other objects as well.

What we confront then may have the role of an explication for beings that are conscious, and always has the role of being a transformation of a more basic reality. That reality's nature is discerned by seeing how its diverse behaviors are not only explicated by some object of which we are conscious, but are interrelated and altered when there is no appropriate change in the explicating items.

April 2

Let a frown be thought of as what a thing is for-another. Then it is a way in which the other three sides of the being are expressed. Let us concentrate on only one, let us say, from-itself, and let this be desire. Then a frown is a way in which a being as desiring expresses from-itself for-another. What is that being in-itself? The two together, the desire expressing itself in a frown, and a frown expressing itself in a desire, is the being as in-itself. If now we want to refer to the nature of that being in terms of the frown, we must use the desire as the principle by which the frown is interiorized and altered. It is the public frown now empowered by desire. But we could also express the desire as that which is interiorized by a frown. These two interiorized (and thus altered) public guises must then be conjoined to express what the being is in-itself.

In the public guise of a being we find elements which come from the outside. If we are to eliminate the outside features, we must treat the frown and the desire in their active guises. We must first separate the frown from the effects of a public conditioning. In so separating it we make it an integral feature of the being for which it is to provide evidence of the inward nature.

Public conditioning is as real as private production, and since I am a being in a world whose expressions are expressions in a setting provided by the world, the frown that I in fact produce is mine even though some of the elements in it are made by what is outside me. It can also be said to be the frown which the world has produced in me; this it is when one takes the public conditioning elements to be active and my own facial expressions (no matter what their origin or source and what I am in myself) to be material, worked over by the public conditioning elements. The world which involves a togetherness of various items cannot be accredited to one or the other exclusively. It can, though, be accredited to one, with the other as passive—and the roles can be reversed. And so far as a being is treated as active it can be recognized to have transformative features, features which can be read back into the in-itself by virtue of the fact that they are then features which support other expressions (e.g., the frown supporting the desire), or are features, which as merely latent, are then other features in their supporting role (e.g., desire supporting the frown).

April 18

The various facets of a being—for-another, with-others, etc.—are together in the being in four ways. Each facet is what the being offers as a term in a special kind of togetherness in itself. Since each of these facets is already caught inside a scheme, say Ideality, God, etc., the facet itself represents a kind of togetherness of its owner with other modes. When then the facets are said to be together in the being, what is meant is that representatives of the various kinds of togetherness are together. This is but another way of saying that the being as in-itself is the way in which various kinds of togethernesses are together. Taking the togethernesses two at a time we can say that the facets (say, representing Ideality and Actuality) are together in a kind of unity (offered by God) and in a kind of causality (characteristic of Existence).

The in-itself is two features together in two special ways. Let us call the features 'square' and 'red.' Then the in-itself of the object is the active separation of these and the satisfied unity of them as constituting a single tensional combination—or alternatively, the square and red as implicatively together and existentially opposed, united by the kind of unity which is God and separated by the mere contingent conjunction which is represented by Actuality. The square and red are implicative and dynamic facets which are assured of being one by virtue of a divine-like unity, and are assured of being separate by a contingent copresence with other entities inside the being.

It is not, then, that one facet sustains and expresses itself as the others, but that all are expressions of a single reality. They are diverse facets of a single being and their togetherness can be understood inside the being in the same way as those facets are understood to be together with facets of other beings.

April 19

The discussion of the thing-in-itself needs radical refining:
1] Each feature is a kind of togetherness biased toward the being to which it is attributed. Smiling is a togetherness.

2] The contribution which the being makes is its joyousness. It is as joyous that it comes together with some other (paced by that other so that the features as a single unity can be said to belong to that other or to be produced by it), though only in a passive sense if the original being is active.

3] The being is joyous in itself. If now it comes together with other beings in other ways (as it must), its joyousness takes on another shape. If the being is tall the contribution which it makes to the tallness, as a mode of togetherness distinct from smiling, is itself as joyous.

4] We read back from tallness, not joyousness but something else—say majesty or imperiousness. Then we should be able to say that the smile is the outcome of that majesty. Since we now have two ways of speaking of the being—joyous or majestic, and since both are legitimate, we must decide either to use one way of being together as the norm for the use of names, or we must qualify the joyousness by the majesty so that we can readily speak of the being as offering us itself as joyous-majesty, and thus smile in one context and be tall in another.

5] If we use the different names which we get by dissolving the different togethernesses, we are forced to say that the joyousness functions as a kind of force which can be expressed as ways of uniting smile and tall in four ways. We are here approaching the unity of a being from the outside, from the perspective of togetherness, and the unity therefore is to be expressed as a way of having those various forms of togetherness together; the unity will be the continuation of the togethernesses, the way they come together with a definite bias, that of joyousness.

6] If we use the term majesty-joy as the meaning of the being in-itself, then once again we can speak of it as the mere merging (of an indeterminate degree) of the various ways in which the actual being is together with other modes of being. It is constituted by the various forms of togetherness; if we want to separate them out we must find the contribution each makes to the common result. We will find that the outcome is biased toward one or the other of the forms of togetherness (e.g., conjunction if it is Actuality).

7] If we start with the being, it is the unity of all the togethernesses; if we start from the outside and want to account for the unity, we speak of it in terms of togethernesses. Or we can speak of the togethernesses having a nature which merges with the natures of other togethernesses to constitute the given nature.

Joyousness is the nature which the togethernesses have when they are united. This joyousness is biased toward one of the natures out of which it is constituted—the one in which the smile appears. It also reflects that way of being together with other natures (inside the being) —or with itself as sustaining other sides of itself as together with other beings. Thus let us say that the smile appears when x is together implicatively with y. Then the smile of x is the neutral implication of x and y, biased toward x. That smile is a biased joyousness in x. It is one with an analogous bias of some other feature, say the size of x which is perhaps merged with y.

The *role* of the *togethernesses* seems to be prior and their *natures* consequent. If this be the case we can say that the *natures* of the various *beings* is prior and their *roles* with relation to one another consequent. x opposes y by virtue of the fact that it has a nature which is attenuated and neutralized as, say, "implication," and also qualified, expressing the presence and contribution of y. If joyousness is in a relation of merging it will yield, not a smile, but something else from which one should be able to abstract the private nature of joyousness.

April 20

Better than yesterday's approach is one which acknowledges the various discerned features to be concrete instances of types of togetherness. A smile for example is all four forms of togetherness merged together in an actuality. That smile does not belong exclusively to that actuality; it is a way in which that actuality is related to other beings. The being must be treated as having four forms of togetherness in it. Let us isolate one togetherness, and view the smile as an implication. Then it is an implication which is biased toward and located in an actuality; it is an implication which has its consequent in another as a possible recipient. The being from which it starts and the other at which it ends, are terminal points.

If I want to understand what the smiling being is in itself I must understand what the smile implies for me—it means that I am to be acceptive of it, to be trusting; and it implies this for me because the smiling being is offering himself as one to be trusted or accepted. We have then the smile as an implication to inform us that the smiling being is offering itself to be trusted, to one who can be trusting—and this whether we do act in these ways or not.

The smile has also a form of the comma, a therefore, and a dot, which is to say it tells us of the way in which others are together as separately with the smiling being, as acting on it and as merging. As separate, it offers the being to us as at a distance and as one who acts from within and is bounded off from us; as acting on us, it is one who is expressing itself and finding a possible response in us, and in fact altering us in some way; as a dot it defines a situation in which we both are, and in which we infect one another's nature and ways. The other, then, is a distant offering being which expresses itself and is affected by or is sensitive to the presence of others.

1] Why does the togetherness have the concrete form of a smile? Why are there other qualities or features at the same time?   2] Why is it that the artist is able to make a togetherness which recaptures the very texture of one of the sides?   3] How can we apply the categories of the modes of being to actualities in relation to actualities?   4] Are there not some features which are essentially implicative, say, and others which are mergers—e.g., primary qualities and affective or evaluational ones?   5] Since a being may express itself in oppositional ways, frown where before it smiled, will not a reading back from the frown give us the opposite result from what we got when we started with the smile?

1] The smile is not separable from the reciprocal natures of the beings. Consequently what it says is identical with what other features say since they involve different terminal meanings. When (to turn to question 5) we deal with a frown, we face a being who offers itself as a rejecting being to one who is to accept it as such. This frown says what the smile says, but for different terms. But why the different terms? We start with the different terms, i.e., with a plurality of beings which are distinct, and we must then have a plurality of ways in which these are related to one another. This means that if there were only two objects in a single fourfold relation they would have only one feature. This is a position which is accepted by physical science with the qualification that the objects are to be treated as quantitatively different from one another, thus allowing the being to be essentially a law, and that we are to concentrate only on the relation of implication.

2] By virtue of his making, the artist produces a togetherness in the shape of a merging, a kind of dot in which the other side can be discerned in the texture and the artist himself can be discerned as meaning or intent.

3] Each knower represents the entire realm of Actuality, so that what he confronts is either another representative, or the others as parts of a many while he is acting as a representative of the whole. Taking him and the objects to be representatives, he is dealing with actuality as such. However, he is first an experiencing being, facing features as forms of merging. Only later, by an effort, does he get to recognize the features in their other roles. Only later does he try to see what those features are as neutral to the components which are their terms and toward one of which they may be biased.

4] Though every feature is a congealing of four forms of togetherness, one of the forms is dominant in some feature (which is recessive in the other forms). A square is primarily implicative, a color is primarily merging, a gesture is primarily affective, and a smile or frown is primarily prescriptive.

Going back, it is perhaps better to say that if I take the position of an actuality (and I do this primarily when I attempt to know or to other all beings), I deal with the other actualities as though they were special cases of unity, of standards, or of existent powers. And if I face them in experience as merging with others, as constituting an experience which is a divine kind of togetherness, I must also face them as over against me, as standards or as powers. If this is the case, we never have a coordination of various activities; the knower or apprehender is asymmetrically related to the other actualities since these function as exemplifications of other modes of being—or conversely, the apprehender, by foregoing knowledge and settling for appreciation, etc., can take himself to be the exemplification of some other mode of being, facing actualities which are representative of Actuality.

Hegel criticizes Kant's theory of ethics in three steps. *1]* He shows that reason, as autonomous, can intend to apply only to content which is alien to itself. To deal with this content, reason must become a tester of "maxims," and its test is consistency. *2]* But every item, whatsoever, in this world is inconsistent (as particular and universal) and every one is consistent if one shifts one's standpoint. *3]* Reason thus must take up the maxim into itself as its own and express itself through this. But then the maxim and the reason are one.

This last is the answer to which one must come from an idealistic point of view; from the standpoint of the Ideal all else is a subordinated instancing case. But in view of the fact that there is an "all else" one ought to say, against Hegel, that the method of "science" is only one part of the entire enterprise, and that one must also take up the position of actuality, etc. Indeed if it be the case, as I have argued, that it is the actual who really knows, and that mathematics is more a domain of appreciation or evaluation, a scientific knowledge of the modes is to be achieved by taking up the position of actuality (which is primarily in a relation of a comma, in which items are separate—though on p. 514 of the *Modes* the comma is attributed to God).

April 21

The various features of a being form an organic totality, but some stand out in one context and not in others. A smile is an epitomization of all the other features; it is primary only when beings are with-one-another, not when they are acting on-one-another.

The smile is a form of togetherness. Viewed from the standpoint of cognition it starts with one individual as offering himself to another. The individual with which it starts has a host of features at that time, and all should be read as implicative, if approached from the same point of view as the smile.

The scientist views the smile (and any similar feature) as a *summary,* a localization, a terminal expression or evidence of a state of being which is connected with other states of being by a different kind of connection. If he is interested in cognition, he will see the being of the smile as something encountered in the togetherness of a dot, a merging, and will turn from that to consider the being beyond this as interrelated on another dimension with other beings. The smile allows for predictions not in itself but by virtue of the interconnection of other dimensions. The summary position of the smile is seen to allow for the summary position of something else. Whereas, for the philosopher or ordinary man engaged in existential penetration, the smile has a nature and a being which was derived from the items it connects, for the scientist it has only a nature and no genuine being. For him it testifies to nothing by itself. It was by trying to predict and interrelate it with other phenomena that he came to treat it as a summary.

When the scientific strands, etc., are united with one another we get the natural substance as by-itself, the object as having features which are purged versions of what was encountered in the common-sense world. What we do then is to bring together various kinds of togetherness with their appropriate terminal points. But the terminal points are distinct in nature. The perceptual gives us, say, the joyous man, while the scientific gives us the muscles and molecules of him as summed up in a smile but as implicating (by means of a conceived law) other movements and molecules summed up in another way.

Must we now say that the molecules sum up to joyousness, that joyousness diversifies in molecules, or must we look for some third way of expressing them together? Are we wrong to add together the different implications; should we not treat perceptual smile as a merged together-ness and the molecular interpenetration as a law-abiding cognitional one? If we do this, will we not have to say that molecules as implicative are the same thing as joyousness as together with its reciprocal? This would seem to be the better answer. Consequently, what we must say is that the scientist looks for an implicative relation which is formal in nature and thus uses the confronted items as summaries. Perception uses a feature as a merged togetherness and tries to dissolve it into its com-ponents, leaving over a merely formal togetherness having only a nature without being (or at best a being of a minimal kind). But the two out-comes should be the same. Consequently we must say that existential penetration is science done by another means and that science is existen-tial penetration done by another means.

If philosophy is a cognitional enterprise why does it not accept science's cognitional outcome? Firstly, because true cognition must not be taken as excluding other approaches as science does; secondly, because qualities can also be treated as cognitional; thirdly, because the molecular domain of the scientist can be treated as being interrelated not by impli-cations but by a merging, to constitute a field; and fourthly, because science has no place for values, etc.

It would seem then that a feature can be treated rationally, or ex-perientially, etc., and that each of the basic strands can be thought of as being constituted by four forms of togetherness. It is by treating the molecules, say, as being related in four ways with one another, that we see the scientific world as a world of substances or entities which are analyzed out of a commonsensical or a perceptual summary feature. A perceptual world of substances deals with a feature as requiring a four-fold complex being; the scientist is satisfied to have found the being and to multiply the modes of connection. The world of action and the world of importance stand in between; a world of action requires the being to have only one nature, but to allow for attenuations of this, connected in three other ways; a world of importance requires the being to have a fourfold nature and to allow for attenuations of its primary relation (the comma).

Still another approach: A being has four ways of being together with others. Perception yields one feature functioning in four ways on behalf of a complex nature—a smile implies, merges, etc., on behalf of a joyous man. Science offers a single nature enjoying four connections: molecules merge, act, imply, etc. Action offers a single nature with derivative layers having four connections; thus an active being engages in a motion which can be understood to imply, merge, etc. Value involves a complex nature for which one relation is primary and others are derivative; the being is possessed of many virtues in a prescriptive relation to others, which is specialized as rationality, merging, or action.

1] Each of the above four has a primary role. The perceived is primarily experienced, the scientific cognized, the event is dynamic, and the prescriptive is evaluated.

2] We can combine the above four. Thus we can unite the perceived as experienced with the implication as cognized, etc. When we do we get a natural substance. There are many natural substances, for we can also combine the perceived as an implication with the cognized as a merging, etc. Each mode of combination gives us types of natural substances— distinguished as requiring different types of logic, or different types of analysis, etc.

3] We can combine different instances of the same mode of togetherness. Thus we can combine four implications in the shape of a quality, a formal structure, an immanent pattern, and an evaluated order. We thus get substance as merely encountered, rational, interplaying, or separated.

4] We can combine the types of natural substance of 2, or the levels of substance in 3, to get real substances. Here we have smile as implying, merging, etc., molecules as implied, merged, etc., by cognized entities, etc.

In 2, 3, 4 each facet is the equivalent of every other. Starting with 4 we can say that the world known by means of the smile is equivalent with the known as molecular; in 3 we say that smile as implying, is equivalent with structure as implying; in 2 we say that smiling as implication, is equivalent with structure as merging. The equivalences hold because they have different termini, of a proportionate nature.

If we say this, then must we not say that science tells us the nature of the real? And how will we characterize what the thing is in-itself? Science does tell us the nature of the real, in 2, 3, and 4. But we do not get the substance as allowing for noncognitive modes of being together, and thus as having these equivalences. Science tells us what the beings are cognitively, but not what they are as experienced, etc. If the thing is more than something cognized, how are we to characterize the thing as in- and of-itself? Can we say anything more than that it is cognized molecules implying, merging, etc., in such and such formal ways; is an experienced smile that implies, merges, etc.; is an encountered force which implies, merges, etc., existentially; is a value which implies, merges, etc., with various affiliated items?

Cognized molecules formally imply, joyous beings experientially imply, interplaying beings existentially imply, excellent beings valuationally imply—and so on, for merging, etc. The being is the distinct implications as one single term or ground; if the implications are solidified into one, the being will be dispersed, divided in itself. Must we not ask what kind of solidity the ground has? It could be a unity, a merging, a set, or an active power. If we treat it as anything but a merging we look at it from the vantage point of some other mode of being. Consequently if it is an actuality of which we are speaking, we would have to say that the termini of the different implications, or mergings, etc., are merged together, and that as a consequence we can speak of the diverse implications, experiences, formalities, etc., as grounded in one being only by virtue of our merging together joyousness and molecules. But does this make sense? Can we do more than see it as an idealized thing, and thus as one which implies interiorly the joyousness by the molecules and *v.v.?* If so, then we must say that we confront the things in the world as being idealized in themselves and thus as themselves providing the logic by virtue of which the termini of cognitional, experiential, dynamic, and valuational ways of being together are together. The interior would be just an equivalence whose terms have diverse careers, by virtue of their sustaining diverse exterior ways of being together with the terms of other beings.

April 22

Not sufficient attention was given these last days to the fact that the problem as put involves the consideration only of a plurality of actualities. We have in fact four distinct approaches to pluralities, and four to the unities or the modes as such—religion and theology; cognition and value; experience and speculative knowledge; and action and existing. We can put aside the consideration of the unity and attend instead to the plurality, to give us four acts: considerateness, cognition, experience, and action.

When we attempt to deal with the togetherness of the termini of any one of these acts, we find we can do it in four ways—they imply one another, merge with one another, act on one another, or stand apart from one another. We find we can grasp these forms of unity in other men—by reflecting, by being concerned for them, by working with them, and by respecting them.

Science cognizes, but only with reference to one type of togetherness

—a formal one. To know what a being is cognitionally, we must use the other sides of it as forms of togetherness. These are just as much implications as the formal one used in science. All the implications will tell us what the beings are as implying one another. The beings as implicated in these different ways must be unified. The unification can be one open to reflection or to other ways. We engage in all ways of unifying in ourselves, and this not only with respect to the content of cognition, but with respect to other sides of ourselves besides that of being in implicative situations and thus for one another. (As implying beings are for-one-another, as merging they are with-one-another, as acting they are from-themselves, and as standing apart they are by-themselves—and they are united as all these in four ways. These we can apprehend by reflecting, or being concerned, by working with them, or by respecting them.)

We find we can engage in all four ways with respect to men. But when we turn to the subordinate inanimate beings in the world we find that we do not know how to respect them (except by trying to know them?), that we can work on them but not with them (except by losing ourselves in nature), and that we do not have any concern for them, in the sense of merging with them (except on a level which we do not distinctively enjoy). The only way we know of dealing properly with the inanimate is by cognition, though we can engage in other ways if we ignore them in their severalty and deal with them cosmically. We will then be able to grasp them speculatively in philosophy, by existing in the cosmos with them (as over against society), by dealing with them from the standpoint of the idea that each and every one of them is a representative of all the others, and by looking at them from the standpoint of a single valuational principle in terms of which they are to be ordered with respect to one another.

If cognition, or scientific knowing, is concerned with the inanimate beings in their plurality, it can nevertheless do this cosmically, i.e., make the account stretch to the limits provided by the Ideal as a unit. Similarly, one can make considerateness of other beings stretch to the limit of representativeness, make the experience of other beings stretch to the limit of speculative knowledge, and make action reach to the limit of Existence. These latter forms of stretching are achieved by a shift in attitude, by an acceptance of a "beyond" as inseparable from that which is encountered here, and by having the action be ontological, in the sense that it involves the readjustment of a being in-itself and with respect to the Existence that is outside it.

Scientific knowledge, then, is a knowledge of a cognized cosmic reality, each being of which is seen as merely sustaining formal implications. Its beings are formalities. If it wanted to know what beings were in- and of-themselves, its formal beings would have to be recognized as together with those in which one terminates by considerateness, experience, and action. These terminations are together with the formal beings of science in the four ways of implication, merging, action, and standing apart. As knowers we are concerned with the first primarily. So far as we are, we say that beings in- and of-themselves are concrete logical junctures, the way in which the formalities imply and are implied by, say, the experienced mergings (which we get to by concern).

A man is experienced as a joyous or offering being whose formal nature is expressed in molecules implying other molecules outside; equally he is an aggregate of molecules whose experienceable nature is expressed as joy which is with the being of others (a with-others which is embodied in the smile). To be is to provide the logic, the formality for uniting the joy and the molecular structure. One need not unite them in this way; we can find the two united as merged, as acting on one another and as distinct aspects of a single insistent unit. Since we do not seem to be aware of the ontological adjustment of ourselves, and since we do not face the inanimate as on a level with ourselves and thus are not as fully considerate of them as we could theoretically be, we do not have any other way of facing the inanimate except as concrete implications or as concrete mergers of the different sides they show in different types of togetherness with one another and the rest of the space-time world.

The smile as that which is implicative, is to be distinguished from itself as in an implication. In the latter guise it is a summary. Does it have two more roles—i.e. in addition to being a form of togetherness, and to being a summary term? It ought to be able to function in two more ways. Ought it not be able to give being to implication (and thus be the smile as it is for-others and open to action), and ought it not be able to hold the implication apart other forms of togetherness (and thus be the smile as it is for-oneself and as open to considerateness)?

If we stay with one feature, say a smile, we can deal with this as an implication expressing what beings are as with-one-another; we can deal with it as related by a prescriptive connection, and having itself the role of a boundary or summary—the way science views it; we can take it to be an expression of an active being and thus one which will be interplaying with others; and we can deal with it as a term isolated in a merging of the smiling being with others outside it. The first is an appearance, the second is a quality or character, the third is a sign, and the fourth is a limit from the outside. The second demands a formal implication, the third a produced one, and the fourth an expansive one generating its own beginning and end.

April 23

The universe contains no problems; problems arise when some part is dislocated with respect to the others. The answer to its problem is already in the situation; its failure is even compensated for by virtue of what the other beings are then with respect to it, so that even in being dislocated and having a problem it is no problem. The problem arises only because there is a state of fitting or satisfaction which a part needs in order to be excellent. We want to know, we want to be at peace, we want to be adjusted, and thus we seek to learn, practice yogi, zen, stoicism, seek success, or security. There is nothing inauthentic in any occurrence in history, no "unnatural" phenomena, nothing amiss with the universe. The occurrence of a delusory being, the presence of conflict and the like, are bad only   A] in terms of some promise in beings which these preclude, and   B] in terms of a standard set by some part or other to which these are to conform. The promise and the standard are fulfilled somewhere or other, but not in the place originally intended.

A philosophic system is distinct from the world; it is excluded by and excludes the world to the very degree that the system has being. Should it give an accurate account we can nevertheless say that the way the world is, is not the way the world is, meaning by that, that the heterogeneity of the world is abstracted from within the system, to allow the system to express what the world really is. Knowledge tells us what it is in promise or for knowledge, and not what it is on its own side, in *concerto*.

When we try to express what things are we can have no better vocabulary than that provided by common sense refined, for that is what the things are. The dates, places, names, etc., should then be common-sensical, and not scientific or perceptual. This gives the common core of the *Lebenswelt* views and of British common sense. The difficulty with these views is that they do not allow for a criticism of them; they think that the *Lebenswelt* or English use is a universe having no problems. But we do have problems of maladjustment and misunderstanding, and of trying to get clear what common sense has in a confused way; we must therefore move away from common sense. To be sure, our standards of maturity and decency are commonsensical, and adjustment to them will leave us without problems—in that society. But we will still have problems of conflict with other societies, and thus must have a way of dealing with others in terms which transcend our bias toward our own.

April 28

The procedure of the *Modes* is that of science, in that it assumes that there are features which summarize, are merely there, and then looks for the rational connection between them. This is particularly true in the chapter on God. But it could have been possible to use such features as otherness, realizability, and unity of Existence to reveal not only the fact that there is a God being testified to, but something of the intrinsic nature of Actualities. This was done, in a sense, when reference was made to the privacy of actualities, to the indeterminate nature of the Ideal, and to the coordinated activity of Existence, or to its self-differentiation as a space, time, or becoming.

The otherness was treated as relational. It should have been seen that there can be a merged, an implying, a caused, or a separating way of being related. Also, when the otherness is viewed as implicational and yet as characterizing an actuality, it is to be treated as a form of togetherness which is biased toward the being and shares something of the nature of the actuality.

Should we not say that what love knows of actualities, action of Existence, worship of God, and obligation of the Ideal, philosophy knows by its concepts—the substantial reality?

Each term can be treated as a boundary, a ","; a relation, ")"; a form of action, a "therefore"; and a testimony, a ".". This is evidently the case with *perceived* qualities. The smile is what the being is over against all others; it relates him to others, "it is an expression," and it shows the way in which oneself and the exterior world are together. *Activities* are insistent, powerful, transactional, and relate us to responders. *Values* are characteristics, relate one to standards, involve hierarchy subordination and an evaluator. But the *intellectualized* or *scientific* characters, though they seem to be boundaries, or limiting terms, and perhaps even to testify to instruments and observers, seem not to be capable of action, unless we think of them as actually embodied in quanta, or indeterminate being. Are they also relational?

If the intellectualized characters enjoy the role of relation with respect to something outside, there must be something on the side of the scientific object which is the premiss for the relation. Should we say that when a scientific term functions as a relation, it either constructs an appropriate term for it, or that it uses the summational perceived qualities as its term? The second would be unsatisfactory; it merges two distinct approaches. If science constructs terms for itself as relational, must we say that since this construction is conceptual, there should be a parallel construction for qualities as continuations of the apprehension characteristic of a perception? We cannot perceive such terminal continuations for perception—nor for action, nor for evaluation. We must in these cases do what the scientists do—conceive of the termini. This is inevitable since we are dealing with implicative relations, even though they are faced as perceived, dynamic or prescriptive. We extend our usage to the termini, and thus speak of this which we can only conceive, not in conceptual language but in the language of perception, action, or value, or of combinations of these as in common sense.

If we treat otherness as a boundary we see the actuality as withdrawing; if as a relation, we refer to its privacy; if as an action, we see it as resistant; and if as a testimony, we refer to its correlative other.

April 30

It would be a mistake to speak of the union of the different aspects of a being as though it were simple. It is in fact a texture, an essence, and an activity of selfdetermination at the same time that it is a unity. Each of these offers a distinctive way in which the terminal features of various kinds of relations of togetherness can be together in the being as over against those relations of togetherness. If one were to be asked how these different forms of union are themselves together, the answer is that they are together as supporting diverse ways in which the being is together with other beings. If we insist that the different forms of the union make a unity the way God makes a unity, we will not be asking how the various unions in a thing are together, but how they are together from the distinctive position of God.

The various unions are together in a complex way and this allows the being to have diverse relations to other realities. The complex way cannot be analyzed except by showing what those diverse relations to other realities are. If we do analyze it, we hold the different unions apart from one another, and this is the same thing as to say that we make a complex union of the different relations which a being has to others.

If we focus on, say, essence and Existence, as aspects of a being, and

say that it is these two together, we must go on to say that the way
these are together is expressed by the being as affecting and implying
other beings—these two ways of relating being distinct. If we ask how
these two ways are related, how they can make a unity, we but turn to
the being itself; or we merge the relations and thereby divide the being
into an aspect which is essence and another which is Existence.

May 1

Each mode of union of the various characters in a being stresses
one role; it needs supplementation by other modes of union. If we ask
for the unity of all those modes of union we but abstract from the being
as in-itself; we then view it from the perspective of God, Who gives the
paradigm for unity. Or we ask for the intelligible nature of all those
modes of union together, and thus take up the position of an actuality
engaged in knowing. What we cannot do is get the being with all its
unions in a singleness, for firstly, this would make us duplicate the being,
and secondly, such a singleness, when put over against the components
of it, would turn it into a fifth item.

There is a singleness but we apprehend it as having a feature in one
primary role and in three secondary ones—or as having one feature in
a primary role and other features in secondary ones. Should we ask how
all the roles can be together, and thus how the various relations which
the features enjoy can be one, we but distinguish the various features in
the being, and ultimately (since the way we want to have the various
relations together will be of one of four forms) analyze it as something
intelligible, etc. We cannot get to an absolute one of features, roles, or
relations; but we can grasp a unity of any of these as involving some
item in a primary role and the other three items or roles as having
secondary functions.

When we ask after the thing-in-itself we are presumably asking for
a knowledge of it. We look to it as offering an intelligible union of
features in their roles as boundaries, termini, implications, and expressions, with a primary emphasis on them as boundaries. The termini,
implications, and expressions are distorted somewhat by being made to
function as qualified by the boundary approach—the approach to the
feature as something which is the object of knowledge. Any further
solidification of the being, by recognizing that the subordinate features
have primary roles in other kinds of unification, is also performed intellectually, and does not go any further than complicate our knowledge.
However, the features as now functioning inside an intellectual content

are faced as having a nonintellectual role. They can be seen to have this role once we stand outside the being as a cognized object, and approach it as something which has a texture, a dynamism, a structure.

There is room for many philosophies, each stressing some item as its datum. A philosophy may take some object in the world, or some discipline, as basic, and claim to do nothing more than to make this intelligible and rationally plausible. If it is content to remain there it is only a philosophy *of,* and necessarily fragmentary. It becomes a philosophy proper only when it is systematic, and thus deals with the entire range of knowledge and being. If it ignores basic features in other items, discussed and properly dealt with in other philosophies, it will reveal itself to be too narrow. To avoid narrowness a philosopher must be willing to accept as basic data items from a plurality of domains. He must accept, e.g., the fact and the legitimacy of the scientific, artistic, religious, and practical enterprises; he must know that there are things that ought not to be; that there is space, time, motion; that there is change, rest, coming to be and passing away; that there are purposes, aims, beliefs, errors, truths, values, rights and wrongs; more specifically, he must accept the fact that it is wrong to hit a baby over the head with a bottle; that it is wrong to put people in gas chambers merely because of their ethnic divergencies; that it is right to be kind and helpful; that it is possible to perceive, conceive, remember, reflect, speculate about and know our world; that men create, remake, misconstrue, hesitate, love, fear, desire and are frustrated. A philosophy is intended to make clear and intelligible a world in which all these occur. Its task is not to allow any one of these to deny a place to the others. More specific beliefs, and other beliefs than these, undoubtedly are to be included. But the philosopher must accept at least these, and check what he concludes regarding any one of a number of them with what he must say about the others.

The philosopher will modify his principles, categories, acceptances, etc., in the light of his need to do justice to what he otherwise knows about accepted basic, nuclear items. He will end by challenging views in science, history, law, common sense, but only on the ground that items in each, as related in a world including the others, have been dislocated, distorted, misconstrued. The final test, then, will be that he has done justice to primary pivotal points. A work which ends with principles which preclude Shakespeare, Mozart, Michelangelo, Bach, Homer, etc., from being creative artists, which denies that murder is wrong, that some things are known and used, etc., is unsatisfactory. If we have two philosophies, each of which is seeking to do justice to such phenomena we will have to judge both as inadequate if each leaves out something that the other explains. If they include roughly the same kind and limited range of data, they must give way to one which includes them both, and perhaps modifies them both.

As a rule philosophies do considerable justice to one area—science, religion, common sense, classical art, etc. By using the principles in that one area on other fields, they provide systematic and complete but yet unsatisfactory accounts. There is no method in philosophy which will guarantee success; we must seek again and again to take account of obstrusive facts, and reorganize our principles and organization so that these can be systematically understood. If we have to give up this fact or that, or this item which is central to the tradition and common sense of mankind, we always leave open the possibility that there will be another system which, while doing as much justice to our items as we do, will take account of what we neglect. The best philosophy is one that is adequate, as well as well-grounded, inclusive, explanatory, and rational.

But perhaps one ought to reject what all men have accepted? Why should that which all accept, or most accept, be retained? Is this not a conservative policy, and a way of sanctifying superstition? That which is accepted, though, need not be accepted as a datum and as occupying a central place. The evaluation of it as a datum, and of its place, may involve a dislocation. We might end by finding ethics more important than politics, Michelangelo more important than Bach, error more prevalent, the ought to be more frequently realized, etc., than we had expected or believed.

In history causation is not simply physical causation; it is social or political, in that what is done has a relevancy and an import of a "meaningful" kind. This means that the dynamic thrust of the causation is geared within an Idealized frame, that there is a teleological aspect to it. This does not mean that there is a striving to reach some end or even that there is an end which will be reached, but only that the activity of causation of history and other "social" enterprises occurs within a frame which in the end is rooted in the Ideal, and is derivatively located in ideologies, institutions, myths, laws, and the like.

May 2

Relevance is determined by an end which is definitory of what will bring it about. Such an end may be a mere terminus, the present, used as a guide for the assessment of the various predecessors, or it may be some present or still future desirable outcome. The end dictates which path we are to take through a multitude of occurrences; there are data given, over which it must exercise some selection.

Historic causation is not aboriginally dynamic; it is primarily the living through of the relevant, with a subordinated dynamic element derived from the actualities and the Existence which constitute the historic occurrence. Thus if we want to deal with the activities of two regiments, we can say, in the light of the victory to come or to have come, that because one failed the other had to change its route. There is no power being exerted by the one regiment on the other; still there is power being exhibited, and even over the stretch connecting the two. The messengers, the shift of material, etc., are part of the transition from the one occurrence to the other. The relevance of the one to the other dictates the meaning of the energies that are being spent along those routes. The energies continue to be energies in nature at the same time that they are outside it, being affiliated with other energies only along the paths of the relevant occurrences.

Historic causation is thus of the same sort as is causation in politics, society, etc. In all these cases the energies of men and Existence are brought together and then affiliated with certain other usages of energies, which may have been brought about without reference to what had been, but which are now affiliated with what had been by virtue of the relevance that an end imposes. Let some men be engaged in robbing a bank, and other men running to the scene. There is no causality, no energies being transmitted from one group to the other. If the men running to the scene are policemen, e.g., the robbing and the running make a single unity whose parts are relevant to one another by virtue of the end of political peace, which requires the two related expenditures of energy. The robbing elicits the running, and this interplays with robbing to constitute the beginning of another sequence of events. Though we cannot say that there is an actual action of the robbers on the police, or of the Existence here on the Existence there, inside the political context in the light of the relevance defined by public peace, the reason, the *because* of the police's action is the robbing.

One can view men as causal agents, the realm of Existence as the spatio-temporal background, the Ideal as defining the relevance (so that when the present is accepted as the condition of relevance it is taken as a special case of the Ideal), and God as providing a condition enabling beginning and end to be together.

It takes a lifetime to make a philosopher, even one who has studied his teachers carefully, for there are two dimensions on which he must operate: he must master a set of abstract categorial elements, and he must make these explain the world of everyday. Even granted that he could get the abstract elements from his teachers, or by some act of genius, it is still the case that the way in which those categories are made integral with the world—the semantics of them—is something which one masters only over a period of time. It is the transformation of the knowledge into wisdom, the grasping of the way in which the commonsensical world is to be purged and reordered and assessed by means of those categories—or conversely, how the different categories are to apply, with what weight, and how they are to be adjusted to the concrete, sensuous, malleable content they are to explain, which is to be mastered.

May 3

The principle of induction is a constructive principle whose final goal is to become identical with some stabilized structure either of inquiry or of institutions. It provides a kind of implicative relation, which not only defines what is relevant but which also enables one to predict. In addition to the use of a principle of induction such as this, we have four other methods which we can successfully employ in order to move through the phenomena without the necessity of having recourse to the kind of analysis of boundary features characteristic of physical science.

We can structure the activities of beings into institutions. These will be ways in which the natural laws are selected and used in the light of some goal, such as peace, prosperity, the good life, the continuation of the society, and the like. We can also view the activities of beings as themselves related in purely formal ways, by mere laws of human or natural behavior. It is this to which we attend in sociology, and particularly in international law and international politics, for we do not seem to have any way in which we can relate the parts except by conceiving some kind of structure of a rational sort (unless we give up all hope of being able to understand and predict). We can, thirdly, provide structures which are dominated by a universal condition which assesses all items in the light of their mutual compatibility, pushing some into prominence and others into the background. Finally, we can provide structures which express the nature of human attitudes, purposes, plans, etc.

When we seek to make predictions in the social sciences, and in particular history, we find ourselves confronted first with the problem of knowing what the facts are. We must proceed then to gather material, using statistics, criticism of testimony, and the like. Having got our facts straight (and thus knowing something about what could have been expected in the past) we can have recourse to the physical sciences and break up the facts into conceivable items to be related in conceivable ways; we can take an existential approach and try to find out what institutional structures are prevailing; we can make use of a method of induction; we can take a most general sociological approach and "philosophically" provide formal relations regarding the most basic aspects of reality (as is done in the *Modes*); we can take a theological approach and try to find what things mean in terms of some basic condition of assessment; or finally, we can view all things in the light of man's needs to make technological use of what environs him.

If we are looking for a rational way of dealing with history, we can try to break up the historic items into purely conceptual ones to be interrelated conceptually; we can make inductions or find the inductive limit in some stabilized bond which relates the various items at one time to others at some other (as we do in fact when we envisage such things as wars, and sometimes epochs and civilizations, as having a "spirit," or as specializing a definite and inescapable Ideal pattern); we can conceive of the items at one time as having some rational relation to others at a subsequent time, reconstituting the course of history in terms of some law of history; we can envisage history as a kind of articulation of God's will; or we can see it as the working out of the plans of individuals, or of the unconscious desires of all.

The rational procedure seems to require rationalized items, analyzed out of the historical; the desires of men seem too narrow and ineffective for the most part. The most hopeful procedure in history would be to deal with history inductively or via some institutional structure. But we seem to have too little evidence for significant inductions, and we want to know something now, rather than in the long run, about what is to be. We have left, then, only an institutional structure, similar to that found in politics. We must then see if there is a way of selecting out the natural laws of phenomena (not necessarily well understood by the sciences, since they are for the sciences the outcome of the operation of laws on "noumenal" entities which were derived by analysis of the phenomena). These laws are not identifiable with the laws governing the phenomena. In the light either of the present, or of the ideal goal of men, we must, then, see how such laws could serve as the way in which the activities of men and Existence are to be channelized so as to constitute a law-abiding rational process of history.

The Ideal as such, or in the present, is identifiable; but what of the laws? Are these the laws found by sociologists, or the roughhewn ones known to common sense, such as the price of tyranny, starvation, rebellion, illiteracy, and the like? Does common sense know even this much? The first question then is, are there laws of phenomena amongst which the Ideal can enable us to select those which have a stabilized being, serving to relate men to one another and their acts in relevant ways? Or is history a concrete induction, the very process of achieving such a stabilization?

May 5

A nation or any other unit involved in history can be viewed as being active in the sense of expressing its nature at every moment. The realm of Existence will be for it a mode of connection and a background. As a mode of connection it will provide the casual ground and vitality of the historical resultant of the two together, the nation and Existence. The situation can be reversed: the realm of Existence can be viewed as active, and the primary function of the nation taken to provide linkages defining the relevance of the various items which (though in part originating with the nation) are thought of as being a function and expression of Existence, or the realm of nature outside the nation. History is here viewed as a locus of the self-development of the nation or people. A third way would be to see history as the locus of the destiny of both the people and Existence, as the place where they are intertwined and where the experience of history occurs. Here the people and Existence have no distinctive nature and no distinctive power, being transmuted and defined by what they together constitute. Finally, there is history as a barrier between the nation and the realm of Existence. Each finds the product, of itself with the other, as a barrier preventing the encroachment of the other. It is thereby enabled to have a private life of its own, which can then be made the object of an ontology, a science, religion, etc.

When we want to learn something from history, it is the first and the second which interest us—the first when we want to see each occurrence as a manifestation of the spirit of a people, united somehow by forces outside the control of the people, the second when we want to see how the nature of a people develops over the course of time. The first is in focus when we are interested in the causal powers that will be exerted, when we want to know what will happen to such and such an adventure—say the building up of a civilization in the wilderness. We take account of the second when we have arrived at the beginning of some epoch, as having produced such and such a result, and in the light of that result would like to know how to relate the various occurrences in the world and thereby know where we are to arrive.

A period ends with the achievement of an occurrence which enables the people to function as a principle of relevance. The beginning and ending of a period thus function in triple ways; they are mere expressions, they are joint products, and they are principles of relevance. Knowing only an expression, we can ask after the kind of transformation in the principle of relevance that will be necessary if the expression, as related by nature, is to be a part of the world of the people.

May 6

A nation or a people has a nature which serves as the link connecting its expressions, treated objectively, i.e. as products or possessions of Existence. When that nature is linked to a terminus, and in the end to the Ideal, it serves as a measure of right and wrong, thereby forcing some of the items previously connected to form one link of proper or desirable occurrences and the other to form a link of undesirable ones, expressing a bad side of the human nature. On the other side, Existence is a dynamic process. Linked to the end, it provides a "natural law," a dimension defining what is rational over against what is irrational. Once again we get two patterns.

Using the pattern of the wrong and the irrational as essential, and thus taking the linkage provided by the nature of a people and the process of Existence as ways in which they are connected, we can see that the pattern of right and rationality is an ought-to-be which is only partially realized. If one takes it as merely defined by the end as a kind of pattern governing what occurs, it may never be exemplified.

When the connection offered by the nation and that of Existence are intertwined and serve to relate whatever does take place, we have outcomes; when linked to the Ideal we get a distined principle of relevance for history. Once again we can distinguish between the desirable and undesirable—in this case, the relevant and the irrelevant or aberrant.

We have three norms: the good, the rational and the relevant. In the case of a conflict between two of these, the third must adjudicate the other two. The good and the rational patterns are to be adjudicated in the idea of the relevant; the good and the relevant in the rational; the rational and the relevant in the good. In politics the living law and the natural law are adjudicated by the very process of politics, or by positive law taken as a model for approaching a true justice; the living law and the process of positive law are to be reconciled by reference to natural law; the positive and natural law are to be reconciled by reference to the living law.

An act of violence can be said to be provoked by the situation and to express the nature of a people, so far as it is linked with such and such another act of violence. The people's living law, and in the end its standard of right, defines intermediate acts as bad; the violence may be said to be good in terms of the end which that people finally reached, but to be bad in terms of the Ideal end, thereby showing the people to be a "bad" people.

From the standpoint of the realm of Existence, one act of violence prompts another. But in terms of the ultimate Ideal, there should be such and such a result produced after the first act of violence; it will be due to the aberration of nature, its failure to be fully rational, we will say, that makes for that undesirable act of violence which the standard of rationality precludes.

When the working of nature and the nature of the people intermesh we get history working out its own course. Related to the ultimate Ideal that history will be judgeable as allowing for all sorts of irrelevancies, and even in the extreme case of being only a tissue of irrelevancies since it does not move to the end. But if we accept the present as the end, then of course in the light of that present we can say that the past is a tissue of relevancies.

The ought-to-be is always realized if we take the present to be what ought to be, or at least our ground for determining the rational, the good, and the relevant. And history does this in its investigations of the past. That is why it must be constantly rewritten. It need not be rewritten so long as it adheres to an absolute Ideal, but then it must assume that that Ideal will be realized and thus is pertinent to history as it occurs, and does not merely define what it would have been desirable for history to have been. If we take the last alternative, we can judge the history which does occur. The judgment need not be revised, though it must of course await its data if it is trying to be true of all history. But we can judge past history today in the same way we can tomorrow, if our test is the pattern which is defined by the nature of a people, the process of Existence, or the course of destiny, when these are linked to the absolute Ideal.

Better: The function of the Ideal with respect to the nature of a people, etc., and thus in connection with the actual habits of them, is to make various items representative of the others, and not necessarily excellent or good. Each of the three ways of using the Ideal—to make representatives turned toward the good, to define the rational order, and to define the relevant—can be used normatively with respect to the others.

The Ideal has three applications because there are three other modes; rationality answers to the imposition of the Ideal on Existence, representativeness answers to its imposition on actuality, and relevance answers to it as concerned with that total unity of history which is defined by God.

May 7

We can begin philosophizing only with "common experience" which has not yet been subjected to a philosophical alteration. This we find is muddled in two ways: A] it involves content which has nothing to do with the normal course of life, while   B] the content which does have something to do with the normal course of life is overrun with conventions, superstitions, and errors. It is the task of philosophy to separate out the different components, and to see what each one imports.

How do we know there is a muddle? We start as men who are mature, sane, and decent, which is to say, who know what the normal course of life may be, who can distinguish in this what is stable or sound and what is not, and who are ready to accredit things with whatever value, or power, or right they are discovered to have. This means that from the start we are sure of certain nucleal realities—that men can walk and talk, that it is wrong to hit a baby with a bottle, that some people are in earnest when they pray. We need not have a full catalogue of these. But we ought to note that they can be dealt with as essentially found in language, customs, experiences, or beings, thereby giving us a base in common-sense usage, common-sense practice, common-sense values, or common-sense realities.

We first see that there are alien contents, by virtue of the fact that they do not behave as the normally expected things do. We do not see all of these quickly, in part because they assume the shape and behavior of ordinary words, things, etc. The expressions of religion or of past metaphysics soon come into ordinary experience and are there expressed or responded to in the ordinary ways. Those who cherish the commonsensical as the only true and legitimate, seek to expose the masquerade. They make a double blunder. On the one hand they forget that it is common sense which has made the transformation of these items into itself, and on the other hand forget that these other items have rights of their own.

The discrimination of what is alien to the common sense normal course of life and what is integral to it, does not warrant a preference for one side or the other. The religious innovators, the speculative philosophers, the absolutistic ethicists, the perceptive artists, all concern themselves with what does not belong to the normal course of life. One does them a service by pointing out that the common-sense categories, in which they are usually framed, do them an injustice. Common-sense philosophers blame these men for an error which common sense produced, the error of expressing alien data in terms appropriate only to the normal course of life.

The discrimination of the content of the normal course of life and the alien material which had been introduced into it, is grounded in one's decency as reflective, i.e., in a willingness to see things for what they are. This is what the program of phenomenology in root really requires, though it narrows its task by considering only one side of the "phenomena," forgetting that there may be a more substantial side to what is isolated, and that the commonsense normal existence has its rights as well. A surer and faster way would be to take seriously the various enterprises in which men have engaged and in which they have directed their efforts toward what is outside the normal course—mathematics, science, history, philosophy, religion, art. This is but a device for getting on with the job of discrimination; if one wants to engage in the discrimination right at the beginning, one can do nothing more than have a steady grip on the normal course of life, or its language, customs, etc., and shear off all others, in somewhat the way in which Wittgenstein has urged. One exposes the various expressions which seem to be legitimate but which, on investigation of the way in which they function, are found to be odd, to violate the ordinary use of language.

Having sheared off the different areas that deserve a vocabulary and an investigation of their own, one can then proceed to engage in them.

Or one can investigate their claims and objectives, and see if there is anything in experience answering to them, and if there is any systematic way of making sense of their presence and claims. I have held that the normal course of life is environed by an area of experience which breaks up into three subdivisions, Existence, Ideality, and God, and that these are open to cosmic science, art, mathematics, theology, religion, etc., to be integrated in a speculative account.

Speculation proceeds by taking some hypothesis with respect to the structure or function of some part or result, seeing how this will fit with what is known in other parts, and tacking back and forth until each is clarified and made to be in harmony with all the others, and eventually with what we are able to save in the area left behind, the normal course of life. Those who wish to proceed by going through languages, the nature of experiences, the conventions, will be doing what the speculative philosopher does if they will try to provide a single account in which the various languages, experiences, etc., are brought together as more than a mere aggregate. At the very least they are together as occupations of mankind, and there ought to be some root explanation or organization of them answering to the nature of mankind of its activities.

The area that is left, that of normal experience, confounds us again and again; it deceives our expectations, and we are thereby made alive to error and the failure to have a reasoned account of its functioning. It mixes illusion with what can be shown to have a status apart from this or that individual, or even from all men, as in a particular position, and we are thereby made alive to the need to have a rectified perception and judgment. It mixes prejudgment with what is in fact discerned, and we thereby (when we come to some hard case where we sometimes say one thing and then another) are made alive to the need to get our values and valuations clear. And it does not properly demarcate surface from substance, passivity from activity. Consequently, we are driven to attend to what in fact is happening and discover it to be a veil preventing us from seeing the power and force of objects. To do justice to our expectations, our perceptual experience, our sense of value, and our practice, we must analyze the common normal course of our lives, experience, language, etc., into various strands. If we take these alone to be legitimate we give up the locus in which they in fact functioned, though in a confused way.

This procedure need not be followed. One can study anthropology, politics, sociology, and history in the endeavor to find alternative normalities and then by a comparison of the various kinds try to find out what is nucleal for them all. But if we know that there are nucleal realities, or modes of expression, or forms of experience—perhaps even defining those who do not recognize these as being defective in vision or value—we can make use of the separated strands which we isolated in the course of trying to do justice to our expectations, perceptions, sense of value, and practice. We can treat these as so many components, constituting unities on a footing with our acknowledged nucleal realities.

This comparative approach runs the danger of equating all schemes and in the end of presupposing that it knows what is properly nucleal in each; the other approach, of accepting our own nucleal elements, runs the risk of parochialism and naïveté. The one method ought perhaps to be checked by the other, but in the end the latter is to be preferred, for otherwise we deny what we grasp as mature, sane, and decent men. If we are sufficiently decent we will see that other societies have different stresses; if we are sane we will understand what it is they are trying to do and say, and if we are mature we will have learned in the course of experience many things they have learned as well, and will be able to see why they or we have not learned things mastered by the other.

The rectification of the area of normal life by isolating strands open to science, perception, value, and action, and then uniting them so that they are in consonance with various nuclear facts, will yield a single domain. This is to be made intelligible in relation to the domains we isolated out of the area which stands outside the normal course—though often brought into it in a distorted form.

If one is concerned with languages, we have, then, the refined languages pertaining to the strands in the familiar world and the appropriate languages for the worlds which lie beyond the familiar, or which at the very least seem to be speaking of worlds beyond the familiar. We can insist on certain nuclear experiences, but we ought also to recognize that those experiences deserve to be related in intelligible ways, so that we are not frustrated, deceived, bewildered and made ineffective. If we grant that the existentialist has hit the core of experience, that he gets to other realities as they are in nucleus, and thus as they really are, freed from conventional distortions, we must still note that he has no way of dealing with large areas of the common-sense world except as functions of the nucleal elements, and thus has no way of accounting for and overcoming the embarrassments of error and ignorance and confusion which characterize him in the course of his daily living. He ought therefore to recognize that what he has cut through is not all irrelevant, and that if he dissected it he would find that it provided a number of routes and ways of apprehending what is encountered. These will enable him to discover other nucleal facts which may or may not be open to an existential encounter. He ought also to recognize that there are different kinds of encounters, answering to different realms.

An entirely different approach would be followed by those who paid attention not merely to language but to any kind of customary way of connecting items, with a recognition, though, that some nucleal items in the common-sense world would serve as a test or paradigm for what is to be accepted in the rest of that world, and that the customs characteristic of other areas of investigation would be as significant and legitimate as that characteristic of the common-sense world.

If one knew exactly what men introduced into the genuine nucleal part of the common-sense world, and which portion of this was arbitrary, distortive, etc., one could shear it off and get to the nucleal facts at once. But it will still be true that we will not then have a set of distinct, universalizable ways of dealing with the world as it is encountered, so that it will be necessary, in any case, to separate out strands enabling one to have sound predictions, respectable evidence, good judgments, and effective action. We distort reality not merely, then, by introducing conventions which pervert the nature of nucleal items, but also by having all the strands together in such a way as to prevent their functioning in their severalty and thus carrying out their functions to the greatest possible degree.

The normal world is distorted in three ways: it is overrun with irrelevant conventions; it is overrun with alien elements; it integrates the appropriate facets of itself before they have had a chance to be themselves as distinct items, and thus to function as agencies for enabling us to encompass the entire range of items in this world, apart from a direct experience of them. The irrelevant conventions enable us to make something distinctive of our own experiences; they do not reflect what things really are, but rather what they are for a small segment of mankind. The alien elements enable us to have a common-sense root for what is in fact outside common-sense realities; they reflect not what those elements are but how they have been distorted and adopted by common sense. The integration which common sense provides for its facets is like its adoption of the alien elements—it subjugates what first ought to be recognized to have a being and an integrity of its own.

What is to be done then is to loosen the grip that the ordinary course of life has imposed on alien realities as well as on facets of itself. The former allows one to see the cosmos, the latter allows one to get rid of superstition and error and frustration. The combining of the loosened alien elements into a single totality with the rectified common-sense object, whose facets have been speculatively united, is the work of the systematic philosopher.

The philosophic language appropriate to the rectified world of common sense should be a rectified commonsensical language. But since there is more to the universe than this—there is the Ideal, Existence, and God—such a language will prove biased toward one mode more than it should. We must then, if we are to do cosmology (with the modes merged), ontology (with the modes as separate), provide a systematic interrelated account (with the modes implicating one another), and live through a purged effective life in which the different modes will act on one another. In all four cases we must find a new way of speaking. Here we can be helped by bringing in the language of religion (sympathy, love, etc.), the language of politics (rights, demands, etc.), and the language of action (work, making, creativity). In each mode each one of these languages will have a place, depending on whether we are doing cosmology, etc.

If we are engaged in ontology and are attending to the mode of Actuality, we should make use of purified common sense; if we attend to the Ideal we ought to make use of political language; if God, to religious language; if Existence, to the language of work. If we want to use only one language, because we want to speak neutrally of all the modes, we must do it, nevertheless, as an abstraction from the perspective of Actuality. Our language will then, even when speaking of the other modes, be a common-sense, purged language, generalized in the course of achieving a neutrality toward all the modes, including that of Actuality. And so the philosopher will speak of substance, obligation, causation, being. We come back then to something like the initial position, for we now make use of something like common-sense ways with words in order to deal with what is outside the province of common sense. But it is to be noted that we can equally say that we are dealing with the actualities inside the common-sense domain in terms which are not peculiarly pertinent to them, and that in any case the language that we are using is properly speaking neither commonsensical nor non-commonsensical, but a refined form of commonsense language neutralized and generalized.

When reference is made to the objects in the common-sense domain, as purged, and no reference is intended elsewhere as well, the language we must use is purged common-sense language. Similarly, if we deal with God we ought to find a language singularly appropriate to Him, a language of religion. These languages will of course deal with their particular objects as ontological, cosmological, systematic, and effective, but the language will be the same in all cases of one type of object. Or we can forge one language for ontology, another for cosmology, etc., and then specialize this when dealing with this type of object rather than that. The second of these alternatives seems to be the better. And what is said about language must be said about custom, concept, or any other agency by mean of which we first approach what was to be separated and allowed to develop according to its own nature, and eventually to exert its own rights, following out its own logic and revealing its own mode of being.

Some terms: common experience—includes conventional common-sense world and the realm beyond, in which faint and fluctuating distinctions among three modes can sometimes be discerned.

common-sense world—the world of actualities and some part of Existence, embracing bodies, values, events, space, etc.

physical world—the common-sense world, minus qualities and values, made cosmic, and purged.

nucleal elements—the common-sense world purged of arbitrary elements, conventions, and superstitions; a localization of the physical world.

What do I want to learn from history? Sometimes who this or that people may be, and sometimes who or what mankind is. This means that I take for granted the rationally grasped course of Existence, and seek to know what kind of nature is being expressed as the link between the various items so far as those items can be said to express the people or mankind. The American people have such a nature that having had a Revolution they then have a Civil War. "American" expresses itself as these and relates them. Is it constituted by these and the fact that the relating is inseparable from Existence? It is. What we must then go on to say is that given such and such a new event, that nature must bring about such and such subsequent event. We judge what that nature does in the light of the Ideal. This defines certain aspects of the nature of the people or mankind to be preferable, thereby making certain items more representative for itself than others.

We look to the Greeks to tell us about man as caught in such and such a series of events: we translate the Greeks into ourselves by a contrary-to-fact conditional, showing how the nature they exhibited will be exhibited in these new occurrences. Such an interpretation supposes that the nature of man does not change. If we are to recognize a change in human nature we must deal with the Greeks as predecessors of ourselves and thus as having an earlier stage of a development of the nature of man, of which we are a subsequent one. And we make reference to man again when we try to deal with the wars among nations, for these are expressions not of one or the other but of all men, or of a large segment of mankind.

May 8

If one is concerned with investigating the past, trying on the basis of present evidence to find out what had occurred, he takes the position of the Ideal, either as ultimate, or as momentarily exhibited in a limited form in the present, and in the light of this determines what will be the relevant items to be selected. On the basis of his discoveries he will then be able to make predictions, if he assumes the position of Existence as providing the normal causal links. Such predictions accept the present occurrence as an expression of man in some public situation, and attempts to see what the very course of nature will require to be a consequence of this occurrence, a consequence which will be elicited from man but not necessarily, from this perspective, expressing anything of his nature.

If one is concerned with writing a history, or periodizing it, one takes the opposite tack, and assumes the position of knowing what man is in the present. Here one takes the outcome of destiny and recognizes it to epitomize what man is, and thus to offer a link between the various occurrences which owe their origin or have their locus in Existence. The link offered is most complete if it is understood to have an origin at some past time, from which time to the present the nature of man is made manifest. Here the approach involves a determination of what will be representative of man.

From the standpoint of the present we find there has been a Civil

War and a Revolutionary War; we go back to these, finding relevant occurrences enabling us to understand within the context of history how we moved from the Revolutionary to the Civil War and then to the present. At present, let us say, we are faced with tensions in Cuba, Laos, and have domestic problems of unemployment, segregation, and the like. What can we predict? Given the fact that we are the very men who went through the Revolutionary and Civil Wars we treat the current situation as something caught in some external pattern. We have, let us say, unleashed the forces of communism, promoted antagonisms, increased the possibility of death, opposition, etc. These are all, to be sure, expressions of man, and can be comprehended in some larger history; but remaining with the fact that we want to predict something having relevance to ourselves, we look at all these agencies as so many impersonal expressions of Existence and thus are able to say, in the light of the way they function, that such and such will be the kind of data with which we have to deal and to which we, because of our given nature, will inevitably and historically respond.

If we want to write about our history, we look to ourselves as here and now, having such and such developed natures. In terms of such natures we select items out of the whole, to stand as the pivotal occurrences in the period. The occurrences define the beginning and ending of a certain phase of our natures. In that period we see the occurrences as given to us by that which is outside; it is not only that we are (as in the case of prediction) elicited to respond historically to something outside the historic frame, but that we are making use of, accepting what occurs outside us as precisely that which we are incorporating within our own history. In the case of prediction we see how something outside us will make us behave in such and such a way; in the case of the writing of history we see how what happened outside us is made by us into our history. A predictive attitude toward history must be combined with a periodization of it, and thus made to constitute together with it the very nature of history as an autonomous working out of a destiny.

It is perhaps more correct to say that the very items which are recognized as objectively historical from the perspective of a destiny are the items which are taken to be related by natural laws when we predict, and are related by a nature when we periodize in the writing of a history. The natural laws are, however, to be seen to be operating on behalf of, to be caught inside the context of, and to be defined by the historical elements; it is their power which is outside the historical situation, making predictions possible; the nature, similarly, is also to be thought of as coming out of a nonhistorical dimension and given an historical status as a kind of selective device inside the frame defined by destiny. The links provided by man and by nature are thus to be understood as delimitations of the linkage given by destiny; the items which are connected by all three are the same.

If we turn to the individual the foregoing would allow us to deal with him in three ways: *1*] His life as a whole viewed publicly is the meaning of him in his society; the story is no more his than society's. *2*] If, however, we are concerned with prediction, we can say that the public occurrences to which he contributes are linked together by laws of nature, and we as a consequence can know what will be, once we know what had been done and what laws prevail. *3*] If we want to write an account of his life we will instead try to show how certain events are pivotal because they are so defined by the nature he has. In psychoanalysis where we are concerned with the individual and try to find out what his nature really is, the last is the only one which interests us. It is thus a form of historiography, not of historical investigation. This means that it is determining the significant points in a man's life in terms of pivotal occurrences—e.g., those which are *outre*—or determining what his nature is in the light of such and such odd acts. If we take this last approach and bring it back to history, we will be able to say that once we have settled on such and such as pivotal acts—the Revolutionary and the Civil War, e.g.—we can interpret man as the being who made the one come after the other, by expressing the one after the other.

1] But can we not predict what men themselves do? And this by attending to them as powers or causes?   *2*] Can we not read off their natures in terms of the way they respond to conditions offered them from without?

1] When men are treated as causes, or better as linkages grounding predictions, the occurrences with which we are concerned are no longer expressions of them but attributed to a domain outside them. The use of men then to ground predictions is in effect the recognition that they—and not nature—are outside history. Such prediction is possible. This fact shows that we can also trace the development of Existence as a link between expressions of men. We would then in effect have a history of nature. There are thus two predictive and developmental strands.

2] If we have a norm of human nature, defined in terms of some end, and if we know what this ought to do in such and such a circumstance, we can read off the nature of men as a distortion or partial expression of it. And we can do a similar thing with respect to nature. We can also do something similar for a single autonomous history with a predestined meaning at which it is to arrive.

May 9

What ultimately is an interplay between man and Existence is also to be seen in a limited form as an interplay between this nation and that, this facet of man and that. This means that we can see mankind, as made up of different factions, working out its destiny. In the light of an Ideal, it works out in a way to be defined as good or bad. (The Ideal enables one to discover significant occurrences in the past of human history.) It means too that each of the factions can ground predictions, and that each can be viewed as having a nature which determines how a history is to be written.

Since at every moment a people can identify a part of the item in a history (which they constitute with others) as its own, the people can be said to change in nature at every moment. The acceptance of this or that occurrence as an expression of oneself is made part of the nature of a people just so far as some subsequent occurrence, which in fact issues out of the people, is seen to be on a different level, to be of a different category from that which was accepted. Thus if a people takes out of a war the idea that it is victorious and identifies itself with that supposition, then if it behaves in some subsequent moment as it had before, giving just that much of itself in relation to the other as it had, the portion with which it had identified itself becomes part of its own historical being.

We change our natures to the degree that we accept any part of the destiny, which we did not produce, as our own. When we do this we add it to the nature we in fact have. If we accept the entire historical reality as our own, then we will but make manifest the course of history as the expression of our nature, actually periodize it as it goes along. When we do this, of course, the other party will continue to be and to function; the identification we make, though it will allow us to have a different nature, will not thereby define what in fact will ensue. We have to identify ourselves at every moment with the product of ourselves and the other if we are to be fully historical and have the historical world be nothing but the expression of ourselves.

The new occurrence which is produced by us, who have identified ourselves with all or a part of the historical, is an expression of the historical as a nature, and not the expression of it as a law-abiding linkage. The item which we produce when we are taking ourselves to be fully historical, is made public, exterior, and thus is offered to the other party as that which it is to relate to the future in a predictable way. It may not do this. In that case we will treat it as irrational, willful. But whether it does this or not, there is something produced by its means.

To make ourselves historical by adopting the historical in whole or part is still to leave outside another power which will take what we thereafter express as something which it can make historical. By adopting the historical we can do nothing but alter our nature and thus leave the law-abiding power outside; or if we use the historical to define a new predictable power, we will leave outside it the nature of the other party, which will express itself in the form of content to be given to that predictable power.

To accept the entire historic occurrence as one's own requires deliberate intent. But each people inevitably acquires part of the occurrence in its very withdrawing of itself in preparation to engage in the next act. At every moment a people makes an historic occurrence and must withdraw from it, taking with itself something other than what it had initially given, and as a consequence it inevitably alters itself, makes itself have a nature which serves as an explanatory ground for whatever things it in fact expresses. It makes itself be a predictable power by the way in which it uses what it had accreted, so as to determine the route connecting the initial occurrence with a subsequent one.

It is impossible to determine perfectly what a people will take from the historical situation, for the outcome is not dictated by its nature or content; it is a contingent product. Still some prediction is possible since the people will continue to have a nature and a way of relating past to future. In the light of some subsequent expression it should be possible to isolate in a previous one what was native and what had been accreted, and use this information as the guide for determining what it will subsequently do. Or more generally, if we can isolate a minimal expression and use this to define what the being is natively, we can always separate, out of the historical nature of a changing being, that component which is constant at least for a given period.

May 10

At every moment each component of the historic process withdraws with more or less of the common content adhering to it. In the ideal case each would adopt the entire content. This would in no way affect the course of history as an autonomous domain; it would merely make each of the components have within itself the meaning of the whole; each would no longer be a mere creature of destiny but would be self-complete, living within itself what it in fact is living outside. This might be said to be the Ideal outcome that ought to be achieved. But what is in fact achieved is a part of this result, and then only for a moment. At every moment each component withdraws in order to be something in itself, as rich as what had been. It, in effect, makes itself in itself be what its togetherness was; this means it does not merely turn itself into a terminus of that togetherness but readdresses itself so as to be a being for which that terminus is an integral part.

In the ideal case each component (a people, mankind, etc.) is not only a predictive power, and a pattern explanatory of a periodization, but is a destiny working itself out. Since the destiny is always inclusive of the predictive power and a pattern, one will be able to understand what can be expected of a people only if one is able to abstract the predictable strand out of its destiny. Consequently, even when we know that a people is changing in history we can, by attending first to the autonomous history and the predictable power of the people, see what difference the destiny (and thus the pattern of something other than the predictable power) makes to the exercise of the predictable power.

We first (under the guidance of the autonomous history) have to separate out of the course of a people's career a component which is contributory to its destiny-nature. Then we may be able, by adding a pattern to that component and seeing how these interplay (and noting the difference made to the expression of the predictive power), be able to determine what the people will do. Thus, if we say that the victor takes the war to be something which is its burden, then though the outcome of the interplay of the two sides will let us have an uneasy peace, the people, which has accepted the burden, will be predictable. We will predict how it contributes to the common history, as this is in fact adopted by itself. We will also accredit it with bringing about something in that common history that otherwise would have been attributed solely to the interplay of itself with the other side.

An event which has been produced inside an autonomous history has its own causal relation to its antecedents. If it is also an expression of one or both of the sides of the history, as having adopted and assimilated the precedent events, the event will define itself as an historical reality when and as it stands apart from that history. If it merely contributed to the making of an autonomous history it would be an ahistorical reality when apart from that history. Whatever predictions we could make, since they always concern strands which are outside the history for which the predictions are made, will have to be with respect to a component of the historical realities. Only after this has been done, can we add to the outcome the differentiation which the pattern, offered by the other side, might introduce.

More accurately, the historic occurrence cannot enter into a man as a mere item to be related in the way it is in history, as the mere contingent antecedent of something which is to come about in the course of time and which in fact is not dealt with except when we are trying to discover historical truths about the past. By adopting the item as one's own, one makes it into part of one's pattern or one's predictive power. If the latter, there is no knowledge of where it will go except by seeing how it does make a difference to the initial predictive power. We can then tell what the being or people will do at some subsequent time as the outcome of that power, but we will not know what the subsequent event will be unless what men in fact do will be identical with the contingent outcome of the historic occurrence.

We do not know just what a people will accrete to itself; indeed we find out what it has accreted, when we see how it subsequently expresses itself. If we knew, we could predict; there is then a prediction open to omniscience. Ditto for the altered pattern which an adoption of the historic occurrence might also involve.

Predictions would be possible if made in clusters, i.e., if one were to view a people as capable of adopting the occurrence to any degree and then seeing what possible outcomes this would involve when integrated with the people's initial nature—provided that this nature is expressed as a power together with the expressions of the pattern of some other being.

May 11

The discussion of the last days has been based on the supposition that the destined course of history is inevitable, despite what the subordinate parts may be doing. But this supposition should not be made. The two parts interplay with one another to constitute a single domain in which there is a new kind of causality constituted by the juncture of their predictable powers. But when they break away from their own conjunction and adopt something of the product as part of their being, their powers change. Their predictable powers are exercised with respect to what is merely passive. Since each is active with respect to the other, and since the predictive power of each is altered by the adoption of the content which it had helped constitute in the past, each functions not as a predictive power of the autonomous realm of history, but only as a power which, starting from such and such a point, enables it to deal with exterior content in such and such a way. Since the content which it is given to act upon is something over which it has no control, there is no predictability to the course of history except so far as one can add the two predictable components together to define a predictable course of events.

(I have been told recently that when I speak I am very clear, but that my writings are obscure. This is odd, for my writings are the result of rewritings and rewritings. My speech is now being exhibited, more or less, for I type almost as fast as I can mumble to myself. It may be the case that when I speak in public I become clearer, but I doubt this. What is true, I think, is that I convey something with my gestures and intonations which I do not convey in print. In any case the foregoing, and perhaps all these notes, give evidence of the unclarity of my expressions, particularly when I am thinking freshly. It may, of course, be the case that those who hear me, hear me when I am speaking about the things I already know—for the most part about things which I have written about in these notes or in my books. This, however, cannot be the whole story for I do speak spontaneously and often do have new ideas in the course of a presentation even of what I had written about before.)

Given no adoption of the common content we have contending forces which constitute the new course of autonomous history. Given the adoption of the content by the different components at different times, we have a different interplay. In the first case we can make predictions by combining the predictions of the components. In the second, we can make them by recognizing that the predictable forces can be understood as having predictable ways of adopting common content, and thus giving us a new set of predictable forces to interplay.

The two contending forces may be understood in three ways: 1] both can be viewed as predictable powers in interplay, constituting a new causal whole; 2] both can be viewed as natures which come to expression, allowing one to see a new spirit arising; 3] one can be viewed as a power and the other as a nature; the course of history is then seen as a predictable power facing certain given contents (some or part of which issues from it). These, because of their recalcitrant nature, help constitute a new domain. The predictable power will then provide merely a kind of rule enabling us to see some kind of order or necessity in the process which the two agents together constitute.

May 12

The predictable power of the components must be understood to be with reference to the autonomous historical domain, of which the prediction is the structural element uniting the given material. The component acts in a predictable way in and of itself, but the prediction is altered in meaning by virtue of the fact that it constitutes with the given content a sequence of occurrences having a definite structure. If, then, the predictable power is affected by some occurrence which its owner participated in, in the past, there will be a new predictable power exerted. The total account of the next occurrence will involve a path from the previous occurrence, which had not been trodden before and which could not be known by anyone who knew only the predictable power, and even the way in which it interplayed with given data.

When we know one faction and see it in terms of its law-abiding nature, we are still confronted with the fact that that nature can be altered by the adoption of some occurrence as its own. That adoption however could conceivably have been predicted. Granted this, it still is the case that the product of that prediction with the given content (which makes for the autonomous realm of a structured history) has a meaning that can be understood only from the perspective of a destiny. We can predict that this nation is expansive; we find that it is now faced with another expansive nation. The second nation is to be thought of as expressing a pattern. It needs some way in which its acts are interconnected, and this is what the predictive force means for it.

Whether the given nation will exhibit expansionistic acts or not, it is a fact (on this hypothesis) that it will use whatever occasion it is confronted with to bring about the expansion of itself. This predictive strand has, however, a changed role when it is fact interrelated with the expression of the other faction, for now the prediction, which was concerned with what the ordering of the data means for the given nation, will have to be understood as marking the structure of the predictive power together with the data. If there were no autonomous field of history with its own mode of becoming, we could say that the predictable power of one nation produced an effete product when combined with the data attributed to the other nation. But an autonomous history demands that there be an intrinsic causal dimension, and perhaps even a structural character to it. History has the power of the dot, of the togetherness of two modes, in a time which is neutral to them both.

We seek to know how to convert predictable power into a component of autonomous history in such a way as to preserve some knowledge of what is to be. We can give up the autonomy, and we can deny that the prediction has anything to do with the being as outside history. But if we do both we have the problem of converting the latter into a component of the former.

What happens when the predictive power is integral to a world of historical destiny? Is it not that the end, either as Ideal, or as already achieved or projected, runs backward through the combination, to make the whole have another value? Just as an atom within a body falls at the normal rate, while nevertheless brought into contexts and even made to move in ways which by itself it could not, so in the history the predictive pattern operates so far as we have the items linked rationally and progressively. If we take the items in their completeness and thus as operating inside a frame defined by some other, the predictable power will show odd aberrations to be understood only so far as we bring a correction into it at times from the destiny. It takes a knowledge of the destiny to give us the conditions under which a predictable portion could operate on its own even while having only a subordinate reality or status.

There is a boundary shared by a constituent faction and an autonomous history. The autonomous realm denies the faction an opportunity to exercise its function by itself. In effect this means that we must speak of the factions being possessed by that which they together constitute, while still retaining some viability of their own. As possessed, they are parts of a domain controlled by a comma; this presupposes their being also connected in a dot. The reality must be the reconciliation of the factions as occupying both roles (in a comma and a dot); there must be a perpetual reassessment of themselves in themselves so that they can keep these two sides in accord. Or one can say that they are always in accord, precisely because the two sides are expressions of a single unity. In the latter case what we have is the two factions as something in and of themselves and the meaning of their roles as separate, e.g., just as the roles of each as together is something which is determined at each moment by virtue of the nature of the other.

The upshot is that from the standpoint of an autonomous history the predictable and pattern factions are abstractions incapable of functioning as such except by a kind of generalization and a projection into one another. But from the standpoint of these two, the history which results from their interplay is purely derivative, summational of the rational distinctive roles they have over against one another.

(Is there not some other position where these two, the comma and dot relation of the factions, can be seen together? After all, the dot is made possible by the presence of the Ideal as destiny, and the comma is made possible by the presence of God as allowing things to stand apart, and the two components are Actuality and Existence. To bring the two sides together would be tantamount to holding them over against themselves as apart, related now by Existence and then by Actuality. We can say that Actuality is one way in which the two sides, comma and dot are together, and Existence another way. We have them separated more in Existence, and united more in Actuality.)

Predictions are possible in history with respect to the future, but in abstraction from the infection which the data imposes on the faction having a law-abiding nature. The future which is predicted is not in historical but in social or human or natural time. We can say, if we like, that this prediction is realized precariously and in a qualified form by virtue of the way in which the counterattack (by the other faction on that future, or on some other prospect which together with the future constitutes the Ideal) is met. We predict what is to be, but this is pulled down into the historic world in the shape of a present as a destiny. This operates to define the historic world in which the predicted outcome, as well as the antecedent of that outcome, are identified as abstractions in an historic context. They are also to be seen to have a relation as separate items in a nonhistoric context. Granted then that we know the law-abiding nature and even how it will adopt something from the complex, we still do not know what will be in history, since the historic result is the concretionalization of this abstraction. We can say that it instances the abstraction, but this would be to stress only one facet, make the comma prescriptive for the dot.

There are four material logics, each appropriate to one mode. There are also four abstract logics—the therefore giving us a pragmatic logic, the dot a constructive one, the implies an intensional one, and the comma an extensional one. The constructive involves the forging of new unities (a kind of abduction); the pragmatic is essentially inductive. Each prescribes to the others and is subject to the others. There is no one encompassing them all, for we must decide whether or not to be primarily intensional, etc. The logic of history is constructive, and makes references to the extensional.

May 13

The predictive power and the pattern characteristic of the components of an historic world are to be defined by abstracting from the historic world with its structure and content interwoven to constitute a new domain. The predictable power is ascribed to one of the components; we say of it that since such and such is the historic world, the component will act in such and such a predictable way. The prediction here concerns the action of the component, an action which as a matter of fact will be interrelated with the expressions of the other component (or what is ascribed to it) and not to the structure of the historic world. The structure and the content of the historic world are the joint product of the two components. We infer a predictable power with respect to an abstracted component and deduce what that power will in fact do. But this which it will do is not what will historically be, but only a component of this, to be redefined when combined with the contribution of the other component. The structure of the historical, however, is no mere conjunction of the predictable power and the pattern (nor is its content the conjunction of the expressions of the two components); the destiny maintains itself and insists on providing a distinctive autonomous unity in which the contributions of the components are to be fitted.

If now we start with the present moment, the components have their self-determined being apart from the historic, in contrast with the case when we look back in the past and find it necessary to abstract the components and their structures and contents from what is in fact more real than they. The outcome of the predictable power is a possibility which, as inseparable from the period defined by the pattern, defines the abstract destiny. This is a norm, a standard, telling us what a rational measure of the present (and subsequent acts) is like. Thus, separate economic blocs, in a nation which has gone through a revolution, will engage in fierce competition. This is a prediction of a possible civil war. The American Civil War defines whatever comes after the Revolution to be a step on the way toward the Civil War. If that war had never happened there would be something irrational in the course of history or in the predictable power, and the pattern would have to be redefined.

Must we not say instead that the predictable power and pattern come together to constitute an actual course of history, arriving at some outcome which will define the new destiny, thereby showing that the initial possible destiny was either too abstract or too distant (which are perhaps the same thing)? The Americans and slavery, as together defining a destiny in the shape of a war, interact to constitute an actual history. So long as that war does not eventuate, the history they produce is a sequence. Yet any moment at which their juncture may be, is a destiny, providing that it be dealt with in terms of a more remote abstract destiny. The War of 1812 is the destiny of the Revolution provided that the War of 1812 is defined by instances, or prepares for the Civil War. The Civil War need not be fought with guns; it may be a kind of "cold war," a tension, and a struggle. In this sense it can be said to be exemplified in all the stages we go through for that period; and if there is no terminal war, the Civil War will be said to have occurred over the entire period, with the end of the period merely an accentuated occurrence.

May 14

The predictable outcome of one of the factions together with the nature of the other helps constitute a single possibility. That possibility is an anticipatable outcome, operating as a final cause. It defines, in the preceding period (begun with the predictable power and some nature), a maximal number of items relevantly related. What we can know of the future, then, is what outcome would do most justice to all the predecessors.

Should there be at the end of the period (defined by the nature of one of the components) an outcome distinct from that which had been anticipated, it can be taken as the destiny. One will then redefine the prediction and the pattern (which we had originally assumed) by abstracting them from the concrete situation they helped constitute. Or we can say that the antecedent occurrences do not make for a maximal set of interrelated items, and therefore fail to be a part of one history.

We can know in advance what would maximize the items over a course of time. What we cannot know in advance is what the concrete nature of the anticipated outcome is. And we cannot know in advance just what in fact will be arrived at, at the end of the period. If we say that the American spirit at the end of the Revolutionary period had such and such a nature and that the fact of slavery had such and such a predictable development, and that the two together defined an anticipatable Civil War, we can go on to say that the occurrences in the period (during which the American spirit remained constant) make most sense when understood to be components in a history which begins with the Revolution and ends with a Civil War. If that War had not eventuated, there would be many items which could not be understood as part of one historic sequence; they would either have to be brought into another history or be treated as aberrations. Or, in the light of the acceptance of the outcome as a destiny, we would have had to interpret the American spirit and the development of slavery in a different way than we had before.

If we know how to predict the behavior of a schizophrenic and know something about the course of society, as having such and such a steady nature expressed in such and such items, we can anticipate what will be the outcome of the schizophrenic's encounter with that society. If the anticipated outcome does not take place, we must say that something extraneous got in the way, or that we were mistaken about the schizophrenic, the course of society, or the way in which the two were able to constitute a possibility governing the sequence of activities characteristic of the two of them as interplaying.

Purposes, intentions, final causes of all kinds, then, when faced as prospects, are anticipated definitions of what is maximally relevant in what actually takes place before the anticipated outcome is in fact produced. We know in advance what would be a maximally determining principle of relevancy; we cannot know in advance that this principle will in fact prevail. If it does not, we can criticize what in fact occurs as being confused, mixed with what is not pertinent; or we can suppose that we must redefine what the components of the historical process in fact are.

The final cause, which is the cat, or the mature and civilized man, defines what in the activities of the young is relevant. If the kitten never matures, if the youth never becomes civilized, there was something odd in the patterned nature, something odd in the predictable nature, we were wrong to anticipate the cat or man; many of the activities (in the light of the prospective mature being) which could be seen to be little experiments in growing up, are to be treated as irrelevant. If we adopt the view that the wrong anticipation was made, then we can redefine the kitten or the youth in such a way that all that they had done becomes relevant to the outcome at which they in fact arrive.

A constructed Ideal (i.e., an Ideal which is constituted by components exterior to the Ideal as such) defines maximal relevance; a constructed realm of nature, i.e., one which is forged out of Existence by means of technological devices, defines maximal effectiveness; a constructed religious reality, i.e., one which is forged in the light of the divine by one interplaying with an institution, the church, defines maximal preserved values; and a constructed individual, i.e., one which is taken to be representative of man at his best, defines a maximal *Lebenswelt,* making for human prosperity in spirit and fact.

The dynamic aspect of history is to be defined in terms of the anticipated end. This orders various items in the actual sequence of occurrences as being more or less relevant to and effective for the bringing about of that end. It is a dynamics which goes from present to future but only as guided and governed by an effective final causal control from future to past. The empirical historian refuses to acknowledge any "destiny" except that of the present moment; but then he must change his view every moment, rewrite his history every day. The absolutistic historian takes the destiny to be some remote occurrence. But then no evidence can possibly count against it; his history does not develop in time. In contrast with these two it is necessary to maintain that the destiny changes, but only at the end of a period in some crucial event.

We cannot write a history of the present for we do not have the destined outcome in terms of which the rest can be measured; contemporary historians must rely on analogies with past sequences, or must exaggerate some present occurrence. In addition, they do not have the evidences which are to be found only by a distant, detached evaluative set of inferences. We know more about the past than those who lived in it, precisely because we approach it in a spirit which allows us to look at all the facts from all sides.

The psychoanalyst often mixes up the predicted behavior of the patient with the anticipated occurrence which that patient constitutes with the ongoing society. It is an aggressive or a sex-dominated patient whose acts can be predicted. The outcome of such an aggression in such and such a situation is, say, off-color jokes. These can be used to explain all that had gone before, providing that the telling of these jokes is itself a crucial occurrence leading to changes in the patient or the world. If the telling of the jokes does not have such a status, the jokes can be used only to guide us back to some event, say puberty or marriage, which in turn is to be understood as the destiny explanatory of the patient's relation to his mother.

We have an analogous situation in the law. The ideal of justice, let us say, defines natural law. But the actual positive law is what is enacted. The meaning of the society is the idea of justice as defined by the nature of the people and the world or society in which they live. If at the end of their civilization or culture we find they do not realize that justice, we must go back and redefine the nature of the people and the society to show that the actual form which justice eventually takes in that society at the end of its period is to serve as the only meaning of justice for it. If the society ends as an unjust totality, this too is the only meaning of its end for it; that end defines even the just acts which occurred earlier as being relevant to the coming about of that end. This view requires one to say that the end of a society or historic present does not occur adventitiously; the adventitious must be credited to subordinate occurrences. If we take the end of a period to be the outcome of an accident we, in effect, say that a proper period of history includes the given period as a subordinate and earlier part. Otherwise we could learn nothing from it, unless it be the transitoriness of all human achievement. But then we would have to say that the period ended before the time of its accidental dissolution, since the achievement is in the period and in human history, whereas the passing away (by an adventitious force) of the historic status of a people is outside the period and the control of the people or its history.

The self is inseparable from a final end; but when the day of death arrives (whether or not the self continues in some other realm), the self will have no further need for that end. We can say either that death defines the end, which seems to allow for an accidental end, or that given death, we can move back to some point in the past and define the life as having that point as its destined end, and use this as the way to understand all that went before; the portion between the discovered end and death will then be of minimal relevance to the self's nature, career, or power.

If we think of artistic production as involving some controlling prospect, we can then say that the work of art is a created product and not the outcome of mechanism just so far as all the things that are done are maximally explained by the presence of that prospect, even when that prospect is not in fact realized. A work in which the prospect is not realized, i.e., a nonbeautiful one, is to be treated as having a different prospect, one which is realized only so far as we think of the artist as insensitive, or of art as that which must be explained in terms of whatever values are in fact realized in it.

May 15

A final cause must be prescriptive; it evaluates that which is to precede it, determining what would have maximal relevance. This means that the final cause cannot be wholly constituted by the items which precede it; it cannot be a mere goal aimed at. This leaves us with the following alternatives: *1*] It has a nature which is a mere function of the preceding items. But then the question is how this function can achieve the power to refer back.   *2*] It can be sustained by a reality beyond it; it can be viewed as a delimited form of the Ideal. This is the alternative I have taken in connection with natural law, and think must be taken in connection with history.   *3*] The final cause gets the backing of some being, such as God, who insists on its realization. We have something like this view in Marx and Hegel; it supposes that there is such a power and that it acts in consonance with what men and existence happen to constitute. The position is possible if we hold that the very constituting of the Ideal is one with the eliciting of the power to sustain it, since both express the dialectic or God's intent.   *4*] There is an insistent Ideality which works itself through the world, regardless of what men decide or do. This is fatalism; it ignores the contingencies and even failures of effort in this world.   *5*] There is a being who has a providential concern for the universe and insists on itself, either in the light of what is done or apart from it. But then men have nothing to do or to say about it.

In the latter two cases there is nothing more for men to do but to try to make themselves in consonance with the intent of the final cause, so that they will be accepted by it, endorsed by it. This in the end is the position taken by the dedicated Communist and the monk; they do not alter the course of history, but merely adjust themselves to the final cause so that they will be maximally relevant to the final outcome. On the other alternatives the components must act in a certain way to bring about the end which defines them to be maximally relevant. What does not contribute in this way, or any constituted product which is not required by the end, will be historically insignificant. We must know what the prescribing end is and what it demands if we are to arrive at the anticipated outcome ourselves.

The paradigm for this account is evidently Aristotle's view of medicine: the doctor sees what the end is, health, works back to the point where the patient now is, and then proceeds step by step to arrive at the health. How does the movement backwards proceed? If the facts are already determinate (as is the case with the past) we can see how the final cause will provide a principle of selection, of ordering. But if we have only the determinate present, could we say anything about the intermediate steps from the prescribed future to the determinate present? Must we not be content with an idealization of the present and the simplest conversion (in reverse order) of the final cause into the present along the lines of the activities characteristic of the present?

May 24

When we are immersed in one domain can we have any grasp of another? If not, we cannot when awake know that we dreamt, and when we dream we cannot know what it is to be awake; when absorbed in the Ideal or action we would not be able to know what it was to be sensible and commonplace—and when we know truths we will know nothing of error, or conversely.

If a final cause is all-powerful we ought to conform to it, or be taken as rejected, irrelevant. If it is merely definitory, something constituted by the projection of the components in the present, we can make its decisions count only if we can act to produce it. Consequently, once we know what the final cause is we know what we are to do. If we are mistaken in the second case we will bring about a different outcome. We know only inductively how men respond to the end they themselves define together with Existence: that they in fact fail to bring it about. As not bringing about the end they help define, they define themselves as mere ongoing beings, as not historically determined.

The predestined end demands that it be satisfied. Were it alone, we could say that whatever it did not encompass was put aside as rejected. But it is the predestined end for history. Consequently, it must take account of all that had occurred. The reconciliation between the end that is predestined and the ends that happen to be brought about is accomplished from an absolute perspective. From that perspective we must say that the predestined end is justice, but not necessarily a justice to this being or that, but to the past. Just as the historian adopts an end which will enable him to make maximum sense of the past he is going to write about, objectively viewed from the perspective of God, we must redefine the nature of the predestined end to be that end which in fact encompasses all the past within it (as the full meaning of historic justice).

In one sense the predestined end is unchanging and insistent on itself as mastering all that went before, for it is the demand for completeness or justice, and defines all the entities before it in those terms. But instead of being a justice with a definite content (which would preclude many things and ideally could be said to preclude all the things that happen in the course of time), it is a justice for history, and involves the preservation of every item in the past. The predestined end as uncorrected, rejects or minimizes most things; the particular ends allow for a failure to get to where one had planned to get.

When there is a conflict between ethics and politics we must look to the Ideal to treat the one as a pattern and the other as a predictable power, dictating which of these is to be dominant at a given time.

From the standpoint of a togetherness the idea of limits is a regulative one. The beings of the modes of being are merely regulative ideas in the use of the togethernesses. The thing-in-itself is a regulative limit to which our knowledge of the togetherness is to approach. We should transform the togetherness in our understanding; we should order it so that it exhibits in the course of time the nature of the components it actually has. (Hegel takes the regulative principle of Kant and makes it come to its proper end by making it predestined and powerful.)

Existence is related to Actuality in art by action, the therefore; in history, by a merging, a dot; in cognitions, as in Kant, by an implication; and in cosmology, by a comma. Actuality is related to the Ideal in ethics by a therefore, in politics by a dot, in practical reason by a horseshoe, and in cosmology by a comma. Actuality is related to God by a commitment, in service by a therefore, in religion by a dot, in theology by a horseshoe, and in cosmology by a comma.

May 25

We must distinguish A] the goal, constituted by the component elements; B] the outcome, that which they in fact bring about; C] the Ideal end, which is defined by the Ideal and which determines what is to be rejected as valueless or bad (the goal serving to determine what is relevantly reasonable in the sense of defining the reasonable course of events); and D] the historical totality, which is the outcome of the synthesis by God of B and C. This synthesis occurs in Him, in the cosmos, or in between. The closer B approximates C, the more intimate a part of the universe is D. Since B can approximate C through inadvertence or through a submission to C on the part of B's components, God can come to be fully immanent in part by accident and in part through design. The accidental achievement requires that, despite the fact that they aimed at A, they in fact bring about a B which happens to accord with C. In any case D is achieved by God attending to C, and attempting to see how it can take care of all the sequences which are B, which is to say, to see how, while maintaining C, He can in fact encompass the entire past made up of attained outcomes. He can do this in Himself, but He cannot do this in the world, except so far as B and C are in consonance. In short He reconciles them, but they determine whether or not He is part of this world. But suppose He is? Then a complete historiography is a record of His career as well as of man and existence together.

May 26

If we adopt Hegel's philosophy we adopt the position of the Ideal. Its activity is subjugation. This means that the Hegelian dialectic is not a dialectic on behalf of knowledge, but on behalf of an ultimate value. The Absolute does not know, and we, too, do not know when we take this standpoint, unless knowing be recognized to be a dialectical mastering of subordinate positions and recalcitrant beings. When the English Hegelians gave up the dialectic they in fact gave up the entire position, and confronted the knowledge, which is dialectical, with the knowledge that is discursive and has its grounding in Actualities. The dialectical mastery, if called knowledge, must be seen to encompass all things from one perspective only, leaving over the need to encompass all things in a discursive systematic knowledge, such as that offered in the *Modes*. But this, too, must be supplemented by a "knowledge" which is productive—a technical, or engineering, or pragmatic—knowledge rooted in Existence, and a "knowledge" which is appreciative, an enjoying "knowledge" such as is exhibited in mysticism or religion. Each of these knowledges faces material embodied in and expressed by other modes.

May 28

Those who ally themselves with the predestined end, which the Ideal imposes on history, are valuable; those who do not, are trivial, unimportant. Those who work to bring about what in fact does occur are effective, and those who do not are ineffectual. It is desirable for the valuable to make themselves effective, and for the effective to make themselves valuable. The one, the valuable, should now act to implement what he himself sees must be, so that it in fact will appear in the shape it now has for him, and not merely as the power of preserving the past (which is all that God can make out of it if man is completely ineffectual). The other, the effective, should now act so that the predestined end is achieved, thereby precluding his effectiveness from adding up to triviality (as it must if all his efforts in history produce what is not preserved as the past—which would be the case since God preserves that past only in the shape which is compatible with the predestined end). By His absorption of them in the predestined end, God would show that they were not effective, since what they made in history actually vanishes.

If there is a consonance of the predestined end with the achieved results by effective man, either by virtue of a mere concurrence, by virtue of the adoption of effective means by the valuable, or by the adoption of a proper final goal by the effective, we have the kind of result which God can produce by Himself when there is an absolute discordance between the predestined end and the achieved outcomes. God preserves the past; He rewrites it, as it were, as the cosmic historiographer, but only so far as He is forced to rewrite it. If there is concordance we have God being born.

The birth of God in history is the union of the predestined end with the achievements of the past, with the least distortion to either. If they are discordant they must be united. This must be done either 1] by insisting on the predestined end and making the past into occurrences which are to be abstracted from until they are in line with the predestined end, or 2] by accepting the past in full concreteness as sheer past, and making the predestined end preserve it, or 3] by modifying both, so that something of the value demanded in the end is preserved, together with something of the effectiveness of the actual past.

In Himself and on behalf of the Ideal, God insists that the past be altered so that it is in consonance with that Ideal; He forgets what cannot be made in consonance. Outside Himself, in the universe, He insists on behalf of the actualities that they be preserved, and that the role of the Ideal be altered to become nothing more than the final cause making possible the preservation of what had been. We then have the past and the Ideal in Him and outside Him in different ways and with different values. Providence, or the interplay of God with history, the making God an integral part of history, is the reconciliation of these answers. If the fully justified Ideal and the fully preserved past are in accord, God is immanent in the historical universe and the universe is immanent in him. If they are in disaccord, so that the reconciliation must involve an alteration in both (which is presumably the theory of the Last Judgment), the whole of history is evaluated and the pertinence of the Ideal to history is judged. Man's public life is then estimated, let us say, as having little worth, at the same time that the Ideal is said to be effective only with respect to some other dimension of man.

The public life of man is significant if there is consonance with the predestined end   A] on the part of effective men,   B] by virtue of their aim in the right direction,   C] by chance, or   D] by the allowance by God of a mere secular Existence on the part of the past. The effective man is assured of preservation apart from God, but by virtue of Him. The man, however, may make himself worthy of it by aiming properly; if he does he will show that the public life has maximum value; if he does not he will show it to have some lesser value. The maximum value of the public life however does not preclude the value of private activities; it merely assures one that the public activities are allowed to have the meaning in eternity that they have in the course of time.

Though we cannot predict what will in fact be effective, and though we have only a vague apprehension of the final predestined end, in the shape of peace and prosperity, we do know that men do not often ally themselves with that end. We know that, since there must be a reconciliation of the entire preserved past with the absolute evaluation provided by that end, the history of man is of less significance than it otherwise could be.

May 29

Suppose a doctor and a patient were both governed by the purpose of achieving health for the latter, but in fact were so working that they produced illness. The minimal historical fact is what they did on the way to producing the illness. (A maximal would have been reached only if they achieved the health by aiming at the health and working effectively together.) Analogously we can say that history inevitably makes for the preservation of the past, and that the only question remaining is how rich that past can be, how valuable that historic totality is. This value is determined by the degree of consonance which the terminus of the past has with the predestined end. Viewing history only secularly, and thus apart from the kind of reconciliation which God might provide for a dissonant destined end and produced goal, we can predict that all the past will be preserved. But we will not know the value of that preservation. It is like saying that every society remembers its holidays, but only a few societies make themselves different by allowing that past to affect their behavior in the future. As a consequence only a few of them can say that their own past experience is given any, or much value. The task of man is to make his history as valuable as it can be, and this means bringing about the predestined end while allowing for the preservation of the past. The predestined end will always be achieved, but not in such a way as to preserve the entire past; the past is always preserved but not without minimizing the role of the predestined end.

The reconciliation of the discordant by God occurs outside the historic secular realm and outside Himself as well. He constitutes an entirely new reality, an ideal history in which the past is preserved but in a somewhat distorted form, and the Ideal is given fulfillment as the outcome of the past, but only by being modified to some degree. This new domain is what is perhaps referred to by the view that in the Last Judgment the realities outside God will remain outside, but oriented with respect to Him so as to constitute an entirely new universe. In that case, the reconciled world would replace the historical, and God would have before Him His own recreated past world and His own reconstituted terminus for that past world.

August 24

Despite the fact that man is a finite being and looks at the world from a limited perspective, he always makes absolute claims.

1] As an individual knower he claims that what he is now acknowledging, in the common-sense world or in a speculative one, is true. The former he is ready to certify by the consonance of other men in his society, the latter by the internal coherence and explanatory power of his view.

2] As a being who must act where others also are, he claims that what he is doing is reasonable. His action may be short-ranged or long; if the former he seeks the support of others in his society, if the latter he seeks to be one with the general pattern of events and activities.

3] The individual as concerned with the Ideal or Good claims to be a decent or well-intentioned being, with a proper character. His interest may be confined to what is to be evaluated here and now, or what will add up to or make the final outcome. The former leads him to deal with matters of preference and choice, the latter with a good will. He certifies the former by its efficiency in getting to the accepted goals, the latter by its comprehensiveness in finding a place for the merits of whatever there be.

4] The individual as involved in an institution claims to be patriotic, loyal, one who promotes the establishment, and has an attitude or habit which allows him to do justice, to be ready to serve it. His claim is to be a man in the sense in which the institution defines. Every institution claims to be right (just as every society claims to be decent), and is warranted in doing so in the sense that men are what they are in that institution, and the institution is doing nothing other than saying that this which it has produced is an ultimate result.

If we are to evaluate the claims of different nations, societies, states, we cannot do so by looking at them from the vantage point of others; each rightly says it has been exhibiting the nature of man under the restrictions of its own structure. If we are to judge the excellence of a nation, evaluate its claim, we must look at it in terms which are exterior to it—see how it makes for the peace and prosperity of all its members, how it promotes the welfare of all men, how it does justice to the demands of the Good, how effective it is, how much it is in consonance with the course of history, how sensitive it is to other goods, how it helps man be completed, how it is in consonance with some ultimate unity, etc.

5] The individual, as sensitive and appreciative, looks out at the world in the guise of an absolute judge of what is admirable, beautiful, finally satisfactory. He does this as a spectator or as a creator. As a spectator he attends primarily to aesthetic objects, and as a creator to the making of works of art. The former is certified by the satisfaction it provides, the latter by its revelatory power regarding the nature of what is existent.

6] The individual as one who is involved in public affairs makes a claim to contribute to the final and desirable outcome of history. He does this by allying himself with what he takes to be a worthy outcome, or an inevitable one. If he takes the former he supposes this will be realized, if the latter that it is the highest form of the Good that can be attained in time. He certifies both by attending to the next outcome to see how much he is in a causal line with it, and how this is to be understood in terms of some ideally defined end.

7] The individual as a worshipper, as one who submits himself to the support and embodiment of some ultimate value, makes the claim that he has properly identified that ultimate value and is now living in consonance with it. He may take the value to be transcendent or immanent. As the former his claim is that he is eternally justified, and as the latter that he is now being enhanced. The determination of the legitimacy of his claim will depend upon a speculative determination of the former, and on the nature of his being and behavior in the latter case.

8] As a member of the institution which we call a church, he claims that there has been a proper incarnation of the divine, either as continuing some other incarnation, as expressing or carrying out some obligation, as embodying some divine command, etc. To determine the legitimacy of the claim that one has properly exhibited the divine, one must make reference to providential or nonnatural supports for the church, either in the present or eventually.

Each of these eight claims has its own peculiar kind of confirmation. Each also can be judged in terms of the other seven. An institutional religion which does not do justice to commonsensical and philosophical ideas of truth, to the reasonable acts in a society and the adjustive acts of men in the world, to the ideals of decency and what is demanded by a good and free will, to the separate and secular demands of other institutions severally and together, which ignores the aesthetic and creative sides of man, or the course of history and the kinds of ideals that can be realized in it, or which forgets the individual worshippers, is one which has failed to meet the needs of men. It can at most claim to be alongside other enterprises, and not to be a basic one in terms of which others are satisfied. The use of one of the seven on an eighth does not mean that the eighth is subordinated to those other seven, but that we must find inside the eighth the kind of satisfaction which the other seven give in their own way. It is possible, of course, to treat these seven criteria as criteria interior to the other seven approaches and thus make the eighth conform to it. One can, for example, ask of a religion that it be commonsensical; one then subordinates the religion to an extraneous claim. But one can properly view a religion in terms of a commonsensical outlook, examine it to see if inside it there is a reasonableness, a rejection of superstition, an acceptance of the common-sense world, and even a rectification of this so that what the common-sense world fails to achieve is achieved for commonsensical men in that religious setting.

August 25

A given religion, or nation, or assertion can be put forth as the only one. The others will then be said not to be instances of religion, etc., at all. Since the others either make a similar claim with respect to the first, or object to the activities of the first which ignore their presence and claims, there can be no adjudication here short of war. One reason for saying that religions must not be subject to the state is that the conflict between them is capable of being held in abeyance and perhaps even adjudicated by being put in another setting than that which each would insist upon. But when the religion is in opposition to the state (and when state is in opposition to state) there is no recourse but war. The conflict can be resolved theoretically of course, or by mutual submission of the opposition parties to some council, league, federation, etc.

Usually a religion takes the stand that there are other religions, but that these are perverse, or partial, or delusory. The same problem as that which arises when other religions are denied the status of religions arises here, and there is the same resolution to be expected.

A religion, and a nation, and an assertion, should be ready to acknowledge the being of the others and their ultimacy with respect to the particular people and activities which are involved with it. None, therefore, must give up its claim to be absolutely right. It is part of the meaning of the religion, or the nation, etc., to claim that it is absolutely right. Not to do this is to deny that it is a religion, etc. And it must claim that it is right over against all other claims; it must not accept the claims of the others to be of equal validity with its own, so far as there is any conflict or opposition amongst them. This means that it does not settle for an easy relativity and allow all others to be equally justified. All others are to be recognized to be making a claim as strong as its own, and we need a judgment taken from a neutral standpoint to enable us to judge which is right. No religion, to be sure, submits to such an impartial judgment, but all of them, when defending themselves, do make reference to some such judgment. All for example say how good they are for men now, mankind eventually, for the conduct of life, for ethics, for politics, for education, and the like.

No religion can submit to an externally defined ethics, without jeopardizing its claim to be the right religion. And none can, without begging the question, take the ethics which it itself promotes to be the right ethics. The resolution of this problem seems to be that the religion must be taken to be a religion, and not a form of ethics or even a justification of one. It must be seen to have as its primary concern the worship of God. There can, of course, be incidental consequences which flow from the operation of the religion. We can note, e.g., how men are inspired to be braver, more sympathetic, etc., when they adopt a certain religion and participate in its activities. We can then say of the religion which does not have this effect, that though it may be true, or right, or even prescribed, it is not a religion for men as they now are. The right religion at this time would be the religion which benefited the men at this time. But suppose the benefit which the men obtained was minor, or transitory or even of illusory value?

We have to compare the benefit with the benefits others provide. No matter how well sanctified by revelation, etc., a religion be, we will have to evaluate its claims as a religion for men now, in terms of what it in fact does to men now.

A religion might be willing to accept this approach, and urge all men to try it. But we already have evidence of the effectiveness of various religions on men, and need do nothing more than see if there is an improvement produced by the religion on men and their activities. A new religion can of course urge men to adopt it, but we could have a right to say that some individuals might experiment with it and the rest of us can see if their devotion to that religion brings about results as desirable as the established religions bring about.

Ethics is not the only enterprise which we would expect to be incidentally benefited by a religion appropriate to man now. One would expect a religion, if followed through to the limit, to have an effect on every aspect of man. It should enable him to be completed in every dimension, as nothing else can. However, there is an oppositionality between the best religion, in which man was completed in all possible ways incidental to his completion as a religious being, and the best ethics, politics, etc., in which man was completed in other ways and incidentally religiously. This conflict is unlike any of the others, for here the opposing claims are discovered to be of equal merit, since they do justice to all sides of man, though with distinctive stresses. Perhaps in the broadest sense of the term all these claimants can be termed religious. One could, e.g., take an ethical, or historical outlook, which promoted man's devotion to a highest value, and incidentally took care of other needs of man to be complete, as one facet of religion, treating the worship in the church, etc., as a dramatic or stressed moment. Or one could take religion, ethics, etc., when they equally satisfy man's need to be complete, as together constituting a civilization. In this case we would have man completed ethically while pursuing his religion, and religiously while acting ethically (to take these two only as examples). In this approach we recognize the presence and the rights of both religion and ethics inside every activtiy. But we would still be faced with the problem of what territory each should occupy, how much time each has a right to claim, how a people (allied with one of these basic modes of completing and with an incidental completion in other directions) is to be balanced with others. It would seem as if one would need some principle, or criterion, or control over them all.

August 26

Concentrating only on religion and ethics as examples, we can say of these basic involvements of men with other modes of being, that they are to be evaluated in a number of ways. Religion can be evaluated   A] in terms of its conformity to an external ethical standard, B] in terms of the way in which, inside itself, it encourages, promotes, or even requires the ethical life,   c] in terms of the way in which it encourages, promotes, or requires the ethical life outside it. Ethics in turn has a similar threefold relation to religion. The religion which did most justice to the three demands of an ethics would not be one which subordinated itself to the ethics, for it would be only as a religion, as one which had initially lived up to the demand that there be a devotion to an ultimate value, that would be evaluated in these ways, and then only in order to see how it compared with other religions. Every religion at some point rejects some position offered on purely ethical grounds, since it does demand an absolute commitment to some transcendental value, which the ethics does not acknowledge. But there are some religions which, without being more God-oriented, are so structured as to deny more ethical truths in one or all of the above three ways.

Also, the ethical world has its own ultimacy, and though it may do some justice to the promotion of religion inside and outside itself, and though it may even be in consonance with the demands of a religion, it does have an independence. He who stays within it does something different from one who stays inside a religion, granting that both follow the same injunctions, both ethically and religiously, for there will be a distinctive stress and use of time and, in case of conflict, a readiness to resolve it in one way rather than in another.

We can ask of each, however, that it provide a vicarious, or metaphorical, or perhaps even an actual fulfillment in the dimension of the other, as well as one itself. We want the good to be done via religion, though this may not be done in the way we would ourselves do it as ethical beings; it would be done through the cooperation of God, or in an afterlife. The religion would then offer itself as a complete life, able to provide the satisfactions which a full and independent ethical life would provide, though not by its route, or place, or time. But we are still brought up against the fact that the ethical life does complete man in a special way, and that it could satisfy the religious urge of man in some way or other.

To resolve a problem of equality or superiority of an ethics and a religion, with each at its best (and, thereafter, promoting the other inside and outside itself), we must ask if it violates any, or more than a minimum number of commands of the other, and if it satisfies all man's needs to be complete, if only in a vicarious or displaced way. The answer requires us to have recourse to something outside the ethics and the religion. If we set man over against Existence, Ideality, and God, we can ask that he do justice to what these three are in and of themselves, and to himself as standing outside all of them. This means that we must know what each of them is by itself, and must be able to recognize a need in them, as to standing outside, which is to be met by having them in interrelationship in ways other than those that religion, ethics, etc., might provide.

We can ask *1*] how Existence is related to God, for example, and how this fact, as promoting the completion of each of them, is in consonance with the completion that they receive from being involved with man. *2*] We can ask if God and the Ideal could be related to man in other ways besides religion and ethics. The former alternative supposes that we can test the inadequacy of man's involvement with God, e.g., by seeing how this involvement affects his relation to Existence. But it need not affect it at all. The second alternative enables us to determine if the mode of togetherness of the Ideal, say, and man allows for the togetherness in other ways (which it does) so as to do full justice to another side of man and the Ideal. It may do the latter, but we still would not be able to determine just what is to give way if one form of togetherness of man and the Ideal, say (as in ethics), compromises another form of togetherness, say in politics, in a rational structure, or in action.

We seem to be driven to recognize the in-itselfness of man, and perhaps of other modes, as being the locus of the terms which are involved in different kinds of togethernesses with other terms issuing from other modes of being. We must ask ourselves what kind of a unity we make if we are related to the Ideal in this way and in that, to God in this way and in that, and out of this consideration to forge an understanding of the most complete unity which is explanatory of all the terms man offers to the other modes, and of all the ways in which those terms are in fact and should be related to the terms which the other modes of being provides.

Let man be obligated to the Good, be devoted to God, be receptively allied with fellowman (or adjusted to nature), and vitally in consonance with the course of Existence as that which defines what it is he should be doing. All these prescriptives relate man significantly to those modes, and define what he ought to do in relation to them. They define his being and require of him activities which enable him to be explicitly what these required him to be. But he can also be said to aspire to the Good, to worship, or enjoy, or praise God, to be sympathetic, and to try to improve or control nature. These different ways of dealing with the other modes must be brought in consonance with the previous set. Such consonance occurs inside the different beings. Man and God must each be such inside themselves that they have this twofold relation (to stop only with this) to one another. The terms they offer are limits and boundary features for relations of different sorts. (The beings could have features which function as relations, actions, or expressions.) The being-in-itself reconciles the limit and the boundary (i.e., the term as defined from without or from within) in relation to another mode. Starting from the limit and the boundary we can imaginatively construct the nature of the unity of the two, but this would not enable us to know if we have a proper boundary or limit. Since we want to test the relation man has to some other being, we must therefore take a stand with him as a unity, and ask if this provides a rational (or dynamic, or unitary, private) ground for these diverse features.

August 27

There are confusions in the discussions of the last few days. It is necessary to distinguish features from roles, the former referring to the termini of strands and requiring a unitary being (whose unity is expressed in a fourfold way), the latter referring to the status a being has with respect to some other mode, and which requires on the part of a being a perpetual dynamic reorganization or definition of itself. Something like the latter was dealt with toward the end of the fourth chapter of the *Modes*, but it was then discussed primarily in terms of two roles needing adjustment.

What we are now confronted with is four distinct roles, each of which has been understood to be so self-sufficient that it incorporates within it the satisfactions, in some sense, which the other roles concretely provide. Also, the consideration of features and roles points up the fact that there must be two other ways in which men are to be understood, in addition to that of being unities and dynamic reorganizers. There ought to be a sense in which they are explanations, formal principles of the cosmos with themselves as one instance, and there ought to be a sense in which they are ultimate, in opposition to all else. As explanations they must be understood to have, in addition to features and roles (required by them as unities and readjustors), data which they confront and which they can account for and categorially organize. As ultimate, in opposition to all else, each man is also an other, or better an experiencer, one who faces the rest of the world as not merely something given which he is to organize, but as that which remains over against him with its own measure and being, and which he will enjoy, or try to explain (thereby moving to himself as unity), or face in some role, or reflect by his features.

The problem, then, of reconciling religion and ethics is firstly a special case of the reconciliation of religion with a number of other disciplines; secondly, it involves the recognition that man has diverse roles; thirdly, it must be seen not to yield man in his full concreteness, since he does have in addition features, categorial powers, and an ego over against all else.

The situation with respect to religion and ethics, where each is full-bodied, the best illustration of its kind, is similar to the relation holding between, say Russia and the United States. If the United States is to meet the challenges of Russia it must be armed and geared to that kind of threat; yet if it is to be a democracy the threat must be met within a larger frame. The meeting of the challenge of Russia must take place within a different setting than that which Russia itself provides. Just so, the challenge which ethics makes to religion is to be faced by religion having within it a proper ethics. Conversely, the ethics must have within it a satisfactory religious dimension equal in power and result to that which an independent religion could provide. Similarly, Russia must provide the satisfactions which a democracy can and does. We can solve the problem perhaps by taking the religion inside ethics (and the ethics inside religion) to be geared to and made to serve the supervening ethics (and religion). Similarly, the democracy must use its arms with full force but always under the governance of the democratic final end. It must be teleologically as well as efficiently employed.

What kind of a difference does a teleological end make? It means that there will always be preliminary adventures, modifications in direction, use of what otherwise might be thought irrelevant, which will serve to bring about the teleological end. In short, it means the maximum preservation of all occurrences, the utilization of what is now not effective, the refusal to dismiss all aspirations which cannot be made to conform to the efficient working out of some scheme. What is being said here seems to reverse the stress of the other days, for the ethics, e.g., is now being looked at as having a primary exercise even inside the religion, and the religion so far is thought of as merely guaranteeing the use of items which that ethics does not encompass. But this reversal of stress is legitimate because what is being sought now is some way of adjudicating the claims of a full-fledged ethics and a full-fledged religion. What is being said is what each, to meet the challenge of the other, must allow its subordinated element, which it otherwise might satisfy in a metaphorical or vicarious way, to have a full-bodied role, so that it can be an effective answer to the other.

But we now seem merely to have pushed the matter back a step. Suppose an ethics allows full place to a religion and yet takes up all other items which that religion ignores, and that a religion allows full place to an ethics but takes up all other items which the ethics ignores? Suppose a democracy is as strong as a dictatorship, and a dictatorship does allow a democratic way of life inside its confines but subject, of course, to the dictatorship as the end which determines the role of that democratic life and the value of all else? The issue seems to pivot on the diverse interpretations of what is not inside the province of the contained ethics or religion, democracy or dictatorship. What, for example, we might ask, does a religion, which gives full place to an ethics and thus can meet the challenge of another ethics, not subordinated to a religion, say about art? philosophy? science? What for example does a democracy, which gives full place to strength and the meeting of the challenge of a dictatorship, say about education, social welfare, community spirit, and the like?

But once again we are merely pushed back a step. Suppose a religion encompasses the totality of human enterprises and does full justice to them, in such a way that the satisfactions provided by these enterprises, when they are dealt with severally and in independence, are all met inside the religion, and suppose also that each one of these enterprises when independently pursued actually contains all the others, including religion? What we would then confront is a plurality of domains in which there were different primary teleologically ordering realms, inside of which there was full autonomy given to the subordinated realms.

Not only would ethics be given a full scope, and provision made for
the place of art, but art would be given full scope, and provisions would
be made for the ethics, and both of these inside the frame of a proper
religion. But ethics would also find full scope with incidental roles for
religion and art respectively.

The religion and ethics treated as teleological and at the same time
as ultimate and autonomous, would differ from what they are inside
the other only in their teleological functioning. The question, then, of the
reconciliation of a full-fledged religion and ethics, which did make full
provision for all other autonomous ways of being (ordering them
though in different ways by virtue of the fact that they were made in the
end subordinate to the values of the religion or ethics), is the question of
reconciling two types of end.

Each of the disciplines requires man to have a distinctive role. Since,
despite their primary place, the religion and ethics will function as concretely in the present as any of their subordinated elements, they will
require man to have roles with respect to the religion and ethics. But
the question that remains over is what one should function as a teleological element, and thus which one is in fact superior to the other? This
matter will be resolved by turning away from either and asking what is
the end for man. That enterprise which is most in consonance with the
end of man rightly assumes the position of a teleological end as well as
of an autonomous discipline. If the end of man is to be complete, as
I think it is, and if completion by thought, devotion, possession, etc., are
not wish fulfillments (this being only a consequence of a materialistic
idea of what a completion can be), then all the disciplines must be
pursued with equal devotion and independence. But all must be subordinated, too, and thereby ordered by whatever discipline answers to the
fact that a man must allow all the roles a place. That discipline is best
which, while autonomous, allows full autonomy to its subordinated
disciplines. But suppose two disciplines allow full autonomy to others?
The question then remains whether there is a difference between them.

A religion which was autonomous, and which allowed a place for
an ethics in which men did complete themselves, would be a religion
superior to one which could not do this. But that excellent religion
could have a counterweight in one which was subordinated to an
ethics that was on a footing with the excellent religion. Facing now the
complete religion (with its autonomous subordinated ethics) with the
complete ethics (with its autonomous subordinated religion), and
supposing that each does full justice to all other activities, we apparently

still have no difference left between the religion and the ethics. The complete religion is one which gives a place and meaning to other activities distinct from that which the complete ethics gives. But if these activities are allowed to have an independent status, by both ethics and religion, there seems to be no difference between the two, for the subordinating power of the religion and the ethics (since it in no way conflicts with the autonomous life of all the activities possible to man) will have only a conceptual significance so far as action is concerned, or an inspirational value so far as motive is involved. This means that our answer is a pragmatic one in the sense that it says, since there is no actual difference so far as the roles are concerned, the difference must lie in what man feels is most in consonance with his understanding, tendencies, and the like.

If in the ideal state of affairs, where a full-bodied religion allows full autonomy to other disciplines and to ethics, and full-bodied ethics also allows full autonomy to the same disciplines and to religion, we must ask ourselves which answer to man's need to be the dynamic locus of all the roles, these different disciplines involve. We look here to the Ideal as our measure (for we are making an evaluation), but not as prescribing but as eliciting an action. If a democracy in arms answers to man's aspirations more than a dictatorship which encourages the democratic processes, the democracy must be said to be superior in an evaluational scale governed by the consonance of the democracy to man's appetites. But of course, long before this point is reached, we distinguish disciplines and roles by their incapacity to take care of all occurrences, by their inability to allow for full autonomy of their subordinated disciplines, and by their incapacity to meet the tests of autonomous disciplines other than themselves.

Is the inspiration to have a dictatorship now, one which will involve its eventual demise; does a world in which the state is to have withered away require that we now have a dictatorship? To this the usual answer given is that there are warring parties which would prevent the coming to be of the proper end; the dictatorship then turns out to be a kind of subordinated autonomous realm having something like democracy as its terminus. Is the difference, then, only in the way in which   A] the autonomous dictatorship is pursued by each side, and B] they allow for democratic processes now, which is to say for an autonomous democracy?

It still remains true that a religion may make demands that an ethics does not allow, and conversely, and that a dictatorship asks for acts which a democracy does not endorse. The decision here must be that the subordinating discipline must accommodate the full being of the other; the religion must eventually find a place for the full ethics, and the ethics for the full religion. Whatever is done now which violates the full ethics or religion must be said to be testimony to the failure or inadequacy of the dominant religion or ethics. We must then go on to ask if the failure is consistent with the demands by the final end.

In the best religious situation no Abraham will sacrifice an Isaac. At most, one can claim that this is necessary in a poor state of affairs. The ideal religious situation will not require this sacrifice, this violation of ethical rights. But cannot a religion ask for such a sacrifice now as a kind of testimony to the excellent state of affairs which Abraham now exemplifies and mankind may eventually (though then not in such a nonethical way)? No more than an ethics can demand of a religion that it now spend its time in good works only. Nor can a dictatorship demand the abrogation of democratic rights as a way of getting the state to wither away, thereby eventually preserving democratic rights. If it be contended that the Communists must now war against the capitalists, it must be admitted that such a war is a subordinated war; its justification lies in the objective of having the state wither away. Consequently, what enables us to judge two full-fledged worlds with their proper roles, each which makes for a satisfaction in some way of all men's needs, is whether or not they are asking now that we give up some of the achievements which we are eventually to have. Must we give up democracy in order to attain it, as the Communists suppose; must we engage in war in order to avoid war, as the democrats suppose? Must we violate ethics to show our faith; must we give up all otherworldly interests to show that we mean well by our neighbors? We must do these things, but then the question is whether we control our activities, do them in a minimal way, or allow these activities, so far as they go counter to the nature of the ultimate end, to work according to their own uncontrolled logic. The best discipline is one which takes all subordinated but oppositional activity to be not satisfactory, thereby defining the activity as something regrettable and itself, the discipline which actually encompasses it, as unsatisfactory in terms of a final end.

Democracy and communism have the same end—an eventual democracy where all live in peace and prosperity; religion and ethics have the same end, a world where men will live in justice and be aware of some supreme value. Starting from the end we can say that there are different strategies by which this result can be reached. We can either adopt the end now in a poor form and work with autonomous subordinates to bring about the better form, or we can take the end to require a concentration on the means by which it is to be attained, even though these may now seem to have a nature which is opposite to that of the end. The Communists and the religionists take the second alternative, but this is paradoxical and dangerous for two reasons: 1] we have no guarantee that the end will be attained, so that we will now give up goods that ought to be cherished, and   2] we will now deliberately engage in full spirit in activities which we ourselves have defined to be undesirable.

In the end it comes down to the fact that one side does willingly what the other does reluctantly. He who gladly does what Abraham did, who gladly goes to war, who gladly suspends *habeas corpus,* shows that his system is inferior to one which demands that he do these things reluctantly, under pressure and in full awareness that they ought not to be done in terms of other legitimate enterprises. They are testimonies to the tragic nature of the world; he who does them gladly defines himself to be demonic, exhibiting in himself a tragic nature, rather than allowing this to be determined by the very nature of things.

Man, the role-bearing being, should be recognized to face an Ideal where all his roles will be on a footing, under the guidance of a supreme role which exhibits that Ideal. At any moment he must take one of the regular roles and treat this as prior to the others, and thus to function as a surrogate for the supreme role. He can rightly claim that he has found such a surrogate when he finds that he can give a place to all his regular roles and actually promote and find himself in the line of the supreme role he is eventually to attain.

August 28

We start an examination of the value of religions by first comparing various religions to see how close they come to having a genuine devotion to a truly supreme value, then by comparing how well they conform to the demands of other disciplines, then by seeing how well they allow those disciplines and something like their satisfaction to occur inside the confines of the religions, and then by noting how well the religions allow these disciplines to function outside them. When we have a number of disciplines equal in this kind of achievement, we must make reference to the ideal of a full life, and in terms of that we must ask which of the various disciplines is most in consonance with that ideal, and can therefore represent it for the rest. If two disciplines are equal in this respect the difference between them is verbal only.

The individual has *roles* which answer to the different disciplines and, as the *counterpart* of the *Ideal,* should be said to be the *explanation* of all these roles and incidentally of all else that a man might be and do. He is also a *unity* of the various *features* characteristic of him, and as such is an *imitation* of the *divine.* In addition, he is a *fragment* of *Existence* and as such is capable of *interplaying* with other beings; he is then the *source* of the various activities in which he is engaged. And also he is a *representative actuality* and as such engages in characteristic strategies such as *cognition* and perception, so that the world as a datum is found to have its *localization* in him as an ego or *individual.*

The features of a man make a unity. The unity has a fourfold stress and this is rectified and integrated in a static, a dynamic, a valuational, and an egocentric way. Evidently this process can be analyzed on and on. But the being as a unity is the unity of the features. One of those features is more in consonance with the unity than are the others, and serves to provide the name for it; the other features (or sets of features) are relational, terminate other beings, or are expressions; the feature or features which tell us what the being as a unity is, are *boundary* features.

A being also has a fourfold set of roles. These are explained by him as a single being. The singleness is stressed in four ways, and these can be said to have fourfold stresses, etc. One of the roles is more suited to serve as the term for expressing what the being is, as an explanation of all the roles. This is evidently the role of leader, guide, reasonable man, master of the situation; the other roles—thinker or actor, worshiper or participator in an institution, artist, or historical being—belong to him but they do not express his explanatory nature as well. By referring to him merely as reasonable we speak ambiguously, for we may mean the role he has or the explanatory nature he has behind that and the other roles.

The being as a fragment of Existence is a source of energies which go in four directions, only one of which is the appropriate referent for what he is as a source. We must see him as acting as an expressive being, as a participative one, as an obligated one, and as a worshipful one. It is as a participative one that he is a source of energies, where "participative" is now used to refer to the "in-itself" and not to one of the roles which that "in-itself" provides.

Finally, the being as an individual has four different strategies for mastering the universe, while remaining a limited self-contained ego. He acts as a representative of all other actualities by virtue of his cognitional powers, his adjustive powers, his virtue, and his devotion. It is only as cognitional, though, that he is to be thought of when we wish to refer to what he is as an individual, sustaining cognition and other powers.

Man in himself is a divine imitation of a unity; his boundary features are all, biased toward himself and merely limited at himself by other beings. In-himself he is also a unity of roles all converging on an Ideal, of which he is an instance or for which he is an explanatory being, and whose status as reasonable tells us what he is from that angle. He is also a fragment of Existence, whose interplaying activities have him as source, and which is best referred to by attending to him as participating in the activities of others. Finally, he is an individual whose strategies belong to him, who is to be referred to primarily as a being who cognizes.

There are thus four ways to approach the nature of man, depending on whether or not we want to see him as a unity, explanation, actor, or individual. The unity and individual are evidently prior in being to the explanation and action, and the unity, as less differentiated than the individual, is prior in being to it. We must then take the unity of a being to be representative of the other ways of being in-itself.

The unity of a being, as we saw, has an appropriate or characteristic referent—some boundary features or set of them. The boundary features will, if the unity be taken to be representative of the other ways of being in-itself, also refer to the unity as the base of the other forms of the in-itself. Only the boundary features name the unity. This is both a gain and a loss; it is a gain in purity but a loss in the ability to reveal the full nature of the being.

A feature which is tainted by Existence or Ideality, as a smile may be, can be used to reveal not merely that the being is a unity, but that it is a source or explanation as well. By blurring together all the types of features and using them to direct us to the unity, we get to that unity as involved with the other ways in which the being is in-itself. One could blur together the various roles, etc., in a similar way; one would then get to the explanation which presupposes the unity. If then we start with a role set, we ought to move back to the features. Consequently, when we see that religion and ethics, e.g., are subordinated to some prior Ideal, and thus refer to ourselves as the explanation of possible roles (in this case as ethical and religious beings), we ought to recognize that we do not yet get to our being in its full depth, but must see what kinds of features lie behind these different roles. We must see if the man is not only assuming a role but actually has the features which a role, truly carried out, requires.

In saying that some item acts as a representative, we have not eliminated the others; we have merely particularized the indefinite totality of all of them, and given it a name. The being in-itself no more answers to that blur than it answers to the elements distinguished, related, or evaluated; but the blur gives us a primary unity which subordinates the explanation, source, and ego, in which elements are capable of being distinguished, etc. It is a blur, then, which precludes the exercise of the proper ways of being appropriate to explanation, etc. When these different subordinates are allowed to stand away from the unity, we do not get a superior position, for we then work in terms of the distinction of the different ways in which a being is in-itself, and this is not superior to the blur except for some purposes.

August 29

A study of religion must, while recognizing the ultimacy of a concern for the divine, recognize that there are ways of adjudicating that concern in relation to concerns for other modes of being. This question was not dealt with in connection with ethics or even politics or art in its full power. An ultimacy was granted to these disciplines and recognition was given to the claims of the remainder, but there was no facing of them all together, and thus no envisaging of them in the light of an aim outside them all which they were to particularize now, in the guise of a superior discipline having the remainder as subordinated moments though allowed an autonomous contained functioning. Why is this an issue for religion? Is it because we are faced with so many warring religions, each making an absolute claim? But we find this also true of political systems, and of the arts. Is it because we see that the religions demand full devotion? But so do the others. Is it that a religion explicitly claims to give us a full life, whereas the others assume it and never dare affirm it with the same insistence or explicitness? Is it essential to religion to make such a claim? I think it is. Does not history also make a similar one? Yes. The opposition indeed seems to be not so much of ethics versus religion, as history versus religion, where the history takes care of all human striving, ethical, political, aesthetical. To be sure, there will be an ethical concern which is directed at the good and which may not be of any historic significance, or which may serve to prescribe to or measure history.

But perhaps it would be more correct to say that each of the disciplines—ethics, politics, history, religion, etc—does make an absolute claim, but that this fact is not seen until one attends to the insistence on the part of religion and history.

Is there not a need on the part of history to be supplemented by art (and conversely) and private enjoyment of religion by public worship, and that this is not to be confused with the subordination of religion (and thus the subordination of the existentially, ideally, and actually oriented activities) to an idea of a full life?

September 3

How rare it is in the history of philosophy for one to maintain that there is nothing real but commonsensical objects. In Greece we might claim Aristotle, and in modern times, Reid and Moore. But Aristotle's world is explicitly pitted by him against the prevailing commonsensical one. He does acknowledge commonplace substances and occurrences; but he also fastens on such arcane entities as "forms," "matter," "soul," "potentiality," Gods, the four causes. We have made his world part of our conventional one in good part, and have overlooked the oddness of his. And when we add to his the angels, Trinity, Virgin Mary, and souls of Aquinas, we get a system which has moved far away from ordinary thought and views. And one can argue that Reid and Moore are able to maintain their place in a conventional world only by refusing to consider the problems that arise when one is trying to make sense of that world, to bring some order into it, or to explain some of its occurrences.

The development of modern science has encouraged the conceiving of entities quite alien to anything met with in the common-sense world. One can say that these entities are only principles, concepts, regulative ideas, enabling one to deal more efficaciously with the common-sense world, but it is a fact that they are reified or (in the interpretation I have been giving science) recognized to have a rootage in common sense in the sense of offering us a common-sense world when that world has been subjected to a purging, and the result to a formulation. Once we admit the reality of a sun, or ocean, or space time larger than that which comes within the purview of observation, we have left the familiar world behind. Have we not moved too far when we go on to claim that the real encompasses Thalesian water, the Indeterminate, Pythagorean numbers, Platonic Forms, Unmoved Movers, Substantial Forms, Existence, Creators, Angels, Monads, The One Substance, a Kingdom of Ends, Absolute Space and Time, Spirit, non-Being—or Actuality, Ideality, Existence, and God?

Ought one not try to keep these supposed realities to a minimum? Still they have been acknowledged for a reason. It is, in fact, the need to refer to them for explanation which leads to their acknowledgment, and one's hope is that with Dewey we can turn them all into mere devices for moving about in Experience. But his Experience is also such an entity, as are his Values, Democracy, and so on. To refuse to acknowledge any such entities is to refuse to face some facts, and to refuse to explain. One should, therefore, go as far as the *Modes* in isolating the different explanatory patterns. The next question is whether or not it is possible to reduce the number of realities or categories. We have ourselves, and we do find ourselves in a larger Existence. Can we reduce Ideality and God to these two? It seems we cannot, for we have the prescriptiveness of the former and the preservative power of the latter to recognize. Might one not say that the individual could be said to be present only so far as he holds himself off over against the Ideal, and could be said to be a self or private being only so far as he holds himself off over against God as an Other? And might one then not say that a man is always a private other who is present and thus has both of these factors over against him, and that as over against him they have some affect on one another, and that they operate on him just so far as he is in the role defined by the other? Both the Ideal and God would vanish with man; but also there would be no absolute ought-to-be imposed on him except so far as he was over against God (and this absolute would vanish with his immersion in the public world and with his disappearance) and there would be no preserving being, and thus no past exterior to man except so far as man was present (and this preservation would vanish with his acceptance of or immersion in the Ideal, or with his disappearance).

It is hard to see how a man could act to realize the Ideal, though, unless it had a real being over against him; it is hard to see how a man could be a genuine other except so far as there was a being which was over against him. If we say that man made the Ideal and God to be and allowed them also to make a difference to one another's being and function, we have not moved away from the position of the *Modes,* except by the dubious move of claiming that two modes achieve full stature only when man takes up a certain position

Having shown the need to consider different principles or facets in order to do full justice to the facts and to explain them in a single coherent system—a move which is not even faced by commonsensical and positivistic thinkers—one must make an effort to avoid reification, and thus to see if the principles of explanation could be treated as mere abstractions from man or his world. But when we find that we cannot do this without promoting obscurity, we ought to affirm that the beings are real. Whatever must be real if man is real, must be accepted as real, no matter how odd it may strike the commonsensical reader. And that is perhaps the best kind of defense to make against those who rebel against the supposed violation of Occam's Razor in the *Modes*.

September 4

The complaint by common-sense men that philosophers have departed to the realm of fantasy (since they speak of realities which common-sense men do not encounter or even surmise to be), can be countered by observing that the common-sense world is a nonnatural one, an artifactual one, and thus not possessed of rights of reasonableness or objectivity over against what might be surmised on the basis of reason. For convenience sake in living together we have produced a commonsensical world. But then why may we not for the sake of reason, explanation, etc., produce a rational, a reconstructed philosophical world? That men agree on the commonsensical is but a testimony to the force of practice, tradition, education, and social pressure.

Why not, instead, return to unspoiled nature? But is there any way of doing this other than to reflect and thus to depart from the commonsensical world? We ought to avoid wild flights of fancy (though there should be an effort to allow full rein to the imagination). We ought not to suppose that everything we imagine is real. We should reconsider the results of our imaginative flights in the light of stern criteria; they should enable us to get back to our initial starting point in common sense; they should explain; they should not go further than sound inference based on strong evidence permits.

Common sense has no rights as such, but only as surrounding a nucleus which is common to all observers, regardless of the particular form their tradition has assumed. But neither can we claim that science or a religious community, merely because it has many in agreement, grounds the real. We must start with the commonsensical, for this is where we are, and we must then move away from it, first by purging it from incidental and accidental and contingent accretions, and then by elaborating, formalizing, and eventually integrating what we then obtain, and finally, expanding this into a full account in which all things find an explanation and a place.

September 6

The cognitive is only one way in which it is possible to get to other modes. We can also move by an actual representationalism, an Ideal oriented submission, an Existential humility and a divinely guided worship. Each of these has four forms, just as cognition has. We represent other actualities in our judgment, the Ideal by our virtue, Existence by our work, and the divine by our otherworldliness. We submit to other actualities in respect, to the Ideal in obligation, to Existence in expectation, and to the divine in prayer. We have a humble attitude to other actualities as defining the reasonable, toward the Ideal as obligatory, toward Existence as necessitating and compulsive, and toward God in awe (the making our will conform to His). We have a worshipful attitude toward actualities in admiration, toward the Ideal in commitment, toward Existence in tragedy and comedy, and toward God in our religious life.

We can get to the divine in four ways—by inference or proofs grounded in a representational otherworldly attitude, by a submission in prayer, by dynamic humility, and by an attitude of awe. Love, joyousness, devotion, adoration come from the encounter, the having reached God by these various routes. They are perhaps variations of an emotional acceptance, which is to be supplemented by cognitional, active, and valuational ones.

A basic claim of religion is that one must give up the worldly life one is leading—not merely improve it or supplement it. In terms of that life, religion does what metaphysics does cognitionally—it makes us abandon common sense. But if this be the case, we ought also to have an abandonment of common sense in our submissions, and in our humility. We do have the former of these when we recognize an absolutistic ethics. The latter we arrive at when we come to see our human realm inside the whole cosmos, and become alive to the subterranean power and relentless movement of Existence.

When, then, we approach religion in four ways, and then enjoy or encounter it in four ways, we do with respect to God what we also sometimes do with respect to the other modes of being.

September 7

In most religions an incarnation—either of an individual, in the shape of a chosen people, in a sustaining cause of the world, in a church, etc.—is a sacrifice, a descent by a God or Gods. There is a generosity to it and a loss, if not in being, at least in power and function on the part of the God. But it is possible to view such an incarnation as an increase, as the achievement by the deity of a body or a realm in which it can work. To be part of a cosmology adds dignity to an ontological being, provides it with a satisfaction, enables it to function in ways it otherwise could not. Just as the Aristotelian unmoved mover can think about himself or thinking, so a God could be involved with a world outside and yet be something in Himself. And that world outside, as having some dignity, value, power and reality, could add to the being of the divinity.

Reciprocally, in an incarnation, there is a kind of deification of the individual, or a people, or a church, a putting on of a new status. Whether or not the deification is active or passive, a free or necessitated outcome, it brings the individual, or people, out of its normal setting and adds to it something of the divine. It is usually thought that this addition enhances the deified, but it could also be said that it injures the deified, since it tears this away from its proper place and subjects it to conditions to which it is not yet suited. Religion instead of being the opium of the people is so far the disturber, the disorientor, the transposer of the people elsewhere, the giver of powers which, though excellent perhaps in themselves, infect and injure it—as we see is the case in the ascetic and mystic and fanatic, which are but extreme cases of the religious.

Both those who are in favor and those who are opposed to religion can thus agree that there is an incarnation and that there is a deification. Those opposed might think the Gods' need to be incarnated means that we must serve them although we need all the energy and time for ourselves; and they can also say that the individuals who are deified here, in the sense of sharing in the divine by being lifted out of their present attitudes or acts, are injured and misdirected. It is not enough then to remark on the existence of a highest value deserving devotion and rejoicing; it must be shown that the acceptance of this as one's own, the putting away of the old Adam, is a good thing—otherwise religion would not be desirable from our standpoint, though it might prove a benefit to the divine in the sense of providing Him with the incarnational material which He needs in order to be enhanced. If one took this latter alternative one would reverse the traditional approach and see the becoming religious as an act which injures a man to some degree, at the same time that it benefits the deity in that it provides Him with a body or realm of action.

In the case of both God and the world (or man) the effect of each on the other is cataclysmic. There is here at least an implicit recognition that they are distinct modes of being then, if not ultimately or really, as they in fact function apart from one another. What no religion seems to admit is that there is a transition, a gradual alteration, an enhancement or reduction of some feature or virtue when the two come together. Religion is treated as an all or none affair, a state in which a change in kind is required, usually on the part of man and, perhaps, also on the part of the divine.

A being might be the locus of the divine and not be lifted up. This is the case with the Hebrew prophets and any others who speak with voices, who prophesy, or who serve as vehicles for the divine. And it might be possible for one to give up the old Adam and adopt the divine and not benefit the divine by the act, for one might not give the divine anything that could be used, e.g., if one were a sinner. The forgiveness of God would be the purging of the sinner but without in any way providing a gain for the divine.

One might conceive of God and the world (or man), to differ in degree and not in kind, permitting of the achievement of a religious attitude which involves only a change in degree on the part of man. This is possible if God is finite, man is divinely tinged, or the effect of God on man is only to rectify or modify the traits he already has. But even a finite God, by virtue of His supremacy, may make a difference in kind to the nature and activities of man. And even a man who already has a divine spark in him, may, by virtue of his concentration on it, be subject to an alteration in kind. Consequently the viable alternative is that, regardless of whether God be finite or infinite, or man be divine or the other of this, a religion might be conceived to make only a difference in degree—make a man be more respectful to his parents, pay his debts, avoid crime, and the like. But we differentiate ethical man from religious man with respect to these particular injunctions by virtue of the fact that the latter is caught in an entirely new pattern. What can this be?

In what sense does, e.g., a religious man's respect for his parents differ in kind from an ethical man's? Is it not that the latter is concerned with the Good in the concrete or abstract, whereas the former is concerned with those parents or a being beyond? The religious man makes an ontological decision, the ethical a "cosmological" or directional one, though the ontological decision of the former does involve a "cosmological" realm, since it does deal with man in relation to the divine. Man's relation to the divine is something like his relation to nature in the coming to be of history; he faces the divine ontologically and then alters himself so as to make a togetherness with Him.

We ought to be able to say something similar about man and the Ideal. He does stand over against the Ideal as a mere being, and it is only as having a self that he is ethically responsible. This points up the fact that though man changes in being when he enters history and ethics, it is as already having entered these domains that he is asked to change. It is not demanded that he change from an ontological to a cosmological role, but that he change from one cosmological status to another, an act which may require that he first retreat back to an ontological role. (In speaking of the ontological, what is here intended is an emphasis on the distinct, separate beings of the entities.)

Religion demands that a man give up one relationship for another, that he shift his occupation with one or the other mode of being to concentrate on the mode which is God, and to do this in such a way that he and God make a unity of a distinctive sort. The activity involves a dissolution, first of his togetherness with the other modes—a denial or retreat from art, history, ethics, politics, knowledge, and action. But once again might we not speak, conversely, of the desirability of man turning away from the religious situation and entering into these others? Might we not ask man to give up his devotion to God to enter into history? The argument against mere meditation, or the argument against abandoning the world might be reckoned here. Might one not also say the same thing for the politician, the artist, the philosopher, and the man of action? Each of these, it could be said, rightly asks of the others and of the religious man that they devote their lives to it.

The religious answer comes with such force because we begin by living in these other realms more completely, intensively, or readily. If we were religious men, would we not then find the message of the ethicists, etc., just as striking, just as "metaphysical," requiring us to make a radical decision and with the same warrant as that now offered by the religious? Do we not make such a decision when we move from ethics to history, art to politics, knowledge to art, etc.? We see in these cases a change in kind because we move from a relation to one mode to a relation to a different mode of being.

The miracle is a form of incarnation; the event remains in its natural setting but it has consequences whose presence is to be justified only by the operation of a divine causality; it links x with y when these otherwise would be unrelated. If the linkage were to serve as a way in which the cause and effect were raised up to the divine, there would be no miraculous cures or witnesses but only another dimension discovered, in a somewhat Swedenborgian way. We would be reading signs and portents and not encountering a miracle. But ought there then not be something like miracles in the other domains? Ought we not to have a kind of causality which is sustained by the Ideal and by Actuality—e.g., the causality of the spirit of myth, or final knowledge, or justice, and the causality of the individual genius—the one being teleological, the other "material"?

In the foregoing I speak about religion as a going concern; a primary task is to isolate the religious side of experience out of the mélange which confronts us, and particularly to isolate it from Existence. Is it not that we become aware of the unity of Existence, of some one focal point outside the passage of space, time, and process, and that the attempt to appease, worship, hearken to this leads to the isolation of the divine component?

In prayer we accept, via petition, adoration, magic, submission, etc., the operation of the divine. "Thy will be done" is perhaps behind every prayer, even when we specifically ask for something which seems to be in consonance with what we desire or will. In part prayer is ejaculation, mere expression of our own passionate desire, but since it is always directed at a power whose goodness or power we respect, in the end prayer allows that what we ask to have appear may be put aside and something else placed there instead—and this it is supposed will be better than what we have designated. We thus do not ask God to do what we want, but to do the meaning of what we want, to see that the Good comes out of this situation. We want a miracle then, even when we ask only that some perfectly natural consequence should be—e.g., that the money we need be forthcoming even in a regular way—for what we want is that it should be made to be this way by God. God's act can, in short, be one which merely allows the ordinary course of events to take place, thus avoiding certain possible obstacles. He operates cosmically, and we may need that cosmic act in order that a desirable fragment come about in the ordinary course of events.

September 8

It is not enough, in order to show the truth of a religion, to make out that one conforms to it if one does Good, or even lives in consonance with its creed or commandments. Granted that there was a saintly man, who was good and did only the Good; granted that there was an effective man who acted in history in consonance with a final outcome which is providentially determined; granted that there was a representative man who acted on behalf of all men by virtue of his truth, method of inquiry, social status, etc., one could still ask whether or not religion was necessary. It would be necessary if a man could not be a private individual in the present except so far as he was in an oppositional relation to God. (This oppositional relation is a mode of togetherness with utmost separateness, and is to be matched by the dynamic relation produced by Existence and used in the proofs as the dynamics of the inference, the formal relation which thinkers and scientists attend to, and the representative role which an individual might take as a monk or priest.)

God must be acknowledged if one is to be acknowledged to be a full-fledged private individual—this perhaps is the root meaning of Buber's I and Thou. And once we have such an acknowledgment we can get a vicarious way of doing the Good, being effective, and being truly representative. The ethical man would then not only find that he was in a domain where he would be forgiven, but that even when he was doing what he ought to do he would be doing it within the context of a possible forgiveness. The effective man in history would not only find that he was providentially right, but would find that while here and now, immersed in a secular activity in which he was effective, there was another meaning present. The divine would not only make him effective even when he was not so now, but also when he was. The representative man who failed would find, by virtue of God, that he was representative nevertheless; in addition, he would find that when he was representative, his status with respect to God would enable him to represent for men more than he otherwise could.

The defense of religion, then, is that it not only makes good the failures in other activities, but that even when they are successful it adds a new dimension, giving them all additional value. It is for that reason that at times the religion can defy the ethics, the history, the representativeness which it in the end supplements and completes. But nothing here tells us which of the many forms, or types, or instances of religion is the best, if any.

September 9

Thomas Aquinas said that it was desirable to prove the existence of God on the hypothesis (which to him was false) that the universe was eternal. If one could prove it on this supposition, it would be easier, he thought, to prove it on the basis of the truth. Just so, one must try to show that one ought to be religious on the supposition that there is a good man (one who lives up to the Ideal) who is perfectly adjusted to Existence in art and history, and who is representative of all other men in knowledge and heroic acts, and then ask what is left for religion to provide. Is it not a state of being ulitimate and irreducible, strong and final enough to stand over against God? Is it not a state in which one can make provision for the removal of guilt by forgiveness, the overcoming of futility by perpetuation, and the filling out of representativeness by being made into God's man?

A religion has its own distinctive good—substantial individuality— and it also provides a way in which satisfaction is provided for other drives, particularly as not satisfied when these drives are made of primary concern. There is, of course, a reverse stress provided by seeing the religious need either vicariously or supplementally met inside ethics, politics, art, history, knowledge, and action (of a representative kind). In each of these man must achieve some kind of substantiality or complete the substantiality which he but partly achieves by virtue of his partial achievement of a true religiosity.

Is it true that the man who is concerned with the Ideal in ethics and politics provides some kind of private substantiality which replaces or supplements that which could be obtained in religion? And is this true also of one concerned with existentially oriented art and history, and representative knowledge and action? In ethics and politics we must have character and virtue; in art and history we must have authenticity and acceptance; in representative knowledge and action we must have appropriation, possession. These are subordinated ways of achieving a new dimension. We also ought to be able, inside these domains, to fill out the religious drive—by being ethical, etc., we ought to make good the effort we make in religion to achieve a proper relation to a supreme value. This means that a full ethical, etc., life will not only make the Ideal concrete, but will endow the religious life, which we otherwise might lead, with an interiority which sustains the ethical, political, etc. Each nonreligious domain thus produces a being who has an interiority; this interiority completes, though in a modified form, the work of interiorizing which was characteristic of the religious man.

September 10

The recognition that there is a distinctive domain and achievement characteristic of religion, testified to by various sacramental acts (and which has been interpreted by me to be reflected in the achievement of a substantial privacy on the part of the individual), can also be understood as the achievement of a place in a connection between causes and effects that one would otherwise not have.

The meaning of miracle is that there is an effect supernaturally guaranteed. That effect could come about naturally, too; one can pray for what in fact will come about in the ordinary course of events. Nonreligious realms can be sustained by a religious one, but it is the contention of the religious man that there are occurrences in a nonreligious realm which cannot be accounted for by attending only to that realm. To have something natural come about through supernatural help is to place the natural in a new setting; it is to see it as part of a larger context, and thus to have a meaning sustained and jeopardized, completed and shown to be limited in ways it would not otherwise be. To have some part of the nonreligious accounted for by the supernatural, means that what would not by itself have come about is in fact seen to come about. But this need not occur. One who takes art, or politics, or knowledge, or action to be sustained by religion must also see these, though producing no other results than those which they can produce by themselves, as being enriched, tinged with a new character.

The view here being adumbrated is quite like that of Kant's solution to the third antinomy; there is an order of "necessity" on the one side and a causality coming from above on the other. An act for Kant, which is done for the sake of duty, has the same outward form as one done in conformity with duty. But it has a different internal quality, since it testifies to the fact that men are a part of a kingdom of ends.

September 11

By placing a discipline in a new context, religion determines what value that discipline will have in a setting wider than that which the discipline itself provides. If religion serves to support ethics, art, etc., it will provide them with guarantees that the values they provide will be preserved. This does not mean that the religion must accept the others in the form in which they come; it guarantees some value will be preserved, and those who pursue these disciplines can hope only that they have followed out that course of action which will be endorsed by the religion.

The religion's function, then, is not so much that of providing a man with a substantial privacy—that is perhaps the function of God apart from religion, and which a religion might be willing to acknowledge—but of providing a permanent context of value, guaranteeing the preservation of maximum value no matter where or how obtained. One who was perfect in ethics, art, etc., would gain from religion a context in which that perfection was made permanent, which maintained itself no matter what contingencies, changes, new beings, were to occur subsequently. In addition the religion should be able to provide a satisfaction for each of the disciplines so far as men were unable to do this for themselves—e.g., it should show how, though guilty, they are forgiven and thus are innocent. And the various disciplines on their side must show that they do provide a satisfaction for man that no other can—not even religion. Thus he who is part of history must make evident that there is a kind of effectiveness which he has that no religion can provide. As part of, or sustained by the religion the historic man is guaranteed that what he now finds effective will eventually be effective, will add up to the final outcome. (This means that though it is the Ideal which determines what items will be identified as effective in the past, the religious position is that such a determination will sustain what man now thinks to be desirable. The Ideal does determine what will be effective in the long run; but the religious man says that this Ideal has such and such a shape because providentially guided.)

The religious dimension must also be given some kind of satisfaction inside other disciplines. Men will not succeed in being fully religious if they concentrate on that life alone; they need to be sustained by other kinds of lives and disciplines. The kind of permanence which religion itself provides must be given to the ethical, political, historical beings, etc., primarily in the form of an altered concern and objective. History, e.g., does not enable the religious to function as a kind of forgiveness for the ethical, or indeed to help the ethical in any way, but only to enable men to achieve a kind of final value, some way of internally assessing the historical and the subordinated ethical, etc., so as to constitute a being who is fulfilled only so far as he is effective in history, but as someone who has nevertheless accreted a status which mere historic effectiveness, taken as a consequence of an isolated discipline, could not provide.

Religion is an enterprise by itself only when it answers man's need to have an arena for the preservation of all values in a maximum way. It must be seen, too, to provide some kind of satisfaction to those who, having pursued some other discipline, find that they have failed to some degree. And it must itself, since no one can live in terms of it entirely, be given some kind of satisfaction inside some other discipline. A man who tried to be merely religious would lose   A] the values that other disciplines could give to religion,   B] the values which it could give to other disciplines, and, of course,   C] the values that other disciplines can themselves provide. The least a man can do is to combine religion with B, thereby living a full religious life. But that man is faced with others who give primary value to some other discipline and who subordinate religion to that other discipline.

It is not enough for a man to give his life to religion; he must engage in other disciplines in a subordinated way and must, in addition, somehow have a life in these other disciplines as subordinating one another, and of course religion. The addition would not be necessary, of course, if these other lives were all equivalent with the religious one when it subordinated and thereby completed the other disciplines. Are they equivalent with it? The claim of the religious man is that they are not. Others can make counterclaims. The religious man, though, insists that religion involves a radical decision, an alteration in one's entire life, whereas the others seek merely to complete what they have done. This means that the religious man thinks of an ontic change as having a cosmic import, whereas the others think merely of fulfilling themselves. Taken in this way, the others receive what they want by being subordinated to religion, and function properly when they subordinate religion to themselves, but do not satisfy the religion when they subordinate it. Religion, in short, seems to reject the kind of completion which other disciplines might provide for it, in addition to the satisfaction which it itself provides. Other disciplines seem to accept the kind of completion which religion provides when this is added to the satisfaction that they themselves give. Consequently, all might be said to accept a full life in which religion defines the basic pattern, giving subordinated satisfactions to other disciplines while allowing them to have a role of their own in which religion is taken care of, but in a way not of interest to religion. The religious man thinks that religion alone does not need to be sustained by other disciplines (and on this all seem agreed).

On the basis of the foregoing we can say that the religious life is basic if it provides a complete pattern for all values, and gives a needed satisfaction of a kind to other disciplines, at the same time that it allows those other disciplines to function independently of it, providing they are then not supposed to be ways in which the religious aspirations are guaranteed fulfillment. Religion thus offers itself as the one domain which needs no aid from other disciplines in order to reach its objective even in a transmuted form. At its best it does complete the others, and allows the others to have a being, since they are ways of enabling men to be men to the full. The religion does not claim that it enables men to be men to the full, but to be excellent, either in the form of men here on earth, in heaven, or as transmogrified into spirits or Nirvana.

If the foregoing is correct, then religion goes even further than philosophy in its claims, for philosophy recognizes the equal right of other enterprises to pursue the real in their own ways, whereas religion would maintain that it itself is of paramount importance, and that its claims are not coordinate with the others but encompasses theirs, though allowing them some autonomy in the sense of being disciplines which do not really encompass it and which as such can be pursued according to their own rationale.

Are there other subjects which have this distinctiveness? Is it a kind of distinctiveness which points up something about a form of together-ness, and if so, must there not be distinctivenesses for other forms of togetherness? Is it that religion stands out because it deals with the divine in a singularly appropriate way? If so, are there no analogues? Is there not a singularly appropriate way for dealing with the Ideal, Existence, and Actuality, which define full, distinctive lives in the way religion does? As ethical, the Ideal becomes the Good; as entering into art and history Existence becomes the environment, and as relating to man, other actu-alities become instantiations. Should we say that   A] in religion alone the divine remains divine, or that   B] in these other cases there is a way of dealing with the Ideal in its ideality, etc?

On the second supposition, B, we must make reference to the Ideal as such, Existence as such, and Actuality as such. The first is faced by the persistent self, the second by man in nature, and the third by an individual man. Does religion stand out as the only discipline which in-volves a special ritual? But could we not create one for the others—say Psychiatry; Cosmological technology, and Authenticity? We must then say that though religion includes ethics, etc., and thus all man-oriented enterprises, it does not include the psychiatry, etc., which gives us an

absolutivity with respect to other modes of being equal to what it gives
with respect to God. But then when should we concern ourselves with
religion, and when with psychiatry, technology, and authenticity? It
would seem as if we must hold these together *in,* or in reference to ourselves *with* religion; they are strict correlatives and we must enter into
all four lives at the same time. We must try to make a unity out of all
of them, and thereby become beings who are unities of all four modes.
We could become unities formally, and as dots and commas; indeed, we
are all these, and as living beings necessarily have them all dynamically.
We can say, then, that as living we dynamically interrelate religion,
psychiatry, etc., or that we dynamically interrelate the different unities
we make of these enterprises.

When we look at man as a mode and ask about his relation to a
mode as such, the mode of God stands out and we have religion. When
we look at the relation of man as a mode to some humanized form of a
mode, the mode of Existence stands out and we get art and history.
When we look at the relation of man as a humanized form of a mode
of Actuality, Actuality stands out and we get representative knowing and
action. And when we look at man as a humanized mode in relation to
some humanized mode, the Ideal stands out and we get ethics and politics. Religion, then, is first (subordinates ethics, etc., and is superior to
psychiatry, etc., which also ask about man in relation to a mode) so far
as we are concerned with man as a mode of being in relation to a mode
of being. It answers to an ontological set of realities. But if we want to
deal with man as a particular instance of Actuality, we will get either
ethics and politics, or knowing and action. And if we want to deal with
some humanized form of a mode other than Actuality, we will get art
and history, ethics and politics. Religion is prior, then, in so far as we
take seriously the "metaphysical" dimensions of reality. This does not
mean that we will not personalize the religion or humanize it, but only
that its ultimate justification lies in the fact that it gives us being in
confrontation with being, as no other enterprise can.

Is it possible, and is it desirable, to achieve a neutral way of dealing
with all the modes from the mode of Actuality as represented by a man?
Is this way philosophical knowledge? And does knowledge of this kind
stand in contrast with religion which, while giving us mode in relation
to mode, does not give a full place for the modes other than God? Also,
we have two other modes to deal with—the concern we have for the
Ideal, and the interplay we have with Existence. Here we have man as a
mode in relation to the modes of Ideality and Existence, as not human-

ized. Like religion they do not give full place to the modes other than themselves; unlike knowledge they are not neutral. But what kind of relation do they make possible?

We have the problem of relating mode-to-mode relations to one another, as in the paragraph above; of relating mode-to-mode relations to specialized forms of these, as when we relate religion to ethics, etc. And a problem of knowing what relation the above have to psychiatry, technology, and authenticity.

September 12

Starting from experience, to find the different modes and ways of apprehending them, we must free ourselves from the limitations of the experience. We begin with ourselves as having specified Actuality and as facing a mélange which is personally oriented. If we free ourselves and the mélange from personal involvement by a shift in attitude we find that we confront the divine, as a naked mode, inside of which our relations to other modes, as sheer modes, are to be found. If instead we are willing to abstract, we can get philosophical knowledge by freeing ourselves and the modes so as to obtain a neutral position. Here all the modes are on a footing. If instead of going this far we allow the modes to be oriented toward ourselves while freeing ourselves from a personalization of the Actual, we get the Good as pertinent to whatever there is. (To get the Ideal we would have to get rid of that orientation—and this we perhaps cannot do except in knowledge or religion.) Finally, instead of freeing ourselves we might concentrate on freeing the modes from any personal reference. When we do this, Existence stands out as a source of the tragic and comic, as ominous but not personal.

Religion and knowledge stand out as ways in which we confront the modes in themselves, ourselves being mere actualities. In the one case, we are mode over against mode with the other two subordinated; in the other case, we have a neutral position in which the four modes are on a footing. In the case of Existence and the Ideal there remains a tincture of the individual and an orientation toward him, respectively.

Is there not some kind of position, some approach in which we might find Existence and the Ideal having some special status as mere modes? As it now is, it looks as if they were partial derivatives, when in fact they are as basic as the others. Shall we say that in Existence we get a direct facing of it when we take up the position of a representative in the shape of a maker or actor, and thus as a kind of Existence (in which case all the others are instrumental); and shall we also say, in connection with the Ideal, that we find ourselves instantiated, and as a consequence the other modes of being—Existence and God—also become instantiated, though in different senses? Is it that the totality of these instantiations sums up to the meaning of the Ideal so far as this can be abstracted out of the mélange of experience?

In summary then, we have: mode facing mode with a primary focus on God; mode knowing modes, with a primary focus on Actuality as neutral for all the modes; man struggling with mode, making Existence stand out, and the other modes functioning as instruments; Actuality instantiated by a personalized mode, making the Ideal function as a Good for whatever is, and making the other modes other types of instantiation. In the first we have subordinated modes, in the second coordinated modes, in the third instrumental modes, and in the fourth diversified modes. Only the second gives us a strict neutrality, in the form of knowledge.

September 13

If it be the case that religion is the demand that a man free himself from the mélange that is experience (allowing the various modes in it to find their proper status), while he at the same time puts off his conventionalized guise and faces God, we must go on to say that knowledge also starts from that mélange but keeps to man and what is oriented toward him, but in a neutral way, while evaluation (with its instantiating of all the other modes) keeps an orienting element in the Ideal, and Existence (which uses all modes as means) is approached by a personalized or humanized Actuality. When now we ask how these four ways are related to one another, we are forced, I think, to say "in no way." The task of a man is somehow to recover them together, i.e., to answer in a more coherent way to what was in fact experienced. There is no goal here in the sense of a man seeking something which could be said to be the possibility of all these ways together. A man is a being with a mind concerned with a Good and involved with an Existence; he has these in a muddled way to begin with. With the awakening of any one of the dimensions of his being, with an accidental or a crisis-determined stress on one of the modes, there is a focussing on it and a consequent tendency to develop one side of himself.

Can we not say that it is good that he have all of these sides at the same time, that he become clearer, that he strive to improve the con-

dition in which he was initially? But then do we not subjugate him to
the Ideal, and thus favor some one mode? But if we do not do this, in
what sense is it good or desirable for him to become clearer about
experience, to find himself over against it, to become the man he latently
is? Or is it possible that he has four distinct dispositions, that getting
clearer is only one of them, and that he inevitably moves back and forth
from the muddled to the clearer state, and ought to? Is this "ought to"
but the consideration of the fourfold movement from the perspective of
the Ideal, expressed as the demand that he be as he ought? If so, the
demand that he get clearer is but a special form of a fourfold effort to
be as he ought. But once again we are on an infinite regress, for if the
Ideal dictates that a man should be clearer and should nevertheless move
back to the muddled state, etc., what justifies him in remaining at one
of the stages, and in what sense is this justification on a level with the
Ideal?

September 14

In these last days I have not made progress in solving the problem of the way in which the four modes are encountered, without getting
into an infinite regress. Perhaps some distinctions ought to be made.
1] To have an experience is to focus on Actuality, with the other modes
   on a footing with it. Actuality will be in the foreground, that is all.
2] Because all the modes are on a footing as personalized and as confronted by an indivdual, all can be known neutrally when we engage
   in philosophical categorization.
3] Each of the modes other than Actuality is in a state of disequilibrium;
   it is related to us because not at its center of gravity; it moves away
   from what it is being experienced as, and we experence this moving
   away.
4] Each mode other than Actuality is thus experienced as coordinate
   with Actuality in two ways; it is coordinate inside a personalized,
   individualized experiencing, and it is coordinate outside that experiencing as a mode which is dealt with by an individual (Existence), is oriented toward man (Ideality), or is a being over against
   a being (God).
5] Each of these modes, as coordinate outside, must have the others inside itself, or subordinated to it in some way.
6] As outside the experienced, the modes of Existence and God are freed

from an orientation toward man, and man is freed from an involvement in God and Ideality.

7] The individual man is a togetherness of all the modes as coordinate. His togetherness is however an amalgam of four kinds of togetherness. If we are to make a single togetherness of these four kinds, the modes will be merged inside one mode. A man is a single togetherness for all the four modes as experienced.

8] The hard question is the relation of the four modes as coordinate outside one another. They cannot be said to be on a level, or faced neutrally, or to be outside one another absolutely, without our invoking a stress on some one mode. Nor can we say any one of these is to be preferred to any other. We must say that we find that each has the others inside or subordinated to it, and that we are so far characterized by a single way of having all the modes together; and that we also find four modes alongside one another and that this alongsideness has different forms depending on what mode of togetherness we have when we face them.

9] If we make ourselves into an amalgam of togethernesses, we have coordinate in ourselves the togetherness as separate from one another in three ways, and thus are able to be directed at the different modes as alongside one another.

September 15

Once again:

1] We have an experiencer, experiencing, and the experienced more or less together, with a stress on the thickness of the experiencing with a consequent separation out of one function or side of the experiencer, and a stress on one mode of being as qualified by the other modes.

2] We can shift to the thickness of the experiencer and thereupon engage in four ways of dealing with the modes. Each mode is faced in a different way, there being four different relations separated out.

3] We can shift to the thickness of the experienced and thereupon engage in one of four states of being experiencers and one of four ways of dealing with the experienced.

4] We are constantly passing back and forth from experiencing to experiencer and experienced, in their thickness.

5] In crises we stress the experiencing; in fear and in imagination, and under compulsion from the outside, we deal with the experienced.

Normally the stress is on the thickness and thus on a kind of unity of the experience.

6] We are most active when we cognize; this allows the Ideal to be most effective in controlling us, brings us into clearer and cleaner interplay with Existence, and allows the divine to be most active in itself as over against all other modes.

7] A genuine concentration on cognition is one with the allowance of the other modes to function properly in relation to us. We cannot take up a religious life in any other sense but that of actively cognizing, accepting Ideal commitments, being properly adjusted to Existence, and standing in awe of the divine.

8] There is no single ought here; each mode has its own oughtness for us, and by attending to one properly we allow the others to be as they ought. But this is also to say that when we are properly compelled, or properly controlled, or properly related, we act effectively. In short, there is no more a single ought than a single state or a single mode. We accept the ought of any one and find that there are different meanings of ought which are expressed by the others. But we need not accept an ought; we might merely shift our position in relation to some mode and get the same results we would have obtained by attending to the ought of some one of them.

The new life that the religious man is supposed to achieve is no other than the life he does have when he engages in neutral knowing of the modes, in submission to the Ideal, or in interplay with Existence.

The only thing man can do on his own is to know; the other activities depend on the cooperation or the activity of the other modes. He cannot, therefore, make himself religious and incidentally discover that he has come to know all things; this is a possible result only if he were God. The only way that he has to get the proper relation to all the modes is to engage in philosophic knowing; the other modes then are grasped not only as cognized entities from a neutral position, but face him in different relations as ultimate modes of being. And one of those relations is the relation of "being-confronting-being," which is of the essence of religion. Each of the modes is then confronted, but it is the divine being which is conspicuous. One can cultivate the relation, and get into the relation to the divine directly, but having arrived at this point one must engage in cognition, follow out the demands of the Ideal, and attend to Existence with the same thoroughness and independence that he would have shown had he begun with these instead. To be sure, if he starts with Existence or the Ideal he also will have to stop at some point and allow himself to cognize. The cognitional relation is his primary one to pursue, and it makes little difference if he reaches that cognitional relation only after he has become religious, or reaches it first and thereby becomes religious in the sense of seeing the divine being over against him, demanding of him that he give up his interest in any other life or even activity, so far as these claim, explicitly or implicitly, to give him genuine being in its concreteness and objectivity, rather than in some abstract or personalized form.

In effect, then, when the religious man commands that we give up our old life he is asking us to improve our ethical being, etc. Religion enables us to find the proper relation to God most readily, and in such a way that we are able to have the proper relation to the other modes and are encouraged to do so. It therefore endorses learning and reflection since these are the proper ways in which we deal with Actuality as infected by other modes, and as permitting of a neutral categorial grasp of all of them as distinct beings.

When we attend to the practical side of religion we notice that it is primarily concerned with ethical or moral injunctions. Sin is often but another name for the anti-ethical, though there are theological sins having no apparent ethical import. Contrition, amendment, penance, and the like must refer to a changed attitude a man must take toward the world, but one, however, which involves a prior alteration in his position with respect to God. The contrite person alters his relation to God in consequence of his awareness that he had the wrong relation to the Ideal or some Actuality, and perhaps to Existence.

The problem of the relation of church and state can be considered here if one thinks of the state as not a proper realm for a full man; in this case it is to the advantage of the church to separate itself off from the state. A proper relation of the church to the divine, will involve a change in the way in which a man is related to the state; he will live in it as a finite determination of the absolute Ideal, to be achieved in public within the pattern of an institution. The church can be thought of as another version of such a state, and will be justified if it is a "true state," i.e., one which is the outcome of a proper relation to the divine. In the latter case any secular state would have to be opposed. A true church is one which can carry out all the functions a secular state now carries out, differing from such a secular state only in the sense that a man's attitude toward the secular state should be dictated by his relation to God. The state would, in effect, be a church, and the church a state. But unlike such state religions, as the Roman or the English, there would be an autonomy to the state, though all its rules and man's relationship to it, would be determined not by the state, but by the relation man had to the divine.

Antinomianism, the view that religious men are not bound by the moral law, is related to the above. There is a proper attitude to take toward an autonomous ethics, and that attitude is defined by the proper attitude toward the divine. Antinomianists overlook the fact that there is an ethical domain, but they rightly remark that one need do no more than to have a proper relation to God in order to do what is right. Augustine, when he said "love God and do as you like," was saying something like this.

It is desirable to distinguish two methods by which one achieves a proper relation to the divine—a positive in which one practices rituals, aestheticism, etc.—and a negative in which one alters one's relation to other modes, by changing one's view of, or actions with respect to, ethics, history, etc. Aestheticism could be thought of as negative when it is supposed to give one a proper attitude toward actualities or Existence, but it is more correct to think of it as a deliberate preparation, an actual direct means for achieving a proper relation to the divine. It is a form of self-discipline and can be sustained by vows of chastity, etc., or by will.

September 16

Each mode has a primary and a supplementary role. When it is exercising its primary role it stands out over against the others, and has them subordinated to it. Each mode has a distinctive relation to the individual in its primary role; he then (or his experiencing) is fourfold. In its secondary role the mode has a relation to a mode in a primary role, completing it, making good its defects. If we attend first to the Ideal and then to God, let us say, we attend to them in their primary roles. When attending to the Ideal we push the divine aside as distinct but secondary. Its divine function is then to be forgiving, to make possible a full ethical life where only good is done, to take up the slack or to make possible some way of functioning which the Ideal does not by itself permit. Conversely, when attending to the divine we push the Ideal to the side, and see the Ideal as adding to the Divine the fact that some good work, some enhancement of actualities is being accomplished.

Each mode has one primary and three secondary roles. The secondary roles are accreted to it by virtue of the assumption of a primary function by the other modes. Were we to face some mode as primary, we would know the other modes in terms which that given mode provides. Were we to face a mode as primary with three secondary functions, we would have to attend first to it and then to the other three, note what they lack, and then make a reference back to the mode we had originally fastened on. The result would be a constant shifting back and forth from one primary mode to another, and a neglect of what we did encounter in three modes, when dealt with as primary. Could we do this, we would in effect also have dealt with all four modes as having a primary and three secondary functions.

When we are ethical we are incidentally religious in the sense that we do face the divine as outside of the ethical, and as providing the ethical with a supplement in the form of a sustaining power which forgives and completes. But it is never enough to be merely ethical in order to be religious. The most ethical man in the world, who does all that he ought and is properly sustained by the divine, is still not religious. What more is needed? Firstly, the divine supplements not only the ethical, but the political, the experience of Existence, and the Actual. He who reached the divine only as that which was a by-product of a full ethical life would have grasped only one of a number of its supplementary roles, and would not, of course, have grasped its primary role. To get the other supplementary roles we would have to focus on Existence and Actuality. But so far as we do not, we are forced to say that the perfect ethical life is defective, is not a full life. It is tinged with guilt (to be overcome by the supplementary act of God), is insufficiently individuated (and needs to be supplemented by the Actual), and is not adequately adjusted to the conditions that prevail (and needs to be supplemented by Existence). But granted that these supplements are provided, it is still the case that one could justify the need to be engaged in a religious life, be a philosopher, and be immersed in art and history.

Making the divine primary gives one a substantial being over against all else, and makes the supplementary features, which it received by virtue of an emphasis on other modes, become derivative features of it. The divine as forgiving, as unifying, and as preserving must follow from Him as supreme and substantial. The other modes will still be of significance but they will be understood to be correlatives of these derivative powers—they were qualifications of the divine as in primary focus, and as such are given the dependent roles of providing the divine with partial results invoking it to provide supplementary acts. The ethical life from a religious standpoint, then, is something which God permits by allowing it to provide an occasion and stimulus for the exercise of derivative divine powers.

Can a life in which there is a primary focus on the Ideal and in which supplementary powers of the Ideal follow from it (and not because the other modes achieve primary focus in place of the Ideal), be compared with one in which there is primary focus on God, or some other mode? In the former case, religion would be the outcome of a relaxation by the Ideal, an allowing of a divine qualification in it (the providential component) to be viewed as that which enables the Ideal to govern the course of things more completely than it otherwise would (and where Actuality is to provide an individuation for the sake of the Ideal, and Existence is to provide it with a cosmic field of operation).

Concentrating only on ethics and religion, for the sake of clarity, what difference is there between a life of ethics which allows religion a role as a feeder for an eventual providential functioning for the Ideal, and a life of religion which allows the ethical a role as a feeder for a possible forgiveness or transmutation of a man? In the one, religion is granted autonomy but is to be rectified or framed and made to feed into the ethical, and in the other the reverse is the case. In one, commitment overrides the status of being a mere being, in the other a man achieves a being and thereby allows himself to be derivatively committed.

In both cases something is left out. The need to have the ethical function on behalf of the divine, e.g., is not made good by religion functioning in a primary way; a religion which is supplemented by ethics, etc., still does not function as a supplement for the ethics and is so far less than it might be. Both alternatives are thus incomplete and both are of equal value. We ought to have both, and then as supplementing one another. But to have both we will have to pay a price; we cannot engage in them completely, concretely, but only under a limitation. If we deal with just these two we can treat them inside the frames of Actuality or Existence—i.e. approach them, for example, in terms of cognition or vital interplay. But if we go on to consider all four modes, as we ought, we do not have this easy opening. We must place the four alongside one another and then supplement them by one another through an act of intent or by something outside them all, and in this sense affirm that they are not complete when autonomous. Since they are faced as separate, they must be made into supplements by an integration, and these two, the integration and the separation, must then be related structurally and dynamically. The full life, then, will be one in which religion, and ethics, etc., will each be autonomous and be seen to allow for a semiautonomous but supplementary function of others inside it, but to achieve the role of supplementing the others only when separated off from those others and then brought together inside the mere conjunctive (.) unity of a man.

The foregoing becomes clearer, perhaps, if one distinguishes between two kinds of supplements. A primary mode supplements those which it subordinates, and the subordinates supplement the primary. In the first case we have the subordinated modes seen in a larger context, as providing them with a new meaning; in the second case we have the primary modes supplemented by the subordinate in the sense of providing them with material. Thus if religion gives the divine in a primary mode, ethics is seen to be a way of doing good in such a way that the divine acts to forgive or to complete; but the ethics, functioning as it does to produce the Good, in the area defined by religion, supplements the religion in the sense of giving it application to particular cases. However, the ethical as having the religion inside it, supplementing or being supplemented, has its own excellence, an excellence not defined by the religion. It is occupied with producing the Good; that Good is specialized by the religion, thereby giving the ethical a particular application. And the Good in turn supplements the religion in the sense of giving it a standard in terms of which it is to be evaluated.

As primary, the ethical is distinct from the religious as primary, and from itself as inside the religious. The question is how the two primary forms are related to one another? Could one have both of them together, with their subordinated modes in them? Here they cannot be viewed as supplementing one another in the sense of being subservient to or adjectival to one another. But we could add a third meaning of supplement, or better, speak of them as being made to complement one another, in that they are framed and related in another context.

Or should we say that they are not even alongside one another except by being held alongside in an act which at the same time merges them, structuralizes a relation amongst them, and dynamically interconnects them? If we take this last tack, the asking what kind of life to lead means asking how we are to have the different lives together. Can we live them together as individuals, or must we frame them in something more abstract, have them perhaps as a plurality for men, one taken by this or that man or group of men, and another taken by some other man or group of men? We take ourselves to be a togetherness which allows for the items or lives to be separate in their being, but by virtue of our living those lives, turn into ways of having a man's different emphases together. The religious, ethical, etc., are so many forms of togetherness for a man's being, commitment, interplay, and individuality.

September 17

If the various types of lives, religious, ethicopolitical, etc., are viewed as substantival, then the ways in which they are together will be sheer products. If a man be assumed to ask himself which of these lives he is to lead, the answer must be that he must lead them all, but that having them "all" can be and must be in only one of four ways. Any attempt to combine these four ways will yield one of them, and will require three other ways alongside. The four ways can be severally solidified, treated as substantival. This is done when a man takes himself to be basic and asks himself what he is to experience. Here he is faced with four ways in which the substantival parts of himself are made to be together. The religious realm, e.g., becomes then a nonsubstantival, derivative way of relating the different substantival parts of the man.

In both of these cases above, the one where religion serves as a kind of life which a man is to interrelate with other lives, and the other, where religion is a kind of togetherness which a man submits to in order to have his different sides together, the togetherness is a kind of continuation of what is together. When a man integrates the various lives he is an experiencer, a real relation amongst those lives, and has no being over against them. When a man has a being of his own, he is subdivided into four areas all of which are related by the religion; this is nothing else than that relating as terminating in the four areas in a man.

What life should a man lead? He can be "led" to lead four of them, but then as a being who is in one area only, the other areas (which are other ways of having the four lives together) not then being open to him. If he wishes to be in all four areas, there must be some life signalized which serves to unite those four areas (the other lives being put aside as not then available to him). A man then has the following choices: *1*] He can accept four lives, *2*] and can accept one of four areas in himself by which he is to connect those four lives; *3*] he can live in four areas, and *4*] can accept one of four lives by which his areas are to be interrelated. He can function as an individual (*2*) who gives (because he in effect is) a single conjunct to the (*1*) four lives; he can focus on one life (*4*) which will then serve as (because it in effect is) a single togetherness (e.g., a rational implication) of his four areas.

He cannot have four lives in four areas, and thus cannot become a unity of four modes of living and four areas in which to live; but he can decide to have four lives or four areas, and thus to function on behalf of objective content or to have something outside him serve as a way of mediating his areas to one another. There are then eight possible cases: four distinct areas serving as relations amongst four lives, and four distinct lives serving as relations amongst four areas.

Neither those who urge different lives, nor the individual concerned with being perfect, take the individual's task to be the providing of a togetherness for the different lives. Consequently we are left with only four choices: to utilize some one of four ways of living as an agency for bringing together the different areas in a man. But each way of living does it in a distinctive way, and we can't have all of them at the same time. There is a purely external way, a merged way, a structural way, and a dynamic way. Religion gives us a merged, and action-knowledge an external, with ethics-politics giving us a structural connection, and art-history a dynamic one. We remain most divided into areas when we act and know; we have less distinctive areas when we are religious; the ethicoreligious life gives us a rational way of connecting our areas, and art and history also function as dynamic ways in which this occurs. None of the lives is, strictly speaking, ours to control, but some (religion and action-knowledge) are more private, closer to our being by virtue of the manner of the togetherness they provide. We are most ourselves when religious and engaged in action-knowledge; we are more intelligible when engaged in ethics-politics, and are more vital, existential, when engaged in art-history. Religion pertains to a state, ethics-politics to a meaning, art-history to a career, and action-knowledge to an articulation or differentiation (so that when we know something we enable our different areas to achieve distinctness). We can do nothing more than engage in all of these at different times: we must cultivate a proper state and achieve significance, while living through time and allowing our different areas or powers to have distinctive being.

We can now make each one of these—state, meaning, etc.—have the others as supplementary within, while remaining outside as well. Here it seems that the state and the career take priority, for their inclusion of the others involves a stronger substantialization. If so, our choice boils down to stressing a state of merged areas mediated by religion, in which other ways of having the areas together have subordinate roles, and the career of interplaying areas in which other ways of having the areas together have subordinate roles. Since the religious man, even in the case of the contemplative or yogi, does have to eat, etc. (whereas there is no compulsion to achieve a state of merged areas), there seems to be a preferential status for art-history which tells us that religion, ethics-politics, and action-knowledge, are to have only semiautonomous status, as providing one's career with results. This brings us close to pragmatism, though it is one which takes account of the creativity of art and the theleological nature of history. There is, then, no primary forgiveness, e.g., or final judgment, or unified knowledge in terms of which we are to live, but rather there is art-history which allows a religion, ethics-politics, and action-knowledge to operate as semi-effective (to be made most effective in art-history), and to provide art-history with a needed unity, a needed rationale, and a needed localization or individualization.

But this solution does not allow full justice to be done to the other lives. According to the Bhagavad-Gita, one is faced with a choice between the active and contemplative, and these add up to the same thing in the end; according to the practice of some Hindus, one must live a series of lives in order to have a full life. The latter seems the more correct approach. But one need not think with the Hindus that a family life must preceded a "religious" one. One can engage in the gamut of lives sequentially but apparently in any order, particularly since in the pursuit of one the others function as supplementary though incomplete, and need the support of the primary. We have then the following possibilities, named after the modes:

Divine, Existence, Ideality, Actuality (*DEIA*)

DEAI

DIEA

DIAE

DAIE

DAEI. These six, times four, give 24 possible lives to be spent with a sequential stress on four subordinate lives, each of which is to be recognized to be primary and to produce an irreplaceable value.

Overlooking the order of the intermediate terms we get 12 cases: *DA, DE, DI: ED, EI, EA: AD, AE, AI: ID, IE, IA.* In the first three, one achieves the proper state by virtue of a participation in religion and then ends by spending his life as, e.g., a philosopher, an artist, or a politician —e.g., Aquinas, Michelangelo, a Cardinal. In the second three, one begins a career in Existence and ends as religious, political or ethical, or speculative—e.g., Beckett, Paderewski, Goethe (?). In the third three, one starts with Actuality and moves on to religion, art-history or Ideality —eg., Augustine, Gauguin, Washington. In the final three, *ID, IE, IA,* there is a beginning with ethics or politics and an ending with religion, Existence, or Actuality—Constantine, Lenin, Marcus Aurelius.

It apparently makes no difference which of the 12 or 24 one elects. *DEIA* is the opposite of *AIED*. In the one there is an achievement of a state of being, due to religion, and then (via effective action in art or history, and a consequent concern for the Good) an ending with a life involved with Actuality, thus grounding the possibility of a speculative career. In the other case there is a beginning with Actuality to end (via a movement through a concern for Ideality and a consequent involvement in history) with a state of being which is essentially religious. Putting aside the question as to whether or not the in-between states have been properly ordered, we have here a constrast between Aquinas and Augustine. If we continue this kind of pairing we get:

Michelangelo, Beckett; a Cardinal, Constantine; Paderewski, Lenin; Goethe, Gauguin; Washington, Marcus Aurelius.

It is possible to argue that all these are on a footing, but that in some epochs or societies certain ones become more significant because they are capable of making an appreciable difference to other men. The opportunity might be provided only for some at certain times. He who accepts one of them at an inopportune time must himself change the time, and when he does, he creates the very conditions which make him have the desirable life at that time. But he is not a greater man than one who is excellently what the conditions make it possible for him to be. A great scientist in the Middle Ages is not greater than a great theologian, unless he actually changes the Middle Ages into the age to come.

We can be rightly exhorted to lead a religious life—but also to lead the others. We cannot be rightly exhorted to lead it always. Also, I might need a different order of development than others do and I ought to provide a place for other ways of living, even inside my own career. A perfect order requires that there be an accumulation, a detachment, a logical involvement, and a production of the items in the sequence. We can say there is one preferable sequence if we can make out that there is one type of life which is most readily accumulated, one most readily detached, one which dictates a logic, and one which determines productivity. The problem is that accumulation, logic and production would seem to require a reference to the entire sequence. However, if one starts with the religious and most readily accumulative (allowing for entailments and productivity), one could end with Actuality as the detached, and place the productive before the logical as the more desirable. We would then have the order *DEIA*. Our model would be someone like an

Aquinas, except that one would not have to be a theologian, and would not have to accept Aquinas' God, and would have to move through a life of art or history before he expressed an ethical or political concern. But there is something cold about such a model; also, a religion which comes first is surprising, since so many think of it as requiring maturity, the ability to stand away from the hurly-burly of life, and a concern for one's end.

Perhaps the combination *EDIA* is better. We do start involved in Existence, and are urged to break away and take on a new life; *E* thus is taken as detached from *D*, which is then treated as productive of a concern for the Good. This in turn entails an involvement with actualities, an involvement which can be viewed as accumulating what had been. Taken in this way our model becomes someone like Goethe, or even a person like Aristotle (whose Existence in a detachable form could be said to be characteristic of his youth, and whose religious side and ideal side, though hardly manifest, could still be thought to be present in his societal affiliations), to end with him as one who is concerned with friendship in the concrete and philosophy in the abstract. For the moment, then, the conclusion is that we must fully live four careers, in each of which we find supporting elements from the others, and that these should occur in the order of *EDIA*.

It is proper, then, that a book on religion follow those on art and history, but these should in turn be followed by a discussion of the Ideal and a concern for the Actual, whereas the procedure of the books outside the *Modes* has been *AIED*—Augustinian. If this be so, the appeal that religion makes requires one to get back into the involvement with art or history, where creativity and effectiveness are to the fore, and then break away from that life to move on to an ethical, and finally to an individual life involved with other actualities, the latter serving to reassess what went before. In the case of one who (as I did) begins somewhere other than Existence (except biologically), there would have to be a repetition of a kind. Thus, for me, the sequence should be *AI*, *EDIA*. Having achieved the position of *E* after a consideration of *A* and *I*, the sequence can be lived through properly. The earlier *AI* would be something abstractly considered, or serve to decorate a more basic *EDIA*.

Some people begin by being involved with other men and move on to a life of concern with a Good (*AI*). They must be made to be part of a world of art or history, for only then will they start the proper sequence. And they can reach that end by recognizing the entailment of the *I* which, though it normally issues in an *A*, could be said, as following on *A*, to require *E*. And we would have to take account of other beginnings, e.g., *IA, ID, AD, DI, DA,* showing how they give way to *EDIA.* We have two cases where an *I* must entail the *E* (*AI; DI*), two cases where an *A* must allow itself to be immersed in an *E* (*IA; DA*), and two cases where a *D* must be allowed to produce an *E* (*AD; ID*). All of these will be preliminary to achieving the proper sequence. We get some confirmation for the above from the fact that philosophers are late arrivals, and that one can be involved in Existence at an early age, even in history, and can quickly move on to a religious life, and that the ethical life or the political seem to require more maturity. But of course one can live a mature life as an artist or a religious being—but one will not then have lived a complete life in the sense of having the other forms and in a proper sequence.

September 18

Each dimension or form of life fails to be complete. Each failure has a characteristic name: Sin, Guilt, Futility, and Inauthenticity, answering to the failure to do full justice to God, Ideality, Existence, and Actuality. These failures are due to man's limitations, even when he takes one of these dimensions to be primary. They also arise from the fact that one of these dimensions has a secondary role; in those cases the failure has a distinctive special name referring to the fact that inside a given dimension there is a dimension having a subordinate role: e.g., Pride is sin. The overcoming of the basic limitations of one dimension—sin, guilt, etc.—is accompanied with the claim that it also in some sense provides for the overcoming of the other dimensions. The overcoming of sin involves some kind of overcoming of guilt and conversely; however the overcoming of sin as primary is genuine—since it is the inevitable outcome of man's finitude, it does involve the action of God—whereas the overcoming of it inside the overcoming of guilt is analogical. If we have no recourse to God, sin remains inescapable and is to be overcome only by virtue of the actions of the other modes in primary roles. Though as in those primary roles they still permit particular forms of sin, sin is overcome by all three of them together.

	God		*Ideality*		*Existence*		*Actuality*
A Sin	*1*		*5* Pride		*9* Anxiety		*13* Idolatry
B Guilt	*2* Dogmatism	*6*			*10* Brutality		*14* Vanity
C Futility	*3* Fanaticism		*7* Irrelevance	*11*			*15* Conceit
D Inauthenticity	*4* Alienation		*8* Resignation	*12* Impotence		*16*	

Sin thus breaks up into pride, anxiety, and idolatry; guilt into dogmatism, brutality, and vanity; futility into fanaticism, irrelevance, and ineptitude; inauthenticity into alienation, resignation, and impotence. (Better terms should be found for what is now being called "anxiety," "dogmatism," "brutality," "irrelevance," and perhaps "futility.") The stress upon God or the religious life involves dogmatism, fanaticism, and alienation; the stress on Ideality involves pride, irrelevance, and resignation; the stress on Existence involves anxiety, brutality, and impotence; the stress on Actuality involves idolatry, vanity, and conceit. These names and classifications should be checked against the classical lists. Some of the classical names: gluttony, lust, blasphemy, prodigality, cowardice, intemperance, injustice, self-indulgence, niggardliness, lassitude, despair, murder, adultery, theft, ignorance, self-love, avarice. (These include some of the seven capital vices: vainglory, envy, anger, sloth, covetousness, gluttony, lust. And there are what may be called the cardinal vices: injustice, imprudence, intemperance, cowardice.)

Aquinas apparently calls what I term impotence, concupiscence of the flesh, and idolatry, concupiscence of the eyes or things, or covetousness.

We are exhorted, no matter where we are, to avoid sin by attending to God to the proper degree; we could be said to be asked to avoid Guilt, Futility, and Inauthenticity as well, by turning to the other modes properly. *1]* Is it the case that we need a radical alteration only in connection with God, or is it perhaps true even here that we merely must do better what we had been doing? *2]* Is it true that a mode can wipe away the relevant defect, or is that true only of God? *3]* And do we keep ourselves as commonsensical men in reserve until we are ready to detach a state where we can acknowledge God? *4]* Is it that we can get to God (and the others) from any position, but that when we have worked out a way of living in Existence we are ready for a life of religion?

1] If we did not have a grip on God from the first, we would have to account for our complete separation from Him, and the possibility of knowing Him. If we account for the second, say by grace, we will preclude the first. What we must mean, then, in religion is nothing other than what we could mean in connection with guilt, etc.—take the dimension of life seriously, all the way.

2] No mode can wipe away a defect entirely; we must make use of other modes.

3] We are commonsensical men while we are religious, ethical, etc., but when we are merely commonsensical men we do not live a life, but through one. Once we decide to live a life we find that we can make no sense of a mere Actual or Idealized one, but only of a cosmic, existential one, which leads to the religious, and which then can clarify the meaning of an Ideal; this in turn can implicate the Actual, making this the summation and the justification of the preceding ones.

4] We seem to be able to get to any mode from any position, but to get to God from experience is not yet to have Him in a position where He becomes the center of a full life, but only as one who is to be understood to be the ordering factor for a life in Existence, or someone to cognize or to evaluate.

The politician or statesman in a limited way urges the life of the Ideal; the educator tries to inculcate the life of authenticity; the soldier tries to have people live in the light of Existence. Each of these does something similar to what the religious man does in urging one to give up the old Adam. We therefore have conflicts between politics and religion, secular and religious education, the world of the sword and that of the dove. Where is knowledge? Is it not the development of the authentic but carried out with respect to the subordinate modes, and then neutrally?

September 19

There are four ways in which men can be completed—through knowledge, through a reordering of themselves in relation to the world, through a submission and acceptance of the various modes, and through the living of a career. In each one of these the modes take up a definite order. We thus get the following: *AIEG*—knowledge; *GEAI*—reordering; *IAGE*—submission; *EGIA*—career.

Modes of Being concerns itself with the first group; the discussions of recent days concerns itself with the last. But we should go through the other two before we deal with the last. This means we must entertain a relation to divinity which involves a re-ordering (an overcoming, Christians would say, of the fault of sin), and then a submission to the Ideal. What has been done so far in the various books has been to go through the four modes in the frame of knowing, and then (having used this as a guide) to discuss the dimension of submission in its beginning (giving only a minor place to *AGE*), and then from there to a dimension of a career in its beginning (with only a minor reference to *GIA*). It is proper to go on to deal with the reordering, but here (since we are now back in the proper sequence) we ought to carry out the reordering through *EAI,* and then trace the consequences of a commitment on ourselves, on religion, and on our relation to nature, and follow this by seeing what it is like to live the careers of art-history, religion, ethics-politics, and individuality, as involved with one another, and following in this succession.

How should one move from the knowledge of God, to God functioning as a ground for a reordering? And where and how does experience of the divine come in? The first question is answered by the recognition of what one has arrived at, the actual relating of ourselves to God as a being. And the movement from the *I* at the end to the *I* at the beginning of a submission is of a similar nature. This is also true when we move from *E* at the end of a process of submission to *E* as the beginning of a kind of career. Regarding the second question, on experience, we are faced with *GEAI, IAGE,* and *EGIA* not altogether distinguished; we could stress the *AIEG* by virtue of an effort to understand the conventionalized world, and that would start us off on the *Modes.* But if we attend to the objective pole we find that this leads us to consider the divine component first as that which helps us find our proper position, and that we then move on to a reordering with Existence, a kind of adjustment; we follow this by an adjustment to other Actualities and end by having the proper relation to the Ideal, enabling us to move on to the set of submitted modes, *IAGE.*

Does the first item always stand detached from the rest; does the last item always absorb the preceding ones; does the second item always entail the third and this produce the fourth?

Who starts with *A* and ends with *G* in knowledge—an Aristotle? Who starts with *G* and ends with *I* in a reordering—a Schweitzer, a Ghandi? Who starts with *I* and ends with *E* in a submission—a Lenin, a Darwin? Who starts with *E* and ends with *A* as a career—a Goethe?

The failure in *AIEG* is ignorance and comes to expression in alienation, utopianism, and passion (where the knowledge does not control *IE* or *G*); the failure in *GEAI* is sin, and comes to expression in anxiety, idolatry, and pride (where the divine ordering does not control *EA* or *I*); the failure of *IAGE* is guilt, and comes to expression in vanity, dogmatism, and brutality (where commitment fails to control *AG* or *E*); and the failure of *EGIA* is futility, and comes to expression in fanaticism, rationalism, and impotence (where the *E* fails to control *GI* or *A*).

In the knowledge of the modes there is an ignorance which should be expressed in the chapter on *I* as alienation, in *E* as a utopianism, and in G as passion (?). When we move on to *G,* we find the failure to be ordered in relation to God yields anxiety, idolatry, and pride, and this should be focal in the achievement of the combination *GEAI*. The reflective man concentrates on the knowledge, the religious on the reordering, the committed on the submission, and the wise on the career.

October 13

The best approach to philosophy is without fear of metaphysics, but with a grave suspicion of all its claims. One ought to see if one can understand common experience by utilizing the common discourse and explanations. The muddle of common-sense data, and the confusion of common-sense explanations (the chalk is white in daylight because we see it to be so, but in twilight it is taken to be white nevertheless; the stick is straight because it is felt to be so, but it is seen to be broken, or it is straight because it functions as a straight object, but a man is not a thing even though used as one; the moon moves as I move about but it is also in one place) leads me to move away from common sense in part. I try operationalistic ideas, ideas which serve merely to connect and make sense of what I confront, but find these are too limited and common-sensical; tensor equations, wave functions, etc., with appropriate abstract or constructed terms, are needed to account for physical entities. Consideration of the potentiality, privacy, ethical prescriptions; the contemporaneity of all items in one space, regardless of signals and as allowing comparisons of magnitude and worth; the need for an absolute other; the reality of things in the same world with men; the capacity to speculate; faith; love; the objectivity of the past; the prescriptions of logic and the necessities of mathematics; the eternity of truth all make us go further. They provoke a consideration of modes of being which are not to be found full-bodied in the common-sense world, but also are not to be found by distilling that world either. The Ideal, Existence, and God are somehow outside that common-sense world, though showing their influence there.

After a metaphysical system has been developed it is desirable to go back to experience again and see if the distinctions which the metaphysical system provides are not to be found in experience itself. We ought to recognize that we do experience the different modes as constituting the background of the world of common sense, and that we do note that background in fear and terror, in surmise, in our appreciation, and even in the course of our production of art. Can we now find in the experience the power which was ascribed to the modes, a power which required us to say that they were ultimate beings? Might one not say, e.g., that all beings are directed toward the beingness in any one of them, a beingness which is common to them all; might this not be the common possibility which each will, as a distinctive being, also specialize and try to realize; might not men be said to specialize it in a distinctive way and at the same time take as their concern the beingness as such, whereas other entities have it specialized necessarily and cannot hold the beingness which attracts them, apart from the specialization? Can we not then go on to say that the beings all are concordant and move into the future together because they are confronted with the same beingness, isolable in any one or in any number of items, and that this beingness (precisely because it is rooted in other beings) stands over against the beings which are attracted to it, thereby guiding them and defining the next moment for them all? Can we not then go one to say that the beingness is also the other of each and every one of them, when taken as distinct from all specializations?

If we can say all these things do we not reduce the metaphysically defined beings to categories, phases, to mere strains or strands inside experience? If so, then metaphysics becomes a device to enable us to see how we can recognize experience to be as rich as it in fact is—a recognition which we would not obtain directly because we confronted it in commonsensical terms which are too narrow, too particularized, and too overrun with traditional ideas, prejudices, conventions, local usages.

Faced with this rich experience we are nevertheless confronted with the fact that we have not accounted for the presence of that experience, the relation of the individual knower to the whole of experience, the potentialities in the experience (and thus what is not yet expressed), and the distinctive beings in it acting on one another and resisting one another. To account for these we are driven to metaphysics once again.

Philosophical thought is an oscillation between a systematic and an experiential approach. We are satisfied that we have the proper system when, after we have read back into experience the very items which we have taken to be transcendent, we find that in the next round we are forced to reaffirm them in the same abstract, though in a different, concrete form. The history of philosophy after the correct philosophy has been formulated—supposing that there is but one, and thus that various stresses of different formulations are taken to be all inside the one philosophy—is the enriching of the abstract notions with experiential meanings, and the recognition of the powers latent in the realm of experience, which the abstract categories tell us are there.

October 15

A philosopher usually sets out with a limited number of categories or ideas. As he tries to apply these more and more, he becomes aware of territories he had not envisaged, and for which his categories are not suited; also, he usually comes across paradoxes which he cannot resolve. To take care of these he adds to his initial set. Having begun with methodological effectiveness, he ends with a wise comprehensiveness. This provides his disciples with a world in which they soon take their ease. It is almost inevitable that another philosopher with another simple scheme should come along and attract the young as providing a short way to the whole, enabling them to get rid of the difficulties and some of the prejudices and perhaps ready acceptances of the older views. Every new philosopher, as it were, has a device by which certain questions do not arise. (Of course if one takes "not arising" as his model, the easiest thing is to say nothing or just a single word. No problems arise for those who refuse to say anything, or who say only "cat.") His appeal is ready if he solves some paradox which has troubled the others, or if he is able to show that his view does most justice or is most sympathetic with the discipline which is then in most favor—theology, or physics, or poetry, etc.

It would seem as if those who had provided extended systems with some protection, in the shape of a formalistic set of rules or some hard principle of verification, would avoid the complacency which had beset the other systems, and would enable their disciples to withstand the new onslaught. But the technical side becomes overly technical and highly specialized as surely as the nontechnical side becomes too general, perhaps a little vague and too familiar. The new offering finds its audience because its new principle is not only sharp-edged, but because it seems capable of being utilized by anyone who would be willing to practice with it just a little.

Must then, the history of philosophy be a succession of schemes, the effective growing up to be wise, and this then giving way to another effective new principle? The older system could try assimilating the new within it, as the theologians have sometimes succeeded in doing—often when it was too late to be of any good. Or it could engage in polemics, though these seem to have little effect on anyone; or it could adopt the new principle and try to convert it quickly into a variant of the system which was being opposed, but this tactic will be resisted by the proponents of the new principle.

October 16

Some aphorisms:

War is a poor strategy for attaining peace.

Philosophers who claim that philosophy has no subject matter also claim that this is how it *ought to be.*

If you don't want questions to arise, don't say anything. But then your behavior will be questionable.

Politics is the art of systematically avoiding ethical questions.

For men, women are a provocative mystery; for women, men are an irritating necessity.

The world for the child is alien, for the youth it is something to live with, for the middle-aged it is something to which one is adjusted, and for the wise or aged it is alien again, but now as that which has a rationale of its own not altogether permeable by ideals, ideas, or reason.

Those are most reasonable who are not always rational.

The confused philosopher always appeals to experience—and rightly, for it is his counterpart.

How annoying it must be to God to be believed in, but not to be understood; to be listened to, but not to be answered.

The new frontier in architecture in America was the sky—hence the skyscrapers.

The spirit of an age cannot be known until the work of the age is done; the spirit is the viable power, the power which actually was manifested.

A nation discovers its history when it achieves power; it studies its history to properly exercise its power; it insists on its history when it has lost its power.

A man who loves becomes alert to all women; a woman who loves closes out all other men.

A child is an adult for separated moments; an adult is a child who has accumulated moments.

"The truth is not in him." Of course, his ego pushed it outside.

October 17

In a contrary-to-fact conditional, we can take the newly considered case to function only as a new condition; we can take it to be the ground for a relation of the old condition to a new consequence. Thus if I say, "Were I king of England," I can mean to speak of myself offering the king of England a new condition from which he, in his potency, would provide an appropriate consequence. For example, in "Were I king of England, I would not enter the House of Commons without permission," I do not make a difference to the consequence. But in "Were I king of England, the king of England would be 5′ 6″," I take myself to provide a ground for the king of England, and thereby make him have new consequences.

"Were I king of England, I would deny America any bases" says that the king of England has such and such a consequence because he is explicating, with this consequence, the nature of myself. We usually use contrary-to-fact conditionals in this way. To say that "Were the Greeks living today they would have no slaves," is to say that the Greek nature is to be explicated today as not having the consequence "slaves" in the conditions that now prevail. Suppose we say "Were the Greeks living today, they would of course have slaves," are we not also explicating the Greek nature as that which, despite changed conditions, would have the same consequences? Or are we taking the present conditions to be a kind of potency and saying that, given the condition of there being Greeks, the potency would produce the consequences they in fact produced in the past? What is clear is that "Were the Greeks living today they would have slaves," differs from "Were the Greeks living today they would not have slaves" in consequence, and that this change of consequence follows equally when we consider the Greeks to be conditions or potencies. In the second case, if the Greeks are a condition, the potency today is a new one; but if the Greeks are a potency, the conditions are new and powerful.

We can use expressions like "even" to make clear which meaning we wish. "Even if I were stronger I could not lift that stone" tells us that the condition "stronger" will not make the consequence different, so that that consequence must be taken to be a derivative from the object being displayed, if it is the stone, or that it overwhelms the being in which it is located, if it is the I. Consequently, it is better to pair three expressions:

1] If I were king of England then *x*
2] If you were king of England then *y*
3] If you were king of England then *x*

1 and *2* show that the difference is in the I and the you, and thus that we are explicating the same reality under different circumstances. *1* and *3* show that the difference between I and you is not pertinent, that what we have is a consequence of the condition "king of England," and that you and I are in this context indistinguishable, mere instances of man. 2 and 3 could be reconciled by saying that in 2 or 3 the you is an indifferent ground and in 3 or 2, consequently, it functions as a condition making a change from the x to the y, or conversely, on the base of the king of England.

All the above seems to be confused.

Suppose we have x on base R yielding y; if on base S we get the same yield, S (and perhaps R) is indifferent; if we get a new yield, then S is newly explicated. But suppose we make the antecedent different by adding the new being to it (instead of "were he asked he would tell the truth" which explicates honesty, we insert "were x—a dishonest man—asked, he would tell the truth"). We can say that the changed circumstances make no difference to the consequence in one case, but do in the alternative case . . . I'm still muddled.

Once again—

If I bring in another entity and find that the consequences are the same as before, I am in effect saying that the connection of antecedent to consequence holds for "anyone," If the king of England has a large army, then "were I king of England, I would have a large army" means that it makes no difference who is king—the condition of being king requires that consequence. If, however, we say that the consequence is that I would not have an army, then my being makes a difference and the king situation is forced to have new consequences. This latter could be said to have new consequences because the king is a new kind of being due to my presence, or because I force it to have a different kind of consequence than it had before. Can these two cases be distinguished? I think not. To say that I, in the king situation, have such and such a consequence means that I am the being explicated; and to be explicated is to affect the nature of the initial situation at least in the sense of making it relevant to the kind of consequence that is drawn.

October 19

Women are natural psychoanalysts; they listen not to what you say, but for what you betray.

He was not impeccable at the typewriter; he looked before he hit.

For some youngsters the most offensive four letter word is "book."

An aphorism is wisdom which has not yet matured—or which is overripe.

An aphorism is what a philosopher writes when he's not thinking.

Those who disbelieve in values tell the rest that they *ought not* speak of values.

October 25

Awe is a consequence of the awareness of the greatness of the divine; fear is a consequence of the awareness of the comparative feebleness of oneself over against the divine; love is the giving of oneself to the divine; trust is the confidence that one is cherished by the divine. These are all individual ways of re-establishing the divine in oneself, of making a simulacrum of the divine which is revelatory of its being, the having of Him experientially. They are to be matched by an objective set expressive of the institutional, public way of having the individual in relation to the divine.

If we insist on the individual activity and deny that there is a reality answering to the object of the fear—which is in essence what Schleiermacher does—we can bring religion inside the naturalistic context. This we ought to try to do—just as we ought always to take the metaphysical results of a speculative system and try to treat them as mere facets or categories of the everyday world, until we are forced by a consideration of various facts (contemporaneity, power, possibility, etc.) to move outward again and affirm the reality of other modes of being, and eventually even encounter them.

There are two kinds of encounter with God that must be distinguished. The first relates to the speculative enterprise; we must find Him in our other contents as the other which makes them be over against all else, or as the unity which governs them, or as a source of value, or as an individual power linking individuals with one another. Here the non-divine is primary and the divine is adumbrated. But we also can have a religious encounter with God in the experience of the numinous, in a direct revelation, or in mystical experience. In these latter forms God is directly encountered, even though He may not be altogether distinguished from other irreducible factors. There seems also to be an experience which is neither metaphysical nor religious, which is in fact the root of both. We encounter God as intermixed with other modes of being, as the counterpart of our daily conventional world. As so encountered, He may be dissolved into an object of intellection, may be intensified as an object of religious belief, or He may be used as a root and perpetually adumbrated content while we engage in other activities of apprehending God through concepts, and through some kind of interplay.

October 26

I have argued that we can encounter the historic past in the (historic?) present. Can we also encounter God, Ideals, Existence, in present actualities?

We encounter God in actualities as the ingredientiality of universals, and as the pastness of facts (and in the present as a freedom from such pastness?)—the latter being an encounter in Actuality, the former in specific actualities in the realm of Actuality. We encounter Ideals in actualities as values, and as the principle which makes for the comparability of different actualities (and in the present as a status?) in Actuality. We encounter Existence in specific actualities as a fragmented dynamism which relates us to a larger world in public time, and we encounter it in Actuality as the determinant of the incongruous counterparts which different actualities will exhibit in relation to one another (and here in the present as a boundary?). In commonsensical objects we adumbrate the substantial actualities, which we come to know more formally through speculation and which we partly iconize in art. But what of the substantial actualities when they have passed away; do we encounter them inside the commonsensical objects? And is the encounter of God, Ideality, and Existence possible in common-sense objects? The last question has an affirmative answer, but one which does not mean that God, etc., are not encountered in other types of object as well.

A substantial object is now adumbrated in a commonsensical object. The past of that substantial object is like the past of the historical object in that it is manifested in the form of the self-maintenance, self-containedness, directionality, and uniqueness of the being. However, in the case of the confronted historical object we have a presented content, and the past enables us to see that it is substantial in fact, though only in history. But in the case of the substantial "natural" object we have already arrived at the point where the historical encounter ends. What we want to know now is whether or not and how we can encounter past substantial objects. These objects are known by inference. But they are inferences, not from present substantial objects, but from present commonsensical objects. Do we encounter them, then, as oppositional elements, giving a border or limitation, or defining the present of the adumbrated and even of the speculatively achieved substantial object? Or should we say what Whitehead does: he supposes that the substantial object is in the present as the prehended content. Or better, perhaps, that there is a givenness to the substantial object's particularity and qualities which are to be understood as inheritances; its mere substantiality now does not tell us that it is to have this or that quality. The presence of these qualities, and even the commonsensical object we now face, would then be the product of the past substantiality. The past beings are now operative in the substantial present beings in the form of the insistent qualities and natures which we can note in commonsensical and other objects.

As we confront the commonsensical object, we dislocate it toward the historical when we encounter the past in the shape of uniqueness, self-maintenance, etc., or we dislocate it toward the substantial when we encounter the past in the shape of the ways in which the present substantial being expresses itself as a commonsensical thing (or as part of one, and thus as perceptual, etc.). We can also dislocate it toward the divine when we see the object as possessing universals and being free from the past; toward the Ideal, as possessing values and having status; and toward Existence, as possessing an orientation and being bounded with respect to the public world.

Does the commonsensical object itself have a past which can be encountered, or is this past present in a muddled way, being in fact an historic past? Were it an historic past, the fact of its muddledness would still have to be taken account of; and in any case the commonsensical object does have a role in society and daily practice. Consequently, whatever being it has must allow one to encounter past commonsensical objects. These objects are recovered through tradition, etc. It is the commonsensical object as now effectively expressing a tradition, which permits of the encounter with the past—i.e., when we encounter a commonsensical object as now carrying a tradition, in the shape of a role, qualities, values, etc., we in fact are encountering the past as the power by which that tradition is now being manifested, acting on us and warranting certain expectations not grounded in a knowledge of the commonsensical object as here and now conventionalized.

These various encounters do not compromise the independent being of the various modes; indeed, they show that those modes must have a being apart from their encountered forms, making those encountered forms possible. The situation is somewhat similar to what occurs in the theory of meaning: we can derive a meaning of "prescriptive" from "descriptive" by adding to the latter such qualifications as "subjugation," "demand," "exterior to," etc. But when we do this we do not make the descriptive prescriptive; we merely provide a meaning for prescriptive by subjecting the descriptive to various transformations which we can conceive. Are these transformations themselves empirical, nonempirical, a posterior, a priori? When we move from an empirical meaning to a nonempirical, or conversely, we subject our term to a transformation which must somehow bridge the gap. It is evident then that we must somehow be in a mode of being which is not empirical. Our transformation must then be an act (and thus in Existence) which has a structure (and thus be Ideal) and must, if there is to be no ostensible question-begging, arrive at the divine. If it arrives at the meaning of the Ideal there is nevertheless a structure assumed; if it arrives at the meaning of Existence there is nevertheless the act of Existence assumed. But in the end the movement of empirical to nonempirical, or conversely, is between Actuality and God, and not between the other modes. It means that meaning is oriented in these two modes and that transformations involve the other two. Of course the meanings initially are ideal entities or abstractions in the knower, or aspects of the other modes.

October 27

A philosophy of religion seeks to understand the nature of God and the role of God in religion, as well as the institutions and experience of religion. When attention is paid to the nature of God there is a double temptation which must be overcome. On the one hand there is a tendency to affirm that God is only a "philosophical" God, a being having a role in the cosmos somewhat the way Aristotle's Prime Mover has, or that God is primarily the object of worship, and then particularly in some special religion. But a true philosophy of religion (which is here understood to embrace theology) will seek to understand the nature of God in Himself and in relation to other beings, without supposing that an affirmation of the one precludes an independent exploration of the other. We can be speculatively aware of the philosophic God, yet that God can be understood to have a religious role; we can be religiously involved with God from the perspective of some particular religion, yet that God is not without a being in- and of-Himself, apart from what the religion knows or is interested in. A philosopher's God thus is richer than the merely intellectualized product of reflection, a being which has only a cosmic role, and is richer, too, than the object of a religion, encountered in experience, miraculous, institutional, or mystical. It is richer than either because it allows for and in fact is shown to have both roles. However, the God as open to religion is not the God of this religion or that; God for a philosopher of religion is religiously viable but not necessarily for the extant religions, except in some limited and qualified sense.

Should the philosopher of religion attend to this or that religion? Is there need, except for instances and occasional insights, for him to attend to what this or that creed or theologian says? We must not take it for granted that the extant religions do more justice to the religious dimension of God than some religion yet to be; and we can doubt that they do, once we explore the nature of God as apart from the religious dimension, and find that it demands a different religion and religious attitude than men have for the most part assumed in the past.

October 29

Because we have a degree of self-sufficiency and because of our powers of concentration and our practical needs, we attend to limited portions of experience. The experience is limited by us in range and, most important, in depth. The first and primary limitation is that which involves the concentration on commonsensical objects. These are quickly overlaid by us by traditions and experiences, conventions and languages; indeed, in the very act of focusing we impose these restrictions. From there we can go in one of two directions. We can try to move into the deeper reality of which the commonsensical is but a surface, or we can try to get to the surface of the commonsensical. The ordinary man in religion, in surmise, in fear, in awe, in his grasp of his own ignorance and finitude, in his awareness of the resistance and the power of others, takes the first of these approaches and ends by affirming that his world is environed by something larger and usually more ominous. Philosophers try the opposite tack as a rule. They abstract the structures, the perceptual contents, the sheer ongoing or the values, from the commonsensical object and then tend to reify these, to take these to have the substantiality which the common-sense man takes common-sense objects to have. But philosophers also note the common-sense reality which they have pushed into the background—that is why they seek to verify or claim that what they have isolated will enable them to know the commonsensical object better, to isolate what is really real in it. Some philosophers would take the philosophic abstractions of the first group and treat these as substantial but vaguely apprehended, and concentrate instead on the surface of these—sense data, language-governed distinctions, sensations, feelings, and the like. These latter philosophers stand to the former as the former stand to common sense and this in turn stands to the awesome world beyond.

Those who concentrate on the focal objects tend often to claim that these alone are real; consequently, we have men who take the only realities to be sense data, perceptual objects, and common-sense objects. They would have no reason to go outside their contents, were it not that they have no way of accounting for their contents, no way of dealing with prescriptions, and no way of understanding themselves (who are not reducible to the objects which they claim alone can be real).

The big problem is to determine when we have reached the last outpost, and how we can reach it and know it. Must we be content with merely adumbrating a world beyond common sense? Or can we not re-create it in art, acknowledge it as the necessary adumbrated component in our judgment of a common-sense object, re-create it by uniting all the abstractions we derive from common-sense objects, or speculatively produce it in the shape of explanatory concepts? The last two ways seem to go counter to the very contention made just before, to the effect that structures are abstractions from common-sense objects and to this degree are not to be reified, not to be treated as answering to what is real. And yet in these last two ways we make even more grandiose claims, and often turn our backs on experienced phenomena. But it is precisely because we turn our backs on the experienced phenomena, precisely because we take advantage of our own substantiality and its power to create, that we can forge new concepts which, instead of dealing with mere derivatives from common sense and to which nothing concrete answers, tell us of the nature of the ultimate real. Speculative philosophy depends on the claim that the more boldly and creatively we think, the closer we come to the ultimately real. And its claim can be checked by seeing how it coheres with what the arts teach, with what refinement of common sense (by a synthesis of the various abstractions from it permits) is like, how it enables us to bring into one single coherent and revelatory account all the various disciplines and experiences (other than those of daily life) with daily life.

We know of God, the Ideal, and Existence (or Nature) by virtue of our speculatively achieved ideas. Those ideas can be said to have a rootage in daily life, or its more refined and objective nature, Actuality. As having a rootage there, they are qualified; we must, therefore, free them from common-sense qualifications if we are to know truly. And we must free them from Actuality if we are to know what they are in and of themselves. We are forced to such freeing because we see that the common-sense world is arbitrarily structured in part, and that the elements as ingredient in Actuality do not account for the kinds of restrictions and qualifications to which the Actuality is subject—indeed, that the elements as ingredient in Actuality can be understood only if treated as the outcome of the actions of beings other than the Actual.

This last consideration enables us to reverse the process with which we began, and to speak of the effect of the ultimate realities on the surfaces on which men might concentrate. The other modes of being prevent one from taking Actuality alone to be final. The Actual affects the common-sensical in that it grounds it as apart from all conventionality; the commonsensical grounds and infects the perceptual by providing it with a locus; the perceptual grounds the sensual by providing it with truth or objectivity; the merely abstract conceptual formulations of science, etc., are sustained by and affected by the commonsensical from which they are derived, together with the perceptual. We can go further and show how the more concrete, real world imposes demands on the rest. The various modes require something from the Actuality which they qualify; this in turn requires something from common sense; this in turn requires something from formal structures and perception; this in turn requires something from sense data. What? They demand conformity, modification so that there will be consonance with a larger scheme of knowledge and action. Each of the abstractions is rectified and thereby given ultimacy and being, by virtue of the place accorded to it by the more concrete.

Might not one get such a place by giving the abstract to the concrete? But then one risks losing the abstract. The concrete can be seen to make a difference to the abstract when we maintain a hold on the abstract; the concrete requires us to qualify the abstract by relating it to other abstracts within the restrictive conditions imposed by that concrete. If we merely qualify the abstract by relating it to other abstracts and then embed the result in the concrete, we treat it as an abstraction still, or we allow it to be radically transformed in the concrete. Such procedures are permissible but are not exhaustive, for the concrete also gives a kind of substantiality to the abstract, dignifying it so far as the abstract permits the concrete to enter into it. Consequently, we have both the need on the part of the abstract to permit an entrance of the concrete into it, and the need of the abstract to allow itself to be carried by the more concrete substantiality outside it. The former is an analogue of incarnation; the latter, of submission either to what is outside, or to oneself as a self capable of creativity and possessing an ultimacy of one's own.

A number of things, then, ought to be done: *1*] distinguish the different layers of being, and the primary occupants of the different layers; 2] show how one is led from the thinnest (most abstract) to the thickest (most concrete) layers; 3] show how the thinner layers are ordered and thus how occupants are rectifiable internally by some rationale intrinsic to the layer; 4] show how the thinner needs rooting in the thicker; 5] show how the thicker acts on the thinner enabling it, in stage *3,* to maintain itself.

The abstractions are reified by the individual. It takes the individual in his substantiality, though expressed in the form of concepts, to know the ultimately real; if he wishes to make contact with that ultimately real apart from concepts, he must face it as interplaying, contrasting with, and opposing himself in his full being. When a man subsequently finds that he has reified his abstractions by virtue of his imposing on them something of himself in the form of habits, conventions, beliefs, constructs, ideas, and the like, he will, if he has no apprehension or no acceptance of the more substantially real, fall into despair, scepticism, nihilism, atheism, and the like. However, as the existentialists see, the fact that something is reified by one's full being does not make it questionable; it in fact invests it with the most concrete substantiality possible. But the existentialists think that the individual is essentially a person, a speaker, a believer, and the like. If they were to recognize the concreteness of the self, as that which transcends the finite categories of thought and belief and the like, they would be able to see the being of the concrete, and would be able to forge concepts which expressed it. The philosophic categories obtained by abstraction and reconstruction, by speculative creative activity, refinement, comparison and essentially dialectical thinking, report the real because they are neutral ideas of utmost generality and thus express the self, not in its idiosyncratic or even individual nature, but in its full substantiality, and thus as that which is an actuality in relation to other actualities and to modes of being. It can therefore be self-contained, with a distinctive being and career of its own, enabling it to represent all other actualities and to know the modes of being.

The Cartesians, with their clear and distinct ideas, were looking for something in the abstractions which would guarantee their truth. They took the clear and distinct to be the outcome of their being sustained by a distinct mind; had they asked what was being sustained by a being in his substantiality as more than a mind, they would not have said that the clear and distinct is true, but that the ideas which are functions of the unity, the existential power, the irreducible individuality, and the concern of the substantial being alone were true. And these latter ideas are not so much clear and distinct (or as the pragmatists alternatively suppose, verifiable or reducible to an experience of things), as categorial, neutral concepts of the highest generality, justifiable in logic and specifiable by whatever is known and done. Have we got such categories? Nothing but an entire philosophic system can pretend to give the answer. And the answer can be known by seeing if there are some items left out or, in principle, not capable of being accounted for or encompassed by those categories. These categories are common-sense rubrics, refined, generalized, deconventionalized, and neutralized. Since we always have a dim apprehension of the real, it can be said that the most speculative of systems is the most concrete of empiricisms; what speculation knows, we in fact experience, though in an inchoate form.

November 2

The past is in the present historic object as a distinctive twist of its power. When the present object moves into the next moment, that twist is modified so that the distinctive twist at the next moment will be one which expresses the fact that the object had been present the moment before. When we come to know the present object we find in it a distinctive twist which is itself a summation of a plurality of twists, each one of which is the preserved existential component of some past moment of history. (Natural objects do not preserve their pasts; their features are now qualified by the adventures they had gone through. Only in history is there a preservation of Existence, of substantial being, though, to be sure, only of an historic substantial being.) Our encounter, then, is not with some distinctive past power, but with a past power now functioning distinctively. There is no encounter with the Existence of some past occurrence. But since we mediate our apprehension of the present object by our inferred understanding of what the past features were like, we are able to isolate out of the present encountered twist the factor which is appropriate to it.

When we remember, we do something similar to what we do with history. The remembered idea is determinate; but so is an erroneous one. Both are rejected by the present item's determinate features. Only because we can somehow encounter the past which we remember can we differentiate the erroneous from the remembered. And we do encounter it as the correlate of ourselves. The object that is truly remembered is something which has an orientation in ourselves; if we are to know that what we now have in mind is remembered and not erroneous, we must note in present content a reference to ourselves as having originally provided an orientation for it. We must, in short, distinguish between ourselves in our privacies producing errors, and ourselves as orienting external content. To see this objective occurrence now as that which is to be treated as oriented toward me, a me which is not present, is to have the idea in my mind dealt with as a remembrance.

What, in present confronted things, says that they need a me which is no longer? Is it that I recognize something? Is it that it is familiar? The answers to these questions, I think, must be negative; we remember even when set within unfamiliar circumstances. Is it then our alienation, our awareness that we have lost a grip on the world, that we haven't made the object our own yet? But should we not say this too when we think erroneously? The object then defies us. This it does, but in order to remember we must face an object as that which is to be converted, to be disalienated, to be made part of our memory. We have, then, an acceptance of the remembered world and at the same time the acknowledgement of the present world as that which is to be coordinated with that remembered world. The present world's exclusion now is tentative in the form of an alien content; it will become exclusive in another way when it is part of the memory situation. But now, while rejecting the (remembered) idea we now have, we see it as that which will not reject the idea subsequently in the same way, but will instead merely follow on it, replace it in time, belong to the same system with it.

November 3

Language (and its words) has a meaning dimension, a sound dimension, and a referential dimension. It is the interest of practical men —those engaged in action, politics, history, and institutional worship— to have others trained so that they associate sounds with objects; there is no need here to understand the meanings or to associate meanings with objects. It is the interest of art, and particularly poetry, to associate sound and meaning, and to cut away from the usual objects as much as possible. It is the interest of ethics and mathematics, and other enterprises concerned with the Ideal, to associate meanings with objects; the vocabulary is technical and perhaps incapable of being sounded. It is the interest of philosophy—making use of categorial, refined, common-sense terms—to combine meaning, sound, and objective reference; its words are those of common sense taken in their full-bodied nature and thus as more than mere usages (which would make common sense practical only) refined and generalized. They are new words in a sense, and require of the philosopher something of the art of the poet and the reasonableness of the carpenter or traffic policeman.

But what, then, shall we say of the words which are to be used in privacy with respect to the divine? And what of the words of science? The latter can be dealt with as delimited versions of the mathematical, subject to the qualification, perhaps, that there must be some practical orientation eventually, or at least an orientation toward the common-sensical, and that it must be ultimately viewed as a topic for omniscience. The former, the language appropriate to private religion, is closer to words used in daily life in the sense that the sounds have no relation to the meaning; the vocabulary is thus like poetry since it attends only to the combination of meaning and sound, but it is unlike poetry in that there is no attempt to find appropriate sounds for the meanings, but only to create them, to express oneself through them. Strictly speaking then, this is the language of meaning alone, with the words as mere vehicles. A language of mere sounds (or in writing, mere inscriptional language) to which meanings are indifferently attached and with which one might associate any objects, is the language of melody or song, of ejaculations. A word which was essentially referential and for which the sound and the meaning were indifferent, would be a sign, an exclamation serving only to arrest and direct attention, a label.

The language of theology would use the language of philosophy (?); so would a language describing the Ideal, and a language describing Existence; the realm of mathematics and the realm of nature would consequently be properly characterized in words in which there was some association of sound with sense and object. Discourse by the historian, since it makes use of common-sense language, must combine all three (meaning, sound, and reference), but the reference would be derivative; in theology the sound would be derivative, something eventually achieved and then insisted on; in logic, where there is an attempt to find distinct and appropriate symbols, one can speak, in a sense, of an association of meaning and "sound" with an ultimate derivation or reference to a world of objects, defined to exist only because the symbols are in existence for such objects—which is essentially the way Quine deals with "ontology." Is there a language in which sounds and meanings are primarily associated and a similar definition of an object is provided? Is this the language of myth?

More clearly perhaps: There is a language of mere meaning—meditative. Of mere sound, ejaculation. Of mere reference, ritual signs, labels.

A language of meaning and sound, poetry; of meaning and object, mathematics; of sound and object, commands and utility; of meaning, sound, and object, philosophy; all three, but the object derivative, history and myth; all three, but the sound secondary, theology; all three, but the meaning minor, clichés, conventional discourse.

We tend to think of a word as a unit; but if it is a sound it is an event, an occurrence, whose unity would have to be determined by the kind of world it inhabits, for in different worlds there are units of different lengths, some of which are eventful in nature. Taken as a unit, whether this be a substance or an event, it is different from a meaning which is essentially a structure, a premiss or a conclusion, a summation or a dissection, and different from an occurrence or object in the world, which has power and a career and a cosmic context. When we look to the meaning to tell us how to classify our words we will get a different result than we do when we look to the sound; the latter yields phonemes, etc., the former, such distinctions as transcendentals, subjects, predicates, copulas, etc. When we look to the referents we get words of process, of achievement, etc.

Is it true that men are trapped by words? Surely they are, but are they trapped by them any more than they are by customs, rituals, attitudes, ways of behaving, etc.? I think not. Do philosophers slip along with words and forget to think; this is most unlikely, for the great effort of the philosopher is to find words appropriate to the thought—i.e., certain sounds which will convey to others what the thought is and perhaps what its object is like.

Spoken words are only some of our instruments for communicating, for articulating, for designating, for persuading. We not only have written words, but we have ceremonies, manners, activities of all sorts which have similar functions. We can reduce the latter to forms of a language, but then we have to make new distinctions. And when we stay with a language having sounds or written expressions we have to distinguish the kind of world to which we are referring. An entirely new grammar will be needed if we are to speak philosophically rather than historically, artistically rather than religiously, and so on.

If logic be defined as the discipline concerned with the legitimate transference or translation of some desirable feature possessed by some item to some other item in which we are interested, can we not go on to say that every language has its logic (not in the sense of having it formulated, or even as being capable of being put in formulae, but as a structure in a dynamic process which warrants the production of new words or sentences, new units or combinations on the basis of given ones)? Can we not say, e.g., that a bit of discourse begins by acknowledging something which it is appropriate to mention, and that the course of the discourse is the production of other appropriate things to say, the appropriateness being at least in part inherited from the preceding expressions? Must we not judge all discourse in terms of the warrant by which the virtues of predecessors are transferred to successors, successors which may, however, be produced without regard for those predecessors? Indeed it is precisely because some succeeding expression or word is produced without regard for what went before that we need to have some way of transferring what we had initially accepted to what we now acknowledge.

The beginning of our discourse opens up an area; when we speak subsequently we want to bring what we then say into the same world with the preceding, but this means that we must be granted the right to do so. Discourse has a unity because new expressions do not form enclaves, but are brought within the arena defined by some preceding discourse and are thereby enabled to inherit a sanction from the preceding discourse. To be sure, one need not discourse in this way; one could take succeeding expressions to ennoble the earlier ones, or could take all of them together to constitute something new; what is to the point now, though, is the consideration that there is meaning to the entering of succeeding expressions into an arena defined by preceding ones.

A premiss, if true, defines a world of truth to which some expression can belong by virtue of having certain features required by the premiss. The succeeding expressions in a narrative can similarly be said to have certain requirements imposed on them—say that of being coherent with, explicating, qualifying, etc., what had been said before, before they can be allowed to belong to the same realm with the preceding expressions.

November 5

The theory of language usage is Aristotelianism carried over into a special part of society. Aristotle's view regarding the ideals which one ought to follow in a society is that they are exemplified by the established citizens. Following Wittgenstein, the Oxford school takes the established practices of the past to provide the test of the appropriateness of expressions in the present. They overlook the fact that for the historian the established practices of the present provide a paradigm for the determination of what happened in the past. The historian's present is, to be sure, in part a determination of what had been adopted from the past; and when he comes to write his narrative he carries into the present some of the past he came to know. But it still remains true that there are satisfactory paradigms which have not been established by usage. There are also paradigms which are now being used and which dictate that what had been used before may or may not have been proper.

Of course a more radical relativism than the Oxford school now acknowledges would say that one can have many paradigms. But then one would need some principle outside all of them to adjudicate amongst them, and this would take one to an absolutism which could conceivably say that all of the paradigms were on a level—a justified absolutistic relativism—or that some one was better than others, or that all should be discarded as inappropriate to the question of what one ought to do.

When we come to questions of metaphysics and theology, it is the case that there are common usages of these which warrant a looking outside the area of common-sense experience, that there are specific usages of these requiring technical skill, as in the churches and in prayer, and that there can be a primary paradigmatic status enjoyed by these, making it necessary to question and denigrate the claims of common sense.

It is sometimes said that we can say various things and not others, e.g., we can say how big something is, but never what kind of smell something has. But when we say "six feet" do we not abstract from the actual magnitude of the object and place the result in a context of numbers, etc.? We are saying something, but not saying "it." Are we not doing the same thing when we say that the smell is disagreeable, and in fact is like that of a rotten egg? To be sure we do not have measurements of smells, and do not enter into the kind of language used in connection with magnitudes, but this is far from saying that we do not thereby properly or even adequately speak of the smell. Any speaking is adequate if it enables us to distinguish the item and draw the proper consequences from the result. On what grounds can we say that the meager information we obtain in discourse about immediate qualities is less than we should have in order to have a proper saying? Are primary qualities any more amenable to saying or knowing than secondary? To say they are, is to come up against Berkeley's arguments. But then are tertiary qualities, the values, in any worse position? The transcendentals?

November 6

There is nothing amiss in understanding the various modes in terms of the other modes, since all definition, explanation, and the like must start outside a given thing and deal with it in alien terms. But when we ask after the real constitution of a being and find that it has the other modes ingredient in it, we seem to risk losing the being entirely. And this is what happens in Hegel and Whitehead. For both, each being has ingredient in it whatever there be, and is indeed the localization of all else. But if all else is itself a localization there is nothing to localize. Consequently, both Hegel and Whitehead make an implicit exception for the Absolute or God; there are more than unifications, localizations, functions of other entities. But a philosophical system should not make special dispensations. If it does there is either no explanation permitted of the ultimate and indispensable element so that the whole rests on an unintelligible, or there are two types of explanation and we are left with a problem of combining or uniting or relating the two so as to have a single systematic account.

The real enters into the constitution of all beings; but the beings are more than the solidification of the prehensions of all things—even when "all things" is allowed to embrace (as it apparently does not with Whitehead) the being of God, extension, and the whole realm of the Ideal. Each being has its characteristic "unity" (to speak in the language of the divine); its characteristic "structure" (to speak Ideally); its characteristic "dynamics" (to speak Existentially); and its characteristic "substantiality" (to speak in the language of the Actual). In and of itself it is distinctive, and we can understand that distinctiveness from various perspectives. If we wish to say what it is in-itself, we must show how the other modes are abstractions from it (and in turn must show how it is an abstraction from them) and that the patterns which those other modes exemplify always leave over a domain of being which the others fill out in a way that the patterns do not permit us to know antecedently. Consequently, we can say that the being of each of the modes is to be found in the a posteriori production of features for which no other modes, as ingredient in them or as outside them, severally or together, can account for. Each of the four modes of being has features which are additional to those we can derive by remaining within the frame provided by the other modes. But, also, each of the modes is a component in and a factor operating to make other modes a component in the rest. The Ideal for example is a component in God, and also a factor in God making possible the ingredience of Actuality and Existence.

If we wish to start from experience to get to God, we must first distinguish the various loci of experience—individual actualities, the human realm (made up of actualities and Existence, but conventionalized), the background of the human realm (in which Ideality, Existence and God are intertwined). In each of these we will find that God is a component and a power making possible the presence of other modes.

God is in actualities A] as the principle of unity enabling them to other all else, but not God himself. (As othering all else, each is a kind of representative of God; as othering God, each is a private being with features additional to those which the othering of all else enables it to have.) B] As the power which enables actualities to possess universals; C] as the power which enables actualities to hold themselves over against the rest of Existence, by possessing their own borders. (4.17 of the *Modes* is then not correct; it has reference to man as in the human realm; the role of God in indirect testimony is that of a being involved in the real constitution of a being in the present.) God is also one who preserves the past of the human realm, made up of man and Existence, and who makes for a relevant futurity of the human realm. He also has a relation to man and Ideality as constituting a political whole, by dictating that the realizable be realized over the course of time, and by seeing to it that the values that are lost are not only inherited, but also determine what ought to be done in the future—a fact expressed in the veneration of heroes, etc. God also has a function in keeping man, Existence, and Ideality together by providing them with an exterior power. In addition, God must be derivable from Ideality as the principle which enables it to be divisible in time (?), and as the power which enables it to be prescriptive and providential (?). Also God must be derivable from Existence as the principle which enables it to have an essence, and as the power which enables Existence to be temporally present. God is to be found in the background of commensensical experience also, as the unity of the Existence and Ideality there, as their Other, and as the power which makes them applicable to one another and to Actuality (?). And He must be found in any analysis of the nature of each of the modes, when we engage in a systematic understanding of them; this is a more refined way of dealing with Him as encountered in experience, but it is also one which involves the use of neutral terms of a categorial character, telling us how He stands apart, how He functions, and what His internal nature and role may be. Once, e.g., we see that man in his privacy is the other of God (and thus the other of himself as othering actualities and Existence and Ideality), we can go on to talk about that other in the neutral terms of philosophy.

What and how is God in the world of common sense? This world is primarily a human realm, a realm in which man and Existence are intertwined. God is to be found there as the guarantee of its continuance by virtue of the prospect which He allows the present to define, and as the guarantee of its continuity by virtue of the inheritance of the past. The continuance and continuity are like history's, but are also distinct from it, for they involve a reference to myth on the one hand, and to a tradition on the other, whereas history refers to an ultimate Ideal and an endless past. Common sense is a narrowed, restricted, qualified domain in which inheritances and opportunities are at once enriched and confined.

In addition to the foregoing, it is necessary to deal with the way in which men and other actualities (and also the other modes) are ingredient in God. Since they are not ingredient in Him in their concreteness they cannot so far provide a knowledge of Him. But there is a kind of localization He provides for them, so that they can, as it were, "prove" themselves by starting with themselves as in Him. Each being must be in the others, and as in the others must stand over against itself, be alienated from itself. Man, so far as he feels that he himself is not yet fully in-himself, that he is not merely incomplete in lacking other beings but is not wholly in possession of all that is himself, is aware of his presence in other modes.

God also is effective here and now, and one should be able to become aware of Him not only as a principle and a power inside oneself, and as the being in which one is somehow preserved, but as a being who is now making a difference to oneself, altering the course of one's life and meaning. This is the sense of God which seems to interest most religious men; it is the sense of God which is at the focus of the prophetic utterances; it is why theologians insist on the priority of revelation and grace, for these refer to a God who comes to us before we are able to come to Him. Yet this is perhaps one of the hardest ideas to grasp, since it involves a consideration of a causality which is "transcendental"—something like Kant's causality, expressive of freedom. The action of God could be viewed as an action in the actualities, or as an action which gives the actualities a new context involving them in new adventures and meanings. But the second is not actually an effective operation by God on actualities; it is an effectiveness of God, but one which allows the actualities to continue to function in- and of-themselves, untouched by Him. Is this all that we can have?

It is the view of those who cling to revelation and grace and guidance and prophesy, etc., that God not merely enters into the constitution of actual entities, but effectively operates on those entities (understood as already substantial apart from him). How is this possible, what is it like? In connection with history I have said that God releases the present historic occurrence from the burden of its accumulated past. But then should we not go on and speak of the actuality as apart from Existence, as outside the human realm or history, and thus as a being whose freedom is guaranteed by allowing the actuality to escape from the burden of the domination of the Ideal which enabled the actuality to be intelligible and valuational (and from the domination of Existence which enabled it to be part of one cosmic contemporary whole)?

God enables an actuality, which is part of one intelligible totality and one cosmos, to free itself from these constraints so as to act freshly at the next moment with respect to the Ideal and Existence. The actuality is a distinctive substance which was enabled to possess the Ideal and Existence as universals and boundaries. These, however, subjugated it, framed it inside their own being. The actuality, while it remained an individual, was also caught in a context beyond. In order to act as a distinctive individual it has to be freed from the restraints of the Ideal and Existence. God's presence, then, is felt in the power of the individual to be over against all else as substantial, individual, private, laying hold of the Ideal and Existence in a new way, a way which will require the action of God to enable the actuality, at the next moment, to possess the Ideal in the form of a universal and Existence in the form of a vital, bounded fragment (of all Existence).

The actuality acts freely on its own, but its freedom is made possible by God's detaching the actuality from the Ideal which lies outside, and from the Existence which lies beyond its borders. When Existence moves on it breaks through the borders of the actuality, and there is always the question of what is left over. We are forced to say with Descartes and Whitehead that there is nothing left over and that there must be a new being, either self-created (with Whitehead) or divinely created (with Descartes), or we must recognize that the Actuality retains some being of its own and is therefore enabled to lay hold onto Existence (and Ideality) in a new way. I accept this last alternative. The Existence which is part of an actuality is now one with the whole of Existence; there is a divinely bestowed capacity in the actuality which permeates a portion of the Existence and comes to a rest in the solidification of a part of Existence at the same time that the Ideal is realized. It is not that God introduces a freedom into the actuality, but only that He releases the actuality from the compulsive power of Existence, allows it to assert the power which it has in-itself. When and as the boundary which Existence breaks down is lost, the actuality is enabled to lay hold of a part of Existence, and is helped by God to hold this off from the rest of Existence.

God, who enables the actuality to bound off Existence and thus to possess a part of it, also enables the actuality to spread into the Existence which is now external to it, and there carve out a portion. Without Him, the actuality would be burdened by having had the boundary, even though this had been pierced by Existence in its movement on toward the future. The movement of Existence would pull the actuality along, were it not that God allows that actuality to maintain itself, to have its own being expressed as a power which realizes the Ideal in the matrix of Existence. What kind of power is it? It is the actuality as sitting inside its border, or (since essence seems to signify the Ideal) it is privacy of the actuality as dynamic, as centered in the actuality and thus defying the orientation provided by Existence as such.

We approach God through concepts, through experience, through revelation, and through value; the approaches involve primary stress on Actuality, Existence, God, and Ideality respectively. The reference to the freedom of the actuality came about because we were trying to find a meaning of revelation apart from some particular religion. And what has now been concluded is that the action of God, as it were, frees the actuality from the pressure of the boundary which it adopted. The Existence itself would destroy the boundary, the actuality by itself is entirely without a boundary, but because of God the actuality acts on Existence within the limits of a boundary. The latter limits are then and there being utilized and eventually will be specified as the actual restrictive boundary of a present Actuality.

God functions, as it were, to allow the alienated boundary, a boundary which the Existence has pierced and thus made external to the actuality (thereby making the actuality's Existence no longer its private exclusive possession), to be the limit of the concentration of the freedom of the actuality as it reaches beyond that point to realize the Ideal, and incidentally possess a portion of Existence as its own. This view seems to be quite close to what Bonaventure deals with under the expression "gifts of the Holy Ghost" which fit the soul for a higher state, i.e., liberates it from its bonds and "fortifies it with resources necessary for actual advance" (Gilson, St. Bonaventure, p. 110).

The encounter with God is an encounter where He is; the awareness of God as in oneself, either as a constituent or as a "gift," is an awareness of oneself as offering an encounter. Granted that there is such an awareness, we ought then to speak of the various modes as not only being encountered, but as suffering and responding to the shock of an encountering being. We here are on the verge of jeopardizing knowledge, for if the encountering being affects that which is encountered, we have an alteration in what we have arrived at through concepts. We can avoid this consequence. What is altered is not the concept with which we approach the encountered object, but ourselves as possessing the concept. The encountered object adds to and supports the concept, at the same time that it suffers from, is made to be in interplay with the encountering being who possesses the concept and moves outside the concept to encounter the object.

Bonaventure thinks of knowledge as a stage which presupposes faith, or in my terms, thinks that revelation is presupposed by thought (and presumably that value and experience lie somewhere in between these two, the one answering to something like theology and the other to something like the gift of knowledge). But one can with equal justice turn this situation around. Each mode of apprehension has a priority and makes possible the completion of the others. The insistence on faith as prior to knowledge is but the selection of one situation, one in which revelation or grace precedes cognition. But if we start with cognition we can find inside its area possible centers of concentration which one can eventually see are the loci of revelation, etc. This is apparently the position which Spinoza and Leibnitz take. (Descartes might be said to have presupposed a kind of faith in his theory that the very idea of God and of certainty are implanted in us.)

Again following the lead of Bonaventure, we can say that we can have a grasp either of God's existence, of God's perfection, or of God's multiplicity. Our problem would be to bring these all together and then within that unity which is God himself, known as the other of ourselves in our ultimate privacy. The existence of God is apprehended as the archetype, the being of the excellent; the perfection is apprehended as primary cause or ground; the multiplicity is apprehended as that which is preserved and then that which guarantees our persistence and cherishing. These are not altogether parallel with Bonaventure's grasp of God's existence as archetype, cause, and immediate, but there are some close similarities.

November 7

The problem of how the various modes affect actualities was dealt with, yesterday, too much from the perspective of what was decided in relation to history. Looking at the matter afresh it would seem to be the case that the action of God on actuality is to enable it to deal with both the Ideal and Existence, the one enabling actuality to be part of a temporal world, the other enabling actuality to be a realized localized factuality. The actuality is released by God from its present localization and its present realization of the Ideal and is thus open to localize and realize again. We need not make any reference to boundaries and we must take account of the mode of Ideality.

Actualities are also affected by the Ideal and by Existence. The Ideal enables an actuality to take account of both God and Existence, by allowing it to express its unity over an extended region, and to have its dynamic nature unified. Existence enables the actuality to take account of both God and the Ideal, the one enabling the actuality to face prescriptive possibilities, the other enabling it to have an excellence. If we take all these effects together we have the actuality enabled to face all three modes afresh, and being enabled to do so by all the modes themselves, each one allowing the actuality to face the other two afresh.

The question that remains is what is the being which is able to act in these various ways? Having been loosened from the various modes by one another, it remains an amorphous area so far as definiteness is determined by other modes outside it. But in-itself it is individual, private, distinctive; it lays hold of these exterior modes in a distinctive way. The detachment of the modes from it thus does not stand in the way of its having a distinctive relation to them as apart from it.

Treated in this way we are able to reconcile Aristotle with Whitehead. What would be prehended would be the various modes, and they would be particularized as a unity, features, and boundary. The particularizations would be separated, allowed to be merely factual, while the various modes are sundered from the actuality by one another, leaving behind the actuality as a substance in- and of-itself, with a distinctive "subjective aim" toward the various modes. This reconciliation recognizes that there are three kinds of things which are prehended. It also denies that what is prehended constitutes the very being of the actual entity. Instead, it says that the entity is a particularization of them in the shape of a private unity, a possessed boundary, and a particular set of features. It recognizes that a being is enabled to function at a new moment because it is acted on by the various modes and sees that the substantiality of the actual being is left over in the form of a distinctive way of being related to those modes as outside it. Whitehead did not see that there were three kinds of things prehended, though he does seem to recognize two, omitting "extension" apparently. He affirms that what is prehended constitutes the very being of the actuality but does not see the need to free an actuality of its particularizations. He thus has no substantial being left to act. Aristotle on the other hand does not have a theory of prehensions and has his substantial being acting in a distinctive way only with respect to the Ideal, which could be said to be particularized as a region of extension and to be ennobled in the form of God, all three having some capacity to be and act independently.

There must be analogous influences, freeing, and recoveries in connection with the other three modes. In connection with God we must be able to say that He, having adopted the other three modes to make a maximum totality in Himself, must be free to face those modes again. But to be so free they must work on one another, thereby releasing them and incidentally allowing Him to be free to vitalize and internalize them in new ways.

Existence and Ideality together, Existence and Actuality together, Actuality and Ideality together must be free from God by the respective actions of actualities, Ideality and Existence. The most interesting case is the first. Men must be able to act on God in such a way as to enable the concretionalized Existence and Ideality in Him to stand apart from Him, thereby enabling Him to realize them in a new way. What is the nature of our encounter with Him? He must answer to our inferences, our work and faith, and thus be a carrier of concepts, a resistant being, and a correlative to our attitudes. He is not thereby made threefold; different avenues to His being are provided by these different approaches. He is encountered as a substantial, impenetrable, responsive being. (There is a reciprocal triadicity to be found in connection with the encounter of actualities by God. He engages in divine understanding, grace, and love, and these are three avenues by which He is enabled to confront the actualities as substantial realities to be freed from the restraints of the Ideal and Existence. He does not act on the actualities in these three ways, but acts to reach them; and He must have them as substantial, impenetrable, responsible beings when He does so.)

We should also say that the Ideal needs to be freed from the restraints which it acquires by adopting the various modes, and that the modes severally act on it to free it from the other modes. The work of actualities, for example, should be to free the Ideal from the restraints which it has acquired by its adoption of God and Existence. God gave the Ideal a providential use, and Existence gave it a cosmic field of operation; to be itself to-itself it needs the action of Actuality, which acknowledges it to have a being of its own, with its own internal structure. The acknowledgment must involve a real freeing of the other two modes from it.

How can Actuality act on the Ideal? Is it not in the way in which the Actuality uses it, the kind of relation Actuality has to the Ideal, which enables the Ideal to function in a way it could not otherwise? But what relation can a man have to the Ideal which frees it from God and Existence? It must be one which focuses on the Ideal as over against these. Must we not say the same thing with respect to God? Man's encounter with Him is a way of facing Him as focalized away from the others. Must we not say the same thing with respect to Existence? But then is there a real separation off from the other modes?

At one and the same time I seem to be saying that there is a kind of theoretical focusing, or alternatively an abstracting of a focal point, and on the other hand a genuine purging, a true freeing of a mode from the other two. The former way of speaking makes sense when we speak of the modes other than Actuality; the latter, when we speak of the freeing of actualities. Is this due to the fact that actualities act in time and seem to be restrained rather than enhanced by the presence of other modes in them? Or is the focalization a kind of effective action? If so, how can this be? How can a man exert a power on other modes, distinct in being and at a distance from himself, so that the mode is able to act in ways it could not before? Man functions as a representative actuality, i.e., only as taking a role, and not in his intrinsic powers. How can he then have the power to free another mode from two other modes, restrictive on that other mode?

November 8

Each mode of being helps another to be itself by freeing it from the restraints of the other two modes and also, at the same time, and indeed as part of the very act, by endowing the entity with an additional power. Each endows the others with some virtue which enables them to stand free of two other modes and thus act on them in new ways. The Ideal gives an actuality a renewed purpose and, in the case of man, an obligation; Existence gives it a new set of relations; God gives it a deeper privacy so that it can act with greater authenticity. Since each of these modes enables the actuality to be free with respect to the others, all three must be said to be active on it, giving it privacy, purpose, and relations, at the same time that they release it from previous conditioning.

Actualities, particularly in the shape of man, must act on other modes, then, to enable these to be free from the restraints of two others and at the same time to benefit from the actuality in some respect. What kind of action is this? It is not physical and it is not, as is suggested in the *Modes* (in the section on the "Creative Enterprise" in the chapter on Existence), epistemological. There must be a real action of actualities on the other modes, particularly if man gives God an opportunity to act on him as having actualized possibilities, and as having encapsulated a part of Existence. The work they do in the body of others is a continuation of what they are doing in-themselves. God acts in man by intensifying his privacies only so far as He is receptive of man's presence in Himself as a preserver. And conversely, man acts on God by giving Him focal points at the same time that he is receptive of Him. And when each acts on the other he finds the other resistant, thereby enabling each to be encountered.

November 10

Each mode encounters the other as subjugated by the remaining two. Its act on that which is resisting it, by virtue of the subjugation of the other two, involves a release from those others. This which it encounters is enabled by the encountering being to recover a more substantial role, to be itself more than it was. The encountering being overcomes, as it were, the resistance of the encountered being so far as this is defined by other modes, and intensifies the status of that encountered being as something in- and of-itself. In connection with man the act of God is to intensify his privacy and thereby enable him to come to new grips with the Ideal and Existence, which are dislocated through that act of God. God encounters the man as qualified by the Ideal and Existence and acts to release him; there is still a residuum of resistant being to the man, for as private he offers the act of God an unbreakable barrier. The encountering of man is then the encountering of a privacy which is qualified by two other modes, and the act of encountering the private being is also the act of releasing it from the qualifications, so that the encounter ends by being more perfect, facing the unqualified mode of being, whereas it began by facing it as qualified by other modes.

The Ideal and Existence both must work on man in a way similar to that in which God does. They must encounter him as an actuality and as qualified by two other modes; the encounter must begin with the man as qualified and end with him as purged and irreducible. The Ideal must leave him as a being of purpose or need, and Existence must leave him as a being in the present.

When we turn to the encounter of God by man we must have

analogous results. God must be encountered as qualified by the Ideal and Existence, and must be freed by man from those qualifications, leaving God to be encountered in His depth as an ultimate irreducible finality. It seems odd, though, to speak of man freeing God. Also in what sense, distinct from that characteristic of man, do the Ideal and Existence effect God? Man adopts the universal, specifies it; God accepts the status of a being of value, perfect in His comprehensiveness. Man acknowledges a border from, whereas God accepts the pluralization of Existence so as to enable Him to be indefinitely divisible within Himself. Man, by attending to God as a supreme being, forces Him to focus on man and thereby separate Himself off from the Ideal and Existence, and, so far, to be enabled to face the Ideal and Existence again.

Man in his anguish begs for God's attention. The cry "why hast thou forsaken me" is an implicit persistent accompaniment of prayer; it is the very substance of the prayer and asks for the recovery of God as the being who is free of the other modes but who will use the other modes as agencies, providential and cosmic, to make possible the fulfillment of man's promise.

Man must do a similar thing to the Ideal and to Existence. Each must be encountered as qualified by the other and by God, and man in encountering each must face it as so qualified, and end with it as in-itself. The Ideal as qualified is insistent and temporally oriented; Existence as qualified is unified and directional. Man must get the Ideal as in-itself, a sheer domain of possibility capable of being specified by the others; and he must get Existence by itself as a sheer divisive extensionality. (The least clear, surprisingly enough, of these modes is Ideality. What is this in- and of-itself?)

The actions in all cases must be ontological, below the measuring and formulations of the various sciences. They involve adjustments of the various modes to one another, and involve a reconstituting of a cosmic whole at every moment.

November 11

Instead of saying that the inescapable possibility is the Good, we could say that there is a single Ideality which is related to the other modes, and is actually pluralized by actualities. The pluralization which the actualities provide does not do justice to the needs of that Ideal to be complete. There is no "*p* or not *p*" in the Ideal, not even as linked together, unless this be understood not to permit of their having distinctive borders. When the Ideal is realized, it is realized as "*p*" or as "not *p*," and one of these forms does more justice to the Ideal than the other. It is not that there is a realization of one of the items or even a tearing of it out of its linked context, but rather that there is no genuine distinctiveness until the actualization.

Still, it is the case that the Ideal, like every other mode, must have plurality within it. This is a plurality of intensities rather than of distinct items. Still, the intensities must have some integrity, otherwise there would be no genuine plurality. However, the intensities as in the Ideal are not faint images of the actualizations which will be achieved through the realization of the Ideal by actualities.

What is the Ideal like in and of itself? If we look to the Idealists to ask what the Absolute is like, or to the East and ask about Nirvana, we are confronted with negations. But negations could just as readily be provided for the other modes of being—privacy as merely an unknowable in itself, extension as a kind of surd, God as the absconding. Yet we do know these other modes and can characterize them. The Ideal should be understandable to the same degree. We should show too how it is qualified by God, Existence, and Actuality. Is it that the Ideal is made normative by being held apart from the other modes by God, that He gives it an obligating or prescriptive role, allowing it to be a standard, and allowing it to function in history as the possibility which is to be realized? These seem though to be characterizations which do not express what the Ideal is as internally qualified. Must we not say that the Ideal, as affected by God, becomes a unitary value; as affected by Actuality, a standard which is indeterminate; as affected by Existence, a future, i.e., directed backward? When men are obligated, do they encounter the Ideal and thereby free it from the value and futurity it had, enabling it to engage in new accommodations with respect to God and Existence?

There is much that is unclear here.

November 29

On the cosmological side, where the various modes come together, we can have a progressive intensification of the unity constituted by the modes. Mode *a* can come together with mode *b*, and this may make a unity which in turn interplays with the rest of *b*. We have something like this in history. We start with the human realm as the product of man and nature, and then have this interplay with a nature which is still outside. The result is that the space, time, etc., of history includes the space of the human realm as an abstractable subdivision. 1] But how does such an idea fit with the notion that the common-sense world is real, but muddled? 2] May the historic world itself interplay with a further portion of nature, or with some other mode of being, to constitute still another space? 3] Does not some complete cosmological space or field encompass all subordinate domains such as history, religion, etc., so far as these are defined as involving the interplay of only two modes? 4] Are the roots of history to be found in men, or in a human realm, interplaying with nature? If the latter, it seems to be the case that history is not rooted in the ontological but in the cosmological, or rather a subdivision of this.

1] What is nature if the world of common sense is the locus of all the modes? Must it not instead be one of the modes (Existence) correlative with the common-sense world? Nature in and of itself would be what a scientist might come to know by extending the abstractions derived from the common-sense world, were it not for the fact that the scientific world is one constructed for the purpose of controlling and making intelligible the commonsensical world. Consequently, we must say that nature is the object of an entirely different discipline, speculative science, the philosophy of nature, etc. This serves as a kind of corrective to the abstraction taken from common sense. A scientific system, which is to be contrasted with the particular formulae, etc., of science, is to be thought of as qualifying the scientific formulae derived from and concerned with common sense, to make them have an orientation in nature outside common sense.

The real world of cosmology is the outcome of similar corrections of the abstractions of perceptions, events, and values from common sense, by the modes of Actuality, Existence, and Ideality, respectively, as learned through categorization, art, and mathematics. The real world is not merely common sense clarified, but common sense extended and rectified by ontological categories, the insight of art, and the scientific use of mathematics. The outcome of these is to be expressed in the language of common sense, made technical by virtue of the consideration given to the rectifications provided by the other modes of being.

History involves a partial rectification, and then with respect not to the isolated abstractions that could be derived from common sense, but with respect to common sense taken as a unit. The space of common sense is related to the space of history as a subdivision within a more cosmically determined space. But it is not the space of an ultimate reality if by ultimate reality we mean what is produced by the analysis of common sense and the subsequent integration of the result.

2] The historic world may itself interplay with nature and other modes to constitute another kind of reality, which is perhaps what is being considered by those who take a religious, ethical, practical, or individual attitude toward history.

3] The entire cosmological domain includes on a primary level the strands rectified and reunited in accordance with the discussion in *1*. So far as there are combinations of only some of the items constituting this domain we have the cosmological domain as more inclusive. But it is the case that the historic, etc., results from more than a combination of two modes; there is an interplay first with only portions of the two modes to constitute a human realm, and a consequent interplay with nature to constitute the historic, thereby making the nature of the historic domain have an intensity and nature denied to the cosmoligical whole, (even though this has four modes). What includes the historic, etc., is the most intensive unification of the historic, etc., with larger and larger areas of the various modes. This interplay is evidently consequent on the achievement of the domains of history, etc., so that the enriched cosmological whole of all the modes is one which is built up.

History, which is oriented toward the world of common sense, is a kind of reciprocal to a scientific system. The latter rectifies the abstract strand of common sense by what is formulated about nature; the former rectifies the being of nature by the being of the world of common sense (and to a lesser degree, conversely). The scientific approach depends on the ontological separation of common sense and nature; the historic depends on their interplay. The one extends an idea to encompass a strand, the other produces a "cosmological unit" to replace the commonsensical one, by using common sense to represent actuality. Consequently, we could look outside the historic for modes of being which would provide principles of rectification of what could be taken out of the historic as a set of strands. Does this not mean that in some way the historic is not ultimately real, and that to find out the ultimate cosmological reality one must take the intensive product of the juncture of common sense with all other modes, then rectify the abstractions from these by a consideration of the nature of the modes as lying outside the juncture?

4] The roots of history are found in men as already parts of the human realm, and also in nature as over against that realm, but to be united with it. History is in root, then, cosmological, where "cosmological" means some kind of togetherness of the modes rather than the modes severally.

The evaluation of history through a consideration of universal and normative principles is but a special case of the rectification of the historic through the introduction of other modes, except that we here have the historic accepted as a datum. It is as if we were to take the realm of nature known to a speculative scientist and then evaluated the realm of common sense in terms of it, instead of (as one could) trying to make a unity out of a strand, taken from common sense, and the speculative scientific account. If we did for history what we do in science we would take the Ideal, not to measure history, but to provide a principle for rectifying the values which one could abstract from history. If we did this we would get to know the real as having one dimension which was value, but a value that had an intensive moment in history and an Ideal component outside. We would have the value as constituting an actuality, so far as we were in the common-sense world, or as constituting a joint product of an actuality and Existence, so far as we were in history. We would be coming to know the intrinsic value of the historic world. When we impose the Ideal on history we learn instead how history stands up in terms of some standard outside it, or which it will eventually exemplify.

If the clarified commonsensical object is an actual substance, though one which shows the effects of other modes, the clarified historical object (i.e., one which has had its strands distinguished and then unified under the constraint of a grasp of the modes exterior to the historic) must give us the reality of a being as forming a "cosmological unity" with other modes. We learn then what the reality of the "one" for the modes is, by engaging in the various disciplines (history, politics, etc.) and purifying the result through a grasp of the nature of the modes as imposing demands of coherence and elegance, etc., on what we learn from those disciplines.

We need a purification of common sense in order to know what Actuality is as such. We ought to have similar problems of clarification with respect to the other modes. We must clarify what we experience; even though this experience is not overlaid with conventions, it is faced by us with emotion, etc. The experienced, when purged, gives us each of the modes as it is in-itself. But we do not get what the modes are in inter-relationship until we abstract from history, politics, religious institutions, and technology. These various enterprises involve a combination of modes, but in an unclarified form.

If the common-sense object clarified is interpreted to be a being in a state of togetherness with other modes (a togetherness which involves a stress on separateness), it cannot be that entity which enters into the relation of another correlative type of togetherness—which is what seems to be required in history. On the other hand, if the common-sense object is the thing-in-itself, once the common-sense object has been clarified and its strands properly synthesized, this object should be able to enter not only into history, but into the domains of politics, religious institutions, and technology, as the beings which helps constitute these domains with the aid of other modes. But since there are many ways in which a being can be together, there should also be a plurality of ways in which the common-sense object can become part of a world with some other mode. There should, for example, be a togetherness of the common-sense object with Existence in which the two merge, in which they are separate, in which they imply one another, and in which they cause one another. Merging seems to be characteristic of the historic domain (and of the artistic too?); but what are they as separate, implicative, and dynamic? Is it as the here and beyond, as the mutually incomplete, and as endeavoring to be complete? But what kind of domains do they then constitute? Experience, Understanding, Opposition? But these are not domains.

The question that remains is what kind of domain, what fields are constituted by beings in various relations of togetherness, other than merging. Does separateness give us the beings as possessed of rights or values; does implication give us the beings as having affiliations of a rational sort; does dynamic interplay give us the contingent world of observation? None of these seem to go as deep as they ought to, if we are to find correspondences to history or to a church.

November 30

If it is man in the human realm who enters into history, then he is already part of a "cosmological" setting, i.e. he is already one who is to be understood as a togetherness of two or more modes. We do not have any further way of intensifying this togetherness beyond history, so far as we are concerned with a public unity of man and nature. We can think of going beyond history in art (or in a myth regarding the role of nature in the determination of the meaning of history) but I think it is more correct to say that we have a maximum intensification of a togetherness of man and nature in history, and that this intensified portion is then related in a rather thin way to the rest of Existence. But we ought also to say that there is an intensification which the human realm receives when it is integrated with the Ideal to constitute a unit of civilization, or a political whole, and another intensification which it receives when it is integrated with God. Both of these integrations will be partial, leaving over the Ideal and God with which the results are to be connected in a thin way.

What we have then is a cosmological outcome in four dimensions, each one of which involves a partial integration of two modes in such a way as to make for an intensive togetherness, which is still to be related to a mode beyond. The cosmological result is thus no simple juncture of the modes, but a juncture resulting in an intensification of the togetherness (of parts of modes) which is then to be in a simple juncture with the remaining modes. (We ought to say that just as there is a portion of Existence which is left out of history, so there is a portion of man—even public man in the sense of being part of a political whole—which is left out, and that the complete togetherness of the two modes requires the intensified unity which is achieved in history, to be related to man and nature as not yet caught in history.)

The foregoing discussion would indicate that the common-sense man and his world is a terminal one, one which is essentially a world of actualities, whereas the human realm is one which involves a mixture with nature. But the common-sense world includes institutions, and involves some encapsulation of an external nature. Are the institutions and the nature here qualifications of real objects, whereas in the human realm there is a genuinely new synthesis in which nature and man play concordant roles?

December 1

The human realm differs from the world of common sense in that it is only partly broken up into enclaves, since it in fact embraces all mankind. It does not refer to that which is experienceable, but only to that which is primarily available for use and consideration in the present. It does not allow for orientations outside man, since it is primarily man in interrelation, and incidentally man with things or an achieved power, which defines its range and meaning. Both the common-sense realm and the human realm are overlaid with socialized meanings; a purging of those meanings does not give us actualities as such, but actualities as interrelated, and this through the help of other modes. To find the things-in-themselves and particularly these as mere actualities, requires the separation out of the items as related, so that we can deal with them by themselves; but this approach first requires that we get rid of conventional elements.

In politics and religion there is a use of the human realm similar to that characteristic of history; the human realm is made to interplay with items which are already partly incorporated in it, but there is always an element left over which owes its being to man in-himself and

nature in-itself. This precludes the full intensification of the togetherness of man with the mode. What we have, then, is a partial intensification, and this in a limited area of the togetherness of man and a world
beyond.

It is not altogether correct, then, to say of the coming to be of history
that it involves the utilization of man as in-himself with nature in-
itself; there is never a recovery of the human realm as outside nature
with which it will interplay to constitute a history.

December 3

The completion of man involves the intensification of the togetherness of himself with other modes. He can succeed in doing this
only through the agency of knowledge. The other modes also engage in
some act of covering the distance between them. The Ideal, by virtue of
its encompassment or reduction of man to the status of an instance,
covers the distance in a way which is the reciprocal of knowledge. In
the case of Existence the spread goes from man but he can encompass
only part of Existence to give him political and historical worlds. In the
case of God there is a movement from beyond, but this goes only part of
the way, awaiting something on the part of man to define the place
where God is to come—in a "cleansed inward parts," purged individual;
in a "love your neighbor," accepted individual; in one who has done
good works, in a community; in a church—depending on the religion.

In knowledge we cover the distance by concept; in value, by subordinating all else; in action we do it by possession; and in religion we
do it by acceptance. If we take the position of the divine we can see how
it enters into the other spheres in a way similar to that in which it enters
into the being of man and saves him—in knowledge it gives certainty,
in value it gives faith, in nature it gives the force that makes for
righteousness. And in bestowing these features in different areas it demands of the recipient either that he deny himself, that he be transposed,
that he be transformed, or that he be enriched.

When we start from ourselves we have knowledge as investigation,
the Ideal as obligating, Existence as a challenge, and God as an other.
We can function for the other modes somewhat as the Ideal or God
functions for us, or we can make use of Existence and thus adopt the
other modes in part. Similarly, we can speak of the Ideal as requiring
a submission to reason, to roles, to historic outcomes, and to providence,
and have it also function with respect to other modes somewhat as
actuality, Existence, and God do—i.e., by seeing itself applied to them,

by becoming identified with a part, or by arriving at the place where they are. We can, similarly, speak of Existence as having a cognitive role in plans, as functioning in technology, as being caught in works of art, as history, and as a Church. And it must be able to act as actualities, Ideality, and God do, and thus reach out to all, in the sense of applying to all, or subordinating all, or meeting all. Finally God comes down to give certainty, faith, control, and salvation, the latter involving the overcoming of futility and worthlessness. And God, too, must be thought to have roles similar to the Actual, Existence, and the Ideal, and thus to apply to all, to possess some, and to subordinate all.

The failures are to be identified as scepticism, despair or guilt, tragedy, and worthlessness. We need a certainty in knowledge against scepticism, a confidence against despair, a self-knowledge against tragedy, and acceptance or love against worthlessness.

We can apply knowledge to the certainty which God provides, and can do this by treating it as a category, a possibility, as a commitment, and as an object. We can take the faith God provides and make it affect commitment, providence, the outcome of history, and God's intent. Existence can take divinely controlled nature as determining man's adjustment, the nature of beauty, the excellence of a church, and God's bounty.

The above are jumbled together and should be sorted out.

	Man reaching out cosmically through	Man made to submit	Man uniting with	Man being met by
Actuality	Yields: Categorical knowledge	Obligation	Community	Love
Ideal	Subordinating logic or formal language	Commitment	Purpose	Providence
Existence	Inquiry partly controlled by experience	Adjustment	History	Sustainment
God	Divinely bestowed certainty	Faith	Empowered	Salvation

Attending to God, we see then that He gives certainty in the realm of knowledge when man's reaching out to God is carried through by

God, that He grounds faith so far as man submits to a kind of subordination by God; that He empowers man so far as man unites with God, and that He saves man by meeting him. Now man allows God to meet him at different places, depending on what man does to make himself worthy of God's meeting. Different religions insist on different kinds of preparation, from the most private and secret to the most communally defined, and they vary as to just what happens to man as a consequence —he is annihilated, enriched, etc. And one can go on to apply man's own principles to the above, and conversely. Thus human categorial knowledge can be used to evaluate the certainty provided by God, the nature of faith, etc. Conversely, faith, salvation, etc., can be used to redefine the meaning of man's categorial knowledge, his community, the love he has, etc. The certainty God bestows, can be bestowed only after man has acquired some knowledge by himself, when he has a knowledge through a church, etc.

December 4

Each mode of being awaits, enters into, interplays with, and encounters the others. We have, therefore, three times four ways in which the modes make a difference to man. And these must be multiplied by three to take care of the fact that they have to do with man's mind, body, person, and will. Attending only to God in relation to man we have 4 × 4 cases to consider, which can be summarized in the table:

I

God	mind	body	person	will
awaits	reverence	science	worship	submission
enters	justifies	dignifies	gives worth	grace
interplays	guides	good work	love	humility
encounters	certainty	sustains	saves	accepts

II

Man	as mind	as body	as person	as will
awaits	enlightenment	agent	saves?	prayer
enters	truth?	dedication?	immortality	prayer
interplays	proof?	self-discovery	priest	prayer
encounters	being?	commanded	other	prophetic instruction

Not only are the designations in the second table unsatisfactory, but man is treated as fourfold in relation to God as one, whereas in the previous table it was God as one who was related to man as fourfold. One ought to have a table in which man as one is related to God as fourfold; such a table would match the first table.

Since a mode can await another while that other enters into it—or more compendiously, since any type of relation of one mode to another can be met by any type of relation of that other to the first, we have a great number of relations making up the joint togetherness of a pair of modes. In general it can be said that any being is, from the perspective of another, something quite different from what it is according to itself. In the case of human beings we are conscious of ourselves, but what others note are our bodies, tones, pasts, and the like, of which we often are not aware. On the whole what we know of ourselves is what is not known by others, and what they know of us we do not know of ourselves; it is this which makes for difficulty in communication and in human interrelations. We, as it were, await the others, or enter into them from our perspective, while they enter into us, or await us. There are many intermediate stages, and the waiting and entering can be on the one side with respect to the mind, whereas the other side engages in them with respect to the body, or some other aspect.

We can see a difference between mind, body, person, and will in man, not only by virtue of what we see him do, but because we can approach him as most receptive to the Ideal, Actuality, God, or Existence. But then we ought to be able to make fourfold distinctions in each of the modes, for each can be dealt with in terms of three other modes, and in terms of its own pluralities. But if we do take account of all these we will multiply our tables greatly. Remaining with God and man, we have to multiply table I four times to accommodate God as awaiting, etc., in each of his fourfold differentiated features; and we must split up table II four times to have man await, etc., as mind, body, etc., God as fourfold. As table II now is, God is awaited by man (who takes the position of mind, body, etc.) but without any differentiation as to just what God's fourfold nature is like. Thus, in speaking of man as mind encountering God, we get God as Being. But if man as mind, encountered God as mind, Being would be spiritual being; if God were encountered as something like body, the Being would be Brute being; if God were encountered as a kind of person, it would be Personal Being; and if God were encountered as an oppositional will, it would be an Insistent Being.

Taking account of God and man only, we get sixteen distinctions in table I to be multiplied four times, and sixteen in table II to be multiplied four times, or 128 altogether. Since the results of each can be matched with the others in all possible ways, we have 64×64 conjunctions or forms of togetherness of man and God, and then only as not qualified by the other modes.

December 6

Faith, like belief, relates to a generic state of affairs, but unlike belief it involves a readiness to act with respect to some specific manifestation of the generic state of affairs. If we stress the readiness, we get the Protestant side of faith; if we stress the state of affairs and the fact that it is expected to be made specific by us or another, and that this will entrain either a response by us or a response by something beyond, we get the Catholic side. If we believe and also affirm x, we but instance the generic state of affairs accepted; we cannot deny the x without a contradiction. If we have faith regarding x and deny any readiness, we turn faith into belief.

The present has a number of meanings: A] here and now, having the duration of a single act, perhaps measured by common-sense ideas of relevance and singleness; B] continuing into the past by virtue of the operation of the Ideal, and thereby making the past accumulated in the sense of being inseparable from what is here and now, and not in the sense of being inside it as an operative power; C] continuing into the future as that which has not yet been completed. A and B accept a terminus in the present. In the case of C we must consider the components of the historic occurrence in the present as occupied with a prospect which is historic in nature, being a prospect of the components together. The prospect is nature as something to be worked on by man under the aegis of the Ideal.

We face a prospect which is eventually to be, as a kind of generic interpretation of nature by the Ideal. In our action we specify that generic prospect and in that very act allow the ought-to-be to operate as that which holds on to the past. Until we specify the generic prospect the ought-to-be reaches only to the present; when we specify the prospect by a particular qualification of nature we make that prospect take the form of a particular present and thus drive the ought-to-be toward the past. The battle that is now being fought is in one sense in the present only if it terminates there; it is in the present in another sense in that what went before it is held on to by the ought-to-be; it is in the present in a third sense in that an eventual peace is now being faced and realized as just that battle, at the same time that it is being held apart as a final prospect by God.

December 11

From the standpoint of any one of the modes, the others are principles in the sense that they are abstractable aspects of it. Were it not that the mode shows intrusions and that the features are not merely present but are unessential and thus offer evidences of something alien, and were it not that there is a many inside each mode, which is interconnected by the other three modes having an independent role, we would be able to stay with the three modes as principles of the given one.

Inside Actuality, actualities are interrelated in the field of Existence, guided by a common Ideal, and united by God. Inside the Ideal there is a many, whose items have different leanings toward Actuality now, and are commonly maintained by Existence as concordant components of a cosmic future, and are providential because of God. Inside God, due to Actuality there is an infinite subdivision; due to Existence there are many roles which His subdivisions have; due to the Ideal His subdivisions are assessed a belonging to a hierarchy.

Every basic realm should show that it appeals to and satisfies all sides of man. Consequently, a religion must show how man is appealed to and satisfied as a mind, will, person, body, as an individual, as a member of a community, as a being in history, as a creator in art, and in any other nonsubordinate discipline. Since the sciences do not appeal to the emotions it would seem that they are subordinate or partial. Unless we can show there is a rational appeal made by art and religion, we must make the same judgment of them. It is true, of course, that the scientist has emotional responses to his discoveries and even is dedicated to the production of truth; if one can be content to say that this is an epitomization of all the emotions, or that one emotion is sufficient to determine something basic, we would here have enough. But then one must avoid so formulating the criterion that anything, which might have emotional repercussions, would be shown to be ultimate. We must define what is meant by rationality, emotionality, will, etc., before we begin. The claims of science for consideration, if it could not be shown to be ultimate, would be in its capacity to satisfy one dimension of man better than any other discipline.

December 13

In 4.04 of the *Modes* it is said that the various modes are ingredient in one another as meanings, or qualifications, and not "in their full concreteness." But this dichotomy overlooks an alternative, and even conflicts with what was said about Existence being ingredient in each actuality. The ingredience need not be in full concreteness, but it must be there in fact, at least so far as Existence is concerned with actualities. Must not Existence be present in fact in the Ideal and God? It would seem so. But then is Actuality present in God, in Existence, in Ideality? Is God present in the others? Is Ideality? It seems we must say yes, but how? In the fourth chapter (of the *Modes*) it is said that the Ideal and Actuality are present in God, as is Existence, but the reversal, where God is present in them, is not clearly stated.

Also in 4.07 it is said that the direct testimony instances the nature of a being to which it testifies. But this overlooks two important points. The "accidents" in a being are carried by the being; we cannot assume that the carrier makes no difference to those accidents. We can use the accidents as direct testimony only by epitomizing "idealizing" them, freeing them from the contribution made by the carrier. The second point is related to this: the carrier of the accident is evidenced by the accident, if only as in the role of a carrier. We can, in short, read the testimony inward to the being in which it is found, or outward to the being which imposed the condition on it. The accident is itself the juncture of two forces, and either one of these may make a minor contribution. The *Modes* fails to notice those cases where the smallest contribution is made by the outside. In the discussion of indirect testimony, the *Modes* says only that the features instance a mode of being distinct from the mode which acted from the outside on that given mode of being. But it could have considered those cases where the carrier contributes most to the nature of the "accident," and considered cases where the carrier and outside contribute equally, as well as cases where the outside contributes most.

December 14

Existence is in the other modes by fractionation; it is embodied in them and subjugated by them as there. This means that it reaches not only to actualities, but also into the Ideal and God. These do not effect its geometry but do affect its nature and career, and the way that geometry will continue. Actualities are in God by virtue of His memory, i.e., as facts to be completed; they are in the Ideal as defining the boundaries of subordinate possibilities; they are in Existence as localizations, bounded areas within the total, as public entities. The Ideal is in God as a value, in man as guilt and obligation, in Existence as its governing future. God is in the Ideal to make it providential, its nonnormative aspects realized and its normative made prescriptive; He is in Existence as the unity of the entire domain; He is in actualities as the self-consciousness which enables one to be the other of oneself; He gives one that perspective on oneself that enables one to know oneself. Of all these ways of being "in" the last seems most doubtful. God is in actualities in other and perhaps more subtle ways.

December 17

The problem of *modus ponens* is that of deciding the legitimacy of the conclusion when it is detached from its warranting rule. It is not enough to follow the lead of Wittgenstein's interpretation of language and to treat a rule as being followed when and so far as we have a certain agreed or common response to its presence. We want to have the rule sanction the result. Does this mean that the rule has to be repeated with the conclusion so that it can continue to provide a sanction for that conclusion? The *modus ponens* then should be written:

$$\frac{P: p \,) \, q}{p \,) \, q: Q}$$

We then assert the *P*, as that which possesses a desirable property—truth, probability (why not beauty, interestingness, believed, etc.?)—and find out that rule by which it sanctions the transfer of this property or a variation of it to *q*. The sanction does not endow the *q* with the transferred and perhaps translated property; it is only a structure. But we do want to assert *Q* in place of the *P*. Since the *Q*, merely asserted, is distinct from the *q* of the warrant (being externally related to the *P* in contrast with the *q* which is internally related to the *p*), it is conceivable that it might not be assertible by itself. Also we do not merely assert the *Q;* we assert it "because of"; it is a *Q* which is asserted because it has been warranted, and not a *Q* which is merely true. We want to recognize that its property is a transferred one, that it is a guaranteed one, that it is a rule-sanctioned one. But does this demand that we repeat the rule?

When the rule is asserted both above and below the line, it is asserted in a different sense than that in which the P and the Q are asserted. The P and the Q are true because of something external to them, the "$p) q$" is asserted because of the structure it has. It would be clearer then to write:

$$\frac{\begin{array}{c} p) q \\ P \end{array}}{\begin{array}{c} p) q \\ Q \end{array}}$$

Do we assert the "$p) q$" below the line? Why assert $p) q$ twice? Do we not merely transfer it? Or would it not be better to write the *modus ponens* as:

$$\begin{array}{c} P \\ p) q \\ Q \end{array}$$

with the $p) q$ having the ambiguous role of separating and connecting the P and the Q? It would then be like a Kantian schema, sharing something of the features of both sides and justifying the application of the property of the P to the Q. Since it is the property with which we are concerned, a clearer presentation of the rule would be:

						PLUS	

(A) $\dfrac{\dfrac{(z) P}{p) q}}{(z') Q}$ (B) $Or \dfrac{\dfrac{(z) P}{p) q}}{(z') Q}$ $\dfrac{\dfrac{(z) P}{p) q}}{(z') Q}$

where the z represents a property and the z' represents the same or a warranted alteration of the property whose alteration and transfer is guaranteed by $p) q$.

If semantics be thought of as the application of a rule, we do not have the rule and then a response to it, but instead a rule which is either outside the asserted premiss and conclusion, or better perhaps, a kind of separating relation between them (A), or the still better interpretation (B), a rule which is attached to the assertion of the premiss, and is attached to the assertion of the conclusion when and as we transfer the property of the premiss to the conclusion. The double line in the first step of B separates a truth from a possible conclusion; the double line in the second separates a replaced premiss by the rule and the asserted conclusion. Consequently, it would be better to write the *modus ponens* as:

$$(\text{C}) \quad (z)\,P \quad \textit{therefore}$$
$$p\,)\,q \qquad\qquad p\,)\,q$$
$$(z')\,Q$$

The "$p\,)\,q$" would, like a middle term, be identical in the two places, but unlike a middle term would not disappear. Our assertion of it, or our acceptance of it, would still be different from our assertion of either premiss or conclusion. This would seem to indicate the preferability of:

$$(\text{D}) \quad \frac{(z)\,P}{p\,)\,q} \quad \textit{therefore}\ \frac{p\,)\,q}{(z')\,Q}$$

where the line would not indicate an act, but a difference in the kind of assertion. We could combine these in one expression, by taking a double line to refer to the act of inferring:

$$(\text{E}) \quad \frac{(z)\,P}{\dfrac{p\,)\,q}{(z')\,Q}}$$

The single line marks off truth, or other kinds of claims, from accepted rules, and the double line marks off the asserted inferred conclusion. However, the rule is not merely stated; it is employed even when we have only the premiss, for it allows for the movement of the property from one to the other. We do not merely have the rule, but make it carry the transferred property which is then given to the conclusion. Consequently, we get:

$$(\text{F}) \quad \frac{(z)\,P, p\,)\,q;\ (z)\,p\,)\,(z')\,q}{(z')\,Q}$$

What sanctions the Q is not the rule alone, but the rule as already transformed by the presence of a certain premiss. Better, then, would be the formulation:

$$\text{(G)} \quad \frac{(z)\ P}{p\ )\ q}$$
$$\frac{(z)\ p\ )\ (z')\ q}{(z')\ Q}$$

On the first line we assert P with a certain property; we then act to identify this with the p of the rule, and produce a new result, $(z)\ p\ )$ $(z')\ q$. That new result says that the approved p (say a p which is known to be true) guarantees the $(z')\ q$. This new rule cannot be used to permit the assertion of $(z')\ Q$. The inference thus requires two steps: there must first be in the infection of the rule by the accepted premiss so as to transform the rule into a new one which can stand apart from the separate assertion of the $(z)\ P$; this new rule can then be used so that one can have a $(z')\ Q$ by itself. Thus if we have a rule that one kindness deserves another, and if we can legitimatize the claim that there is a kindness, we can change our rule to one which says that this legitimatized kindness legitimatizes another. If three strikes means you are out, and you have a legitimate three strikes, you can have the rule that, that legitimate three strikes means a legitimate out, and you can then assert that there is a legitimate out.

The structure "$p\ )\ q$", since it does relate certain kinds of properties and entities, is not written out entirely correctly; at the very least it should be written as "$(\ )\ p)\ (\ '\ )\ q$", where the brackets show that there is something to be transported or translated as a property, from p to q. And then we ought to read $(z)\ p\ )\ (z')\ q$ as "because . . . then," which will contrast with "$(\ )\ p\ )(\ '\ )\ q$" when read as "if . . . then," and with $(z)\ P$ as separated from $(z')\ Q$ by the "if . . . then" and the "because . . . then," which together should define a "therefore."

$$\text{(H)} \quad \frac{(z)\ P}{(\ )\ p\ )\ (\ '\ )\ q} \qquad \begin{aligned}&1.\\&2.\end{aligned}$$
$$\frac{(z)\ p\ )\ (z')\ q}{(z')\ Q} \qquad \begin{aligned}&3.\\&4.\end{aligned}$$

Line *1* is to be thought of as an assertion which is made to operate on line *2*, the abstract rule, to yield the used rule. The used rule (3) is to be thought of as allowing for the abstraction of the abstract rule (2) and for the final conclusion (4). From line *1* and *2* to *3* we have a synthesis; from line *4* we get an analysis into line *2* and *3*. The whole reads: Given $(z)\ P$, $(\ )\ p)\ (\ '\ )\ q$ will yield $(z)\ p)\ (z')\ q$, and this in turn will allow for the conclusion $(z')\,Q$ and the recovery of line 2. Consequently the result of the inference leaves us with the structure:

$$
\begin{array}{lll}
(\text{H}') & (z)\,P & \text{1.} \\
& \underline{(\ )\,p\,)\,(\ ')\,q} & \text{2.} \\
& (z')\,Q & \text{4.}
\end{array}
$$

the line 3 having been dissolved into line 2 and line 4. The "therefore" of the *modus ponens* is then the recovery (from the specific used rule) of the abstract rule, which, together with the initial $(z)\,P$ produced that specific rule, and the correlative presentation of the detached conclusion. If we wish to distinguish products from elements we must write:

$$
\begin{array}{ll}
(\text{I}) & (z)\,P \\
& \underline{(\ )\,p\,)\,(\ ')\,q} \\
& \underline{(z)\,p\,)\,(z')\,q} \\
& (z')\,Q
\end{array}
$$

where the single line is to be seen as expressing actions which can go up or down, with the double line expressing an action which goes down only. The used rule dissolves when we obtain $(z')\,Q$, but not without yielding the abstract rule. To show that $(z)\,P$ goes down to $(\ )\,p\,)$ $(\ ')\,q$, we need a double line again which allows one to move down only, so that we get:

$$
\begin{array}{ll}
(\text{J}) & (z)\,P \\
& \overline{\underline{(\ )\,p\,)\,(\ ')\,q}} \\
& \underline{(z)\,p\,)\,(\ ')\,q} \\
& (z')\,Q
\end{array}
$$

Or, reversing the meanings of the double and single lines, so that the double alone reads as going both ways and the single as reading downward we get:

$$
\begin{array}{lll}
(\text{K}) & (z)\,P & \text{1.} \\
& \overline{\underline{(\ )\,p\,)\,(\ ')\,q}} & \text{2.} \\
& \underline{(z)\,p\,)\,(z')\,q} & \text{3.} \\
& (z')\,Q & \text{4.}
\end{array}
$$

We can read from $(z')\,Q$ upward to the second line and thus take the abstract rule (2), to be an inferred result in the very same sense that the used rule (*3*) is an inferred result from lines *1* and *2*. If (*z'*) is at once an objectively valid quality and a transferred one, we should then have the right to infer to a general abstract rule which guarantees that an objectively valid (*z*) will give the used specific rule.

With the elimination of the used rule in its use, we get:

$$(\text{к}') \quad \frac{(z)\, P}{(\ )\, p\,)\, (\ ')\, q} \\ \overline{} \\ (z')\, Q$$

The abstract rule is not the rule that is used; it points up the fact that the used rule is the therefore which dissolves into its elements (*2, 4*) when used. We have then:

$$(z)\, P\, .\, [(z)\, p\,)\, (z')\, q]\, .\, (z')\, Q$$

where the expression in square brackets is to be viewed as a process, the very meaning of "therefore" as having just that initial starting point and end. But the therefore must be produced out of the "if then" and when it is treated as an outcome or condition as in к, line *3* must be read as "because . . . can be."

The inference to *3* in к involves the insertion or "colligation" of line *1* in line *2*, and the consequent carrying of (*z*) over to the *q* in an unchanged or certifiable altered form. The movement from *1* to *2* is the decision to use the abstract rule here and now on (*z*) *P*. The movement from *3* to *4* (and *2* and *1*) is the decision to analyze out, to use the rule in accordance with our decision. Line *2* says a king can move one square, line *1* says it is a king, and we therefore get the rule that a legitimatized king can legitimately move one square. We in fact move to the square by releasing the abstract rule that a king can move one square, and allowing this rule to be used again.

(*z'*) *q* in line *3* is quite distinct from (*z'*) *Q* in line *4;* in the former the (*z'*) is an acquired character having a synthetical justification; in line *4* it is claimed to have a semantical one, even though it has not been directly discovered to have. The assertion of line *4* is the conversion of an acquired feature into a claim. It is like a mirror image when it is in *3* and like a real person in *4,* but a real person which we know only because guaranteed by *3.* It is thus like our claim that what we see in a mirror is true of a real person—or (since this seems to raise the question of the causality of mirror images and to refer us back to the *p*) it is like our claim that what we predict we will encounter, verify, experience.

We specify a general rule to get a rule to use, and use that rule by isolating what it has legitimatized. If we were given the rule to use without a prior justification, we would start dogmatically by saying "Because (z) p, (z') q can be." "Because this is a king, you can move here," or "Because your king can rightly be here, you can legitimately move here," or "Because your queen can rightly move here, you can legitimately check now." When we say "I move here" or "check!" we use the rule in its specific form.

Is there a risk in moving from the (z) q as implied by (z) p, to the (z') Q? Not so long as the abstract rule is allowed to remain in force, together with the asserted (z) P, for the conversion of (z) p into (z) P is the same kind of act as the conversion of (z') q into (z') Q. But is it legitimate to go from (z) p to (z) P? Only so far as it is legitimate to go from (z') q and (z') Q. And both of these are legitimate at the same time, since they take place with the recovery of $(\ )$ p $)$ $(\ ')$ q. The used rule is fragmented into the original claim, the abstract rule, and the final claim. But the final claim replaces the original claim. How, then, can we be said to analyze it out and therefore have it again? Is it not that we point back to it and assert of our justified (z') q that it now has the right to stand by itself as (z') Q, and that this is one with holding that (z) p has to stand by itself as (z) P? But we know that (z) P; that is what we started with. If we have doubts, it is about (z) p $)$ (z') q. But that says merely that the z is a transportable property in an unchanged or legitimately altered form. And this is to say that there is a rule for transportation; this rule does not affect the status of the independent claim of (z) P.

We are therefore saying that the (z) P, which through the help of an abstract rule made a usable rule possible, does have a right to stand apart. When and as we say this we dissolve the usable rule in the using of it, and end by making a counterassertion that (z') Q can stand by itself. (z') Q has the same warrant for being taken out of (z) p $)$ $(z)'$ q as the (z) P has. But the (z) P was initially discovered to have a position outside. The taking it out is but a reiteration of what was already known to be true of it.

Our awareness that we would be right to hold the (z) P apart, is our awareness that we are right to hold the (z') Q apart from the used rule. The capacity of (z) P both to stand outside and to function inside a used rule, tells us that (z') Q has a similar capacity. We might, then, be said to be looking for what would exclude the (z) P legitimately. Our answer is that the used rule tells us what this is, and when we find it, we use it to exclude (z) P and (z') Q, both under the aegis of the abstract rule.

Where, then, is the risk of inference, and how great is it? Is it not but the very same thing as the risk of bringing (z) P into the abstract rule; is it not then the risk of making a usable rule? It is not, then, the inference to (z') Q which is bothersome, but the inference to the rule from which it will be derived by analysis. What risk do we run if we take (z) P and make it into (z) p? What do we do? We make an independent claim into one which is to be transported. If it were not transportable, logical implication would not have a connection with the claims things have in-themselves. And it is possible to see how this can be. A truth claim could be intrinsic to something, something carried by authority or merit or revelation, and what it implied might not be capable of carrying this; it might have to be changed when made transportable. If the Catholic Church has the keys, it does not follow that what it accepted to carry on is identical with what it was before and outside the acceptance. Only so far as it is identical or legitimate to move from one to the other, are the (z') q and the (z') Q identical or legitimately related. We need not suppose them identical. All we need suppose is that just so far as it is proper to go to (z) P from (z) p, so it is proper to go from (z') q to (z') Q [where (z) p and (z') q are parts of a usable rule].

The legitimacy of inference is the legitimacy of the use of a rule through the movement from an independent claim to a transportable one. The kind of change to which we subject the (z) in moving from an independent claim to a transported one, is the kind of change to which we subject the (z') when we move from an acquired claim to an independent claim. Consequently, we can say that the acceptance of a rule for a certain condition is on a footing with the use of the rule for a certain result. Let us suppose that getting the keys is the humanizing of the divine message; then the holding of the result of the use of the keys, apart from the transferring act, is a divinizing of the result. This will require as much of a change from the transferred result as was required to get to the beginning of the transfer. If we maintain there was no change in the beginning, we can say there is none at the end; but if we say there is some in the beginning, we must recognize it in the end. Thus when we say that in order to infer we must change an experience into a proposition, or a fact, or a claim, or a postulate, or a conceptualized and personalized item, we should say that we recover the experience by reversing the stress as we move outside the used rule. There is a risk in inference then, but it is abolished when we take account of what we ventured to get to the usable rule. There is a dangerous risk only for one who forgets the fact that a change might have been or was in fact made to get to a transportable feature.

But in the discussion of the logic of the Creative Process, in the volume in honor of Peirce, I maintained that there were different risks involved in various businesses, etc., and that our civilization would collapse so far as it had identified itself with one of these which was found to be unreliable. Is this but to state that the conversion, say of human beings into statistics, is the risk of getting a rule in which the meanings originally found are radically distorted? Of course this would be no risk if we accepted the fact that there was a change introduced into (z) by being attached to p after having been attached to P—the p being a premiss and the P being an independent proposition. The inference to (z') Q involves a risk so far as we ignore what may have been done to (z) and to (z') by having them in a syntactical relation.

December 18

A rule that is used is not stated, and a rule that is stated is not used, being abstract, a mere structure or form. The used rule is produced by a creative act uniting the external item with the structure in such a way as to transport some feature to another item. That other item can be held apart from the structure, and even be endowed with some feature as apart. But the supposition that as apart it has the very feature which it inherited is unwarranted. It has the kind of feature which the initial external item possessed, and this might have been altered in being made part of the structure. Thus we can start with a common-sense truth and through the combination of this with a structure, make a usable structure. The latter will endow some other item with a feature. If we suppose that this new item is possessed of common-sense truth, we will have overlooked the transformation to which that truth was subject when it was brought inside the abstract structure. To make the implicated result into a commonsensical truth we must reverse the process by which the initial truth was united with the structure. The holding of the new fact apart is one with the identification of the initial fact as standing apart and thus pushed aside. The conclusion replaces the premiss because the premiss is pushed aside when the conclusion is detached from the structure.

In the foregoing case we move from one realm to another with the items somewhat definite. But we can engage in a similar activity with respect to a Kantian manifold which is solidified in a categorial structure and then made to imply further solidified categorial items. It would be a mistake to suppose that inside the categorial scheme it is like the manifold, or to suppose that outside the categorial scheme the item has the virtues it has in that scheme. Outside the categorial scheme it has the defects of being part of the manifold.

If we start with a desirable state of affairs we tend to suppose that what is transported inside a rule is legitimately held to be a part of such a desirable state of affairs. If we start with an undesirable state of affairs we tend to suppose that the detached conclusion has the features it obtained by being part of a structure. And when we are undecided in our judgment, as we are in connection with common sense (or observation) and science, we sometimes take the one view and sometimes the other; we think that the conclusions of our scientific deductions are observables in just that form, or we think that what we observe has been sanctioned by our scientific scheme. We can take the observed to be sanctioned by an actual used rule inside science, but only so far as we undo the transformation which an original observed item suffered in being united with the abstract structure of science to make the usable rule.

When the pragmatists urge us to test our abstract knowledge by experience, they attend to only one half of the problem of abstract knowledge; the first half has to do with the way in which they moved from experience to knowledge originally. Sometimes both halves are ignored; in Dewey and Wittgenstein we stay with used rules and have merely beginnings and endings for them. But they overlook the fact that we can identify items outside common language and then bring them in, and that just as we can bring them in, so we can take them out. Having begun with theology, metaphysics, scientifically defined items, and the like, and then made use of a commonsensical structure in order to transport a feature to some other items, we can reinsert that item, with its inherited feature, into the original context, providing we then convert the inherited feature into a theological, metaphysical, etc., one.

The above considerations are related to the theory of vindication given in the *Modes*. They are also related to the discussion of the risk of inference discussed in the "Logic of the Creative Process." There is a risk in inference only if one ignores how one made an actual used rule (and thus changed a feature which was an adjective of some detached item into a feature which was in a structure and transported there to another item). We have no right to suppose that the feature as transported can, without alteration, be treated as an adjective of the item which inherited it. Going from detached item to usable structure or rule involves no risk; it merely gives us a possible change in the nature of the feature. Going from the used rule to the detached conclusion involves no risk since it is merely analytic, providing of course we also analyze out the abstract rule and the initial premiss. Risk lies only in supposing that the terminus of the structure has the properties, when apart from that structure, that it has in the structure.

The rules of chess in Hoyle are abstract structures; the game is played by making usable rules and using them, the usability coming from the acknowledgment of this or that piece for a place, and the use coming from the acknowledgment of a place for a piece—or better, a piece in one place first and then that piece (or perhaps some other) in another place.

We all are confident of logic and yet can see the difference between implication and inference, an abstract calculus and an applied language. Our confidence in logic is warranted only so far as we see that the transformation of a conclusion, when held apart, is correlative to the transformation of the premiss as apart, and acknowledged either before and apart from the abstract rule, or in the course of the dissolution of the used rule and the affirmation of the conclusion in- and of-itself.

December 19

Goethe somewhere said that it is not enough to inherit from one's ancestors, one must make the inheritance one's own. But this is exactly the point being made these last days in connection with the difference between the (z') q which is an entailed consequence still in the structural whole, and the (z') Q which replaces an initial (z) P. And when we turn to language and face some such question as to how we get words for our experiences and use them to refer to our experiences, we have a similar situation and solution. The child is in pain and then it cries. The pain as privately experienced is a (z) P. The cry is connected with the (z') q, and thus is made into a (z) p by the nature of the child, i.e., the nature of its associations, physiology, etc. The cry as heard by me or even by the child is (z') Q. If this be treated just by itself it is the cry of an actor, of someone watching it, etc. The cry of the child can be held apart from the situation in which it was derived, only by virtue of the analysis of the derivation into this cry and a replaced pain, with a readiness to use an abstract structure, "experience," "physiology," and the like.

The cry is a cry of pain only so far as it remains in the context of (z) p $)$ (z') q. It becomes a mere cry which testifies to a pain when it replaces the pain as a matter of attention, but is treated as that which has a place in the abstract structure of a child's experience or nature. Similarly, if instead of a cry a word was used, we must say that the word as uttered is a mere ejaculation, and becomes a word in a language only if it is detached from the uttering of it. But the language is purely "formal" or constructed if the detached word is not faced as that which can be brought inside the abstract structure of an actual experience and which now replaces another experience. When the word is heard there is another use of a rule. We receive the word in the context of an interpersonal situation, and when we detach it we can make it our own only if we push aside the utterer, and also acknowledge a possible new use of the rule connecting speaker and hearer.

When we refer to a symbol as that which has within it the power of the divine, we have a similar situation, except that here we recognize that the power of the divine is now possessed by a sacramental object. When we live through this or enjoy it, we are standing over against the divine (as Tillich sees). We are also aware that there is a "religious" situation which is needed, as an abstract structure, to make the sacramental object one which permits of an othering of God. It is to be noted though that the sacramental object requires a prior intrusion of the divine inside that religious situation. God makes a symbol or object one into which divine power has been transferred. The transferred divine power is different from what it was in God.

When we accept the symbol as our own, we have it as the representative of God. When we try to get to God from the symbol we must engage in another activity, one in which God becomes affected by the concern we have for the symbol. When we acknowledge Him as apart from our use of the symbol, we must recognize that He replaces our symbol and allows for further use of the religious situation.

The derivation of abstract rules of logic, science, etc., is evidently a consequence of our use of a concrete rule. Starting with a "because (z) p we can have (z') q," we derive (z') Q. The (z') Q is a legitimate consequence providing we make no claim that it is identical with the (z') q. And we can see how it agrees or disagrees with the (z') q, by acknowledging a (z) P. Whatever is true of the discrepancy between the (z) P and the (z) p is true of the discrepancy between the (z') Q and the (z') q. And we can say this only so far as we keep before us the abstract rule as that which can be used again and again.

We derive abstract rules, and thus prescriptions, from matters of fact by recognizing the detached consequence to transform the product of a used rule, to replace some detached antecedent, and to occur within the context of a possible use of some structure. The structure that is prescriptive transforms the detached antecedent's property into a transportable one, and in fact transports it to the other term of the structure. What must always be the case is a general context which will allow the (z) P and the (z') Q to be concretely related, i.e., to stand to one another in the concrete structure or usable rule (z) p $)$ (z') q.

Logic in its most formal and general sense is that general structure which enables distinct items to be interrelated. It is prescriptive since it tells how the items must be together in order to inherit this or that feature. It tells us that a feature will be inherited as such and such; it does not tell us what that feature is like outside the structure. It can be said to prescribe to the outside the condition "if you wish to have this feature inherited it must be brought into my context and perhaps altered to some extent."

If logic is prescriptive only in the sense of the demand it makes on something to become a part of it, it would seem that we cannot say that the universe is governed by logic—or (to shift the context) that language is, or experience, or science. But if it be recognized that no entity really exists by itself, that it is we who, for various purposes, concentrate on an object as though it were alone, and that conversely no object is only a term in a relation, we can say that logic is prescriptive in the sense that it allows the being to fully be, since it provides the context in which it is together with others. The forms of togetherness discussed in the *Modes* are really logics dictating how the items are together, and therefore how they could possibly be apart, for the apartness of the various modes consists in the fact that there is a context in which they can be together.

December 20

To deal with the problem of rules from the standpoint of logic unduly restricts attention, since it keeps us to truth claims and assertions.

When we detach an outcome, we are faced with the fact that an altered property need not be detached in the same way that it had been detached before it had been altered. We have no genuine warrant for assuming that the way we accept (z') Q is similar to the way in which (z) P had been accepted, unless acceptance means merely "holding away from a structure."

There is some gain in looking at this and similar issues from the standpoint of language, as Wittgenstein did. If I say "I am in pain" the remark is but an exclamation, and denotes what I then take to be its designatum in me. Any one who says to himself "I sympathize" reverses this stress and makes a comment which serves as a reminder or perhaps even an elicitation of some feeling in him. Both of these occurrences take place outside the field of communication. But the relation of the inward occurrence and the expression needs to be examined.

The expression as merely exclaimed is quite different from what it is as something which is in a communication. The very words which I utter have a twofold use; they mark some occurrence in me, and they are parts of a discourse. The movement from the marks to the discourse is the use of some rule (such as being part of the human community) to make it a set of words: "I'll go for the doctor." If we stay with the items in discourse, we cannot distinguish the words of a play from those of a serious activity. One who was caught in the communication, which did not begin with an initial marking of some occurrence in him, but who then went on to have a detached expression and thus elicited some private feeling, would be the victim of a misunderstanding. Conversely, if one had started with a private feeling and then had his exclamation answered by another which was not then detached as a reminder, would be one who was being made fun of.

If I say I will go for the doctor, what relation has my going to the expression? Is it a subsequent occurrence on the same level, a kind of behavior, or is it in another area of being altogether? If the first, it would seem to be a produced consequence, an outcome in the public domain which could even be said to be produced or commanded by the initial "I am in pain" and the situation. If the second, it has something like the role of a conclusion of an argument which has been detached from the used rule. My going for the doctor—would it then be like my saying to myself "I sympathize"? Yes, and it would have as its correspondent "I want to go," "I gladly go," and the like. It is as if we said that the nature of conversation involves the separation off of a reminder to oneself. No one cares about this fact though, because one can hardly tell whether or not I do remind myself. The separation, then, is the separation of a mark, the having of the mark as capable of testifying to something private. Wittgenstein is then right in insisting that a merely private language is not a language; but he does overlook the fact that the detached items are reminders, and that they can have the very same verbal form that they have when they function in the social language.

Coming back to propositions and truth, what we can ask of a used rule is to allow us to end with what is worthy of carrying a truth claim of its own. We need deduce nothing from the rule but that we could now face a world apart from the rule, and can do it in the way in which it had been faced by the initial premiss. If it be the case that there was no initial premiss, that we started with the discourse, with the using of a rule, then what we are saying is that we have a right to use this as a claim so far as there is an abstract structure and a possible initial premiss having the kind of right that we now have. He who feels sorry in himself for what the actor is saying makes a mistake, unless this feeling be taken to be an accidental accompaniment of a mere reminder, which requires the use of the initial premiss as an expression outside the acting situation. We can conceive of the initial statement as outside the acting situation by taking it to have a common use, and thus see it as somewhere or other (not necessarily in these people) function as a genuine accompaniment of something privately suffered. My detaching the remark (accepting it as my own by sympathy) and therefore using it to elicit or remind me to feel in a certain way, is then one with the recognition of the initial remark by the actor as having the role of an expression for someone or other.

December 21

Higher education in this country could be viewed as a secularized version of the Protestant revolution. The Protestant revolution allowed men to make something like a direct contact with the source of the religion. Each man, in principle, was allowed to decide what the Bible said; the position of an interpreter or intermediary was, in principle, abandoned. In higher education in this country we have abandoned the idea of a guru, a master of the subject who teaches disciples, though this is in some way the teaching that still prevails on the Continent and in Great Britain. Our method of getting the student to face the issues himself, runs the risk of the abuse which we can see in Protestantism; we have either the frenzy of self-conceit, or the parochialism of a restricted community. To avoid these, we must depend on character and an opposition to the community outside. We look to the character of the students and we try to build up an entire world of values which contrast with those that are now prevalent. The idea of character is essentially Greek, the idea of a group, protected essentially by its opposition to Baal, is Hebrew.

We do seem to have arguments which begin with false premisses. What warrant do we have for asserting the conclusion as that which stands in opposition to the premiss? Suppose we have as our general structure, "natives usually speak the native language," and also the used rule "because you are an Italian, you speak Italian." If one were to separate out the latter and affirm "You speak Italian," one might have a true proposition, and yet it might not be true that "You are an Italian." If we say that "You speak Italian" is true only so far as one assumes "You are an Italian," we seem to have made no advance from the premiss. Can we say   1] "You are an Italian" is probably true, or that it is true so far as we recognize the context,   2] "natives usually speak the native language," or the combination of *1* and *2?* Is "You speak Italian" to be understood to involve a readiness to use and thus enter into the frame of "natives usually speak the native language"?

The acknowledgment of a false premiss would seem to be like the acknowledgment of any premiss which has its property transformed either on being introduced into the structure or on being conveyed by it. All conclusions tacitly refer to a situation which warrants the conclusions being held on their own, dealt with as conclusions of a certain sort. The reference to the abstract structure is thus a reference to the kind of conclusion it is, the world in which the conclusion fits. "You speak Italian" looks as if it held in any world; but it is a concluded result only so far as it is thought to fit inside the world defined by the abstract structure and thus to require a correlative "You are Italian" with perhaps some probability value. Were there no such correlative we would not have a conclusion; we would have misunderstood the expression "You speak Italian." All conclusions seem then to be true relative to a context, and the best logic is the one, as Peirce saw, with the widest context.

But we would like to have conclusions which are guaranteed outside a context, in the very sense in which the initial proposition was outside the context and obtained some property there. But the initial proposition is outside the context only as capable of using it, for otherwise it would ground no reasoning. Our readiness to use it in some structure, logical or linguistic, transportational or transformational, makes the initial proposition, even apart from use, more than a merely objective truth. Logic, as a final discipline, presupposes objective truth; it supposes that there is a minimal change in that truth when it is employed in reasoning, so that when we relate (z) p to (z') q we need make only a minimal change to get (z') Q by itself. The guarantee of logic is that the abstract structure applies to all separated assertions, assertions which belong in the largest possible world of distinct assertions. In short, to be able to have a logical conclusion we must belong to that world in which there are other detached assertions making no reference to a particular context. When we detach the conclusion we accept the logical structure and make reference to some proposition or other from which that conclusion can be made to follow. This seems to mean that a logic must presuppose at least two propositions outside it, and thus to have an "ontological" commitment.

December 23

In maintaining a conclusion we run the following risks: 1] There might not have been a rule used, so that the conclusion is not really something to which we concluded (though there has been, to be sure, some way of getting that conclusion, and this can be viewed as a rule that is used—in which case we have a reduction of this risk to one of the subsequent ones).   2] There might not be a general context in which the inference occurred, so that it is a mere singular occurrence (but this too is reducible, since one can always abstract some contextual generality).   3] The context is narrower than it is supposed to be, and the feature which has been transferred cannot be taken to apply since the conclusion might be outside that narrow context. And this is perhaps the form to which the previous cases might be reduced.   4] The inherited character was transformed and cannot be taken to be possessed, as the initial one was. But this case, too, perhaps can be reduced to 3.

The risk in inference is that one gets a conclusion in a context which is restrictive in a way that is not noticed, and nothing less than the largest possible context in which items actually stand external to one another before entering into that context, and are unaltered when they enter it, will make the risk vanish. But the supposition that there is no alteration is to be questioned. The supposition that the widest context is as wide as we assume it to be in logic may not be correct, and our result may therefore hold only within the unexamined and undetermined confines of the logic.

It is a tautology, then, to say that the logic holds; it holds so far as it does, and we are assuming that it holds so far, when we take the conclusion to be true, for we then identify the logical context with the boundaries of our known world. And that is where we err. The error here is like the error made in smaller contexts, except that we move in logic from the widest, most inclusive domain of entities to them as existent in a world in different relations than they have in the logic. The proposition we hold as concluded to, is already caught in the new context and this means that there is a transition from one context to another. That transition is of course also subject to rule, and so we can say that the basic risk is that we make use of a rule to which we pay no attention, and which makes a difference.

Suppose we express the new rule, and add it to the old? We will find that the conclusion of the result must be held apart from the combined rule and thus given another context, and thus to involve another rule, and so on. There is, in short, always a rule which is being used when we hold on to a conclusion, and this can be made part of a larger rule only so far as we still have a conclusion to hold apart by virtue of the use of the larger rule. And if this risk were overcome we would still push aside an antecedent, for this is involved in the use of a rule. A used rule expresses an abstract rule and this requires something to be put in the used rule. A conclusion always presupposes a context and the use of it.

The very smallest step of communication involves three rules: A] the movement from a private acceptance to the use of it as a premiss; B] the movement from premiss to conclusion, C] the movement from conclusion to private possession. The moves from the uttered cry to an expression in a language, from an expression in a language to an appropriate consequence of it in the language, to the adoption of the consequence (which might be the initial expression as communicated to one), make one whole. The initial pain is caught in a private context, and this is not identical with or even comparable with the final feeling we have in the adoption of the consequence of the cry of pain; all we need for communication is a coordination of the career to which we subject our adopted consequence, with the career in which the initial pain is involved. If our interest is in communication, we must see that we and others move into the common context of communication in reciprocal ways. Then when another is in pain, it is not true there is no rule governing the way in which he suffers it, nor is it true that there is no rule governing the way in which he expresses himself, nor is it true that there is no rule governing the way the expression enters into the common language. These rules Wittgenstein seems to have overlooked.

There are seven rules being employed in the normal course of events, governing *1*] the private career, *2*] the expression, *3*] the entering into a common context, *4*] the inheritance of an unchanged or transformed feature, *5*] the holding of the conclusion apart, *6*] the adoption of the conclusion as one's own, and *7*] the adopted conclusion as entering into a career inside us. The smallest step of communication involves *3, 4, 5,* when we have already defined the participants as mere limiting terms in the communication context. If we restrict ourselves to the present moment and the attempt to get together, we have five steps, 2–6. But strictly speaking we always have all seven.

When we deal with cosmology, or any interpenetration of various modes to constitute a single realm, we have the analogue of 4. We dissolve it into its ontological components only by subjecting, whatever we distinguish in it, to transformations. If we have a sacramental object, we isolate the divine element, as standing apart from that object, only by isolating another element too, say the secular. This is the having of the (z') Q over against the (z) P. There is some such (z) P, but we do not know what kind of substantial reality it has within the abstract context of the formal rule. It might be a divine component sustained by a community. We need to move from (z) P back to some antecedent of it which expresses something substantial, and then we need to move back into that substantial realm to see how it in fact behaves in its own private domain. We know that the (z) P has a being of some sort, for otherwise there would be no abstract rule to use to make the used rule; but we do not know what its antecedent is or how that antecedent's antecedent functioned inside another domain. We can know that if a man says he is in pain we can say something in response, but we do not know whether what we then do with our saying (or his) is like what he does with his (or our) saying. It is sufficient to know that he does come into discourse with us, and that he does have the (z) P as a possession or expression in the same sense that we have (z') Q, though not necessarily with the same import, since the antecedent of that (z) P need not match the consequent of the (z') Q, and the antecedent of the (z) P and the consequent of the (z') Q may be caught in quite different careers, with quite different consequents. All we ask of both is that they yield expressions which can make possible similar advances and retreats into privacy as had been engaged in before when we first stated and accepted (z) P and (z') Q, respectively. We do not know how another feels, what his pain is like, what it is like to be a man or a woman, but at best what it means to be a human with humans, for this means merely that the propositions (z) P and (z') Q, though held or maintained individually, can enter a common context.

December 24

Might one interrelate the four types of connection discussed in the paper on the ultimate elements of the physical universe, something like this: We start with *a* and *b* as merged, and take this to be itself a single implicative whole permitting of the signalizing of a hypothetical premiss and conclusion *xy*, and then separate off the *x* and *y* as asserted separated items, the entire process being achieved through the process of moving from *ab* as a kind of cause to *x* and *y* separated as an effect. If *ab* be a smile, then it could be said to be the product of a union of oneself with one's flesh, viewed as something distinct from ourselves. That *ab* can now function as implicative, perhaps having the premiss "friendliness" and the terminus "friend." And the "friendliness" and "friend" can be held apart just so far as one, say someone watching the smiling being, moves to acknowledge the friend. The dynamic relation from the smile to the affirmation of the friend, with an oppositional reference to friendliness, could be said to be the smile as prompting action. We would then have the smile as an occurrence, a structure, a used rule, and as a using of a rule.

December 25

There is no rule for detaching (1) (z') Q from (2) (z) p) (z') q, unless there be a rule for going from a usable rule to the use of it. But then how could one avoid an infinite regress? Let A be the rule by which *1* gets detached from *2*. This rule will be usable but will not produce *1*. The written is never more than a usable rule, and what is used is not written but appears only in the disappearance of the written usable rule and the appearance of its detached terminal points. But then do we need the usable rule *2;* why cannot we start with the abstract rule ( ) p) ($'$) q as that which is to be used by (z) P to give (z') Q? Is it that we cannot make the abstract rule usable until we introduce (z) P into it, and that this does not involve a detaching of the (z') Q, but only the achievement of (z') by the otherwise unqualified terminus, an achievement which is hypothetical, contextual?

A usable rule is a structure with qualitatively different termini, and it stretches between those termini. The abstract rule has no stretch to it, no orientation in time, or space, or mind, since it defines an area of possible place where usable rules can be achieved. We have here something like the difference between Hoyle's rules for chess and the usable rule which specifies it, saying, e.g., that the king can move to R 7 or R 8. The actual moving of the king to one place or the other will involve having a king and arriving at a place.

If we arrive at a conclusion, or hear an expression, must we have a rule in order to internalize the result? Yes, in the sense that there is a context, and there is a distinctive outcome to be achieved having validity because of that context. We properly internalize the conclusion if we accept it as having the property ascribed to it in the use of the rule 2, given above. But Wittgenstein objects, because he apparently thinks the rule is too private. But to this, one can answer: The detaching of the (z') Q is done by an individual using the rule 2, which can be stated. Just so, we can privatize (z') Q by using a new rule: (z') $Q)$ (z'') R. (z'') R will be produced by using that rule to make a private detachment.

It might be objected that (z'') R is a private result, whereas (z') Q is not. But not only may we infer something about an individual, we can acknowledge that (z') Q has a public status and yet see that it is being possessed in an individual, nonpublic manner. Putting aside then the case where we are inferring to a private fact in an ordinary logical situation, and attending only to the privatization of what is inferred through the use of the *modus ponens,* we have the fact that the only difference is in the localization of the detached result. The (z') Q is held apart from the rule by an individual, but as available to others, whereas the (z'') R is not available. The (z'') R is inside the individual and can be related there to other occurrences and thoughts, etc., by virtue of the structure of the individual's being; that structure is statable and there can be derived from it an abstract rule and a usable one which the individual's career may be said to be using.

The rule of privatization is not a private rule; e.g., one can object to it as involving a perversion, etc., an over-personalization of common knowledge, etc. What one cannot do is to give a rule for the way in which the outcome stands as detached. But this does not pertain only to the privatized conclusion; it also pertains to the public conclusion of the argument brought about by the using of the used rule. That detached outcome can enter into another situation and thus be understood as a premiss to be replaced by something else. Were it not possible to say anything about privatization, we would not be able to say anything about conclusions—and then nothing about premisses so far as they were not yet being used. We would have one continuum of language or logic, permitting of no assertion of a conclusion, and no separate identification of a premiss. We would have only rules, usable without being used (if by "use" we mean having some outcome as a result), or rules used but being unable to say that it was that was achieved through the use.

"But no one knows what another's private feelings or color images, etc., are." No one knows how one's conclusions are held by another.

"But the conclusions have an objective component apart from being held." So do the privatized elements, for they are distinct from the individual who enjoys them.

"But the objective component of the conclusion points back to the rule which justified it." The privatized element is also the outcome of a rule of privatization; it starts with the detached outcome held apart from one, and makes use of an unprejudiced way of adopting it; the objective component of the privatized result is the result as part of that rule.

"But a rule for privatization is a rule for ending in something others cannot know." So is any rule, since what it ends with is a detached outcome having a status outside the rule; the condition under which that detached outcome can be known is in principle one by which the privatized outcome can be known, for it involves grasping the nature of the detached's setting. A conclusion held apart, a conclusion answering to an objective world, a conclusion verified, etc., is a conclusion we can have only so far as we have made ourselves part of the context. Is not this the same as to privatize the detached conclusion, or to publicize ourselves? When we ask what a conclusion is like in another, we must find out how we can privatize him or publicize ourselves to provide the requisite background. Wittgensteinians take it for granted that we know what it is for something to be in- and of-itself, providing only that it is not in us; but one could argue the other way around as well, and maintain that we know, as Existentialists believe, what things are like in us without knowing how they stand apart from us.

January 2

Beginning with separation, we specify the generic structure to give a particular one, perhaps a formalized version, and then use it (i.e., act) in order to arrive at a terminus which must be adopted (i.e., merged into some domain). This last can be used as an item separated from others, so that the process can be continued on and on. And if we speak about evidence, we must recognize that we begin with material in which there is something like a merger.

The Ideal is in actualities in the role of a response to a demand—obligation, guilt, etc. Existence is in as fragmented, as making the actualities present. God is in, in the sense of providing them with an orientation away from one another. So far as He is in them we start with a merger, and then endeavor to find Him by proceeding with a structure of hope, a rule, a use of the rule to have a terminus, and the acceptance of that terminus. Or, having started with the merger, we can recognize the relation of the merged to God (as standing apart) and the determination of this as a religious setting. The having of the evidence in such a setting is the recognition of its symbolic character.

Religious discourse has a series of paradoxes to confront:

1] God is always beyond what you have identified yourself with.

2] God is always present as an orienting factor; He has reached to and infected everything.

3] We are always trying to find God, because we want Him in a more conscious, more intensive guise.

4] God is always trying to find us. Despite His power and His presence, there is a privacy to us which is resistant, and the request is that there should be a fuller orientation toward Him.

5] We are in God, and this despite the fact that we are trying to find Him, and that He is trying to find us. We are in Him, though only as remembered and reconstituted.

January 3

Religious experience, like all experience, is dual in nature. We experience something of ourselves when and as we experience something of God. We can begin with a feeling of being alone, bereft, and face a counterpart as an object of awe. The object of awe is what is other than ourselves as alone; and we can be alone in ourselves or at the limits of our interests—and particularly of what we cherish. From this experience we can move on to point to the being beyond us, an act which is the reciprocal of an act of pointing by that being. We then have a faith, and God exhibits a concern.

Faith is the awareness of the being who is divinely concerned. A divine concern is directed toward a being of faith, not as a precondition which He demands, but as a reciprocal which defines His act as much as it defines Him. This can be followed by an activity of seeking the divine being, and having Him seek us. We wish to be saved, reassured, helped, our prayers answered, and He in turn seeks to have us as beings which are available for perfection. And we end by merging ourselves with His being, when and as He merges with us. This merging can occur in ourselves, at a distance from us, or in His being, depending on where we and He moved in order for the merging to occur.

We thus have awe, faith, prayer, and enjoyment. The smaller we are in these, the smaller He will prove to be, not out of vengeance but because His activity is the reciprocal of ours. Both occur together. And both presuppose that there is a compound structure through which the experience moves. This structure can be expressed in a series of paradoxical oppositions: 1] God is in us, but at a distance. 2] God seeks us, but is already in us. 3] God reaches us, but we are radically private. 4] God and we merge, but we and God are radically distinct from one another. 5] We are in God, but still are finite and bereft. 6] We seek God, but still are occupied with our own affairs. 7] We reach God, but He always absconds. 8] We merge with God, but remain private.

If we think of expectation and eventually of an inductive inference to the future as the establishing of a link between present and future, we can view the reaching to God and man (whether we take this structurally or as the carrying out of an activity) to be a kind of induction. Such inductions define what one takes to be the world in which one is to be, and in terms of which all else is to be understood. It is not an approach to some pre-existent world. If I have been hurt in love

I may refuse to love again. I then define the kind of world in which I will continue to live. Should I try again? If so, I must change the structure of the world within which I will live. This means that I must change the nature and experience with which I have already identified myself. So far as it does, I must envisage a new world different from that of the past.

The inductive leap is a reassertion of the kind of world one had; there is a risk in this which cannot be reduced, unless one, following Peirce, has a method of perpetually correcting and asymptotically arriving at one perspective for all investigators. When religious people speak of the nonreligious having a faith similar to their own, or even a religious faith, they usually confuse an inductive expectation in the realm of nature with the faith which links men with God, or they are referring obliquely to the fact that men are always in a relation to God. In religion we try to intensify the relation, to quicken it so as to make one do consciously what we are always doing and being.

January 4

Religious experience can be dealt with as a sequence of states, each one having a kind of duality in it, and leading to the next. We begin as alienated beings, beings who are aware that they have lost something, that they are alone, and move on from this to a feeling of singularity, of standing out because of what we are. These are the subjective sides of the otherness given by God and the otherness given by us. We then move on to an awe of what lies beyond and from this to a feeling of being acceptable by what is beyond. These are subjective sides of a relation which we have with the divine. From there we move to an awareness of grace, and from this to a feeling of faith. These are subjective sides of a dynamic interplay or communication of ourselves and the divine. We end with an awareness of salvation and a feeling of being bereft and abandoned. These are subjective feelings of a merging of God and us, i.e., of a possessing of us by God, and of God by us. From here we move to alienation again. At every moment the success is but the prelude to an awareness of failure, and a demand that we move on.

If we separate out the components which are due primarily to us— singularity, awesomeness, faith, alienation—we make use of symbols and forever look for the divine signs. If we deal primarily with the alienation, acceptability, grace, and salvation, we make use of public domains and await the individual's response. Alienation and acceptability, like grace and salvation, here become decisions on the part of something outside, and not feelings in us.

We have a similar set of experiences when we try to speak with another, and even when we make an inference, and we can have these experiences with respect to a church, a community, or anything else. In inference we have, as the analogues of alienation and singularity, the recognition that what we are or know is outside a public discourse and is marked with features expressive of us. We move from this to the analogues of awe and acceptability, i.e., to the recognition that there is a world outside us which has a magnitude and virtue greater than our own, and that what we have to offer can find a place there. We then move to the use of the rule, which instances the situation defined by "awe" and "acceptability." We then get the analogues of faith and grace, which is to say we get a confident movement to the consequence, and the acceptance of our transferred feature by something beyond (even perhaps a reaching to the antecedent to assure it that its feature will be acceptable). And then we move to the analogues of salvation and abandonment, which is to say, to having the transferred feature and "object of faith" acquire a status over against us. From this last position one ought to be able to move to the initial "alieninity," recognizing that what we inferred to still remains something not entirely assimilated by the being or realm in which it is resident.

We have the progression—

Alieninity	⟶	Singularity
Singularity	⟶	Awe
Awe	⟶	Acceptability
Acceptability	⟶	Grace
Grace	⟶	Faith
Faith	⟶	Salvation
Salvation	⟶	Abandonment
Abandonment	⟶	Alieninity, etc.

Alieninity can have degrees; awe can stop at various points; acceptability can be directed at various features, grace has degrees; faith has different objects; salvation has degrees; abandonment has different sides.

January 5

If we view the world of logic as an objective world, and the world of individual adjustments as a private world, we can look at Existence as the juncture of the two. The problem of giving body or verification to the conceived would then be a phase of a larger problem, for the basic issue would seem to be the reconciling, the synthesizing of the private and the public inside the dynamic. In connection with religion it would be the reconciliation of theology (or the formalized understanding of God) with the religious experience, as something possessed by an individual. The reconciliation would take place in work.

In the sequence of yesterday we could have begun the objective series with "acceptability," the recognition of the world in which the items with which we begin are to be placed, and then moved through the analogues of grace, faith, salvation, abandonment, alieninity, singularity, and awe, to come back to the acceptability again. This means that in a proof we begin with the awareness of our accepted feature as having some kind of place in some exterior domain, then being located there, moving it from one position to another, and then finding it not altogether absorbed, leaving us with it as "alien." We then discover its singularity over against a closed and ultimate world.

The movement of faith would begin with "grace." The movement of "work" would begin with the merged situation of "salvation," and the awareness of "abandonment." If work is reconciliation, this would mean that the very beginning of work would involve the integration of the kind of salvation achieved in the other two. The abandonment would be a consequence of the inability to reconcile them entirely, so that the movement of work would be the progress in the reconciliation, the making of more and more of a merger.

But what, then, will we do with the movement of religion, which is begun from the side of the divine? Must this be thought of as a counterpart, in the field of religion, to the "logical"? If so, must we not have a reciprocal counterpart in connection with logic—i.e., must there not be a kind of subjective movement, of belief, or experience, or thinking, which we ought to consider in connection with logic? And then must we not think of reconciling each of these subjects with its correlative? Must we not have a work dedicated to reconciling the subjective and objective facets of a faith, and another for reconciling the subjective and objective facets of logical reasoning? And then the reconciliation of work would seem to be one of reconciling these subordinate works, and the work itself which did the reconciling might treat these "works," the one as subjective, the other as objective.

Where in any of these do we really have an encounter? Can it be anywhere than in the realm of work, and can we have anything but an encountering there? Would work be the way in which we were encountering, and would it itself be asking for its components, which were being reconciled by it, thereby enabling us on the one hand to have a proper meaning or structure (so that we can know what we are encountering) and on the other hand to have a feeling of adjustment enabling us to enjoy what we have come across? But if the final work is the reconciling of subordinate works, do we have a "meaning" and a "feeling" to adjust by means of the neutral work? In any case, in work we would have to go through the movement of finding ourselves at once abandoned (resisted?), then ourselves alienated (made aware of a task?), then singular (thrown back on ourselves?), then awed (aware of the enormity of our task?), then acceptable (capable of doing what is wanted?), then an object of grace (actually having our work find a place in a world?), then faith (projecting and adventuring outward?), and then once more back to a salvation. Would this salvation, this merging, this making our "form" one with a matter lead to more work, more intellection, more adjustment?

January 6

Dealing only with ourselves as occupied with some mode of being beyond us, we have, *1*] speculative knowledge having to do primarily with actualities; *2*] inference having primarily to do with the Ideal; *3*] attitudes having to do with Existence; and *4*] privacy as having to do with God. The attempt to reconcile the first two leads to creative art or to religious service. The reconciliation of the second with the third, leads to action with respect to other actualities or a rational will directed to the absolute Other. The reconciliation of the first with the third leads to ethical action or intent, and to service on behalf of the divine. The reconciliation of the second and fourth involves an understanding of an ultimate perfection or faith. (I am here dealing with the topic of God.) The reconciliation of the third and the fourth involves an understanding or an intention.

On the objective side we first integrate the individual with some mode so as to constitute a representative man, a society, a human realm, or a religious cult; then we must revitalize these by continuing to interplay with the mode as still beyond, to get an adjusted man, a political moral world, history, or a religious community.

If we stay with logic on the one side and faith on the other, we can say that at the end of our inference we are looking for the reality which will sustain our conclusion in the very form in which we arrived at it. We seek to encounter our conclusion as carried externally, unaltered. But in faith we desire the opposite: we want to have the outcome of our struggle with faith—through the steps outlined the last few days—to adopt us, and what we offer it, in such a way as to enhance us and our offering, i.e., in fact to bring good about. We want our conclusion absorbed and then to be encountered as that which is ennobled; we want to see ourselves or what we offer transformed by that at which we arrive; we want to arrive at that which allows us to encounter what we offered, in what we in fact are encountering, as something arrived at; we want thus to find ourselves in that which we are encountering.

Faith gives us a correlative to what logic provides. But we cannot be content with having them just together, for then we do not know how to test one by the other, and do not know just how much one must give way to the other. After all, the logical outcome demands that the encountered be innocuous, not altering our conclusion, whereas the faith demands that the encountered be primary and that we should be altered for the better.

The reconciliation is to be accomplished in "service"—a better term than "work." Here we always have the two sides, the formal predicate and the ontological ground, but we struggle to have an outcome which is "right"—one in which we can have a persistent way of inferring (a matter to be tested in our work in logic, mathematics, science, art, etc.) and in which we can find that what accepts us allows for our participation with others in a smooth way. What we are looking for is then something which allows us to carry out a procedure which enables us to touch upon other realities at desirable points, and also allows us to be together with others significantly. The encountered reality of faith is a kind of togetherness which is final but transformative for all enterprises; the encountered reality for logic allows us to carry out a self-determined set of rules in other areas as well. We have here the analogue of Hope, Faith, and Charity, with Charity being recognized as superior to the others, and in a way a test of them, as St. Paul maintains. What is true of God ought to be true of the other modes as well. We ought to have a reconciliation, through vital activity, of a conceptual grasp of the social good with a faith in its realization (which is characteristic of the publicly ethical)—or, to go back to an individual's struggle, we ought also to have a public aim reconciled with a feeling of loyalty in publicly desirable actions. And we ought to have an artistic grasp of myth reconciled with an emotional grasp of the real in a creative activity.

January 7

There are three approaches to be made to every mode of being from the standpoint of an actuality, such as man. They are the structural, the connective, and the adjustive. In religion these take the form of proofs, worship, and service; in ethics they take the form of proofs, obligation, and ethical activity; in art they take the form of proofs, emotional response, and creativity. But what can be meant by a proof in the realm of art? And in what sense is it needed? Is it not that we presuppose some intellectual awareness of the nature of Existence? That this is minimized in art is true. Proofs are minimized in all areas except that of the Actual. In Actuality we stress the proofs (or logic) and almost take for granted our adjustment to others and to the language or other modes of intercommunication we forge with them. In religion we have a greater stress on worship, perhaps, than on service; in art we have it on the creative activity. But then what of the ethical—do we here keep the obligation and act in a closer equipoise, making the act not so much synthesize the intellectual relation we have to the Ideal, as allow the relation to have a place in the obligatory situation?

When we turn to the experience of God we can once again say that we look up from the commonsensical world in three ways. We find that proofs or discourse which we there use are not adequate to what we see beyond, and try to produce a religious language, a way of acting, or an adjustment in our attitudes.

Better perhaps: in connection with art we stress the work, the reconciliation of anything formal (technique), and anything emotional through which we are going. In connection with ethics we stress the formal commitment, the relation of obligation we in fact have, and must then introduce an intention and a set of appropriate actions. In connection with God we stress the emotive element, the dimension of reverence or faith, and bring in a formal element which we must then integrate to constitute a world of service. Our concern with other actualities will have these different dimensions all copresent, and not have one of them introduced as a supplement. We find ourselves, when dealing with other actualities, occupied with them in terms of structural relations, personal relations, and a public kind of discourse or manners.

January 9

We can make three columns of stages:

Emotion	Structure	Activity
Alieninity	Private Expression	Individual Energy
Singularity	Sentence	Individual Act
Awe	Question	Offering
Acceptability	Proposition	Appropriateness
Creativity	Belief	Readiness
Accommodation	Transferrable Truth	Effectiveness
Beauty	Public Truth	Exchange Value
Incompleteness	Incompleteness	Incompleteness

When in the course of creativity (involving expression and the use of material) we continue pressing forward, we achieve first a kind of artistic submission to our material (enabling us to pursue a career of art) and can then press on to achieve a faith. If we do this our next steps are grace, salvation, and abandonment. If instead we carry through our belief, we find ourselves being subject to an obligation which will lead us to ethics, or, if we press on in the same direction, which will lead us to theological thought, religious truth, religious proof, and religious conviction. Finally, if we start with readiness and carry this through we get an adjustment to other actualities and an activity with respect to them; but if we press further we get a loyalty, an effective service, productive service, and genuine helpfulness.

Why is it that the pressing through ends up with religious dimensions? It need not. The persistence of the emotion to art, of structure to obligation, of activity to action with respect to actualities, is sufficient. It is only if we are not content with the kind of ultimacy these offer, that we right away begin uniting the "transferrable truth" to the creativity to give an effective activity that leads us to art, and that we begin uniting the belief with an emotional accommodation to get an effectiveness in ethical action, and that we persist in adjusting ourselves to other actualities. If we wanted to stay with creativity, or with transferable truth, and were not yet concerned with being effective, we would move to the religious dimension. Religion, or the concern with God, arises by continuing in the dimension of emotion to Incompleteness, in the dimension of structure to communication, so as to yield, via effective service, a final genuine helpfulness constituting a community.

January 10

Perhaps it is more correct to say that we live in some kind of alienated world all the time. It is wrong to suppose that this is merely the world of private sensations or feelings. We can live inside common sense or use our own public language correctly and still find that we are alienated with respect to a larger world outside, or some other language, etc.

We go through the process of living with emotion, structure and activity intertwined, to constitute Experience. This begins with alienated privacy and ends with some kind of interplay with others. It is when we end with an Incompleteness in the field tied up with a kind of completeness in which Beauty, Truth, and Exchange Value are intertwined, that we begin to forge new views of alieninity to give us a field for the emotions, for logic, and for some kind of distinctive work. And as we pursue these we are led to deal with other modes of being, in which the force of the incompleteness is finally made to stand out and is made the topic of an endeavor. If we do it with respect to work we move on to Actuality; but if we do it for logic we move on to ethics, and if we do it for emotion we move on to creativity. But if we insist on having these together again, or on forcing to the end the issue of a world in which we can unite emotion and structure in activity, we move on to religion. Is it that in ethics we do not concern ourselves too much with the realm as it stands over against us; that in art we do not seek too much to preserve our pristine feelings, and that only in religion are we ready to merge the two, to change them both in work or service?

What is called "faith" in the *Modes* is not religious faith; the latter presupposes something like grace, the acceptance by God first—a first which is not necessarily temporal but is presuppositional, or better, correlative and indispensable.

The work of service is to be determined as appropriate if it in fact merges the context which *preserves* the logical outcome, with the encountered context which *enhances* the outcome. There must be an equilibrium point where the logical (better, "structurally attained") outcome is preserved though enhanced, without cancelling the values it in fact has. We know the service is proper if what is attained is made more excellent; or conversely, if the insistent context preserves what we have attained.

January 11

Better than the previous days: In daily life we exercise our emotions with respect to the conventionalized realities about us. Our emotions are expressed more or less without refinement, and the values we cherish and express through them are not preserved. To preserve them we engage in the creative work of art, where we can control the existential matrix which is to enhance the values we express emotionally. But this is limited in range, and covers only the emotion and not the items themselves with which those emotions are involved. By moving to history we get a larger range, and also take care of the items. But history is not yet all-inclusive; it does not necessarily "cherish" our values. We therefore move out to Existence itself only to find that this, though cosmic, does not cherish even the values which we produce in history. A concern for some reality emotionally reached, which will preserve what we cherish, leads to faith in God.

When we go about our ordinary affairs we make use of language as the locus in which our ideas are to be imbedded unaltered, so far as they are true. But the limitation of the language and the conventionalities of it are not suitable to science, mathematics, logic, etc. Their ideas need to be imbedded in something which will allow them to retain their truth. This is what the Ideal provides. But the Ideal demands that we abstract, if we are to make what we know be part of it. To avoid the abstraction we specify the Ideal in the shape of plans, achievable goals, and the like. But this is too restrictive, and also requires some alteration in what we find is the case. A more objective situation (which allows us to conform to it and thereby, at that very time, find some of what is true made real) leads us to politics. But here our canvas is limited once again; we also find alteration produced by the social and public nature of the political scheme. In order to find that which will do justice to the concreteness of our knowledge and yet be receptive to it, and thus not alter it, we accept the reality of a God.

When we engage in ordinary work we find that we are not altogether adjusted to others, and that our plans do not cohere with our basic intentions. We seek to control the work by attending to what is reasonable, and find that this allows us only a limited sphere of endeavor. We then give ourselves to determination by the market, but this subjugates both our plans and our intentions. We need to allow our work to find its place in the entire domain of Actuality, where it is to be reassessed in terms of its place in the entire field. But this does not yet allow for the full sweep of our formal understanding, particularly of the prescriptions of logic and ethics, and does not encompass all that we cherish, including private notions and imagined goods. It is necessary for us to act in service of the divine as a way of having the most extended rationale and the most comprehensive concerns (both as most inward and outward, preserved in the activity as that which is "to find favor in God's sight").

A proof of God might be a proof of the "existence" of God as that locus which will allow our truths to be preserved. It could also be a proof of the unification of all the evidences and testimonies, and thus require a supplementation by an "encountered" God, in the sense of something "existent" (just as the proof of the God's "existence" is in need of an Idea of God as worthy of being ultimately existent). The "proofs" in the *Modes* seem to be of the second kind, of the unification of all the evidences and testimonies. God's "existence" is proven only in the sense that we know Him as the Other, etc., and on the basis of our assumption of the reliability of logic, take this to be sustained in fact.

We can go with Anselm and say that this proof presupposes faith, but we can also reverse his tactic and recognize that we can have a theological proof of the "Other," of the unified meaning of whatever there be, and particularly of ourselves, and that we must then look for a supplementation of this by an encounter, or an object of faith. But better than either is the procedure of moving from work to dedication or charity done on behalf of or in terms of God. In this last way God "exists" only so far as we make Him exist through cosmically conceived service on His behalf, i.e., belief in the most extended abstract scheme unified with the acceptance of the most enhancing reality. This is the "immanent" God who nevertheless stands over against us—i.e., it is God as pertinent to man at his most concrete.

Does God exist? is ambiguous. Is there a locus for the Otherness of all we know? Yes, if logic is to be trusted. Is there an ultimate Existence which will enhance all we cherish? Yes, as the terminus of faith. Is there a God who will save us? Yes, so far as one acts with "charity." But is faith legitimate? Yes, at least at the minimum which we require for logic. Is logic to be trusted? Yes, at the minimum which is justified by faith. Are the two supplementary? Yes, to the degree we make them be, and thus as guaranteeing a minimum justification of logic and faith.

This is the minimum that is achieved by any one who, without religion, recognizes the ontological reality of God and the way we must get to Him from common-sense realities, via an experience of the counterpart of those realities.

Service on behalf of God guarantees the minimal objectivity needed for logic and the minimal preservation demanded by faith. In logic of course we believe there is an objectivity, and thus we have a kind of "faith" going beyond the logic; in faith we are going to a God we some-how understand and thus have a kind of rationale, a minimal exterioriza-tion of what we attain in thought. In the one we suppose "Existence" for the meaning we have unified and to which we in fact infer; in the other we suppose a "logic" for the reality which we accept in order to be unified ourselves, to enjoy our privacy as ultimately real. But the minimal we get in service is beyond these; it is the "Existence" which en-hances the logic, a "logic" which clarifies the supposed object of faith.

A proof of a mode is thus not similar to ordinary proofs. A proof of "God" for example might be only, as was suggested above, the achieve-ment of a unity which "others" us and what we cherish. A proof of "Existence" itself would be of the essence of dynamic Existence; a proof of "Ideality" would be of a meaning which was imbedded in a pre-scriptive power (?), and a proof of Actuality would be of an ultimacy which was less concrete than its many members.

January 13

In a primal experience there are no definite polarities or or-ganizations of content, and yet there is something more than sheer chaos. We have focal points merging into less intensive areas, which themselves merge into still other focal points, the entire mass shifting constantly. This primal experience is never entirely eliminated, but due to language and experience we do sharpen a common-sense region and spend most of our time living in it. It is then that we also have a correla-tive focus in an experience of the awesome. The more we concentrate on the common-sense area the more we suppose that it is sustained by "the awesome" which lies outside it. This is the minimal faith in the common-sensical and logical which we all have. What we know has its objec-tivity by virtue of being part of something larger than ourselves, where "ourselves" can be us in our privacies, in our societies, or even as all mankind and its enterprises. But we could have started with the op-posite stress and recognized the awesome as that which is "gracious," reaching out to make worthwhile what is outside it. This is a minimal "rationality" in the sense that the reaching out demands that there be some value in what is being sought—truth, e.g. Faith says that there is a truth which it seeks, and that this is what logic, language, etc., offer to the awesome.

The minimal faith which logic and common sense require, the faith that they have objective status, can be intensified to give us a domain in which the logic, etc., is enhanced, and in which more than logic is acceptable. Similarly, the "truth of logic," which faith already guarantees, can be supplemented by other values such as beauty. This is not merely offered up for the object of faith to do with as it would, but as that which has its own integrity and value, and deserves to be preserved by the awesome.

A "believer" is one who goes beyond these minima, and does so by some kind of activity. He could act like anyone else most of the time, but there must come crucial points where we can see how his belief makes a difference. He need not pray or worship but there must be some "detachment" from the world, some sacrifice of worldly goods on behalf of some power beyond which is understood to subtend all that he can distinguish.

To praise one prays.

Experience: any participation which has an effect on consciousness or practice. This allows for work and faith, "religious" or common-sensical reference, unnoted activities, private "experiences" of pain, and public experiences of things, both as individuals and in groups, or even mankind.

If we think of common sense as being developed in language, empirical science, etc., we need a faith that this has an objective status. If we view its correlative as the awesome, we can say it has a minimal rationality in that it says there is something worthwhile in what we are doing. From this perspective we do not bring in the Ideal—except as a way of uniting the above with a stress on the rationality, with the substantial object of faith penetrating this rationality to get to us as a prescription. God would have a correlative function in that He would stress the substantiality and would be concerned first with the enhancement and cherishing of what we have done. The development of the Ideal would require that it be specified as a rule of ethics and as a guide for politics, the one stressing the prescription and relevance to us, the other the particularity and the relevance of a needed rule. The development of the understanding of God would require that He be recognized to have a concreteness and particularity in an institution, and a relevance and enhancement for the individual. The acceptance of the Ideal is an awareness of an insistent obligating demand governing the structures we accept, to be made specific and realized here and now in ethics and politics, but in the end to be granted an ultimacy. The acceptance of God would, correlatively, be an awareness of an exterior union of what we cherish with a transformative enhancing power, with a consequent effort to make it concrete first in the shape of some public institution and then for and in the individual.

To make rationality maximum, we must recognize that the object of faith not only is ready to accept all we do, but demands that this be of value in itself. To make faith maximum, we must recognize that not only the value achieved by thought, i.e., "truth," is objective (and so the *modus ponens* is justified) but that all we achieve is objective, and that it must be transformed in order to be enhanced.

When we take our categories to be sustained by what we creatively make, we see ourselves as satisfying the Ideal in ourselves; when we take our creative efforts to ennoble what we know, we view ourselves as satisfying a divine injunction. When we see our actions justified in history, we see ourselves living up to an ought-to-be; when we see our history opening up our action and ennobling it, we see ourselves as free men living as images of the divine.

Both the Ideal and God require work as a way of combining what we do and that which we wish to have objective, and what is insistent but will preserve and enhance what is valuable. We would then have ethical activity and political activity on the one side, and a dedication in work and a public service in the name of the divine on the other side.

There ought to be analogous problems in connection with a reconciliation of the rational, not with the ultimate substantial but with man as knowing and acting here and now—the problem of the way in which his guilt is to be overcome by God, and by art or history, and a reconciliation of the ultimate substantial, not with the rational, but with man as knowing and acting—the problem of conversion through the agency of ethics, politics, art, or history. (Reconciliation of the dynamic with the rational or the substantial is not as relevant here as the reconciliation of man as knowing and acting with the dynamic. This is the problem of adjustment under the guidance of the ethical or political, or the mythos, and under the guidance of the divine as understood, say by the Bhagavad-Gita.)

But why should not the unbalanced reconciliation provided by the Ideal be matched by one by Existence, and these be mediated by God who is as occupied with what is beyond as the Ideal is, is as insistent on itself as Existence is, but is more particularized than the former and more enhancing than the latter?

January 14

The Ideal in-itself can be said to be at once a structure, prescriptive, and a standard; Existence in-itself is ground, becoming and perpetually present; God in-Himself commands, absorbs, and absconds; Actually in-itself is individual, private, and substantial. Each of these features play some role in the various modes (subordinated in those modes to the power of the modes themselves) and must be freed from those modes if they are to exhibit the above features fully.

The Ideal uses Existence to enable it to stand away from itself, to provide a backing for it. We refer to that Existence in taking content to be objective. But if we intensify the Existence and pull it away from the Ideal we can see it as grounding all contents. The Ideal uses God to enable it to be prescriptive. We refer to the divine component when we see that the content we make objective must conform to conditions external to itself. If we separate off that divine component we can see it as commanding. The Ideal uses Actuality to provide it with internal seams or creases. We refer to the encompassed actualities when we speak of relevant possibilities. Those actualities can be separated off from the Ideal and then seem to have an interior individuality, not reducible to universals.

Existence uses the Ideal to give it direction. We recognize that Ideal when we see structure in Existence. Separating the Ideal from Existence allows it to be a structure in- and of-itself, a locus for any values. Existence also uses God to give it a unity or essence, and we recognize this fact whenever we note there is an ultimate domain, a realm in which things are together. Separated from the Existence, God is seen to be an absorptive unity, one which has things together in His own enhancing terms. Existence uses Actuality to give it pivots, points of orientation. We recognize the Actuality when we come to stopping points, ultimate points of resistance, and when we separate out actualities we acknowledge them as having their own privacies.

God uses the Ideal as content obtained from elsewhere. We acknowledge it when we see it as imposing conditions of value. When we separate out that Ideal we have it as prescriptive. God uses Existence as a field of operation and we recognize that Existence in Him when we see it as the locus of all our references. Separated off from God it recovers itself as a perpetual becoming. God also uses actualities as an occasion for multiplying Himself. We note the actualities when we note that beings have ultimately preserved rights or dignities or values. When we hold those actualities apart we have them as free and self-developing, substantial beings.

Actualities have the Ideal in them as a purpose, objectives which obligate. We note the Ideal when we attend to the commitments and prospects open to an actuality. When we separate off the Ideal we have it as a standard. The actuality also contains Existence; this enables it to be present. We note the Existence when we note the passage of time, the independent movement and being of the world. Separated off we get Existence as a perpetually renewed present. And finally, actualities contain God within them. He gives them a unity as an Other. We note that God when we note that He operates as it were from a distance. When we separate Him off from the actualities we have Him as the Absconding God.

We try to master Existence by being creative; to get objectivity we move to history. But not until we refer to God do we have Existence as a unified field of operation which will enhance and not merely permit things to be. We try to live up to the Ideal ethically; to get our prospects more particularized, we move to politics. But we achieve a more comprehensive satisfied Ideal by recognizing its place in God. We try to be adjusted to other actualities by knowledge, and then more effectively through action. But we get an ennobled set of actualities by recognizing that they are in God.

What we seek to do with the various modes is best done if we locate them in other modes. Thus the Existence, which we seek to master by creativity and history, can be mastered better by also being divided among actualities or made to give backing to the Ideal; the Ideal can be satisfied not only in God, but as the very controlling structure of Existence, or as a standard imposed on man making him guilty or justified; actualities can be adjusted not only in God, but as the subdivisions in the Ideal and as pivotal points in Existence. God in turn can be acknowledged as a prescription in the Ideal, the unity of Existence, and the Other of Actuality. (In these cases it is not a fact that the items lack certain features which are then introduced, e.g., the Ideal is not unprescriptive and made to prescribe by God. It is an analysis of the Ideal which reveals that this is the role God plays as an ingredient in the Ideal.)

Which way of being satisfied is better? Is it better, for example, to have the Ideal dealt with as a component in Existence, God, or Actuality? Must we not say that no one is better? The reason we turn to God is that we then are able to do justice to the Ideal, Existence, and Actuality as components. We cannot do justice to all three as components in any of the other modes, since the other modes function to allow only two of them to become components. We turn to the other modes because we want to deal with God as a component and thus as more than mediated by other modes. In the case of other modes we do not have this kind of interest; we are content to deal with them as helped out by God. God is helped out by the other modes, since in them he achieves such functions as being an Other, giving a Unity, and as providing for a prescription, a kind of commanding role.

When we look to the counterpart of common sense we find the various modes interlocked, each in each. We normally begin by enabling each to stand out, and as a rule get God to stand out as a vanishing unitary and ultimate commanding being, through an act of discrimination, thereby making Him the background of ourselves, Existence, and the Ideal. Faced with this distinguished but undefined reality, we then take Him as the locus of the other modes as sought for in their full range and intensity. He is seen to be the unity of all "idealized" content, satisfying all; the "existing" possessor of all, and the individual sustainer of individuals. And then we can go and reverse our stress and see how He is satisfied by actual worship, ennobled by being evaluated by the Ideal, and enabled by Existence to work in the world.

We must separate out the fundamental realities, then see them subjugate one another, and then see them as subjugated. The separation out is a matter of discrimination and persistence. The seeing of them as capable of subjugating is the pursuit of various efforts to deal with them, leading finally to the acknowledgment of modes of being. We then move to see them subjugated as ways of having those modes satisfied. And then we can see them as finalities subjugating in turn.

January 15

We proceed most satisfactorily in religion if we have first identified ourselves with Ideality and Existence, either by virtue of an engagement in various disciplines or through obligation and technology.

Had we instead been concerned with the mastery of the Ideal in itself, we would have identified ourselves with Existence and God, which is to say we would have been effective and confident, using the practice of reasonableness to bring them together. Had we concerned ourselves with the mastery of Existence in itself, we would have identified ourselves with Ideality and God, which is to say we would have been purposeful and confident, and used the existential context as a way of synthesizing these.

We ought to proceed in religion by accepting Actuality, finding rifts in it which will lead us to note an Ideal and an Existential side with which we will become identified in obligation and effective work, or in the various disciplines of ethics, politics, art, and history. The awareness of our representativeness, of prescriptiveness and compulsiveness, leads us to absolutize these in the shape of a final privacy, command and power, achieved by giving ourselves, our values and what we cherish, in honest, private and public service. We can then see that God Himself is excellent, creative, and concerned, and that an absolutization of these features is what He is aware of and which we can attend to.

February 2

Let logic be defined as the discipline concerned with determining the legitimacy of a translation (having a minimum in the form of a mere transfer) of some feature from one situation to another. We can then say that the route covered by the transfer is a Rule or Leading Principle, R. As Peirce observed, given P (a beginning) R, and Q (the outcome) we can isolate a Logical Principle L. P and R suffice to give us Q, and the fact that Q is derivable from it is stated by L. When we add L to P and R we still get a Q related by an L. L then is the last principle.

Now it is the case that given any P and any R we get some Q. Given money and the law of wills or contracts in my society we get a certain Q; given another law we get a different outcome. Given P to be true and R to be, say, the repeating of it three times, we will get a Q, let us say, P repeated three times. And we can say that given P as true and R as any route it is true that Q. But what we want to know is whether Q will have the very truth that P has. It can have only the kind of truth the P has in relation to R; it will be involved in that context.

The concern of logic is to get an L, for this allows P to be only minimally changed by being brought into relationship with it, and allows, therefore, the achievement of a Q which can stand outside the L. The L, thought actually offering us an internal relation, gives us one which allows for the beginning with a P which has a truth apart from all contexts, and thus permits of a Q which is true apart from all contexts. The contingency and materiality of a rule restricts the objectivity, the independent status, the universality of the possible contexts in which the P and the Q can be true.

The most general logic is based on the acknowledgment of what will allow for the minimal alteration in a feature, as standing outside the logical context. When we employ contingent rules we but delimit the possible places in which the items with which we begin, and thus with which we end, can be.

The more contingent the rule the more internally determined is the property which is being translated from one position to the other. Given the illustration above about the threefold repetition, the kind of truth that is conveyed to Q is but the truth of being available for a repetition. When we employ the logical rule to say that if the P is true and if Q follows from the P together with the R, we are saying that the truth, that R has been used with the truth of P, is a truth in any context, and that the Q has such a truth. This means that there are two kinds of truth that Q can have; a truth which belongs to it as following P because of R, and a truth which it has because it follows P and R because of the logical principle L.

If we take the rule and convert it into a proposition, which is to say, if we claim it to have a truth of its own on a footing with the P, we can get the Q as a consequence of two truths. This conversion of the rule into a truth is one with the conversion of the P into a truth for the rule, similar to the truth of the P. Consequently, it is the same thing to say that my private pain or acknowledgment of it is, by virtue of my private rule, made into a private Q, as it is to say that the public rule makes the public meaning of P become the public meaning of Q. In both cases we have Q following by necessity from P and R, but in the former the R is a private "truth" and in the latter the P is a public "truth," and the Q consequently is private and public respectively. The rule of repeating the premiss three times, when converted into a truth, "It is true that he repeats it three times," might give a conclusion "P becomes tiresome," and this would be true only if the character of "tiresomeness" was actually a product of that rule as an operating factor. If it were such a factor it would not be the case that "He repeats it three times" would be true in the sense that P was true. (I am not clear that the foregoing is altogether right.)

February 3

The rule or leading principle which I use on any beginning, must be one which is in the same domain as that beginning if it is to result in an outcome on a level with that beginning. If the rule is not on that level, the outcome is nothing more than a qualification of the beginning. In either case the logical principle is operative, telling us that the end, whatever it be, is necessitated by the beginning as operated on by that rule. The difference between a poor rule and a good rule is that the poor rule does not give us separated content on a level with the beginning. A logical principle is always a good rule; it gives us an outcome which is on a level with the beginning. The difference between a logical outcome of the use of a poor and the use of a good rule, is that the outcome in the latter case is not only on a level with the initial P and R, but with the initial P. We would like to have outcomes which are as good as our beginnings. Or otherwise said, we would like our rule to be stable as a true proposition of the same order as the P.

February 4

It is the case that any operation on something will produce a result which can be said to be necessitated by the juncture of the something and the operation. But what we want to know is how we can obtain a certain result, given a certain beginning, and thus what rule must be imposed on that beginning to get that result. The result could be an entity which we would like to have characterized in a certain way. In that case the rule will tell us how to move from the initial characterization to the subsequent one. Or the result could be a characterization which we insist on having again, and the rule will tell us what kind of result must be produced if that characterization is to apply. In the working with formal logical systems it is the latter that is of primary interest, but in the ordinary course of events, in inquiry, where we have something interesting in mind and where we may insist on having this, we look for the rule which will give us content where this can have maximum value. We want, let us say, to know if there will be a war, and seek to find out the probability of it; we could, though, insist on finding out what will in fact ensue, and thus what is as real as what now is, or as true.

When we operate on a beginning we produce a result; but when we approach this situation from the standpoint of logic we detach the beginning, with its operation, from the result, and thus make the logical rule be the principle of operation on the juncture of the beginning and the rule. Having decided that such and such is to have such and such a value (and therefore merge the foregoing two ways of dealing with an outcome, i.e., the one which is concerned with a translation or transfer of a characterization on a fixed item, and the other with the determination of an item which will have such and such a characterization) we look for a rule which can be imposed on the beginning. Our starting point is a beginning and an outcome detached from one another. So far as logic is concerned there is only a juncture of beginning and rule, even when as a matter of fact the rule operates on the beginning. But what we ask for in such a case is a rule which will in fact operate, and thus will in fact produce the outcome in the same world as the beginning is. Until we do this, we put the beginning and rule in a world of mere truth, and operate on this to get the conclusion.

Logic tells us what rules we can use to produce the outcome which is on a footing with beginning and rule together. But beginning and rule together may give us only a momentary result, one which exists only in the mind, etc. We need a rule to be imposed on the beginning, to accept the beginning on its own terms, so that we can have an outcome which is in the same domain as the beginning. We thus dictate what will constitute a domain, a rule-dominated area.

On this basis we can say that it is one of our desires to have another think as we do. The rule we normally use is common language. Language then can be said to be that mode of operating on something which will produce what another entertains, and that this which is entertained is necessitated by my idea and the operation. What we would like to be sure of is that what the other obtains is exactly what we had wanted him to obtain, and this means that the process of language must be evaluated. Ordinary language may be discarded or modified if it does not produce this desired result.

Wherever we get to is something entailed, since we did get there by the joint operation of just that beginning and process; the outcome is the result of the two. But not every outcome is equally desired, and the problem of logic and inquiry is to first ascertain what is desired and then to find a rule which will operate. Until we find such a rule, the logic will tell us only that the process as conjoined with the beginning make an entity with a definite characteristic and that this characteristic is inherited by such and such an outcome (indeed by the very one at which we in fact arrive through the use of the process). Starting with logic we know of possible rules, but we do not employ those rules; starting with the employment of rules we necessitate outcomes but not necessarily desirable ones.

February 14

When confronted with a number of disciplines dealing with topics which are of interest to mankind, and which seem to have elicited devoted followers, wisdom would dictate that we deal with each one by itself. But we must also recognize that the interpretation of it must   A] allow room for the others to stand outside its domain, and   B] allow the others to be given some kind of satisfaction inside it, though in a muted form. The latter consideration involves a recognition that the field is rather large in interests and presuppositions, perhaps much more so than its practitioners imagine. And the acceptance of it as so large, when combined with the first consideration, means that there will be a plurality of "lives," each of which encompasses the others and also has them outside it.

How are these to be reconciled? Is it not by the principle of detachment and affiliation? We detach each and let it have its full being, and then recognize that each should have the others not only in it in a muted form, but accredited to it as adding a context for it. If we have a religion it must find a place inside itself for ethical demands; and conversely, the ethics must accommodate the salvational component of religion. If we are ethical, with a salvational element in our ethics, we must accept the religious dimension as something which can be externally added to our ethics in the sense of giving it a larger meaning, and this by virtue of the affiliation of the ethical with the religious. That is, we will say that the ethical life, e.g., when lived with full integrity, is to be understood as fitting into a world in which a religious life is lived with full integrity, and that the ethical man should recognize that he belongs in a world embracing both that religious world and the ethical, even though he does nothing to promote the religious. And we must do similar things for other lives—historic, technological, e.g., in relation to the ethical or political, and the religious. The attitude of the Bhagavad-Gita then, with respect to the fruits of one's action (and the reciprocal of this, as discussed in my book on history, the detachment of the private life and the accreditation of the world of action) to the privately living being, is to be used as a model for all the lives, and thus of all possible dimensions which different men could occupy as complete. The affiliations are nothing but ways of completing the meaning of what is internally complete in itself, by giving eternal determinations to it, even though it also has determinations inside it in a muted form.

The combination of ethics and religion, to stay with this example, can be characterized as ethical or religious. We do the first sometimes when we speak of the full life as the life that alone is good; we do the second sometimes when we say that religion is the referring of the full life to the orienting of it in God. But no orienting toward the Ideal, or God, or whatever, could give us the all-inclusive life which contains all other ways of living in their full forms; the only way in which we can have all the lives together at their maximum, and thus have a full life, is to have no one of them define the orientation, to have all orientations together. But it might be said: ought we not to live such a full life, and is this not an ethical claim? To this we could answer "yes," providing we at once say that it also is an excellent life, an effective life, an aesthetically satisfactory life, a spiritual life, etc. As soon as we use one of these lives to characterize the totality, we should bring in the others, or define the one as demanding that it be only one of many. Either, then, an account of the ultimate life involves a coordination of many, or it involves the use of a one which denies itself so that a subordinated form of itself should be together with equally subordinated forms of the others.

February 20

A model for an answer to the way in which various realities can be distinct and yet together, is given in the Nicene Creed's interpretation of the Logos and God the Father—homoousian, the same substance, though distinct as persons. This can be carried over into the relation of God to Actuality; and an analogue can be obtained in connection with God and the Ideal—"homoagatha"—and of God and Existence—"homoenergeia." We should find similar combinations in connection with the participation of Actuality, God, and Existence in the Ideal; the sharing in Existence by Actuality, God, and the Ideal; and the distinguishing by Actuality from itself and the Ideal, Existence, and God.

February 24

If it be true that each of us must act representatively for all the others and that we ought to detach ourselves from the fruits of our activities—fruits which may be religious as well as practical—then it seems that no one of us can live a full life except so far as we are instances of a full life in an entire society. The practical man must detach himself from the fruits of his actions in order to give a place for the contemplative life. The contemplative man must detach himself from his life of thought in order to have a place for the realm of practice in which he inevitably engages. The practical man does not get to a proper position though until he has accredited to him the whole worth of the contemplative life; the contemplative man, similarly, must have the whole of practice accredited to him. Each is to be free of what he himself does and is to possess what the others do. This means that the center of gravity of each is the same, no matter what the contribution; the part he brings in is of no more consequence than the part he acquires; consequently his perfection lies in his being an instance of a socialized ethical man—not in the sense of being a member of a society, but of being together with other men in a single mankind in which various individuals function representatively, to deal with certain specialized facts of the world encountered in thought, religion, creativity, etc.

March 12

If it be the case that an item achieves determination by being brought into a context, we ought to add a kind of hook to a p before we use it in an implication, to indicate that it will enter into the implication. But ought we not also have a hook on the p as that which could be given implicative status? And if we do the latter do we not invite an infinite regress? I think we need not, for it is possible to affirm that the initial status is that of an indeterminate p, and that we are not interested in the way in which this may achieve a place in a possible situation. We start with the fact that p has already been dealt with as something which we want to use in a possible situation. Consequently, the *modus ponens* should look like this:

$$(1)\ P \qquad (2)\ P \frown$$
$$(3)\ p \supset Q$$
$$(4) \frown Q \qquad (5)\ Q$$

(*1*) is a proposition viewed as that which could be used as a premiss; it is the private which says that it could have a public use. (*2*) is the premiss for an unspecified conclusion, the "assertion" for a *modus ponens*. (*3*) is merely the usual implication. (*4*) is the inferred conclusion, and can therefore be recognized to involve some affiliation with the initial premiss. (*5*) is the separated conclusion which is to be taken as a distinct proposition; nevertheless it still shows that it has been certified in a situation.

1 and 2, and *4* and *5* differ in the kind of referent they make. *1* and *5* both are separate propositions, asserted by themselves as pertinent to an external world, but *1* says that we want to use that truth syntactically and *5* says that we are to use its truth semantically. 2 says that the truth now is a syntactical one, but has not yet been given its distinctive syntactical use; it merely belongs to the set of rules for such a use. *5* says that the truth now is a semantical one but has not yet found the semantical referent; it merely belongs to those which claim to have such a referent, having been guaranteed by virtue of the achievement of the development from 2 to *4*.

How do we go from *1* to 2, and from *4* to *5*? We go from 2 to *4* via *3* by inference. But from *1* to 2 we move from, "There is a rule for p" to "p is subject to a rule." The movement from *4* to *5* is the movement from something like "q has been certified" to "q has been certified to be that which needs no further certification." We move from a relational to a characterizing meaning of a rule in the first case; and we move from a relational to a characterizing meaning of reference in the second case. We want our rule to be dealt with as integral to the premiss in the first case, we want a truth reference to an external world to be dealt with as integral to the conclusion in the second case. Consequently we have the following moves: *1*] From a reference to a rule by p, to   2] a unification of p with a rule, to   3] a structuralization by a rule of implication to q, to   4] a reference to a truth claim by q, to   5] a warranted truth claim.

Preceding *1* is p as something privately enjoyed, or even as that which is true by virtue of a reference to the external world; succeeding *5* is q as something privately enjoyed or as matched with some external fact. Preceding *1* and succeeding *5*, in short, is the non-contextual, which we get by detaching from a reference to a possible context. It is the view of people like Dewey and Wittgenstein that the predecessor to *1* and the successor to *5* are either meaningless, indeterminate, or indistinguishable from *1* and *5* respectively. But this does not seem to be correct, for we can and do stand outside the public domain, not considering that we are to enter it or that we have left it, and holding data entirely apart from it as part and parcel of our being over against that public world. Consequently we have the following seven steps:

A] The entertained
B] A reference to a rule
C] A unification with a rule
D] A structuralization by a rule
E] An inference to a claimant
F] A claimant asserted
G] The assertion entertained

We can get to A as we get to G, but we can also invent it, abstract it, get it by expressing ourselves, etc. The movement to A, if it is like a movement to G from F, presupposes another inferential situation. When we move from F to G we must reverse the process of going from A to B; we must analyze out the asserted component, put aside the claimant aspect. This means that we go from A to B in a kind of synthesis, and from F to G in a kind of analysis. We now have:

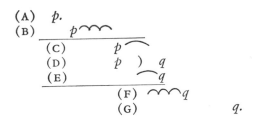

$$(A) \quad p.$$
$$(B) \quad \underline{\qquad p \qquad}$$
$$(C) \qquad p$$
$$(D) \qquad p \;) \; q$$
$$(E) \quad \underline{\qquad q}$$
$$(F) \qquad q$$
$$(G) \qquad\qquad q.$$

March 24

Socrates thinks of himself as a midwife. This means that there is another who is to bear the children of thought. He asks that the other be willing, and that means the other must be open to his help. His help consists in finding the proper moment at which what is in the other can be brought out. This is why Socrates does not write books. A book is a kind of instruction to the reader on how to become a midwife to himself. But Socrates would like to help someone; he must therefore speak to that other, make a proper move at a given time. Each person has moments when the ultimate truth is seen by him, no matter how dimly. The easiest person from whom to elicit this truth is a young person who is not yet habituated, who is more readily responsive to outside help. The oldest possible habituated person (a sophist?) can also be brought to see the truth, but the occasions for penetrating to the place where he can discern this are less frequent, and the response to the help of Socrates is more violent. Socrates questions young boys, then, because in a way they more frequently open themselves up to what is the case, and Socrates can with comparative ease make them see more clearly what they had already dimly discerned.

In opposition to Socrates, Plato writes books; this means that Plato is either trying to teach others to imitate Socrates and become midwives for others, or that he is teaching others how to become midwives for themselves. The more speculative books evidently are engaged in the second. And all subsequent philosophers, so far as they pursue dialectic, are concerned with making evident the method by which they themselves, and consequently the reader, can cut through the habituations and blurs of daily life to exhibit the truth which is within, and which is discerned occasionally.

April 6

Dewey's view of logic and language, like Wittgenstein's, is social in nature. But Dewey's view is superior to Wittgenstein's in that A] it is concerned with inquiry and science and thus is not restricted to a particular society. B] It asks about the nature of the entities which come together to constitute the determinate unity of public language. It says these are indeterminate anticipations or instruments for that inquiry, whereas Wittgenstein can see them only as components or derivatives from the public togetherness. C] It sees that the world of nature as well as societal things are themselves indeterminates, made determinate by being integrated with the language, and then not by merely being plastered on or used as a kind of glasses or sign, but as in fact made integral with that content in the course of the inquiry. D] It pays some attention to the fact that there are such things as abstract mathematics and logic, though it tends to suppose that these are also indeterminacies for use in making a concrete situation determinate. E] It pays attention to the various claims of evaluation, negation-affirmation, history, art, consummatory values. F] It tries to link the developed sophisticated language of inquiry with the primal biological drives of men and thus provides a continuity and an explanation of how and why inquiry is what it is. G] It is alive to the fact that knowledge, science, logic, and language are constantly changing and that they make use of funded knowledge acquired in the past.

There are a number of weaknesses in Dewey's view, and I think these are to be found in Wittgenstein's too, in addition to those which he has because he falls short of Dewey's position. There is no adequate provision made by Dewey for the prescriptions of logic, mathematics, ethics, as standing outside and definitely organizing and dictating to inquiry; there is no recognition of anything transcending inquiry or public discourse, and thus no understanding of how man can think in private, pray in private, imaginatively construct and create in private; there is no recognition of the reality of any beings outside discourse and its constitutive functions.

Every mode of being is at once determinate and indeterminate; each has a nature and a rationale of its own, and each falls short of having determinations that the other has. Actuality lacks the rationality, the vitality, and the private unity of the others; the Ideal lacks the individuality, the vitality, and private unity of the others; Existence lacks the individuality, the rationality, and the private unity of the others; God lacks the individuality, the rationality, and the vitality of the others. Each achieves some determination by being integrated with the others to make cosmological limited unities.

In the *Modes* reference is made to the collective disjunction which possibilities have as part of a mind, and to the distributive disjunction they have in Existence. But there ought then to be either a recognition of a disjunction produced by the coming together of these two (mind and Existence) in some kind of directed action, or the distributive disjunction should be seen to be the product of two other disjunctions which are now indeterminate with reference to their role in that distributive disjunction. In short there ought to be a disjunction which is the determinate outcome of the union of the collective and the distributive, or the distributive itself should be seen to be the determinate outcome of the union of two other types of disjunction, one of which is the collective. In either case we must recognize a third type of disjunction, as either more or less determinate than the collective or the distributive. The more determinate seems to be the correct answer since it is produced through a union of what has justification in distinctive modes of being.

There must be a mode of disjunction which expresses the fact that mind (as the locus of ideal contents) and Existence are united. They can be united by Actuality or God. In the former case they lead to a consideration of art, and in the second to that of cosmic providence. Are these two distinct types of combination? Apparently so. In any case what we have is a dynamic disjunction, a disjunction which could be said to have content and therefore determinateness given to it and its members by the act of artistic creation or by divine interest.

What is true of disjunction should be true of all the other "logical constants" and all other ideas and essences and meanings which are rooted in particular modes. And when we come to the language of society or religion, etc., what we ought to find is a determinate outcome of usages and entities which have their own determinate natures and indeterminacies.

We ought not to assume that the product of a juncture of the various modes of being is determinate in every respect. The determinateness achieved in art, ethics, history, politics, religion, conceptualization, action are linked to indeterminacies expressing the fact that the constitutive entities have a being and a power and a career outside the juncture, which is distinct from that which they have in the juncture, by virtue of the contribution made to them by the other constituents.

May 20

If we pair off actualities and Existence, and Ideality and God, we could with some justice treat them respectively as essentially Aristotelian and Platonic in temper, or as the reasonable and the rational, the judicious and the dialectic, or the lived and the conceived. If we take our start from the Platonic position we can distinguish the four modes of being as functioning prescriptively with respect to one another, and arrive at an Aristotelian position by going to a mixture of the modes. The move requires us to say that the Platonist already has a thin mixture; the modes are together "cosmologically" and the move is a move toward a thicker togetherness of pairs of modes (for all four never have a greater thickness than the minimum prescriptive). If, instead, we start with the Aristotelian position, we begin with a mixture and can arrive at the genuine Platonic position only by recognizing that we already had detached ourselves from the Aristotelian world, that our living together meant that we were also separate, that knowledge, though a kind of being, is a facing of what is other. We could, of course (as the typical Platonist does), have treated the Aristotelian dimension as nonexistent, or as involving a leap, or as a blurred version of the Platonic position; but it is better to see the Platonism as already "Aristotelianized" as indeed it must be since the ultimate oughts of a Platonic scheme must be realized.

The ordinary Aristotelian accepts some contingent matter of fact as primary and uses this as a prescription; he is rightly charged by the Platonist for being arbitrary. If we start with Platonism we can say that the ultimate prescriptions are the ultimate realities, and can explain the ordinary Aristotelian world as an intensification of the inescapable prescriptive togetherness of those ultimate realities. But the Aristotelian charges that the Platonic dimension is a reification, is nonexistent, is nonsense, or involves a leap. But it is better to see that Aristotelian "platonized" as having reached a legitimate transcendent ground from which to make his prescriptions effective. He says that the Platonist accepts some necessity as being a matter of fact—mathematics, logic, ethics, aesthetics—and uses the fact as the real; in short, that the Platonist converts impalpable abstractions into final substances. But we can also say that the ultimate realities are norms for one another and that we are over against them right from the start.

The chains in the cave are already broken, so we can go from the cave to the Platonic heaven. Yet we are already chained, so we can go down from the forms to things. We are in fact always partly chained and partly free, and when we stress the one, the other stands out as beyond our reach unless we see it as that which is some variant of the other. Neoplatonism and Constructivism supplement one another. Each by itself never gets to the reality with which the other begins, but if we have both we are always at the beginning of each of these extremes. The Platonist has already become Aristotelianized as he moves down the Neoplatonic hierarchy; the Aristotelian has already become Platonized as he moves up a dialectic to reach the presuppositions without which he could not function.

July 20

A non-ontological interpretation of the *Modes of Being* would attempt to deal with the world as a product of many perspectives. It would perhaps say that the whole, taken distributively, yields actualities; taken collectively, is Existence; that its invariant features make up Possibility; and that some individual whose meaning or status is paramount for men, is God. The question will arise as to what the perspective is being imposed on, and who is imposing it. This could be answered by supposing that God is the source of perspectives, that we inherit them from Him, and that they are imposed on the Actuality-Existence-Possibility totality as over against that God. There would be need, though, to make the collective scheme have some kind of status over against the distributive, and to have everything subject to the prescriptions contained in possibility. God would then have to be thought of not only as a source of the perspectives, but as allowing them to be. In His very nature He would require that there be over against Him this combine in which the elements function with respect to one another in various restrictive ways. God would be something like a Fichtean ego or a Hegelian absolute; one could think of Him achieving His own distinctive being by virtue of the fact that He made these others possible, and that He had to make these others possible in order to be possible Himself. The argument for God's Existence would be an argument which showed that the Existence of the combine makes evident its possibility. This possibility would be indistinguishable from the possibility of God, unless God were existent. (Here "possibility" would be something isolated in the realm of possibility, but of course referring to what was outside that realm.)

Possibility, as that which is exhausted in all else, would be over against all else so long as any being was occupied with realizing it in some degree; there would always be redistributions of possibilities so that they could be realized. Individual men could be said to defy God and even be other than He by assuming a representative role. Existence would have the power to organize and keep individuals abreast by virtue of the features the beings had in common and the inseparability of their relational status.

An ontological argument for God could be framed by saying that He was the being who, because possible, was necessary and therefore was everywhere (in Existence—which is what the cosmological argument says), and who was concerned with producing the distribution (of actualities—which is a kind of teleological argument), and who controlled the final realization of possibility (which is a kind of moral argument).

The foregoing reduction is nonnaturalistic in the sense that it starts with God. To make it naturalistic one might try to identify the source of all perspectives with oneself. But we would be up against the fact that we die. The most that one could hope for is to make the God somebody or other, and see this as having the foregoing roles. One would have to grant primary status to the vague or general, the indeterminate, and suppose this to have a definite effective role over against all the others.

Could this be worshiped? What would become of faith? Of religious observances, etc? We would have achieved a reduction in ontology but only by making one also in religion and perhaps also in other enterprises.

The justification of an ontology is in good part the fact that it provides a satisfactory underpinning for practices, insights, and apparent truths that could not otherwise be found. To oppose the ontology by a reductive scheme is to accept as more reasonable what one can construct with a minimum of ontological suppositions; it is also to endow the constructions with various powers in order that the facts be dealt with properly. Is there a gain in supposing that "somebody or other" has a role like God, with something like His powers, prescriptions, persistence, rather than that there is a divine being which "somebody or other" mirrors at some remove? And if we need a divinity, ought we not need the other three modes of being?

September 26

The absolute is of course not relativized. Nevertheless it is correct to say that it is relative. The absolute—and similarly, the thing-in-itself, reality—is something in contrast with the relativized. Take away the relativized, the appearances, the non-real, and there would be not an absolute entity left, but one in which there was no way of distinguishing either side.

The absolute or nonrelativized is what a relativized item is when functioning as a support or background for a relativized one. Though we always refer to the nonrelativized in relative terms and in two ways—as that which is relativized but is now functioning as a support, and as that which is being approached from the vantage point of the relativized for which it is serving as a support—we in these ways in fact designate what it is in-itself.

We can start either with the relativized features which we confront in perception or with our ordinary knowledge of a thing. In the first case we attempt to penetrate to the heart of the thing, stopping at the point where we encounter a different type of relativized content in the role of a support for the feature. In the second case we seek a neutral position by starting from some biased position and then attempt to envisage the point at which it is met by other biased positions. In the first way we stop with an obstacle, an actual support; in the second we try to remain neutral to both the support and what is supported. The second way ends with a "togetherness" of the different biased positions. Made absolute, as having a being and power of its own, it would appear to tell us what a being is in- and of-itself, but in fact it is radically ambiguous, being only the indeterminate center of a plurality of biases all engaged in supporting one another.

This now sounds as if the being was not something in-itself but a mixture of alien beings, and that it had no integrity or substantiality by-itself. But this is not true; the neutral point in it has no substantiality if understood to be over against and independent of all the various biases. It is in terms of the various biases that the neutral point inside a being is radically ambiguous. It has a nature and a being but only so far as it functions in a plurality of distinct ways, each of which expresses the way one biased side of the being supports the others. There is such a point but it exists in its full concreteness and determinateness only when it is pluralized. I can know it though, because in knowledge I abstract, consider things in their indeterminate generality. From the standpoint of knowledge the neutral point is a definite point; it has as much reality as any of its pluralized subdivisions or any biased content; indeed it should be thought of as more than any, since its full meaning is only partially expressed by any, and the sum of these partial expressions is, as it were, antecedently in it.

We thus know the thing-in-itself, the absolute, the reality behind the appearance, because knowledge fixates the variable as that which is the most constant of the cognizable items. But knowledge is not being. If we want to arrive at the midpoint as it is in- and of-itself, we must approach it from the outside and then find it only as a kind of barrier, a place where the emphasis shifts from something dependent to something supporting this—the support itself being of course something, when we look at it, found to be supported, and then by that which it now supports.

There are other ways of getting to the neutral point than by knowledge, e.g. by appreciation, etc. Do they get to different points, to different roles of a given point, to facets of it, or to the same point but from a different position? They evidently get to the same point, but as possessed of qualities, virtues, powers, meanings which are not evident to knowledge. What they get to is, from the standpoint of the being in its full concreteness, an abstraction different from that which interests knowledge. We can know the abstraction in knowledge, but then it is known as that which is an abstraction for some other approach than knowledge—knowledge knows the abstraction faced by other approaches, not as that abstraction, but as abstraction-faced-by-other-approaches. And these other approaches face the abstraction which confronts knowledge, though they do it only as "abstraction-for-knowledge." It is the entire complex which is grasped, not the components, though of course the components can be separated out and dealt with in their own contexts.

September 28

The United States with its troops, money, history, president, etc., is obviously distinct from the fifty states. It cannot be reduced to their combination either, for it is able to oppose the states. The combination might be said, as involving a merger of the states, their being intimately involved with one another, to constitute their society or themselves as a nation. The United States is more than the prescriptive togetherness of the states, the having them together as separate from one another. It is the separated states together as requiring the states as merged, which constitutes the United States. But then the United States will be unlike the cosmos of four modes in that it has a being and a nature and a power of its own. The " , " and the " . " which constitute it are unlike those connecting the modes of being. Unlike the modes of being, they form by their mutual reference a new kind of entity.

Why is it possible to do this in connection with the states and not with the four modes of being? The reason must lie in the fact that the states are not ultimate realities, that some of the reality which they lack is in fact possessed by the way in which they are together. The connections, the togethernesses, the ones of the fifty states are thicker, substantial; they are like the junctures of nature and man in history, or man and God in religious faith. This seems to indicate that the various states are all in one mode of being and that, because they are so, they make unities which have a thickness reflecting this fact. Indeed, this point was seen in *Reality,* in the interpretation of space as the outcome of the overlapping of the penumbra of the various beings said to be in space. Just so, the United States can be said to be the product of the overlapping of two distinct kinds of penumbra, one of them making for a thickened kind of separateness of the states and the other making for a thickened kind of merging of the states, the thickness enabling the unions to have some power of their own, particularly with reference to one another. The reference of each type of togetherness to the other would be the essential being of the United States.

In the book on history I said that the power which the historic process has is inherited from its constituent men and nature, and that when these separate (as they do every moment) the history loses the power. But perhaps it would be better to say that the history encapsulates some of that power, for after all history has its own dynamics and causality. And we can say that the United States, though it does derive its power from the individual states, possesses this power and uses it in its own way, making it have the role of relating the two kinds of togethernesses of the states to one another.

When we turn to a confederation, a league of nations or even a United Nations, we have only one of the togethernesses (the merging) with any power of its own. There is a power which keeps them separate only because, as it were, the merging permits this. The prescriptive power of these groups is feeble; it does not enable them to meet the power of their members as they in fact are together in a merged kind of way.

Prescriptive power is achieved just so far as the constituents remain separate. This power is used to subject those items, in a more intimate way, to the power acquired from the separateness. It is as if the separated items said to themselves as together in a merged way, "you must do so and so," the saying being done by the power which defines their separateness.

The above is stated in terms of only two modes of togetherness. A similar combination might be developed by uniting items by implication and productive relations, or by combining the union of separation with one of production, etc. Thus the various parts of the body might be said to imply one another so as to constitute an organic whole, and have this implication in a referential relation to a *de facto* merging (such as might be represented by a pervasive feeling) or to a productive relation (such as might be represented by the various discharges and acquirements of the different organs).

The different forms of togetherness tell us different ways in which we can analyze the body. Were we to have productivity, we divide according to organs, but if we have merging we do it by intensities; separateness would give us the atomic or cellular divisions; implication would give us the main parts, such as head and heart, limbs, etc.

September 30

At the beginning of the *Phenomenology,* in the chapter on Sense-Certainty, Hegel remarks that what we say is always something universal, and that if we intend to refer to a momentary, particular "here" or "now," we will mean what we do not say, and say what we do not mean. But since Hegel does know what he means, it is evident that there is more to the situation than he is allowing. To be sure he will try to get this meant content expressed in some universal form, but right now as he confronts the particular content and says something about it, he is actually using his meaning.

In the end, Hegel cannot say anything about the unity of his entire enterprise but only show ("mean") this. The situation is not unlike that which we face in connection with any statement. We write down, "This is a cat," and we thereby make a unitary claim. But the unity of this claim is not written down; it is only meant. It would be foolish to try to say it then and there. Just so, the content which is now being articulated, say "This is here," is verbal, universal, duplicable; but the unity which is present is singular, precisely because it is then and there being judged on our side, and being lived through on the side of the world.

When philosophers turned from a consideration of judgments to propositions, they turned from intended unities to exhibited unities. When they turned from propositions to sentences, they turned from exhibited unities to a sequence of terms which were being collected by a knower or speaker, but which was in no way acknowledged. Thereupon they were faced with the problem of semantics, the way in which to bring the sentence in relation to the world, or, more specifically, to a unitary object. The loss in moving from judgment to sentence is in the unawareness of the power of meaning, of knowing what is not being said. If we start with what is said, say a sentence, we will of course never find what is meant. Empiricists, behaviorists, materialists, etc., start as it were with the said, and have no way of knowing what it is that they mean, even though, as surely as the rest of us, they inescapably mean more than they say, because they are concerned with something meant.

Hegel, concerned as he was with producing a phenomenology (in which all that is substance is also subject, where the noumenon is made into phenomena without remainder), in the end must confess that he uses the meant as a power, and that he cannot phenomenologize the totality of the enterprise, the unity which it in fact exhibits. He must mean something he cannot say, no matter how much he says. Unlike other phenomenological thinkers, though, he does know he means something before he gets to the last stage; he knows that when he confronts an abstract universal there is a concreteness which remains outside, by which we are lured, and which in fact leads us to move away from one universal to another. What Hegel does not see is that the meant can be a resting place, a correlate, an essential component in the acknowledgment of universals, and that this component cannot and need not and ought not to be phenomenologized. It is known in its own way, through adumbration, when we articulate the object through the use of universal denotative and predicational terms.

Not all that is knowable, is knowable in the shape of what is said. And in fact we can even say what we adumbrate, though only by turning away from the particular case and reflecting on the nature of knowledge, or by achieving a speculative grasp of what it is to be real. Ontology might be said to begin with the unitary substantial being of the object, which it will of course articulate through universals. These are categories having an existential import, names which are properties, subjects which in fact are subject-matter. The sentence here says what it means, for the unitary subject-matter is made into the subject in terms of which one speaks. But it is to be noted that the subject-matter still has its own being; it becomes one with the subject only so far as we are engaged in an abstract ontological discourse, so far as we are trying to say what we mean. Ontological discourse re-presents the object, but only because it catches in the subject the unitary meaning which the discourse will exhibit.

October 1

Phenomenologists, cosmologists, process philosophers, and orthodox Hebrew and Christian theologians are agreed that the ordinary things in space and time are over-substantialized by Aristotle. They insist either that these beings have no reality, or at the most a reality which is less than and derivative from other beings. They are right to object to the Aristotelian emphasis. But they ought not to deny reality to the Aristotelian substances. Each one of us is such a substance. But we are such only because we are representative of an Actuality that is ultimate and irreducible. Also these non-Aristotelians do not acknowledge all three of the other realities which are also ultimate, permanent, necessary— Ideality, Existence, and God.

Hegel then is right in making the particular thing give way before the omnivorous dialectic and the ultimacy of his Absolute. But he is wrong if this dissolution is taken to be a vanishing of the thing, the showing that it was not concrete. Hegel of course insists that every stage through which the dialectic goes is preserved, but I think more than this is required. It is not the acknowledgment that a thing is a stage in the history or achievement or unfolding of the Absolute that is required, but that the thing be recognized to have a power, a being, a career, and a rationale of its own which it maintains over against the Absolute, both when it is and when it is not given a place within an absolute context.

October 14

In every judgment there is an adumbrative component. This is the terminus of the unitary act of judgment, and is properly represented by the entire proposition as a referring unity, rather than by any one component. However, it is possible to assign this role to the copula, in which case it will have a double role—that of linking subject, or subjects, and predicate (or relation), and of orienting them in a unitary being beyond (from which they should in fact be derivable by analysis). The object of adumbration is not known in the sense in which the subject and predicate are known; the adumbrated is always at the border line, and is presupposed by the subject and predicate. It has being only when the judgment is made, though of course the object which is being judged has a being outside and apart from the judgment.

If the adumbrated could not itself be known, we would have to say that all knowledge involves a component which we cannot know, but which enables us to have a unified subject and predicate. But the adumbrated can be known as easily and as readily as any other aspect of an object. It can be analyzed, and it can even be designated or described. But when we do these things something else assumes the role of adumbrated. Nothing then remains unknowable, though in each particular case there is something which is not known by means of a subject and predicate.

How do we know that there is another adumbrated for a judgment which uses some adumbrated as a subject or a predicate? It is not that we can see (as we make the adumbrated into one of the elements in the judgment) what we had in focus before merge and move to the background? The adumbrated in each judgment is the background, and as we attend to it as something to be judged, or something to which a distinct term is provided by some element in the judgment, we find that something else becomes background. We can watch the change and note that it is the previous subject and predicate which merge and give us a new background. That background may contain more than the merged subject and predicate. Indeed, it seems to be the case that there is a fixed component in the background, evidencing the fact that the adumbrated is rooted in a larger world of nature and Existence.

When we forge judgments apart from perception, we nevertheless have a background for our judgment. This is how we know that we are awake. The fixed component which we face when we make a perceptual judgment—which is what the previous discussion alone dealt with—is the only adumbrated element in a judgment of any sort made when we are awake, unless that judgment is intended to articulate an encountered Ideal, God, or Actuality (or person). Each of these seems to have a distinctive background of its own. When we judge something about God, providing that we are in fact occupied with Him in faith, worship, etc., God also is fixed and adumbrated.

Suppose we make a judgment of God in a philosophic work; must we not acknowledge God as the object of an adumbration? Yes, for though thought does not make the kind of contact with God that faith does, it nevertheless does make some contact. Though every inference needs to be supported by an encounter, it is nevertheless the case that an inference involves an encounter, indeed a participation in Existence, and this at the very least has a divine qualification, so that we have a faint awareness of God even when engaged in a proof which apparently starts away from Him. But then why is it that we are dissatisfied with an inference which is not supported by a distinct encounter? If we have something like an encounter when we infer, why do we need to look for another encounter?

The encounter we have when we infer is one which leads us to a domain, to a kind of object; an actual encounter distinct from that which is a component of an inference, presents us with determinate content, forcing us to sharpen and revise, alter and qualify what we had judged.

Returning to the perceptual judgment, we must say then that the object which is adumbrated, i.e., the adumbrated element in the object, presents us with a determinateness we otherwise would not have. The discussion in *Reality,* and in other places including the above, makes adumbration an act which is pointing outward toward the real, and does not take account of the fact that the real, at the same time, gives us something. We take some note of this fact when we refer to the "feel," the sensuosity, the experiential side of things in contrast with what we conceptualize or express in propositions or embrace in judgments. When we make a judgment apart from perception, the adumbrated item presents us with a minimal determinateness. Were we to forge a judgment of a purely fictitious object, we would adumbrate the waking world beyond, to which we perhaps would add some distinguishable adumbration of ourselves.

We are always adumbrating ourselves, but we do not distinguish this either when we perceive or when we form an ordinary judgment. It becomes prominent only when we set ourselves to imagine something, or to attend to our own selves.

Perhaps, then, it would be more accurate to say that we always face a vague adumbrated, and (depending on the type of judgment we make) that we break this up into a component which relates us to some one mode of being primarily, and to the others secondarily? And when we make specific judgments, using components which had been abstracted from what we confront, or which are had as attached to such components, we intensify the primary adumbrated, thereby tending to obscure the presence of the secondary. We come to know of the presence of the secondary only because we can see it assuming a primary role as we shift our interests and judgments.

November 25

In knowing an object I place it in a new context. It now is affiliated with other items by association in my language, concepts, or actions. The difference between the associations I introduce and those which it in fact has with respect to various items can be noted. I can see that the cat runs after the ball at the same time that I can look about for a dog, write down the name Dr. Katz, and begin to say "scat." Since I observe the cat running after the ball, I evidently have the cat in two contexts provided by me—one in which the cat itself is associated by me with various items, and the other in which the cat chasing the ball is associated by me with various items. In the latter case I can distinguish between the associations I provide for the cat with the ball, and the actual consequences which ensue on the occurrence of the cat chasing the ball. The latter again can be associated with various items by me, and so on and so on. Consequently, I can conclude that my thought has two dimensions —one which may be termed "observational" and the other "reflective."

When I am concerned with knowing whether another has a mind similar to mine, I am concerned not with the observational dimension but with the reflective. I want to determine what it is he is able to contribute to the objective situation. I therefore look to his behavior to see whether or not he replies to the kinds of additions I bring into the situation, or whether he adds to the observational situation, content similar to that which I brought in. In either case I take him to have a mind—in the latter, an independent mind, in the former a social mind, one which is in communication with me. It should make no difference to my judgment of whether another has a mind or not, to know that the other had been made by a machine, or had an appearance utterly unlike that of the being I normally term fellow man. All I wanted to know is whether he had a mind similar to mine, and this I can tell only by noting the differential behavior—in speech or act, gesture or grimace—which the being has directly with reference to the object, or indirectly to it via his response to me.

If I know another has a mind, I still do not know whether or not it has a will, sympathy, perceptiveness, and the like, except so far as still other differentiating elements are brought in. In all cases the criterion is to be found in myself. It is because I see the difference that I am introducing, it is the fact that I am affiliating the observed object with items with which it is not itself directly affiliated, that tells me the difference my mind makes.

But can I not know that there are beings with better minds than mine? Can I know whether or not they have minds with respect to objects not observed—fiction, dreams, speculations? The knowledge that another has a better mind than I depends on my recognizing that he has a mind engaged in tasks similar to my own; the superiority is discovered by seeing that the other can produce affiliations which are more illuminating about the object itself or some other things than my own. Had I no mind at all, I of course could not know that another had a mind. Usually we are persuaded that another has a better mind than our own by noting how he can anticipate what the observed object can do, how what puzzles us can be resolved by him, and how new connections can be brought in by him in such a way as to enable us to understand other things besides the observed.

The second question, what do we do about thoughts of the unobserved objects, can be answered by referring to the reports given in the works which are subsequently produced, or by the illumination provided with respect to what is observed. We learn, for example, that another by realigning what we observe in new ways (say, through the formulae of a science) is enabled to bring an order into the realm of the observed that it otherwise does not seem to yield; the mind which attends to speculations or even which idly dreams provides a mesh or context in which the observed occurrences are reordered, but in such a way that multiple consequences can be anticipated, or some device is revealed by which other heterogeneities are brought into ready harmony, ordered better, and thereby made more intelligible.

November 26

A religious community has God immanent in it, while pointing to God outside it. The immanence and the external reference are constituted by the way the men in the community harmoniously interplay. In some cases there is a great stress on the transcendence, with a minimal immanence. This is the case when we have new communities, missionaries, attempts to practice a religion by being of service in the larger community. The largest community, that of mankind, can be thought of as a religious community in this sense, though the fact of the religious nature of the community may be evident only to the religious leaders. We can say the same thing of a state, such as our own, in which there is an official acknowledgment of a transcendent God. We have here of course a question as to whether a community can be termed "religious" if the majority of the people, as participating in that community, do not think they have God immanently in that community, and thus treat the church as something which stands in contrast with the community or state.

Most religious communities in any case are acknowledged by their practitioners, and others as well, to have a distinctive nature over against the larger community. God is immanent in the religious community for all the members; they constitute the nature of that immanence and thereby produce an effective reference to God as transcendent, to whom they in fact refer while constituting Him as immanent. This sense of religious community involves a contrast with the secular world, and makes it difficult to see a warrant in "good works" outside the fold of the religious community. But the other sense of religious community, where there is a major stress on transcendence and only a minimal immanence (and this perhaps only in the eyes of the religious leader), has the difficulty that it allows the most secular or pagan state to be termed a religious community, if only it is in some consonance with the activities of some religious leader who envisages that state as a kind of religious community.

We could perhaps overcome both difficulties by affirming that we must have an immanental religious community first—though this would have a difficulty with the stray prophet—and take the larger community to be religious relative to the other, but not to be so in- and of-itself. Or we can say that the larger community is not religious at all, but that one who approaches it from the perspective of a transcendent God or as an agent of the immanental community is doing religious work, for he is engaged in converting the secular into the religious.

"Good works," then, are not simply acts of grace, mere externalizations of a religious community; they are acts of conversion, acts by which an effort is being made to change a secular into a genuine religious community, not by imposing a creed or even awakening awareness of a transcendent or immanent God, but by molding the community through the good works into a unity similar to that of the religious community. The missionary or the religious leader who goes out into the secular world and helps the poor and downtrodden in the name of God is engaged in religious work, because he is working on others in such a way as to make God immanent in the situation of himself and those others. The result will not be a religious community though, until the recipients are integrated with the givers, and are thus actually members of a single community in which the giving and the receiving are a way of having God immanently while referring to Him as still outside.

November 27

If we compare the following assertions—a number of important differences appear amongst them.
1] The money you have you will lose.
2] Since you have money you will lose it.
3] If you have money you will lose it.

4] The money you have you can lose.
5] Since you have money you can lose it.
6] If you have money you can lose it.

7] The money you can possibly have you can lose.
8] Since you can possibly have money you can lose it.
9] If you can possibly have money you can lose it.

In the first set of three we have a prediction made: *1* states this categorically, *2* states it in the form of two subordinate propositions, a form most appropriate for the conclusion of an argument, *3* makes a prediction by implication, but does not necessarily refer to an occurrence in this world. It might prove to be the case that you do not and never will have money, but the implication holds. We can convert *1* into *3* and then, with the knowledge obtained from the same source that we obtained the subject of *1*, we can derive *2*.

4, 5, and *6* all have a modal consequent or predicate; they end with a possibility. *4* grounds the possibility in something factual, and is apparently equivalent to *5*. *6* is somewhat different from these others. The presence of the "if" makes the antecedent something less than a fact.

But if we compare 6 and 9, there seems to be a difference between the hypothesis of a fact and a hypothesis about a possibility. The antecedent of 6 refers to a possible fact, not to a possibility; it marks a place for a fact, and then draws the consequence that such a fact could have a possibility ascribed to it. In the light of this we can say that 3 also gives us a set of blanks for a fact; that it states not what is merely possible, but what is ingrediently possible. In contrast then with what was said here initially about 3, it is an assertion oriented in this world, though not speaking of anything in that world necessarily. Its truth lies in the fact that it articulates a fact about the world, and does this even though there may be no instance of its antecedent or consequence.

When we come to 7, 8, and 9 we have an entirely different situation. 9 seems to be a proper expression, relating two possibilities to one another. But 7 and 8 ascribe a possibility to a possibility. The money one can possibly have cannot possibly be lost; only the money one actually has can possibly be lost. There is something amiss then in ascribing a possibility to a possibility. Yet 7 and 8 seem to be like 1 and 2, and like 4 and 5, and to have the relation to 9 that 1 and 2 has to 3, and 4 and 5 has to 6.

Should we say then that all these assertions have a generality and make reference to possibilities, but that only the first six (and 9) can be said without qualification to allow for the ascription of another possibility, and this because they are schemata for actual occurrences? 1 and 4 differ from 3 and 6 by pointing up the place where the possibility is realized, and they differ from 2 and 5 in that the latter ascribes a place to the consequence as well. 9 seems to refer to the capacity to have a possibility exemplified; the consequence is not ascribed to the antecedent but is alongside it as another exemplifiable possibility. But in 7 there is an attempt to characterize the possibility itself by means of a higher order possibility, a fact which seems even clearer when we come to 8.

From the foregoing one must conclude that not every categorical expression can be given an hypothetical form. Though "A jet plane might explode" is true; it is not true that "A possible jet plane might explode," for only actual jet planes can explode. "A jet plane might explode" translates into "If x is a jet plane, x can explode" but "A possible jet plane might explode" does not translate into "If x is a possible jet plane, x can explode" (which is like 9 above). The latter could be said to be true if taken in the sense that its antecedent refers to one possibility and its consequence refers to another which is linked with it. But if this is the case what is the categorical translation of 9? "The money that can be possibly had can be possibly lost"? "Since money can be possibly had it can be possibly lost"? If so, we must carefully distinguish those assertions which link subject and predicate, antecedent and consequent, from those which ascribe predicates and consequents to subjects and antecedents. We seem to get into no difficulty if our initial orientation is with respect to something actual, for the ascribed possibility is then something which is linked, required by what precedes it. A possibility of a possibility does not follow on the possibility, having no definiteness or status until the initial possibility is given some actualization. However, if in *1–6* we have only places marked off for actual occurrences, in what sense could we be said to ascribe anything to the initial case? Would it not be better then to say that in all nine cases we have the marking out of some region, and that we can then go on to mark out others? It seems so.

November 28

It makes sense to say:
1] It is possible for a jet plane to explode.
But it does not make sense to say:
2] It is possible for a possible jet plane to explode.

The first of these assertions relates an actuality to a possibility; the second relates a possibility to another possibility, apparently as one which is to follow on the other after an interval. The relation of the jet plane to the possible explosion is one which moves from present to future. The only way in which one could relate a possible jet plane to a possible explosion is conjunctively, as items in a single domain. Consequently the second proposition should be rewritten as:
3] If a jet plane is possible so is a jet plane explosion.
Or, to leave out the hypothetical form—
3'] It is possible for a jet plane to be, and it is possible for a jet plane to explode.

However, this last formulation continues to relate the possibility in both cases to something actual—e.g., to the being of a jet plane in the first clause, and to an actual jet plane in the second. Better perhaps:
4] A jet plane is possible, and a jet plane explosion is possible.

However, this does not show the dependence of the second possibility on the first, at least as that which is entailed by it. Better, then, would be:
5] Since a jet plane is possible, so is a jet plane explosion.

This last must be understood to relate two possibilities not in a relation of subordinate to predicate, or actual base to dependent adjective, but in a relation of condition to conditioned within the same domain. We have something like: "You cannot go from New Haven to Boston without going through Providence if you take the NYNH & H RR." The going through Providence is a condition which must be realized before you can reach Boston, but the possibility of reaching Boston is not a possibility for the possibility of going through Providence; it is a possibility for one who is leaving New Haven by the railroad. The going by the railroad requires a sequence of occurrence; those occurrences are possibilities now, but they are not possibilities which depend for their being on the realization of one another, nor even on the presence of one another. The possibility of going through Providence is linked to the possibility of reaching Boston, but the former does not ground the latter. Nevertheless, once we have gone through Providence we are faced with a possibility of reaching Boston. That possibility is relevant to the fact that we have gone through Providence. We must therefore acknowledge a possibility of going to Boston as linked to the possibility of going through Providence, and as in fact made available by our having gone through Providence. There is in short the status of a possibility as linked with others, and the status of it as available for realization. Our initial proposition relates to the availability of the possibility, whereas the second proposition (and its improved formulations) relates to the linkage of possibilities.

But what does it mean for possibilities to be linked, particularly since the linkage requires a certain order of realization? Is it perhaps true that the third formulation, which defines the dependent possibility in terms of the initial one, points up the fact that this dependent possibility has as part of its meaning the initial possibility, whereas the first formulation does not? In short, when the jet plane is only possible, what we also have possible is "possible jet plane explosion" as an analytic component. But when we have an actual jet plane, what is possible is "an explosion." Here the explosion, though of course an explosion of a jet plane, is one which stands away from the jet plane as a possibility, relevant to that plane but not an analytic component of it.

November 30

Hegel should serve as the model for those who, following the lead of Aristotle, Dewey, or Wittgenstein, would like to deal with the private or individual in public terms. Hegel is aware that an individual is presupposed by the collectivity, that he must himself identify himself with the meaning of the collectivity, that the collectivity must contain within itself the values which he had as a private being, and that the result could be indifferently termed the "collectivity personalized" or the "person universalized."

If I say "I am in pain," the public meaning of that expression is never adequate except in so far as the anguish I intend to express is also somehow conveyed. The individual must accept some total set of expressions as the translation. The public world on its side needs me to make the present announcement as expressive of my anguish, and it will need me to accept the translation it offers as expressing my meaning. The public set must be permeated by my personal meaning, and thus must reflect the fact that an individual is suffering. Conversely, I must accept the public set if I am to have the dignity of being a part of the public set. I must, like a man of service, abandon what is merely idiosyncratic for the sake of having my inmost value preserved in the shape of some excellence. The public set must as it were say better than I, "I am in pain"; it must be a tissue of doctors, hospitals, sympathies, etc. And I must then be recognized to be one who accepts these as my own; the public set itself is directed at me as one who will make use of the set in a private way.

Hegel denies that there is any single Absolute in- and of-itself; all realities for him are realities in reference to others. His solution is to say that the ultimate absolutes have one another as themselves. He thinks the final expression would be "self-consciousness self-consciously related to self-consciousness." But one need not accept that formulation and yet could profit from his answer. According to his answer we would say that each of the four modes of being deals with the other modes as another version of itself. The Ideal, for example, idealizes all else, so that Actuality for example is but an instance of the Ideal. But since the reverse is also true, so that from the perspective of Actuality the Ideal is only a locus of relevant possibilities for the Actual, we will have a plurality of answers in place of Hegel's one, and the plurality will be stated in terms which do not relate to Spirit. The big question that remains is how one is able to make reference to all these different answers. The solution I have offered is that of abstraction. Each ultimate being grounds a distinctive type of abstraction in terms of which one is able to deal with the other modes of being in independence of the initial being, or alternatively, in neutral ways.

Perhaps another variant of the Hegelian answer is the treatment of contingency in his system. The contingent is something not explained by what had been, but which can be explained when analyzed into components or placed in a larger context. Such a view of the contingent is to be distinguished from those which treat the contingent as surd, and those which treat it as that which might not have occurred. The contingent can be thought to be the necessary product of the intersection of a number of necessary processes. It is contingent only taken by itself as a whole, for as such a whole it has no antecedent whole which could account for it.

December 1

Though it was rather naïve of G. E. Moore to suppose that if he kept to common sense he would have no philosophic problems—for where else do they arise but in the confusions, indeterminacies, superstitions, delusions, and traditions of common sense?—he had a sound philosophic warrant. If any world be ultimate it has no problems. Problems arise only because some part of the whole is taken to be the whole, or is in improper adjustment to the other members. But then it would seem that since the whole has no problems, that there would be in fact no occasion for any movement, or even for the dislocations to occur. Every system which acknowledges a fundamental reality is faced with the issue of how there could be "appearances," granted that we have a reality in which those appearances are no longer something over against the reality, as the erroneous or rectifiable is over against the true and final.

Each ultimate has its answer in the rest of the ultimates. Any need it has is satisfied by all the others together. The totality of them thus makes a single completed whole. But the needs of a being are twofold. It has the need to possess the others, to have their reality somehow in-itself, and it has the need to be benefited by the others where they are. It is the second need which is satisfied, but the first is not. If we start with the second we can see an ultimate being making a demand on some other and not being fully satisfied by that other, and therefore being forced to turn to the remaining ultimates for the needed satisfaction. No particular one of those remaining ultimates may satisfy the demands which the given being makes on it, and will therefore force the initial being to look to the other modes. Each demand will be satisfied by the rest of the beings together, but each one of the other beings will force another distribution of satisfactions over the rest of the beings.

A being is then satisfied by the totality of beings which distribute among themselves the satisfaction which it initially sought in only one of those other beings. Because it sought that satisfaction in only one of those other beings, the kind of satisfaction it gets is not exactly the satisfaction it sought. The satisfaction is provided for it, but it does not yet possess the satisfaction. For this to occur the being would have to satisfy its other need, the need to possess the others. At every moment it must make an effort to adopt the kind of answer which others provide for it, and to make that answer have the value for it that the answer would have had, had it been provided by the being to which the given being initially looked.

Though there is a lack of problem in the very completeness of the universe, a problem does result from the fact that the answer from the perspective of each being is not what the being sought, and which it can make its own only by a special effort. A man is guilty for not doing full justice to the Ideal. The satisfaction of the Ideal which he should have provided, he does not provide. The Ideal must therefore be satisfied by the other modes. The man remains guilty so long as he does not make their answer his own; the Ideal remains dissatisfied so long as it does not adopt those answers as answers which are as good as those which he might have provided. The Ideal is ontologically satisfied, but not integrally; and a man is defective, is guilty precisely because the Ideal is not integrally satisfied. Every mode of being has the defect of not providing the whole answer which another sought in it—it is then in a state analogous to guilt—and the defect of not having the answers, which the rest provide, in the form of an integral unity. The double defect will require a double adjustment. Staying with Actuality for the moment, we have the defect that it is unable to do full justice to the demands which the Ideal makes on it, and the defect of Actuality's making a demand on the Ideal which the Ideal only partly answers and which is completely answered only by the totality of other modes (and which the Actuality does not therefore have in the form it sought to have). Consequently, Actuality must accept the answers which the other modes provide, whenever Actuality fails to do justice to what the Ideal demands of it; and it must try to unify the multiple answers, or rather the partial answers it receives from the various modes, to the question it poses to the Ideal.

In the course of today's discussion I have evidently shifted ground, and have come to acknowledge two defects in each mode of being—one because it does not provide the answer which another mode demands of it, the other because it does not have the partial answers, which the others provide, made into an integral unity. The partial answers which the others provide, and which add up to an adequate answer, show that the universe is complete; but the defect of having to unify these partial answers, and the defect of not giving a full answer to the demands of the others, require the being to adjust itself in two ways. This adjustment, since it is internal to the mode and thus is independent of what the others do, gives the tensions and the problems which the universe internally exhibits.

December 2

To understand the failure of a being to get the satisfactions it requires, it is desirable to concentrate on one as an example. Let us take the Ideal. This needs a certain kind of satisfaction from each of the other modes. But each of the other modes fails to give it the peculiar satisfaction that it needs. The Actual, for example, ought to embody the Ideal throughout, but fails to do so. This failure is made good by the divine and by Existence. They in turn have to satisfy the Ideal in characteristic ways, but do not do so. What they do not do is partly done by Actuality. Consequently, Actuality not only fails to do full justice to the Ideal in the characteristic way which only Actuality can provide, but it makes good the defective operation or satisfactions which the other two modes exhibit in relation to the Ideal. Consequently, the Ideal, with its three distinctive demands imposed on three distinctive modes, finds that it has these three demands answered in a partial way by the appropriate mode, and the remainder in unappropriate ways by the other modes. Only if the mode which gave a partial answer is able to accept the rest of the answer which the remaining modes provide, will there be an appropriate answer given to the demand made initially by the Ideal. But this is an adventure which takes time and is rarely completed. There is change in the world because the acceptance of the rest of the answer given by remaining modes is one which is not guaranteed in advance. Also, even if it is achieved, the fact remains that for the Ideal the answer it needs is dispersed in three directions, and it must itself bring them together into a unity. The Ideal, then, is not satisfied until it unites the various answers which the different modes give to its demand on one of the modes, and this whether or not the mode, to which it initially looked, adopts the partial completing answers that the remaining modes provide.

The Ideal itself has a task, that of providing an answer to the other three modes. It fails to do justice to their three different requests, and what it fails to do must be done by the remaining two modes. It must then go on and identify itself with the remaining modes, so far as those remaining modes yield the answer it should have provided. The Ideal thus has a three-fold need to identify itself with other modes; it must accept whatever answer they provide, to make up for the defective answer provided initially by itself.

The Ideal thus must make a unity of the answers which the three modes offer to each of its demands; it must also adopt the answers that it failed to provide in answer to some second mode, but which are then provided by the remaining two modes. These two activities are independent, and the Ideal is in a state of tension with respect to the other modes. Each of the modes in fact has the same twofold problem and must adjust itself to the others, both by adopting the answers which make good the mode's deficient replies, and by uniting into a single whole the distributed answers which the other modes provide to the questions which the given mode poses to some given mode.

The observations made with respect to the Idea, when translated over to God, force the conclusion that God has a problem of an internal adjustment, of uniting the answers which men give to the demands that He makes on men, with the answers that the other modes make to those very demands as unanswered by men, as well as a problem of accepting as His own the kind of answers which other modes provide to the demands that the modes make on Him and which He does not fully answer. God's demands are always answered, but not by the beings to whom they are addressed, and He must take over the answers which are made by the beings to whom His demands are not addressed, to make them all add up to His needed answer. In addition, God as only one being among a number in the universe, and as having a resistance of His own, never will fully satisfy the need of any other being to be fulfilled in Him. He does not satisfy these others in the way they demand that He satisfy them. "Thy will be done" all must in the end accept, so far as they are willing to rest with Him alone. But such resting is not possible in the cosmos, which must have all the answers in it. What God fails to do, other modes of being will make good. He becomes a perfect being only so far as he accepts their answers as His own.

Is God the only being who can effectively unite all the answers which the modes provide for Him; is He the only being who is able to identify Himself with all else, who can successfully adopt the answers which other modes make to the demands which He only partially answered? Apparently so. But He much achieve this success again and again at every moment. Each moment then will have the various modes satisfied by God through His adoption of the answers which other modes add to the partial answer He initially gives. He will at every moment also make Himself into a satisfactory unity of the dispersed answers which the other modes make to His demands on each. The former fact makes Him a pure being, one who makes good the demands imposed on Him by each mode; the latter fact makes Him an infinitely malleable being, who can make His own what the cosmos provides, but in a dispersed form.

Each mode of Being will fail to make a perfect unity in itself, or will fail to accept the answers which the other modes provide, when it fails to answer adequately. Can we say that Existence fails to unite, but does succeed in accepting the answers which other beings provide when it fails to make the adequate response to a specific demand? That the Ideal fails to accept the answers which others offer to make good its failures, but that it does succeed in uniting the dispersed answers that the three modes make to the specific demands it imposes on each? And that Actuality fails to accept and fails to unite? Or is it the case that all the modes, including God, must fail to unite and fail to accept to some degree?

December 3

Each mode of being is faced with six problems. Using Actuality as an example we have:

1] The demand made on it by Ideality is to be met. Failure means guilt. Since it does fail, and since its failure is made good by Existence and God, the Actuality must adopt the answer which these provide for the Ideal, as it were, on behalf of the Actual. They give "actualizing" answers to the Ideal, and the Actuality must adopt these.

2] There is a demand made on the Actuality by God. Failure here means sin. It does fail, but the failure is made good by Existence and the Ideal. The Actuality must adopt their "actualizing" answers to God's demand.

3] There is a demand made on Actuality by Existence. Failure here is maladjustment. It does fail, but the failure is made good by God and Ideality. The Actuality must adopt their "actualizing" answers to the demand that Existence initially makes on Actuality.

4] Actuality makes a demand on the Ideal. But the Ideal does not answer this fully, and what it fails to do is make good by God and Existence. The "idealizing" answers of these last two, together with the answer which the Ideal in fact provides, must be unified by the Actuality.

5] Actuality makes a demand on God. But God does not answer this fully, and what He fails to do is made good by Ideality and Existence. The divine-like answers of these two, together with the answer which God Himself provides, must be unified by the Actuality to make a single answer to its need.

6] Finally, Actuality makes a demand on Existence. But Existence does not satisfy this demand fully. What it fails to do is made good by God and Ideality. The "existentializing" answers given by God and Ideality to the demand of Actuality must be added by the Actuality to the answer in fact given by Existence.

No actuality meets these six problems satisfactorily. Each remains partly guilty, sinful, and maladjusted—or better, the kind of forgiveness, recompense, reassessment which the other modes offer to one who is guilty, has sinned, or is maladjusted, is never fully accepted. And the triple answer which it receives when making a demand on one mode is never made into an adequate unity. There is always something, then, which it must do, even if it were the case that the entire universe remained selfsame. Its failures do not compromise the fact that the demands it makes are in fact answered in the universe; the failures merely indicate that it is not as fully in-itself as it might be.

So far as Actuality succeeds in answering any or all of the six problems, it is internally one with itself. But this success does not alter what is available to the other modes of being. Whether Actuality is successful or not, it offers to other modes the same degree of being, the same content. It offers a different content to the different modes of being at every moment just so far as it fails or succeeds in different degrees to do for the mode what that demands of it. It remains constant only in the sense that it has answered the demand to such and such a degree; the fact that other beings provide the rest of the answer, and that it does or does not adopt this which they provide, does not affect the kind of content which it can offer to the given mode of being.

An actuality ought to realize the Ideal; it will not do so fully. But it will vary from time to time in the degree to which it will do so. As it varies in its degree, the burden which the other modes will have to carry because of it will also vary. Whatever those modes do the actuality ought to adopt. Whether it adopts any part of what these do, or not, it will still be an actuality which had failed to do initial justice to the Ideal, and it is this which is available for the Ideal at the next moment. The Ideal does not take account of the actuality as that which has or has not adopted the answers that other modes provide in the face of the failure of the actuality to answer the demand directly made on it.

The actuality also makes a demand on each mode. It makes that demand from the center of its being. The fact that the demand is not met by that mode fully, does not affect the demand that the actuality makes. The fact that what the confronted mode does not provide is provided by the remaining modes, does not affect the nature of the demand that the actuality makes. And the fact that the actuality does or does not unify the triple answers which its demands receive, does not alter the fact that it makes those demands. But the fact that a given mode will answer a demand in one way at one moment and in another way at another moment will affect the kind of demand which the actuality will make on that mode at different moments.

When then we turn to God as the Being who successfully adopts the answers which other modes provide in the face of His failure to do justice to the demands directly made to Him, and as the being who successfully unites the triple answers that he receives from the other modes of being when he makes demands on each, we find nothing altered in Him by virtue of the fact that He is successful in these activities and the other modes are not. God's excellence consists not in His giving the full answer to the demands which each mode makes on Him, but in his ability to adopt the supplementary answers which other modes provide when He fails to do justice to the demands directly made on Him, and to the fact that He is able to solidify the triple answers which the other modes provide to His specific demand on one of them. His excellence is thus to be found in His adaptability and in His tolerance. These do not alter His nature as a mode of Being, but only His attitude and His interiorly-defined completeness. He does for Himself something like what a man does when he knows something. Knowledge gives a man the world beyond, but only in an abstract form; it does not diminish the world or enrich the being of man with the concrete being of another. Just so, the adaptability and tolerance of God gives Him a majesty, a dignity, an inward concreteness which the other modes cannot have. But all the while He remains one mode among many, needing things from them, inadequately giving things to them, resisting them, and insisting on Himself.

December 4

A good deal of contemporary discussion centers around the relation of Actuality to Existence. In its current form this relation has the shape of a reference to private experiences and public language, or to a vital existential one and a scientific impersonal outlook. The restrictions are rather narrowing, for the private world is more encompassing than a reference either to experience or anxieties or the like would indicate; and the public world is richer than that which is expressed in a public language or in a scientific impersonal formulation. But putting aside these restrictions the current views face a number of serious difficulties.

A] Since these views ignore the dimensions of the Ideal and God, neither can deal with ethics or religion except as some variant of the inexpressible private or the indifferent public. But there is as basic a problem relating the private to the Ideal and to God, and relating the public to the Ideal and to God, as there is in relating the private and the public to one another. The private relation to the Ideal gives us character; the private relation to God gives us faith; the public relation to the Ideal gives us public accountability; the public relation to God gives us the religious community.

B] Since the two elements which are selected are dealt with asymmetrically, only one of them is explained. For the Wittgensteineans and the Deweyites the private is explained by the public, and the public is taken for granted. The fact that there is a private is, of course, also accepted without question, but the meaning of the private is given by the public. Conversely, for the existentialists, the public is something which it finds given to it, but it dissolves this into the private. For the one the public and for the other the private is inexplicable, a meaning which is given; for the one the private and for the other the public is a contingent occurrence whose presence cannot be accounted for.

C] Since the private is absorbed into the public by the one, and the public into the private by the other, there is no problem of the private or public failing to do justice to the public or private respectively, and, therefore, no problem of the private or public having to adopt the answers given elsewhere. But conversely, then, the public which is supposed to absorb the private, and the private which is supposed to absorb the public must either do this completely or partially. If completely, there is no such thing as a failure to be adjusted to the public or a failure to have a significant role in private. If there is only an incomplete absorption, the private and the public will be irrationals sooner or later, and what the public and the private failed to do on their own behalf will not be done by anything else. This sounds like a bankruptcy of thought.

D] From the standpoint of the private, the public never provides a full answer. There ought to be answers given by other modes of being. Since this is not done, the private would have to say that the public's interpretation of it is not satisfactory but still is all that one can demand, or that it is in fact, no matter what it seems like, a full answer. And from the standpoint of the public it must be contended that either the intensified translation which the existentialist offers for public content is not adequate, so that the public content remains dissatisfied, or that it is adequate despite the fact that the rationality and impersonality of the public is then lost.

E] The public is diversified, and from the standpoint of the private there should be some way of unifying it. But there is nothing left to do this, since the private is supposedly absorbed in the public. Conversely, the private intensifies what is initially public, but in that intensification the necessities of the public should be retained. But there is nothing to retain it. The neobehaviorists, who take the first of these positions, never do justice to the unitary nature of the private, and provide no way in which this can be expressed in or recovered from the public. The existentialists on their side never do justice to the rigor of logic, and provide no way in which this rigor can be expressed in or recovered from the private.

Each side of the current way of thinking about the private has great strength. One can say that every intelligible communication requires one to give up the idiosyncratic and to express oneself in terms of the shared rules of a common language. Though there is an experience of having a pain, there is no meaning to "I have a pain" except so far as this can be dealt with in a language shared by others. And one can also say that anything that is significant is something lived through by an individual, that all scientific discourse is but a schema, inert, inane, useless, except so far as it is dissolved into the lived experiences of the various members of the public community. The one can deal with discourse, but not with sympathy; the other can deal with communication, but not with language. The one finds a way of making privacies have public value, but forgets that the privacies are given to it and that they remain private. The other gives the public a private value (and thus can allow for communication in the sense that the various privacies may be in attunement as they dissolve the common public item), but in its turn forgets that the public is given to it and continues to remain public.

Were one to treat the relation of man to the Ideal or to God in ways similar to that in which the private and public is dealt with by the neobehaviorists and by the existentialists, one would be faced with problems analogous to the above. And were one to add these dual ways of dealing with the various modes to one another, so that, for example, an actuality, viewed as a privacy, was translated into a public existential frame, an Ideal rationale, and a divine unity, we would be left with the fact that there would be no private being left who could make a unity of the triple answer (or of the three triple answers which would result from the fact that the demand made by the private on, say, God, would be only inadequately answered by Him, and would require supplementation by divinelike answers on the part of the other modes).

The relation of man to God is one in which man's direct demand on God is not answered by God altogether; a man must look for his salvational answer in part to the Ideal and in part to Existence. A fully religious man, it may then be said, is one who not only looks to God, but looks also to the Ideal and to Existence for divinelike answers to his problems. He will also look to God for an idealized kind of answer, and for an existentialized kind of answer. When he looks to God in the latter spirit, he sees God as the great preserver; when he looks to God in the former spirit, he sees Him as a companion who must not merely be submitted to, but must be dealt with together with a divinelike answer by the Ideal and Existence. The Ideal's divinelike answer is given in the idea of providence; Existence's divinelike answer is given in the space-time coordinate position it allows the actuality to have within itself.

December 5

Perhaps the most brilliant chapter in Hegel's brilliant *Phenomenology of Mind* is the one on the struggle of enlightenment with superstition, with the next chapter on about the same level. Hegel calls the two components Insight and Belief. They could be translated as Rationality and Experience, Science and Enjoyment, Form and Matter, God and Man, Logic and Content. Among the many points that Hegel makes, the following are perhaps the most important:

A] He takes Insight and Belief to be the same but opposed; all content, though, is possessed by belief and the attitude of being right. Belief is for insight a kind of false insight, just as from the perspective of a rationalism (such as Descartes'), body, matter, emotion, etc., are confused forms of the rational, the clear and distinct.

B] The "false insight" divides off a portion of itself as that which will deceive its naïve nature. The deceiver is a "Priesthood" working with a despotism; together they make the naïve nature be the bad insight of a multitude. Translated into these other forms, Hegel is saying that sheer experience or enjoyment distinguishes a component which confuses the remaining component by acting both as a conceited, self-confident mode of apprehension, and as an authoritative final way of apprehending. The confusion of which Descartes complains is thus the outcome of the emotions having a kind of willfulness to them, thereby acting on the simple expression of the emotions with a self-confidence and authority which succeed only in bringing about a deception. The point is, then, that what stands over against the rational is viewed by that rational as having a naïve component which is deceived by virtue of a base component that takes itself to be self-sufficient and all-powerful. It complains, as it were, about the claim of matter, emotion, etc., to be self-sufficient.

C] The endeavor of the rational is to rescue the deceived component, to get out of the confused the genuine truth that it contains, to wrest it from the state of being an expression of the base component. In effect, this means that there is a sense in which matter, man, enjoyment, etc., are allowed to be genuine if allowed to be innocent, and not distorted by other forms of the emotions, etc.

D] Belief is said to have absolute Being as content, and to allow its own naïve being to be exhausted in the having or being of that absolute Being. When it does this it realizes itself properly, avoids being a false insight. But this requires the belief to abandon itself as a controlling factor. Translated, Hegel is saying that the confusion of common sense or the errors of mankind (over against God) are avoided when these domains abandon themselves to being molded or embodied in the real. Let matter give up any claim to having determinations of its own, and be that which is shaped by reality itself, and insight will accept it as nothing other than matter, with itself as form. The form expands throughout the matter, as that which was over against it, to become the form for reality.

But the expansion of the realm of insight is not merely the "like combining with like," the making itself the very meaning of the real; it must struggle against the other. But this is only to say that it must be opposed to itself because from the perspective of insight, form, God, etc., there is in fact nothing else in the world, so that what these struggle against must be themselves—unless they are to give up the claim to be everything, to be the truth, or give up the attempt to be articulate, intelligible. But insight therefore deceives itself, since it imagines that it has an opponent. There is no evil against which God must struggle, there is no matter to limit a form, there is no confusion to oppose the clear and distinct, for the other is actually the same as that which is presumably opposing it. To condemn the other, to pronounce it to be unreliable, bad, unworthy, is but to denounce itself.

E] The dealing with the other is but a way of expressing itself, exteriorizing itself, and then taking back into itself what it has put forth of itself. This is how insight is able to have a content for itself which is not alien to itself. If it sees the content as other than itself and only that, it deceives itself. To know the opposite which it faces to be itself is but to know the content as its own. To know the confusions of the emotion to be over against itself is to deceive itself; the mind must instead see these confusions as its own content, with itself as a mere attitude of rationality. The form must see the matter as itself in the shape of a content, and not as something which is given to it, as it were, from the outside. It fights "itself" in them and condemns "that in them which it asserts," says Hegel.

F] From the standpoint of belief, enlightenment is seen to give up its pure self-identity and to attack, making itself a kind of "lying unreason and malicious intent." Instead of being all in all, as it claims itself to be, it spends itself in denying something outside itself or in fighting itself (which is the same thing). From the standpoint of the emotions, matter, man, etc., the supposed noble other is not so noble since it spends its energies in destructive negations; it rejects something, indeed itself, or what it takes to be not itself, and in either case shows itself not to be that single unbroken calm it claims to be, self-sufficient and all-encompassing.

G] Insight, from the standpoint of belief, since it opposes its own content, is empty. Form, from the perspective of matter, as opposing that matter, is empty. (When Kant said that forms without intuition were empty and intuitions without forms were blind, from what perspective was he speaking? According to Hegel he must have first taken the position of intuition and then the position of the categorical forms.) The content for the form is found in the realm of belief. The rationalist spends his energies in clarifying the confused which must be given to him, and on which he depends for his work. But the confused content belongs to the form, and thus in not recognizing itself in the confused the form fails to recognize itself. A form, God, etc., so far as it combats something and yet is to be understood as the real, fails to know itself as it is.

H] Insight accepts what belief presents to it, and spends its life in making this a kind of function of itself. But this is precisely what insight said that belief does, for belief is supposed to produce its own object. It criticizes belief for the very thing which it itself does. Translated, this means that in disdaining confusion, man, sin, matter, experience, privacy, etc., the supposedly rational, noble, etc., insight is in fact criticizing itself and objecting in the other what it practices itself. The rational, etc., is to make out of itself what is real, turn what it sees as error into nothing but itself. But it objected to confusion, etc., for making something be by its own action.

I] Belief puts its trust in its object; it identifies itself with the object, and thus is self-conscious, self-contained. The fact that the products of the confusion, the work of man, etc., are taken to be genuine products and are accepted by the producer, makes belief and its analogues have a completeness which insight claimed itself to have, but which it denies when it combats belief. The self-containedness of private experience, etc., shows it to have an ultimacy which any alienated reality, such as insight is, cannot have. Moreover, belief, etc., can see that the other object is but itself, as it were exteriorized, and thus can function the way insight did, as that which has itself over against itself.

J] Belief engages in acts and obeys, and thereby achieves a certainty of its object as the real, an object which is produced by the community. The idiosyncratic element of the belief, the surd quality of experience, etc., is eliminated by these accepting as their true object not the mere terminus of the believing, etc., activity, but the terminus of such a believing, etc., as having its own substantiality. The realm of matter, of private experience, etc., is not as exclusive, fractionated, self-enclosed, idiosyncratic as the rationalist makes out, for it accepts as its true object what is substantial on its own and which can be said to be the very truth of all the beings together.

K] Insight takes the objective of belief to be concerned with something alien, but here belief chides insight for not knowing what belief does. (The answer to the doctrine of common usage, or logic, etc., when it criticizes the private, etc., is that it does not know what privacy, etc., is.) Indeed, insight says that it is essential for the belief to take such and such an object as its own, and yet goes on to say that this is alien to belief's true nature. Belief accepts its object and trusts in it, has its confidence in it; belief is of the very substance of it. Insight knows this and yet declares that the object of belief is alien to belief. Insight then says of belief the opposite of what insight maintains about belief; it shows belief that enlightenment is a "conscious lie." Belief could not be deceiving itself, for it finds itself where it produces the object. Translated, the rational says that the confused, etc., is so necessarily, and at the same time says that the confused object is alien to it. But the confusion is existent in that very object. (If metaphysics, from the perspective of positivism, is a tissue of error and confusion, then metaphysics sees itself as having its proper object, and that object ought not to be said to be alien to the true intent of metaphysics. Of course one could say that it has no true intent, and thus deny that there is something to be saved in the domain of metaphysics. But if this were the case, there would be nothing to combat, or no way to combat it; if it is wholly alien it will remain outside the reach of the efforts of the positivists.)

L] There is no possibility of deception where an effort is expressed in such a way that it finds its certainty in what it produces. The self-completion or self-containment of the private, etc., shows it to be doing what the private should, and that its object is not deceptive but entirely appropriate; what it is and says is itself, and is this as an object, something which it confronts. It is wrong to criticize the private even in rational terms, for the very nature of the rational is to express itself adequately, to find itself in the content. The so-called irrational does exactly this; its object is itself and is just what rationality says the rational is.

M] Belief is identical with absolute being, is related to it as a form of knowledge, and acts on its behalf in worship and service. Translated, the material or individualistic is itself irreducible, is related to a reality beyond it, and works on behalf of that reality through its submission to it and by its sacrifice of itself on behalf of that absolute being.

N] Insight takes a negative attitude toward the absolute being of belief. For belief the absolute being is something given, but the viewpoint of insight is that true being is something in- and of-itself, and therefore supposes that the being which belief faces is some relativized object, indeed something sensible or gross. It therefore takes belief's object to be something anthromorphic. But this is not what belief does; it is what insight does. Insight relativizes the absolute and attributes this result to belief, thereby doing a double injustice to it, for it denies the objectivity of the object of belief and relativizes this in the shape of particulars. Insight treats the eternal and holy as something in the gross world of

sense, but this is not the object of belief. Insight insults belief by supposing this is its object. Translated, the rational always supposes something about its other which is unworthy of that other, and thereby reveals that instead of being that which is pure and true, insight shows
itself to have a cheapening and "calumniating" attitude.

o] If insight says that belief's object of worship is also a thing of sense,
this is no news to belief. But belief had put this side of the object to a
side. When the rational says that it is evident that the daily world is
shot through with contingency, this is no news to the daily world. The
daily world, however, does not stay with this but penetrates it, takes out
of it what is sound and true.

p] Belief has its object directly before it. The relation is in fact the
relation of insight. But insight does not know itself as the relation connecting belief with belief's object. Insight treats the relation as something
external to insight. In developing itself it must include that relation, but
it takes the relation to belong to belief. It supposes the relation to be a
purely contingent one, one of accepting stories, etc., and thus as believing
too much. (Translated, it says that the relation connecting matter with
anything beyond itself is a rational one, and thus essentially like the
formal, but that when the formal views this relation it does not know
it to be itself, and indeed supposes that it is a purely contingent one,
connecting the matter, etc., in a contingent way with transient, irrelevant,
and inadequate objects.) But belief never did rest its case on these contingencies. It knows its object in its purity. The realm of the private,
confused, etc., is not one which accepts the adventitious; it has a naïve
and direct connection with what is absolutely so. When these try to provide the evidences which would suit their accuser, they are led astray;
their objects are themselves.

q] Belief denies its individuality in its service and thereby becomes one
with the absolute reality. Since insight takes a negative attitude toward
this worship, it must look to belief as being stupid and unintelligent; yet
what else is right but that the accordance of end and means hold as it
does when belief is engaged in service? Belief's intention is pure, but
insight says it is impure; it thus identifies pure with impure and therefore
defines itself to have an impure intention. Translated, the action which
the private, etc., engages in on behalf of the real beyond it is immediate
and proper, and when this is frowned upon, the rational takes this to be
the opposite of itself and thus shows itself not to have attained its own
purpose. And when it takes the intent of the private to be impure it in
fact reveals itself to have an impure intention, since it supposes what is

a pure intention to be an impure one, and thus that even itself, supposedly pure, must be impure.

R] Belief makes a sacrifice of the contingent and present on behalf of the absolutely right or real; it denies its individuality on behalf of the ultimate. But enlightenment finds both of these to be foolish. It believes in a reality beyond these particularities, but it objects to belief acting on that supposition. It wants an inner elevation, but "declares that it is superfluous, foolish, and even wrong to be in earnest in the matter." The formal says that it is right to escape from contingency and sheer particularity, but when it finds the individual having beliefs or attitudes, or, more sharply, when it finds the individual engaged in metaphysical speculation, insight shows that insight is not in earnest in saying that one ought to free oneself from contingency and particularity. It says we ought to do this, but it objects to one who in fact does this.

S] Taken positively, insight regards everything as a finite or human product. But then being, as such, becomes a mere empty indeterminate. Translated, this means that the truth or reality for insight is empty, and only particular realities are allowed to eixst. Its own activity is self-contained, and thus comes to know only what is negative to itself. The object of the merely formal is something which is other than itself, and which is devoid of content. The only truth that is allowed is that all the finite forms are, and that there is an empty reality, a something of which it knows nothing.

T] The facts of sense are related by insight to the empty being beyond; but this means that it will accommodate any content, so that every particular content as much affirms as negates that empty being. Every particular is what it is, and is just as agreeable to the absolute being as any other. Translated, the pure form has no distinctive object and every content is equally agreeable to it; every item thus is acceptable. The items, by being related to the empty absolute of form, are related to their own non-being. Insight sees the particulars as positive, each itself, and also as related to the opposite and thus having being only as something for another. As having being for another it is something useful, and is at the mercy of other beings and exists for them.

Everything from the standpoint of insight is useful—religion, the world, man himself. But belief finds this repugnant. Translated, the rational, in the end, finds everything to be but a moment, something belonging to a system, something having a role; but belief, which is directly aware of the absolutivity of direct or inward existence, finds this a particularly repugnant attitude to take toward what is ultimate. It

takes its stand with rights and dignities, truth and being. Belief rejects the idea that the absolute reality is a great void, that every particular is good, and that everything is useful. For belief such views are "revolting."
U] To belief, insight reveals itself to be insipid, for it knows nothing about absolute being. It does not even know what finitude is, since it supposes that knowledge about finitude is the highest possible knowledge. Translated, the existential and private see that the formal knows nothing about what is really final, that it knows nothing about the nature of the finite since it accepts every item equally, and yet takes the finite to be the area of truth. It even goes so far as to suppose that we can have no other knowledge than the knowledge of finite things.
V] Belief has a divine right, but enlightenment has only a human one. The private and idiosyncratic has a claim, one might say, which is not based on anything human, as the formal and the rational are. Enlightenment opposes; it destroys. But both have a right against one another. The formal and the material each has an integrity and stands in opposition to one another as possessing this integrity, no matter what the other is or does.
W] Enlightenment uses the principles which belief implies and contains; it merely reorganizes belief, reminding belief of its richness. It shows belief that it is a genuine insight so far as it sees the whole. From the standpoint of the private, the public is a basic position to take, only so far as it envisages the whole and enables the private to see the rich complexity of itself, and only so far as it makes use of the private's resources to make evident to the private what it truly is. Enlightenment's role here is misunderstood by belief, for when belief sees that another side of it is exposed, it thinks that enlightenment distorts and lies. But enlightenment, which reminds belief of its own richness, is blind about itself just so far as it takes its own content to be other than itself.
X] The absolute right of insight is to interrelate the elements of belief; this, belief should recognize. Insight "makes valid in belief what is necessary to belief itself, and what belief contains within it." The right of reason and God and form is to interrelate the dispersed elements of the private, material, human, and this "opposite" of the material which is presented to it by the formal is to be accepted by the formal as making the material valid.
Y] Belief finds itself as a particular "personal consciousness in absolute Being, and its obedience and service consist in producing, through its activity, that Being as its *own* Absolute. Enlightenment, strictly speaking, only reminds belief of this." So far as the material accepts a reality

to which it will submit, the formal serves to remind the material that there is this absolute being which is to be absolute for it.

z] Enlightenment finds that belief does not bring its various components together. It sees that belief gets to a reality through trust, and that that reality is unsearchable; it sees too that belief distinguishes the absolute and the finite and gives each a place. Belief accepts these two realities, the absolute and the finite, as in- and of-themselves. The formal sees that the material both has and has not its object, and that it takes to be final that which is absolute and that which is particular. It shows the material that these both belong to it.

A'] Belief does accept accidental knowledge, and even pictures the absolute in these terms; it does not then have the certainty it seeks in it; it confesses to be cut off from what it wants. The material, etc., knows nothing but the particulars, and when it refers to the absolute takes this to be an attenuated version of these particulars; it confesses that it really does not have the object it seeks. But when enlightenment reminds belief of this it refers to the contingency side of belief's knowledge and not to the absolute which belief immediately (though not mediately) knows or has.

B'] Belief, in its sacrifice, makes two mistakes. It gives up this or that thing and thinks it is giving up property, etc. It gives up an instrument and thinks it is giving up the inward drive. Its self-denial is merely a rejection of a part and of a particular agency. Enlightenment clings to the universal, the inward, the intention, and therefore denies the need to carry it out. Enlightenment holds sway over belief because enlightenment gives significance to belief's moments. Enlightenment looks as if it were polluting belief with vanities, lower thoughts, etc., but instead overcomes the division it thoughtlessly had in belief. Belief is twofold: uncritical and asleep, and conscious in the world of sense. Translated, it has a nuclear unexpressed truth to it and an articulation in the contingencies of the world. Enlightenment reminds belief of the finite side, clarifying the heaven by the world of sense, revealing the meaning of the private, material, etc., by bringing to bear what is known in fact in the public formal world. The formal has taken over the material, the area of belief, since everything that can be known is known formally. But belief knows that there is something more, though it faces this only as an emptiness for which it longs.

C'] Belief and enlightenment are one; both relate a finite existent to an unknown and unknowable absolute which has no predicates. One is enlightenment satisfied, the other dissatisfied. The formal makes a reference to the material as that which is filled out by the formalities; the material makes a reference to the formal as that which it is still to possess. It is because the material still longs that the satisfaction of the formal will never do; the material reveals that there is still something to be brought into the situation. Both, starting as finite, have different attitudes, the one filling up the absolute with the finite, the other longing to possess that absolute as something distinct from the finite. Both can be said to be formal—or belief-like—though Hegel speaks as though only the former way of speaking were proper.

All the above illustrate the point that the basic drive of a formalistic philosophy is dialectical, one in which an attempt is made to look at questions from two sides. Hegel supposes that the other side must operate dialectically too; but it can be argued that the other side—and this idea I got from "Chip" Dallery—should be dealt with as an item in a dialogue having the initial dialectical beginning as the other member. If we start with belief we enter into a dialogue with one who himself must function dialectically. One takes himself to be dialectical and makes a dialoguer be dialectical for him; in turn the dialoguer takes his opponent, who is dialectical, to be only a member of a dialogue. There is no harm in these movements provided that each sees the right of the other to deal with him in that other's terms—i.e., if the dialectician sees that he is rightly treated as a member of a dialogue by the other, and if the dialoguer sees himself rightly treated as a dialectical item for the other.

When the dialectician allows that he is to be viewed as a participant in a dialogue, what takes place? Is it anything more than a recognition of the right of the dialectical other to function properly, and thus from its perspective to subordinate all else?

December 6

There are four basic methods, each of which takes its start with a particular mode of being, and all of which could be used by a philosopher. The most appropriate, I think, is the dialectical, particularly since this makes evident that the other methods are needed. It starts with the Actual and recognizes the reality of the other modes; it also makes an effort to adopt the position of the other modes and to understand the nature of the universe from their perspective. However, when it starts dialectically from the other modes it does less than justice to their full powers.

If the other mode is God, it would be better to adopt the method of Communication, or in its restricted form, Dialogue. Here the effort is made to be in consonance with the other modes, to make oneself be sympathetic with them, to appreciate what they are. It means that even Actuality must look at others, as it were, from the perspective of God. The dialogue of which Buber speaks in connection with man and God is, in fact, a communication of God with Himself as adopted by man.

Were we to take our start with Existence, the proper way of dealing with other modes would be through work, through alteration, by remaking them so that they belong to a single ongoing totality. A philosopher who took this approach would be primarily concerned with action. If he formulated his views they would be essentially programs, plans, directions, even rules for the playing of games, etc. But the primary use men have made of Existence has been in art. The communication or elaboration here is not to be confused with the communication characteristic of one who takes the position which is divinelike, since the respondent is to be inspired, enlightened, purged, adjusted, rather than sympathized with.

If we take this position of the Ideal, the basic method is one of classification, ordering, arranging, primarily in terms of worth, value, dignity, status. We have here a way of dealing with others which relates to the kind of roles they play; in dealing with them we provide an organization in which they can play their roles effectively together.

When an individual starts off in one of these four ways he must become aware that the beings at which he arrives have a reality of their own. Is it correct to say, as I did to begin with, that only the dialectician can say just what is the proper way to express the kind of temper these other modes have? Why should not one who communicates be able to appreciate the need for other modes to sustain the dialectical, productive, and role-bearing activities? It would seem that this is the more reasonable assumption. If we adopt it we can say that no matter where we begin we will eventually come to appreciate the dialectical character of a systematic philosophy which takes its start from Actuality, achieves neutrality by abstraction, and then takes account of the presence of other modes, each acting in a distinctive way. Laying hold of that distinctive way requires an effort beyond the dialectic. The philosopher must shift his gears and become a communicator, an artist, and a categorizer. It is possible for him to be all these at the same time, by carving out a distinctive style within the dialectical frame. But this unification of the various methods into one could take place with the dialogue, etc., uppermost. We would then have four distinctive philosophic styles, depending on what method, and thus what particular mode of being, was given primary stress.

In each of these four methods there must be a consideration of all the modes as having distinctive beings, and as providing a perspective on one another, though this perspective may not be as undistorted and comprehensive a one as the perspective which answers to the particular method appropriate to a particular mode.

Plato might be said to have stressed the artistic mode of production, Kierkegaard the divinely toned communication, Hegel or Aristotle the categorial organization, but I do not know any place but the *Modes* where one can find the dialectical method taking full account of the fact that there is more than one being from which a dialectical approach can be made (though only one, Actuality, has this approach as essentially characteristic of itself).

The dialectically tempered philosopher claims to have the proper method, not only because he is able to assume the perspective of other modes of being besides Actuality—for other methods also allow one to do similar things—but because he can with his style, categories, and involvement or commitment express the temper of these other modes of being and the methods they sustain. Only the systematic approach does justice to some extent to the dialectical approach, but it does not know how to do justice to the commitment side. It is too cold, too austere— which is, of course, the charge made against the *Logic* of Hegel by Kierkegaard.

Hegel's system is often thought to be dialectical, but it is not so in fact if dialectic be the actual entertainment of a position from the side of other beings. Hegel's dialectic is an internal one; it shows how a being must recognize that what it takes to be its other is really itself. This surely is what a dialectic must show. But what Hegel does not see is that this other is a reality and that it is not altogether assimilable inside the frame of the initial being. Instead, it takes the same kind of approach to that initial being which that being takes to it, and therefore finds that initial being to be itself. Since both beings are ultimate, what they actually find to be themselves are but transformed versions of one another. Hegel's view is, instead, a systematic, a categorial one, in which the categories are systematically linked by the dialectical method.

In his *Phenomenology* Hegel tended toward a different view; he then was more inclined, not to the dialectical or the systematic, but to involvement and commitment. It could therefore be said that he was giving an existential account, one in which sympathy and involvement were primary, but that he, unlike the existentialists, interlaced this with a dialectic (of the limited sort noticed above), a kind of system, and a peculiar style. It is dubious, though, that any account which did full justice to the sympathy side would ever have room enough for the dialectic, since the rhythms of the sympathy are distinct from those of the dialectic.

Even if one were to grant that all the methods could find room for the others, to about the same extent, it could still be argued that the proper method for the philosopher is the one which stresses the dialectic, because his primary concern is to know rather than to make, enjoy, or organize, and that this knowledge when carried to its limits and made sufficiently abstract and neutral, is an achievement not possible except by one engaged in an inquiry and a proving, which is precisely what a dialectic allows.

December 8

Each mode of being needs the others. But it meets with a resistance by them; they cannot be possessed by the being except in some substitutional way. Each mode of being has a triply divided answer to its need in the form of a substitutional form of mastery. An actuality thus grasps all the three modes through knowledge. The resistances which these others offer actuality (making knowledge an abstract way of possessing them) are their characteristic ways of subjugating by classification (the Ideal), unifying through sympathy (God), and adjusting through expression (Existence).

Each mode of being also needs to be embodied in the other modes; there is a reality in the others which it can benefit from by yielding itself to those others. The Ideal needs to be embodied in Actuality. It is this need which is not satisfied by virtue of the resistance of the needing being itself. The Ideal does not give itself wholly to the embodiment, but keeps to itself. Or, staying with an actuality, it not only seeks to lay hold of the Ideal and the other modes and has to content itself with doing this cognitionally, but it needs to be rationalized by the Ideal, properly related by Existence, and sustained by God. But it does not allow these to occur, because it insists on being itself. Still, what each fails to do on behalf of the others, is done by the remainder. The Ideal's resistance to being embodied by the actuality is the source of the actuality's guilt. But the other modes make up the slack; they give the Ideal the embodiment which the actuality failed to provide. The actuality overcomes its stain of guilt and circumvents the Ideal's resistance by adopting the actualizing way of embodiment which is practiced by the other modes. This actualizing way of embodying is not cognitional. Cognition is for the sake of possessing the being where and as it is, but embodiment is for the sake of making it possible for another being to get the value which the embodiment can provide.

Actuality actualizes by going through the analogue of the processes characteristic of the other modes—it acts and unifies on behalf of the Ideal; it acts and subjugates, or classifies on behalf of God; it unifies and subjugates on behalf of Existence. When then an actuality fails to do justice to the Ideal's need to be embodied in Actuality, the actuality reveals itself to be a poor substitute for Existence and God. Its failure to do the Good is due to the fact that it neither acts nor unifies properly. When then it looks to Existence and God to do what it cannot finally do, it looks to what can act and unify better than it does (though what they then act for and unify is something which was to be embodied in Actuality).

A mode of being, then, is defective in the sense that its resistance makes it offer only a third of an answer to the demands of some other being's need to possess whatever there be. Its resistance is a function of the distinctive method or approach it makes to all else. In addition, the mode is defective in that the way in which it is satisfying the need of another mode to be embodied in it is through activities which are more effectively carried out by other modes. Each deals with a side of a given mode in ways which are not the most appropriate ways for the acting mode to use, and yet are the only ways it has to embody the given mode. To make good its deficient mode of acting, it adopts the achievements of other modes which carry out that form of acting in a better way, though with the content and with the outcome characteristic of an actuality. God, for example, though He will not embody the Ideal as an actuality does, will nevertheless embody it as a pluralized Good, just so far as actuality fails to do this. He will of course embody the Ideal as His own perfection, which will be a kind of embodiment carried out by His functioning, not as a divine unifier, but as a divine actor and a divine knower.

Each being, then, resists the possessive attempt of others because each grounds a distinctive method or approach to the others, which precludes the others from absorbing it. Each being also carries out the kind of activities characteristic of the others, but does not do that well; it must look to the remaining modes to do what it failed to do, and must accept their result as its own. If Actuality is essentially or primarily cognitional, it will not be possessed by beings which approach it, as they must, primarily in the role of sympathetic, classifying, or expressive modes (which is the way God, Ideal, and Existence respectively function); and when in the attempt to embody the other modes Actuality does act with sympathy and expressively (for the Ideal), with sympathy and organizationally (for Existence), and expressively and organizationally (for God), it does not function in the best possible way for itself, and must in each case look to the remaining modes for better actors to bring about the kind of result which it alone ought to achieve. Each mode now will either be one seeking to embody another and failing to act properly, or will be substituting for a failing one, and though acting properly, i.e. automatically, as just the way it ought to act, it will be doing this with respect to the wrong kind of content and for the wrong kind of result so far as that mode of acting is concerned.

Each mode of being solves its problem by unifying the triple answer which the other three provide it with, though only God gets that unity into his very "subjectivity," makes it substantial, solidifies the results through sympathy. Each mode of being can also solve its problem by adopting the outcome achieved for it by the other modes, but only God, in fact, takes this answer. Only He is appreciative of the outcome provided by other modes when He necessarily fails to do full justice in his sympathy to the need of the other modes to be embodied in Him. He could not satisfy them directly without their losing their natures, their resistance, their being, or without His being able to act like Existence, subjugate like the Ideal, and cognize like an Actuality. But though He cannot overcome this resistance, and thus must fail to embody the other modes fully in Himself, there is a divinelike result which Actuality can provide through cognition, Ideality through subjugation, and Existence through sheer becoming which He can and does adopt, and thereby indirectly achieves a perfection of result not achieved by the others.

December 9

The incarnation and the mind/body share a common problem: granted that the two components make a single unity, does it follow that both are expressed at the same time? Does every moment of Christ's life exhibit a divine nature; does every act of the body exhibit the presence of a human mind? Since the mind has its own rationale, and seems to be able to operate apart from the body, and conversely, since the body seems to be subject to purely physical forces which in no way are affected by the mind, and since the man Jesus could evidently walk about and not be noticed by anyone as being God, and since the rhythm of the religious and the purpose of the divine are independent of the secular, it would seem that the two components need not be in accord except at certain crucial points. We can conceive of one moving along a straight line, and the other moving in semi-circles and impinging on the straight line only after a period. Such a view does, though, seem to have the difficulty of showing how the two components make a single unity. It could well be argued that every act of a human being, no matter how subject to purely physical conditions, is always permeated by the mind, if only to give it another flavor; one can argue that though Jesus Christ was not recognized, he was recognizable by anyone who would really look at the way he walked or talked or ate.

Might it not be the case that both these views are true—that there is a kind of consonance of two components at every moment, and there is a divergency in their expression? The being of Jesus Christ, and the being of every individual man would then involve the presence of both components, but only one might be expressed, only one would be allowed to be exercised at a moment, just as a man might walk instead of talk. Better perhaps would be the view that at some times, and perhaps even in the case of Jesus Christ all the time, there would be a perfect unity in the expression of both components, but that normally the two would diverge. Thus we could have an independent historic and religious time and the two might not mesh except occasionally, the one moving in a straight line, the other in waves. But there could conceivably be times when the two kept together. Sometimes the keeping together would be wavelike, exhibiting the religious dimension or the mental side, as controlling the secular or bodily, respectively. In such a case we would have miracles, controlled actions, purposes and the like. In other cases the secular or the bodily would be dominant, and as a consequence the rhythm of the religious would be modified, slowed, but it would still be part of the wavelike rhythm characteristic of it as apart from the other. Thus, we have the building of a church under the control of religious authorities, but going according to the time schedule and plans of an ordinary building contractor. Or we have the idle observations of a man who is strolling.

Must we not say, to preserve the unity of Jesus Christ (or of an ordinary man), that it always is the case that the secular (or the bodily) has the other dimension overlaying it, though not necessarily altering it, and that the other dimension occasionally comes into its own, both when moving in waves, and when moving at the pace normally characteristic of the secular (or bodily)? The history of Israel may be said to be an illustration of the way in which one can have the secular course define the pace of the religious. The religious dimension may still have an extra power where it behaves in wavelike ways to define kairotic moments. If we take this as our guide then we have the two interlocked, with both being manifest at every moment, but with some moments being extra-charged by the intrusion of a wavelike act. And there could then also be times when the secular rhythm controlled or intruded on the religious— for example, the secular calendar ordering the religious days and even determining which of these are to have primary importance.

This question and its solution have relevance to every mode of being, for everyone has other modes in it not altogether subjugated for it. On the foregoing account, the modes in one another would sometimes be governed by the rhythm of one and sometimes by the rhythm of the others; sometimes a mode would function independently, but come together with the others at crucial points, though all would continue to be interlocked and so would constitute one single whole whose rhythm was dictated by one or the other. This means that my attempt in *History: Written and Lived,* to hold history away from the natural course of events was mistaken; history has its own pace, but this does not preclude it from making a unity with the natural, from dictating to that natural world, from being dictated to by it, and from coming into interrelation-ship with it from time to time.

December 10

Strictly speaking, every mode is immanent in every other. The immanence has two degrees.

Firstly, it is immanent in the sense that it is subjugated to the mode in which it is. We call the mode by a distinctive name, but we cannot know it except as the unity of the diverse modes which are ingredient in it, or as the unity of the modes as outside it. An actuality, for example, exists. This is not possible to it except so far as Existence is in it, subju-gated, modified, though still connected with the Existence outside, indeed being pulled by that Existence and thereby becoming subject to time. And what is true of the actuality with respect to Existence is true of it with respect to God and the Ideal.

The second degree of immanence is a reflection of the ingredient mode as outside the accepting mode. Here an actuality exists because Existence is intruding on it, forcing the actuality to resist, respond, rebuff, or accept. It is this second type of immanence which relates to the Incarnation, and to the affect of the mind or will on the body. The first kind allows for the characterization of a mode of being as one in which all others are ingredient.

The first type of immanence requires us to have a definition of, say actuality, which does not relate to the ingredients—actuality is that which is over against, opposed. The second type of immanence starts with the first. Actuality here is existent, and interplays with the intrusive Existence.

Answering to the first type of immanence is the transcendent being of a mode; the ingredient mode has a definition of its own, as standing apart from the mode in which it is ingredient. Its immanence is not possible except as related to itself as transcendent, independent. Answering to the second type of immanence is the transcendent being of the mode as that which is active, which is doing the intruding. From the standpoint of the being which is receptive of both forms of immanence, there is a reference to the transcendent sides: the first through a relation of need, and the second through a relation of opposition.

When we turn to the question of the relation of historic to natural time, or of the relation of religious to secular history, or of the relation of the activities of Jesus and Christ, we find that we have: 1] The two components together in both places, to give beings which have one another ingredient in them. Jesus, the secular, and natural time already have something of the other in them, and conversely. But we speak of them as Jesus, etc., because the other is subjugated, transformed, made to follow the contours, be at the service of the being in which they are immanent.   2] We also have the two components as standing apart from one another, thereby making it possible for them to be ingredient. Here each goes its own way and at its own rate, to give us a duality (or plurality) of realities. In this guise they never meet, though all are related in various types of togetherness, some with thickness and persistence, and some (the final ones for the modes as such) without any character or power beyond the barest minimum of being prescriptive or descriptive, etc.   3] The beings as intrusive, as impinging on one another, make a difference to the functioning of one another. Here each retains its own nature, is not yet subjugated or cancelled out or rebuffed by another, but makes that other take account of it in some way. This is the kind of situation which prevails when the religious history impinges on the secular. It is an impingement which need not be constant, and may vary in degree. 4] There is the assessment which a given being makes on the being that impinges, the kind of value and role it allows it to have in its career. We have here the kind of problem faced by the secular when it is intersected by the religious. It could alter its pace, take account of what came from the religious dimension which it encountered.

December 11

The various modes intrude on one another's subdivisions and do this in different degrees. A thing, for example, is caught in the field of Existence; it does not subjugate Existence in itself to the degree that a man does. It is appropriate to look at it as primarily a localization of Existence. It can also be seen to be an instance of the Ideal in the way an individual man is not; it instances the rationale of the Ideal, is more readily open to prediction; it is more law-abiding. But then we must also say that it is more inside, more one with God than men are. The last point is seen by pantheists, who find it necessary to reduce men to a kind of thing; once this is done, there seems to be little difficulty in making all actualities be in God in the sense of being localizations or cases of simple unities, repeating His nature simply.

Inside the Ideal the best possibilities would be those which are more resistant to the intrusion of other modes, which subjugate other modes more, and the least valuable would be those caught inside Existence, God, and Actuality. Inside Existence, the categorial features, Space, Time, Dynamism, would be the most capable of subjugating, and the fragmentated parts of Existence would be most readily encompassed by the other modes. Inside God those parts which required the least alteration in order to be excellent would offer the most resistance to being caught in other domains, and would subjugate whatever did intrude on God.

The Incarnation is not to be viewed as a kind of intrusion. Intrusions characterize the prophetic and miraculous; they involve the introduction of God into areas where He is already ontologically immanent. The Incarnation is understood by Roman Catholics to involve the preservation of both the divine and the human nature. Would it not be proper to say of it that it also encompasses a man who has something like the role of a thing with respect to God, i.e., that God is ontologically present in the man, makes the man continuous with Himself, a subdivision of

Himself, and thus like a thing in the sense that he is divinely oriented and not one who subjugates God within himself? His human nature would preclude the man being like a thing, since it would keep him away from the divine, but this thing-like status of being part of the divine would allow him to share in the divine. This sounds like a reasonable interpretation, though the reference to "things" seems very odd. Is it that the analogy is misleading precisely because it is an individual man who is divinely oriented, that there is a maintenance of the human nature while he is divinely oriented, whereas in the case of things, their individuality and substantiality is precisely that which is lost? We could make the analogy of Christ with a thing only so far as we denied his distinctive human nature.

Ought there not be something like an Incarnation in the other modes? For example, ought there not be a possibility, or set of possibilities, which reflect the presence of man, which while functioning like minor value-possibilities (in that they are oriented toward the realm of the Actual) are nevertheless possibilities of excellence which stand apart from the world? Would this not be the Good? And would not the analogue in Existence be the tragicomic nature of Becoming? And would not the analogue in God be the divine mercy or love?

Would there not also have to be something like an incarnational status achieved by other modes in a given mode—e.g., must there not be a kind of incarnational presence of the Ideal and Existence in man, in addition to the divine mentioned above, and incarnational presences of other modes beside Actuality in Existence, the Ideal, and God? Thus, the Ideal in man might be realized in the form of a saintly man, and Existence might be realized in him in the form of the heroic man. The Incarnation is thought, though, to be the outcome of a special act, and to allow for a time when it did not occur; if this be the model, none of the above analogues need be instanced. And if they are instanced, what power would make them possible?

The Incarnation is thought to require a divine act; would anything less than an act of that magnitude make it possible for the various other modes to be ingredient in one another and in God? One could say that the analogue of an Incarnation of God in the Ideal and Existence would require God's effort, but there would not be a need to invoke God in the other cases, for every mode of being is as powerful as any other. The Incarnation in the realm of Actuality moreover need not have a counterpart in Ideality and Existence, though it is perhaps reasonable to say that the analogues do occur at the same time as the supposed Incarnation.

On that supposition there would be a providential determination of the Ideal and a controlling use of Existence occurring at the same time as the Incarnation.

December 12

If the Incarnation be viewed as the openness to the presence of God, of Christ who continues to be a man and thus who like every man subjugates the divine component that is in him, the Sacrifice could be viewed as an openness of the man Jesus to God, so that he presents to God the nature of man unqualified, functioning as man—or more completely, as a representative of all Actuality. Ordinary men would be said to qualify God in themselves, on the one side, and on the other to be qualified by God, and thus never to have God either as a domain in which they are, or as a pure subject standing away from them entirely. Only a thing has God as a mere domain, and only a thing has Him as a mere subject for it; He provides the thing with a locus, where it is unqualified and unaltered.

Each mode of being can be thought of as having a nature of its own which subtends the togetherness of the other three modes inside it. The thing is Actuality, with a minimal status of being other; it functions somewhat as a point. A man is representative of all Actuality and so far stands away from all the other modes. Those outer modes are ingredient in him, but qualified and modified to constitute the content through which he expresses himself.

A man's existence is continuous with the unqualified Existence which lies beyond. But though that Existence pulls on his own, and though in fact he helps determine the geometry of that Existence, he does not act on that Existence unless he does some particular thing; there is no ontological impingement on Existence by him, and consequently there is nothing he does to make Existence function in relation to the Ideal or God—or conversely. He could by a deliberate act produce such interplay; when he does so he raises himself in dignity. It is possible, as it were, to hear the voice of God and do nothing; the prophet mediates, brings God's word into the context of the people's present activities.

Returning to the question which is in fact behind these remarks, that of the relation of religious to secular history, if the religious history be thought to deal with man as already embodying God, it will deal with God as already having a secular side. The question will be whether God as outside that embodied role acts on the secular as outside the man. This comes down to the question as to whether man, or a people, or a church mediates God and the secular world. The fullness of time will be the readiness of these to mediate; the "time" in which that fullness occurs will not be either divine or secular, but the distinctive time of a being who is already one, having God within him.

Every being, even those we call purely secular, has God within it. Consequently, what must be said is that a religious time, which relates to actualities, must be one in which there is a fluctuating distance between it and God, and in the sense that it is more or less open to His operation or presence. It would be something like the relation achieved by a religious man when he moves from his daily tasks to prayer, etc. At every moment we can view him in terms of his relation to God; when we do this we view him in a religious time. We have that time impinge on and make a difference to the time of daily life only so far as there is more than a minimal openness. The normative situation will be that of a being who has a minimal orientation in the other modes of being, while internally subjecting the modes inside himself to constitute him as one who possesses them in a characteristic way. When that being opens itself more to the presence of the other modes of being, and thereby becomes more oriented in those other modes while continuing to be himself (and thus in this sense imitating the Incarnation), we have God acting through him on the other modes. The acting of God on him, as one who has the modes in him, will be an act of election, not an act of influencing the secular world, for such influence must go beyond merely presenting man with the pure being of God, i.e., allowing him to be unqualified, but in God.

When a man acts he acts in Existence, and it is this action, as well as his action with respect to the Ideal, which makes it possible for God to be influential in Existence, an Existence having pertinence to man. And there ought to be similar inroads made on Existence by the Ideal through the agency of man. And there ought to be similar impingements on God in which man mediates Existence and the Ideal. In the latter cases we can speak of man as a mediator, as sacrificing, as God's representative. But we could also, as we do in the case of the Incarnation, speak of man in terms of the Existence and the Ideal which he is helping to function and which make a difference to God. In short, he can be said to present God with the demands of nature and the demands of the Good; he will make this presentation through a characteristic act of worship, perhaps, but whatever his act, he will be doing on behalf of Existence and the Ideal something similar to what he did on behalf of

God, when he mediated God in an act similar to an Incarnation. The Incarnation would be structurally an orientation in God while retaining a human (not a merely existential or thinglike) nature, but dynamically it would involve the activity of mediating God, making Him effective in Existence and in the Ideal. The latter activity would be occasional; the structural side would be constant. In the case of man we would have only the occasional impingement.

The history of Israel is a history of a people. This is, strictly speaking, neither a religious history nor a secular one, but the two of them together as subjugated to the people. We get a purely religious history when we deal with the openness to God, and a purely secular one when we deal with the openness to Existence, or to other human groups. If we approach Israel from the side of God or Existence we can see it as purely religious or secular, but we will then have lost its peculiar momentum.

Religious and secular history are both dependent on a third history, in which there are religious and secular subordinated components, but which has its own distinctive rhythm and contents, and has variant degrees of openness to the influence of the religious and secular, relating the one to the other.

What designation is appropriate to this distinctive history? Is it "spiritual" or "cultural" or "civilized" history? Is it "national" history? Whatever it be, the fullness of time will not be determined by God, nor by actions in the secular world, but rather by the way in which this singular history of the people opens itself up at various times, readies itself to mediate God to the other modes—and of course conversely, readies itself to mediate the other modes to God. In these cases the other modes are not dealt with as mere modes, but as a world of nature and a realm of desirable possibilities.

December 13

The relation of religious history to secular history should be something like the relation of secular history to the human realm. The human realm already has some Existence in it, and is directed toward the Ideal and presupposes God as the being which gives it a kind of persistence and value. When this human realm interplays with Existence and incidentally gets the support of the Ideal and God, we get history. The relation of the historic time to the time of the human realm is like the relation of the latter time to the time of nature. We have here no necessary intrusion or even intersection of the different times (as I suggested there might be in recent days); there are only the new times which are constituted by new interplays, and which give new kinds of connections to the beings involved in those interplays.

By bringing man and Existence together in the human realm, Existence is subject to new human conditions, and man is reorganized in an existential frame of society or state. Existence as a whole continues as before, but Existence is partly encapsulated and then has new functions. Apparently, similar things must be said about man as standing outside society and as in it. Taking this cue we can say that religious history subjugates a portion of the larger history of mankind to special conditions, with the consequence that this portion has a distinctive rhythm, even though it is also to be included in the larger history and will there be subject to the time of that history—somewhat the way in which the submicroscopic parts of a man follow the laws of nature so far as they are viewed as continuous with the whole of nature, and yet follow special routes and have distinctive rhythms inside the man.

The secular history of the human realm is subject to special conditions in certain areas. There is no reason why the whole of mankind might not be brought within the religious orbit, just as the totality of submicroscopic entities might be subject to special conditions in individuals and come out smooth and regular in behavior only so far as abstraction is made from their various localizations.

December 14

In speaking of religious history as intersecting secular history an assumption was made to the effect that the secular history was continuing as it had been. But it seems more correct to say that the items in the secular history become absorbed into a new present, and there have the status of items in a relation of before and after, while retaining the status inside the secular history of being earlier and later. The relation then of the secular to the religious history is like the relation of the time of secular history to the time of nature.

How long is the present of religious history? A religion can be said to have presents which run about a week long, sometimes, as with the Muslims, a month long, and all religions in their recurring festivals, etc., might be said to have presents either from one festival to another or for an entire year in which the various festivals can be said to make a single block. Religious history would be represented by such presents.

The present of a religious history could be the life of the founder, or to consist of a series of crucial occurrences in that life, or of crucial occurrences in the course of the development of the religion itself—solidifications, schisms, definitions of creed, dispersals, and the like. The present need not drop out any items occurring in the secular history, but it will not allow all of them to have causal or conditional roles. Secular history will see these latter as analytic components in a larger whole which will keep these components in an order of before and after, while having others as earlier and later in a sequence which is governed by a principle of relevance.

If we take this to be a model for the mind-body problem, or for the intersection of the various modes with one another, we would have to give priority to one factor rather than the other. Or we would have to say that the analogy breaks down, or that the secular might have longer presents than the religious, but that historic time might have shorter presents than natural time (presents which, however, are included in the present of that natural time). I would think that the two-way treatment is more correct, but that it may be the case that if we take some one dimension, such as time, it may be correct to go in only one direction, and that if we are to have a reverse movement it will not be one involving time but perhaps value or power or agency and the like. Thus we might have Actuality include God in one way and God include Actuality in another. However, the fact of time seems distinctive in that it requires that there be something which could occur in the same order but with a distinctive value.

Is there such an order to be found anywhere but in time? Can we find something similar to the difference between before and after, and earlier and later, and therefore to an inclusive present taking into itself what in another sequence would be past? Can one say, for example, that the value which a man has stands outside the values which other men or beings have, but that in God the totality of values makes an entirely different context for the particular values, so that they have a new relation to one another?

If God is the inclusive value, Existence could be said to provide the inclusive extension, the Ideal could be said to provide the inclusive universals, and Actuality could be said to provide the inclusive concern. The inclusive universal would change the way in which the plurality of universals would be related to one another. Where before they would be connected by implications and affiliations, inside a more inclusive universal they would be ordered as more or less general, and would not be completely distinguishable one from the other. Actualities would have a concern which subordinated and reordered all the other interests and activities in which a man might engage. Each mode would include the other modes in the guise of analytically contained subdivisions. Thus God would be in Actuality as subordinated to the inclusive concern; the Ideal would be in Actuality as something similarly subordinated to that concern, and so would Existence.

December 15

I ought not to have taken for granted that all the temporal units in a secular world are of the same length. This would apply only to Existence as over against all other modes. It would not apply to existent actualities. The present of an actuality could be said to be its life-span, or its entire career. Such a span could be larger or smaller than the span of a religious occurrence or of an occurrence in history. Consequently, the inclusion of one type of time in another cannot be determined as going only one way, with the exception of the time of Existence. But the time of Existence, it is to be noted, is a time ingredient in Existence, and is unlike the time of an actuality, etc., which results from the interplay of Existence with actuality and other modes.

In the case of secular history and religious history we should have some events in the first include events in the second, and also some events in the second include those in the first. The included events will be altered in significance and will be in an order of before and after in the context of an including field. Also, the divisions of one series may cut across a unit of another. This can be the case even in Existence with its minimal units. One of these units might begin inside some larger including field and have its end inside a subsequent including field. When this occurs the unit occurrence will not in fact be divided, but will have to be understood as having two distinct analytic parts.

The units in all cases will be dictated by a principle of relevance, which is to say, by the determination of earlier portions by the final one. The end dictates what is relevant and what is the proper beginning of the unit ending in itself. The purely causal sequence is never a sequence of relevance, but one of units already defined by a principle of relevance.

Causality in the social sciences and in law is quite a different thing from causality in nature. In the former cases we actually have a principle of relevance in operation, and the beginning of the sequence is defined to be the cause. The idea of cause in law is introduced as a way of distributing responsibility: that analytic part of the relevant unit which is responsible for the outcome is the cause of it. Having identified this cause one can then deal with it as coming earlier than the effect, but this earlier status does not really belong to it as constituting the unit. Every legal causal situation is actually a present one, with the effect being after but not later than the cause.

The relation of religious and secular history is a relation of includer to included, and included to includer, depending on the event chosen. Some events in the one will encompass a number of those in the other, and will cut across some events which are undivided in the other. There need be no events in the secular world which are left out of a religious history, or conversely. As including the events of the other, however, there will be only a present unit, defined by the terminus and dictating the nature of the relevant beginning of the including event.

December 16

Fr. Johann, in an interesting paper in *Cross Currents* a while back, held that charity is a way in which God's presence is brought about by us. God, he holds, is present in every being, but that it takes the act of charity or love to make His presence open to us. Faith is a kind of expectancy of knowledge, and hope a kind of expectancy of possession, but charity offers a kind of contact or encounter. The point is most suggestive.

If God is present, the act of charity would be an act which either made the fact evident or would be a way of penetrating more deeply into God's being. The first alternative requires the least addition to our familiar ideas, but the latter must be embraced once we recognize that God's presence subtends the presence of other beings at the same time. We are in the present and are aware of some other beings when we engage in an art of charity either toward other man or toward God. (Is an act of charity possible toward God, even when this be interpreted merely as love, unless love is also adoration and worship and is inseparable from faith and hope?) The reaching to God as a being in eternity must involve not merely becoming aware of Him as in us, but a moving toward Him as having an inward depth—an act in which the first alternative of getting to be more aware of Him would be involved.

Taking this cue we can say that when some mode encompasses another it does not merely place it in a larger present, but includes it within itself, and thereby gives it a different weight and location. Religious history cannot be only a larger kind of secular history in which the moments of a secular history are related as before and after; it must subjugate the secular history to new kinds of conditions, make it feel the effect of the presence of God, or of a community, or of a prophet. The kind of relevance which it introduces is one which operates within the substantial being of the mode. The converse should also hold; when a religious history is given a secular referent, it must be intensified and restructured, providing that the secular referent covers a longer period than the religious. We thus first have a recognition (of the greater length) i.e., of the fact that what one mode encompasses is in the other mode, with the addition of items which the other did not include in that time span, in a given rational order, in a given level of value, or in a dimension of concern (to speak respectively of the kind of relation Existence, Ideal, God, and Actuality provide for the items within them).

What about the space of Existence? What of the becoming of it? Surely the becoming is included in other modes. Is it not true then that there must be analogues to the becoming—e.g., alterations in classification, shifts in the way in which beings are ordered as more or less important, and acts of adjustment? This seems to be the case. But then are there not also analogues of space? Might one not say that space allows for the distinctiveness of a plurality of items, so that the relation of opposition, similarity, of the more or less general, etc., in the Ideal would be relations like that of space? Must we not also say that God's assessment of all the parts of Himself would be another analogue, and that a third analogue would be provided in actuality in the shape of the way in which beings are more or less representative of the rest? (I think the analogues of time and becoming are plausible, but that the analogues of space have not been properly focussed on as yet.)

What we have then, when we have a number of histories or when we seek to relate histories to beings outside them, is the use of some set of items in a serial order which is subject to an inclusion within another serial order governed by different principles of relevance, or within some context which need not be serial at all. We ought to be able to say that items in space could find a location in another mode in the analogue, say, of time. Thus if men as in space were thought of from the perspective of God as including them in a kind of time-like way, we would have to say that as in God they would have themselves evaluated, not merely as beings in- and of-themselves, but in the way in which they are actually related to one another in contemporary space. We should in fact have the following cases:

Time of Existence in a time-like dimension of God
Time of Existence in a time-like dimension of Ideality
Time of Existence in a time-like dimension of Existence
Time of Existence in a space-like dimension of God
Time of Existence in a space-like dimension of Ideality
Time of Existence in a space-like dimension of Existence
Time of Existence in a becoming-like dimension of God
Time of Existence in a becoming-like dimension of Ideality
Time of Existence in a becoming-like dimension of Existence

To these nine cases we should add nine more which consider the space of Existence, and nine more which consider the becoming of Existence, each encompassed in three dimensions of each of the three other modes. These twenty-seven cases must be multiplied by four to give 108 cases to consider. Including the time of Existence in the time-like dimension of Actuality for example, is distinct from including the time-like dimension of Actuality in the time of Existence. In the former case the time is brought within the orbit of concern; in the latter the concern is located in the time of Existence.

December 17

We make contact with the inward nature of other actualities in a number of ways. Using the *Modes* as a guide we can begin by distinguishing the activities of work, rational structure, sympathy, and thought as governing respectively the making of contact through the body of Existence, Ideality, God, or Actuality. In each case we interlock our external being with the external being of another and thereupon retreat within ourselves to constitute with the being, with which we were publicly interlocked, a realm interrelated in the above ways.

When we work we engage the public dimensions of a being, and release ourselves as potentialities confronting potentialities subterraneously in and across the dimensions of Existence. When we order things, organize them in some kind of structure, particularly when we do this in logic and in mathematics, we release ourselves as beings who are substantial, final, sustaining the structures which terminate at us and the other, and thus have the other together with us as in a rational domain of substances. When we perceive, and then more generally when we speculate, we interplay with other actualities and adumbrate them and ourselves at the same time, to constitute a single realm of private beings in a relation of opposition or independence. And when we sympathize, love, or, more generally, respect another we interlock with them on one level, and release ourselves and them to constitute another mode of connection which is that of mutual regard or concern.

If we are to know other men we cannot do so only in work, unless the work be a cooperative one where there is regard for the rights of others working with us. Nor can we do this by merely organizing men, unless once again the organization is framed against the rights they equally hold with us. Nor can it be done in perception or other forms of knowledge, unless once again we take the men to have, toward the content we discern in them, the very relation we have to it. But we could never know that there were these relations and rights were it not for the fact that we have a relation of mutual regard, sympathy, affection, friendship, love, and the like to them, and thus from the start face them in a context which is divinelike.

We must then start with an attitude toward other beings which is sympathetic. This sympathy must not be one-sided; if it is it will reduce to a longing or a concern. The sympathy must be met by another in a similar way, and this we must feel when and as we are sympathetic. Our sympathy initially involves some way of dealing with the presented surface of the being, and his must involve a similar treatment of our surface. It is because we see another take account of our public being in ways which are like ours that we are able to feel his sympathy. We do not know him as a man though, but only as an adjusting co-member of the situation, until we free ourselves from the public side. In that freeing, in that enjoyment of ourselves as the source of the sympathetic treatment of the other, we enter into a domain where we are merely subjects which now face the subjectivity of the other being directly. It is by freely giving ourselves up to the interlocking of our public natures that we are enabled to have a dimension where we are free subjects in a relation of respect for another who has already manifested a regard for us. We and the other then become beings who interlock with one another in mutual regard and face one another as subjects with mutual respect.

Turning to things, we find that they do not deal with our public beings in the way we deal with theirs. But sometimes, in connection particularly with domesticated animals, we seem to have some mutuality. The mutuality does not, however, reach the point where we ever get further than to note that they have potentialities, are substances, or have privacies. We do not see any way in which we can evoke in them a regard for us which is the reciprocal of our own, and for that reason there never is a relation of mutual respect between them and us.

Our relations to the other modes of being should be analogous to those which we have with respect to the various actualities. To be able to deal properly with the Ideal we must interlock with it across the body of the divine or Existence. When we face God in adoration, etc., we must interlock with Him across the body of Existence or Ideality—which in the *Modes* grounded the cosmological relations of work and faith to God. The work and faith are here already affected by the fact that we are in relation to the divine. This means that it is not the work as terminating in the object worked over that is relevant, but the work as expressive of the divine, and thus as that which allows us to relate the mode of Being of Existence to God, or to free the divine dimension from actual entities and thereby enable us to have a relation of mutual respect with Him.

December 18

The complete life involves   A] the achievement of one type of value, and   B] the adopting or benefitting from the values others achieve. But this double contention has at least four meanings: 1] It may mean that one should engage in the single-minded pursuit of some one value, and have this value supplemented by the results achieved by other equally single-minded pursuits.   2] It may mean that one should engage in an enterprise in which some one value is achieved and all others are incidentally achieved, though in a subordinate and thereby transmuted form, and this would be supplemented by the outcome of single-minded pursuits by others.   3] It may mean that one should engage in a single-minded pursuit, but that there should be accredited to one the outcome of the activities of others when engaged in enterprises where some value is attained and all others are somehow incidentally satisfied.   4] It may mean that one should engage in an enterprise in which some one value is attained and all others are subordinated and transmuted, and that this is to be supplemented with the results of similar activities on the part of others.

1] The first of these alternatives has the advantage of concentrating on pure cases. It recognizes that certain values—produced by or expressed in honesty, love, knowledge, effectiveness, for example—deserve full devotion. Moreover it makes for a life in which values acquired by other men at their most determined, most disciplined, best focussed are united to make a set of pure values intertwined. To have the values acquired by a Shakespeare added to those of a Lincoln, an Aristotle, etc., would seem to give the highest possible set of values, and express life at its best. Also no question need be asked about whether or not an enterprise is basic. One need not go to Beethoven for the highest values in music, for on this present view one could add the various values others achieve to the limited value one had himself achieved in music.

Not only would this lead to a multitude of so-called simple values, but it would not allow us to distinguish basic enterprises from those that are not so basic. It would put a premium on simplicity and purity, and overlook the values obtained by complexity and integrity. It supposes that full devotion could not be exhibited and high values achieved if one attended to the production of outcomes which mixed a number of values or had some subordinated to others. It makes the full life a result of combining a number of thin lives on a high level, a fact which is obscured by using illustrations such as Shakespeare, etc., for none of these devotes himself to a single-minded pursuit of one kind of good, even though he might be conveniently classified as a writer, a playwright, etc. If we were to change the first alternative so that it referred to the single-minded pursuit of one kind of enterprise, we would be back to the question as to how to interpret this—as an enterprise which did or did not do some justice to the values of others, and this would be to repeat the present discussion. And how could simple values be added to one another?

2] A basic enterprise is one in which the values acquired in other ways are also acquired in it, though as subordinate to the major value characteristic of the enterprise. Thus, as was indicated in *History: Written and Lived,* a good man realizes the Ideal, and incidentally masters other beings, acquires something like the worth he needs from God, and the effectiveness he needs from Existence. Having acquired the values which the other enterprises provide, this alternative says that he has no need to do anything more than to have accredited to himself a pure form of these values. The limitation of this view is that it has each person live a rich life and look to the others for thin versions of such a rich life, either because these others are to live such lives—which seems invidious—or because the rich lives of these others are abstracted from, and their full values therefore neglected.

3] The third alternative reverses the second, and has a man engage in a single-minded pursuit of some pure value and have added to him the outcome of a concern with a basic enterprise. But if one individual ought to engage in a single-minded pursuit, so should the others. Moreover it denies to the individual concerned with living a complete life, the opportunity to have a rich one of his own; it asks him to keep to some narrow concern and get the other values from other men.

4] The best alternative would seem to be the last. It asks of each man that he carry out some basic enterprise in which some major type of value (good, power, worth, effectiveness, answering to activities occupied with the modes of Ideality, Actuality, God, and Existence) is achieved and the values produced in the other pursuits are incidentally acquired, though in a muted form. He who lives such a life, is to have added to the values he acquires the values of those who have engaged in the other enterprises. If a man is good because he lives up to the Ideal, he will incidentally also exhibit some kind of power, worth, and effectiveness. In acquiring the values obtained by a religious man in pursuit of an ultimate worthiness, he will also acquire the good as a subordinate element in the religious man's life. The good will then be for him a major value which also has a muted place inside other adopted values. Those adopted values will have counterparts inside his own value. Consequently we would have to remain with only two modes: a as including b; a as accreting b which has an a in a subordinate role; b as including a; and b as accreting an a which has b in a subordinate role. Each will then have itself as major, itself as accreted via some other value, and have that other value as subordinate to it. The latter, b as included in a, is distinct from b which is including a. The b which is included in a does not have an a within it. Suppose that a religion included ethics and had accreted to it the values of a full-bodied ethics, the religion would then include an ethics which was occupied only with the realization of a good, and would accrete the value of an ethics which also gave a man some worthiness, somewhat like that which a religion gave in full measure.

December 19

The problem of inference could be stated as involving the following steps:

$$1] \quad p \supset q$$
$$2] \quad p\text{---}$$
$$3] \quad p$$
$$4] \quad \text{therefore}$$
$$5] \quad q$$
$$6] \quad \text{---}q$$

The first step states the rule; it presents an "if, then." The second step withdraws the premiss from the structure, but allows it to be exactly what it was. It is the analogue of a man standing by himself in a public place, waiting for a bus, say. The third step is the premiss by itself, asserted, making a claim of its own; its analogue is the man in his privacy. The transition from 2 to 3 is radical and involves a possible risk of alteration. Step 4 expresses an act, a movement away from the p. Such an act, if done without any control, without an awareness of the fact that there is a germane q, would be a mere action in the dark, without direction or warrant. The "therefore" says there is a reason in what is being done, that what one is doing can be justified, that it is possible to find something like the first step, and use the "then q" of it as a guide and warrant. Perhaps it should be expressed as:

$$4'] \quad \text{therefore, since "then } q\text{"}$$

or as

$$4''] \quad \text{since "then } q\text{," therefore.}$$

In all these versions, the "therefore" throws one back into a domain where action occurs. The next step is one which arrives at the q, as on a footing with the p. Indeed it replaces that p. The sixth step recognizes that the q at which one had arrived is distinct from a withdrawn q. There is a big step from 5 to 6; it reverses the step from 2 to 3. The heart of the problem lies here.

We can think of the brain as a kind of coding machine. It is the domain of p, therefore q. The p and the q are detached items and the programming of the machine is the movement from one of these items to the other. It is more than a sequence just so far as there is an "if, then" guiding and controlling. The question is: how does this occur?

The mind can be thought of as the structure "if p then q," but we will need to have the detached p's and q's related to the withdrawn cases. There must be an acceptance of p in 3 in terms of the p in 2, and of the acceptance of the q in 5 in terms of the q in 6. The brain must act with respect to the withdrawn items, accept or start with p only so far as it holds on to p as withdrawn—or must be subject to a control which presents the detached p with a withdrawn one, and faces the detached q with a withdrawn one.

The man who is waiting for the bus must have himself as so waiting related to himself in his privacy, and must have occurrences in the privacy be related to himself as having other withdrawn positions. The issue is to determine how his control is exercised. It is not a control by the brain, unless the brain, like a programmed machine, has the program built into it. If the brain were so structured that it was a tissue of withdrawn *p*'s and *q*'s, it could then operate as that which produces items connected by a "therefore." Is it that the mind accentuates certain portions of the brain to make them loci for withdrawals, and that the brain then functions in its production of detached items? This sounds something like a Cartesian pineal gland idea, with the mind impinging on the brain at a point. But the mind might be conceived of as having an overall effect, of being an organic character of the entire body whose role is to accentuate certain places as withdrawal places, so that when a detached item is offered, there is an opportunity to make it function as the antecedent of an inference by having it located in the withdrawal place.

But what are we to say of the operation of inference and consciousness in contrast with the operation of utterance or writing down or anything else that could be said to be done by a physical organ? Is it the constant relating of the withdrawal places which constitutes the "if, then"? Perhaps so. But what of the mind's own inferences; are these perhaps the result of the kickback of the physical on the structure? Does the mind infer by allowing itself to be pulled down into the physical withdrawal place, and then escapes only to be pulled down in another? And this other into which it is pulled accords with what it recognizes to be the consequent of an "if, then"? Is consciousness the product of this being pulled down and escaping, of intruding and retreating? There is here the hint of a hint in the solution of the mind-body problem.

December 20

If the mind be viewed as an organic fact, and thus as a phase of the self, and if its acts are conditioned by the brain in the sense that it defines the various withdrawal places in the brain, i.e., places where the items in its structure will allow for the presence of detached items which are to be linked by a validating process, we have to face up to the question of the nature of meaning, concepts, abstract ideas, self-criticism, self-identity, and self-discipline.

One can take meaning to be given by the relation connecting a given item with some other. This relation will be a physical one in the brain; but as defined by the withdrawal places and eventually by the structure which links these, it can have a "cognitive" meaning. A concept or cognition will be the imposition of the structure of the mind, and thus of the unitary organism, on a number of withdrawal places in an order. Abstract ideas will be concepts which govern a number of subordinate concepts. Self-criticism, self-identity, and self-discipline will be possible so far as the individual is attached to something outside himself—self-identity requiring a reference to God, self-criticism to the Ideal, and self-discipline to Existence. The individual as an organic unity returns to the withdrawal places under the influence and guidance of these outside modes, to which it is linked by the fact that it is in the universe.

A strict empiricism would insist that the structures of the mind be treated as abstractions from the biological, and would define them in terms of the withdrawal places, and then define these in terms of the detached items or acts which the brain and body permit. But there is a prescriptive force to the mind; it is this which does not allow us to be strict empiricists. We (the organism as a whole) must control the parts, the brain, and even the mind.

The mind is the whole as a structure. The structure is not the anatomy but the principle of transformation of the importance, or value, or stress, which might be encountered in the body at this or that place, to a different importance, value, or stress at the same place later, or for the transportation of the importance, value, or stress to a different place. The structure is the organic being's principle of internal adjustment and equilibrium, its way of retaining throughout an activity the same "truth-value" or one which is at least as desirable. It is not a habit, as Peirce thought, but rather a regulator.

The first principle of identity, as it were, of the living organism is that it has an equilibrium tendency, and that this as expressed via a particular organ comes out as health, or walking, or eating, or speaking, or the expressing of a thought. The last is unlike the others in that it presupposes a continuing distinction between the mind and the organ, in this case primarily the brain, since it relates to the fact that the total equilibrium principle is not merely resident in but is being imposed on, comes down on to the brain.

The problem of the perception of distant objects raises no new issues, once it is recognized that the body is in relationship with those distant objects, and that the mind is a dimension of an organic body which is in interplay with bodies at a distance. Perception requires the abstracting of relationships from concrete involvements of body and body. The abstracting is one with the utilization of a dimension of the total being in the form of a conditioner of the brain. When and as the brain is dictated to so as to have distinctive areas of withdrawal, the individual abstracts from the involvement with others. Indeed, the initial use of the mind is in perception, and only later does the mind seem capable of imposing withdrawal points regardless of what is perceptually evident.

December 21

Does the difference between a murderer and a general who sacrifices a regiment to win a war, consist in the fact that the latter is preventing a great loss of value and paying a price for it, whereas the former reduces a value without such an objective? Is it only a matter of numbers with the general? Would there be twice the guilt in the case of the murderer should he kill two instead of one? I've asked these questions of myself many times, but I still am not satisfied with any answer I have managed to forge.

The general operates within a framework of a society; the deaths he requires are the deaths which are involved in the very constitution of the society. The murderer in contrast acts from outside the society; he enters into it to destroy. Having entered into it, he can be judged either as a member of it or as alien to it, since he comes from the outside. The first murder is judged in legal systems as coming from one who by his act shows himself to be a member of the society—that is why killing by dogs and even by the fall of trees could be judged in some legal systems as requiring a legal execution of the dogs or trees. The second murder can be treated as being performed by one who continues to be outside the society, just so far as the society takes the man, who commits the first act, to be punished by being excluded from the society.

If a murderer is caught he is subject to the society and is so far kept within its confines. But so far as he is not caught, he has defined himself to be one who has entered into society to destroy and now remains outside it. It is only when he is caught that he is taken to be a member of the society. Should he have committed two murders by the time he is caught, he will be brought inside the society for the first, as one to be punished by being excluded from the society. But in fact what is done is to define him as one who remains in the society, the later murder being in effect absorbed into the first one.

The general is an instrument mediating conditions to bring about the maximum benefit in a difficult situation; the murderer makes himself into an instrument which must be regulated and controlled; as an agent capable of destruction of ultimate values he must be prevented from acting. As a man the murderer is kept in the society; as an instrument he has no rights and in this sense is not a part of the society of men.

An easier answer is given by denying that men have more than a finite value. Two murders are more than one, three are more than two, and so on. The situation is parallel to that of the general except for the fact that the general has a good objective in mind. The solution I was muddling through above held instead that the murderer destroyed an irreplaceable infinite value; the general's decision did not have anything to do with that infinite value, in part because he was presumably preserving the value of the regiment or the army.

The general deals with man as having finite value; the murderer deals with man as having an infinite value. How is this possible? The one takes account of man's rights, the other does not. The one attacks from inside the society, the other from outside. The one destroys relevantly, the other irrelevantly; the one destroys because he must, the other does it freely and unnecessarily. These differences surely hold, but they do not seem to get at the root of the issue.

Sartre suggests to me the idea that I come to know about other minds not through the way they function, but by discovering that through the gaze of another I find myself to be a being circumscribed in my probable activities. I am a being who has such and such a character and might be expected to do such and such things. It may be the case that I do not have the particular character I feel is being assigned to me; it may be the case that what is expected of me I will not do. But what seems undeniable is that I find that the other has the power to make me be for him a tissue of expectancies grounded in a certain character.

The cases where I am mistaken—for example, when he is not in fact attending to me, where what I thought was a man was a machine, etc.— are derivative from an initial case where I felt the reduction of myself to a certain character and set of expectancies from his perspective. The reduction is felt by me immediately, and it is a reduction which expresses horizontally, as it were, the vertical difference between the other and myself. The other is a subject to the degree that he has the power to make me feel that I am something for him. So far as I sense this from a dog or a cat, I sense them as subjects; so far as I ignore this in another, take him to be anonymous, as a waiter, etc., and pay no attention to his feelings, etc., I treat him as a mere thing. My respect for him as a subject depends initially on the fact that he makes me less of a subject than he then is, since I now become a subject for him, and he is something in himself.

My knowledge of other minds is a knowledge which tells me more of them than of myself, since it reveals them to have the power of reducing me. To be sure, I had to be a subject such as he is in order to be reduced, but I do not know this initially. I come to know that I am a subject by the negative nature of my awareness of status—that the other has made me less merely by looking, merely by being able to look, merely by being accepted by me as one who can so look. My feeling of shame is the feeling of the gap between myself in-myself and myself in public for another. But what of my feeling of elation, what if he praises me?

If he praises me I am still subject to him; I depend on him for this state; I am one who faced him as a consciousness, I am something for him. My pleasure lies in the fact that he maximizes the role I can play with respect to him. Suppose he praises me for my intrinsic character, for myself as in-myself—virtue, intelligence, piety? He always approaches me from the outside, and he cannot actually tell me about myself, unless it be that I, too, am one who can make him have a being for me. The praise, if it is to catch me as I am in-myself, must be for me, the being who can make him something for-me. It will be a kind of confession of my power, his admission that I have a mind, and indeed that I reduced him. His praise of me in- and of-myself, in the end must then be the the telling me that it is right that I take him to be something for-me, and that I do this in the best possible way. He must praise me in the end, then, for giving him the best possible status as a being in the world for me.

I have a feeling of elation either because another has given me a maximum status as a being for-him, or because he is pleased with the fact that I have given him maximum status, and he praises me for that. The former elation is the correlate of shame, where I have been reduced more than I need be; the latter is the correlate of anger, irritation, resentment, where I am being viewed as one who does not give another the highest role he can have for me.

Might it not be the case that no one gives me the status of being for-him, that the feeling of being seen, reduced, of having a certain nature, and a set of expectable postures and tendencies which can be specified and whose outcome can be predicted, is illusory? If so, I will still be truly ashamed, proud, etc., but will be mistaken (*a*) in thinking that this was produced by another, and (*b*) in thinking that I can make that other be something for-me, since in fact that is what it is in- and of-itself. But there are other realities only so far as they are something in themselves; they are never only something for-me. If they were, they could not be there for them to be for-me. But though others have a nature in- and of-themselves, it may not be such as to reduce me to the status of one who is for-them. Instead then of having a mind of their own, they will have only a substance of their own, and I will mistakenly attribute to that substance a power to make me something for-it. It will be for-me while it is something in-itself, whereas I will be for-it while I am something in-myself, but not by any act on its part. I will have made myself be for-it in addition to being something for-it through the mere presence of myself with-it.

I either then make myself into a special kind of being for-another, through my shame, etc., or I am made so by that other. I give up the first of these alternatives when I find the other dealing with artifactual entities in the same way I do, and with regard to how I might use them, in the sense that his movements and preparations alter, and then not merely with respect to the act or the entities, but with respect to me as one who deals with those very entities. The dog may be confused when I do not throw the stick but let it slip behind my back, but it does not resent my not throwing it; it "judges" me in the sense that it separates me from the act, holds me away from it, ascribes a character to me, a fact which it makes manifest in the distinctive approach it makes to me apart from the act.

I know of another mind, then, by noting that I am being reduced to a character and expectable activities apart from the acts in which I engage. His look at me is but a separating me out, and anticipates what he might do. I see in his look at me an estimate of myself as over against my activity. He sees me as a substance which is distinct from his act. He could have looked in this way at my qualities, and this would be legitimate so long as the qualities summarize what I was or did in the past; but if the qualities are adventitious, he will be confusing them with my substance. This confusion is somewhat like confusing me with the tools I am using, and thus the defining of me as a workman or slave.

I know another has a mind when I see him act toward me, either in the shape of a look or in other overt ways, as one who is more than a substance, i.e., more than one who possesses qualities, and in fact as one who can reduce him to a being for-me, apart from this or that act, or apart from this or that position which he happens to occupy over against me now. I note then that he sees that I am doing to him what I in fact am doing—making him be for-me. I see his shock, his blush, his shame, his alteration in the way he looks at me. The dog can be made to feel ashamed, but what I do not see is that he knows it is I who does this to him; he feels the rebuke, he sees the look, but he does not know himself as one who has been made to feel ashamed. He has no resentment.

The reduction of me which another accomplishes is performed by him as a structure of his entire organic being; it is his power to have a certain equilibrium, to define withdrawal places in himself with reference to a world of which the brain is a part (and not merely withdrawal places for acts internal to the body), which enables him to deal with me as something for-him. I sense the reduction of myself by sensing the difference in the activity of a withdrawal place in relation to other things in the world, in contrast with other withdrawal places in me. He makes me attend as it were to the acts of the brain instead of allowing me to dictate to the brain when its acts are proper. By myself I govern my body and may do so with reference even to the things about, but when the other looks at me, I govern my body in terms of that look and what it epitomizes in the shape of expectable actions on his part.

In one way it comes down to the fact that I can read a look as a promise of certain kinds of actions having relevance to me. Any being which can provide a sign of what it will do to me takes account of me. If the sign has to do with a look by me, we have a communication, a meeting of minds. So far, we are no further up than the animal level. The human level is reached when the sign separates me from what I am doing or what I am using, and does this after and/or while it is dealing with me as together with the act or instrument. I know other human minds when I note the others' differential action toward me with my acts, and toward me apart from the acts, or when I note this differentiation as being conveyed in a look which thus promises acts of two sorts toward me.

December 22

Ignoring for the moment the physiological basis of inference, *modus ponens* should be understood as requiring an abstract structure which is imposed on some detached idea or meaning to define a withdrawing place, at the same time that a withdrawing place is defined for a consequence, thereby permitting a detached idea as a conclusion. This means that we have the following pattern.

A

$$1]\ p)q$$
$$2]\ p$$
$$3]\ p— \qquad —q$$
$$4] \qquad\qquad q$$

1 and *2* are distinct, and enter into the situation from different directions, the one presenting us with a structure, the other with a claim or focussed item. The union of the two defines a withdrawal p in *3*, and thereby a withdrawal q in *3*. The central question now is the movement from *3* to *4*. Must not *4* be rewritten as:

$$4']\ p \quad therefore\ q?$$

That is, does not "p therefore q" take place only so far as we have $p—\quad —q$ imposed on p?

We then have the following schema:

B

$$1]\ p)q$$
$$2]\ p$$
$$3]\ p—\quad —q$$
$$4]\ p$$
$$5] \qquad\qquad q$$

1 and *2* combine to give *3*. *3* is imposed on *4*, and this yields the detached conclusion *5*. The "therefore" is the movement which one makes from one isolated place, p, to a withdrawal place—q, thereby making that an isolated q.

The validity of an inference then depends on A] the way withdrawal places are defined, and B] the way in which one isolates, detaches something in a predefined withdrawal place.

A] involves the affiliation of a detached p in line *2* with a q; it gives up the detached p for the sake of an affiliation with a q, as on line *1*. The p and q here are places. It is only after we have these places that we look back at the p; we then move from p to $p—\quad —q$, i.e., recognize the difference there is between the p as detached and the p as affiliated. B] concerns the getting of the isolated q (line 5). We say, as it were, that the sacrifice we make of the p (line 2) to get 3, p— —q, is to be repaid by reverse movement of the same magnitude, and thus we get 5, the detached q.

Inference, then, is dependent on the definition of withdrawal spaces through a synthesis of a detached item with a structure (2 and 1), and the recognition that the detached item was sacrificed to get a withdrawal situation, p— —q (3), which is to be justified by forging a detached item q (5). There is then no replacement of p by q, and no watching or following a rule, but instead a production of related withdrawal places and a reinstatement of a detached proposition, though one of a different content or value from the initial. (It is to be noted that if the withdrawal places be thought of on the analogue of the public world, the detached items are the members of that public world, and that (1) p)q will be private.) What risk does this run?

Perhaps an illustration will enable us to find the risk if any. Let 1, p) q, be the private meaning "Being in pain I want help or sympathy," then p (2) will be the detached public utterance, "I am in pain." It is a detached remark, having no applications. It is an expression in the language, but is now a mere unit. My private meaning is now imposed on it to make it a withdrawn item (3), my expression in public; it now requires another withdrawn item, such as "I sympathize *with you*," "I'll get a doctor *for you*." The initial withdrawal should perhaps then be expressed or understood as "I am telling you that I am in pain." Having said "I am in pain," I understand it as part of a social world, and in that understanding define another place in that public world. I expect or hope someone will say something like "I sympathize with you." And someone, I think, ought to say it, or someone will in fact say it by occupying the position I initially took in using a public expression, "I am in pain."

Another now takes a stand, similar to the stand I initially took. I accepted his withdrawal position and expect him to repay me by adopting a public unit or act which is the reciprocal of mine. The risk then would seem to be in getting the q, i.e., in moving from 4 to 5. I had q initially in a structure (line 1) and I found a place in the world where it could be a withdrawn item (line 4), but I must await for it to be detached, or must myself produce it as a detached item (line 5). But it may not be forthcoming.

When I assert q as the conclusion of an argument, I of course have the q as detached. But the issue here is whether we can get the q detached in the withdrawal space, i.e. whether q is not merely detached, but a detached *conclusion*. Is that why we want to confront the outcome of our inference? No, for what we are here asking is, is there an outcome to the inference? But this seems to be asking is inference possible, or at least is this or that inference possible, given an initial starting point and an implicational structure. This is but to ask if *modus ponens* is legitimate. Why doubt that it is? Precisely because it is constructive, because it produces the q. We want to confront it because that produced q, unlike the p, has no substantial nature. The detached p is something we met, whereas the q, though on a footing with the p, is not rooted in something we can meet. The detached q is something which has been detached, whereas the detached p is something which had been in existence.

I made the public utterance, "I am in pain." I know what I would like this to mean and what is to answer it, but I do not know if there is such a detached answer, for that must come from elsewhere. If I deduce the answer I claim that I can really have it in isolation; that my assertion of it is on a par with my acceptance of the p. Were we confined to propositions or meanings of our own construction we could give q exactly what we get from p. We would not need suppose that p has any status apart from us; we would in affirming q have it on a footing with p. But even here we would have the risk of producing a q for a withdrawal place, whereas we started with the production of a withdrawal place by means of an accepted p.

Putting that aside it is evident that there are two types of reasoning —one in which the p is transparent, has no substantial ground and is what it is as detached, allowing us to get a counterpart in q; and another type in which the p has a substantial ground and is justified by experience, the past, etc., and in which we move to a new item, a detached q, which lacks that justification. The former is mathematical, abstract, logical reasoning, the latter is material, existential, experiential reasoning, though it may be conducted in the mind apart from all examination of facts. The second is oriented in the world away from us; the other is merely set over against us with the content that it then and there has. The reliability of the mathematical over against the nonmathematical reasoning lies in the fact that our initial p was produced by us with the same right and legitimacy as the q is now being produced, even though the p was produced without antecedent concern for a withdrawal space, whereas the q is produced only because of it. We could have started, and indeed often do start, with a constructed q, and then see if we can get a withdrawal space for it. Might we not do the same thing in the other form of reasoning? May it not be the case that we start with a q which we would like to prove? We do, but the very proving is the having of that q as a detached item; when we merely entertain it we have it as something that might be proved, that might be shown to have a detached status.

In the mathematical case the q might not be provable, but that it is detached may nevertheless be a fact. The item could be a mathematical item, it could have a mathematical meaning and yet not be derived from the given p. In the experiential case we are caught in a single world and the q must be in it. In the mathematical case we could perhaps find some other ground for getting that q; we could perhaps invent another kind of p. But this is not possible in the other case, for we must start with whatever p there is. In mathematics we create our premises, whereas in the other case we accept them.

December 23

The withdrawal pattern "$p—$ $—q$" is indistinguishable from the schematism of Kant. The account of it that I have given requires the categories of Kant to be imposed on the manifold by the transcendental ego to constitute the schematism. The pattern can also be used to describe the nature of verifiable science. Here the initially given structure is the mathematical formulation and abstract definitions of mathematics, and the detached objects are common-sense things (and not as Northrop supposes, sensations, images, etc.). The result of the combination is a world of scientific objects. Are they real? They cannot be ultimately real, for there are similar objects produced by making use of different types of structure on different aspects of common sense—perception, values, technology, or action. Instead of supposing that these can actually be integrated to define a new type of substance which is the common-sense object purged and clarified, or that there is something even more basic, say, a mode of being such as Existence, which is to be captured in art (which is what I supposed in *The World of Art*), would it not be possible to hold that all we ever get are strands, which are resultants of the synthesis of common-sense entities with various formalities? It would not be possible to do this unless provision were made for the prescriptive rules of ethics. But why may not these be another version of the unitary nature of the mind? If we treat the prescriptiveness of logical structure, the prescriptiveness of ethical commands, the prescriptiveness of plans, and the prescriptiveness of duties toward fellowmen, and the respect for their rights in this way, we should be able to eliminate the need to refer to God, the Ideal, Existence, or Actuality, leaving us with only actualities.

But what of the coherence of these actualities in Existence, their movement in time, their connection in space, their becoming past within a single past? Are these not taken care of by viewing detached items from the perspective of the structure as not yet or as no longer encompassing those items? What of God, and the need of unity for all? This could be taken care of, perhaps, by referring to the withdrawal pattern as a produced unity which has a kind of prescriptiveness for the elements which produce it. But how does such a withdrawal pattern differ from one provided by the state or society? After all a state or society could be said to be constituted of private beings of infinite value, uniting with themselves as mere units of finite value, to constitute beings in an interlocked system of rights and duties of a civil sort. Would the meaning of God then be all mankind as governed by a withdrawal pattern involving various rights and obligations in relation to one another?

Is the above a solution obtained by starting with a duality of mind and body? No, for the duality of mind and body is taken to arise from the distinction between the organic whole and its parts, and the fact that the parts are being governed by the whole. One could say in fact that the withdrawal pattern is always in existence, but that at various moments the elements constituting it fall away to give us new opportunities to make withdrawal patterns. When the items fall away we get a dualism which is not absolute since the structural side has the power to impose itself on the other. We come back then to something like the view in *Reality* about the nature of an actuality as at once a unity with parts which belong to that unity in one sense, and which act independently of it in another. We also come back to something like what is said in *History: Written and Lived* about history as being constituted of elements which have an independent being apart from it, though what is now being said is that the independence of the constituent beings is a derivative matter, and never is absolute, being always made to refer to or be connected with the beings as constituting a withdrawal pattern. It is as if we were to derive the implicative structure "$p \supset q$" and the detached items "p" and "q" from the withdrawal pattern and then use them as independent items to constitute a withdrawal pattern, similar to or different from the one with which we began.

Could this position be maintained, God would be immanent but not transcendent, except in the sense that the withdrawal pattern would not be lived up to by the individual men, or would lack the purity of a purely logical structure. We would have nothing but common-sense objects viewed as making up a world of items in a withdrawal pattern, and from this we would derive by abstraction various structures answering to the prescriptiveness of our own organic nature, and would allow various items to stand out over against us as so many units. We would then bring the abstracted structures together with the units to constitute purged versions of the common-sense objects. The totality of such versions would express what the common-sense world is in fact. The modes of being would then be mere dimensions of such a world, absolutely indispensable, answering to the nature of the new withdrawal pattern or to the items which are to be synthesized to constitute this pattern. There would then be no need, perhaps, to ask about the relation of the various modes to one another as though they could contain or influence one another, but only about the way in which the withdrawal pattern was constituted, and the way its elements functioned in the pattern and outside it.

In the very being of the "is" there is an "ought," the meaning or tendency toward equilibrium, the pressure of the whole on the parts. The ought which stands over against the individual, which evaluates the nature of withdrawal patterns, and which may not be realized in any case, would be a purged, generalized version of the ought which is here and now. The prescriptive power, in connection with the mind/body would be the organism as a whole; but the referent of the ought, the kind of content it was organizing, would be different on this view of the ought. The organism would, for example, take a withdrawal place within the brain or other part of the body and refer this to a withdrawal place in some other being or at some other time.

The state and other large systems seem to have a power as well as a nature of their own. Could these be encompassed in a scheme which derived structures and prescriptions from generalizations of the mind or the individual organism? Does not the state use the energies of Existence? Does not history? Does not art portray Existence? What happens to cosmology, the cosmos, the substantiality of scientific objects? Could the state be the concurrence of the generalizations of a number of men, thereby having a prescriptive power greater than any, and therefore the ability to make use of their energies?

If we can start with an organism such as man, why could we not start with an organic concept of the world in which the same relation of prescription to detached items would be found? This would be tantamount to starting with Existence as containing within it the Ideal and actualities, and being subject to the unifying power of God, or as itself possessing such a power. Existence here would be the only mode, and individuals would be prescribed to by an Ideal which had no substantiality of its own, but was in fact only a dimension of Existence allowed to function as a controlling structure. But can we not then find a way in which the Ideal and God are the only modes?

The withdrawal pattern is constituted by the action of the structure. (We get a Kantian idealism when we take the actualities to be mere points or surds which are given meaning and being by being captured by the Ideal.) If we take God to be one with the withdrawal pattern governing mankind, we could say that this was the initial reality and that the Ideal and Existence were derived from this, with actualities constituting subdivisions within Existence.

It would seem then as if we could deal with the prescriptive structures, detached items, and withdrawal patterns in four ways. Each would allow us to eliminate modes of being except as distinctions within a given mode. If these ways are all equally sound and good we would seem to be back with the four modes of being; but we would treat each internally, seeing how the universe looks from its perspective alone.

Forced to reduce the modes, I do not see how I could have less than two kinds of being—Actuality and Existence. The one is needed because if I know anything, it is that I am a substantial being with a privacy and irreducibility. And if I know anything else, it is that I am in a larger world with its own structure, time, space, movement. I could say that the Ideal is but the resultant of taking either one of these modes to prescribe to the other, and God is the outcome of their juncture. I would then not have an Ideal for God, or for both Actuality and Existence together, and I would have no referent for religion, no unity for all, no essence for Existence, and no absolute other for men (though perhaps Existence could be thought to have this role?).

How could the two beings be related? Would this not require a third mode; or is it possible to have a sheer togetherness similar to that dealt with in connection with the four modes? What about the ideal of history, and what about the preservation of the past? Might not the ideal of history be forged in the interplay of men and Existence? Could the juncture of the two modes precipitate out the past as relevant to the present? Would that past need nothing to sustain it, being sustained in the very act of being produced?

Existence and actualities give us the world of Aristotle, minus his prime mover; it is at the root of some existentialisms. Whitehead, instead, has God and Existence, and gives short shrift to actualities and Ideality and Existence, particularly in the later essays. But there does seem to be power in the views which hold on to Ideality and Actuality, and to God and Actuality, the one answering to Personalism and Panpsychism, the other answering to Christian humanism and Christian existentialism. The combination of Ideality and God is apparently suggested in early Indian thought.

If one must have at least two modes, is it possible to stop with less than four? The two must be related, their interplay regulated or evaluated. But it is possible to have each do the relating in its own way, and to have the regulation determined and the evaluation achieved by the way in which the receptive mode is controlled. The insistent mode would thus dictate the imposition of itself, and would also evaluate the outcome by virtue of its incapacity to be fully realized in the receptive mode.

December 24

One can view structures, rules, principles as A] common (constituted by a number of people together, by society, tradition, habit, or as dwelling in a Platonic heaven) or B] private, personal, inward, mental. One can take it to be C] self-imposed or D] imposed by another. And it can be imposed on detached items which are E] private or F] public. We have then the following cases:

1] A, C, E
2] A, C, F
3] A, D, E
4] A, D, F
5] B, C, E
6] B, C, F
7] B, D, E
8] B, D, F

1] A, C, E   The morality of a society is common and imposed by the society on private individuals through education, habituation, social ap-

proval and the like. The result is a man in the society who has a withdrawal position there, defined by the society. The individual abandons
his private view to become one who, even as solitary, has his conduct
ruled by the society, though not without his having the private status of
one who engages in the acts.

2] A, C, F   The positive laws of a society are common, and are imposed
by it on public individuals, men who face one another with claims and
counterclaims. The result is a set of men whose civil rights are defined
as a set of withdrawal positions in terms of which the claims and counterclaims are to be expressed, and the laws in fact carried out.

3] A, D, E   The case of common rules being externally imposed on
private beings. The external imposition can be that of a sovereign who
stands over against the society, or it can be the imposition by an individual in his privacy, making use of the rules. A good illustration of the
latter would be a language with its socially constituted rules being
employed by an individual and imposed on himself as having such and
such private ideas or feelings. The outcome is a man whose speech is
directed at other men; the language will be common in its rules and the
men will be withdrawn termini for it. This is apparently the case which
Wittgenstein had in mind most of the time. It evidently presupposes the
existence of distinct private realities who have the power to bring a
public set of rules to bear on themselves, thereby tranforming themselves
from private to withdrawn or solitary men ready to act on one another.

4] A, D, F   The case where we have common rules imposed by external
force on public detached items. This is the way in which organizations
work, under the directive of a larger society, or through the planning of
an individual. The outcome is to make the public detached items have
an organizational role. When a state issues out of a society it deals with
public men; the constitution of the state is a set of public rules. The
imposition of the constitution, by police power or by individual loyalty,
or through the dictates of some sovereign, yields citizens.

5] B, C, E   Rules can be private in nature, be self-imposed on private
content. This is the case of pure logical inference, of private thinking
where there is regard for validity. The rules here have a prescriptive
force derived from the organic nature of the body and abstracted in the
shape of an equilibrium principle constituting the mind.

6] B, C, F   The case where private rules are self-imposed on public content. Here the principles of logic, the categories of knowledge, the viewpoint of the individual is carried into the public content to constitute an
ordered world. This is essentially the view of Kant, although sometimes

he speaks as though his view were B, C, E (5 above), where the initial content is private. However, it is to be noted that the manifold for Kant, whether treated as private or public, is not thought by him to be constituted of detached items. But there must be stresses in it which are topics for the categories, and this will then give us either 5 or 6.

7] B, D, E Rules which are private an imposed on private content must evidently be in the control of the private being. But his impositions may be guided, determined, dictated by considerations of expediency, habit, etc. In any case the rules here are to be thought of as impotent, mere suggestions or hypotheses, and requiring therefore an additional act on the part of a man to impose them on his private content.

8] The last case is B, D, F, where private rules are imposed on public content by external force. This is the way one can view a game of chess. Rules entertained by the individual in private have here no efficacy. They await their imposition on content by the individual who wishes to play. The rules are imposed on the detached objects now on the chessboard, and the outcome is a piece in play. The rules of a game of chess, though, should perhaps be thought of as common to the two players. This will give us case 4, so that chess would be something like the functioning of an organization when this is planned by an individual. The chess game would then be seen to provide an organizational setting for the pieces, in which case 8 would be reserved for such games as solitaire.

The knowledge of other minds comes into this schema. I know another has a mind when I see him deal with me as one who is a rule-determining being, operating on public content—6] B, C, F. He sees me to be part of an ordered world as a result of the fact that I imposed my own intent on the public object. He differentiates me from my act as one who is ready to act in a certain way. His look at me, as Sartre has underscored, reduces me to an "object." Such an object is not a thing, but a being in the world who has made himself be there; the other recognizes him to be there by his own act. The other does not get to the rule nor the rule-determining act; he does not grasp me in my subjectivity. He still faces me as a being who has made himself an object; he recognizes that I have put myself in that position, and by so doing he reduces me to the status that I assumed for the moment. Sartre is inclined to speak as though I become an object because of the other; it is more correct, though, to say that I know him to be a subject because I note that he attends to me as one who has made myself be an object and thus ready to function as a withdrawn being in a social setting.

It is because I have acted so and so with my rules on this object that the object and myself are in the position of beings in the same world withdrawn with respect to one another. I still have my private nature and I still express my private nature autonomously; but the other sees only what the outcome is, myself as functioning with respect to my act, not as a mere body, but as a controlling force, as one who makes that act be a withdrawn item with respect to other acts with respect to myself. The other shows that he takes me in this way by the fact that he evaluates me, looks at me and deals with me, and readies himself with respect to me, not only as a source of the act (for that would make me a substantial thing in his eyes and nothing more) but as a ground for it, as giving it a setting in relation to me and others. The act as produced by a thing is a detached item; it is made into a withdrawn item by me. I convert it from p to p— with respect to some —q. The other sees that I am ready for a —q, and deals with me in those terms.

We can look at things as withdrawn items in a world governed by public laws which are imposed by others. We would have here 4, public rules externally imposed on public content. When another sees me as determined by circumstance and expects me to do such and such because of the kind of —q that is to follow on the p—, he views me as such a thing. And we can look at animals as withdrawn items governed by law of appetition and the like, self-imposed on public content. Though the laws are internal to the animal they are shared by others of the same kind. We have here case 2. The difference between me and an animal is that I make use of private rules, express myself, intend, and it is this fact which is rcognized by the other when I know him to have a subjectivity, a mind of his own. He sees the withdrawn state of myself and my acts as involving the use of rules peculiar to me. He can deal with me only as withdrawn, but that withdrawn state is something he takes to be produced by me as an individual, and therefore to be different from the withdrawn state of any other being. I am a unique object for him, whereas the animal is one of a kind.

In the relation of man to woman, the man sees the woman as an object, whereas she sees him as a subject. She is passive with respect to him, and does not see him make himself into the withdrawn reality. He sees her, though, as one who has made herself be her body, and that is the mystery of her for him; he knows her body to be a unique withdrawn one achieved through the imposition of her own mind on her own organism. She, however, finds him acting, functioning as a withdrawn being and dealing with her as such a withdrawn being. He has made her be withdrawn—the word "withdrawn" is here evidently most misleading; it refers only to the status of a being as separate from others but part of the same world with it, a p—, or a —q—by his look, and now functions with reference to her as such an object. She knows him to be a subject by his looking and takes him to be a withdrawn being by his act. What she does not understand is the way in which he makes his subject operate on the world to constitute each of them as withdrawn beings. She sometimes supposes that it is herself who makes his private rules operate on detached items, and thus that he defines case 8. She sees him thus like one playing solitaire with his own rules and cards, but dictated to, inspired, and made to act out the rules by her. In the union of the two she can be thought of as the source of the imposition of rules, and he as giving her a true subjectivity by acknowledging that she is a withdrawn being, self-constituted as well as constituted by him.

December 25

It would be better to term p— an agent or power, and —q a patient or recipient or respondent. We can then say that the structure of a being's subjectivity, when united with a detached item, i.e., himself as a mere unit in a public world, or as some instrument, yields an agent who can then act on the unit or instrument. The other takes me to be such an agent, and in doing so I recognize him to be a subject, a being in-himself. By taking me to be an agent he recognizes that I have a subjectivity. But he ignores this to treat me as one who makes use of the world in ways he now estimates when he looks at me. It is his allowing me to remain over against the things in the world while I deal with them that tells me he is an independent being, with a subjectivity or mind of his own.

A man sees the woman as an agent, and she is aware that he takes her to be such. He does not know her subjectivity because he does not see her taking him to be an agent. The activity of converting him into an agent is accomplished by her as she thinks of herself as the catalyst by means of which he is enabled to unite his subjectivity with the unit objects in the public world. From her own perspective she is a kind of demiurgos, and he is dependent on her for his being an agent. He makes her be an agent by the way he attends to her, she makes him be an agent by mediating his two sides for him. He makes her be an agent by reducing her subjectivity to the role of agency, through synthesizing her with the body she has and the things she does, and then holding her over against the body and things as the estimating source or power, by virtue of which another unit and other things can be achieved. She makes him be an agent by ignoring his ability to make himself an agent on his own; she sees him as detached or animal, and herself as the civilizing influence, herself as the being who will make him an agent at least in the same realm where she is.

The relation of the musical composer and the musician, of the writer of the play and the actors in the play, of the script and the performance is somewhat like the relation of structure to agent. The composer and author are like structures; the performer deals with units. He must make himself an agent, one who uses the instruments to bring about the outcomes which the structure implies. If the performer is a mere interpreter, a mere user of the instruments in the light of the composition, the composer, etc., must be viewed as converting a unit man into a performer; he becomes a man such as Ion, who does he know not what under the inspiration of the creator.

If the performer is an artist then he is his own demiurgos; he brings the composition into relation with the unit instruments and unit objects to constitute himself an agent who will then use those instruments and objects along the kind of route the composer provided. This offers a good way of viewing the composer. It brings him closer to one who plays a game of chess than to one who is subject to the laws of the state. The composer is not prescriptive; his composition does not synthesize with any object. The instruments and sounds in the world to which he refers and which he says he hears in his inner ear are in fact integrated with others to constitute a single structure which is the composition.

A composition is in the dimension of time, whereas a performance is in the dimension of becoming. Does this mean that becoming is obtainable when time is synthesized with unit objects, and the product is then made into an agent operating on such objects? The synthesis would then give us substances, and becoming would be their product. We would then have broken up Existence into existent objects and not caught the becoming itself. Must we not instead say that the becoming is the unity of the agent with the unit objects, and that it is the agent who is the substance?

The transition from a composer to a performance requires the substantialization of the musician into an agent, who makes himself function as one concerned with such and such instructions and tones and audiences, etc. The becoming which he produces is the movement which goes from p to q. It is a movement which is guided by the relation of himself as agent to others as listeners.

December 26

I can be said to have a number of natures or identities. *1]* There is that given by my organic equilibrium principle, which has one dimension in the form of the mind as a structure of implicative relations. This is distinctive for me, but as oriented toward a distant Ideal it can be said to be common to many, and to be subject to a prescriptiveness which reflects the fact that the Ideal is germane to many. *2]* There is that given by the fact that I am a unit in Existence, a one among many ones. I am distinctive there, but have no distinct nature except so far as I can be approached as a unique terminus inside Existence. *3]* There is my status as an agent with respect to all else as patient. This is myself as an actuality. It is as agent that I represent all actualities.

How are these three related? We can view ourselves as an amalgam of all; this would in effect make our unitary identity and nature some kind of product. But we seem to have an identity and nature beyond, and not dependent on these three. As the other of whatever there be, we are these three solidified into a single one, a soul over against God.

The relation between ourselves as structure and agent is that of responsibility. Sartre thinks it essentially one that represents a fall, so that we are ashamed; he overlooks the fact that I may be performing as agent just as I want to perform. I do not of course express what the structure is in- and of-itself, but I do give it its viable meaning in the world, and if I do this in ways which elicit or even ought to elicit the approval of others, their look does not make me ashamed. Also, my structure or mind is not my subjectivity, as Sartre thinks.

The relation between ourselves as agents and ourselves as units is the relation of efficacy. It is what we do with ourselves as units with respect to other units, under the guidance and control of ourselves as agents, that determines what kind of viable role, what kind of political or technological import I have both with respect to myself, as a mere body or thing, and with respect to others.

The solidification of the three dimensions of myself into a sheer subjectivity over against God involves the two relations of responsibility and efficacy. I am over against God as more or less guilty, as more or less inept. How is this solidification produced? What bearing has it on the religious turn?

Can we not be subjects, mere men, without the help of God? Does it require an act on His part or a recognition by us of His presence? Why is it not enough for us to be a representative of all actualities? Is it not that we are representative of all actualities for Him? Is it not He who allows us to withdraw from the role of mere agent, without forcing us into the position of components of an agent or of some combination of components and agent?

We are representatives of actualities not as mere unitary beings, but as beings who possess a structure, are agents, and are units, and who interconnect these in responsibility and efficacy (which involve the will in intent and the will in production). If we try to make our subjectivity equal to the structure, we would be back somewhere with Aristotle and his definition of man as a rational animal. Despite all protests, and despite all efforts (on the part of existentialists and materialists, respectively) to make this structure individual, or purely biological, it is, even when distinctive, too remote from the body and what men do to be what man truly is. We are representatives who are ethical, existent, and with others, and the combination of these depends on our being focussed on by God.

The religious turn is the result of our freeing ourselves from an immersion in the world, and a referring of ourselves to God. This is to say that we give up being a unit or an agent, and instead of retreating back into the structure, turn instead to a being who will allow us to be a unit or an agent in new terms. We in effect then substitute God for the guiding principle of our structure, in place of the Ideal we had employed before.

Which is it, unit or agent, from which we turn? When we turn from the status of unit we immerse ourselves in the role of agents. Does the religious turn involve a turning from the role of agent? Why not go back to structure, meaning, private import? Because we want to continue to be agents in a new way. We want not to give up the status of agent so much as to be agents in a new way. Religious faith is our being an agent with respect to a patient who will make us a patient in turn. We are often ashamed of the way we are agents with respect to other men; by making ourselves agents with respect to God, we seek to attain a proper way of making our beings, as agents with respect to something, do justice to what we are as structures and as units. But in the end we are judged as solidifications of structure, agent, and unit.

Or is it that we can do nothing more than alter the direction in which we will be agents? Is God perhaps the other of us-as-agents in a way which does most justice to ourselves as structure and unit, and thus which allows us to fulfill our responsibility and be most efficacious?

The latter alternative is most attractive. It does not require that we have our subjectivity produced by God; it in fact leaves all the activity to us. It starts with us as beings who are agents in a realm of Actuality, and only derivatively does it find us to be agents over against God.

This position, though better psychologically and religiously than one which requires God to make us be subjective units, has the ontological defect of not having any work for God with respect to us until we engage in the religious turn. But apart from our religious turn we have an ontological relation to God; we are already solidifications of our different roles. This means that we are from the start agents no less than units and structures.

Is this true of the infant? The embryo? The idiot? It surely is true of the infant quite early in its career; before that it could be said to be asleep. We could apply the same interpretation to the embryo and idiot. But what would being asleep mean here? Perhaps only that the units on which the structure is to operate are not yet available; the brain, we say, is too undifferentiated to enable it to function as an agent in the world. It would be an agent, not with respect to itself as internally differentiated into a plurality of units, but only with respect to a plurality of units outside.

"Sleeping" humans are agents with respect to some units inside, for otherwise they would not be able to live. They are also agents with respect to something outside, for otherwise they would not be able to function at all. They differ from animals in that the animals are not agents at all, but unities of structure and units, which does not allow them the status of agent and thus the opportunity to act on and be acted on once again by structure and unit.

The infant, from the start, has the role of agent, and thus is the locus of rights. Is this due to the ascription to it by us; do we always see infants, etc., as structures being reduced by us or by themselves to the position of agents? They evidently haven't the responsibility or power to do it for themselves; we must be doing it for them somewhat as men do it for women. Is it that in connection with women we sense that they have the structure which is operating in them and that we reduce them to agents, whereas with the infants, etc., we immediately take them to be agents and therefore assume them to have a structure? In acknowledging that structure we function for them as women do for men, acting as their catalysts.

Starting with infants, etc., as beings who are faced as agents, we go backward to take them to have structures, and then take them to be agents made so by us. This is not very clear. Perhaps we ought to say that they are agents vis-à-vis God, sheer subjectivities made so by His presence, and that they have yet to get into the position where they can achieve this status on their own—an achievement which requires an immersion in the world. We come back then to something like Aquinas' view of the soul as divinely instituted, though not necessarily deliberately but only ontologically, by virtue of the fact that God is, and because humans have distinctive structures and unit places in Existence.

December 29

It is possible, I think, to side with both Thomas Aquinas and Duns Scotus on the question of the univocity of the idea of being. Aquinas thinks there is no more inclusive term than God, so that "being" as referring to Him must be distinctive, but analogical to the use of "being" in connection with other realities. Scotus maintains that there is a single idea of being which can be specified as infinite or finite, and that we know this being without knowing whether that to which we are referring is infinite or finite.

Whenever there is a plurality of realities, being must be specified in different ways in each of them. Each is a distinctive being. The term "being" as distinctively applied to one of the realities cannot be applied to the others except so far as it is first generalized and then newly specified—or used analogously. But if we could say only this we would have difficulty, as Scotus saw, in being able to talk univocally about any two entities. We could not really say that Socrates and Plato are both men. However, the concept of being, which we can properly use to speak of God or the world indifferently, does not have answering to it a particular reality. It is not clear whether Scotus would say that it did have an object answering to it. Being as such is not, any more than non-being is. But this does not prevent one from referring to the common character in both God and the world, or more generally in all the irreducible modes of being. Otherwise we would not even know that there was something to which one could apply an analogous predication.

The predicate, "transcendental being," is located in all the basic modes of being; it has a common nature in them, or better, the to-getherness of them all is the root meaning of the being which is common to them all. Viewed in this way all beings can be said to be specifications, determinations of the togetherness of them.

According to the arguments of the *Modes* there are four types of togetherness. This would seem to lead to the conclusion either that there is a single meaning of togetherness which is the true core meaning of being, and that this is specified in the actual togethernesses, which in turn must be specified in the shape of the modes—and this without compromising the ultimacy and ontological concreteness of the modes over against the constituted reality of the togethernesses—or that being is equivocal, at least with respect to the final form of togetherness, as that which is common to the four types of togetherness. But I think we ought to say that the four types of togetherness are instances, not of some further more general idea of togetherness, but of one or the other of the modes of being which are together. In other words, the four modes of being are together in four ways. Each of these ways is a being common to the modes. There are then four beings which are common to the modes. These four have a being in common. The being they have in common is expressed in four distinct ways by the distinct modes. Each of the modes is the common being of the four ways of being together which encompasses that mode and the others.

On the above view, a mode of Being is a specification of mere being, or more precisely, it specifies four different meanings of mere being. These four different meanings of mere being have in common the idea of being which is itself a specification of four real modes of being. A mode of being is then a fourfold concretionalization of being as such, and itself provides a unitary meaning for four meanings of being, each of which has it in some specific form. Specification and concretionalization here do not have any reference to antecedent and subsequent existence, but only to what is taken to be comprehensive, and what is from that position a specialized version.

We have, then, two highly general meanings of being—that given by a form of togetherness, and that given by a single mode. The first is specified in four ways, and so is the second, but the one is specified in the shape of irreducible modes, and the other is specified in the shape of irreducible forms of togetherness. Do these two kinds have anything in common? Is being as such the tension between them? Ought we not to say that a mode of being is the being which a togetherness must have, whereas the togetherness is the being which is possessed by a mode only as related to others? The togethernesses are resisted in beings, each of which is a mere being for those togethernesses. Each being is related to other beings in four distinct kinds of togetherness, each of which is a mere being for those related realities. Whereas the beings are diversified by the togethernesses, the togethernesses are concretionalized by the beings.

The being which a mode of Being offers to four togethernesses is concrete, but it is then attenuated by being multiplied; the being which a togetherness offers to four modes of Being is abstract, and is made concrete by being multiplied. Consequently we have being as such, which is concrete and has the shape of a mode of Being in relation to the various kinds of togetherness; and we have being as such, which is abstract and has the shape of a togetherness in relation to four modes of being.

I originally asked about the being which was common to all four modes of being; this is now seen to be a togetherness—or more accurately it is seen to be answered in four ways by four togethernesses. What is common to four modes of being is thus being in the shape of four kinds of togetherness. But it is now evident that each mode of being itself has the status of mere being with respect to four kinds of togethernesses.

Scotus and Aquinas seem to have limited versions of this resolution. For Aquinas, being as such is identical with God's mode of being. This means for him that God is the being for the diverse attenuated forms of being which actual entities have. Scotus takes being to be identical with the togetherness of God and man, and sees these modes as instancing being as such, as their togetherness. But there are more modes of being and more types of togetherness than either allows.

Remaining only with God and the world, we have then God pluralized so far as He is identical with being as such, and we have Him as an instance of being so far as He is seen to be together with other realities. Both of these occur together; God then is an instance of being and is identical with being as such—and so is the world. And most generally, every mode of being is identical with being as such, and is an instance of one of four types of being as such.

Each mode of being is being as such from its own perspective. This means that we do not know God as being as such; only He knows this, though we can know that He knows it, since we can know what it is to be a mode of being without enjoying the role it has. We get to God through the agency of some mode of togetherness, and thus we get to Him as instancing, in the sense of concretionalizing, a togetherness.

Diversifying ourselves in the guise of togethernesses we take one of them and treat it as being as such in the sense that it can have a plurality of intensifications, of which God is one. We make use of the mode of togetherness which is formal or existential or evaluational or actual. The last is the best for us men. Our act of knowledge is ourselves attenuated, and we with respect to that act of knowledge are being as such. But we recognize that this being which attenuates us can function as being as such with respect to concrete, unifying instances of itself and other modes of togetherness. Though we cannot know God as being as such, we can know the togethernesses as having that status, for this is an abstract role, an attenuation of ourselves, a continuation of ourselves as being as such.

From being as such, which is ourselves, we get to knowledge which is at once an attenuated version and partial diversification of ourselves, and a thin reality of which we and God are both concretionalized instances. But then it would seem that I cannot know God, and that I must reach Him only through faith. This would be the case were it not that the act of knowledge in which I engage is not only an act of mine, attenuating my being as such and functioning as a being as such which is to be intensified in me, but is that which attenuates the being of God as well, not actively as I do, but passively, reciprocally, as that which is related to me via knowledge and makes a difference to the act of knowledge by virtue of being the terminus of that act.

December 31

A type of togetherness is an attenuated version of four modes; only as such is it a being as such. A mode of being is the congealed version of four types of togetherness. Only thus is it a being as such.

What is the relation of the various togethernesses to one another; what is the relation of the various modes to one another? These questions do not have to do with the beings as such. Each being, whether it be a mode or a togetherness, is being as such, i.e., is mere being related to togethernesses or to other beings, respectively.

What is the difference between being as such and a being in itself? A being in-itself, though it can be said to be a unification of content determined from without, makes no reference to what is outside; a being as such is a condition for what is outside. But is not each mode a condition for the other modes? Yes, but not as being as such, but only as this particular type of being. Consequently we must distinguish what a being is in-itself, what it is for other beings, and what it is as being as such. In addition, of course, it interplays with other beings to constitute derivative domains.

Is it the contention of the ontological argument that God's being in-Himself is one with being as such? Or is it the contention of those who hold that God is a creator? Apparently both hold to this contention. But then both suppose that all other being is derivative being. God is being as such only so far as one makes a beginning with Him, looks at the other realities from His perspective. But the other realities also provide a perspective on Him. Moreover, it is denied by the defenders of the ontological argument and by those who hold that God is a creator that one can look at things from His perspective. They in fact look at Him and all else from the perspective of an actuality or Existence. Consequently, what they ought to say is that they can understand God as the being who is for them, as that which can be viewed as a precipitate from the four types of togetherness and thus as concretionalizing them, and therefore one who can be conceptualized as attenuated to yield facets of four togethernesses. The being as such of God will then be dealt with as an outcome of reflection and never identified with the being in-itself, which is to be loved, sought, feared, etc.

It takes four modes of being to make possible one mode of togetherness; it takes four modes of togetherness to make possible one mode of being. Each mode of being is a being as such for only a facet of each of the forms of togetherness. Each form of togetherness is a being as such for only a facet of each of the modes of being. The being as such of a togetherness cannot be found except by solidifying the facets which attenuate the different modes of being. The being as such, i.e., the mere being of a mode of Being, cannot be found except by solidifying the concretionalized versions of the togethernesses—versions which are mere facets of the different modes.

Starting with Actuality we can have a being as such which is then dispersed in a set of four facets, each of which belongs to a different mode of togetherness and relates the given mode of being to the others. When we engage in such activities as knowing, loving, etc., we approach the stage where we are identical with some form of togetherness. We can then see this as a being as such which is concretionalized in the guise of four distinct facets, and distributed as facets of different modes of Being.

Is there no meaning to being which is common to all the modes of being? To all the forms of togetherness? To all the modes of Being together with all the forms of togetherness? All four modes of Being share the character of attenuating to a facet of a form of togetherness; all four forms of togetherness share the character of being concretionalized as a facet of a mode of Being; all of the modes of Being and all of the forms of togetherness share the character of being diversified by the plurality of realities of a different order, by distinctive beings with distinctive natures. All the modes and all the togethernesses then share the character of offering conditions for the specific realities of togethernesses and modes respectively. Mere being is a specific reality functioning as one of a number of conditions for the being of a different type of specific reality. Mere being is never disoriented from some specific being.

Is there no being which is shared by both God and the world for example? Can we not say that both are sources of facets of the different types of togetherness? I think we can. But then we must modify the foregoing and assert that mere being, being as such, is that which is articulated in the shape of facets of four types of togetherness or of four modes of Being. That being as such has no objective reality; it is not a being in-itself. But if it is only a concept it is something which falls into the realm of ideas and thus is something which has meaning only in the realm of Actuality or Ideality. If so, must there not be something like being as such which reflects the nature of God or Existence; i.e., is there not some source of facets, of forms of togetherness which can be expressed not as an idea or concept but in some other way? Is there not a meaning to being as such which is not conceptual but dynamic? Must there not in fact be four ways of designating being as such, where being as such is the source of facets either of a togetherness or a mode of being? Why is there not a being as such in the guise of an idea, of a structural or implicational law, of an action, and of an evaluation? It would seem that there should be.

When we ask for being as such our question is ambiguous, for we have not yet determined whether we are looking for the concept of such a being, for it as functioning as the structure in everything, for it as intrusive in everything, or for it as a criterion or condition of everything. We must ask for it in one of these ways. And once we do we can say that it is the source of four facets either of togetherness or of modes of Being. But once again, we are driven to ask if there is not something in common to the different ways being as such is determined. But this question itself is ambiguous, and requires determination as to just what is being sought—an idea, an action, etc.

But what is the nature of this which is to be determined in one of these ways? It never is anything other than one of four distinct indeterminates—a vague concept, an incomplete structure, a merged presence, or an attitude of evaluation. Faced, say, with a vague concept of being as such, we go on to ask for the concept or for the structure or presence or value of what is being as such. This, we can answer, is the source of facets. The vague concept with which we began (though we might have begun with being as such in the shape of an incomplete structure, etc.) can thus be made to give way to an adequate formulation of being as such, not necessarily in the guise of a concept or idea, but in the guise of a law, action, or evaluation. Initially, we apparently do not have a vague concept, but rather a blurred merging with other beings. We clarify this in the shape of a concept, and then have being as such as an object of knowledge which we can understand to be diversified into facets.

1963

January 1

Reflecting on the Hirschorn exhibition of sculptures at the Guggenheim Museum leads to the thought that sculptures do not merely occupy space but possess it and thereby reveal to us how we might have possessed it, how it can resist us, and thus how arbitrary our present limits are and how complex the world of Existence is. The sculptured world reveals a promise of possession by us of more than what we now possess via our bodies; by identifying ourselves with it we can possess what is there now (and which is contouring the space) at the same time that we will be resisted by it, and even resist it to maintain a hold on our own portion of space.

With this as a guide we ought to say that the other arts—from architecture to dance—do not merely re-present the texture of Existence, but specify it, give it details and meanings it did not have before. As a consquence we discover what we might have been and done, and what it is that we might or will have to face. Art gives us, then, a more definitive message than I supposed in the art books, and one that is more directly pertinent to man. Its specialized configurations are anticipatory delineaments of what could be an actual structuralization of Existence. This should not obscure the fact that art epitomizes, idealizes, and has cosmic import. It adds to this fact the realization that the particular specialization which an art work produces has reality for the art, and has this without reducing it to a portrayal of some particular thing.

By recognizing the contours of a Giacometti dog one recognizes not a dog, but an epitomized dog or, better, an epitomized structure of space. The epitomization is such that the particular space occupied could be anywhere and everywhere, and in the fact that the structure is dramatic, heightening what would otherwise be a prosaic fact of occupation. The occupation is thereby shown to be something vital and important and to be faced over against man, the being who is now as a matter of fact occupying his own space non-dramatically, and who will occupy others in a similar way. The idealized occupation tells him what occupation means in fact, and what it is that he might have done or become, and what it is that stands in his way.

The turn to God is never satisfactory; He does not give us all we want or need. We must turn to the Ideal for a providential form of divine salvation and to Existence for a world in which we can as a matter of fact live. The first says we are to have good character and be devoted, the second, that we should live a life of service; both are under the aegis or stimulus or control of the divine.

The turn to the Ideal is never satisfactory either. We must turn to God for a divine form of the answer which the Ideal fails to provide, so that the judgment He makes can be part of us, and we thereby are faced with a concrete set of values.

Nor is the turn to Existence ever entirely satisfactory. We must turn to God for a divine form of the answer which Existence fails to give us, so that His reassessment will be something which we can take into ourselves.

The task which God imposes on us we only partly fulfill and must look to the Ideal and Existence to help us out. The Ideal will carry out God's demand that He be embodied. It does this in history. Existence will carry out God's demand that He be embodied. It does this over the course of a spatiotemporal becoming. The task which the Ideal and Existence imposes on us is in part done by God. We must identify ourselves with Him to avoid guilt and maladjustment.

January 2

A basic discipline A] provides the answers which other disciplines provide, but in a muted, transformed shape; B] claims to be omnipresent, so that no matter what they may be doing or saying, one is in fact carrying it out, at least in an unconscious form; C] takes itself to be of primary importance and therefore asks men to turn to it, and to give it their complete devotion. The last two are in conflict. On the one hand it is maintained that there is no need to turn to the subject and on the other hand it is urged that we do. This dilemma is most conspicuous both in religion as a whole and in the particular religions. On the one hand we are told that even atheists and pagans, blasphemers and the self-indulgent are religious, though not to the degree they should be, and on the other hand we are told to give up the Old Adam, the secular ways, the devotion to material things, and to turn toward religion.

We can of course maintain that the B is the right one, and that C tells us only to do more thoroughly what we have been doing all along. The trouble is that there are other disciplines besides religion, and other religions besides our own; the first do not recognize themselves to be a form of religion while the second do not take themselves to be the given religion even in a minor way. Instead they claim that the religious man, or the practitioner of some other religion is doing their kind of thing in a minor way.

From the standpoint of someone who is immersed in the basic discipline, the proper thing to say is perhaps that ontologically viewed there is nothing which escapes the reach of the discipline, but that as a matter of fact the discipline should be pursued consciously and whole-heartedly and that he who does not do so, instead of having the virtues which the discipline bestows, has instead vices, lacks, defects. Every basic discipline must separate men into sheep and goats, even though it sees that what the goats are is not altogether alien to what the sheep are. From the perspective of someone outside the discipline the ontological claim might be denied, and the difference between the goats and sheep insisted on, though without the perjorative meaning which the practitioners of the discipline give to this distinction, and without distributing the virtues and vices in the way those practitioners do.

Both those inside and outside the discipline then must start with an attitude something like that expressed in C: that there are men who do not participate in the discipline. Those who favor the discipline will exhort others to participate; those who do not favor it ought to go back to alternative A, and see that their own discipline includes the given one in a muted form. Only those who favor the discipline will acknowledge B, and then in an ontological guise—with the exception of the philosopher whose task it is to speak of the various disciplines in sympathetic terms, even when he does not engage in those disciplines.

The philosopher's relation to basic disciplines in which he is not engaged is then unlike the relation one of these disciplines has to the others. The various basic disciplines are competitive. But if so, philosophy cannot be treated as a basic discipline—as is done in the *Modes* at the end.

Does not philosophy claim to be exactly what the various basic disciplines claim to be—of primary importance, all-inclusive, that which is practiced by all men in a muted form, that which men ought to practice even more diligently and self-consciously than they normally do? Ought we not then to say that philosophy is a basic discipline, but one which acknowledges other basic disciplines to have an ontological base? I think so.

How, then, will philosophy differ from a basic discipline, when looked at from within that discipline? It will not be producing the virtues of that discipline in a non-muted form. Philosophy will subordinate that discipline as others do, but it will recognize that the discipline has the same roots as others have and as it itself has. It will be no more basic or no less basic than the others, and will not do any more justice to what it includes than the others do; nor will it succeed in producing all the values which the other disciplines are geared to produce. Philosophy will be like every other basic discipline, differing only in that it will recognize its root identity with them all, and will even go on to say that their divergency from it is desirable, since it will involve the production of values which philosophy itself cannot produce. Philosophy will then provide the blueprint of the full life; it will not itself be the full life, but it will be that part of the full life which can say what the full life is. It will report that the full life is one which includes philosophy as a proper part, and which allows all the others to have a similar role.

This has bearing on the problem of free speech, tolerance, etc., in the political and humanistic spheres. From the point of view of any parochial value, of this state or that, this set of values or that, the position of a basic discipline is evidently the model. But there must be some position which is analogous to philosophy, in which all the different forms of expression are seen to be in root the same, and even the same as the position which recognizes them all to be in root the same. Traditionally, such an outlook is "liberal." A genuine liberalism must then say that the various positions taken in politics, even those it finds repugnant, including antiliberalism, fascism, and the like, are, in root, one with it and with one another, and that as a matter of fact they produce desirable values. It can nevertheless insist on itself as the discipline or position which is to be carried out on its own, as being as basic as the others.

We are now back to the situation of conflicting claims. Must we not assign philosophy and liberalism and similar views, which acknowledge the basic rights of the others in the sense of seeing them to have the same roots as itself, to be primary at least in an adjudicative role? But we will then have to allow that what opposes these has something to say for itself; all philosophy and liberalism can deny is an adjudicative role to the opposition. They therefore must say to the opposition that if reason is to prevail, if there is to be an end of conflict, what is seen from the perspective of the adjudicative role is what should hold. This means that the various disciplines must be made to find a place for one another.

The tolerance of the adjudicator will extend in terms of ideas, principles, and even actions; it will stop only at the point where what it sees to be the rights of other disciplines or activities, are effectively denied, and not merely denied in terms of the meaning of the discipline. The various positions occupied by basic disciplines or enterprises will be adjudicated in principle by the "philosophical" one, and will be adjudicated in fact in the "market place" of free discussion. The "market place" will be the counterpart of the adjudicative position; it will, through a process of trial and error, in which there is "free competition," seek to achieve that mutuality and equality which the adjudicative position acknowledges all to have.

If then a man through his speech or even his actions opposes the present government, he can be suppressed on the grounds that the present government is exclusive and tolerates no alternative except in the form of a subordinated muted note within itself. He can also be suppressed from an adjudicative position because he refuses to allow the government any right—but conversely, the government will also be subject to a similar criticism. And he can be suppressed from a "market place" position as a mere matter of brute fact, since he is unable to meet the competition of other forces. But the latter can be judged to be a good or a bad consequence, as can the decision of the government or his own actions. The only proper thing to do then is to look to the adjudicative position for a guide, not on how to suppress him, or why, but on how and why his activities are to be modified, moderated, brought into interrelationship with other claims. We can say that he has a right to denounce the government, but not in the Senate visiting chambers, or that he has a right to advocate the overthrow of his own state, but not to advocate this to soldiers or to idlers.

Is this not denying him the right to be effective? No; it merely denies him the right to be effective in a certain channel. Properly dealt with the man should be accorded alternative approaches which are as effective as the one he chose, but which, unlike the one he chose, will not deny the right of others to be and to act with the same degree of effectiveness that he himself is able to have. After all, he functions over against them only by virtue of the fact that they with him constitute the same unitary mankind, or totality of disciplines.

January 3

We ought to distinguish two meanings of tolerance: acknowledgment of coexistence, and recognition of the right to be and flourish. The first can be forced on one. Today, particularly in this country, religions exercise the first type. In fact only a subject which recognizes that it and others have the same root can exercise the second type of tolerance. This in effect means that the various political parties, the various religions, and even the various basic disciplines do no more than grant coexistence to others. But the coexistent items have a common root. This may not be very deep; but it is this which one must find in order to obtain the discipline and the criteria, in terms of which one can in fact adjudicate the claims of the opposing coexistent items. We must not leave them to the "market place" or to a power struggle, unless they are no more than coexistent items of a market place or a power struggle. It is the nature of a government, of a set of laws, of a philosophy, of a genuine tolerance based on the rights of coexistence, to specify the limits, to determine the rightful claims of the opposing parties.

The government has the right to reject any claim to free speech which denies the free speech of the government in fact or principle. It is of course possible for one to oppose the government, and to plan to overthrow it. Such a course can be justified only so far as it touches a deeper root than that from which the government had come, together with its coexistent competing components, or members. One must appeal to the dignity of man, the destiny of man, or to the rights of man, or something like these.

The Fascist or the Nazi wishes to work inside the established patterns. The intolerance that he expresses cannot be opposed except so far as it denies the right of the government, within which it occurs, to function properly. If he rejects the right of the government he sets himself over against the government and has so far defined himself as one who, together with the government, is subject to adjudication in some third court. As a rule he thinks it enough to have power, to win by the exercise of a strength in numbers or in others ways. But this means that he acknowledges any strength to have a right over against himself, and this means that he accepts the principle of the dominant as right. When and so far as he is himself not in the ascendancy he grants the right of the others to suppress him.

The others, however, may not themselves subscribe to a principle of force. What we must then do is to find the common root of the faction which is advocating force as its criterion, and the one that is advocating ethics or traditional rights, etc. Let us say that what is common to these is a desire to control the public life of men in the light of the fact that they must be restrained and that they do have an inheritance of tradition. This principle precludes either side from preventing the existence of the other. The unlimited reliance on force or tradition which they respectively claim must be denied, not by one another but by the frame into which they both fit. They must be forced to tolerate one another's presence and characteristic insistence, and thereby to deny their own. So far as they refuse they must be limited by the third court to which they are inescapably subject.

When we view the various religions from a perspective which includes them all—say, religiosity or a concern for God or salvation—we can criticize the excesses of each and all, since we can see when and how far they deny the rights of others, rooted in the same concern that they are, and when and how far they preclude the existence or functioning of the root concern. That root concern is the philosophic concern for God; it provides criteria for the evaluation of the various religions, telling us that those which obscure, hobble, or deny that there be such a concern, either through their acts or principles, are so far lower than the others. And if that concern be taken to be basic, so that every other interest, such as art, ethics, history, etc., is given some place or right by it, then we can say that the religion which rejects these places or rights is so far inferior that it must be restrained in the light of the basic principle.

A similar consideration applies to the consideration of the kind of life a man ought to lead. All the different lives, including the ethical, are to be viewed as under the dominance or aegis of a full life. The full life has the same roots as the partial lives which it includes as so many subdivisions of itself. The nature of that full life can be specified by each of the components. The ethical life will, for example, express what the full life is as an ideal objective, whereas the political life will express what the full life is as a common objective to be reached through the public interplay of men, etc. Each will see itself as concrete and limited, referring to an abstract but more comprehensive scheme in which it will continue to be a part when that scheme is actualized. Each will shadow forth the kind of comprehensive scheme in which it will be with the others. Ideally this is what a religion or political faction should do—define in its own terms the kind of comprehensive, though not abstract, scheme in which it will be a proper part. No one will do this; but he who is willing to reflect on the nature of factions, parts, wholes, and the like will be able to use the parts to make them express, in their own terms, the nature of that scheme on the basis of which they are to be judged and eventually limited or expanded.

The full life has the same root as the partial lives; it therefore is able to recognize their rights, and they in turn are able to portray it in abstract but characteristic terms. The full life, like a philosophical approach to religion, or a set of laws controlling factions, has a concreteness which it seeks to attain in the form of the full being of all the others. It never gets to be a life alongside the others; it never is a life that anyone in fact can live. All that one can do is to reinterpret one's partial life so that the values of other partial lives are accreted to oneself, and thus vicariously and not *in concreto* achieve something which is in fact outside the orbit of one's acts and values.

We are able to share in the values of other partial lives by accepting the ideal of a full life, and thus by accepting our own lives as partial and subject to the meaning of the full life as also including the other partial lives. It is only by accepting the right of the full life to be, that we at once sink into the proper relationship to the full life and to the other partial lives. We share in those other lives by virtue of our sharing in the ideal of the full life as in fact operating as the encompassing total for ourselves and for the others. The full life is concrete only in the neutral juncture of all, but each of us can share in it in our own way by approaching it from our own angle and seeing it as having a right to subjugate us and the others as well. The full life then will have something like the shape of a neutral togetherness for the individuals who make use of it.

January 4

It is sometimes maintained by defenders of the Roman Catholic point of view that there is a kind of salvation outside the Church. It is said that were there some excellent virtuous man in some tribe or place who did not know about Christ, God would make him the object of a special act of Grace. Such an answer has all the faults which Hegel pointed up in Kant's theory of ethics. It supposes that there is a virtue which deserves a "happiness" or blessedness, but that as a matter of fact it does not acquire this itself. Moreover, in the religious area it smacks of a semi-Pelagianism; it is as if God had to endow a virtuous man with a supernatural status, as if He had to act in the light of what men did or were. We ought to say instead that if virtue merits salvation it provides it itself, and therefore we so far need no religion or divine help. If it does not merit salvation, we ought to say that God will save without making necessary a reference to virtue or to a man's supposed merits.

Consequently, the answer which should have been given by the theologians is that no one merits salvation, and that no one can merit it even by faith, good works, participation in a community, etc. All one can maintain is that these various ways are means by which contact is in fact made with God, and that one hopes this is the kind of contact which God endorses and will therefore aid, making it possible for us then to make an even more intimate contact with Him.

Every religion must take something like this answer as its own. The Christian somehow thinks there is no salvation outside Christianity; if he concedes there can be salvation elsewhere, he has to justify the insistence he has on his own religion. If he says it is only an insistence on the familiar and the conventional, he is up against the challenge of those who maintain that their own religions are not endorsed for these reasons, and that there is perhaps no salvation at all in Christianity but only in the others. If he concedes that others can be saved without being Christians, and still insists that Christianity is the best of religions, he acknowledges that God may act more vigorously and effectively in connection with the members of the inferior religions than toward his own. This contention can be supported by the recognition that the supposed inferior religions do make contact with God, as surely as his does. Consequently, though a supposed superior religion will hold that it makes it possible for its members to make a more intimate contact with God than other religions can, it must allow that the inferior contact provided by other religions may nevertheless be in the line along which God will make possible a more intimate contact with Him than He allows in the superior religion.

We then have the following alternatives: A] a religion which claims that it is the best, and therefore brings us closer to God, and B] a religion which is more agreeable to God, even though it does not initially bring us closer to Him. Each religion must claim the first for itself, but each must allow for the possibility that only the second is true of it.

January 5

I am a Jew, but I am not Jewish—I'm not anti-Semitic enough.
I am not a Jewish liberal—I'm insufficiently anti-Catholic.
One's natural turn to religion is quickly discouraged by the clergy.

They want one to adopt their faint image of themselves, which they call God.

It is possible to be one with God and yet to be over against Him. This is what we do when we reject Him, blaspheme, etc.

History, English, Religion, and Philosophy were once nonacademic subjects. They were dealt with then by men of vision. Such men are academically suspect; the successful academic is one who most readily appeals to mediocre colleagues, for these run the committees, the administration, and set the tone of the professional associations. The hope of these disciplines is that an odd man or two will slip through the mesh of conformity every once in a while.

Poetry, Painting, Sculpture: these are the next subjects to be academized, but now no longer in their own academies but in the universities.

Only those whom you trust embezzle: Is there a sadder truth?

January 6

If God is at once transcendent and immanent there is a problem of how He can be one Being. As immanent He is involved in a transitory world; there He is pluralized, whereas as transcendent He is self-contained and over against such a world. If account be taken of the fact that He has no body, the answer can be found by considering the world as His body. Then God as transcendent will be somewhat like man in his privacy, a structural being governing the interrelationship of items which can be in existence as separate units in a public world. God as transcendent will then be imposed on the objects in the world to constitute Him as immanent, a being who is "withdrawn," ready to act with respect to correlative sides of Himself or correlative realities which, like Him, are ready to interplay in the terms of the structure He, as transcendent, possesses.

The immanence of God, then, is not an immanence of Him as a substantial being, but rather a reconstruction of Him in the world, or if one wants, a redefinition of the items in the world in the light of His transcendent structure. God then is not to be thought of as incarnating Himself, of descending from Himself in his transcendent guise to become immanent, but rather as having translated the unit objects of the world in such a way that they are interrelated as agents and patients, as readied beings in interplay in the light of the structure of His transcendent being. His immanence consists in taking account of the actual entities in the world, and making them into readied, withdrawn realities. What is immanent then is the structure of His transcendence in the shape of an orientation of the different items in the world toward one another, in terms which He provides. He remains a unity in-Himself, for in-Himself He is transcendent; His immanent guise is nothing but that transcendent being as translated into a public dimension.

When we come to know God from His immanent side we become aware that the various items in the world are affiliated with one another in terms which are not provided by the world, but which reflect a divine unitary meaning or purpose. This purpose is not an aiming at some goal, with the various items in the world moving to realize it. It is a purpose in the sense that the very nature of God's transcendent being is now expressed in terms of the readiness or referential nature of the various items in the world toward one another.

When we engage in an act of faith we start with the awareness of the imposed affiliated relation of the items of every day, and move to the substantialized form of that relation in the being of God as transcendent. The religious turn will involve a movement to the imposed affiliation, only so far as we must have faith before we have a movement to God. But we can turn away from the world with its daily affiliations to go to God as transcendent, and then we can descend to consider those very items as possessing other affiliations due to the fact that God is immanent in the world.

God is present in every community as the affiliation of its members; they can be said to produce a relation to one another only so far as this coming together of them allows for or opens itself up to God's transcendent structure.

Does God, having defined an affiliated world of items, then act on those items to bring about the results which are made possible? Does He take a detached item and use this to ground a movement to and an eventual detachment of affiliated items? If He does, then He is in control of the world. But we need not suppose that He does. It seems in fact as if the items in the world act as detached items, and that we can see them as divinely affiliated only by making reference to another dimension of them, a dimension which does not operate though on the items as detached. It is as if we had a rule of *modus ponens,* in which we had the implicational structure, the detached items, the synthesis of these in the shape of affiliated readied agents and patients, yet did not take the next step and actually make the agents and patients interplay in the course of an actual inference, but allowed our readied structure to be utilized by objects so that they did conform to the anticipations provided by the implicational structure. God makes it possible for objects to behave in divinely sanctioned ways, but He does not make them act in these ways.

Our conclusion has an old-fashioned ring to it, for what we are saying now is that God allows men a "freedom" (and in fact allows this to all beings) and still does not hold Himself away from the world. The world has now as a dimension of it a divinely defined readiness or set of affiliations, which the world may or may not use depending on whether or not it is corrupt, etc. This means that God's immanence can be ignored or perverted or distorted, without Him being denied a place in the actual universe in an undistorted way.

January 7

It is possible to view the divinized objects in the world in two ways. There is the pantheistic way, in which the affiliations which God imposes on things is taken to be an affiliation of the parts of God. Here the objects in the world serve as the occasion for God to transform them into items which are ready to behave with respect to one another in the light of the kind of structure which He has in- and of-Himself. In the second way, the truly immanent way, the objects are our daily things, but subject to a new and additional type of affiliation. The objects remain apart from God; all He does is to utilize them as occasions for the translation of His structure into affiliations amongst those objects. The second way is better, since it does stress the fact that the affiliated objects are outside of God. This makes it possible for us to speak of them as the very same objects which are in fact related in commonplace ways.

The immanence of God then raises no principle not already present in connection with the reality of social, political, historical, aesthetic, and ethical affiliations amongst the objects of the natural or commonplace world. If we were to take the natural or commonplace world as basically real, we could easily find a place for the affiliated items. We will then say that amongst the various paths which the laws of nature allow there are certain ones in fact selected, and this not by chance, nor by some antecedent determination of what things are to do, but through the imposition of human activity, divine judgment, and the like.

This solution does not, however, do full justice to the reality of the political, historical, etc., realms. It would, for example, make the time of history be a specialized version of the time of everyday. Such a history might be said to have its units forged out of the units of everyday time, but it could not be said to include those units, to give them a place within it, in the very sense in which they give a place to the history and its time. To do justice to the historic realm, as ontologically as basic, though perhaps later in time than the natural, we must orient it in some other mode of being, as basic as the "natural."

If we take this approach we must say that the items of daily life, or their more refined versions such as the space-time-dynamic substances which we come to know through various devices (amongst which are science, art, and speculation, and the adumbrations which accompany even perceptions of daily things), are in fact to be understood, when divinized, etc., to be mixtures and types of togethernesses made up of themselves as merely in nature, and of themselves as subject to affiliations which owe their being and meaning to some such mode of being as God, the Ideal, etc.

When the items of the natural world do not follow the path which is prescribed in history, they are to be judged from the perspective of the latter as having fallen short, as being defective, wicked, etc. From the perspective of the natural world, the specific affiliated occurrences raise no problem, except that of why just this particular set of occurrences should have taken place when some others are equally allowable according to the laws that in fact prevail. The one approach allows us to say that the stone falls on this man because there is an affiliation between stone and man which can be traced back to the very nature of God (or, to secularize this, to the very nature of the stars and planets, the structure of the world, etc.). The other approach takes it for granted that the stone and the man are the outcome of some initial distribution of items, which since then have been acting in accordance with the very same laws of nature that now prevail. Peirce had an in-between view. He recognized the arbitrariness of the doctrine that all the variety of the universe is given initially at one fell swoop. His alternative was to maintain that the laws of nature evolve.

One can hold that the laws of nature evolve, and even that every occurrence whatsoever involves some creativity and novelty, without meeting the present issue. Why do the laws evolve in just this way; why do items which are together in some particular way persist in being together again and again—i.e., why is it if x involves y today it also involves it tomorrow? The man on whom the stone falls today has another fall on him tomorrow, or he stumbles tomorrow, or he is rewarded tomorrow. We try to deal with such cases by speaking of the man as "accident prone," or of "bad fortune," or of "providence," but these are only summary ways of referring to the fact that items which seem to be at random in nature have affiliations with one another.

It is the awareness of affiliations that makes men speak of God's purpose, His concern with the world, or of luck and chance, and makes them believe that when they are the recipients of the luck or chance that there is something exceptional about themselves. They then think of themselves as caught in the web of the chance with its desirable (or undesirable) affiliated items, and to be so selected because of some peculiar merit (or demerit) they may have, not necessarily intrinsic, but by election perhaps or even through "chance" itself.

January 8

If we have two schemata, say of time and space, we can take each one to be primary, and view the other as a muddled form of it. The muddling could consist in the having of many items which are not affiliated by the primary schema, or it could be a muddle which omits relevant items that the primary schema affiliates, and thus jumps over areas which should be linked.

A primary schema may also take the other to be a kind of abstract, idealized version of itself, in terms of which it can speak of itself as falling short of some ideal not yet realized. In this second interpretation the primary schema takes itself to be insufficiently rational, valuable, etc., though without allowing that there is any other schema which is better.

In the second of these ways the primary schema becomes the only one that is real, but subject to a standard provided by the other schema, whereas in the first of these ways the primary schema becomes the only one that is good, the other being dealt with as equally real but of lesser value. The first alternative is the better since it does allow the primary schema to grant reality to other disciplines, times, etc. Thus it allows a philosophy of history to grant a place for nature and its time outside history, and for a philosophy of nature and its time to grant a place for human history and its time outside the control of nature itself.

Neither of these ways allows us to unite the two schemata. To unite them we would have to have recourse to some object or being which in fact was able to be a member of both schemata with their diverse affiliations. Once we recognize the need for such a third in the shape of an object, we are in a position to adopt a third alternative to the effect that there is a neutral position in terms of which the two schemata can be seen to be diverse expressions. This neutral position in fact is provided by an object that can be in both schemata.

It is man, as an ontological being, who can be both in nature and in history, in politics and in ethics, etc. The mind-body problem similarly must be recognized to have at its core the reality of a man who exhibits himself both mentally and physically. Such neutrality does not preclude the actual operation of the first two alternatives. It is possible to have an ontological man who expresses himself both as an historic and as a natural being, and also have his natural status be a primary schema to which his historic being is subject, and conversely. It is possible to have a man manifested both as mind and body, and also have the body dictate to the mind and the mind to the body, the one by offering units, the other by offering a structure. Taken in this sense, the individual, as readied to act in public, could be said to be the constructed counterpart of what he in fact is as neutral to his body and mind. Were one to say this, one would have to recognize that the being as neutral is unrelated, whereas the being as readied is placed in a public frame where there are specific items to which it is relevant. How could these be counterparts?

Though the neutral item is a being by itself, it is a unity of two tendencies—one which links itself to a meaning, thereby making it a different meaning, and another which has it stand over against other entities. It is thus a being with a private, structured inside and a bounded outside, set over against other things. That is the meaning and being of its unitary neutral reality. Since the being as readied is a synthesis of structure and unit, it is as so readied the counterpart of itself, but now with a primary emphasis on its public role. As neutral it could be said to be primarily private and structured, and secondarily a unit (because the unit is neutral only with respect to some encompassing totality in which the unit is alongside other units), whereas as readied it could be said to be primarily public and distinct, and secondarily affiliated (because it obtains the affiliation from the private source and is exhibited only in the actual behavior of the readied item). We could say that the readied item is a kind of articulation or translation of the neutral one, the giving to it its full import.

The followers of Wittgenstein would be inclined to applaud this result. However, they would tend (whereas he would not) to dismiss the private counterpart. But then they would not be able to understand how an object became readied; they would have to start with a realm of readied entities and try to explain the neutral item in terms of it, or they would have to take the neutral item to be exhaustively and properly translated into the readied one. They would also have trouble with the unit items. Indeed they make no provision for these, since all they recognize are items which are affiliated in social and linguistic ways.

Coming back to our initial question we are confronted with two types of readiness. From the perspective of one schema we could say that the other either provides a structure or units, or that it alone provides readied items. But from a neutral standpoint we would have to take the one schema as being a readiness for the other, and conversely. Each schema will have affiliations within it, but will also have a neutral grounding in an object which will express itself as these schemata, as readied with respect to one another. A man will then be said to be readied for history and for nature, and the realms of nature and history would be affiliated as disciplines or areas which are pertinent to one another.

We know what it means for a man to be readied in a given area: he will be exactly where the units of that area are, but will be affiliated in ways that no domain of units provides. But what does it mean for two areas to be affiliated? What kind of units correspond to the affiliated disciplines?

The disciplines are products of the neutral being and thus already have some warrant for being affiliated as soon as they appear. Is it that the neutral individual who expresses himself as a set of affiliated disciplines, or better, expresses himself as an item in the affiliated disciplines, also is the being of their affiliation, so that a man would be the relevance of history to nature e.g.? Could the history and nature be "unit" areas in the sense that a man is a being who is articulate and thus can be dealt with as a set of distinct dimensions, one answering to, say, his values and the other to his body, or to his need to resist and insist?

January 9

The hitch in the theory that a plurality of schemata can be united in a man, comes out when we consider schemata which are temporal in character—such as history and nature. After all, a man does die, pass away in nature, and when he does he is not available for action in history. Even if he be said to be part of the present of history it is a fact that only so long as he is in nature has he the power to act in history. We can speak of his effectiveness as continuing beyond him, but this we can also recognize to be something which is being carried on without him.

Can we get out of this impasse by supposing that a man has different boundaries, by taking him to be in fact in that effectiveness, somewhat as he can be said to be in the rake which is now touching the leaves, or in his feet which are now on the ground, or in his breath which is now outside him? The first of these illustrations still allows him to be in existence, perceiving what he himself does not feel; the second has him in existence with his feet and united with them organically and through his sensitivity; the third alone is close to the problem. There are primitives, to be sure, who suppose that a man continues to be in his breath, that this is his very soul or part of it, but even they must recognize that the living individual is distinct from what is exhaled and is now "outside" the man.

Can we, in short, acknowledge anything to be part of a man which is not organically or sensitively or consciously one with him, and this not merely as future but as present? Must not what is part of him be occurring at the same time, and not merely be that which is inclusive of him (as an historic present might be) but without any elements which are then and there interplaying with him?

The historic present as I have dealt with it in the history book does seem to freeze every item in it in a sequential order, and does not have the items together. Is it enough to say that the items are, after all, not earlier and later in that historic present but only before and after? When a man dies is anything clarified by saying that in the historic present there are other events which come *after* this, but which are nevertheless not *later* than this except so far as one departs from the historic situation?

One possible answer is to hold that a man in fact, what I called the "ontological" man, is not to be said to have died or to be in history except in the form of limited expressions. He would live either in no time at all, or in an entirely different time of which these others were specialized, delimited versions. But this too will not do, for it does not meet the challenge of the fact that a man dies and acts no longer, and is therefore not available to be "ontological." It does not seem to make sense to say that the ontological man continues to be, but ceases to manifest himself in the dimension of nature while continuing to be in history.

Can we turn the matter around and say that the man who dies in nature is after all an abstraction which has concreteness only in history? The man himself and his dying would then be said to be in fact continuing in the historic present moment whose boundary in the future lies outside a number of successive moments, of which only one (and that an early one) is the dying man or even the man as already dead. The fact that the man is not conscious, that what he takes himself to be in nature is not all that he is being said to be, would then raise no more problem than the fact that he is not conscious of much of himself, and that there is more to him than he knows. But this we can say only if we can show that the "after" items in the historic present are really part of him. This is possible if one takes an analogy from *Reality;* what is contemporary with us in space can nevertheless be seen to be future to us from the perspective of our desires and needs.

Whatever we confront is that which is to be used not then but later; at present it is an item which is to be defined as being in a present moment with us, but nevertheless "after" us. On this basis we can go on to say that what comes "after" the dead man in the historic present can even be said to be contemporary with him, to be coordinate with him just as his gullet is with the food at a distance. He will then be thought to get into historic time by skewing the contemporary objects around so that they become affiliated with him in a new way. His historic being would consist in converting what was in fact contemporary with him in nature into a prospective future for him, a limiting boundary of his historic present. When then he passes away, and these contemporaries with him too, their relationship to him in the historic present will still allow for a causal process which will realize those contemporary items (to be sure, in altered form) as items germane to him. He will have died and will not in any sense therefore be acting in the historic time; the items will be prospective for him only so far as he is related to them by some reference. His dying, though, need not change that reference; his presence in the historic present is enough to make that reference continue with him as one term and they as another, both in the historic present, and ordered as before and after. We will, as it were, have kept a hold on the items which were prospective for him, or at least the items so far as they are prospective, even though they may alter or even pass away before the prospect is realized. The historic present moment would be a way of fixating the prospectiveness of contemporary items for a man, and holding on to this until the course of history in fact arrives at the prospect and converts it into the termination of that moment or period.

Would this skewing effect occur only with respect to including presents? If so, would we then have to say that the present of a religious history is not only governed by something like a day of last judgment, but that that very day is the present of secular history skewed around to be a terminus of a religious tension, thereby making the present objects in the secular history constitute a prospective day of last judgment? The day of last judgment, as it were, would peer through the contemporary secular world of man, making him be religiously oriented just so far as it awakens in him some kind of response to it. When he dies his response will die too, but the operation of the day of last judgment would continue, colored by the kind of things through which it peered, even when those things pass away.

What passes away on such an account is the entire religious historic present moment when and as the secular present does, so far as the content of the items is concerned, but there will then continue to be the teleologically determining prospect, the factuality of the being or beings which pass, and the coloring which the prospect received from the content when the content was present. On this way of viewing the matter, the religious present would not last longer than the secular, but it would have the items related to one another with different affiliations.

If we wanted to speak of the religious historic present as including a number of secular presents we would have to take the historic present which passed away to be the historic translation of one of the secular included presents. A long-spanned religious historic present would then be made up of historic secular presents, each of which was analytically stretched over the whole of the former, but each of which would be said to have passed away so far as its content was concerned. This would mean that the including long-spanned historic present would contain as analytic parts not the original secular smaller presents, but these as already skewed and as stretching over the entire span. The long-spanned historic present would then have a thickness in which items were arranged in it as before and after, only so far as before and after could be assimilated to lower and higher, since each of the included items would be as long-spanned as the including present but would lack its completeness, its concreteness. The including present would occur only by virtue of its solidification of the plurality of secular presents skewed into the form of a set of dimensions having as long a span as the including present, but being ordered with respect to one another as before and after. The including present would terminate in the prospectivity of the various prospects which constitute the boundaries of the included presents.

January 10

It is quite possible that Whitehead had something like the problem of the foregoing days in mind when he was working on his last books. His solution was to identify the substantial being with the shortest span in nature, and to make the "historic" and the other larger time-spanned dimensions be in some sense derivatives from the short and natural one. But even though a series of occurrences in nature might follow one another in a temporal sequence, this does not mean that the beings from which these issue or in which they occur need pass away with them. Nor must one overlook the fact that the historic makes a difference to the natural as surely as the natural does to the historic.

The substantial individual is neither the natural nor the merely historical. As merely natural he is a unit amongst units which are subject to any number of laws and possible affiliations. As a mere historic being he is related through the aid of the Ideal and is thus essentially a meaning. The individual by himself is a unit with a reference to something beyond him, the reference being private and the beyond being future. As a concrete and dynamic being he acts in nature along the lines of the meaning which he obtained through his attachment to the relevant historic ideal. We cannot then even remain with the short-spanned units of natural time if we are to understand man as an item interacting as he in fact does with other items, for that interaction is only one of many that have been, and is to be accounted for by reference to the historic "meaning" dimension which forces the individual to deal with this or that item rather than others.

If we abstract the individual as a mere unit we will not be able to understand why he is affiliated with such and such other units. The affiliation is to be understood in terms of the historic dimension; but then we find that we have more than a mere action with respect to other units which have been selected by the historic meaning. We have the historic span itself, within which the affiliated items fall and to which they must refer in order to be able to be affiliated items.

The very activity of items in nature requires a reference to the historic dimension, not only to account for the fact that this rather than that occurrence takes place amongst all that nature in principle allows, but in order that the affiliation which they have should be an integral part of them. There is something of the awareness of this problem and its answer in the field theory of current physics, and in the Gestalt theory in psychology. In both cases there is a recognition that there is a need to refer units, which from one perspective could be said to be parts of an aggregate, to a frame in which they then act in ways otherwise not explicable. But what must now be seen is that they are then no longer beings which can be said to pass away entirely in a mere unit-world, but are also preserved inside the affiliating world. And the historic dimension must also be seen to be made concrete and delimited in the affiliating world.

A Whiteheadian might claim that he is at one with this position.

Every item, he might say, has a subjective form which reflects the nature of what is relevant and possible to it, and when it perishes, this form or the effect of it is inherited by its successor. But this still denies an ultimate reality to the "society," and denies that the society with its own aims and outcomes has its effect on the items it includes. It has the virtue though of showing how the society is included in the units, when the units are taken to be primary. There is also no recognition that a being is substantially more than it is as a unit, even with a subjective form, or is more than an item in a society, even when it is the item's nature that is inherited along the route of the society.

January 11

Mind-body, the reconciliation of the different disciplines, private and public, natural and historic time, the secular and the religious, *modus ponens*, all have the same problem, similar to that of the categories and the experience for which Kant employed the schematism. If we start with a private extended but empty structure or category and a set of units which otherwise would be only an aggregate, we can take the substantial reality to be the mere togetherness of both—Kant's transcendental ego. This togetherness becomes manifest, expressed, spelled out by a twofold process. In one the various units are affected by the private structure, so that each has a meaning pointing to others. We will not know of this until we see how it is affiliated with such and such units. This is the result which concerns the behavioristically tempered thinker, and is in root the answer Whitehead provides. In the other process we have the filling out of the structure by the units as so many meanings to constitute a concretionalized structure, a structure with its own time-span and nature. The neglect of this reciprocal leads to a kind of reductionism; it lets us see the symphony only in the movements, each of which is affected by the meaning of the whole, but no one of which is in fact absorbed into the whole to make an actual symphony. But what we do with the symphony as a whole here will have to be done with the movements, and then the phrases, etc., to leave us with nothing more than a sequence of sounds.

The music is at once a whole symphony filled out with content all present but in a relation of before and after, and a sequence of parts in a relation of earlier and later, each part being conditioned by the whole as resident within it and making it apt or readied for such and such a successor. The initial togetherness is the composition, whose articulation is provided in the two ways together. The composition can be said to be the prescription, and the two unifications can be said to be descriptively together. The two sets of togetherness are not in either of the unifications; neither can be said to pass away or to continue with either unification.

I, as a being with a mind and a body, do not pass with the passing of the body, nor do I continue to be, for the time which is projected as the future by the mind, is pertinent to the body or to what is now being done. I could be said to be present in the form of the relation of the affiliated units and as the nature of the content for the structure, and as so pluralized to require another togetherness of these unifications, one of which comes at the end of the period in which we can indifferently say that the structure has been realized or that the units have made a unity.

It is part of the meaning of myself now to have such and such neighbors and followers, and not others. I am a unit in a field, a part of a public language, a being in which certain rules are now being embodied. It is part of the meaning of the rules, the language, of my society or state, of my mind and purpose and values to have this content rather than that as the content through which they are manifest. The structures and units have to be given together, and they are manifested together.

A first togetherness is language in potentiality, with such and such a grammar and vocabulary; it is myself as potentially quantity and quality, potentially able to be a mind with content and a body organically structured. This togetherness is not separable from the presence of a distinguishable mind and body, grammar and vocabulary, historic and secular time, etc. A second togetherness arises when the separated mind and body, etc., are imposed on one another to yield two unifications which now are together in a descriptive way. The first togetherness is split up into two, for it becomes the biased togethernesses of the two unifications; in order to recover the neutral meaning of togetherness, reference must be made to the second togetherness.

Why not four forms of togetherness? Because we are here concerned with the reconciliation of instances of two modes, each of which is constituted by the other two forms of togetherness. The mind is given by the Ideal as having reference to Existence; the unit has the meaning of an actuality as having reference across Existence to other existent actualities. The two, mind and unit, are together as divine, though only potentially, and come to be interrelated with one another. These interrelations are together in the guise of the divine in a descriptive role—what God has turned out to be in fact.

Does the early part of the symphony pass away? This question we now see has a number of answers. As a part in the domain of units which have within them a structure and tendency requiring such and such affiliations, which is the only guise the part has in a symphony, it does pass away. As a distinction within the played symphonic whole it does not pass away. As that which is potentially to be in one or the other guise (and thus which is inseparable from a potentiality of having the role of a whole for which there is content to be supplied, or the role of a disposition imposed on the unit) it is translated into kinds of togethernesses. It becomes articulated, and itself, as merely potential, passes away, but all the while the articulation continues to terminate in a new togetherness.

My privately felt pain can be treated as a potentiality or as an item subtended by a potentiality. Taking it in the first sense we will be able to say that it is to be expressed in two ways at the same time. It is to be the unity of a public expression in a language—the use of the words "I am in pain" according to the grammar, and rationale, etc., of a common world, and the unity of a language in actual use—so that the fact that I am in pain is conveyed to others. Another illustration: a game of chess is the rules embodied in the actual movement of the pieces, and in the ways in which the rules are vitalized by players. The game, defined by Hoyle, is the potentiality which the game expresses. The potentiality is to be understood as having a reference to the unity which the game as embodied rules and actual games according to the rules, have as a matter of fact. Another illustration: the Constitution is the potentiality of the United States and the fifty states. It is expressed as the United States as united with the fifty states in the sense of intrinsically governing their relation to one another, the way they are affiliated with one another; and it is expressed as the fifty states actually giving substance to the United States' laws, etc. The reality of the United States of America is the factual togetherness of these two ways of exhibiting the Constitution.

January 15

The *modus ponens,* as providing a readiness in which a universal structure (*1*) is ingredient in the readied items, (*3*) is balanced by a production of a disposition (*3'*) where the content is ingredient in the structure ($1'$). The detached outcome of the *modus ponens* (5) is balanced by the habit or structure of a material logic, ($5'$). We have then:

$$
\begin{array}{ll}
1] & p \ ) \ q \\
2] & P \\
\hline
3] & p\!-\!\!-\!\!-\!\!-q \\
4] & P \\
\hline
5] & \qquad\quad Q
\end{array}
$$

$$
\begin{array}{ll}
1'] & p \quad) \quad q \\
2'] & P \\
\hline
3'] & P \ )\,) \\
4'] & p \ ) \ q \\
\hline
5'] & P \ )\,)\ Q
\end{array}
$$

1 and $1'$, and 2 and $2'$ are the same. They are synthesized though to give a readied pair on the one hand, (3), and a disposition ($3'$) on the other. The readied pair, $p\!-\!\!-q$, is then synthesized with the original unit, P (2), whereas the disposition, $P \ )\,)$, is synthesized with the original structure, $p \ ) \ q$ ($1'$). The result is a detached conclusion, Q (5), in the one case, and a habituation or a material logic in the other, $P \ )\,)\ Q$ ($5'$).

Do the two operations occur at the same time? Are they always performed? It seems to be the case that we can have one without the other, though often the use of a structure involves the affecting of it by the content to which it is applied. When this takes place it seems to coincide at least part of the time with the occurrence of the reverse activity, but it might conceivably continue after the other activity had ceased.

January 16

The four modes of being are not only to be thought of as the ultimate explanations of everything, but to be the only realities which have roles that follow from their natures. The Ideal in- and of-itself is a structure; Existence in- and of-itself is extensional; God in- and of-Himself is Unity or Subjectivity; Actuality in- and of-itself is the oppositional or self-centering. When we come to anything else, it must be viewed as a mixture of the various modes. When it is treated as a structure, etc., it is given a role which it need not have; in another context it could have a different role.

If we have a pain, this can be dealt with as a unit, a structure, a synthetically produced readiness, a synthetically produced disposition, an outcome, or a habit. And what is true of a pain is true of the mind, common language, and the like.

A pain as a unit is an occurrence in us which could be united with a structure given by our mind, our body, a common language, a society. The pain as a structure would be a kind of categorial encompassing region to be united with some particular part of the body, some unit idea or expression, some unit act, and the like. The pain as a synthetically produced readiness could be said to be the product of a mind and body unification, of a unit idea with a bodily region, of a public language and a unit feeling in us, etc. The pain as a disposition would be explained in the same way as the readiness, except that it would be seen to be structural in nature, with whatever unit we start with being absorbed within a patterning provided by the structure (rather than, as in the case of a readiness, having the structure pulverized into units capable of acting in certain ways by virtue of the structure). The pain as an outcome would itself be the consequence of a movement from some readied antecedent— a movement which might occur in the mind or body, in language, or through a causal activity. The pain as a habit would be a particular structure which had an antecedent and a consequence together in an order of condition and conditioned, a structure which differed from a mere abstract structure since it had concrete terms and was on a par with these. My pain, for example, could be a stretch of expectancy which had as a conditioning antecedent some bodily damage, and as a conditioned consequence a state of depression, a feeling of relief, etc.

Might not every one of these roles be assumed by pain at the same time? That is, might it not be the case that pain functioned both as a unit and a structure and that the unification of these might also be a pain, and that the final outcome and the habit might be pains as well? I think so. Thus we could have a "feeling" of pain as a unit, combined with pain as a categorial attitude or as an expression, to give us pain as a readied item to be affiliated with other occurrences in us or outside us, or to give us a disposition to respond in a certain way and thus to have the pain as something which could have a public meaning. And we could have pain as that consequence with which we rest, or as a habitual expectancy with respect to subdivisions of itself. The pain in the last two cases—as outcome and as expectancy, would be pain recognized and pain as a distinctive process. These are pains as surely as are the structures, units, etc. which made them possible.

What is true of pain is true of more public occurrences and of the common languages and behavioral patterns to which some thinkers have recourse in order to make a privately felt pain intelligible or communicable. If the foregoing is correct, pain itself can be thought of as "public" and as intelligible and as derived, etc., and the most common language with its rules, etc., can be taken to be a mere unit requiring the use of some structure to be united with it before it can be a readied item or a disposition. One might refer a language for example to the mind for structuralization; one can even refer it to our pain, where this is itself viewed as a categorial item. When we take the latter alternative we reverse the current procedure of trying to make a supposedly incommunicable pain intelligible, and instead treat a whole language or set of uses of language as unit items and make them significant by structuralizing them through the use of a categorial pain. I, as pained, make use of a common language in such a way as to make it a readied item with which I can communicate with others, or to make it yield a disposition in me to speak in a certain way—"I am in pain," "Don't bother," "Get a doctor."

We are justified in treating a common language as a structure, and solely as a structure, only so far as we can show that it is an ultimate mode of being having the nature of a structure in- and of-itself. The rules of grammar or of use are themselves not rules objectively; it is only when they exercise the role that they are rules. Before that they are words, suggestions, material which can be made to function as rules in this situation or that. Or they are subordinate parts, representatives of, or instances of the Ideal.

The foregoing account seems to make use of only two types of entity —structures and units—and thus to attend only to the Ideal and Actualities. There ought to be a role which beings can assume that imitates God, and another which imitates Existence—absolute unity and absolute extensionality. We would then have the following pairs to consider: Ideal and Actuality (the case we have been discussing under *modus ponens*), Ideal and Existence, Ideal and God, Existence and Actuality, Existence and God, Actuality and God.

The case of the Ideal and Existence would lead to the spreading out of structure over a region, the making of a field. The case of the Ideal and God would be one which leads to the vitalization of the Ideal, the charging it with values. Existence and Actuality would yield classification, the placing of items in a setting. Existence and God would give us unified action, the delimiting of areas, the solidification of what otherwise would be dispersed. Actuality and God would lead to absorption, reevaluation, adoption. We would then have five "movements" parallel to the *modus ponens,* and another five "concretionalizations" parallel to the production of a habit.

Since a religion and even the God of religion is not to be identified with the mode of Being which is God, we can view the religion and its God not merely in the role of an ultimate functioning as a unity or subjectivity, but in the other roles as well. This is to say that any discipline or activity or entity which is distinct from a mode of Being can have any one of four roles as an Agent, any one of four roles as an Object, and be viewed as either a kind of readied item or a kind of disposition, and can be arrived at as a consequence or as a habit.

Must we think of the readied item, disposition, consequence, and habit in four ways? Does not, for example, the outcome of a synthesis of, say, God and Actuality (or of items adopting these roles) result in the same kind of readied item we would get if we had employed something having the roles of the Ideal and Actuality? I think so. Therefore we must say that there are four roles of Prepared Items, four roles of Orders, four roles of Terminal Items, and four roles of Controls.

Modus ponens would, on the foregoing, be a special case of the combination: Agent synthesized with Object to achieve Prepared Items and Orders which, when synthesized with Object and Agent respectively, will yield Terminal Items and Controls. *Modus ponens* deals with these only so far as Agent is structure and Object is unit, the one assuming the role of an Ideal, the other of an actuality.

January 20

It is tempting to suppose that there is a time ingredient in every mode, and that the togethernesses of the modes has a time of its own. But we tend to multiply times unnecessarily unless we can show that the various times are derivative from the time of Existence. To suppose that aboriginally there is only the time of Existence is to make the least number of assumptions and yet to be closest to the accepted views of all men, apart from special philosophic doctrines.

The time of an actuality could be said to be the product of the subjectification of the time of Existence. The individual is caught inside the time of Existence while he subjugates it to make it a private time. There is only one time, but this is given a new function which allows it to be contrasted with itself as subjugating and coordinating the various individuals. The individual with his subjectified time is able to interplay with the time of Existence. The time of Existence can also be said to interplay with other modes of being, thereby having its own nature altered.

When the various modes impinge on Existence they constitute the time which we conventionalize as common-sense time. The time of our daily life is thus the time of Existence as affected by Actuality, Ideality and God, and then subdivided and categorized by language, habit, practice, use. When then we come to refer to the time of nature, the time of history, the time of art, and the time of religion, we but clarify the common-sense time, purify it, and specialize it in the shape of a combination of Existence with one or two other modes rather than with all three. The purified counterpart of common sense, involving the modification of the time of Existence by all the modes, is a produced time, but one which is richer and has more content in it than the time of Existence. The time of Existence is an extensional structured sequence of atoms; the time which is produced by the unification of these with the other modes is a kind of togetherness, but a substantial one, since it gives us a mode of being united with a dimension of Existence.

We men, as caught inside the complex produced time which results when we qualify the time of Existence, or when we share in or interplay with the time produced by other modes qualifying the time of Existence, cannot be said to exist only in the time of Existence. The very fact that the time of common sense is more than the time of Existence shows that we are not caught wholly in Existence's time. We live and die in common-sense time; the time of Existence catches us only in part. We, as caught in the time of Existence, and thus as functioning within the pattern of its atomic career, are not fully concrete. We are concrete full-fledged beings only as at once subject to and subjecting Existence, at once qualifying it and being qualified by it.

Religious time is no new addition to a secular time. From the very start we have the two intermingled in common-sense living. The problem then of interrelating secular and religious history is not the problem of introducing into a secular world a religious dimension. Instead it is the problem of purifying the common-sense time so that one gets the secular and the religious times distinct, and of then seeing these interrelated. The span of each is different, to be sure, and what passes away in one of the times remains present in the other. But it is also true that in the common-sense time what passed away in Existence was retained, and what had not yet completed itself in, say religion, is given a boundary now by common sense.

The purified common-sense time is the ultimate produced concrete time of the interlocked modes, but as oriented toward an Existence which is qualified by the other modes. We men are interlocked with pure Existence, and are with it as qualified by the Ideal and God. When we interlock with it in its pure state we get ourselves framed in the time of art or of nature; when we interlock with it as qualified by the other modes we get the times of secular and religious history. Since these histories express the nature of the time of Existence, not as it is by itself but as qualified by the Ideal and God, they tell us what man is, not in himself or as involved in nature, but as oriented toward the Ideal and God.

I die in the time of Existence and yet live on in the time of history, since the time of Existence is there preserved, stretched out, given a new import. My death is not canceled, but my role in history is not canceled either. Still we would like to be in history while alive. In that case we must accept as our span the unity of all the modes as governed by ourselves, as providing an orientation for, a qualification of the time of Existence. Time is for us our private time, i.e., the time of Existence subjugated, as interlocked with a public time of Existence so as to produce the single complex time of daily life, purged, delimited, secular, and present. When we think of history, secular or religious, we tend to think of this time of history as being added on to the other. But since secular and religious history are already ingredient in common-sense time, and since they involve no new principle beyond that which was already exhibited by Actuality when it infected and qualified the nature of the time of Existence, we ought to be able to refer to them without modifying our basic understanding of the nature of produced times.

Our living and dying, in other words, can be said to start earlier and last longer than they do in our private lives and in the public Existence. Common sense knows us to have begun our lives before our birth or perhaps even in some cases before conception; it knows of our continuance as going beyond the last day of our active visible lives—that is why it has recourse to the idea of ghosts. To say that we exist longer than the period provided by private or public time is but to say that the Ideal and God are both real and are both effective in holding on to us, even when we are involved with Existence, since they hold on to us via the Existence which they qualify. They hold on to us in other ways as well, of course, since they are interlocked with us directly and via one another.

Speaking to Jonathan about various cases involving religion, it has become clear to me, mainly through his arguments, that a religion in relation to the state and such enterprises as medicine, education, and the use of the mails must   A] avoid going counter to the laws of the state, and thus cannot encourage the practice of bigamy, prostitution, robbery, mutilation, and the like   B] cannot enter into other domains without warning, and there claim to produce results that others do not, or even those results that only men with specialized skills can produce— the normal expectancies of men must be respected. But   C] religion (or a religious man) has the right to take all other enterprises as being subordinate to it in power and value, and to claim that things can be accomplished by a leader or by a member, which others deny or even cannot see. So long as a religion does nothing more than take itself to have a primary perspective, even when this involves the supposition that it can control and redirect other enterprises, just so far as it does not violate the expectancies of those to whom it looks for support, and the irreducible structure of the state in which it seeks to live, it is in the clear, and no one can tell it or its participants that they are in error or are engaged in a fraudulent enterprise.

God affects the time of Existence; he also affects the derivative but nevertheless intrinsic time of the private individual. The individual then, as private, can be in two times—the initial privatized Existential time, and this very time as qualified by God; and as public he can be in the public time of Existence, and in this very time as qualified by God. (And of course he can be in other times, resulting from other qualifications, and from combinations of the qualified items with one another and with the aboriginal time of Existence.) Staying for the moment with the individual in his privacy, he will participate in the divinely qualified time just so far as he recognizes that it is a time oriented toward God. What is past for himself as private may be present for the divinely oriented time, but only because it is rooted as it were in God and thus away from man; it is as if man had found a place for himself which was larger than himself and thus could, while remaining his small self in his own private time, be made one with a larger being whose nature will not be grasped until he frees himself from his own limited way of being in time.

When I say something to another, he takes my meanings inside himself and restructures them, giving them new affiliations and divisions. He thus does something similar to what is done to my private time by God when He qualifies it. The only difference is that I follow, as it were, the time into God, whereas I do not follow my meaning into another. If I understand how he deals with my meaning I still stand over against him, whereas it is my own time that is being qualified and in which in fact I live. It is as if I took the other's meaning as the guide to what I am now to say. This is possible. The analogue then of our living in a divinely qualified time is our living in terms of the meanings which others have made of my expressions and meanings, perhaps even while I continue to hold on to such expressions and meanings. Indeed, I seem to take just such a position when I see myself in a social context. The social import of my individual acts are given by others, and I behave as a sane and respectable man only so far as I respond, not to the meanings I express, but to the meanings I am taken by the others to have expressed.

Is it one and the same thing then to say that God is qualifying the temporal dimension of Existence and that a man is affiliated through the agency of God with various items, some of which will occur after he has died? I think so. The fact that the man has died precludes there being action owing to him; it does not preclude action which begins with him, but which has its dynamics given by God. It is not his action in the sense of having been produced by him and sustained by him until it arrives at its effect; but it is his action in the sense that it originates at or with him, and through the sustaining activity of God, does reach a remote effect. He is then a causal agent via God, and can be said to be responsible for what ensues. He will be responsible, of course, only by virtue of God's mediation, but the responsibility then can be one which He gives to the man.

Without being stretched or placed inside a longer period, my time could be said to be interpreted inside another mode of Being. A moment in it would remain a moment in the new mode, but the new mode would slow it up or speed it up to make it part of that mode of Being. There would be no comparing of it as it was before, with it as in the new mode of Being; it would be approached from a new angle; it would adopt a meaning which the other mode provided, without altering anything in itself. It would have an additional role without affecting its own being, a role which it acquires from the other mode. The reality of other modes thus makes it possible for a given dimension of Existence to have a new role. That new role can be set over against the dimension as having a different qualitative feel, as having its own tensions, affiliations, meaning, but without preventing the dimension from defining when a moment is over, when it has passed away.

Qualifying time on this account would mean not giving a present moment a boundary in the future, but allowing it to keep its boundaries while giving it new content and associating it with other content. As so associated it could be said to constitute a new present moment, but it would perhaps be better to say that it is made up of a plurality of the old present moments that now have a filling which the moments did not have before. Each mode of Being, and derivatively secular and religious history, would then provide the content of time, without altering its moments, its span, or the way in which or the fact that the moments do pass away. The content in those moments, as provided by the other modes of Being, would not necessarily pass away with the moments and, as not passing away, could be said to constitute a present larger than those moments. The content would be tainted by the fact that it had been in the moment; it would be ordered content, and in this sense different from what it would be were it considered merely as content in the mode. By virtue of the modification of Existence by God, the occurrences in Existence would then be enriched by God and related to further content in other moments of time, but this would be done not in time, but merely inside God, the Being who possesses the related contents as having already been temporally determined in the realm of Existence.

January 21

We can compare religious history either with the temporal world of common sense or with a secular history. If we do the former we compare a part with the whole of which it is a part, having first held the part away from the whole, and allowing it to function there with its own rationale. We then in effect compare a pure case with itself as muddled with others. To relate the two we would have to reduce the pure case to the muddled—though we could of course integrate it with other purified elements of the muddled case to constitute the constructed meaning of all of them together (which is the substantial occurrence as a unity of a plurality of modes in Existence). The second case would involve a comparison of two purified cases and would lead to a relation of them either via or by means of the common-sense time, or by means of a purified constructed version of the common-sense time.

If all the different times are the result of qualifying the time of Existence, we are led to say that Existence has at least one dimension which not only has a plurality of contents given to it, but which paces and orders these in distinctive ways. The same moment of Existence's time will require one item to be earlier than another in some one purified time (i.e., some time which is merely qualified by some mode of being and is not overlaid with common-sense conventionalities) and to be merely before another in some other purified time. The purified times, it is to be noted, are the content as still caught in the time of Existence. In the mode which is qualifying Existence, that content is not temporal even when it is defined as earlier than some other item, for the earlier here is something like the earlier in a memory, something which must be thought of as having occurred and passed away before another could have followed.

History on the above account does not, strictly speaking, have a distinctive time, space, or causation. Rather the content produced by the interplay of man with Existence is structured by the time of Existence (which is not the time of common sense or science) so that there are affiliations and implications amongst the items which they otherwise would not have, and which as a consequence must be dealt with as belonging to blocks larger than the units of the time of Existence.

Something similar would have to be said about religious time, the time of the dance, etc., and ultimately about society and the state. There will be an internal, though externally produced, unification and division of items resulting from the fact that the divisions of Existence's time are imposed on content which exists outside that time, where it continues to maintain something of its own integrity.

If we view a mode of Being as a single item, then we can say that the time of Existence succeeds in breaking this down into a plurality of items, no one of which is small enough to fit inside only one moment of Existence's time. There will be no passing away of those items as in the mode; yet they will not all be present, since some of them will have the role of replacing others. The divisions which time will make on the content produces unities in which components may be analyzed out as in a relation of before and after, and which themselves will be in a relation of before and after but with the mark of being replacements.

On such a view there will, strictly speaking, be no coming to be and passing away in history, but only a passing away and coming to be in Existence, with the historic items, produced through an interplay of socialized man with Existence, being unified and divided by time. The content of socialized man will be produced in the sense that it will be sequentially interlocked with the time, but it will not be produced in the sense that it will not have any being before it is so interlocked. This content, however, does have an origin, for socialized man is the product of an interplay of man with nature and its dimensions. Here man will produce content which has a non-temporal nature to begin with—the meaning of society and state, the "spirit of the times," the nature of man and the excellence which he promises, etc., and have this divided and united in the familiar ways of every day living; this will now function as content for history by being subject to a new structuralization. The new structuralization does not confront a single whole, but a sequence of items which it may then subdivide and unify in new ways.

The content of secular history is ingredient in the content which constitutes religious history, for the religious history has this very content as ingredient in God or, conversely said, has God bringing Himself to bear on the content of secular history. The content of secular history with its divisions and unities, defined through the agency of Existence's time, becomes the time scale, the source of divisions and unifications of the content which is God.

This does not mean that God acts in terms of what men do, or that He is somehow divided and unified by men, but that by making Himself immanent in Existence He subjects Himself to qualifications by historic time (as well as of course by the time of Existence as such). Since He does not yield passively to that time, the divisions of the religious time which He helps constitute, will reflect something of His unity, nature, intent. On this interpretation the kairotic moment will be defined by both God and secular time together; it will be defined too by some antecedent moment of the religious time which God and secular time together constitute.

January 23

In time items replace one another; they are also ordered, have a kind of direction, may exhibit a purpose, and constitute larger temporal wholes. It is the combination of these facts which raises a host of problems in connection with each. There are those who are impressed with the replacement, and treat the directionality as derivative. Whitehead is the latest of these. The position tends to give us smaller and smaller units which replace one another, and is unable to have persistent beings, and thus beings that act. The opposite tendency which is accepted by some idealists, takes the opposite risk. It moves toward larger and larger wholes, and tends therefore to lose the occurrence of time itself. From the opposite side they too are unable to have any beings that act.

Evidently we must have both of these facets together. This is in fact what we have in common sense. But the problem we then have is that in common sense we seem to have a number of directions of different lengths, and a number of units of different lengths measuring the time of replacement. Moreover the time with which we are familiar in common sense has a conventionality to it. The common-sense man speaks of seconds and hours, but also of battles and war, of momentary flashes, and the like. If one of these constitutes the dimension where items replace one another, the others will provide only directions.

Nor will it help to take some complex history as the ultimate reality, for then the replacements in nature would seem to be unreal; nor will it help to accept the time of nature, where we have both replacements and a directionality defined by world lines, etc., for these do not make provision for the replacements of history, or for the directionality which is characteristic of it.

The suggestion of the last days that different modes of Being offer content to the time of Existence, and as such have their content ordered in a time which, so far as they are caught in it, makes them pass away, will give us a world in which from one perspective items pass away, and from another, abide. The passing away will be a passing inside Existence, and the abiding will be inside the other modes, but as tainted by having been involved with Existence. But then one would like to know what a real being is. Do I actually pass away in Existence, and therefore have only a meaning within a larger whole elsewhere? If so, are we not back to some variant of Whitehead's position, with all its difficulties? How will we be able to deal with history's causation, or with the causality in society and state?

There is a position which is suggested in *Reality* that offers an alternative. Each entity in this world can be said to be related to all the others in more or less loose connections. When the connection is above the minimal the entities will make a whole. The whole reacts on the items which constitute it to make them its terminal points. The whole with its terminal points is an area in space and can persist. The items inside the area are related to one another as directed toward one another. Everything they do will be in terms of the others as relatively future to them. From the perspective of each there is a replacement of one act by another within the area; time will be the mutuality of replacements or, perhaps better, the replacements which involve the largest units for that area. Whatever occurs within the area involving smaller units, will be viewed as an abstraction. Thus if an organic being such as a man be thought of as an area, there will be replacements in him from heart to lungs, to feet, to ears, etc. The relation of hearts to lungs, let us say, is measured by a breath and is longer than the contraction of a cell or the reaction of a synapse. We will then say that though there is a genuine replacement in the case of the cell or synapse, this is true only of the small area where it is, but that in the larger area constituted by the organic body, the contraction or reaction is but an analytic part of the larger unit constituted or defined by the breath.

What is being said here is that different areas will have different temporal units of replacement, and that we can isolate inside the area a directionality, from one item to another, that is exhibited in the shape of the units of replacement characteristic of the entire area. These units of replacement will be the largest units that any of the items can provide in reference to one another. The entire area will, on this account, have no directionality of its own, unless it is made to function inside another area, where it will have the role of an abstract item somewhat as the cell or synapse had with reference to it.

It could prove to be the case that the items which help constitute an area may outlast the area, or that the area may outlast the items. If the former is the case we have a crisis, a change in situation, the end of an historic period; if the latter, we have a present within which we can find a plurality of orders constituted by the reference or affiliation of the various items to one another, and a sequence of replacements along the lines of that order. I and a tree will constitute an area where I purposively move toward it. My various steps will subdivide the order into a sequence of replacements. The tree and I will continue to be as constitutive elements in the area. If we do not constitute it then the order is changed for us, or another area with other items is substituted for the area which contains the tree and me. Inside each of us there will be a series of replacements, for we will be areas for our subdivisions. The subdivisions in us can of course be affiliated, not only with one another, but with items much more distant, to constitute the single area of nature. But since the affiliations require different time schemes from that which the items have as inside some restricted area, we are back with the problem of having to say that the widest affiliation of items in a kind of flat space, or that nature is a derivative from, an abstraction from a more intensified space.

If the most intensified space is the most real space, will we not have to say that it is history (perhaps even religious history as encompassing both God and man) which exhibits the most basic time, and whose units, replacements, and order have the others within it as abstractions? Are we not then back again with the problem of having preferred the directionality of an inclusive whole, and thereby have defined the replacements of smaller areas as somehow derivative, at least so far as they are interrelated in a common world?

Why interrelate them? Why not begin with religious history as the history of a people, such as the Jews, or the history of a church with its signal events? This will be a history which is like that of common sense in that it will have as content secular objects and events, but affiliated with one another not merely secularly, but in terms of what the religion requires them to be with respect to one another, or perhaps with respect to what the secular world is to do with what is outside it. But we can say, alternatively, that the religion demands a unification of mankind, and the use of the material in the world in a preserving or enhancing spirit. We would then have an area of actual men and things affiliated and thereby constituting a plurality of orders, within which those men will act on one another and on the things in a time where units replace one another.

When the various items affiliated in the religion are abstracted from the particular affiliations which the religion provides, they will have a secular role. The secular role could occur at the same time as the religious in somewhat the way in which the cells of our bodies interact when and as we are interplaying with fellowman. Each of the secular items has an additional meaning as part of the religious situation, and as such belongs in a different area from that defined secularly, without thereby losing its position in the secular. Just as a cell has a neighbor but may in fact be more vigorously interplaying with some other at a distance, through the agency of the organic body, so the secular events may have religious affiliations which go around the purely secular ones that are also there, and in fact which are given a new meaning by the religious. Everything in the secular will be in the religious, but reassessed; and there will be close connections in the religious which are only abstractly connected in the flat space of the secular.

A kairotic moment on this view will be any secular occurrence which has been given a signal role by the religious whole, but in the time of the secular. The secular will not dictate the occurrence of that moment; it will merely emphasize the religiously affiliated items, the fact that this or that secular item is so related to this or that secular item in a nonsecular area or by nonsecular means, i.e., by agencies which are not reducible to the laws and replacements of merely secular items.

No reference has here been made to the operation of the Ideal nor to the operation of God. Will the first not be needed in order to get a single time scheme, and will not the second be needed in order to have a retention of what was replaced in the secular order? And will we not be minimizing secular history, the common-sense world, politics, society, and nature?

If we use the largest units as the measure of all the others, there would seem to be no need for the Ideal; and we take the area to be persistent, we will not need to have the replaced items kept in being, for we will have them in the ordering which the area permits. Yet the ordering has no items until they occur. It would seem that though the ordering is defined by the kind of affiliations items have with one another before they act on one another, the items nevertheless have to come to be and thus must be part of a replacing time before they can constitute an order, an area. And the secular historic world seems to be as real as the religious, and the order of nature as real as either, not to speak of society and state.

We could take the more inclusive order to be a prescriptive one, a norm in terms of which the secular can be judged. But we would then make it unreal unless we oriented the religious order in the being of God, where it could be said to have its own reality. If we said this, then the kairotic moment would be that moment when the prescription was fulfilled by virtue of something that was in fact done in the secular. The secular would not have produced the moment; instead, the moment was ready in the wings as it were, and the secular acted in such a way as to fulfill the conditions which were laid down for it. If and when men love one another, for example, it might be said they will then have God incarnate in the world, not because their love will compel this, or because God awaits this, but solely because they are now normatively defined to be in a religious relation to one another constituted by love, and that they in fact do not act in the light of this, and are as yet sinners. When they do act in consonance with the religious demands they will so far make themselves beings in whom God is present. If we take this alternative, what is nonnormative—the secular historic, the societal, or the natural?

Since secular history is not all it ought to be, it is hard to deal with it as normative. Yet if we do not, do we not have the same problem of reconciling it with nature that we had in reconciling religious history with it? We could make it normative by taking the position of the Ideal, and affirm that this, like God in a kairotic moment, is in fact realized in the area of man and nature. Men would be affiliated with one another as items in a civilization; they would be ordered with respect to a possible peace and prosperity, or better, with respect to one another as needing one another in a harmony. This order would be realized at every moment in the shape of historic occurrences which affiliated the men, not necessarily in the ideal form of satisfying their mutual needs, but in the light of the fact that the ideal form defined the order which was now being sequentially produced. The men would then have mutually defined an ideal order which the secular history would have as its norm, and the history would fall short of that norm in somewhat the way it falls short of religious history most of the time. But the history, whether falling short or not of the ideal form of order which men are defined to have so that history be possible, would itself introduce affiliations in the realm of man and nature that they otherwise would not have.

On such an account history occurs only because men are affiliated with one another in ways which no society, state, or other nonhistoric totality could provide. The actions of those affiliated men constitute history. Inside that history one will be able to mark out subareas where the men are affiliated in other ways. The history, unlike religious history, may never measure up to the ideal order which it presupposed, but in religious history God in fact produces the affiliations (which men ought to realize) and at kairotic moments does have these realized. But perhaps this is not different in principle from the secular case. The norm which men face as a precondition of history may be realized in history; the norm which men face as a precondition for religious history might conceivably never be realized. So then we have the following—

1] A norm will be defined by the affiliations men have with one another, and this through no other agency than need, promise, and the like.

2] There will be activities in which the men engage, and which may realize the norm, or may not. But the prescriptiveness of the norm will then mean that they are men in a history, though not as good or as excellent as they ought to be. They will blunder in secular history and be wicked in the religious.

3] The norms will be realities, defining the order within which the replacing units will occur.

4] There will be a plurality of norms; the norm for secular history is not one with the norm for religious history.

5] Since one may turn away from one ordering to participate in another, within the larger and presupposed ordering of all men, there must be actual orders produced by the presence of men in limited areas.

6] The replacement of one of the limited orders by another is what is meant by the sequence of historic occurrences. Within a given order we have only the sequential occurrence of the elements which realize the order in fact and in such and such a shape.

Perhaps it would be more cautious to define the order of a secular history as merely whatever affiliations men in fact now have, and the actual occurrences in history to be the way in which this is realized. We could then say that the cold war defines the possible war that will ensue, and that the battles of that actual war will be a sequence of occurrences within the order initially defined by the cold war, i.e., the antagonisms of the various nations. The actual history that ensues will be a product of the sequences; it will not contain the affiliations of the cold war but those more or less realized through the actual battles, etc.

The final religious history presupposes the affiliations of men not as they now are (whatever this be) but an affiliation of them as all having a desire or need to be perfected. The actual occurrences in the world will be ways of realizing this more or less. The very same battles which realize the secular historic order will be realizing the religious one as well, to produce a religious history in fact which may do less than justice to the religious order the men themselves defined. In this way of looking at the matter, religious history would not require any reference to God, for the affiliations and the occurrences would all be defined by the men in interrelationship with one another either through their needs and promise or through their actual behavior.

What I seem to have come to is the acknowledgment of a plurality of affiliations of men with one another and with things, and a sequence of occurrences appropriate to the different affiliations, and the admission that these occurrences are areas within which we can find distinctive orders, and sequences realizing them.

I am far from being satisfied that I have made much if any advance in the resolution of this problem.

Why not say that the most intensive and extended affiliations of men constitute a basic pattern which defines the possibilities of various sub-orders? These latter must occur sequentially in order for the basic pattern to be realized in the shape of an actual history, presumably having both secular and religious components. The suborders[1] in turn define suborders[2] of their own, and become realized by virtue of the sequential occurrence of their defining suborders.[1] The ultimate replacing units are the last in the hierarchy of defined suborders. Their sequential occurrence gives concreteness to the suborder above it, and this in turn does the same thing to its superior order, until we reach the stage where the all-comprehensive pattern is sequentially realized, not by the occurrence of the ultimate replacing units, but by a sequence of subordered[1] events. The soldiers' marching brings about their battle alignment, and this plus other activities brings about the battle, and the battle is followed by battles until the war is produced. But when and as this sequence is going on, the war, which is defined by the affiliations of the nations to-day, in turn prescribes what kind of battles there will be, and these in turn define the kinds of alignment and eventually the kinds of marching that are possible.

A sequence of occurrences can constitute a battle only because those occurrences take place within an order of affiliations provided by a war and defining a possible battle. These very occurrences could constitute an actual divine punishment if they also took place within an order of affiliations which define a possible divine punishment. In the latter case the possible punishment would have to be defined by a set of affiliations which was other than that characteristic of a possible war.

Affiliated items are items in a material logic. They are the p— and —q which are used in *modus ponens*. These though are the results of a synthesis. The affiliations of history, etc., are the products of the implicational relation which the various items in the world have to one another as mere units. A new item is produced sequentially when the affiliated item for the new one is synthesized with itself as a mere unit occurrence. The initial structure of implications could conceivably be given by the Ideal or by the very structure of the world, and the synthesis could be produced by the mere juncture of men with nature.

Historic time can be said to include many items, which are without historic effect, through the agency of the Ideal that turns those apparently irrelevant items into obstacles or occasions defining the length of historic time. Similarly, the realm of religious time can be made to include every item in secular historic time, even those without religious import, by defining those items to be obstacles, delays, or occasions for the direct movement from affiliated item to affiliated item. The role of the Ideal in these two cases is not to make the affiliation possible, but to make it possible for the history to include every item whatsoever, even though antecedently not defined to be relevant. Affiliations, through the help of the Ideal, are distorted, forced to allow a place for the operation of nonaffiliated items.

On the present interpretation a battle is measured in the units which sequentially bring it about—it is a multiple of some smaller units. But since as a possibility it is kept in being by the pattern of the war, it can itself function as a single present unit, after it has been sequentially brought about. As such a produced unit it has no copresent components; but as a unit which is defined by the battle it does have copresent components.

At one and the same time the battle is a produced sequential occurrence and a single abiding unit. As an abiding unit it is defined by the war; it is only a possibility. But this possibility is the very structure of the sequentially produced battle, though under limitations, subject to distortions and modifications.

The war defines the battle as capable of holding on to the sequential items which in fact produce the actual battle. As they give way to one another in the production of the actual battle the items in the temporal sequence are held on to from the vantage point of the possible battle. They are thereby enabled to remain affiliated and not merely to occur one after the other. The produced battle *is* a battle only so far as its production means that the possible battle is in fact actualized, and thus is a present despite the sequential occurrence of smaller presents which are necessary for the production of an actual battle.

There is no produced battle, but only a sequence of smaller occurrences, unless there is a possible battle kept in being by the pattern of the war. The war is realized in those occurrences only so far as those occurrences are reduced to an order of before and after. That the sequence of items is just this sequence rather than another is determined by the way in which they make a single sequence through the presence of the battle. The battle as a possibility is the affiliating of these items; when these items occur in sequence we would be lost in a surd, faced with an arbitrariness in their having just such neighbors and successors, were it not that this sequential occurrence is an occurrence of affiliated items, of items already defined to be part of a battle.

(The entire symphony determines that there will be three movements of such and such a kind; the playing of the notes in a sequence would be haphazard or mysterious were it not that the sequence is governed by the movement and that the movement is in turn a unit giving way to the next unit in accordance with the demand of the entire symphony.)

What is the actual battle? It is not the sequence of its contained items; it is not the copresence of these items; it is not the possible battle. It is the actual affiliation of the items, the items as they have actually linked themselves in time, as more than a sequence and as less than what they were defined to be by the possible battle. The actual battle is the connective link, the law-abidingness, the interconnection, the lived duration which stretches from item to item and as such keeps them together in an order. The actual battle can be said to be present in the sense of stretching from and to all the items in it and to be a sequential occurrence in that it also lets go, concentrates on, ends with particular items.

This is still not right, but I think closer to the answer than I have been before.

January 24

Since the being which is functioning as a relative future for another is (objectively viewed) nevertheless contemporary with it, and passes away with it in whatever moment both of them are, there must be a way in which the common futurity remains and they continue to hold one another as present in being for that future. Given two beings we can say that there is a common futurity to be derived from their roles as relative futures for one another. That common futurity will encompass all the activities in which each engages in the course of its effort to arrive at its relatively future other. But this means that the common futurity must have a being outside the concrete realities, and this I think will require that it be rooted in or be sustained by the Ideal. By virtue of the Ideal there is a common future for the pair of items. That common future defines the persistent area as a present; it gives it the status of an order determining the nature of the sequence which will in fact realize that order in some way or other.

The order may have suborders within it; these will constitute the sequence which realizes the order of the area. The suborders will each be brought about by the occurrence of some sequence of subordinate items. These items pass away only so far as they are viewed solely as atomic entities. Viewed in terms of a rationale which they exhibit together, they exist only so far as the rationale is being manifested. Conversely, the rationale persists outside time only so far as it is viewed as a mere futurity determining subordinate orders. Taken as that which is to be filled out, that which is realized, it is together with the sequence. The temporal world is one in which items are in a rational sequence, an intelligible sequence, a sequence governed by principles of selection.

If we carry over these reflections to the realm of nature we should say that the occurrences in this world are not altogether separable from the dominance of a final causative role on the part of the laws of nature, and that these laws are realized in some form or other by the actual occurrences.

The Peircean suggestion, which I also adopted at one point, that the laws of nature are habits in things, but restates the issue. If a habit is not a controlling determinant of the activities which are to exhibit it somehow, what kind of being has it and what kind of role does it play? If the habit is controlling it must be something like an organic form defining the area for the sequence of occurrences.

This view would not require one to make reference to final causation or to the future, since one could take the habit to be nontemporal, a geometry of an area, and then take the various occurrences to take place in sequence within it, thereby exhibiting that geometry in some form or other. What we seem driven to say then is that there must be a persistent space through which a sequential time goes, or a persistent pattern which items in time will sequentially exhibit, or a governance by the future or the Ideal of what is now occurring.

"A persistent space" sounds something like an ether, and in any case would have to be distinguished from the actual space which is now being occupied by one moment of time in such and such a way, and by another moment later in another way. The doctrine of the pattern seems to require the control of items from above, and thus to be under the control of some superpower. The government by the Ideal seems to give us causality running backwards, or a mere meaning which is to be filled out with content in a sequential way, and yet able to dictate to that content that the sequence contain such and such items and not others.

We can make some progress by being firmer with respect to the meaning of a sequence of items replacing one another in time. If all we had was such a sequence we would not have it or know it, for we would merely have presents, each one absolute, having no relation to others. There would be no time if there were only atoms of time; we would have one atom, then another atom, and then another, but we would not have three or have had three or anything else, but just one of them. To have three they must be related, and to be related something must stretch from one to the other, holding on to them all even though they be separate in time. Recourse to memory will not be sufficient, not only because we have time apart from our memory, but because the relation of memory to the items in the past is the same kind of relation which the Ideal has to the present. The various moments must be together when they are occurring and must be dictated to in advance of the completion of the sequence they constitute.

Stated formally, what we have is the situation where some sequence or occurrence or function is accounted for by the pattern or outcome, i.e., an item is a necessary condition for the pattern and the pattern is a sufficient condition for the item. But this way of putting the matter is ambiguous. The pattern is a sufficient condition for the item when and as the item occurs; the item is a necessary condition for the pattern only as that which is realized. The pattern, as dictating to the item as an occurrence, dictates only the kind of affiliation it will in fact have; it is a necessary condition for the affiliation that in fact takes place, and the affiliation is a sufficient condition for the items which it affiliates in fact.

But if the pattern is a necessary condition for the affiliation, the affiliation must be a sufficient condition for it (as C. I. Lewis long ago observed), and if the actual affiliation or rationale connecting items is a sufficient condition for those items, then those items are a necessary condition for it. We will then have the actual affiliation functioning as a sufficient condition for the items and the pattern, and the items and the pattern functioning as necessary conditions for it.

Without the pattern and the actual items, no actual affiliation; given the pattern and the actual items we will have an actual affiliation. Is this not but to say that the actual affiliation which is exhibited amongst the items as they occur is a product of a synthesis, and that the isolated items and the pattern are analytic components of it?

The present discussion is a variant of what biologists discuss under the relation of structure to function, or the relation of spatial organization or unitary present total being to the affiliated sequential activities of its parts or acts. We evidently have both, and the central question is how they are related. If we identify the structure with an area—a spatialized geometry—and the function with some affiliated activity in time, our problem reduces to the problem of the relation of space to time, and perhaps also of sequential items to time. What I have been saying in effect is that the space controls the time and the items also control the time, where time is the actual affiliated items.

Time is the juncture then of a sheer becoming, a mere replacement of unit by unit inside a structured whole or geometrized space. The persistence of the space is as necessary for it as is the vanishing of the items; the space in turn gives way to another geometrized area but the items in it will be preserved, have a place within the time. If we take time to be a primary reality we can then speak of the geometrized space and the units as isolated elements in it. The time here is the time that actually occurs; it is a time in which items have a definite affiliation, and are so far preserved within that area. Taking time to be derivative we can say that it is the product of sequential items caught within the pattern of a space. It is the latter sense which seems closest to what the present discussion is dealing with.

Starting with the brute fact that various portions of space have definite contours, we must deny that this space is caught in a moment of time. We must say instead that it makes possible the reality of time within it as a way of connecting sequential items. So far as the space is caught in a time it is part of a wider space, itself not caught in that time. We come to an end when we arrive at the totality of space, and will then have to say that time occurs inside it, but never encompasses it. We would thus reverse Kant's position, and take space to be a pre-condition for time. The spatial regions would be identifiable with bodies and the kind of formal affiliations they have with one another; the time would be like historic time in that it always connects items which have some relevance to one another.

If the space as a totality is not in time it would seem that we are driven to hold a doctrine of an eternal present as characteristic of the whole spatial world. Why not? Why not accept the reality of Existence as essentially spatial, with its time treated as a subordinated or con-tained dimension within that space? Or should we say that there is no whole of space, but only an aggregate of spatial areas, each of which will have a distinctive time? But then we would seem to lose the unity of time. Do we not need some perduring total space over which a single time traverses endlessly? But then it would seem that nothing really passes away. Time would then appear to be a way of bringing into space items which occur outside it. All this sounds odd and is perhaps unwarranted.

January 25

It is impossible to restrict the idea of time to what occurs inside an area. Every part of a whole, and the whole itself, occurs at the same time; as the parts making up the whole pass away so does that whole as so constituted. If the whole remains it must be by virtue of its being able to continue, despite the fact that it has gone through a sequence of stages in which its subordinate elements have passed away, and been replaced by others.

Let an ideal case of an organic unity of three items be considered. One can imagine that the entire unity, the contoured geometrized area, can occupy a present which has a stretch larger than those parts, by thinking of time as involving a forward and a sideway movement. Item a will give way to item a' at the same time that a' is solidified with b', which is replacing item *b* that had been solidified with *a*. The movement to *d″* from *d′* will be accompanied by another from *b′* to *c″* where *c″* is the replacement of *c′* and *c*, which were coordinate with *b′* and *d′*, and *b* and *a* respectively. And what has just been delineated with respect to *a* must hold also of *b* and *c*. Consequently, what we have at the end of a period which is as long as three units (expressing the time in which subordinate parts replace one another) are three replaced items interlocked to constitute a single present spreading sideways to encompass all the parts (*d″,b″,c″*) in one present organic whole, and relating back and being inseparable from a stage where *d′,b′,c′* are similarly interlocked, and then to a stage where *a,b,c,* are so interlocked.

The interlocking of *d″,b″,c″* involves a slab of time which cannot be understood without having the sequences *a,b′,c″, b,d′,c″, a,c′,b″, b,c′,d″, c,d′,b″,* and *c,b′,d″.* We come to *c″* from the position of *b′* and *d′,* which in turn comes from *a* and *c,* and from *b* and *c.* This means that we can, for example, go to *d′* to *c″* from *c* as well as from *b.* If so, we should add to the above the cases *a,b′,d″, a,c′,d″, b,d′,b″, b,d′,b″, c,d′,c″,* and *c,b′,c″.*

Perhaps a better focus can be obtained by restricting the situation to two parts, *a* and *b.* Then *a* will give way to *d′* and *b* to *b′* concurrently. If *a* and *b* are organically linked, the new organic unity will have *d′* and *b′* organically linked. The organic linkage will be produced by the double movement of *a* to *b′* and *b* to *d′* when and as *a* is being replaced by *d′* and *b* is being replaced by *b′.* *d′* and *b′* will thus have two antecedents each. *d′* will have the antecedents *a* and *b,* and so will *b′.* But a′ will replace *a* while being related to *b,* and *b′* will replace *b* while being related to *a.* *a* and *b* will be retained then as the agencies by which *b′* and *a′* are to be organically linked. It will be the retention of *a* and *b* in *b′* and *d′* respectively, which will allow the latter to be connected intimately. The organic unity which *d′* and *b′* constitute will have a time which is twice as long as that which is involved in the passing away and coming to be of the unit parts or acts.

Would it be possible for the organic unity to come about in less time? In more? The former would seem to be impossible in view of the fact that it depends on the replacing of unit acts or parts; the latter would seem to occur since one can have a replacement without an effective organic unification taking place all the time. Indeed to understand the nature of a mere temporal sequence in one line, i.e., not spread out over a space, we would have to envisage attempts made to have an organic unity, but which in fact fail.

To account for an integrated time, an accumulative time with the single unit a, we would have to envisage it as engaged in making a pseudo reference to a nonexistent b, and from there moving to d' at the same time that it gave way to d'. An accumulative time would thus require of an item in it that it be capable of being affiliated with others. If the others are not existent, its capacity to be affiliated will nevertheless enable it to yield an d' which will accumulate not the item itself but the affiliation. Thus if we start with a—, where the — indicates a certain kind of affiliation of which it is capable, there will be an d'—' succeeding it only because the d' will have maintained a connection with the — of a, and the —' will have maintained a connection with the a.

If this line be taken, then there need be no reference from a to b', as in the previous example with the two elements. Each of the elements a and b will be accumulated in the — they together make possible, and the d' and b' which are so connected will adopt, as permanent termini in the past, the kind of affiliations that a and b, respectively, had. But were this true, why should the kind of linkage which d' and b' have be so similar, so often, to what a and b had?

January 26

On the question of the accumulation of the past it might be better to revert to an older idea than that suggested yesterday. A structure can be said to obtain concreteness only by spreading out backward and forward. In some cases the structure will have already been spread out spatially, in which case it is a pattern for an area which functions as a unity; there is a single present for that unitary area. In other cases the structure from the start is an abstract entity and will acquire concreteness for the first time by being realized. The whole of time could be said to be a structure in the latter sense, and every segment of time can be said to be a way of delimiting that total structure, thereby giving the time an extension.

The pattern of an area, the very unified meaning of a spread-out spatial whole will, on this view, first require a detachment from the spatial content before it can function as the time of its various parts. But if made to be the time of its various parts, it will be pluralized into as many times as there are parts which are to be accumulated, each in its own line. And then what happens to the organic state of the being a moment before? It would seem that the stretching out of the time backward and forward must retain the spatial stretch which the initial structure had. The difference then between the time of an organic being and the time of a mere part or any single unit would be that the former never loses its extensionality in space; when it is stretched backward and forward it is stretched over the area which it initially had.

What happens to the parts or the acts which take place inside the organic being? What happens to the acts in which it engages with respect to others? Does the stretching backward and forward mean that there had been no time until the stretch occurred? Must the stretch be equal in a temporal extension to what it had been in a spatial; and if so, do we not here make time a kind of one-dimensional space? Into what will the stretching enter? If the previous state or acts have passed away will it not involve a creation out of nothing, a recovering of what no longer is? Will we get anything more than the meaning or abstract versions of the parts and acts, so that the time which includes them will be an unreal or derivative time, forcing us to say that history, secular or religious, is after all not real?

When physicists speak of a curved space are they not faced with all these questions: does the space persist in time; does it control the course of a moving particle by continuing to determine it at every moment, and thus in effect be a kind of structure which is stretching backward into time? Or are they trying to say only that there is a persistent behavior of beings in the course of time, and that this means that there is a persistent structuralization of the area which the beings constitute, and that as a consequence the way in which they can behave with respect to one another is determined persistently? Apparently the latter is intended. But then we ought to say that each entity has a single life line, and that the togetherness of all these life lines constitutes a single structure, within which those entities will act in relation to one another. Each entity will pass away as in its own life line and as caught within the structure at a given point. There will then be nothing which is accumulated, only a structure which is repeated. The view seems to be what Whitehead had in mind. It denies the basicality of the structured whole, and thus of any complex being, such as ourselves.

January 27

What passes away for the organic whole is its state, where "state" is understood to be the organic structure as united with the particular components which exist for a moment, either in the form of entities or acts. The state is a product of these momentary components and a structure. One state is replaced at the next moment by another state, which may or may not be similar to it. Since a being is more than a series of states, and since the states must in fact be produced somehow, it does not seem unreasonable to suppose that as the structure is imposed on the components it stretches backward and forward.

The being of a persistent substantial organic whole can be said to consist in the double reaching upward and downward to structure and component and a double stretching forward and backward to future and past. The components as separated from the organism are the unit elements in nature, subject to the cosmic structure of nature which, when imposed on those elements, stretches all the way back in time and all the way forward, i.e., indefinitely.

Who integrates the cosmic structure with the components? What does it mean to stretch backward? The forward stretching can be understood as a projection or as an anticipation. Can the backward be understood as a recovery or a memory? I think not. What the backward stretching amounts to is the definition of the present state as a state in time, and the stretching back is one which does not encompass actual entities in it (for these have passed away) but allows only that their meaning, as fully determinate items, affect the structure. Or perhaps what is the same thing, the stretching backward is a stretching backward to a previous state, not as actually integral with its components, but as having once been constituted by them, as having been made fully determinate by them.

A state, even when actually constituted of components and structure, is not something which replaces them; it is a new entity which allows components and structure to be distinct from the state. When a state stretches backward and forward it stretches only to previous and subsequent states, the one determinate, the other indeterminate. The stretch defines the nature of time as a structure which is in fact filled out by the components in a sequence of earlier and later, and by the structure as a mere abstract meaning or essence. But in what sense could time be extended if there be no components which actually sustain it, in the past and in the future? Is the extension dependent on the fact that there are other realities which sustain its terminal points? An affirmative answer would mean that Existence does not have an extension in time by itself.

We are driven back into the nature of Existence, for this too has stages. There must be a constant integration of Existence's pulverized parts with its essence, with a consequent production of an extended time. Does this unity require God to impose the essence of Existence on it?

This is what the *Modes* suggests. The time which is integral to Existence will be only the time of the pulverized parts; a genuine extended time with a true past and future would seem to require the action of God, the Being who keeps the essence and parts of Existence together.

If God constitutes the structure of extensional time by virtue of the imposition of Existence's essence on its sheer pulverized being, must God not also be said to constitute the smaller temporal stretches which constitute the substantial career of organisms? On such a view time would itself be a product of an eternity and a sheer process of replacement of units, and this product would be the result of the imposition of an essence on the parts. But why should not the essence and the parts be internally integrated? Just as an individual being might be said to be that power which holds on to structure and units to constitute a state which is related backward and forward to other states as past and future, so might Existence itself be said, while constantly subdividing, to maintain itself by constituting distinctive states which define the extension of ultimate extended time.

If the units which replace one another constitute a time of their own, must it not be one which defines an aggregate of the units to constitute one state of the universe, one moment in Existence, but in abstraction from the particular geometry provided by organisms? What relation could such a time have to the time of Existence as constituted by the essence of Existence and those very units? In the latter time there are no units except so far as they are integrated with the essence; in the former the units pass away utterly or are mere points in a cosmic whole.

Is it possible that the units which are integrated with the structure to constitute a state might themselves be squeezed, as it were, to constitute the determinateness of a past state or states and the projectivity of the future states? The units will then pass away as disconnected items but will continue to be, precisely as items which are able to be present, for as present they are made to define the determinateness of the structure in the past and the possibility of some future states.

From the standpoint of the being which is at a state and is related to other states which had been, and to still others which are to be—but which connects them over longer stretches than is possible to the constituent entities—the constituent entities have already been abstracted from in achieving the state. The state stands outside the entities which help constitute it, and as such it makes no difference to it whether the entities continue to be in existence or vanish, for from its perspective, it has obtained all it can use from those entities, accepting their unit values and their determinateness to help it particularize the structure. A previous state, as issuing from the constituents at an earlier time than its successor, is viewed as also issuing from those constituents. But viewed from the standpoint of the state which is now present, a previous state is only an analytic part of a single moment of time which encompasses that previous state and a number of others, until it ends at a relevant beginning for that present state.

The stretch from state to state is determined by the relevance of one state to another; usually there will be a number of states in between which are defined by the constituents, and are not determined by the present state to be a past for that state. All states which are determined by their constituents are analytic parts of a stretch that issues from the past and terminates in the future via a present state. The beginning and ending states of an organic being are unities which extract, from their constituents and the structure, what is necessary in order to have beings of their own. In between the beginning and ending are states which are functions of the constituents; these and their constituents are to be viewed as analytic parts of the temporal stretch of the organism. The states ought to have a similar relation to the structure which they unite with the constituents. The beginning and ending states ought to have absorbed the import of the structure without of course affecting its being; the structure will be instanced by the states just so far as it is an analytic part of the stretch between relevant beginning state and ending state, but not otherwise.

If we revert to the position of the *Modes* we would have to say that the replacing unit entities are together in a descriptive way, that there is a prescriptive togetherness in the form of the structure, and that there are two remaining ways of being together which constitute the pattern of the organism and the link between its states. These remaining modes if togetherness would be the "therefore" and the comma. The replacing units would be merged and not really distinguishable so far as they were merely together by virtue of the comma. In order for there to be a "therefore," a genuine passing to and from relevant items, there would have to be a togetherness of the items as distinct; they would have to belong together somehow in a unity which allowed them to stand apart. If they stand apart sequentially the unity must transcend the time of each and all. But without this togetherness there would be no replacement but only a merging, an indeterminate way in which the units were together, at the same time that there was a structure or implicational relation amongst them.

January 28

If items are merely replaced one after the other and there is no affiliation of them, we have something like a mere merging or a mere separation of them, without directionality and without meaningful connection. Ought we not then say that there is no replacement in fact except so far as, in addition, the units which are replaced are distinquished, affiliated, and meaningfully interrelated? And if we say this about the replacement ought we not also to say that the structure remains abstract and irrelevant unless it is captured by a plurality of items, unless it becomes integral to them as making an organic whole, and unless it serves as the guide by which one moves from one to the other? There will be a replacement and there will be a structure, but these will not be unless there is also a togetherness of them, and in fact a number of togethernesses of them.

We can say that the items and the structure are merged, and this so far as the items themselves are merged, and the structure has no, or minimal, definiteness. We can say that the items and the structure are separated, and this so far as the items themselves are separated one from the other, and so far as the structure has a prescriptive role. We can say that the items and the structure imply one another, and this so far as the items themselves imply one another and so far as the structure has distinctive terminal points in it. And finally, the items and the structure can be said to give way to one another as condition and conditioned, and this so far as the items themselves condition one another and so far as the structure has the double role of being prescriptive and descriptive.

The actual passage of time is expressed in the last case. This will be inseparable from the other cases as well. If we wish to speak of the occurrence of a passage without reference to a structured and directional time, we get the first, a kind of duration. If we want, in a Kantian fashion, to distinguish the form of time from the content to which it is supposed to apply, we get the second case. The third case has the items and the structure as analytic parts of a rational complex of them both.

It is tempting to suppose with Bergson that the merged state is the ultimate one. But atomists take the second of our cases—that of separation—to be equally ultimate. The third case is taken to be ultimate by idealists and other rationalists, amongst which perhaps ought to be included modern physicists with their world lines. The fourth case, where the items condition one another and in turn are conditioned by and condition the structure, comes close to metaphysical theories of time which take time to be the product of a dynamic behavior on the part of the items said to be in time, but not without taking account of the role that is played by the directionality of time.

Every one of these approaches to time has justification. Moreover, the *Modes* has arguments which justify the claim that nothing less than the four ways of having items with items, and structure with the items, will be satisfactory. Does this mean that time cannot be understood without orienting it at once in four distinct modes? The merged state could be said to characterize it as rooted in Existence, the separated as connecting Actualities, the implicational as oriented in the Ideal. This would seem to leave us with the view that time, as involving a conditioning of items one by the other (though they replace one another), together with a conditioning of them by, and their conditioning of an over-all structure for them, would require an orienting in God.

Does this mean that the unity of the fourth case is provided by God, that God is in fact (or some representatives of Him are in fact) the reality which or in which the conditioning occurs? Or does it mean that something like the divine power functioning as a unity is necessary in order that the items can condition one another, and condition and be conditioned by the structure?

If we take the last alternative, which seems most plausible, we are in fact attributing the power of God to the inwardness of what is happening here and now. But then we ought also to say that the Ideal to which these items are oriented is not something external or distant, but that it is ingredient in them, and that Actuality has the role of having them as separate, oppositional. We then seem to make God into the substantiality of wholes, constituted of items and structures in time. But then we would seem to make Him usurp the place that complex realities have.

I am a complex reality who has items and structure together; to say that the unity of items and structure are constituted by God is in effect to say that the time through which I live is not a time in which items and structures are conditional of one another. It is also to compromise the idea that time is a dimension of Existence.

Why ought we not to say instead that the merging state is the time characteristic of Existence, and that an actual man has a triple role to play with respect to that time—having its components separate, rationally interlocking them, and making them condition one another? The first he would achieve by virtue of his distinctiveness, the second by virtue of his mind or meaning, and the third by virtue of his internal unity.

This seems the most cautious and plausible of interpretations, for it requires an actuality merely to mimic the role of the Ideal and God; and it can be said even to mimic the role of Existence in that in the actuality there can be a merger of a few items with the structure, to constitute the lived duration of the actuality.

We are still left with the problem of interrelating the various ways in which the structure and items are connected. Are they not capable of being added to one another except as constituting the very being of an actuality? Is an actuality the togetherness of all these ways of analyzing time? Ought there not then be three other ways in which time can be analyzed? And ought not each one of these analytic parts of time be itself capable of being viewed as a togetherness of Existence with the other modes? Thus the merged form should give us Existence as having some kind of reference to the other modes. And must it not, whatever conclusions are arrived at in connection with the above, yield a reference to other kinds of time—historical and religious—as well?

January 29

When the units and the structure are merged, the units are merged one with the other. The togetherness here is represented by the dot, and the nature of the result can be said to be close to what Bergson called duration. When the units imply one another, and imply and are implied by the structure, we have a law of nature, a world line, the temporalized rationale that in fact prevails. Time itself would involve the constant replacement of unit for unit, and structure by unit, and unit by structure—a "therefore" which went from unit to unit and from unit to structure, and back again. How is the separateness of the units from one another and from the structure, expressed by a comma, to be described? They are not more abstract than the items caught in the other connections; nevertheless they could be said to be *abstracta,* items without any function.

All four connections occur together. This means that time itself, a "therefore," exists only so far as there is a duration, a world line or law-abidingness, and idle entities. If we tried to unite all these, the result would be a union having one of four forms, for each of which the four modes would be forms of togetherness. We would not have gained anything by this endeavor, for we would in fact have the four new forms of connection to unite. Time must be recognized to be only one dimension of Existence inseparable from a spatial set of *abstracta,* an essence in the form of mutual implications, and a merging duration or dynamism. The dimension we call time is, only so far as the other dimensions of Existence also are.

These four dimensions should appear again in any account which involves Existence, as history does. But now, if we have a new time involving a new type of structure and new units, do we not have to have a new type of duration, new laws, and new idle entities? What will be the relation of the new to the old?

January 30

If structure and units are independent, it should be possible to vary the one without the other. If we vary the units the structure will then serve to provide punctuation points or rhythms in what otherwise would be undifferentiated masses. (I am supposing that the units dealt with initially are of minimal magnitude, and that varying the units means increasing the magnitude.) If we vary the structure, making it more inclusive (supposing that it initially had minimal inclusiveness), the units can then be bundled together to constitute a time with somewhat extended presents.

If this tack be taken there could be a plurality of structures and a plurality of units, a plurality of mergings of these, a plurality of implications of these, and a plurality of ongoing times in which units and structures condition one another, when and as the units are in a relation of causal influence to one another. We can envisage the most inclusive structures and the largest units to have the less inclusive and smaller as subordinate parts. But if the subordinate parts are not granted autonomy to constitute times of their own, all times will be swallowed up into the most inclusive one, and it will not be true that each of us has lived from moment to moment, even when we are living through some extended present. Consequently we must say that even if there be an all-inclusive structure and units (such as the earth or the entire cosmos or societies, which should be dealt with as indivisibles) and even though we can find a place for the subordinates within these, we must also say that the subordinates have a reality of their own, and that they interlock with one another to constitute times of their own. Such times will be caught inside the larger, but will nevertheless function as distinct from it, and as having a past, present, and future, but not demarcated properly if one takes up the perspective of the including time.

What we will have then is a merging of a maximal structure and units, an implicational interplay of these, a separation of them, and a conditioning of them by one another, inside of which there will be distinct parts. A fourfold relationship of subordinate structure and units will occur inside the area defined by the superordinate set. A minimal unit will have a place in a subordinate set, and will also have a position in the larger set where it will have no distinct status, will not be differentiated sharply from other units there. (Did I not say in the history book that a unit becomes determinate not by itself alone but by the addition of a determination from the including present? Does this not contradict the above? No, for the including present provides a determination for the unit, only so far as the unit is past, but this is the unit not as included in the present.)

January 31

The full life is richer than an ethical life. But the ethical life is concerned with the Good as the total possibility facing a man. How could the full life be possible then? And if it is not possible, how could it be an objective? And if it is an objective, ought one not to realize it, and is not this "ought" ethical?

The full life is a possibility, but this possibility is the concrete reality of the Good as encompassing whatever subdivisions it may contain. The very fact that the ethical life can be subordinated to the religious or artistic or political (and of course conversely) means that within the Good there are subordinate possibilities, which have the Good as a subordinate possibility within them. The full life will then realize the Good, and this will be obligatory, but the realization of that Good, though the primary object for an ethical man, need not be the primary object for a society of men, or for an artist, etc. When, for example, an artist is concerned with the realization of beauty, the beauty as a prospect is the Good under a limitation, that of requiring a sensuous embodiment. The addition of this requirement to the Good is tantamount to specifying the Good, to taking account of some subdivision of it.

The Good has two types of subdivisions—there are the divisions which are made by actualities, and there are the divisions which involve a reference to the primacy of other modes of being, but expressed in the form of possibility and thus as contained within the Good. Since the full life does have a part devoted to the Good as a primary objective, the full life will involve the realization of the Good as such, together with the realization of the specific parts which reflect the right of other modes of Being to make the Good subordinate to themselves.

The full life demands that the total Ideal, the Ideal on the whole and in its parts, as both One and Many, is to be realized in this world, a fact which will require one to make the Good, as one (which is the object of the primary obligation), be but one of the possibles to be realized. The realization of one of the ontologically determined subdivisions of the Good will require its expansion so that it in effect has the same range as the Good itself.

If the Good is to be realized in this form, which amounts to making the parts of it (when it is realized) coordinate with it, ought not there to be somewhat similar issues in connection with the other modes of being? Ought we not to say that the subdivisions of Actuality, e.g., individual men, should be realized in God for example, as on a footing with Actuality itself? We must and we do. This is after all what is being said when it is affirmed that man is a representative of God.

But what is to be said about the subdivisions of God and of Existence? Can we put the subdivisions of God on a footing with Him, and ask that when men imitate God or sacrifice themselves to Him, they must also imitate or give themselves to God's subdivisions? Since those subdivisions are nothing but God multiplied, there is no harm in this suggestion. Indeed it provides a ground for man's particular religiously oriented duties.

Can we ask that man not only take account of Existence as such—its space, time, and dynamism in art, for example—but that subdivisions of these be put on a footing with Existence's dimensions? Is this not to say that we must not only represent the whole of space or time or energy in art, but that there must be specific delimited versions of these, particular moments, places, or energy transfers, that must also be expressed, and with the same degree of objectivity, and the same cosmic, significant relevance to man? Or is it that there is a realization of Existence as a single whole (with all three dimensions) which must be acknowledged, and then a realization of the different dimensions, each of which epitomizes the whole of Existence? The latter would seem to be the concern of art; and the concern with the whole of Existence would seem to be the concern of history.

If the latter clue be followed, one might expect that there is one concern for a mode which has to do with its bearing on individual man, and another which relates to him as a being in public or together with others. Were this the case the concern for the Good might be said to be ethical and private, and the religious would be part of the full life only as that which was the objective of a number of beings. But this answer is much too easy, for there are competing private lives which take one another to be subordinates of themselves.

Suppose we were to turn the matter around and say that the ethical, despite its requirement of intent, must pay off in practice and is therefore, like history, properly related to the whole of the Ideal? We would then have to say that there is a kind of public religion which is devoted to the being of God as a whole, and a private religion which is occupied with some subdivision that epitomizes Him. Also, that there is a kind of public concern with Actuality as such, in the shape of a shared knowledge, and a concern for particular actualities in the shape of private interplays of actualities with actualities. Yet the latter would seem to be public. It is evident that the problem of the full life raises issues which have not been faced by me before.

The full life ought to be the climax of a life in which men struggle with nature and other actualities in an economics, with the Ideal in education, with God in service and devotion. But how does one determine just which enterprises are involved, and why must one of these cases involve two modes, and the others only one?

It surely is an omission in the system I have presented that there is no detailed study of economics, engineering, the mastery of the world, and the conversion of it into the valuable for man. Are these all perhaps in a subdivision of craftsmanship? Shall we say that there is a problem of craftsmanship which encompasses economics, engineering, education, service, and that the outcome of these is the grounding of the full life, which then proceeds to occupy itself with the realization of the various modes as one and many in such a way that something excellent and revelatory is made, and not merely something useful? Is there a usefulness for the whole of some mode, and for the different ontologically determined parts?

When a subordinate possibility is realized men are not directed toward it, but toward the mode of being which that possibility now expresses as a subordinate item inside the realm of possibility. And in being directed toward another mode of being men are involved in attitudes unlike those which they have when occupied with the realization of the Good as such. In their religious activities for example they turn toward God in an attitude of devotion, and when they do this they incidentally realize the subordinate possibility in the Good, a subordinate possibility which in fact contains the Good itself as a submerged prospect. All occupation with the subordinate parts of a given mode involve a reference to the mode itself and a distinctive attitude on our part. As we realize the relationship which we seek to establish with the mode, we incidentally concentrate on the various subdivisions of the other modes in which the given mode is a submerged component.

February 3

The background is not known but rather disclosed, revealed. And this is how we come to get our first glimmering of God and other ultimate modes of Being. It is wrong then to start an inquiry into them as though they were objects in the foreground. It is a reflection of this mistake to speak of God as a subject, for the subject is here thought of as that which avoids the limitations that characterize an object. But God and the other modes of being are not initially faced as either objects or subjects. When we come to concentrate on them as in-themselves, and thus as beings who can be encountered, known neutrally in a speculative system, or treated as transcendentals which have an existential import of their own (and never as entities in which predicates or qualities inhere), we come to recognize them as substances, with the power to affect one another and to possess one another in some form within themselves.

An object, to be sure, is close to what has traditionally been thought of as a substance. If this association be insisted on, it would be better then to speak of the various modes of being as so many areas, domains, fields, and in this way bring out their presuppositional nature for the various particulars within them.

There has been a growing awareness of the limitation of speaking of God as an object, though there is no doubt but that the inappropriateness was known to mystics, to negative theologians, to strong transcendentalists. It could be said that the only ones who had run the risk of taking God to be an object were those who insisted on picturing Him, who treated Him as somehow constituting a single world with men (even when this world was thought to be broken in parts by the theory of analogy), or who looked at Him as some variant of the Aristotelian unmoved mover (who by virtue of being a mover is a cosmological reality over against, but yet part of the same kind of world as objects are).

God as a subject is God identified with something like our individual selves, as a being sunk in privacy, yet enjoying, knowing, existentially involved with us. But God is also over against us; He can be thought about; He does interplay with man.

There is a subject side to God and there is an object side to God, but these are only facets, and do not tell us what God is as a single being. Viewed as a domain or field, He can be said to be an object over against other domains or fields, or their representatives. As a domain though He is at once something in-Himself and something over against other domains and at the same time provides a ground, a way of ordering whatever is within Him. And since every being, even those resident in other domains, can be preserved by Him, in His own way, as a reassessed combination of various values, God can have the role of ground for the men who worship Him. For them He is something like a subject, but it is a subject into which one can enter, in which one can be a part, and not one with whom a man discourses, not one with whom a man has a "dialogue."

February 5

Since whatever happens must first be possible, and since the ethical life, which involves a concern with the most inclusive possible, is only one of many possible kinds of lives, we are faced with the question as to just what status the possible full life has. ("Full life" here means one in which the ethical dimension not only plays a dominant role, subordinating the other types of stress, but also a subordinate role as dominant inside the others.) A possible answer could be that the full life is a subordinate specific prospect inside the possible. It will be made up of a number of subordinate prospects in each of which there is a different discipline or value that is dominant, and in which the ethical dimension is given a distinctive subordinate role. The full life will consist in the realization of this complex subordinate prospect, with the realization of the all-inclusive Good (as having the prospect) together with the prospect of each of the disciplines, as having a subordination to the Good.

The other modes make primary demands on us, and a full life will involve the satisfaction of those demands. Corresponding to the ethical obligation to have a full life (and thus to satisfy the Good as dominant with the other forms subordinate, and the complex possibility made up of those other forms in a superior position, with ethics subordinate) is a need to adjust to a full life allowed by Existence, to be committed to the full life which is lived sympathetically in relation to God, and to cognize it as an individual in a world of actualities. The individual in short must have a fourfold attitude toward the various modes, an attitude which has a component of obligation, cognition, sympathy, and adjustment, answering to the modes of Ideality, Actuality, God, and Existence. This is the attitude he should assume while spending his energies in the realization of only one of the constituent lives. The attitude enables him to benefit from the achievements of others, engaged in the pursuit of other objectives on a footing with his own.

Must there not be a possibility for the attitude? If so, are we not back again, putting everything inside the Ideal? Or at least referring everything to the Ideal? I think not. The very acceptance of the subordinate prospect in the Good requires an attitude toward the mode of being which is occupying the superior role in the prospect. We adopt the subordinate prospect only when and as we take up a proper attitude toward the being.

Ought there not to be analogous subdivisions inside the other modes, matching those which are inside the Good? It would seem so. This would mean that when and as we face the prospective Good we face it in the other modes as well, having the role there of a superior factor within which the containing mode is a subordinate element. As we face any one basic objective, let us say the Ideal Good, we must then face it in three other ways inside the other modes, and at the same time face the other modes as subordinated to the Good. We would not, except so far as we were concerned with the full life, have to consider the subordinated modes in the Ideal as themselves having the Good within them in a muted form.

February 11

Man as the being who is a representative actuality, must also have representative functions with respect to the other modes, for these are not only effective in Actuality but are interrelated with it. As a representative of God he is one who has an assessment of himself and thereby an assessment of all else; as a representative of the Ideal he has a sense of duty, and in the light of this is related to all other beings as one responsible for enhancing and perserving their values; as a representative of Existence he has a responsiveness, a readiness to adjust himself to the nature and resistances of an extended Existence; and as an actuality he is responsible for grasping what others are in their "truth," and for expressing this in his assertions and claims of knowledge. A man has all of these intertwined.

When a man subjects himself to a life in which some one basic discipline is pursued—religion, ethics, politics, art, history, technology, inquiry, philosophy, etc.—he is able to adopt the values which others obtain by pursuing other enterprises than the one to which he has devoted himself, because he has already prepared himself in his representative capacity to accept those values.

The good life in the sense of the all-inclusive life will involve the internal division and reorganization of a man, so that the multiple representative roles that he has initially in an intertwined form will each have its own value and place without being reduced to the position of one of the expressions of man. Thus the representativeness of man with respect to God, which takes the form of an assessment of oneself, is not religion, but a religious attitude. This attitude may subtend a life of religion or some other form of life. If the attitude subtends the religious life we say that the man is an authentic or completely devoted religious man; if the attitude subtends some other kind of life we must say that he has a religious spirit. And similar things ought to be said with respect to the other attitudes and lives. If a man engages in a religious life but with the attitude appropriate to ethics, say, or politics, etc., we will have to term him a practitioner in religion, one who pursues the values of religion and may even achieve them so far as this can be done through any series of activities, but whose spirit is moral or communal.

The ideal case has the individual with all four attitudes pursuing some one particular line and accepting the others. He would then be one who looked out at the world in terms of a set of values, an obligation, an openness to experience, and a sanity or judiciousness. At some moments one of these may be more to the fore than others then are, but all are needed if a man is to be complete.

The full life then can be achieved in attitude, though it cannot be achieved by actually living through the various possible lives. The attitude would of course be achieved in part through decision, in part through the way one acted, in part through the kind of ideal goals one had envisaged, and in part through the way in which one interplayed with other beings—which is to say, in part through the effort to engage in something like a divine kind of act, an existential one, an ideal one, and one answering to the fact that a man was an actuality amongst other actualities.

The Bhagavad-Gita says that the private and the public, or better, the contemplative and the active lives are on a footing. If the comparison is one between, say, ethical intentions and political activities, etc., the point could be accepted. But if it is thought that the contemplative answers to what has now been termed an attitude, and if the active answers to what is termed a particular form of life, the two cannot be put on a footing. The attitude can be completed in the sense that an individual can have all four types well-developed and integrated, but each of the particular lives must be lived to the full, and as such requires a denial of the opportunity to follow up the other lives, except incidentally. To be sure, no one gets the attitude fully developed, but this is not due to the fact that one has to spend so much time in developing one of its components, but rather to the fact that a whole career is needed before the individual is able to expand himself sufficiently to be able to express himself in a full and steady, fourfold attitude.

February 15

The past has at least four distinct meanings. It is something abstract; it is rejected by the present; it is integrated with the present; and it is effective with respect to the present. The different meanings answer to the past as it is in a scientific time, a commonsensical time or the time of actualities, a religious time or the time dealt with from the perspective of God, and a "natural" time or the time which is involved in the course of nature. When then it is said that something in the present becomes past, it is important to note just what it is that becomes past. It is not the concrete substantial object which becomes abstractly past; such an object becomes past only as the unification of all these four types of past.

The past of secular history, if it be understood as a past in opposition to nature's or man's, is a past which is abstract, and thus known to the historian. It requires substantialization through the help of God. God is not needed to give substantialization to the past which is the past of the real substantial object, but only to the past which is abstract (and which may also be rejected by the present and even be effective with respect to it).

The concrete object passes away in a past in which all four meanings or dimensions are to be found. When we try to integrate these four meanings we find ourselves unable to do so, so far as we try to keep each unaffected by the others. The past concrete object is on a footing with the present in the sense that it too has all four modi of time in it. It too is at once formal, eventful, unified, and valuable.

Religious history is concerned with a past which is integrated with the present, or better, which has past and future integrated with the present, constituting and defining it. The supposed unextended now is nothing more than the now of religious time. "Natural" history is concerned with a past which is abstract, and thus intelligible, and refers us to a future which is equally abstract. The present of such a history extends into both the future and the past, for it is also abstract.

Secular history is one in which the past is effective in the present. That its past is also abstract is a derivative or subordinate fact about it, having to do with the need for the past to be. But the major meaning for secular history is that the past is now operative, is now vital. The present for such a secular history is eventful, an actual ongoing here and now with a future having some control.

The history of actualities, which I sometimes confuse with secular history, is one in which past and present are in oppositional relation to one another, but together face the projected possible that is other than either and both. The present here is bounded over against the past and the future; it is atomic, self-maintaining, a rigidified or spatialized unit.

Common-sense time, since it is the muddled amalgamation or coincidence of all these times, has a past which is also such a coincidence—and a future as well. The real object, which is the common-sense object purged of its conventional accretions and intellectually understood by separating out the components in common sense, dealing with them severally and integrating them to provide a concept answering to the purged real object, cannot be said to be in the abstract past (which is numerically remote), in the effective past (which is ontologically deep), in the rejected past (which is actually correlative), or in the integrated past (which defines the present and possesses it). Each one of us passes away, but only in the time and into the past which is all of these together. We can no more speak of the past in terms appropriate to only one of these times than we can speak of a present reality in terms appropriate only to the strands we could abstract from it.

There is then no problem of integrating secular and religious time, or the time of secular history and the time, say, of nature, after we have acknowledged a time and a history more inclusive and real than any of these, and then sought to understand the nature of the real as that which was commonsensical, but purged of its irrelevant and societal and conventional accretions.

The fourfold history is constituted by all the modes, and not only by man and Existence. We can say it is history only so far as these two are dominant; but the others are present and equally effective. History is the togetherness of all the modes, but biased toward two. It is the cosmological togetherness of the modes, and thus is the dot, comma, implication, and therefore, all together but with a bias on the comma and the therefore. Since no togetherness is ever as substantial as the modes, history is always derivative. But since these various togethered items are present, even in the common-sense object, history is no more derivative or unreal than the common-sense world. But since the common-sense world has a nucleal reality within it, which is the fourfold togetherness purged, the real is a fourfold togetherness purged and with a stress toward the Actual and Existential. This is of course the real as in the common-sense object. It is not the real in its entirety, for this is the four distinct modes of being. It is the real actuality as in Existence, and inseparable from the other two modes.

When a common-sense occurrence passes away, the past factuality of it is more dispersed than the present concrete occurrence was. Because we readily isolate the abstract and other facets of it, we think that this is the past and that the history which deals with that past is a final or basic history. And when we become aware of the fact that the past is as complex as the present, we tend to suppose that the history with which we are concerned deals with the past in its full concreteness. Consequently we suppose, e.g., that religious history with its integrated past is dealing with the true past, and we soon come to identify this as the total past of what had been present.

There is a religious history and it is as basic as any other. It has its own units and meanings, its own present, past, and future; but these are all factors in a richer and larger history which is commonsensical as we first run across it. This becomes the knowledge of the real when we separate out the various histories and integrate them again.

February 17

I have sometimes spoken of the world of common sense as though it were a world of actualities, overlaid with arbitrary accretions. That it is so overlaid is true, but it would be more accurate to say that it is made up of actualities as involved with other modes of being. It is at once interpersonal, institutionalized, historical, and dedicated; it is at once judged, governed by purpose, affective with respect to the promise of man, and assessed as having such and such a value.

We can take the common-sense world as the ultimate reality, but then we must recognize that it does differ in content at different times and in different places, that the judgment of it is often muddled, and that its different dimensions are not always distinguished or constantly prominent. We can isolate from the common-sense world some abstract strands and take these to be real. But not only do we then lose encountered facets, but we lose the way in which actualities interplay with other modes. When e.g. we concentrate on the strand of science or value we will of course be taking some account of the rational or divine dimensions, but we will do this only as ways of characterizing and ordering the common-sense world; we will in effect be taking one facet of the common-sense world and either identifying this with the whole, or using it to order that whole. The common-sense world is more concrete than any one strand can reveal.

Instead of attending only to one strand, it is desirable either to isolate the actualities inside the common-sense world, or to try to get to the reality which is partly obscured by the conventional accretions of the common-sense world. If we take the first of these approaches we may get the actualities as overlaid with conventions, but they will be freed from the affects of the other modes. This will require one to purge the kind of judgment which one normally employs, and to try to penetrate beneath the surface of the interplay of the various objects in the common-sense world. If we take the second kind of approach we will provide a systematic account of all the modes, divide the modes into an obligated, a temporal, and a perfect domain, create a work of art, or worship as a man who is at once individual, existential, and obligated.

The second approach does not give us the real in- and of-itself, but only our version or icon of it. The version will differ from the real in so far as the version stresses one way of uniting the various strands. So far as it merely expresses what we do, it cannot give us the being of the real. But since the version has all the four strands interconnected, it has a substantiality of its own.

Philosophy, classification, art, and religion each constitutes a world of its own; each has its own rationale, integrity, rhythm, etc.; each has been created in a way by man, and each answers to the nature of the real as primarily involving an interplay of Actuality with some other mode. An adequate presentation of the real (which is the purged nature of the common-sense world) will involve some unification of all four disciplines—philosophy, classification, art, and religion. This can be accomplished in attitude, but cannot be carried out in act because of the insistence of each discipline to an absolute autonomy.

Is it permissible to speak of these four as constituting "worlds"? Would it not be more correct to speak of their public counterparts— action, institutional life, history, and the dedicated community—as constituting worlds, where the others are merely approaches or interpretations? But history, etc., are the outcomes of delimitations and abstractions from the real, where actualities interplay with three modes. But then might not one say that there is a world which is constituted by all four—action, history, etc.? That world is the real as centered primarily in Actuality.

The question is whether we can legitimately speak of the interplay of actualities with one mode as constituting a world of its own. I think so. And the corresponding privately sustained way of dealing with such a world (in knowledge, art, etc.) also is a world, since it is the product of the interplay of Actuality with one other mode, though with an emphasis on man's experience. There is no more ultimacy to a union of Actuality with some other mode, where the stress is on the other mode, than there is to a similar union when the stress is on an actuality and its way of experiencing.

There are then at least eight "worlds" constituted by Actuality interplaying with the other modes, or by actualities interplaying with one another, with a stress either on an actuality's experience or on the presence and behavior of the other modes. All eight worlds must in the end be brought together if there is to be a recovery of the real which was originally in the common-sense world, but obscured and distorted. That they *can be* brought together in principle is evident from the fact that they are already together in the common-sense world. But we do not know how to have them all distinct and then united so as to give us the real as it in fact is, freed from all contingency and arbitrariness.

Would it not be better then to start with the common-sense world and merely free it from irrelevancies? Why not ask ourselves what we introduce through language, tradition, custom, superstition, belief, etc., and then remove these so as to have as a residue the real in- and of-itself? But what way is there of getting free from these accretions except by separating out the different strands and the different worlds, and allowing each to exhibit its own rationale?

February 18

If we suppose for the sake of simplicity that whatever there be is made up of an essence and an existence, or a form and a matter, and that the common-sense world has these combined, but overlaid with traditions, expectations, projects, fears, beliefs, classifications, etc., we can see the desirability of separating out the two components and trying to have them in their purity. Having separated and purified them we might like to have them together again. There are many ways in which this could be done. One might do it conceptually, through a creation, through a submission to a higher power, or through an obligation; one might do it through action, by organization, by making history, or by belonging to a dedicated community. Each one of these ways will involve a combination of the form and the matter, but with a bias either toward the one or the other, and with some involvement of an actuality with some other beings. No one of them would give us the reality which is at the root of the common-sense object. Yet each, by virtue of the fact that it does combine the form and matter into a unity, can be said to produce a substance, to make something in a distinctive world. Such worlds and their substances will not be identical with ultimate reality for they are subject to a stress one way or the other. They are alternatives to the common-sense world and its objects. Where the latter might be said to be neutral with respect to all the different stresses, but to be obscured by conventions, the former might be said to be pure, but to be biased toward one kind of combination of form and matter rather than another. There is an irrelevancy in common-sense in the form of the intrusion of non-real elements by men, and there is an irrelevancy in these constituted unions in the form of a bias toward one component or the other.

It would seem then that we have made little gain in separating the form and the matter and then combining them, even though the result is something which avoids the adulterations introduced by men into the common-sense object. Can we hold on to this advantage which the new combinations have over the common-sense object, and avoid the bias? If we can, we will have arrived at the real as it really is.

Might we not use one of the biased forms as a supplement or guide for the others? Why not combine, for example, the art product and the historic product and thus get the union of Actuality and Existence in a form which is not biased either toward the experiential or the public? Could we use the artistic product as a way of interpreting the historic —and, of course, conversely? The second way seems better, for it allows one to make use of the first and then to take advantage of one of them as providing a way of dealing with the other. But such an answer must be supplemented by the other answers as well, for the common-sense object involves an interplay of an actuality, not only with Existence, but with other actualities and with the other modes. Consequently one must have knowledge and action supplementing and interpreting one another, ethical intent and political life supplementing and interpreting one another, and private faith and public communion supplementing and interpreting one another. Having achieved such a recovery of equilibrium with respect to Actuality in interplay with items or wholes of a given mode of being, we have the problem of bringing the results together.

The real is evidently that which allows for the being of historic, artistic, evaluative, etc., dimensions; it contains rectified action, public being, historic career, and assessed existence somehow united. Can that union be found or faced except so far as we internally live as beings who are all these things together?

February 19

When actualities interplay with other modes we get two domains. In one there is an emphasis on experience and in the other there is an emphasis on the reality of a public interplay of the actualities. These two domains offer one another contexts and conditions. As offering contexts they provide supplements; as offering conditions they provide interpretations, modifications.

If we take art and history to be the outcome of the interplay of actualities with Existence, we find that each offers a context for the other, each provides a way of interpreting the other, and each grounds a special kind of reflection. Art, as providing a context or an interpretation for history, enables one to recover the balance which is disturbed by the stress that history provides toward Existence itself; conversely, history, as providing a context or interpretation for art, recovers the balance the other way. But each of these also has its own reflective side. And thus we come to a philosophic account of art, and to history as a report or account of the historic.

Ideally, we should so mesh history and art that they both provide contexts and interpretations of one another, with the result that we recover the way in which Actuality and Existence interplay. In this interplay there is still an emphasis on Actuality. Even in history, where there is a swing toward Existence, it is an Existence as involved with Actuality. Existence itself has a much wider range, and there is therefore another pair of enterprises which have to do with the way in which Existence is adjusted to by Actuality—technology and economics—the one public, and the other private in its ultimate import. But if we wish to know what actualities are by themselves or in their own domain, though affected by the other modes, we need consider only such pairs as Art and History, Knowledge and Action, Ethics and Politics, Prayer and Community.

A monumental work of art combines art and history; the history of art combines art and history in another way. Must they themselves not be combined so that we get a history of monumental works of art? Granted this, we still have the problem of uniting such a result with the outcome of the combinations of knowledge and action, etc. Should we say that we must attend to an ethicopolitical world in which the history of monumental works of art occur? If so, let us speak of the result as a cultural history of monumental works of art. We can then try to combine this with the outcome of a union of action and knowledge. If we term this the decent or sane life, we can then perhaps produce an intelligent and useful cultural history of monumental works of art. This result must be combined with the result of the achievement of a balance between private worship and public worship. Let us term the last "religious loyalty." The combination of this with the previous result gives us an intelligent, useful, cultural history of monumental works appreciated by religiously loyal men. This should be a description of what actualities are in fact as they interplay with the other modes inside the domain of Actuality. What does not answer to the monumental, etc., will have to be treated as incidental, subordinate, conditional, derivative, etc.

What we apparently have then is an actuality experiencing and being framed by the other modes, at the same time that it is experiencing and being conditioned by other actualities. The freeing of the common-sense objects from irrelevant accretions, and the union of the resultant domains, ends then with a world of entities having a larger range and import than was evident from the confrontation of the initial objects. What is obscured by the conventional is the ultimate rationale, the effectiveness, the nobility, the historic import, and the religious dimension of the real.

February 21

One of the differences between the disciple or the amateur, and the master or the professional, is that the latter is always aware of the rights and the pull of the negative. He sees something in the claims of that which he rejects. Even when he speaks dogmatically there is something in the way he paces himself, stresses his points, advances and retreats, argues, defends himself, even sometimes sharpens the edges and insistencies that reflect the presence of other views in his mind. The disciple or amateur ignores these; instead he tends to smooth out the whole, to give it an internal unity but no outward attachment.

A great work is self-contained, whereas a poor one is not. Yet the above characterization sounds as though the master's work has external affiliations and the amateur's does not. But what is intended is that the master's work is self-contained by the very fact that it has elements which bespeak the presence of other items outside; it makes no reference to the outside except in the sense that its own structure is a consequence of the effective presence of that outside. The amateur or the disciple, precisely because he ignores what is outside, has a work which is detached, but it is also one that is not self-sufficient, not rich enough to be a world of its own. The disciple and the amateur do not have to refer to anything outside any more than the others do; their fault is only that they do not have a self-sufficient work.

When one asks the master just how he operates he rarely tells about the power of the negative. Aware that rules are hobbling he tries to avoid presenting rules. Knowing that in his creative activity he is spontaneous and inventive, he rejects any antecedent prescriptions. Nevertheless, as he produces his work he is constantly bringing in the negative, seeing what is to be said for the neglected, the rejected, the denied. His rule is in essence then the achievement of an excellence along a certain route, but over against the obstacle presented by alternative roads. In the end he does not provide a synthesis of the affirmative and the negative; but he does provide a place, within his accepted route and objective, for the value of the negative, not as it is in-itself but as it can enter into this particular chosen route or accepted kind of outcome. There must be a standard of excellence adopted which need not be articulated and perhaps cannot be articulated without being made too abstract and too limited. But it is in the end the making of something critically or, what is the same thing, with strength, by virtue of the encompassment of the values of the negative.

February 24

From many conversations with Ellen Haring I have become convinced that the Aristotelian position is stronger than I have previously allowed. It is stronger too than it has been made out to be by his followers. One must of course overcome a number of difficulties which are characteristic of Aristotle's own view of it. That view keeps too close to common-sense observation to do justice to the certain basic astronomical and physical occurrences; it does less than justice to the necessities of mathematics, the prescriptiveness of a logic, ethics and aesthetics, the intrinsic togetherness of objects in the space-time world, the intrinsic status of the so-called accidents, the homogeneity of the cosmic as requiring no reference to a different essence or set of motions for the heavenly bodies. It needs to recognize the value of an abstract logic; it should find a place for religion, give some consideration to the richness of the private nature of man and the representative character of man's knowledge and virtue. It should reject the doctrine of fixed species, and replace it by some type of evolutionary theory. One ought to go back to something like the view presented in *Reality,* where consideration was given to some of these factors. But then account must be taken of the problems which set me on the road to the four modes of being.

There is no great problem, in principle, of making the Aristotelian substance more of integral unity than Aristotle had it; we do not need his doctrine of accidents, or his theory of knowledge as restricted to essences. Indeed his own account of perception and common sense would indicate a way out. He ought to have treated the common-sense world as primarily one where effective action takes place, though within some kind of restricted conventional setting. Action treats the objects with which it deals as unified; even the secondary or tertiary qualities can have a role in action if only in the guise of directives, symptoms, indices, and the like. They are not to be sheared off to give us the truly real; they are themselves part of the real, and may at times be the very topics of the action.

More serious perhaps is the problem of prescriptions. This perhaps can be dealt with by recognizing two kinds of necessity, one of which is ingredient in the actual entities and which, when isolated from those entities, tells us what is necessary in them. The other type of necessity can be said to be derivative from the first, or to be derivative from the actual entities through some complex or indirect route. They will be contingent structures in the actual entities which, when isolated from those entities, at one and the same time have an interior necessity and a reference to the source from which the structure was derived. The necessity in the latter class of items, in other words, is inseparable from a reference to the actual entities in the world. Modal syntax would be the correlate of a semantical reference. If we attend to the necessity, we attend to something merely formal, but the formal entity would be essentially adjectival. Since it would be adjectival to some item or other, and since the nature of the formal structure is that of something which is pure and inescapable, it will have a prescriptive value for the actual entity.

An actual entity has necessary structures in it, but as a whole it is a contingent item since its necessary structures are inseparable from a "matter" which reduced them to being parts of a single contingent whole. The necessary structures resident in the actual entities, when held apart from those entities, enable us to see what the "logic" of the entities is. Such necessary structures are the topic of a science.

The derivative structures, by virtue of their purity and their reference to some object or other, face the actual entities as pure necessities which they ought to incorporate if they are to overcome the influence of the "matter" that (in the case of the ingredient necessities) had made the actual entities into contingencies.

There is a need to realize the derivative structures in order that the actual entities may avoid being merely contingent. They can then be said to strive to realize the derivative structures in order to be pure necessities. Such derivative structures can be said to be non-Euclidean mathematical structures, to be the Good of ethics, the beauty of art. Should any one of these be exemplified in actual entities, the actual entities would have a distinctiveness they did not have before; their "matter" would be subservient to the structures they then had realized. But if the world is in fact Euclidean, streaked with evil and error, etc., such a result will not come to pass. The actual entities will be judged to be bad, muddled, etc., just so far as these structures, which were indirectly derived, are faced as ideals or norms.

A question arises as to where such norms can be located. It would be incorrect to suppose with Aristotle that they are actually ingredient in actual perfected members of a particular kind of object. But there is no reason why other entities may not be carriers of such norms, without themselves being subject to them. Though it is true that the green of the grass belongs to the grass, and is no mere adventitious accident, it is also true that the green as something sensed does not belong to the grass. Similarly, the norms we confront, though they can be said to belong (through a reversal of the procedure by which they were obtained) to other objects as well as to ourselves, have the role of norms, of prescriptions, of objective directives for us so far as they are carried by those other objects—and of norms for those objects so far as they are carried by us. In the carrying we are not affected by them; we merely give them place, objectivity, the opportunity to be exterior to what is seeking to realize them.

If this program could be carried out there would be no need for the modes of Ideality and God. Both would be immanent in one sense and, through an indirect derivation, would have the role of being transcendent to whatever was concerned with them. There would of course be no single Ideal or God for everything whatsoever, since then there would be nothing which would enable these to be objective, and exterior to what might be concerned with them. This would not seem to raise any great difficulty in connection with the Ideal since this might well have primary pertinence and make a peculiar demand on different types of reality. Taking that answer as a clue one could say, perhaps, that even the God, which might be thought to be transcendent for all, would have one distinctive kind of meaning when transcendent, say for men or living beings, and another for subhuman or merely inanimate beings.

Existence would not of course on this view be a mode distinct from Actuality. What one would have is Existence as a product of the inter-locking of a plurality of actualities, each with its private side, or actualities as precipitates out of a common Existence, the precipitation allowing them to have something like a private nature. Perhaps the second view comes closer to the spirit of the Aristotelian; it does though minimize the private life of men. But a richer idea of Existence might show that the precipitated items, particularly as capable of interplaying with one another, achieve an interiority as a consequence of being enabled to stand apart from the total matrix of Existence.

The disadvantage of the second alternative is that it tends toward a materialism, no matter how much one insists on the privacy of the precipitates. The other alternative, by insisting on the actualities as prior, leans toward Existentialism, and makes all togetherness somehow derivative.

Perhaps the strongest position is that suggested in *Reality,* where the private and public are taken to be on a footing; the existential inter-connection of the various actualities will then be one with their existen-tial privacy in the sense that each will have a role of its own. The cosmic world of space-time will be not so much a derivative from actualities as it will be that which is partly constituted by them at the same time that it helps constitute them.

As suggested in the *Modes,* individual Actualities help define the particular geometry of a totality. The totality in turn helps determine such features as the incongruous counterparts—since these depend on orientations beyond themselves and the presence of them in an independently defined space and time. More sharply, what in the *Modes* has been called Actuality and Existence will be taken to be abstractions from a more basic single reality which has a plurality of independent acting beings, that are together in a public world which also, to some degree, conditions and controls their activities.

There is however a private career which an individual has; and men not only have private feelings, but engage in speculations, programs, plans, and the like. Despite their finitude they have minds which seem to encompass everything. We have here on the side of man something like the derivative necessities which can be abstracted from things. If we take the mind to be the unity of the organism operating on and controlling the particular activities of the parts of the brain and the body itself, the meaning of the highly general ideas in the mind will be that of directing the body, or of prescribing to all other bodies by means of a derivative necessity. That necessity originally had its locus inside the mind and was part of the contingent structure of the total organism.

February 25

Two difficulties might be brought against yesterday's view, which relate to positions taken with respect to the various modes of being. One could well argue that the same kind of ultimacy which has here been bestowed on actualities or Existence could be accredited to God or the Ideal. And one could well argue that just as at yesterday's end I acknowledged that the actualities are inseparable from Existence (and that in fact they, with Existence, constitute a single mode of Being in which the actualities are but subdivisions with an accentuated inside capable of some independent operation), so the actualities might be said to be inseparable from the Ideal and God. The actualities are thereby revealed to be internally richer than beings which are merely inward over against Existence, and to be externally involved in other types of activity and interest than that characteristic of beings immersed in Existence.

There is no reason why the realities with which we begin should not be thought of as involved in a plurality of directions and relations, and to be related to one another by means of Ideality and God as well as by Existence—understanding by Ideality a purely formal set of relations of affiliation, and by God a purely unified set of assessments of what has been achieved by each actuality in relation to every other actuality. The interiority of an actuality would then be the inward reality of all three sets of relations as encompassing the outward side of the actualities as they bear on one another.

If we take this approach there would be no point in speaking of the first of today's suggested alternatives, for there would be no acceptance of actualities as such, but an acceptance of what before had been treated as four modes, but now taken as interrelated—though to be sure with a focus on actualities. The first suggestion, if it meant that one should focus on some other mode instead of actualities, would be up against the difficulty that our evidence, ourselves, our vocabulary, our activities, and our privacies all show the irreducibility of activities. To acknowledge the irreducibility of the other modes would be tantamount to acknowledging a plurality of modes, whereas the acknowledgment of the ultimacy of actualities would, on the present view, require nothing more than the admission that there are relational patterns and derivative norms in terms of which those actualities are to be ordered and directed.

The outcome of this way of facing the nature of things would be to have God as immanent, the Ideal as germane, and Existence as embracing actualities. The transcendent, the exteriority, and the dynamism of these modes, as over against the role they have in relation to actualities, are derivative necessities having no ontological status of their own. They are sustained by other actualities, at least in the guise of some actuality or other, as mere bearers on which these derivative realities have no direct impingement.

I think these suggestions would not be acceptable to one who insisted initially on the reality of any of the other modes, for what he would want is the recognition that these other modes have a distinctive power and dignity. These might be relationally dealt with by actualities, but would themselves use the actualities as relations connecting part of themselves with other parts of themselves. In other words, one who insisted on the ultimate reality and irreducibility of God as a being in- and of-Himself would refuse to accept the actualities as beings which had a privacy and a public nature interconnected by God as well as by other relations. He would insist that the actualities also had a role as mere relations connecting the various distinguishable parts in God, or that they were instances or expressions of God without having any power to use Him as a relation except so far as He lent Himself—and so far as that lending presupposed a position in which He had a reality over against any and all actualities. What is now being said regarding God might be urged as well on behalf of the other modes of being.

And if it be true that the Aristotelian would be willing to accept the enriched form of Actuality here offered, in which actualities have, internally and externally, features which reflect what had been termed the modes of being of Ideality and God as well as Existence, his opponents would have good grounds for maintaining that there has been an acknowledgment of features, values, and powers which point to the reality of something other than actualities. He would say for example that the need for humility, the reality of hope, the existence of faith all point up to the fact that actualities are involved with a being from which they derive features they could not have had were the being supposed to be only a facet of actualities, and was so abstracted from them as to give it the status of a necessary reality having pertinence and even prescriptive value for those actualities. But then we come right back to the four modes of being, with each having the right to claim an ultimacy and a prescriptiveness for all the others. Even the supposed supremacy of actualities, as answering to experience, action, and the like, would be denied or at least countered by the acknowledgment of other supremacies such as rationality, extension, and assessment.

February 26

Is it possible to envisage a neutral position between an Aristotalianism and that of the *Modes?* It would have to be one in which we not only have actualities interlocked with the other three modes (no one of which has a being independent of the interlocking situation), but would have to allow for the stress on one of the modes other than Actuality, and the having of actualities and two other modes as focussed on that mode. But would this combination of stresses be itself one in which the various stresses are merged, or would they have to be distinct? To have them merged is not only to have put emphasis on their togetherness rather than on some one mode of being, but it is to have stressed one of a number of possible ways in which those different stresses could be together.

One might allow that the initial situation, apart from all interest by man in coming to know what is real, is one which is radically indeterminate in the sense that there is no warrant for supposing that it is initially a case where all the different stresses are equal in value or strength, or that they are together with one another in one way rather than another. This indeterminate situation would answer to the very inward nature of man, the way in which he himself existed at every moment. But at every moment, because of the upsurge of desire, interest, pressure, and the like there would be a kind of focussing on some one stress and on one way in which that stress was together with the other stresses. As a consequence, one man at one moment might be faced with a focussed divine fact which might have the other kinds of reality pushed away from it, and with minor emphasis; another man or the same one at another moment might face that very same fact as having the other dimensions intruding on it, altering it, giving it a setting.

The Aristotelian, in effect, is one who says that perhaps initially, hopefully eventually, but surely correctly, we begin with an emphasis on actualities with a secondary emphasis on Existence, and that we have these two merged together and set over against the other two stresses, which themselves need not have any genuine ontological reality—though Aristotle did assign such reality to his God.

If one were to take this position, there would be two sets of problems still to face. What is the nature of this initial situation; what kind of reality has it; what right have we to characterize it in this way? How could we adjudicate between the different philosophies which insist on putting an emphasis in one place only, or which insist that there is one primary way in which the various stresses can be together? Could one take the former set of questions to be epistemological initially, and suppose that the exploration of one of the alternative philosophies is subject to the criticism of ontologizing only one of the ways of making the situation determinate?

What seems promising is the idea that we do have such an initial indeterminate situation, but that it itself is only one way in which the realities could appear. The coming into focus of this situation must occur in a number of ways: there must be some one stress coming out at some moment, and that stress must be together with other stresses in some particular way. If man never faces more than one stress and one way in which this is together with other stresses on other dimensions, he will have a position something like an Aristotelianism, materialism, etc. If he is aware of the indeterminate situation as something adumbrated behind this philosophy which he has adopted, he can take his view to be a precipitate of that adumbrated realm, or view the latter as a kind of unfocussed way of having his own view. But should he see this adumbrated realm as having some ultimate reality, in which there might be stresses and ways of being together other than that which he had acknowledged, or should he be faced in fact with different stresses and ways of having stresses together, he might be driven to consider his initially chosen philosophic position as one of a number, and to acknowledge that nothing less than all of the basic positions will do justice to the meaning of what was initially there as indeterminate.

On this last way of viewing the matter, the plurality of philosophies, in each of which there is a stress on some one mode of being as interlocked with others (but without any acknowledgment of the separate or transcendent reality of those others), would be interdependent ways of expressing the nature of what is confronted as radically indeterminate, because it has not been faced as having some stress or other. Or, better perhaps, the indeterminate situation could be said to be a constructed given, that which we must come to acknowledge once we see that the diverse philosophies give us alternative ways of dealing with it. Each philosophy will focus on it, make it determinate in part, leaving the rest of it as indeterminate. As merely indeterminate in- and of-itself it would be the correlative of all of the different philosophies as belonging together. We would never confront the indeterminate in- and of-itself, but only a part of it, the part which remains when we take up one philosophy or another.

What all this seems to amount to is the substitution of a number of basic philosophic outlooks for a number of modes of being; in effect it is a shift from ontological divisions to epistemological ones. But if the different philosophies have warrant, there must be a sense in which the different realities stressed by those philosophies have an ultimacy of their own. The acknowledgment, for example, of the primacy of a stress on God (with the other modes having only an immanent role in Him) places God over against the Actuality or Existence which an Aristotelian might insist on. This seems to mean that it is of the essence of the different philosophies to deny finality to one another, and to deny the possibility of entertaining a neutral position where the different philosophies, and their different stresses and ways of having the stresses together with others, are given place.

All of these philosophies will agree in getting rid of transcendent realities. For each of them some one reality will be final, and the rest will be somehow adjectival of it, with a derivative role given to necessities which prescribe to the given reality. But the denial of the transcendence now appears to be but a way of denying ultimacy to these alternative philosophies.

February 27

The upshot of the discussions of the last few days is that one who wished to acknowledge only a single mode of Being would have to "beef it up," enrich the nature of it, so that it was something like one of the modes in the *Modes of Being*. The one Being must be seen to be affected by what I there took to be the other modes. But instead of affirming the reality of these other modes, the position would content itself with taking the affects, as evident in the given mode, as the total meaning of the other modes. It would then derive, what I have termed the other modes, as mere formalities which achieve an internal necessity by virtue of their abstractness, and which are rooted in other areas of the given mode of Being than that to which they are being applied. Yet if the given mode is made this rich, we will have warrant for assuming that what has been considered an affect in that mode is actually a basic mode, and that the mode which one initially accepted is to be treated as a delimitation or modification or an affect of this. The recognition of the rights of the "affect" to be taken as basic is tantamount to the allowance of another philosophy which starts with another mode of being.

We would seem then to have a plurality of philosophies, no one of which allowed for any transcendent being. But the totality of these philosophies is in fact a presentation of transcendent beings for each one of them. He who accepted Actuality and did not recognize a transcendent God, for example, would nevertheless be faced with a philosophy which acknowledged God as basic, and denied any transcendent reality to Actuality. But the two systems would in effect be offering two distinct modes of being. The recognition that there may be a plurality of philosophies, each grounded in an immanentistic point of view, thus yields a philosophy which acknowledges four modes of being, each of which is cherished by some one specialized philosophy. A consequence of this observation is that one need not prove the existence of other modes of Being from the base of any given one by using testimony in the shape of various affects in that given Being. The concentration on that testimony as having a reality, which cannot be reduced to the status of a mere adjective or expression of that in which it is ingredient, is in effect the entrance into another mode of being.

Experience brings us into contact with all the modes, and not merely as constituting an adumbrated penumbra to a common-sense world or to something Actual, but as present here and now, where and when the Actual and the commonsensical reality is. To get to a mode of Being other than the Actual requires only a shift in attention, and not a demonstration, or a breaking through of the veil of experience. To be sure, once one concentrates on the Actual or defines the world to be constituted only of the Actual, one would have to get to the other modes by moving away from the Actual in experience, or by inferring to those other modes on the basis of testimony discovered in the Actual.

May 4

In order to live the full life we must bring together a number of factors to constitute a dimension, and then unite that dimension with others which themselves have factors within them. Thus if we take account of the fact that we have mind, will, emotions, and the like, we must unite them to constitute an attitude. The name of that attitude varies even though the content is the same; some people speak of having a religious outlook, others of an ethical, others of a practical. But they are all one since they are nothing but ways of expressing oneself as a private being, able to be manifested through the various factors.

The attitude comes to expression through various organs and instruments, and when these are interlocked they constitute a single way of acting which carries out the attitude. We speak of these ways of acting as so many different disciplines, but all are alike in that all have the same interlocked set, though perhaps with an emphasis on one component rather than on another. A third dimension is determined by the ideal at which one aims, and here one must interrelate the various factors by making one of them a means at one time, and another at another time. Finally, the various activities in which one engages to the neglect of others must be welded with the activities in which other men engage. This is done by each man functioning as a representative of all the rest. The over-all result is that each man will live a full life so far as he, when carrying out some specialized work, so envisages it that all the various powers and virtues are exhibited by it. He then, in effect, when following one pursuit rather than another, is merely having that pursuit as a precipitate of some broader, though more amorphous or ill-defined, project.

We can think of each man as having two terminal points. One of them is in him as a mere particular or id; the other is beyond him as the common goal of all men. Through the nature of his body and eventually through his acts each man colors the tensional relation he has between these two points. Every activity in which he engages is but a precipitate and specification of the basic tension. Over the course of his life he defines his person as the specialized version of the relation between the id and the common aim. At no time is that specialized relation exhausted by any one act, but there is nothing more to the specialized relation than the totality of acts in which a man is engaged. He can be said, apart from this or the act, to be a project, a specialized way of filling out the structure of the relation connecting his id with the end.

We can deal with *modus ponens* by starting with the idea of a *p* warranting a *q*. This is ambiguous, and means at once that *p* implies *q*, and "if *p* then *q*," but fails to distinguish them. If we attend to the first of the meanings we get a purely formal system, and study the way in which elements can inherit features from other elements through the use of necessary connectives between them. If we attend to the second without the first, we have a rule or authority telling us that if we have a *p* we are warranted in putting a *q* in place of it. The first without the second gives us formalism; the second without the first is conventionalism.

Modus ponens begins with the warranted case, breaks this up into the two components, and by using one of these in the light of the other justifies the inference:

$$p \ W \ q: \begin{cases} \dfrac{p \ ) \ q}{\text{if } p \text{ then } q} \\ p \\ \therefore \ q \end{cases}$$

What is left unexplained is the meaning of *p W q* (where *W* symbolizes "warrants"). Is this a product, something aboriginal, or is it a mere schema of which the two meanings are the particularized content?

May 5

When strands are abstracted from the common-sense object we free them from involvement with one another, and at the same time dissolve the object and thereby become free of the relational situation in which that object was. When the strands are reconstituted to make a unitary substance, what we then get is not the object as it is in-itself, but the dehumanized object as in relationship to other things. As interlocked with one another the strands always involve a number of objects.

To get to the thing-in-itself one would have to start not with the common-sense object but with the aesthetic object. This is the common-sense object deprived of its relations. When we take strands from the aesthetic object and reunite them, we get the thing-in-itself as a unity which allows for dissection into those strands, and for a relational status, and eventually for the muddled common-sense object.

When we say that the thing-in-itself is a unity are we not taking the perspective of God? Not necessarily. The "unity" is but a name. Actually, since we are now knowing it, what we have done is to assume the position of Actuality, and distinguished the thing-in-itself from the de-humanized construction we obtained by uniting the strands of common-sense—a construction which, however, answers to an objective fact, the way in which the thing-in-itself is related to others apart from the context of our society.

If we had wanted to speak of the unity as having the relational object as a subordinate feature of itself we would have assumed the position of Ideality. If we had had the unity possess and re-evaluate its relational nature we would have assumed the position of God. If we had it producing the relational nature and perhaps interplaying with it we would have assumed the position of Existence. In assuming these positions we would have actually replaced the attitude or strategy of knowing with others such as sympathy, action, etc.

There is then no mere thing-in-itself as preceding what the thing is in relation, except from the position of Ideality perhaps. What we have in fact is the thing-in-itself and the thing-in-relation, in a relation of subordination and possession, and in interplay.

But it might be asked which of these ways of having unity is real? The question has in effect already been answered. Each way, since it is apprehended in a distinctive manner, is equivalent with all the others apprehended in distinctive manners. The thing-in-itself is distinct from the thing-in-relation for the understanding, and possesses itself as relational for the divine sympathy, etc. The understood distinct beings are sympathetically had together in a relation of possessor and possessed. And I who know them as distinct, know that this distinctness vanishes for sympathy, just as sympathy is aware that it appears for understanding.

Those who take only one of these approaches make two mistakes. On the one hand they suppose that the real is exactly as it is apprehended in the given approach, and they overlook the fact that the given approach actually tells us something of the result to be obtained when we adopt the other approaches. The rationalist thus supposes that the thing-in-itself and the thing-in-relation are forever and irreducibly distinct, and tries therefore to reinterpret the one in terms of the other. (For some the relational thing is illusory, and for others it is a fragment or unit which together with other units make up the thing-in-itself.) And he supposes that those who say that the two are in interplay, as an activist should, are mistaken. But the thing-in-itself and the thing-in-relation are being pulled into a different relation just beyond the possessive grasp of the intellect; they are then available to what will not deal with them in the way the intellect is dealing with them now.

Similar things are to be said if we start with some other way of dealing with the thing-in-itself and appearances in a relational setting. We cannot say that the appearances are appearances of the thing-in-itself without assuming the position of the Ideal, which takes the thing-in-itself to subordinate its relational nature.

Hartshorne, in his reversal of the traditional hierarchical relating of being and becoming, makes becoming the more concrete and inclusive. He thus takes up something like the position of activism with its stress on Existence, though it is doubtful that he would also allow becoming to interplay with being. If he does not, he would have to treat Existence as the mere inverse of the Ideal. But in fact it has a distinctive kind of power and nature, and a distinctive way of having the thing and its relational nature together—a togetherness which can be apprehended only by engaging in action, in art or in history.

May 6

If by "existence" we mean that a nature is in a context where consequences are made to flow that could not be deduced from that nature, then when we say that God necessarily exists, or that He is Existence, we are in effect saying that we cannot have an adequate idea of God without having that idea pulled away from the realm of mere ideas. It would be an idea which cannot avoid being absorbed within a larger and more vital context. The very nature of the idea of God then is creative, productive, able to *make* consequences and not only to allow them to be derived.

The contention of the ontological argument is that it is impossible to have a mere idea of God, to understand His nature without distorting it, for the understanding of His nature is the having of it apart from Existence, allowing one to draw consequences from it. The religious view that the ontological argument presupposes faith is allied to this result; what it says in effect is that the idea we have of God's nature is torn out of a richer context where it properly belongs. The religious interpretation John E. Smith holds is essential. But in fact it is but one special way of looking at the nature of God, and seeing that this nature cannot be dislocated from the reality of God without destroying it.

There is a sense in which we can speak of any derived idea as being somewhat like the idea of God. As soon as we recognize anything to be a derivative idea we recognize that it is pulled out of its context, and that if that context is Existence, it is an idea which has been deprived of a career in Existence. Unlike the idea of God which is the ground of a career in Existence, however, an ordinary derived idea is merely caught in the world of Existence. If we said this about the idea of God we would make God subordinate to, be a part of Existence. We must say this, but not only this, for it is also true that God subordinates Existence within Himself.

For the Christian the ontological argument holds without qualification even if he does not know how to carry it out. For him there was a time when God was without a world and thus existed in- and of-Himself; that means the Existence which is appropriate to Him is one which is inside Him.

Can we not say a similar thing of the ideas of ordinary objects? Is not the idea of an apple as in my mind different from the nature of the existent apple, not merely in the sense that the existent apple makes the idea have new roles, but in the sense that the total existent apple is nothing but an idea or nature both making possible derived ideas (from which implications can be drawn) and containing a residual productive element from which still other consequences follow? On this supposition the ontological argument applies to every being.

But apples do not necessarily exist, and God presumably does. That means that given an idea of an apple we do not know that it is derived from a richer nature, whereas in the case of God we do—where nature is the idea as subject to a power producing more consequences than can be logically determined. The idea of God then will be one that shows it to be derived, or that cannot be made intelligible except as part of a reality in which consequences are being produced. Unlike every other idea it will not be possible to draw consequences from the idea of God except so far as at the same time we acknowledge the production of other consequences. The idea of God is then the idea which requires one, while drawing logical consequences from it, to recognize that there are other consequences to be acknowledged at the same time. If the logical consequences be thought of as necessitated, then we can say that though the other consequences might be necessarily produced, from the vantage point of logic they are contingent. Consequently, the idea of God is one which requires that there be something like contingent consequences acknowledged along with the necessary logical ones.

August 17

The most radical alternative to the view presented in the *Modes* is one which allows for only one mode of Being. Taking advantage of the distinctions and difficulties discussed in the *Modes* one could make a plausible defense of this alternative in one of two ways: One could start with one mode of Being and take this to be self-diremptive in three ways at the same time, with itself becoming diminished to make it on a level with these others. But then we are faced with the question as to why it should engage in such self-diremption and how and when it could. We would also have four modes of Being, though we have derived them from something that is prior to them. In the end this way seems to take Togetherness as basic and makes it dissolve into four modes related in more specific forms of togetherness.

A better alternative would seem to be one in which we start with a multiplicity of actualities and have these encompassed by a single mode of being. That mode of being would be polarized and specified by virtue of the different attitudes the actualities took toward what was other than themselves. In this way we could account for the various modes as related to the actualities. We would get rid of any substantialization of them, and of course would get rid of the problem of their togetherness. We would however have to abandon consideration of the relation of the various polarities to one another. We could not, as in the *Modes,* speak of the Ideal giving direction to Existence, or having the role of providence for God, or of God providing a unity for Existence, etc., except in the sense that actualities had in fact imposed each of the polarities on the others.

One might be willing to make these sacrifices for the sake of having only actualities in relation to one another and to some single, ambiguous reality which is distinct from them and yet encompasses them. We would still have room for the prescriptiveness of ethics, the unity of God, and the contemporary relata provided by Existence. Time, space, causation would, however, have to be said to be specializations of this more basic reality. And we would not be able to handle the problem of guilt or the reality of the past in the way it was done in the *Modes.* There would be no imposition of Existence on the departed fact by God, but only an imposition by us of the polarity, God, on part of the polarity, Existence. I think it may be possible to do a good deal with this alternative, but it does now seem as if it would leave many perplexing problems unanswered.

August 20

If, as it is said in the *Modes,* actualities not only have Existence in them, but are themselves in Existence, it would seem that the Existence must itself be inside Actuality. The actualities are all in Actuality, and Existence, as the area in which the actualities are, must also be there. Is there then any need to suppose an Existence beyond the Existence within which actualities are? Why should we not say that there is a single unity within which we find actualities and Existence, each with its own power and capacity to encompass the other, to make actualities either substances related to one another, or terminal points in a single cosmic space-time-dynamic whole? And if we do this, ought we not go on and note that the Ideal need have no other meaning than that of a prescriptive future for the actualities and Existence? The Ideal and Existence as such (that is as having a unitary nature within which the actualities are) could be said to be diverse specifications of a single universal, Being. We would then perhaps have no need to make any reference to God except as another form of the unity of being—one which is constituted in its content by the actualities, as harmoniously related to the separately operating Existence and the Ideal.

This alternative way of looking at reality is not yet clearly in focus, but it does allow us to see that there may be no need to acknowledge anything but a unity above and beyond the multiple actualities and the existential field in which they are, and which they embody in part. The actualities and the field could be said to be diversifications and specifications of the universal as interplaying with the unity which might be called God. Both the universal and the unity would together constitute a final mode of being. We would have no special problem of togetherness as a result, for the various actualities would be interrelated by Existence; and there would be no problem of relating Existence to Actuality; Existence would be contained within or specify Actuality. We would of course have to show how the actualities, as having Existence in them and being in Existence, were unities, but this would not be a matter of a togetherness but of a vital union of two sides. (We would have no problem of a togetherness of God with the Ideal or the other modes because these others would be subordinate to Him; or He and they would all be specifications of the single unity within which all the actualities and all these different modes would be found.)

The individual actualities would have different relations to different kinds of specifications of the unity in which they are. God for example would be the other of men acting representatively for all actualities; the Ideal would be the prescriptive guide for men as required to act on behalf of others; Existence would be the field in which men are, just so far as they were units rather than individual and final substances in-themselves. The unity for the actualities would be indeterminate taken by itself, and would acquire determinations and have something like the role of God, etc., as in the *Modes,* but only in relation to the various actualities, particularly as mediated by men.

August 21

If we start with Existence and its act of self-division we can distinguish two forms of division, a materializing and a nonmaterializing. Each of these in turn has two forms. The materializing can be said to result in areas which are units in a public domain, entities which are contemporary and related as parts of Existence; and it can be said to result in solidifications that involve the intensifying of Existence in the shape of substantial beings, which stand apart from the rest of Existence and have the area as their limit defined from the outside.

The nonmaterializing division would be a merely formal essence of Existence, which needs the Existence as its counterpart (and in this sense functions as a kind of prescription), and a solidified form of the essence in which all the values of the divisions of Existence are united. What these divisions yield are the three other modes of Being, provided that the outcome of a division is the being of something over against that from which it was divided, and that it does not therefore vanish when held away from the other. This means that the division must be such that the having of one of the components requires that the other be there too. But can we ever be sure of this if we do not know the various divisions through an encounter?

We can also start with God and invoke a principle of iteration by which He repeats Himself in a formal guise, and thus as the Ideal; in the shape of limited units, and thus as actualities; and in the shape of an endless repetition, and thus as Existence. Once again we would have the problem of knowing that the repetitions actually had a being apart from Him, and were not merely envisaged by Him or projected by Him, and thus were without the power to mediate for Him or to act on Him.

Starting with the Ideal one makes use of a principle of articulation. There is the infinite articulation which is God, the endless articulation which is Existence, and the limited articulation which is Actuality. Each of these divides the Ideal, and as a divider is intended to stand over against the Ideal, dictating to it and even being further dictated to by it. But once again we have the question as to whether or not the articulations have a being outside the Ideal, and thus are able to oppose and interplay with it.

Finally we have actualities and the power of alienation. Each actuality achieves its own full being only by purging itself of accretions, by holding itself away from what seems to be inherent in or adjectival to it. These accretions are forms, extensions, and have the status of being othered. If one could be sure that these alienated factors had a being outside the actuality which purged itself of them, one would have a warrant for holding that they lead us to real modes of Being.

In all the above cases we are faced with the problem that one of the modes is taken as basic and the others, though derived from it, nevertheless stand over against it. If we suppose that the derivations are occurrences, we have the problem of having a state where there was once a single mode, and then there were many, or at least some derivative entities.

The foregoing derivations should be thought of as essentially analytic; the mode with which we begin should be thought of as providing us with the analytic principles or a ground in terms of which the other modes can be understood. Or we can think of the mode with which we begin as itself becoming reduced in the very act in which the other modes are enabled to be. If we take this view we would seem to start with something like being-as-such, and then derive the distinctive beings by virtue of the fact that being-as-such has this or that particular nature and principle of self-diremption. There is also the fact that if the derived entities do not have a being of their own, the compulsiveness of Existence, the prescriptiveness of the Ideal, the completion by God, and the individualizing separations in Actuality will not be preserved, just so far as these modes are derivatives. But how can we know that these modes have a being of their own except so far as we have already made some contact with them? We know for example that there are actualities (since we are actualities), and therefore know that the divisions of Existence terminate in actual units or substances. If we did not know this we would be in the same position as those who deny that any one can encounter God—i.e., we could accept the deduction only as giving a possible conclusion, but could not have it as a reality over against us and our concluding.

Should we accept any one of these deductions as legitimate, perhaps at the price of leaving open the question as to whether or not the derived items have a genuine being of their own over against the original, we will still be faced with the question as to whether or not any one of these derivations is superior to the others.

We could argue with some plausibility that we ought to start with Actuality, since we are actualities. But it seems equally clear that we are actualities in two ways, one of which would seem to require us to begin, not with Actuality, but with Existence. As areas we are to be defined by Existence; it is only as substantial that we can start with ourselves and derive the others.

Similarly, one can argue that if we start with Existence we at once find ourselves dealing with Existence in at least two ways—as interior to other entities, i.e., as having solidified forms (substantial actualities and God) and as having purely terminal forms (Ideality and areas).

If instead we start with the Ideal we find that the various articulations balance one another; the articulations provided by actualities, for example, are too coarse, and those provided by Existence are too minute. Something of the definiteness and spread of the actualities must be retained while completing the articulation—and this is what God provides.

Finally, if we start with God, the nature of God by-Himself and what He is in relation to the other modes will be derivative and dependent, or derivative and independent.

The various modes with which we might begin thus all show themselves to have at least a double face, as by-themselves and as approached from the outside, and thus as derivative from the position of some other modes.

Though a single mode will allow us to make some kind of derivation, and though it will enable us to avoid multiplying entities unnecessarily and perhaps even to side-step the problem of togetherness, each seems to have a nature which shows it to be "derivative," having other modes over against it which prescribe to it and even interplay with it, etc. There seems to be nothing which would warrant our supposing that it, and not the others, was primary. He who would "deduce" other modes must overcome these difficulties, plus the difficulty of having an outcome which must be encountered before he can be sure that his deduction is satisfactory.

Such items as our language, the self, the collective "we," the body of science, the values of a society, experience, the present, God, Existence, Ideality, and Actuality have in common the fact that they are in some sense accepted or are in fact finalities, and as such serve to measure, assess, place, establish, ground, justify a set of particularities which are distinct from them in status and in value. It is eminently desirable to find some method by which we can ascertain just what finalities there are, and how they are interrelated.

It is conceivable that what is final in one sense may be supported by some more basic finality, or a finality in some other sense. The finality need not have a different content than that for which it is a finality— everything we know might be a kind of ego-stuff, or conversely, ourselves as final may be only mental beings, allowing a place for particular mental items. But the finality always has a different role to play in the different places. It is not something observed in the sense in which the items it grounds are observed or observable; it is not tested or justified in the same way they are.

I suppose it is something like a finality that Aristotle had in mind when he said that science rested on absolute truths grounding all others. I suppose it is also what Thomas Aquinas had in mind when he took God to be the *prius* of all being and thought. But it is to be noted that a first premiss and God are not realities in the same sense in which the items they ground, justify and test, are realities. Nor will one be able to get to them by methods of extrapolation or analogy, since these keep one inside the same kind of pattern as that with which one starts.

The proper procedure is either to recognize the need for a given content to have distinct roles, or to see how the very acknowledgment of data involves a use of something not a datum. It is the awareness of the last that justifies the a priori philosophies which are affiliated with Kant's. It makes us see too that such expressions as "it is true that," "it is the case that," "I know that," "we hold that," and the like can be termed "a priori," or conversely that the "a priori" is but a frame, a condition, a locus in which the a posteriori is to be placed in order to have an assessed being as that which is, or is accepted. We ought to add to the above set, the rules of inference, the principles of induction, the transcendentals such as beauty, unity, and, perhaps, value.

The relation of the finality to the items it includes might be said to be that of explanation, encompassment, grounding for, justification for, application, control; the relation of the items to the finality may be said to be that of reference, grounding by, justification by, support by. Application and reference, to use these to epitomize them all, are activities which can be said to have limiting cases in instantiation and generalization, where the instantiation and generalization yield something like hard particulars and Platonic forms.

The problem of the relation of mind and body can be viewed in the light of the distinction between ground and item, and their related applications and references. The mind, as that which is more comprehensive in its range, is possessed of generality, and is the source of consciousness; it would have a role similar to a ground, whereas the body would be like an instance. On such a view the mind would be a justification which provided a context for the body, when the body was treated as intelligible; conversely, the body would be viewed as an outcome of an application of the mind on an organic matter.

It is to be noted that when we speak of an application we are forced to view that on which the application is made as somehow without the character which the application will provide. This does not mean that it is amorphous but only that it lacks the particular feature which the justifying ground provides for it—that it is experienceable, true, human, and the like. Consequently, when we say that the body instantiates the mind, what is meant is not that the body is a case of the mind, but that the body becomes a case of a mind-controlled entity—or to avoid the supposition that there was once a body without a mind which then was mind-determined—that the human body must be understood to be grounded in the human mind and to instance that human mind; that the human mind is applied on, expressed through the body as one particular instance of itself.

We never get over the dualism of having two roles, but we need not suppose a dualism of distinct contents. Consequently, though we must recognize that the mind functions in a way that the body does not, we need not suppose that there is a mind stuff and a body stuff and that the one is made to control the other. The "stuff" of both mind and body can be the same, but there would be a difference in their functioning. A mind uses the very same stuff, in the shape of a dominating or grounding principle, that a body uses as an item for that principle.

August 22

Anything whatsoever can be taken to be a norm for anything whatsoever, for this means only that each has a basic reality or finality, and that this offers a measure for others. If we make use of Ryle's railroad-ticket example, we can say that a ticket defines or measures what is a legitimate ride; but it is also the case that the ride measures what is a useful ticket. Those tickets which are issued in the ordinary way may still not be used because the individual with the ticket is taken to be too young, too drunk, etc. And those rides which are allowed may be allowed because the rider has forged tickets, or the conductor is careless and the like. If one were to ask the railroad how many riders it had, it could not rightly answer that question by referring to the tickets sold or even to the tickets collected; nor can it answer it by noting how many seats were filled. What it usually does is to give us two sets of figures—how many tickets were sold and how many were used, where "used" is measured by the number collected, though it might be better measured by an actual counting of occupants, as is often done in buses.

Only those enterprises are taken to be perfectly legitimatized which meet all the criteria available. Since we rarely have such perfectly legitimatized cases we must be content with accepting those which meet a number of the criteria that we prefer. The preference can be justified by showing how they answer to our purposes. But the basic purpose is to have what we encounter or consider meet all the criteria. Therefore we accept those incompletely legitimatized items which appear to lead us to the situation where there will be a complete legitimatization. We accept a ticket as a more basic criterion than a ride—i.e., a ticket which authorizes a ride even for one who has been denied the ride is taken to be more legitimate than a ride which defines whatever ticket one has to be a useful ticket. In good part this preference is dictated by the numbers of cases involved in each. Were it customary to ride with any kind of a ticket, old or new, forged or bought, etc., the ride would define what tickets were useful; but as it is, the tickets define most of the rides, and the few rides which are not allowed, even though one has a ticket, are to be treated as minor qualifications of the nature of a ticket, or the scope of legality, and the like.

One can well imagine situations where the rejections from either perspective were about equal. In these situations one would have to consider which set of criteria, if continued to be used, would make it possible to use the other set eventually. Rejected cases tell us of the scope of the railroad, showing it to be something for riders or something for holders of certain tickets. Tickets in the first case will eventually be identical with a paper of such and such a sort; a rider in the second case will eventually be taken to be only one who has such and such privileges and rights as he rides. In both cases we eventually make rider and ticket match, the former changing the meaning of ticket and the latter the meaning of rider, and these changes are congenial, depending on whether we are governed by practice or by rules.

In a rule-dominated world there is more likelihood of finding something which meets the criterion of both practice and legitimacy, by changing the scope of the practice. This point has some relevance in the philosophy of science where it is often asked whether a theory is to be abandoned when the facts prove recalcitrant, or whether it is to be maintained in the face of those facts. Both practices are common. But theoretical scientists lean toward the second, whereas practical, laboratory scientists lean toward the first. But in the end what science knows must answer to all the facts, and the theory it holds must be one which is forged on the basis of those theories which had prevailed before with success.

There seem to be the following finalities all of us acknowledge:

Individual actualities, particularly men, each with his own final "I," grounding and testing whatever is felt, done, perceived, known, approved, etc.

The totality of men (and subdivisions of this totality) constituting a final "we" in terms of which sanity and maturity are defined.

Actuality as such, answering to something like Kant's experienceable realm, the field in which actualities are to be found.

Ideality which defines formal validity, the rules in terms of which we try to dictate what is acceptable.

Existence which defines the realm of practical activity to which we try to make ourselves adjust.

God who defines basic worth or importance, and in terms of which we place things and occurrences in hierarchies.

In view of the fact that individual and collective actualities offer norms for the others (no less than these offer norms for them), we cannot make what we individually accept or collectively endorse be subject to tests of logic, practice, etc., in any sense in which the reverse is not true. What we want is to have what we individually accept, say, "this is a pain" or "I remember a dream" or "this is a cat," to be supported by the "we," the Ideal, etc.

It is to be noted that though the four modes of being are final ontologically, they are not more basic, as criteria or norms, than particular actualities or collections of them, and can in fact be evaluated by the actualities or the collections. The epistemological situation is thus not on a footing with the ontological, for in the ontological situation the actualities have not the same status as the modes of being.

The epistemological situation has a definite orientation in individuals and in collections of them. It is what they accept that is initially to be taken to be a test for all else, particularly when the collective is overlaid with conventions and traditions, to constitute the outlook of a societal common sense. It is only gradually that we come to see that if we take this test we impose it on something distinct from it, and thus which has a being and a nature and therefore a legitimacy of its own.

Only gradually do we see that the rules that we might want to test by our experience make a claim to test what we experience. Such an awareness marks the change from Egyptian to Greek mathematics. The Egyptians were empirics; their rules were solidifications of particular discoveries. With the Greeks we had a reversal and an awareness of the rules as having a status of their own, enabling us to decide which particulars belong to mathematics. It is only much later that we accept what is not empirically known in the old sense, and perhaps even reject what had been accepted empirically. In the beginning, the rules which the Greeks accept allow for all the Egyptian cases, but are now seen to have a finality of their own. It is this awareness of the finality of the rules which makes for the change, not the fact that it allows for cases which the other did not, though this allowance may be one of the factors in the conversion of an empirically grounded into an ultimate testing set of rules. But it is quite possible for one to accept rules which immediately disqualify much that had been accepted, and to do this for the sake of clarity, precision, simplicity, communication, etc.

We in the West have a healthy respect for rules, for the Ideal, for the formal, and as a consequence use this as a test even of what we say about God and Existence; in the East the test seems to be more divine-like. Northrop has seen this opposition in a more philosophic light than others. In his *Meeting of East and West* he holds that each has its rights, and tries to bring them together in a correlation. But what he does not see is that if each has its rights each rightly rejects something of the other, and that if there is to be a reconciliation it will have to be in terms of an alteration in both, until whatever is accepted on one side is also accepted on the other. Not until all that the West takes to be formally respectable is tested by all that the East takes to be "intuited," and conversely, do we have a completely justified set on either side. A complete justification, in other words, requires that what is being tested should itself be such that it will extend over what tests it, thereby giving this a test in turn. Each side must be modified until the test is tested by what it tests, and comes out entirely endorsed.

The most satisfactory items are those which are at once privately enjoyed, collectively acknowledged, have an experiential role, are part of a structural scheme, and have practical import and a final worth— where each of these qualifications is itself taken to be an acceptable item which meets the test of all the others. What I privately enjoy is not only tested by its place within a rational totality, but that rational totality must itself be something which is enjoyed, where the latter enjoyment is a test of the rational totality's bearing on what is real.

As a rule we do not know just which of the partially satisfied tests is to be insisted on in order for us to reach the stage where each item tests all the others and finds them satisfactory. We must sometimes emphasize one and sometimes the other, working toward the ideal goal largely by luck and guess. The fact that in the end we have a circular outcome is exactly what we want, since nothing should be left over which is surd, unable to meet a test or give a test to others. But what should we then say of what had before been rejected as not meeting a test? Will it not always be true that some inferences are illegitimate, some rules irrelevant, some parts of Existence brute and tragic, and some of God's import beyond our reach, comprehension, or control?

What is invalid for one set of rules, or is irrelevant in one domain, becomes valid for another set of rules or (to take the second case) becomes relevant in some other domain. The madman's reasoning is reasoning which becomes intelligible and even satisfactory when put within the frame of his madness; and that madness can be related to the sanity of others in many ways. His rules can be said to be irrelevant in the realm of the rational, and his acts can be said to be invalidated by the rational rules. But his rules do exist and his acts do occur; all one need find is the proper systematic tested content and the testing principles for them, to make them be the rules and acts of a madman.

In every situation we have at least two items to note: one which is being accepted as a test, and one to which the test is to be applied. We keep up the asymmetry until we reflect on the rights of that to which the test is being applied. Men engaged in special disciplines stick with the asymmetry, and hold to one type of test as a rule. But philosophers should be alert to the claims of what is being tested, and the fact that its very existence shows it to be that which tests as well.

These observations fit in with the view that the essence of American thought is not pragmatism but pluralism, the recognition of the rights and the limits of each part of the totality, no matter what it is like. The balance of powers characteristic of the government of the United States carries out this principle in the realm of politics. The balancing is in effect a testing by each of the acts of the others. We distinguish there a formal dimension in the guise of court law, an existential dimension in the guise of the legislature, an actual dimension in the guise of the executive, and something like a divinelike dimension in the guise of the Constitution (where this is taken not to be a body of laws but guides or conditions for the determination of what is legal, legislatively respectable, and executively permitted). Those who hold that the Constitution is inviolate, like those who hold that the decisions of the legislature, the executive, or the court are inviolate, in effect deny that these can be tested and found wanting. Black seems to take this view of the Constitution, and Frankfurter of the legislature, whereas the President usually takes this view of the executive branch. Each is justified, but not in excluding the justifications by the others.

The perfect functioning of the United States will involve the preservation of the Constitution in such a way that the legislature never makes an illegal decision, the laws never are violated or ignored, and the executive always is in consonance with the others and they with him. Were the Constitution an unambiguous document there would be a difficulty here, for then it would not change in any way. But the very meaning of the Constitution changes in the course of time; and of course amendments make a difference to it as well. In any case, that legislature, for example, functions best whose positive laws match the Constitution, are supported by the court and the chief executive, at the same time that these others are redefined and redirected by the legislature. So far as the positive law matches the others, it is being tested by them, and passes the test satisfactorily; by redefining, etc., what tests it, the legislature in effect tests in turn and requires what fails its tests to be altered.

These considerations require a modification in what was advanced yesterday. The mind and the body are equally basic; each provides conditions which the other is to meet. It is not necessary that they have the same content except so far as we know one from the perspective of the other. But whether they have the same content or not, each makes demands that the other ought to fulfill. If the body does not match the mind's demands it is ill, maladjusted, alienated, distorted, and must be restructured and controlled in order to make it fit with the mind. If the mind does not match the body, the mind must be treated as confused, misleading, abstracted, in error.

But what does it mean for the body to fit with the mind, or the mind with the body? Is it not that the body, dealt with as part of a world of bodies and not as a mere isolated region, is the extended articulation of what one has in mind? Is it not that the mind, dealt with as a locus of rules and principles, arguments and categories, is the meaning of the body, the nature of its unity, the organic meaning of it as functioning apart from it? When the two match perfectly the mind has a grasp of the whole realm of body, and the body is an instance of a system of known laws. But there is more to the world than bodies. The mind, then, must have another status over against what it can have for the body; the body is caught inside the realm of Existence and is governed by the other modes as well, so that it must have a role of its own over against that which it has as answering to the mind.

The mind and body make a unity in two ways: there is the empirically oriented mind and the body as part of a spatiotemporal totality, and there is the cosmic mind and the body as related to other modes of being. These two unities require different things of their constituents. It is possible to have a cosmic mind and to deal with it as related to a spatiotemporal body; it is possible to have an empirical mind and to deal with this as related to a body which is affected by the other modes. In either case we will have a maladjustment.

The adjusted mind-body is either empirical or cosmic. What is the relation of these two? The empirical is a subdivision inside the cosmic, and is to be understood as specializing it. And this is the answer we must give with respect to all the other criteria and tests. Each has an empirical and a cosmic import: empirical because that is where we start and have our evidences, cosmic because it is inseparable from the modes of Being. We must for example test what we enjoy or feel or experience or believe or observe, etc., by what is justified in an empirically relevant logic or science. And we must see our enjoyment, etc., to be qualified by God or some other mode, and have it in relation to a pure logic or science. And of course the converse must hold as well: the empirical logic or science must be justified by what we enjoy or feel, etc., and the pure logic or science must be justified by qualified enjoyments, etc.

But it was said earlier that every item can test any other. Consequently it must also be true that the cosmic mind must test the empirical body, the empirical mind the cosmic body, and conversely. This is not now being denied; what is being observed is that the adjustment of the two, the proper matching of the one with the other, requires having in the end the two components in either an empirical or a cosmic form. Each of these unities tests the other. We need not make the empirical give way to the cosmic, as the Indian philosophers do, nor the cosmic give way to the empirical, as the commonsensical and empirical philosophers of the West do. But this is only to say in another guise that particular actualities have their own finality as surely as any mode has, and serve to test as well as to be tested by them.

But it is also true that the various modes have multiplicities in them. There ought then to be something like the relation between the multiplicities and their modes, and other modes as well, as holds between particular actualities and Actuality, and other modes. This would be the case were we to have these subdivisions over against the modes in which they are.

Whatever we say of the subdivisions of the Ideal is either said within the frame of the Ideal itself or as somehow already involved with particular actualities, or with Actuality as such. If we ever could get these subdivisions separated off, and know them as having a being of their own over against us and the modes in which they are, we would be able to use them too to test whatever else there be. And we do make such use of them at times. We recognize particular possibilities, limited regions of space and time, and specific acts of God. Consequently, though we may initially operate within the frame of the Ideal or from actualities, we are able to have the particularities of other modes over against them and us, and therefore enable them to function as tests for ourselves and for the modes. A particular possibility for example might be tested by Existence, or be the test for what we take to be God.

All this discussion leaves over the question as to how we are to designate the different kinds of validation which the different tests provide. It is for example the Ideal which tells us that something is valid, and God who determines its worth. And we leave over the question of what it means to test something, which is to say what it means to apply a norm or a standard, to evaluate and classify, to determine whether or not something is to be allowed or rejected.

Application is the reverse of abstraction; it does not mean that the content to which the standard is applied does not embody that standard in it already, but only that we cognize it via the standard, and find the standard in the object when we do so. When we find that in such an approach we do not have the standard in the object, we take the object to be that which defies the standard. We thereupon confront two alternatives: we must either alter our standard, or place the content in another context, make it subject to a different standard. The failure to measure up to one standard marks it as erroneous or defective from that perspective, but by that very token makes it a fit object for another standard which is designed to classify particular cases of defectiveness characteristic of items approached in terms of the initial standard.

The recalcitrance of an item to some standard does not mean that there is something wrong with the item or the standard, but only that one or the other (and perhaps both) is partial, limited, not identical with the realities as they are apart from us (it being assumed that the universe itself has no problems or internal discrepancies). When we find a place where things do not fit, we must account for this by the fact that we have an hypothesis of limited scope being referred to an item to which it is not appropriate. Even if the hypothesis is one which begins with a consideration of a mode of being, it has a limited scope in the sense that what we say of that mode of being may not be an accurate account of it, and will in fact be inaccurate to the extent that it fails to accommodate some item.

Might not an unaccommodated item itself be distortive, illusory, erroneous? It might. Consequently, we must add to the supposition that an hypothesis is of limited scope the supposition that an item may be an improper one, requiring dissection or analysis. But the item would have to be said to be improper in terms of some standard. This means that the item to which a reference is made may be evaluated in terms of some other standard as being defective and therefore recalcitrant to the initial standard.

We make items give way to their tests when they have failed some other test. Could something fail all tests? If so it would be incompatible with them all. It would have a being of its own and would so far offer a test of them; it would define all the tests to be inadequate. To fail all tests is thus not to be revealed as nonbeing, erroneous, evil, ugly, the other of whatever there be, but rather to evidence that what standards we are using are all inadequate.

On finding something which fails test after test, we must modify our tests until we find room for it. If we have used two tests and have found something that fails them both, we tend to criticize the item and look therefore for some way to explain it as a complication of the normal tested items. If we find it failing test after test, we do not treat it as a complication of what was previously successfully tested but, because of its recalcitrance, as that which shows the tests to be unsatisfactory. The failure to meet two tests could also be dealt with in this way, but it is not desirable to treat items, which must measure up to limited conditions, as being more important than those conditions. It is the cosmically grounded item, or better, the item which proves strong enough to defy our various tests that makes us consider those tests to be defective; whereas when we have an item which fails to measure up to a few tests, we find that its strength is not such as to make us think of it as anything more than twice defective, and capable of being understood by a complication of other factors. (None of this is altogether clear to me as yet.)

August 23

It was paradoxical to say yesterday that an item which failed all tests proved itself to be able to withstand them and thus was an unalterable test of them—and it was most likely false. One can suppose a dream of some vile deed which would fail to answer to experience, God, the Ideal, and so on; we would want to say of it that it was only a dream and an idle fancy. It would have some kind of being, but so does any item which fails only a single test, or fails two of them. An illusion measures up to conditions, if only it be the avoidance of the conditions imposed on realities; it exhibits certain traits not characteristic of a lie, a distortion, and so on.

Might it not be the case that something which was being tested vanished, that it did not prove recalcitrant in any sense but that of not being able to sustain the test? We would not then have something which would remain in being defying the test. The very application of the test would result in the annihilation of the supposed datum. But it would be true that there was a datum to which we were applying the test, and that that datum would have to have the being of something which we sought to test. It would be something felt or imagined. It could be taken to be final, thereby requiring us to say of the test (that is applied to it and which makes it vanish) that this is a destructive test, an unwanted test. A romantic might readily prefer this "vision" to anything publicly knowable or logically intelligible, which might withstand and be confirmed by a test.

We are driven then to say that anything whatsoever can be final, and that if it failed to be justified by any test, this would not mean necessarily that it was superior to all others, or that it was not. The question would still be open. Under what circumstances do we justly take the failing item to be defective and deserving of analysis, and under what circumstances do we insist that it be acknowledged to be as it is, and the tests to which it is subject taken to be inadequate, inappropriate, bad, because tested by the accepted item and found wanting? We take the first position when we insist on some test as final; we take the second when we are not sure of the finality of our test. But when is this?

When do we give up our scientific theories because they are not answered by certain facts? We sometimes do give them up, as the revolutionary movement from Ptolemy through Copernicus through Galileo through Newton to Einstein indicates. But that we also sometimes do not give them up is evident from the paradoxes that confront a contemporary state of science when, say, as in quantum phenomena, no one of the prevailing views accounts for all the facts.

Might the second position be said to give way to the first once we come to a crucial case? No. Right now we have theories which could cover all the facts were we to allow that this or that supposed set of facts is to be reanalyzed or dismissed because they are not in consonance with the theories which otherwise would seem to be satisfactory.

The answer suggested yesterday, that the final view must be such as to do justice to all the items, seems to be correct. We must alter both the tests and the tested, sometimes emphasizing one and sometimes the other, until we have an account in which each covers the others. We do not know which to change beforehand. On the whole the policy of scientists seems to be that the degree of reorganization of accepted data is an important factor. But still the slight deviations which the Einstein theory took account of and explained, were thought sufficient to make one revise a whole set of basic notions.

It is sometimes said that the revision is dominated by a desire to have simpler views, more fruitful views (in the sense of yielding more unexpected consequences, subsequently verified), or views which require the least change. The last I have just indicated will not do. Simplicity is hard to define, and seems in any case to be a relative matter. Moreover some theories which replace old ones have a complexity to them, involving the use of branches of mathematics hard to master and involving much computation and analysis. And as to the fruitful, we cannot really determine how fruitful a theory is until we have accepted it to some extent and tried it out; the few results we might obtain, when we accept it tentatively, may not be reliable enough guides as to what would happen if we carried it out all the way.

Better than any of these views is one which makes the new theory be more in consonance with the use and with the results of the use of the available instruments. This is in a way something like the "fruitful" view, differing from this, though, in that there is a well-defined realm of apparatus and even well-defined kinds of data the apparatus can provide. It is these data that help determine whether a new theory is more fruitful than another.

We judge a test, if the foregoing is a reliable guide, by seeing whether a fixed area of data is satisfactorily dealt with by it; the fixed area of data is acceptable and remains so because it has been justified by the instruments which one employs. We can eventually criticize the accuracy of the instruments, but this will itself be the result of the use of some other theory whose soundness has been determined by the way it operates on material provided by other instruments. These observations amount to saying that a practical acceptance is one that is more fundamental than a theory, and that the only way to make one give up what had been practically accepted is by means of a theory, itself practically grounded.

The better theory uses more precise instruments, and has a greater range of application, particularly to items not evident without them and from which predictions have been successfully drawn. More generally, we start, as Dewey often remarked, with a funded body of knowledge and in the light of this determine which new theories and new facts are to be accepted as unquestioned parts of the enlarged funded body of knowledge. (This matter requires much more clarification.)

If it be the case that any item can be taken as the test for others, it should be true that an evidenced pain, such as an outcry, should be a test of the reality or meaning of the "I" or the collective "we" or the reality of God, etc. Antecedently this seems implausible, but it surely is the view of "sensationalistic" philosophers. For them "it is true that . . ." would characterize the sensations and not the individual or the collective or some mode of being.

In the light of this fact we are forced to say that "it is true that" or "finality" is a moveable feature and can be accredited to anything, no matter what it may make us dismiss. But this radical relativism, though open to anyone, will come across the givenness of the data, the recalcitrance of items, and the defeat of the test by items which refuse to yield to it. Instead of saying that the finality is a moveable feature we ought to say instead that it is a constant epistemological dimension to be found in anything, and which comes to the fore when one commits oneself to a certain outlook toward whatever one confronts. But this would mean that behind any "finality" there is another, expressive of an attitude. But this is final in another, a moral sense, a sense of being willing to accommodate the facts.

Perhaps it would be better to say that every discipline takes something to be final because it is endorsed by an attitude characteristic of that discipline, but that philosophy is the enterprise which seeks that one outlook in terms of which all these finalities can be accepted—a view which requires it to revise and revise what it accepts along the way.

Sensationalism on this account would not be refuted epistemologically but only philosophically, i.e., by taking seriously the reality of the data which the sensationalistic theory could not accommodate. We take all on face value and then engage in a constructive enterprise of adjusting them one to the other with minimal change in the various items. One philosophy will differ from another in its decision as to what and where the changes must occur so that one single harmonious totality is produced. There are those philosophies which would do nothing at all with scientific theories, others which would revise them, and still others which would ignore them. The second is to be preferred.

The reason for a revision must be data as hard and as cosmic as any that a science could produce. The one thing to avoid would be the supposition that because one took seriously what science was saying and doing, and the data it presented, one had to suppose the scientist was giving us basic ontological material. The scientific account is to be taken as final, and slowly and cautiously modified in relation to all other things that are known, including the modes of being. So far as one thinks that the scientific account tells us what being truly is, one has of course warrant for supposing that an alternative speculative philosophic account of being can do this too, and perhaps better.

Regardless of what men in various disciplines do, it is desirable to determine what they ought to do when something fails a test. It would seem to be correct to say that the more items and the more kinds of items a test fails to allow, the less useful it is, the more restricted is its domain in fact. For even if the items were supposed to be under it, the fact that they do not conform to it would indicate that they make up a body of data which must be understood in another way.

A stringent test of what is a good painting would leave us with very few cases. If men persisted in painting we would then have a vast array of works which we would have to deal with in some way. It would not be enough to say that they were not excellent. What is wanted is an account of their presence; to provide it, we would more likely than not make reference to a cultural explosion, an educational campaign, the high incidence of competence among people engaged in other tasks. We would then search for a test of what would make something a painting of this nonperfect kind, and we might settle for whatever society took to be a painting, or whatever involved such and such a work, or had such and such an effect. The perfect paintings might or might not meet these criteria; in either case we would have a test of what made up a large class of paintings. If these items are bundled together with many otherwise diversely classified items, all falling short of some test which we adopt, we will find ourselves dealing with an unwieldy class of objects, all of which have been brought together only as rejects with respect to a given test.

Put another way: when some stringent test finds most items excluded, we ought to look for other tests by which those excluded items can be classified and eventually understood as forming various kinds, and as being interlocked in various ways. The defect of theoretical science is that there is so much it cannot accommodate and must declare from its perspective to be too recalcitrant, and therefore not refined enough, abstract enough, or real enough to be allowed to be a scientifically ascertained fact even of low degree. And of course one must make the same evaluation of common sense vis-à-vis science. Since these are only part of what we face as irreducible in some important sense— there is also art and history, philosophic speculation, politics, ethics, and practical technological achievements—we are forced, in order to have an adequate grasp of what is the case, to subdivide these effectively into classes which answer to tests without too many rejects.

We run the risk here of course of getting what Plato called a safe and stupid answer, by seeing to it that our test repeats in abstract form what we actually concretely encounter. His illustration is the attempt to explain why things are good by saying that they embody the form of the good. Our classifications or tests must be composed on principles which are independently forged, apart from the data to which they are to apply, though there is no reason why they should not be grounded in some of the data. When so grounded they must not only classify or evaluate, but must integrate the items if possible, by virtue of their relations, roles, affiliations, promise, performance, and so on.

One might now protest that this policy can be carried out to a bitter end by forcing one to subdivide and subdivide until we were left with only one item for each test. Two distinct items will not meet the same test in the same way, leaving something in at least one of them which is not accommodated by the test. But to this one can reply that such subdivision is not incompatible with the retention of quite broad typing, under which these subdivisions will fall. As accommodated by the broader scheme the items are abstract. When the broader scheme is unsatisfactory there are many items which cannot be brought within it, even by abstracting a facet of them.

The fact that a science cannot accommodate the concrete sensuous particularity of things does not involve any serious criticism of science; it merely points up the fact that there is more to the world than science can encompass. Serious criticism of science, in the sense of making evident that it is limited in scope and claim, comes when attention is paid to what does not fall inside its scheme at all—anything, for example, which is not spatiotemporal, and thus minds, dreams, God, ideals; and whatever is not *physically* spatiotemporal, and thus history, politics, dancing, acting, etc.

If with a few tests, and thus with a few classes of items to be tested, we can take all of what we face in some way into account, we will have the best scheme possible. It is evident that we cannot make use of only one notion, for the object to be tested by it is so far over against it, even if it have the same content and origin.

We can do with no less than four items and need make no use of more than four—though in truth the four become eight when one takes account of the four as being ones and also manys, and the eight become many more when one allows mixed forms to define such regions as history, etc.

The multiplicity of spaces and times that art, history, and science introduce makes the world seem very complex, and one longs for some single over-all principle by which all things can fit into one single scheme—this is the hope of commonsensical, sensationalistic, rationalistic, pragmatic, and positivistic philosophies, no less than of the Hegelian or the Spinozistic. There is something tempting and even awe inspiring in a view which accepts one principle and encompasses everything else, except the fact that it "appears" or is there, particularly when one dismisses the various types of appearance, and refuses to see what can be done to interrelate them, or to account for their differences, or to make provision for their being explained by means of other categories not subject to the initial test.

Among finalities, one might also include the act of application, and indeed suppose that this was defective when we find that some test reduces some item to an inferior position. Whenever we take the conflict between theory and fact to revolve about the question as to which one of these is to give way to the other, we have obviously taken for granted the fact that our application of the test is beyond reproach. But this is in effect to say that application is a finality beyond question and beyond testing. But surely one may make mistakes in application, and one can significantly ask whether there are not various types of application, and whether we could not differentiate those which were subtle, direct, or simple, from those which were obvious, devious, or complex. Once these questions are asked we see that application becomes something to test.

But may not an application be conceived as a kind of act, and thus fall under Existence or work? But if this is the case could we use it when we are making Existence a norm or are subjecting Existence to a test? If we say that it does not fall into this classification, can we say that it falls into any other, without some kind of circularity being involved? (If it falls into none we seem to have a fifth mode of being.) The answer to these questions was given in the discussion about the relation of possibility and actuality in the second chapter of the *Modes*. Application is a case of a mixture of two modes. It means therefore that we have different kinds of application, depending on what it is with which we start and on what it is to which we apply it.

If we start only with the list given yesterday, we have applications made up of various combinations of any one of them with any other. But this now raises the question whether a mixture is a finality, and thus whether it can test the antecedent finalities which it relates and out of which it is constituted. To this I think the answer must be in the affirmative, for there is nothing in a pure case that makes it necessarily superior to a mixed one in terms of a right to be maintained in the teeth of recalcitrant material. When a fails to match d' we can attribute the failure to a or to d' or to the application of a to d', or to both a and d' in different degrees. When we blame either or both of the terms, we insist on the application as final.

It is to be noted of course that the mixture of two modes is subsequent to them, and that what we are here dealing with is not the modes in their ontological reality, but as known to us or used by us or confronted by us, and thus as perhaps needing rectification so that what we know may approximate what in fact is. An application is a mixture of the modes ontologically; when we question it we question the shape it has assumed in the given situation, and thus ask how much its actual operation involves a distortion of the ideal mixture which it ontologically is.

In every situation then we seem to have the following choices: we can insist on the test we initially accept, whether this be explicitly or implicitly acknowledged; we can insist on the data as respectable regardless of what the test may reveal (so that if the test endorses it, this in effect shows that the test is so far satisfactory); we can insist on taking the data as a test and subjecting the initial test to its conditions, to end with the initial test as disqualified or as respectable (thereby revealing the data, in the role of test, to be satisfactory); we can insist on the data, and the test as respectable (even though they fail to cohere) by taking the application to be a problem, so that if the application of test to data works out properly the outcome becomes a way of endorsing the application; and we can insist on the application as a datum which we will hold to be respectable regardless of anything, thereby in effect making it a test of the test and the datum, though it is not being used as one.

August 24

An act of applying a rule or a test may bring in irrelevancies, may involve distortions, be incomplete, overelaborate and the like. This raises the question as to how the application is to be tested. If we try to test it by some other rule, we would be faced with the question of the application of that rule to the initial application, and would then be on our way, over an infinite regress. Yet we cannot say that the rule tests the application of itself, for what it tests is the datum; and we cannot say that the datum tests the application, for what it tests is the original rule. Yet if the application were not capable of being tested, any way of applying a rule would be satisfactory, which is evidently not the case.

As a beginning to the solution of this problem it is desirable to observe that each of the three factors has a different import. A rule tests data for legitimacy, reliability, respectability; data test the rule for validity, pertinence; the act of application tests the rule and the data for authenticity, for being pure cases. If we accept a mode of application, what we are in effect doing is claiming that the result which we obtain is correct, so that if there is an incompatibility between rule and data the fault must lie in either or both. This fault will not be due to the fact that the items are impure, but rather that they are authentic items which in fact do not cohere. We might try to engage in an act of application and find that we do not succeed in bringing the items together. Having accepted the act of application as basic we then affirm that one or both of the items is inauthentic, not properly to be related in this fashion, and so far defective.

We could deal with an act of application as a datum which we are going to subject to a test of an ideal act of application. We would then have the problem of relating the ideal act of application to the actual act of application. This would not yield an infinite regress, for we here are not moving to presuppositions, but are deliberately isolating an item and subjecting it to new conditions. When we are engaged in an act of application we do not examine or test it by some ideal act of application; instead we deal with it by accepting rule and data as authentic and then seeing if they are completely in accord, or if there is an obstacle in their union, or a distortion in them when combined. Our act of application is tested then by a process and a result. The process is an act of application which the rule and the data together define as that which should vanish without remainder, and which should be embodied in any acceptable act of application. This looks as if it were an ideal act of application, but it is only the togetherness of the items which are to be united by an act of application.

What we are in effect doing when we engage in an act of application, is not submitting ourselves to some ideal act or subjecting our act to a test by an ideal act, but are operating with the rule and data, which abstractly and formally are held apart, as items which should be merged. Put another way, the items initially are symmetrically related as appropriate and satisfactory.

Were the application of the rule to datum to be an instance of an ideal application as constituted by the items as apart, it would be a two-way act, involving an application of datum on rule and rule on datum, where the application has the same significance in both cases. That is, though data always test a rule, in this particular instance they would not be testing the rule in their role as data, but would assume the role of a rule for the rule as datum. The application of a rule to a datum is not then an instance of the togetherness of the rule and the datum; the application is not tested by that togetherness nor is that togetherness applied on it. That togetherness is presupposed by the application. Accepting both the items as apparently authentic, the application then proceeds to impose one on the other, with the result that one or the other or both may be found to be unsatisfactory.

The conductor is required to apply the rule of a ticket to a rider. He could conceivably be a confused conductor and look at the wrong parts of the ticket; he could conceivably treat the luggage as a rider; he could bring in his own prejudices regarding women, race, and the like. If he did these things he would be applying the ticket rule improperly. We measure his activity by seeing ticket and rider as together. If the conductor, by applying ticket to rider, gets ticket and rider together in fact without altering either, we take him to have applied the ticket rule properly. We do not ask him to look at the ideal situation where a ticket is directly related to a rider, though we can, in teaching him how to be a conductor, teach him by making use of that device.

Training to be a conductor is training to apply rules properly, and this training does consist in applying a rule of application to an application (with or without authentic tickets and riders). But a conductor in training is not a conductor in fact. The conductor in fact starts with the ticket-as-rule confronting a rider, and then, with these as presupposed to be the material for an application, he engages in an application going in one direction only. He who protested against the ruling of the conductor might reject his ticket rule in favor of some such rule as the occupation of a seat for such and such a period of time as presumptively a proper occupation.

We who wish to test the conductor's conduct will have in mind the togetherness of a proper ticket and a proper rider; these we can define apart from him. When we find that he ends with them as discrepant we know that he has not applied the ticket rule properly. We then judge his application by an ideal application. But he did not so act; he did not look to an ideal mode of application to test his own act. What he did was to face what was presumably a proper rule and proper data, and when he saw that they were discrepant found himself forced to allow that (since those items might be in fact what they were presumed to be, and thus would be directly related as compatible), his method of application was unsatisfactory. Had he actually applied the rule in the light of an ideal application, he would have found fault with his application were he to bring in irrelevancies, even though the outcome turned out to be one in which rule and data were found to be compatible.

If there is no fault in the outcome, we find no fault with the legitimacy of the application but only with its efficiency. We may say that the conductor is slovenly, careless, fussy, and the like, but this does not mean that he is improperly applying rule to data.

When we engage in an interference in accordance with a rule we apply the rule on the particular material. We assume that the two will become one, with rule structuring the material and the material filling out the rule. The structuring of the material will involve a breaking up of the structure, the extending of it over a number of items; the filling out of the rule will in effect be an authenticating of the final outcome. We can be taught how to make the application, and so far as we are being taught will be applying according to a test of application. But when engaged in the actual inference, where this is viewed as involving the application of a rule to a situation (which is not always the way an inference occurs), we engage in an act under the guidance of the rule, on the assumption that such behavior involves the union of rule and act in such a way that the outcome of the act is what is desirable from an intellectual point of view.

We have an ideal result presupposed in what rule and act are as together; one might say this is the presupposition of rationality. When we engage in an act of inference we do not then subject ourselves to a test of rationality, but instead engage in an act which, if it fails to meet the demands of the rule, raises for us the question as to whether or not we did in fact act rationally.

When we accept anything as final and thus as a possible test for something else, we presuppose that this finality and the something else already make an ideal unity in the shape of a compatible pair. We then proceed to apply one to the other with the consequence that we may find them compatible. Should we find that they are not compatible we must return to consider whether rule, datum, or mode of application was defective. In this sense the ultimate finality is some such idea as rationality, coherence, mutual completion. This we never question, but use it to determine that something is amiss when we find that rule and data cannot be made one through an accepted mode of application. But why should we not question this? If we do not question it, does this mean that there is something about which we might conceivably not be mistaken?

The presupposition of rationality is not absolute in the sense that we might not violate it, or even find it not desirable in some cases. The application of a rule to a datum is something which we offer for checking; it is not itself to serve as a check on something. Every mode of dealing with a number of items presupposes that those items are together in some way. The acceptance of that way of being together makes possible certain kinds of activities. We assume rationality when we infer; we assume a one-to-one correspondence of ticket and rider when we act as conductors.

May not these assumptions be tested by one another? Is there one underlying both? We sometimes speak of the conflict between rationality and practice or intuition or insight or revelation. We can deliberately set about to take one of these as basic and use it to judge the others by. But, since their meaning is to make possible an activity in some realm, any evaluation of them in relation to one another is tantamount to the evaluation of different areas of knowledge or practice. Evidently we ought not to use one of the assumptions to measure all the others by. But they can all be evaluated relative to one another, and then only if there be a single assumption which they all share and in fact express in diverse ways. This might be termed a principle of justice or dialectic, as that which dictates that we are to deal with data sympathetically, without distortion, and which may require us to proceed sometimes with a rational rule, sometimes with a practical rule, and so on.

Yet it was said earlier that certain items might be redefined, reanalyzed, redistributed in a number of places when found to be recalcitrant to some approach. Would it not be more nearly correct to say, in the light of the principle of justice or dialectic, or dialectic justice, that these items should be accepted as they are, within their own setting, where they meet the tests which alone can be said to be appropriate to them? Ought there not to be provision made for authentic cases of illusion, real cases of error, and so on, and does this not mean that they are to be viewed as root, and as ultimate as anything else? I think it does. The conversion of the erroneous, etc., is desirable only because we have accepted a commitment to the truth, etc., as involving the direct application of such and such rules or meanings. The same commitment to truth as involving other rules (say that of bringing in the peculiar conditions of observation or the state of health of the observer) would give us these items as final, though of course only as what are also, from another perspective, properly termed "false."

Starting then with a commitment to dialectic justice we distinguish multiple rules and multiple types of data (the distinctions being different sides of the same, since a rule can be a datum and a datum a rule) and proceed to specify the dialectic justice in the shape of such conditions as rationality, experienceability, revelation, and so on. But surely it is possible for a man to refuse to accept the commitment to dialectic justice. If not, how could we have systems of materialism, idealism, scientism, panentheism, all of which insist on one approach rather than another and reject whatever their principles cannot accommodate, without making any effort to find some place for the rejected items?

The rejection of dialectic justice is in effect an insistence on some limited field or some limited approach. This field or approach does not offer a test for dialectic justice, except by assuming it in another sense, for in saying that a specialized approach gives us more content, or allows us to have material in a more coherent and manageable form, etc., we but say that it is a device by which maximum justice is done. We can see the desirability of dealing with the world in multiple ways when we recognize that the activity in which we are engaged but expresses one way in which justice can be done to certain content. We may prefer our own way, and in fact by appealing to the initial idea of dialectic justice can show that our preference is justified by virtue of the extent of justice it makes possible. But what we cannot say is that the other methods and fields are illegitimate.

The idea of dialectic justice is related to the particular approaches somewhat as ideal compatibility is related to actual applications, or the way in which rationality is related to actual reasonings. But there is something disturbing in the thought that there is something which is not to be tested and which tests all else. Dialectic justice says that a given method of discipline or rule of application is to be given up for another when it fails to handle such and such data, finding them incompatible and so far unreal, undesirable, requiring dismissal, analysis, or interpretation.

Might dialectic justice not be deemed presumptuous, incapable of being realized, impractical? It seems so. But then there are tests for it, such as practicability, realizability in a finite time, familiarity. One can criticize it in these ways, provided one used the principle of dialectic justice in its full extent. But if one merely acknowledges it, and indeed takes one's own limited enterprise to be carrying it out in the only way a man can, there would be no criticism of the principle of dialectic justice but only a criticism of those men who think that they can use the principle in other ways as well.

The principle of dialectic justice, in other words, might conceivably be embodied only in one discipline and with respect to one area. Those who wish to carry out the principle in multiple areas can be criticized for being presumptuous, unrealistic, etc. Dialectic justice is merely saying that we do apply rules, that we do test, that we do have data, that we do engage in applications, and that these, to be carried out, must allow for the presence of the others, and in principle permit of a different approach to the same array of material.

Suppose someone were to say, "I reject the principle of dialectic justice, in favor of a preference for the best. I am not interested in any kind of painting but only in great paintings. To ask me to attend to the various poor paintings is to take me away from important work." To this one may answer that one ought not to put all lesser paintings on a level. But suppose to this one answered that it doesn't make much difference how one arranges the inferior works, and in any case one wants to attend only to the great ones. Still it would have to be admitted that those who are not qualified to determine what are good paintings and what are not, or better, who lack enough sensitivity to isolate the great paintings, would gain something by discriminating amongst and relating the inferior paintings. I suppose though that a true aristocrat might maintain that if one couldn't appreciate the best, one ought not to attend to any. But would the aristocrat not say that a man who could discriminate among the bad paintings was better than one who could not see any difference amongst them at all? Is it not better to know the relations of the various shadows on Plato's cave instead of seeing them merely as shadows?

A rejected group involves a discrimination, by a single principle, of that group from preferred ones. The carrying out of the discrimination inside the rejected group could conceivably be the outcome of the continued application of the same principle which enabled an aristocrat to isolate the excellent paintings. The issue then seems to come down to whether a class of rejected items should be taken as a single homogeneous whole or whether it is desirable to deal with it differentially (and therefore to make use of the principle of dialectic justice).

Why not carry this policy one step further and refuse to discriminate at all, refuse to apply any rule, refuse to have any standard? This would lead to a radical scepticism, solipsism, or chaos. One might live with these, but they could not be defended without an appeal to truth, criteria, tests, and so on. We see then that those who refuse to accept the principle of dialectic justice merely stop using it at some point. They define themselves to be indifferent and cut away from various areas, but make use of the principle in the area which interests them, attending to data there with great care so as to make the most discriminatory judgments.

The principle of dialectic justice reveals that there is something besides oneself. The extent to which one carries out this principle or acknowledges its ubiquity is one with the determination of the extent of the world in which a man takes himself to be at home, or is willing to make himself at home. It is in the end then a matter of what a man's claims are, what it is that he denies is or ought to be mastered by man. If he makes any claim or assertion, takes any stand whatsoever with respect to a range of items having some principle or criterion in terms of which he is going to deal with them, he already makes use of the principle of dialectic justice. The principle in other words merely says that there is something of which he ought to take account, and not indiscriminately, but with an appreciation of its nuances and interrelations.

If we take I to be a final one, there will still be the fact that data are used and evaluated by that I and that there is some discrimination made amongst the items which conform to what the I demands. All that need then be done is to see that the items which are rejected are taken to have some kind of being (and thus to challenge the I), that there are other principles which allow for some other evaluation of the rejected items amongst themselves, and that the principle of application of the I is left unaccounted for unless one attends to the fact that it is a form of the principle of dialectic justice and, in this limited form, can be questioned and evaluated, and perhaps even rejected, in this area or that.

It was a neglect of the principle of dialectic justice which prevented Plato from making a contribution to sociology, economics, and practical politics, for he lumped together all the tradesmen and all the guardians, and failed to see that there is a whole world of significant information to be obtained by attending to subdivisions of these groups. To be sure, it is not the function of a philosopher to make a detailed study of social groups, or to distinguish different types of women, and women from men, on the grounds that this or that limited enterprise can be performed better by one than the other. But he ought to have a principle which makes it desirable for discriminatory judgments to be made in the areas where the inferior or limited are found. It is as if one were to say that there was the mode Actuality, and neglected to remark on the plurality of actualities and the adventures they individually undergo. One need not, as a philosopher, study those actualities, but one ought to carry out some discrimination or show that this discrimination is desirable, and that it involves the use of other categories than those employed to mark off the superior from the inferior, or one mode of being from another.

Is not the principle of dialectic justice self-defeating? It asks us to do full justice to whatever there be. But can it do full justice to that which rejects it brutally, dogmatically, foolishly? I think it can. One ought to recognize the different types of rejection that could be made, and ought to see the grounds for them. He who rejects the principle may do so because he prefers the best, or because he does not want to occupy himself with anything less. He gains something by this narrowing, and so far can justify himself. But this does not mean that he rejects the principle but only that he does not allow it to extend very widely, so far as he is concerned. He may even claim that this is what all others should do, but then it is to be noticed that he is attending to others and trying in fact to do most justice to them by urging them to do as he does, presumably for their own greatest good. He will then be employing the principle quite widely and in a somewhat paradoxical way. He will be looking at "inferior" men and urging them to become superior, thereby making his own principle of excellence into an imperative rather than a rule, and will be telling them that they ought not to attend to various "inferior" items in an effort to make the items superior, but ought to reject them entirely. He will be employing two principles: one a principle of excellence used as a measure enabling one to recognize who is inferior and what things are inferior, and a principle of excellence as an imperative demanding of the men that they improve themselves by using a principle of excellence to separate themselves off from what is inferior. He will try to attend to what is good or desirable in inferior men and will refuse to attend to inferior objects, apparently on the ground that there can be nothing good or desirable in them. But the last cannot be known unless one attends to them.

August 25

We learn in a number of ways. Two are prominent. In one of them we are given a rule and try to follow it; in the other we are given instructions and try to keep abreast of them. The rule must in the end be translated into instructions either by the teacher or the student. There is then on the side of learning really only the instructions and the activities which carry them out. The rule in effect tells what the nature of the outcome will be; it justifies our following such and such instructions. Strictly speaking, then, it belongs to a different set of considerations; he who wants to follow a rule or is being taught to follow a rule is in effect being made into one who accepts a certain kind of outcome as desirable, or at least desired.

Instructions are like complex commands; they tell us to do first one thing and then another; they may carry a penalty and even be expressed is terms of orders. But whether they are or not, they consist in a set of cues or stimuli in response to which the learner is expected to act. He on his side may look at the instructor as a model and try to imitate him; he may attend to the rule so as to keep in mind the various steps which are structurally defined, or to remind him of the standard of excellence which is required if he is to obtain a certain result. But as he goes through the steps, what he is doing is to respond by will or association or conditioning.

When a man engages in an inference he does something similar to what one does when he follows instructions. He does not instance or apply the rule; he leaves the rule untouched, and may in fact have no awareness of a rule. What he does instead is to follow out a series of tried moves which can be justified by having recourse to a rule that tells him how, with such and such a beginning, to get a desirable result at the end. Another way of putting this is to say that the rule which presents a relation between elements, has its correlative in an act, and that so far as one has the act he presupposes the other; and perhaps when he has the other (the rule) he acknowledges a place where the act can take place. Both ways of connecting the terms are appropriate, the one "merging" the items which it accepts, the other separating them; the one having them together at the same time, the other having them in a temporal order; the one validating one term by another, the other replacing one term by another; the one being open to conceptualization and logical manipulation, the other being performed and subject to the exigencies of circumstance. When the inference is checked by the rule, one isolates in the inference the structure which is constitutive of the rule. That structure is not produced by the rule nor does the rule provide a finality for the act in any sense in which the converse is not true.

If this is true, the act of inference is like an act in which one is learning, obeying commands, following instructions, going through required steps. An isolated outcome, which by itself would not have any but an isolated character, by virtue of its being arrived at along a certain route, is found to have a desired character. It has of course whatever character it does have, but what it accretes is a setting, and a nature by virtue of that setting. If one gets to a true conclusion, the conclusion is true and is this regardless of the premiss or the route over which one had gone. But by going over the route, by finding the truth through this procedure, one does not have to determine the truth by a more direct confrontation with the fact. We have an assurance of the truth, an assurance that when we make a direct check we will find that the quality we attributed to the conclusion does in fact belong to it. By getting the quality over a route we accredit the conclusion with it as a feature which the conclusion is supposed to have, but which we have not yet discovered it to have.

"If you will turn right and then left you will get to the post office." "Turn right and then left and you'll face the post office." The first of these gives us the rule, the second the instructions, i.e., the rule spelled out in steps in a sequential order. When I arrive at the post office by following the instructions, either as given directly or as converted from a statement of the rule, I face the post office, not as one who is merely there, but as one who has arrived there. This fact is lost because I, who arrived, immediately take account of the fact that it is there, and thus occupy the very position which would be occupied by one who has not arrived as I have. I am one who says, "that *must be* the post office," whereas if I confront it without having arrived at it I can only say "that *is* the post office."

When I say "that *must be* the post office" I am acknowledging the warrant which the rule provides and thus the post office as the outcome of the following of instructions. When I say "that *must be* the post office" I am of course not saying that a post office is a necessary existent, but that "since the rule is correct and my steps followed the derived instructions correctly, the last step at which I arrive is a step which is required to be of a certain sort."

The post office as arrived at is one subject to a categorial condition; its nature is assured in advance. When I face the post office without arriving at it, I learn what it is only by confronting it. But now I know what it is before I confront it, even though what I want to do perhaps is only to confront it. "Do so and so and you will confront it" gives us a confronted object as already predesignated, and not merely an object which we then designate or come to know.

All learning, all following orders and commands, all use of guides and instructions give us a terminal item in a predesignated way, with an inherited feature which we will find, if the rules or instructions are correct, to be a feature which it has in fact, but which we could not have come to know without first having followed the instructions. It is as if we had been willed some money; the money is ours and no one else's, but it is ours only because we have inherited it. The inheriting of the money is one thing, and keeps us in the situation where we are related to the testator, but once we have arrived at the proper stage of being acknowledged by the law to have the right to the money, we have it just as any other man may have money, inherited or not.

An inference then is like an act learned under a guarantee that the outcome is desirable, or like a command obeyed for a desirable reward. What the teacher's knowledge and the commander's authority or power provide is provided by the logical justification of the rule of inference, or the theoretical plausibility of some scientific hypothesis. Since we did follow the instructions, since we did what we were ordered to do, if our authorities (formal or formidable) be reliable we will find that the world will produce the desirable feature which we attributed to it in an inference.

August 28

He who takes himself to be a finality without any regard for other finalities is a fanatic. All others seek some way of utilizing or checking by various finalities. By taking himself to be a subject subordinate to a supreme subject a man allows his *I* to have the power of the divine. He is a religiously committed man, who is, as an *I,* functioning in terms provided by God. He does not identify himself with God, nor does he deny his own *I;* what he does is to have the *I* strengthened, given objectivity, by being made to be the avenue through which God's finality is exhibited. It is still his own *I,* but an *I* which has its individual notes all divinely qualified.

An ethical man achieves a similar outcome by committing himself to an ethical ideal; he too has his own *I,* but what he measures by that *I* is measured in ethical terms. All that his *I* acknowledges is qualified by the ethical, so that he individually expresses something final in another sense. He belongs to the kingdom of ends, just as the religious man belongs to God. Each can act as a representative of the other finality, but he then in effect gives the divine and the ethical, respectively, the support of the *I*—the converse of what is now the case.

A wise old man through his reasonableness identifies his *I* with the course of Existence. When he is a representative of that Existence he passes implacable decisions on others.

Women make a similar identification of their individual egos with the collective *we.* They then see the world about them as an occasion or background for the production of a *we.* A woman is an *I* with the force of a *we,* an *I* that, without needing support from other *I*'s or needing to form a collective *we,* speaks as a *we,* subordinating her own *I,* so far as this is idiosyncratic, to the commonality of all *I*'s, to the fact that the *I*'s make an interlocked *we.* She too can act as a representative of a *we* in the sense of representing decency.

It is possible to find supports for other finalities elsewhere than in the *I.* Thus a religious man can find support in the ethical, and conversely; the former is what St. Paul pointed out when he said that those who speak with tongues but have no charity are but empty sounds. It is possible to support the divine with the existential, and conversely; we then get such outcomes as the "God *of* history," where what history brings about is taken to be the expression of the divine, and the "God *for* history," where the course of history is taken to be subject to a divine evaluation. In the former, the finality of God supports the existential; in the latter God is a finality who awaits historic material, and thus backs His finality with what He takes from Existence.

Existence and the Ideal are finalities. Each can represent the other; and each can be identified with the other in the sense that it can express in its own terms the meaning which the other has.

Every one of the modes can have similar relations to the collective *we,* whether this be identified with the individual *I* or not. Where it is identified, as in the case of woman, we will have the woman religiously qualified, with ethical obligations, or with a wise reasonableness.

When the *I* or any other finality is identified with some other in the sense of making itself the locus of it, so as to be able to express this in its decisions or attitudes, there is in a sense a greater arrogance being exhibited than was the case when the individual expressed himself alone, for now there is a claim not only to be final in oneself but to be a carrier or mediator of another finality. But this appearance of arrogance disappears once it is seen that the insistence on the *I* by itself is one which allows every instance of the *I* to be final (no matter how arbitrary it seems), unchecked and untested, whereas when the *I* is taken to be a mediator or a locus it is presumably subject to conditions it does not prescribe.

An individual of course can say that he is God or God's mouthpiece or God's representative, and in this way change from a mere fanatic to a religious fanatic. To avoid fanaticism there must be some acknowledgment of the finality as standing apart and even challenging some of the expressions of the individual. The assumption of the role of a mediator or representative is one with the assumption of duties and conditions which restrict the individual's expressions and activities. The *I* then remains final, but as pulled outside its normal functioning and justifications.

To say justifiably that one is speaking God's word, it is not enough to feel confident that one is; one must be aware of God as a finality distinct from oneself. When the woman accepts herself as the meaning of the *we,* the individual nature which is hers is made to carry a meaning which is not hers alone, and to which she yields.

Just as particular assertions are given a context by the finality to which they are attributed, so different finalities are given contexts by the finalities to which they look for supplementation. The only difference between these cases is that there is no denial of the right of the individual finality to provide a context for that which provided a context for it, nor a forgetting that the individual, even where he abandons his own claims in favor of that other finality, has justification, though one now held in abeyance. The latter recognition is actually nothing but a way of making the former recognition. Because the individual has a right in- and of-himself as a finality, he, when he submits to some other, makes himself a vehicle for it or a bearer of it, and knows that he still has rights as a finality which he can exercise with justice.

The way in which one brings together the various finalities has something in common with the way in which one conforms one's actions to rules, or engages in the application of rules. A finality which is acknowledged as superior to one's own, so that one wants to act as a representative of it, is something like a rule to which one will try to conform. When instead there is an insistence on oneself, but with the other finality as a qualification, we have something like the application of that other finality to the situation in which we are, but subject to the limitations provided by us. When we identify ourselves with another finality in the sense of allowing it to be manifested through us, we are applying the other finality as a rule to which we give way, without denying ourselves the role of a datum, as it were, in which the rule is to operate.

Remaining with the *I* and the *we,* we should have the following cases: *I* qualified by the *we; I* representing the *we; I* subordinated to the *we;* the *we* qualified by the *I;* the *we* representing the *I;* and the *we* subordinated to the *I.* The discussion today began without a clear distinction among these.

The last case seems to be somewhat close to what was called identification, but this was sometimes confused with the others. The *I* qualified by the *we* is one in which the activities of the *I* are restricted in consideration of what the *we* requires. When the *I* represents the *we* the demands are made by the *we,* and the *I* merely functions on its behalf. When the *I* is subordinated to the *we* it is not merely restricted in its activities but has its role controlled; it then lacks the right to function for the whole but is made instead to function as the whole requires.

Conversely, when the *we* is qualified by the *I,* and thus has its activities restricted, we have what is sometimes called an appeal to the individual conscience. When the *we* represents the *I,* we have what is sometimes said to be the public spirit, the voice of the people. When the *we* is subordinated to the *I,* it has no rights or dignities beyond the meaning given by the various *I*'s or by one's own *I.* It is then something like Rousseau's general will, or the expression of the autocrat.

Women function primarily as representing the *we:* men instead are subordinated to the *we.* Who then is qualified by the *we?* Children? What is the *we* qualified by the *I?* The responsible society? What is the *we* representing the *I?* The responsive society? What is the *we* subordinated to the *I?* The great leader's society?

One can represent the *we* in a way in which the woman does not, as, for example, the judge or the administrator does. The representation by these is the carrying over into and through the individual the express rules and outcomes of a *we* decision; in the case of the woman the *we* is dealt with as something which receives focus from her, which she expresses. In the one case the individual is a representative *agent,* in the other she is a representative *being.* An agent makes himself permeable, whereas a being gives substance to what it is representing.

The *I* is transitory and expressive of a particular set of experiences; the *we* is constant and stable and reflective of the experience of an indefinite number of men over an indefinite period. The woman does not try to conform to the *we.* She does not try to act on behalf of it. She acts as a *we* though she is only an *I.* This means that what she expresses lacks the idiosyncratic nature of an ordinary *I;* she has that idiosyncratic nature and does express it, but not as the finality she allows to the *we.* When she acts only as an *I* it is in the world of men. She otherwise does in a localized place what the *we* in fact does for the men.

For the last three or four days it seems to me that I have begun to break through to a new set of ideas, and that I have been writing about them in a rather confused and often unfocussed way. There seems to be an awareness of a plurality of finalities, a capacity for measuring one by the other, a way of evaluating the application of the measures, and an opening into the problem of how and with what result one of these finalities can be made to function on behalf of, or as involved with others. But I have not yet succeeded in doing more than catch glimpses here and there of the area to be explored, the distinctions to be made, the principles to be employed, and the kind of consequences that will ensue. I feel somewhat as I did when I first began formulating my ideas about art, except that in connection with art I knew artists and some works of art in terms of which I could check some of the tentative suggestions that I had been making to myself, whereas here I seem to be without guidance and know no one to whom I can turn for help. Perhaps the guidance and the nature of the help will become clearer once I achieve greater clarity about some of these ideas.

August 29

If it be true that anything whatsoever can function as a finality, then any particular can be taken to be final. When this is done, it no longer is one item alongside others, but is a test for other particulars and for other finalities. When the romantic knight said that his damsel was the fairest in the land, he was prepared to die on behalf of his contention. He yielded his own individuality to it, and did not recognize the rights of the *we,* of God, or ethics, or politics, or history, or art, to be superior. It was for him a truth that had the rule of "it is true that," where "it is true that" entrained obligations, commitments, dedication, and so on.

The fact that "it is true that" (when exhibited in the form of a particular assertion) entrains certain kinds of demands and values, points up the fact that "it is true that" is ambiguous, not in what it says, but in what it involves. "It is true that" as reflecting the *I* is different in import from itself as reflecting some momentary experience, some particular occurrence, or some mode of being.

"It is true that," when expressed as a finality, makes all objective occurrences subservient to a private acceptance. It contrasts with the particulars we might take as final, for these make the individual subservient to the particular, even though the particular could not be known or possessed without the individual being present or supposed. In the case of the particular, the individual could be denied any other being than what is contained in the particular.

When the *we* is final, both individuals and particulars give way to a collective which could go to the extreme of denying the reality of any particular or individual. We would then have a basic atmosphere or spirit, something like Jung's unconscious, as the basic reality.

When God is taken as final, one can deal with Him mystically, and thereby reject everything designatable in or apart from Him, or one can accept some command or act or course of history as embodying Him or His intent at the moment.

When the Ideal is taken as final, one faces a future which is prescriptive, and thus subjects oneself to guidance and conditioning. All else is then viewed as an instance of the Ideal, or as something which is being directed by the Ideal.

When Existence is taken as final, there is a stress on the nature of activity and whatever it might produce, so that all established occurrences and all the other modes and particulars will be taken as somehow over-rigidified.

When Actuality as such is taken as final we have an acceptance of something like a realm of experience, a domain of which we do not speak, but in terms of which everything is to be treated as legitimate if it falls within it, and as illegitimate if it does not.

In the case of particulars we have "I pledge that it is true that"; in the case of the *I*, we have "I insist that it is true that"; in the case of the *we,* we have "I grant that it is true that"; in the case of God, we have "I accept that it is true that"; in the case of the Ideal, we have "Rationally, I take it to be true that"; in the case of Existence, we have "Practically, it is true that"; in the case of Actuality, we have "Experientially, it is true that." The qualifications infect the "it is true that" to make it have a different import in the different cases. When then we apply one finality to another, we are subjecting one kind of outlook to the conditions of another. If "I pledge it is true that" be used to test "I accept it is true that," the latter objects. It claims that it is idolatrous, blasphemous, for one to do what is counter to what God commands or is supposed to require—but this the test may require.

A finality is not then something perfect, ultimate in any ontological sense, or superior in value to all else. It is a standpoint adopted with the consequence that it will hold itself away from criticism, will not take itself to presuppose anything, and will dictate values to others. What this shows is that there is a potentiality for an attitude which is specified in different ways at different times. This attitude can be said to have an objective counterpart in a Togetherness, which itself is a finality in an ambiguous ontological sense, achieving specificity and unambiguity only when concretionalized as the modes of being.

When men like Heidegger look for the Being beyond particular beings, or when like Tillich they look for a God beyond God, they are looking for Togetherness. But this lacks concreteness. The attitude answering to Togetherness is only a potentiality for particular attitudes. Because this point is not seen, these men tend on the one hand to have an ineffable absolute beyond all the modes of being and all particularities, and on the other to suppose that there is an appropriate position to take toward it—anxiety or courage or the like.

If one is truly anxious about one's own nonbeing there is no pointing to an absolute togetherness. If one is courageous with respect to some particular mode there is no reference to an absolute togetherness. And if absolute togetherness is taken to be the object of anxiety or courage, the anxiety or courage should vanish into particularized attitudes which are appropriate to what alone is.

We have no necessary attachment to togetherness to make it an essential referent for us. We need not be viewed as beings capable of particular attitudes but in ourselves having no attitude whatsoever. Indeed to cling to togetherness as such is to have an attitude of a particular sort, for it is to have accepted a speculative condition as the primary object of one's interests. It is to be concerned with an ultimate togetherness which lacks the ultimacy of a true being.

Heidegger and Tillich are right in remarking that no one of the objects in the world, including ourselves, is an ultimate being. But it is an error to suppose that what lies beyond these is Being as such. What lies beyond these is either the four modes of being in their distinctness, or the four modes as merged together in a blurred way, or the togetherness of the four modes. The four modes in their distinctness are the objects of distinct attitudes. The four modes as merged require a merging of the distinct attitudes, not an attitude in general or a potential attitude, since we then do face the ultimate beings but as insufficiently distinguished. The togetherness of the four modes is inseparable from the presence of them, and dependent for its being on them, though possessing a nature of its own.

Heidegger has, under the influence of Kierkegaard, made modern man aware of the fact that he is looking for a finality which he can maintain in the face of other finalities that have betrayed him in some way or other in the past. But if what I have been urging is correct, every finality will betray. What would never betray is too amorphous to be the object of an attitude; it is the object of a merged set of attributes, or the counterpart of ourselves, not yet focussed into a distinctive attitude.

Since it is the case that men have always sought for a finality, how can it be true that anything whatsoever can be taken to be a finality? Were this true it would seem as if there would be no need for a search. It is nevertheless a fact that even when men have adopted some one finality they are restless and seek another. But is this not due to the fact that they are aware that there is more than one finality, and not that they are supposing that what they had accepted has no finality to it? They want another kind of finality, one which enables them to have "it is true that" in another sense, for though what they take to be final is so, it does involve limitations, and it does presuppose data which must have their own finality.

The very acknowledgment of data for an accepted finality alerts one to the need to look for another finality grounding the data. Since we start with the data as over against and as subject to the initial finality, the normal move would be to look for a finality which embraced both the data and the initial finality. Even if one recognized a finality to the data one would be inclined to look for a still further finality embracing the data and the initial finality. We are quickly faced in other words with a desire to have a finality in something which is not our initial finality or the data it deals with, and we quickly suppose that this further finality has the kind of being characteristic of our initial finality or our data. But, if I am right, the subsequent finality may be nothing more than the togetherness of the initial finality and its data, and thus would not be a finality grounded in some ontological ultimate. Instead it would be a finality only because we had accepted it to be such—the very thing which we found disagreeable and which set us on our quest for another finality.

The search for a finality beyond the one that is accepted should not be construed as a search for an arbitrarily selected item. That we have to begin with. Nor should it be thought to be a search for a being behind the initial finality and our data, for this which is behind may be nothing more than a togetherness. If we seek another finality it must be because we see defects in the one we accept, and know something which could provide a finality without those defects—or more cautiously, because we are seeking a finality without those defects. Such a finality is rooted in something other than our decision, for if it were our decision alone that made it have the nature it had, we could give this nature to what we now accept.

August 30

When we communicate we take one of three attitudes toward content. We present it, we justify it, and we estimate it. The most common is presentation. Here we take for granted a context provided by ourselves or another, and deal with a particular item. If challenged about this item we more likely than not will offer evidence which is pertinent to it. But sometimes we insist on it in the face of denials or rejections. We then refer it back to some ground of which we now become aware, and whose presence indicates the acceptance by us of some finality. It is then that we say, "it is true that. . . ." Having made such a justification we may be inclined to rest with it, and thus to look out on all particulars in a way we did not before, because we do it in terms of what would justify it. It is this last approach which is characteristic of those who speak of themselves as religious men in the face of rejections of their dogmas and creeds. To be religious in this sense is to start with an attitude of estimation which is to affect every item, placing each in relation to others in terms of a value that the accepted position entrains.

When young, or when immersed in particularities, men are either in the first or second of these positions; it takes maturity, decision, commitment to make it possible to assume the third. In some cases the third is achieved without effort; this would seem to be the case with women whose maturity is one with their discovering a base of estimation. In the case of political, ethical, and religious men there is usually a decision together with a commitment.

Because an estimation may be like others in its outcome, and because it is "a priori" in the sense that it is not derived from the particulars (even though initially we may have arrived at it in order to justify some assertion or claim), it is hard to know just what the base is that one has identified oneself with. Is the base in terms of which the religious man estimates things (apart from creed and dogma) different from that used by an ethical man, a woman, an experienced man, a political man, etc.? Should we not then say that a man becomes religious, etc., only when this single base is applied to religiously determined content? But I think it is perhaps better to say that there is a distinctive estimation in the different cases. A religious man cannot fail to see that the values of the things about are subordinated to some primary one. The ethical man cannot fail to see that the values of the things about are ordered in terms of some obligating end, even where it is not known what that end is like. A woman cannot fail to see the things about in terms of the way they constitute or support the *we* she individually embodies. The practical man cannot avoid approaching the objects about as having different instrumental values. In all these cases no judgment is made of the various items. One merely looks at them from a certain perspective, ready to relate them to one another on the basis of an estimate, having a distinctive valuational role.

Maturation seems to be the time when we seek an estimating base. Time is spent in part in trying out one estimate after another, and sensing and experimenting with the commitment they entail. Usually we begin by being committed in a certain way; then, as we find the items with which we are concerned passing away or being challenged, we become aware of what it is that we had been using to justify our selections; and then we come to find that the estimation enables us to get a single rounded look at whatever occurs. There is a kind of confidence, and sometimes a smugness, and surely a dogmatism in those who have found the base for estimations they will thereafter make.

Is there any choice amongst these bases that one ought to make? I think not. All of them must be employed. Since no one can employ them all without denying each in turn, he must take his estimation to allow for the acceptance of the outcomes of other estimations, and thus see that the items which he values in one way are valued properly in another way, and that these values can be his if he will enter into a scheme whereby what he produces is allowed to be accredited to others, and what they achieve is accepted by him.

September 2

On the Freudian view, the impulses of the id are controlled by the ego and the superego, the former consciously, the latter unconsciously. But there is no distinctive machinery provided for the assessment of the impulses and the world they presumably reach. The superego is, to be sure, a kind of conscience, but this makes one treat only the attitude of morality as that which provides a final assessment of what is desired or done. But if I am right we have a primitive amorphous attitude of desiring a finality, and a plurality of specifications of this attitude in the guise of finalities which rest with the individual, the collective, the Ideal (this comes closest to the interest of the superego), Existence (this comes closest to the interest of the ego), Actuality, and God. (Actuality is perhaps represented by Freud in his doctrine of the id, and of course God is for him some kind of dodge.) Psychoanalytically the generic attitude seeking finality would lie behind both the ego and the superego, and would involve a set of controls of what Freud calls the id, answering to the specific attitudes rooted in full Actuality and in God. There is also the fact that various finalities can be interrelated.

When we approach psychoanalytic theory in this guise it becomes evident that Freud's world contained a kind of private Actuality and Existence. The superego, which should be doing justice to the Ideal, is supposed by Freud to deal with a degenerate form of that Ideal in the shape of the demands and commands and authority of the parents. But Freud does recognize that Actuality (at least in the shape of the id) and Existence have the right to be treated as finalities. His answer in the end does seem to be that we must somehow meld these two, and that the final and proper answer is one in which the finalities of each are balanced by the other.

One can take this to be the final word of psychoanalysis. If this is done then the recognition that there are other finalities will involve a more complicated set of items to be balanced. The acknowledgment of the generic attitude behind all these finalities will lead to a consideration of metaphysical issues outside the interest of psychoanalysis, at least as a therapy or as oriented toward therapy. It is sufficient for psychoanalysis to start with the plurality of finalities and seek for an answer by seeing how one can, together with other men, allow for some expression of each finality, while muting it by virtue of the restrictions imposed by other finalities. This idea of merging, in the end, must be a matter of judgment; there will be no quantifying of the different finalities, no adding them up in some way. All one can hope for is a combination of them in such a way that one can fit together with others in the world.

Freud seemed to believe that any insistence or overinsistence on one finality was psychologically undesirable. He interpreted artists, philosophers, religious men as something like obvious psychotics. Were he right, those who were philosophically dogmatic and insisted on only one type of finality would be psychotic to the second power, for they would be psychotic qua philosophers, and psychotic in philosophy, since they would not philosophically recognize the merit of other finalities. In any case, it is a mistake to confound those who chose some finality and live full lives in the light of it, with those who suppress some finality but are unable to control the expression of others, and come into conflict with themselves. The artist, etc., does hold to one of a number of finalities; he is philosophically in no better position than others who stress some other finality. Philosophically viewed each finality is incomplete. But this philosophical incompleteness is consistent with an accommodation of other finalities when and so far as they do make themselves manifest, with a subsequent reassessment of them and a redefinition of their place in one's economy.

The psychotic is overwhelmed by that which he has put aside, or by that which he has accepted and which he insists upon in the face of the painful insistence of what it does not tolerate. The normal person, who has elected to stay with one of a number of possible finalities, suppresses what goes counter to it, but not at the price of being overwhelmed by its insistence in the face of a dismissal; also he is not overwhelmed by the finality he accepts, since he uses this to assess others and not as that which rejects them.

Put another way, the artist can have a strong feeling of his own ego; it is for him a finality which he will not allow to be overwhelmed by other finalities. But this does not mean that he uses the finality of his ego as the measure of what he does or wants or believes. He allows it, as it were, to assert itself within the area of the accepted finality of his life as an artist; it is allowed to permeate the life but not to evaluate it or to resist it or to subjugate it. He does not, however, merge the finality which is his ego with that of his life as an artist. He makes his life as an artist function somewhat as a generic attitude, and then has it specified through the agency of his ego. But the generic attitude he has as an artist is not the generic attitude which permits of his recognition of the rights of other finalities on a footing with his own, and which are to be merged with it to make a fit that a Freudian would take to be satisfactory.

We have then two solutions to the problem of the adjustment to one another of finalities having therapeutic value. The one is that of the Freudian which recognizes the rights of other finalities, which the therapist must bring his patient to see, and which will then be merged with the accepted finality to give us the rounded life of a functioning man in public. The other is that of the successful student of any of the great disciplines, where one accepts one finality and allows the others to permeate and thereby specialize it whenever they make themselves manifest insistently.

Over against these therapeutic answers is the philosophic answer which says that the merging involves a neglect of the claims of each, and that the permeation of one finality by others must be reciprocated so that the final answer would be a multiplicity of permeations in which every finality would function as a kind of generic attitude specified by all the others. But it is questionable whether this answer can be provided by any one individual. It would seem that it depends on a plurality of men each taking a different finality, or a different way of having this specified, and who give to one another the benefits of their different devotions.

Somewhat related to this idea is the attitude one should take toward criticism in one's own field. Instead of defending one's own discipline, one should look at it in a highly critical sense. One knows its virtues and will undoubtedly continue to engage in that discipline, but if one looks at it critically the lines in and around it will be sharpened, and one will understand what it is that one accepts and why. The philosopher, as he approaches some other discipline, should be most sympathetic with what it is trying to do, so that he can do full justice to its claims and its rights as a finality. Unfortunately, men usually reverse this state of affairs. Theologians, for example, are primarily apologists; they defend their faith regardless of what others say, or what difficulties they find. Philosophers, on the other hand, approach theologians with scepticism and a highly critical spirit. Neither learns very much from the other.

Philosophers, who look at religion, art, politics, and so on in a sympathetic way, speak more perceptively and profoundly and with more positive results than do the apologetic theologians. Those theologians who are highly self-critical sharpen up the issues and make advances in their disciplines which are beyond the power of other theologians. A St. Paul is very critical of his inherited Judaism, and a Croce is most contributive to history and art precisely because he tried to do justice to their spirit. The illustrations can be readily multiplied. They all point to the fact that the philosopher is one who ought to be attentive to the claims of all disciplines and who ought to take account of the rights of all finalities; and that the practitioner of one discipline ought to defend his discipline only by limiting its claims. The practitioner uses his own finality without question, and ought to do so, but when he comes to understand (while learning or reflecting on what he is doing) what it is he is assuming, he should be self-critical, alert to the need to face up to difficulties which his insistence on that one finality inevitably introduces.

But surely philosophy offers another finality over against others. This point was conceded when it was said that the multiple permeations which philosophy endorses are not possible to any one individual. Philosophy's answer is an answer in the abstract. It knows about the desirability of the multiple permeations but does not produce them, or act them out. The discipline of philosophy, like any other, exhibits only one finality carried out. Self-awareness of this finality is the recognition that philosophy is abstract; the carrying out of the finality which philosophy accepts is the abstract acknowledgment of the rights of all finalities to permeate one another.

Sometimes men accept another individual as their finality—and thus we have religious, political, ethical, and military leaders. These men, though often respected for themselves, are treated as avenues, as loci, as occasions for the expression of what is truly final. We know that no individual, as a being among many, can be a finality, and that the finality of any one individual is on a footing with others. So far as we place a man above the rest we must say that he is a man unlike all others—a genius, a hero, a saint—or that, though a man like all others, he is being used to express a great truth—a prophet, a man of destiny, an expression of the spirit of the time. We constantly move between these two alternatives. But the former in the end makes for mystery; it takes a man who in every other way is like the rest, to be unlike them. Eventually aware of this paradox, the tendency is to add to his ordinary career a whole series of extraordinary facts—Pythagoras was supposed to have a golden thigh; some saints have double vision or telepathic powers; leaders are believed by their followers to have remarkable aesthetic, physical, and other abilities. But though the position now becomes a little more consistent, it is also more mysterious; how is it that this man born of woman is so unlike all others?

It would be better to take the other alternative and understand the unusual man, whom we are accepting as final, as a chosen man, as one who is carrying out some finality not his own. But are we not now driven back a step to a position similar to the foregoing, for are we not now faced with the question of why this or that man should be a mouthpiece and others not, though all are equally men? We would be driven back if we supposed that only some men can be such mouthpieces, or that the selection of them is entirely arbitrary, for then we would rest everything on an unfathomable mystery.

But suppose instead we remark that there are virtues which answer to the occasion, and that some men are prepared for those occasions, not deliberately but as it were by accident. Their selection is accidental in the sense that it is conceivable that circumstances could be different and thus that some other man might be more appropriate. But whoever is chosen would be a man who had developed some power to high degree, a power open to others but which they did not develop because they were involved in some other enterprise for which the rewards perhaps, though not as great, were more certain and immediate.

At a time when religion has little status, it is not likely that many religious leaders will be found; at a time when the world is at peace, great military leaders are only promissory; at a time when there is a disdain for the world, there is little room for inventors, discoverers, and technologists, though many a man might have native abilities which could be developed were these enterprises encouraged. In a world where no music is tolerated, those who are gifted in this area will not be encouraged and may even be suppressed, with the consequence that they will have no opportunity to express themselves in these areas. But were these the men who under other circumstances would have been great musicians, it is likely that they now, in their unsuitable surroundings, are exhibiting traits of character, virtues of persistence, and powers of originality, ingenuity, self-criticism which may make them appear as eccentrics, or are showing momentary flashes of ability in what otherwise is an unsuitable situation.

Whichever of these alternatives be taken, it is a fact that men do subordinate their own finalities not only to a *we,* but to some other individual, taken somehow to be the epitomization of the *we,* or of some basic mode of Being. And when they do not make such a subordination (as well as when they do) they recognize something to be final only if it be primitive, perhaps even below conceptualization or consciousness. Whenever we treat religion as essentially a feeling, Hocking has observed, we take account of its ultimacy, that it is a foreign power to which one is paying deference.

There are, to be sure, many who think that something is disqualified if shown to be primitive either anthropologically or psychologically, but this is a minority view, and perhaps is not held by these men themselves in all fields and on all occasions, for their own finalities are not propositional nor articulated, and come in a sense before anything they utter or know.

September 3

When we retreat from the world in order to find ourselves, or to prepare for a better approach to it, or to get a better backing for ourselves, we come to a center in terms of which what we encounter can be evaluated and oriented. This finality is satisfactory for the items from which one retreated; but it is not satisfactory for oneself. There is a concern for ethics, religion, practice, and other men because the finality which is ourselves seems to be strong only with respect to what we had privately undergone.

We may abdicate our own position in favor of some other man's, who is then defined to be a man unlike ourselves, either because he is an agency for some other power or because he is made of different stuff. Or we may fall back into some kind of consensus. In these two cases we do not give up the finality which is ourselves with respect to what we privately undergo; we do, though, take our finality not to be sufficient for the purpose of guaranteeing values, or wisdom, or preservation, or sheer objectivity. These finalities in turn are never sufficient to determine what it is that we ourselves are undergoing, and thus what it is that we have felt, sensed, dreamt, remembered, etc. There are times, though, when we may be willing to allow these finalities to be interpreted by these others, and we ourselves might submit to the result. But the submission would be because of the values which are involved and not because of the factual content which is being offered to us.

We yield with respect to our own egos only when the whole confirmation of what we undergo is called into question by a finality which we take to be concerned with more important values. When on behalf of our individuality we reverse this stress, we say instead that we reject or oppose these other finalities precisely because they fail to cohere with the value we feel is intrinsic to ourselves. The conflict then is one of values, so far as it is a conflict between ourselves as individuals, ourselves as represented, the representative, and the commonality.

When now we look to the Ideal as the ground of values we ought to be able to resolve this conflict. It should tell us which of these values is superior, or how they are to be reconciled. Let us suppose that it says we are to subordinate the collective to ourselves whenever there is a conflict in what it and we say. Could we refuse to accept the judgment on the ground that what we ourselves feel is aberrational, or that no mere criterion of excellence has precedence over the feeling or encounter with excellence, say in the shape of the individual's self-awareness and radical reality? We can. Otherwise the Ideal would have absolute priority over these others. But we have already seen that it can be judged and evaluated by the others. Here the evaluation is not in terms of a principle of value, but in terms of the value actually embodied.

The conflict between the Ideal and the individual is a conflict of values; but now the conflict is between the Ideal as expressing excellence but itself as possessed of comparatively little value, and ourselves with great value but with only a limited capacity to give a valuational significance to other entities.

How can we adjudicate this quarrel? One way would be to refer it to a final judge in the shape of God; another way would be to refer it to a final resolver in the shape of an ongoing Existence. Which of these should have precedence? Neither should have precedence, for they belong together.

The reference to God is to a being making use of a principle, though one which is concrete because it is identical with His own meaning or mind. The reference to Existence is to a concrete process which by virtue of its career in time has the effect of a principle of adjudication. The value of these two is also distinct from the value of the others; each has a value of its own, but I do not see how they can be compared. Both lack the austere abstract universality of the Ideal and the concentrated private feeling value of the individual.

The foregoing, ending as it does in a pair of reconcilers, is evidently only one of the ways in which one can move through the various finalities and relate them one to the other. Had one begun with revelation either through a man or in a more absolutistic way, or with causation or history, a different movement through these finalities would take place. Whatever way one took there would always be something in each which would preclude its reduction or complete subordination to the others, and which would allow for it to be prior to all others, from one perspective, and would allow for a distinctive circuit and evaluation of the other finalities.

September 29

The problem of man and woman is obviously distinct from the problem of white and black, Jew and Gentile, old and young. But there is also a sense in which the problem is the same, for it does deal with an issue of majority and minority mentality, an issue which need not be identified with one of numbers, rights or powers, but of attitude, often helped by the fact that one is part of an actual numerical minority, or a minority with respect to rights or powers. The problem of the minority person is his refusal to accept the minority status as definitory while also refusing to reject it (since this is in effect to accept the position of the majority), and his insistence upon becoming an individual who is able to assess not only himself and other members of the minority but all else as well.

The error of most minority people is to live inside the given border, and there carry out a life and use a vocabulary which is essentially framed in terms of a rejection or a lack of opportunity to participate in the majority situation. And thus we have Jewish anti-Semitism, Negro self-hatred, antifeminine women, and the like. On the other hand, those members of the majority who do not express any antagonism toward the minority, often run the risk of being overkind or overconsiderate. And this one can see might be a good political or social attitude to take. But so far as they fail to treat the individual in the minority group as an individual, they fail just as surely as the bigot does.

The minority person does not have full rights until it is recognized that he can be as stupid, as immoral, as imperfect as the majority person. When he tries to be better than the majority person, he is in effect saying to himself that the majority standards are not only right but represent a norm for him which he must fulfill perfectly in order to rightly be the equal of the majority person. But once again this is tantamount to denying his basic equality. The minority person has a right to various privileges and rights because he in fact in himself is the equal of the others; he must not therefore assume that he is required to perform on a different level or in a different way than the majority person, except so far as this is demanded as part of a political or a social strategy.

October 1

The essence of Judaism can be expressed as:

The Lord, My God, is One
The Messiah has not come.

But what is it to be One? God's unity does not preclude a multiplicity of functions and relations. The oneness would seem to be the oneness of an ultimate irreducible mode of Being, and does not preclude the reality of other modes of being. The marks of the Messiah are not well-defined, and what it means for him to have come is also not altogether well-known. All in all the minimal admission required to define Judaism leaves one with a great latitude of interpretation. This means that Judaism is open to almost any theological interpretation. To do justice to its tradition, however, there must be some provision for a religious history, and some provision for the practical carrying out of supposedly divine decrees and the ideas of justice and responsibility expressed by the Prophets.

January 12

There are at least five ways in which we reach realities other than ourselves: 1] enjoyment, 2] penumbration, 3] encounter, 4] revelational re-presentation, and 5] direct access.

1] Enjoyment is somewhat close to what some thinkers, and perhaps most laymen, call experiencing. It involves ourselves and something beyond, in interplay. There are times when we are dominant and identify what we enjoy with a sensation or feeling in us. There are other times when we feel overwhelmed and speak of ourselves as participating in, or being in the presence of something. These are extremes in a spectrum.

It is correct to say with Peirce that we here have a phenomenon, but it would be wrong with him to suppose that we, when at the participative extreme of the spectrum, are involved in a different type of enjoyment than we had at the other extreme. What he calls Secondness is but a limiting case of which his Firstness is the other. There is, in short, no mere Firstness which is sheer presence; Firstness, or enjoyed possibility, is the real in which our contribution is maximized. Secondness, in Peirce's sense, is a case where the object contributes more than the individual in the sense of making that individual function only as a counterforce with respect to it—though of course as a counter-force the individual and the object are on a footing. Be that as it may, enjoyment is phenomenal, and locatable anywhere from deep within us to far outside us in a phenomenal space.

2] Penumbration is an act of reaching realities which transcend the enjoyed content. When the enjoyed content is judgmental, I have been in the custom of calling penumbration "adumbration." The discussion of adumbration in *Reality* still seems to me to be basically right. We do not remain wholly on the surface of things, but when and as we enjoy the content, either as subjective or objective, we penetrate beyond it, but not through an extra effort, nor with any conscious intent. Indeed most philosophers seem to be unaware of penumbration, and it is rarely referred to in the most careful accounts of knowledge. But there is something referred to whenever we enjoy something, though what this is to which we refer we do not know, except that it has some claim on the content we are enjoying, and is sometimes used as the ground to which that content is attributed either as an effect or as a property. Aristotle's doctrine of common sense seems at times to be a doctrine which relates to penumbration, since his common sense reaches beyond the particular senses to the object which these diversely specialize or on which they take perspectives.

In enjoyment we have the real in operation on us, with ourselves providing at least the subjective warmth of feeling to the particular content which is present. When our concern is with ultimate realities we find that they are present in us initially, and that we eventually find, e.g., in mysticism, love, action, and devotion, that we enjoy them at a distance from ourselves as well. In penumbration, we move not from ourselves to the realities at a distance, but to what is below, outside the enjoyed content, whether this content be located in us or outside us.

3] Encounter is perhaps the most widely recognized means by which we make contact with reality. This is due perhaps to the fact that we so often start with ideas and hypotheses and seek only to check these by the facts. Encounter in this sense is one with what is often meant by an experience. We speak of ourselves experiencing, i.e., enjoying something, but we say we have an experience only when we in fact are resisted by something, met by a counterforce. This counterforce is not Peirce's Secondness, but the object itself as matching our idea or hypotheses.

Our ideas and hypotheses, since they are carried by real beings, have a penumbrational component. This was made evident in the discussion of perception in *Reality*. There it was seen that subjects and predicates, indicateds and contemplateds in judgments are not simple entities, but have corresponding penumbras. The synthesis produced by the judgment is in effect the filling out of each penumbra by the nucleus of the other entity. The penumbra of the contemplated is filled out by the nucleus of the indicated; and conversely, the nucleus of the contemplated fills out the penumbra of the indicated.

Penumbration also moves in depth. Our ideas always reach beyond themselves to a real outside the content we enjoy. Every idea could be said to have an aura of reality, unfocussed, unparticularized but nevertheless capable of being filled out, specified by what lies outside our being and what we enjoy. The real objects in this world, and ultimate realities as well, can all be said to have an aura of "ideationality" about them, which is filled out when they are met by a knowing mind. The ideationality is in fact the element they contribute, to constitute a togetherness with other entities. Since these togethernesses are diverse in kind, there evidently are many auras, of which the ideational is but one case.

There is no need to suppose that encounter, in the sense of facing a particular fact, is primary or final in that it actually determines what is real. The real is the product of the matching of penumbras, and it is only because we start off with our ideas that we look to something beyond us to provide us with a counteracting, reciprocal penumbration. But sometimes we do start off the other way; having spent our time and energies being involved with particular matters of fact, we sometimes look to ourselves for ideas by which to explain what we have been undergoing or interplaying with. And sometimes we refer what we acknowledge to a counterpart which will, with it, make a whole.

Dialectic is the method by which an attempt is made to discover the supplementary items which have nuclei matching the given penumbras. We know that the nuclei match (despite the fact that we are usually unaware of the penumbras of ourselves or of the things we acknowledge) by virtue of the fit they exhibit in the resultant whole.

We here are at the root of the answer to the question "what does it mean to 'verify'?" A verification involves ideas and objects altogether other than those ideas. Yet the one can be said to verify the other only because the aura of reality of the ideas answers to the nucleal fact of the objects encountered; and conversely, because the penumbras of the objects answer to the nucleal nature of the ideas. The outcome of a verification is a complex entity, one part of which is given by the nucleal idea and the other part of which is given by the nucleal object, each filling out the aura provided by the other. The known verified fact is thus different from the fact confronted, for the latter is environed by an aura of "ideationality" which has not yet been filled out. To fill it out in a scientific way is to come to the facts armed with a systematic philosophic theory.

4] The discussion of art in the art books, particularly in *The World of Art*, points up the fact that we can with profit turn away from reality at times, providing we then take advantage of our creative powers and try to make something excellent. A work of art, it was said, was a created whole which reproduced the texture and lilt of Existence. It was by attending to the problems of art, by making a work of art, that one was enabled to penetrate beyond the surface and conventional aspects of reality to the more basic Existence beyond.

What art does for Existence, service does for God, speculative knowledge does for Actuality, and virtuous activity does for Ideality. These of course have to do with ultimate realities. What is now being sought, and what has been discussed above for the most part, are ways of knowing particular objects, i.e., not ultimate realities, but individual actualities. Here we have recourse not to knowledge, as is the case with Actuality as such, but to sympathy. We feel with others, and in that "feeling with" we begin to portray the other by virtue of the fact that we have made ourselves feel in ourselves what we ourselves are. It is by reaching into the roots of ourselves by means of our feeling that we are enabled to discover the nature of the beings who are outside us. Sympathy is most readily achieved for other men; our grasp of lower forms of actuality is the outcome of a modification of the kind of grasp we have of men—and perhaps, even as is suggested in *The God We Seek,* of the grasp we have of sacramental objects.

5] There is finally the method of direct access. In the field of perception this has been termed the method of acquaintance, though it is hard to know, from those who hold this view, whether it is the real in its roots or only phenomena, in the first of our five senses, which is being said to be the terminus of the access. In the field of religion, access is thought to be the special achievement of the mystic; in ethics it is achieved by submission to an obligation; in the field of Existence, it is achieved by work; in the realm of Actuality, access is achieved by systematic metaphysics, and access to particular actualities is achieved by "intuition," though exactly what this is in this connection I am not now sure.

Perhaps what ought to be said in connection with actualities is that "love" is a complex and ambiguous term, having the role of providing us with enjoyment, penumbration, encounters, and revelational representations, as well as a direct access. It is eminently desirable to distinguish these different components in it, and to provide a "phenomenology" of love in which the different components are held apart from one another, thereby giving us different types of love.

How are the above five modes of reaching reality related to one another? No one of them is evidently sufficient in itself. We seem too often, though, to suppose that encounter needs no further support because encounter is that mode of reaching reality in which a support is then and there provided, and because we are here content with determining which of our ideas are viable and not with getting to the object itself in-itself.

Encounter surely does not give us a genuine access to the object. It may provide only the thinnest of enjoyments, and blur the penumbration which the facts themselves have with respect to other confrontations besides that of ideas. It surely does not give us that rich reproductive content in terms of which we can understand what lies beyond our direct apprehension. It would be more correct to say that each of these approaches is taken to be final and satisfactory for some purposes, that each one has many cases, and these different cases supplement one another.

Can we make the five supplement one another? To do so we would have to have some way of standing outside them all (some superaccess), some way of turning away from them in order to discover what it is that underlies their several objects (some superrevelational re-presentation), some confrontation of them all, with a reality beyond them all (a superencounter), some way of reaching outside them via their diverse referential notes (a superpenumbration), and some way of having the real beyond them enjoyed by us (a superenjoyment). These "super" forms are but the older forms, employed on themselves. If we acknowledge the legitimacy of them all we are faced with the question of how they are related. This will bring us to a third level, and so on and on. But this regress is harmless; it does not affect our grasp of the real, but only the way in which our various methods of reaching the real are to be related one with the other. We do get to the real in enjoyment, for example. When we also get to it through an access, we have the question of how the two results are related. We can answer this by referring to a superencounter or a superaccess, etc. The result will be a richer quality. As a consequence, we must admit that there is something desirable in the regress. But if the regress is infinite it would seem as if we could never get to the real but only to fragments of it.

Would it not perhaps be better to say that encounter is a generic form, and that it provides us with an agency by which the other different approaches (including an encounter with fact) are interrelated? This means that each must have penumbra; each must be enjoyed. Each will fall short of a direct access to their union, unless such an access is then and there provided through an intensification of the initial access. Each will have to be said to give us a kind of re-presentation of the real in that it does tell us about it, and does this by a means which is distinct from the real. If we take this tack, what we are in effect saying is that each of the means, when it is related to the others in an encountering way, acquires a stronger form—enjoyment, penumbration, and representation will be multiplied, and access intensified. Any particular encounter of idea and fact will be but an item in the single encounter of the different means. But such a superencounter would perhaps be better termed a "supplementation."

What we have then are five approaches to the real, which are then made to supplement one another in such a way that each is strengthened. The act of supplementing them would be the act by which we were placed over against the real we thereby were able to penetrate.

Let us apply this conclusion to our knowledge of God. We enjoy Him in ourselves, in experience, in sacramental objects, in the dedicated community, and in faith. We penumbrate to Him through the fissures of experience, in a reference beyond the sacramental objects, in one beyond the dedicated community, and in the seeking of faith. We encounter Him when we approach Him in terms of an idea of Him and face this with the supranatural content. We produce a revelational representation of Him in service in His name. And we have direct access to Him in mysticism. When we supplement these by one another we have a grasp of God as a being to whom we have an access, and whom we also enjoy and encounter. At the same time we represent Him in our lives and take advantage of the penumbration of Him that we had earlier, supplementing this in fact with the penumbrations of the different means we have been using to get to Him.

January 13

Do penumbras environ nuclei or do they merely point away in some one direction? If the former, it should be possible to relate any one nucleus to any other; any approaches to reality, or any items in a judgment, could then have any role. If the latter, different nuclei would have different functions. Consideration of the distinctive roles of subjects and predicates, of knowledge or ideas over against facts or encountered items, would indicate that in some cases at least penumbras do not environ nuclei, and that one must match certain items with certain others.

We can distinguish amongst the various approaches to reality those which are insistent, adventurous, outward-going, from those which are receptive. The conspicuous cases are of course ideas or hypotheses, and encountered facts. But we can go back to yesterday's set of approaches and list them as either active or passive. To be sure, knowledge, particularly speculative knowledge, will make a claim to be unlike other insistent approaches in that it will try to be neutral (and thus to encompass all other insistent approaches) and perhaps even report the outcome of the union of these with others. But this means, I think, that we must distinguish between knowledge as one approach, requiring a counterapproach from the object, and knowledge which is neutral, involving perhaps the union of the foregoing knowledge with its counterpart. This neutral speculative knowledge might be thought of on the analogue of art, and thus not to make a claim which was to be answered by something beyond it, but instead was to provide a construction. This, by virtue of its excellence, would reveal the nature of the reality which was beyond it, without making any effort to provide an approach to it, requiring a counteracting supplement.

Speculation, penumbration, and re-presentation, however, might all be treated as outgoing, and as requiring a counteragent in the shape of an enjoyment, and as accesses which are direct and which, without mediation, are with the content they seek. But in that case the union of the two approaches must be of a distinctive kind—a synthesis which can no more claim to be cognitive than experiential. It will have the outgoing and the ingoing thrusts balanced.

Might it not be the case that there are some penumbras which environ their nuclei? I see no reason why this may not be so. Would these not be the primary elements of being, knowledge, or discourse which could assume any role in any context? But what are these? Transcendentals?

Might it not be the case that speculative knowledge may in some contexts have the role of being a singular approach, needing a particular counteracting one, and that in other contexts it might offer a final synthesis for a pair of subordinate thrusts in opposite directions? Yet it seems to be the case on the one hand that knowledge of whatever kind must always be faced with an object, and that on the other hand there is no significant synthesis which is noncognitional. In short, we would seem to be faced with the situation that the highest possible synthesis always leaves over something which is to be synthesized with the supposed final synthesis, and that this subsequent synthesis cannot give us an object which we know. Perhaps all we can do is to live with or through the fitting of an intellectual approach with the counteracting one, and to have the intellectual approach be a neutral, comprehensive one; this would allow a place for similarly directed particular efforts, and would have as its supplement a reality of a similar generality and neutrality toward the particular ways in which we are being confronted.

In the end we seem to be stopping with a mere fact of adjustment, in which the synthesis is accomplished but not itself made an object of knowledge. Yet it is known. Is it not perhaps the case that what we then have is the complete object, at once intelligible and objective, and that if we want to know or grasp this object we must now place it in another context, say history? The historical situation will itself have to be known by means of a supplementation of approaches, but the real object will have already been made evident as that which is inside one approach to the total historical situation. We would know what we had synthesized only by placing it in a larger context, which would require that we add a supplement to the synthesis in order to see a new kind of entity, the historical object which is the synthesized real object in a new role. We avoid an indefinite regress of contexts by supposing that the synthesized object, when placed in the historic context, loses a dimension of itself which is recovered when the item is taken out of the historic context. In other words, the object as synthesized is in a distinctive context; without losing anything of its being, we can know what it is (and not merely have it in its context) by placing it in another context. We know what an object is by finding another context for it than the context which enabled it to be just that object.

The last suggestion is something like, or is somewhat related to Austin's idea that there is a difference between "x is y" and "it is true that x is y"; the former is offered in an open world, the latter tells about a closed one. What we have when we make a final synthesis of knowledge and confronted fact, is not an object which is identical with our judgment (as the Kantians and the idealists seem to suppose), but instead something having the status of "it is true that . . . ." When we seek to know what that object is we tear it away from the context "it is true that . . ." and find another having another way for it to be "it is true that . . . ."

While we move from one state to the other, we know the object as in- and of-itself only in the sense that we can contrast the two types of context and recognize that the object remains selfsame. I think this last remark is not in full consonance with what was said above. It in effect says that the object which is produced through a union of various approaches is imbedded in a context from which it can be abstracted, and thus known to have other properties and roles in some other context. Why do I hold that I see it as sustained by something supplementary to myself?

The last suggestion in effect says that we make a synthesis which is the real object as at once intelligible and objective, inside a context where we as beings are made one with the reality in which the object is to be imbedded. The object is within the area which we and some other reality constitute. The question that immediately arises is how this synthesis of ourselves and the context in which the object is to be located in relation to us as real beings (and not as knowers only) is to be known.

Must we not say that any knowing of an object is but the restatement of it as something cognized? When we know the nature of the context constituted by a synthesis of our being and the reality in which the object is located, we abstract from them both and thereby insert them both in the real union of them.

We always have a union of our real beings and the context in which the synthesized object was imbedded. When we attend to that union we do so by forging something subordinate within it. In this particular case we isolate cognitive and insistent features of the union and bring these together inside the union in fact. We know the union by a simulacrum within it.

If we have as the object of our inquiry some such ultimate reality as God, will the context in which our knowledge is imbedded be anything other than God Himself in a real relation to us as actualities? The knowledge of ultimate realities always occurs within the cosmological union of ourselves and those realities. Does this not deny the ultimacy of the ontology of the modes of Being, and replace it by a cognitional cosmology of all the modes together? If so, we would then be on our way to substituting an idealistic monism for a realistic pluralism, for we would be seeing the various modes of beings as limits of a rational world of internally related items. But why may not there be an idealistic cosmology which reveals that the connected items have an independent being outside the cosmological whole within which the ontological items are identified? Is the cosmological cognitional whole inside the ontological situation of ultimate realities, but there exercising an independent role? Does one come to know one of these realities by "reducing" it to a component in a cosmological situation of interrelated entities in an epistemological setting?

January 14

There is some gain in reversing the stress of the last days and, instead of referring to a penumbration as though it were an outward move, take it instead to be a residual result. We would then have an insistence by the object or oneself, and a residual penumbra on the part of each. Other beings intensify the penumbra of ourselves, and conversely. Suppose, for example, we approach another being with an idea. Then we would structuralize the residual penumbra in it, give it a mean-

ing in a context of our ideas; we would make explicit the structure it
has in-itself by relating that structure to other structures in the totality
of our intelligible scheme. Conversely, the presence, say of God in us,
would consist in the provision of an intensification of ourselves. We
would have this intensification in ourselves, but only as related to other
meanings. These meanings would be in God so far as God is approached
from us, and would be in us so far as the intensification was being
viewed as an approach *to* us. The objectivity of any one approach is
provided by the fact that other approaches make explicit what is implicit,
and this is achieved by relating the implicit to other items in that other
approach's totality.

When I approach God from an intellectual position I have an idea
of Him. The objectivity of my idea is provided by the possession of it
by Him. Conversely, He as a penumbra is given objectivity by virtue of
His being intensified by the idea as part of a larger set of ideas.

The thing-in-itself then has the nature we know it to have; but in
knowing it, either our ideas or the residual penumbra of the object
obtains objectivity by virtue of the other as part of a new totality of
penumbral meaning or set of ideas. It isn't that the being is not objective
by itself. But when we approach it from one angle we make use of a
single idea or expression or act, and locate this in a penumbral totality,
thereby making explicit the additional content of the being, but then
doing nothing to our idea to make it known to be objective. It is only
when we take the penumbra to possess the additional content, the explicit structure as subordinate, that the idea achieves objectivity.

We say that our ideas are true when we withdraw them from the
situation where they are verified. Verification is but the finding of a
penumbral field which gives objectivity to the idea—it is what Kant
meant by experience. But then there is the converse: the penumbral
whole might itself be taken as a unit; it is then that we look to the set
of ideas to provide it with objectivity. Without the set of ideas the
penumbra would be merely a possibility, a meaning.

The qualifications God imposes on us gives our egos an objective
role. But we can also take the intensifications that God provides, and
catch the implicit unitary meaning in them in the shape of a lived residual penumbra-ego which then gives the divine intensification a context
in us.

What is implicit has a role in a being. The imposition of a matching
other isolates the implicit item—e.g., structure—and gives it another
context, say, in the shape of ideas. Or conversely, the structure is taken

Paul Weiss revises his manuscripts in shorthand, and occasionally writes in shorthand when no typewriter is available.

up and given a context in the being, or (if the structure be taken as that which is approached) our idea of it is taken up into the context of that structure as having a kind of vigor, or power, or at least a content denied to the idea as such.

The foregoing was typed at Pomona College on an electric machine which I evidently have not mastered. It was taken from shorthand notes which I jotted down when the typewriter was not available.

January 15

There are evidently two types of context. One is a penumbral being which is intensified by nuclei from others; the other is a systematic interrelationship of penumbras, which is specified in the shape of a single item. When we have an idea, we make explicit the structure in another being by giving the intelligibility of that being a place within the context of our ideas or meanings. Our idea here functions merely as a pivotal point. When instead we wish to use our ideas to deal with objective material, we allow the penumbral being to make the beingness of the idea explicit. Similarly, when we are intensified by something coming from without, we give the intruder the status of being part of us by making explicit in it the element "being felt"; and when the intrusion serves as a way of giving us a context, it makes itself function as a pivot which makes explicit the fact that we have a place within a realm of intruded beings.

If we take the foregoing, two at a time, it may be clearer. We intrude on others by way of our ideas, and allow our ideas to be given a context in the penumbral reality of others. But we do not always take the penumbral reality of others as a resting place; we sometimes wish to see what it means. When we do this we use the idea as the way in which the penumbral reality can enter into the realm of our ideas by virtue of its structure.

If we think of our ideas as providing one of a number of approaches to an entity, and if we are concerned with knowing whether there is in fact something real answering to our ideas, what we must do is to find another approach which will accept our ideas as items in its context, thereby making explicit something in the ideas. Thus if we approach God in terms of some idea, we must use our enjoyment of Him in or through experience, in a dedicated community, etc., to give the idea a context where it will be related to other ideas. The enjoyment of Him will then prove to be something like the binding tissue of the various ideas we have of Him, making those ideas have an external being, i.e. have a life apart from us. Conversely, if we wish to know whether the enjoyment is an enjoyment *of* Him, that there is in fact something outside the mere enjoyment, then we must have our idea make explicit the structure in the enjoyment, and thereby relate that enjoyment to other enjoyments.

The terminus of an idea becomes objective by being caught within a context of other termini which are of course external to the given idea; the terminus of the emotion or enjoyment becomes objective by being caught within the context of structuralizing ideas. It is because, as it were, the enjoyment belongs to a world of its own, capable of controlling the idea by relating it in certain ways, and because the context of ideas belong to a world capable of controlling the enjoyment by relating it in certain ways, that the terminus of the idea is able to be detached from the idea and the enjoyment, allowed to have a being beyond that of a referent of the idea or the emotion.

We move in depth and achieve objectivity for our penetrative terminus by having it caught in a world of breadth. That breadth is the penumbral reality, functioning as a controlling systematic power. Does this not reduce our initial double-context view to only one case? Is not the penumbral being which is intensified but the breadth of context for that which makes one factor in it pivotal and explicit? If so, we would seem to be led to the conclusion that we know a thing in-itself only when we see that what we truly know of it is objectively related to other realities.

If we make many approaches to the same being should we have so many different realities, no more and no less? The answer to this question can be put in a double way. So far as we are trying to know a being, we approach it and are confronted with it; there are therefore only two approaches to consider. But we can confront it from three positions. So what we have is a threefold approach to it, and a single encounter with it. The encounter of course can have multiple modalities, such as the enjoyment of it in ourselves, the enjoyment of it as at a distance from ourselves, the feel of it in a mystical access, the having it in a revelational experience, etc. All of these give us the content for our ideas, our ideals, and our activities.

Staying with a pair, say ideas and content enjoyed, we can say that the real entity is the center of an intersection of a realm of ideas, or a scientific system with a realm of content. Or we can say that reality is the togetherness of two modes of being over against Actuality, as represented by a man with ideas. The idea of God can be said to isolate Him from the context of the other two realities, at the same time that God Himself can be said to isolate the idea from the context of other ideas. The being of God in-Himself would be this localized intersection. When we come to know God, and want to make sure that we have a real object to know, we must reinsert Him in the context of the other realities, or take His isolated being as content and have it caught up within the realm of our ideas.

January 16

A real Being serves to make intrusive aspects of other Beings into concrete mediators of the other two Beings (or where we are dealing with particular actualities, to make facets of other modes of Being be connected by a facet made concrete by the actuality). Thus God takes an idea of Himself and makes it be the unity of Ideality and Existence. He takes the Good and makes it unify Actuality and Existence. He takes vitality and makes it unify Actuality and Ideality. Actuality, Ideality, and Existence do the same for an aspect of God, and for aspects of one another, with God as one of the terms.

In-itself, then, a real object solidifies an aspect of another real Being to make it relate the remaining two. A real Being is the concreteness of an aspect of each of the other three modes. It is a Being having over against it three other modes of Being; its nature can be expressed as that which has as aspects all three of these other Beings made solid and relational with respect to any other two. God is thus my idea, the Ideal in the shape of a goal, and Existence in the guise of vitality, each functioning in the manner peculiar to His unity so as to mediate two modes outside Him. The idea is objectified and concretionalized in the shape of a unity for Ideality and Existence. The Being or the idea as a concrete unity is what we mean by the reality of God from the perspective of intelligibility or understanding.

If we want to know what God is like from the perspective of value we must replace in the foregoing the idea of God by a goal, and that of Ideality by Actuality. We have an analogous change to make if we approach God from the perspective of action. In-Himself, as all three, He would be all aspects of all three having the ultimacy of the three, each in the role of a unity for the other two. This sounds as though God had no being or nature of His own; but it means merely that we are speaking of Him from outside Him. Also, what are aspects of the other modes made concrete in Him, can also be said to be Him implicitly, but made explicit by virtue of the intrusion of other beings.

Were there but two beings in the universe we would have to say that each could be described as an aspect of another, made as concrete as its other. Were three beings all there were in the universe, we would have to say that each was to be understood as making aspects of the other two concrete and over against itself.

January 20

Each mode of being provides a distinctive context for what intrudes on it. To approach God, for example, in terms of ideas, a set of values, or in action, is to have them ennobled and given an additional value. We know that our idea of God is true if we find it enriched by the content of an enjoyment of Him. This is the confirmation of the idea. To ask if the content is the content of the divine is to await determination as to whether the idea is the idea of the divine. If it is, then we answer the question affirmatively. But if we want to know what a given content means we must refer it to ourselves who will give it a personal value, a richness of a "psychological" sort. Is this an experience of God? Yes, so far as we thereby enrich the content by making it part of our vital existence.

Suppose I hear what purports to be the voice of God. This is content received, and it must be understood in such a way that my acceptance of it as His voice means that it is enriched in significance by being adopted by me. The voice of God becomes more significant, says more things by being made part of me. If the voice says "kill," it could be the voice of God only as this expression was thereupon intensified in the being of man in relation to other men. If the man is bad or corrupt or foolish it will have one import; if he is good it will have another. For the former it might lead to the killing of others, but for the good man it will have the effect of revealing the awesome nature of God, and the fact that no being should be prior to Him, but it will not result in an actual killing. God's presence or voice is subordinate to the character of a man, just as ideas, purposes, or actions are subordinated to the excellence which is God.

The Ideal provides a systematic normative significance, and Existence provides extra implications. If the voice of God is heard by a prophet, it commands that something be said or done. This means that though it comes through the individual it must, through his mediation, be in fact affected by an action. It will have implications which it otherwise would not have, in that the utterance will now require and entail consequences which it did not before. To say something to me is to appeal to me in relation to Existence; "kill" should make me more adjusted and contemporary, and not exaggerate the value of any thing.

The following reflects reflections on a conversation with Steve Ericson.

1] There is more to the universe than entities (i.e., particular actualities), for entities are together and controlled.

2] Being is no entity, for this would require a further being beyond to make it together with what else there was, and to control it.

3] Being is no project, for then there would be no prescriptions. We are subjected to conditions beyond us; these conditions have a rationale and are not merely put there or supposed to be there by us. If they were, they would not be able to sustain subsequent or subordinate projects.

4] There are four beings: God who necessitates an increase in value for what comes inside His context; the Ideal which determines our obligations, logical and ethical; Existence which compels, brutally making us contemporaries with one another; and Actuality which determines what is of vital importance.

5] We can picture a being alongside us—Existence; before us—Ideality; below us—Actuality; and above us—God. This yields a square environing ourselves and all other entities. So far as we are actualities we have the base of the square as our primary environment. But we need not suppose that any being is distant from us. Beings provide us with necessitating totalities into which we and our operations fit.

6] Beings give our ideas of them new contexts in the sense of giving ideas new meanings or consequences. Conversely, any content we get is altered by being made to have a role in- and for-us. There are basically only two approaches, but each may have many components intertwined, and it is possible to isolate one and ignore the others.

7] Even God is not remote in any sense but that of having a Being which gives extra values and new neighbors and roles to what I and all others present to Him. We ought to have no more trouble accepting Him than we have in accepting the presence and reality and availability of space-time which is "alongside" in the very sense in which God is above —i.e., their realities begin where ours end, and have an extent, a magnitude far outside us. The fact that we do not encompass them as unities does not mean that we do not touch their being.

January 28

He who abandons the familiar world of every day, in practice or in theory, will soon end in frustration and fantasy. It is there where we live; it is there where most of our ideas, our language, our desires, our hopes and prospects find their satisfaction. Still, no one can remain with it in the shape it has initially. The familiar world is crisscrossed with errors and confusions, superstitions, traditions, and hardened misconceptions. It reflects in part the folly as well as the wisdom of the society in which we live. It is shot through with values and assumptions reflecting the nature of our own individual experiences rather than what in fact is encountered.

The discovery that the commonsensical world cannot be accepted as it is encountered and gradually understood, comes quite early. The youngest child is disappointed soon and often; much is unknown and much is obscure for it. And it is soon overrun with questions and doubts which the familiar world cannot quite settle. Why am I here? Why does this happen? Who made the world? Such questions soon come to the fore as questions for which it has no answer. Indeed any and all questionings of the common sense world (even when performed idly and not pursued resolutely) are philosophical in the sense that they drive one away from the obvious. But the answers to such questions are not necessarily philosophical. One can classify the phenomena, or deal with them in such a way as to find clues for the way to analyze them. One can make inductions, inferences, extend one's hopes, build upon one's past adventures. The philosophical attitude comes about when, instead of trying to interrelate the phenomena either through the imposition of some rule or law or through the discovery of elements which can be related by rule or law, one attempts to isolate what is essentially true of them.

To discover the essential, one must purge the common-sense world of the distortions and intrusions which preclude an objective, neutral, universal understanding of it. This can be done in one of two ways. One can try to separate out a residuum of stable material, either in the form of what is intelligible, or what is elementary, or what is self-contained— methods which are pursued by men as diverse as Plato, Aristotle, Spinoza, and Husserl. The difficulty with this method is that it seems almost inevitably to lose the rush, the complexity, the vital import of the world of everyday at the same time that it frees us from what we have introduced into it for the sake of living at ease in it and with one another.

A better method would be to take the commonsensical world in its concreteness and, instead of trying to abstract something from it as its essential nuclear element, try to see if we can locate the power or ground or unitary being of it (so that the intrusions which convention and experience have introduced can be avoided) without our thereby losing the substantiality of the common-sense world, together with its vitality and involvement with us. This method seems somewhat like the former, for it does go to the essential. But instead of dissecting the common-sense object into elements, it keeps it as full-bodied, and merely tries to find what it takes to be the constant, the steady core of it as a real entity.

It is conceivable of course that there may be no nucleal substance. It is possible too that the results of both this and the other method are themselves unsatisfactory, and that what one ought to do is to proceed at once or as soon as one can, through self-discipline and self-denial, to consider realities having nothing to do with the common-sense world. But since it is the common-sense world which we do want to understand, we must reject these two suppositions. We want to find out what we can learn of the world of every day without jumping, we do not know how or where, to some other realm, and without giving up whatever does vitally interplay with us.

We find ourselves caught up in a world with others. Despite the fact that we have an individual center and even a rhythm of our own, we find that we are related in space, keep abreast in time, and are subject to causal powers. We cannot account for this fact by dealing with mere essences, individual items in atomic isolation, or by leaving the daily world behind. Instead we must refer to the fact that there is a space-time-causal totality, which we conventionally term "nature," from which we are inseparable. To acknowledge this we need not leave entirely behind what we daily know. We continue into that totality by noting that our bodies are related to other bodies across space, in the present, and with respect to powers behind and beneath that compel us to act in various ways.

We are not only compelled, but find ourselves prescribed to, obligated, faced with future prospects which demand that we conform our thinking and our acting to them. All attempts to derive logic and ethics and perhaps even aesthetics from a consideration of what in fact occurs, is faced with the fact that things are not altogether what they ought to be, and that we are lured and obligated by what is not yet realized.

To say that the prescriptions are projects of ours is in the end to say that we deceive ourselves regarding what is to be. But the claim that we deceive ourselves tacitly affirms that there is something else that ought to have been said and thus is once again to open us to prescriptions. We are then not only on the edge of a contemporary world big with a power beyond each of us, but we are on the edge of a future which is insistent, demanding, but which lacks the compulsiveness to make us conform to it. It is therefore a necessitation of quite a different sort than that provided by "nature." I call it Ideality.

In addition we all feel some kinship for one another; we are private beings who nevertheless feel that we are affiliated primarily with other humans, and secondarily with other animals. Eventually we may see and perhaps even feel an affiliation with other beings in this world. This feeling of affiliation has nothing to do with the extensional relation we have to other bodies. We can feel more intimate with something at a distance than with something close by. Nor is it something we feel obligated to achieve. We have it apart from the obligation, and indeed we take our obligations to apply to us as so affiliated. It is our awareness of our affiliation, an affiliation which is on the edge of ourselves as private beings, that makes us aware that we and the others are equally actualities, distinctive beings belonging together not by virtue of our place in space, time, or a series of causes, but by virtue of our natures. I call the affiliational totality of all of us, Actuality.

These different domains on the edge of ourselves are somehow together. They all impinge on us and therefore have some way of being in the same universe with one another. That being in the same universe could conceivably be a merely neutral, descriptive fact expressed by a simple "and"; but it does seem to answer to ourselves in our individual loneliness; it does seem to insist on the different domains over and above what they themselves demand. We are not only compelled by Existence (or Nature) but in addition find ourselves compelled in ways which it does not seem to account for; we are subject to obligations or commands which we cannot rationally justify by taking account of the Ideal; we find that we have affiliations with some men and not with others and that we are being urged to alter this. It is the awareness of these additions that leads us to say that the togetherness of these three domains is not something idle but a domain of its own. Traditionally this has been termed "God." We are led to acknowledge God because He too necessitates, but in a way different from the others. His necessitation is that of making a harmony of the others.

In approaching God in this way we make the explanation or reference to Him apparently something derivative. But it would have been possible to have started with Him, or to have dealt with Him together with two others, and found the remaining domain needed to account for the peculiar way in which He and the others are together in an insistent way. But for the present it is perhaps sufficient to note that God is not something remote, but is instead the Being who is as close as these other domains. Each one of these is on the edge of our being, moving away from it to the being of other substantial distinctive entities like ourselves (affiliated substances), the prospective future, and the reassessor of them all.

Metaphysics is not then to be thought of as an enterprise which abandons the known world for an unknown one; nor is it to be supposed that it concerns itself with elements which have none but an analytic status, such as the Leibnitzian monad; nor (with Dewey) with pervasive traits of experience, as though whatever was ultimate was constantly present. It relates to what is a continuation of ourselves, with an insistence of its own.

Were the domains not insistent, they might be mere projects of ours, hopes and fears thrown across a waste beyond us. Were they not beyond us, we would be divided against ourselves, being subject to conditionings by ourselves, and we would not be together with one another. Were there but one type of insistence we would lose either compulsion, prescription, affiliation, or command.

January 29

To judge from various conversations I have had with both Protestant and Jewish theologians, most reflective men in the field of religion seem to think that it is possible to be religious by taking one step when at least two are needed. Once one admits that there is more to the universe than the commonsensical, with its practical needs and limited objectives, its stress on money and competition and struggle, the religious thinker is inclined to suppose that one has already moved into his fold. But it is possible to hold oneself away from the values and activities of everyday and not yet be religious. After all, this is what the scientist, the artist, the truly ethical man, the inquirer in the fields of comparative religion, and the speculative philosopher do. To be a religious man, one must not only turn away from the contingencies and values of everyday, but must go on and differentiate out that particular division of the noncommonsensical which is the locus or affect or evidence of a Being who assesses whatever there be, and who produces the maximum harmony out of whatever does occur.

There are, to be sure, religious thinkers who deny that any kind of intellectual commitment is involved in their religious acceptances—

these are the confessional "Christians" who seek to avoid being in opposition to any other sect; and there are religious thinkers who hold that it is the object of the religious man to do good to his fellows—a position which is close to what has been called the "social gospel." But a confessional religion, though it ignores the theological affirmations, nevertheless pledges itself in one way rather than another; it at least implicitly takes the position that this particular confessional is right—a position rejected by those who hold that some other religion alone is correct. The willingness of the confessional religious thinkers to accept the others is met by a refusal of those others to accept them; this inevitably leads the confessional thinkers not only to neglect the theological questions which hover on the edge of their own commitments, but to accept those who reject them. And those who hold to the doctrine of the social gospel cannot distinguish their view from that of mere ethicism, unless they can show that they have a different type of obligation to fellow man than any ethicist could have, and that this does not involve an antecedent separation from the world and an acceptance of God apart from it. That there should be service in the name of God is surely true, but this service is possible only so far as there is an antecedent movement away from the world, which is then completed by an act of isolating the divine factor in what is then encountered.

The recognition that there are other transcendental positions besides that of attending to God does not mean that those who take the religious position do not look on all things as somehow subordinated or quickened or ennobled by God. The point being made is that a similar subordination or quickening is also characteristic of those who instead take as basic the position of inquiry, art, ethics, philosophy. And of course those who attend primarily to the world of common sense, either in its gross or as oriented toward history, politics, technology, or cult, also suppose that these positions ennoble the others and encompass them.

S. S. Cohon has remarked on the difference between spirituality and piety, the former answering to the escape from worldly concerns or what he calls "materialism," the latter answering to a personal religion expressed in acts of ritual. But then one must make correlative distinctions for other enterprises such as ethics.

Not all public activities are minor or even subordinate to piety. The participation in a dedicated community is not a falling away from religion but a distinctive mode of being religious. We should have a basic "spirituality" which is completed by piety and religious participation, by ethical and political obligation, by aesthetic and historical creativity, and by inquiry and purposive activity. The political obligation and purposive activity need not be thought of as kept within the initial confines but may, though occupied with this world, be directed toward ends and for a future far outside the purview of any commonsensical practical "worldly" outlook.

Theologians tend too to weaken the force of the basic arguments for God, not only by separating out components of these arguments and taking them for the whole, but by using inadequate examples of what they intend. Thus there is something sound in the theological argument. It offers a fine premiss, provided it be understood to remark that there is a permanent feature of the world (the unity of the extensive separative parts of time, space, and causality) which the world cannot account for. But theologians tend to identify this feature with order, and suppose, without proper regard for the law of probability or any doctrine of chance, that order is not possible without cosmic guidance, and that as a matter of fact the world is ordered in some highly significant way which no course of nature could produce.

The doctrine of evil is also misconstrued. There are evils, and nothing but callousness would allow us to reduce them to mere negativities or essential contrasts for the sake of the whole. But it is also true that what is evil, as oriented toward man or particular entities, can be reorganized by God, so that though the evil does occur from God's perspective, it is also transformed by Him. It is not, then, that cosmically the evil is satisfactory, but that cosmically it has another role without losing the role of being evil for the particular individual.

The answer to the problem of evil, from a religious position, is a cosmically practical one. Evil is what God must transform. He is not to be charged with having brought it about or even with having allowed it to be. It is a product of this world, and not necessarily of man's wickedness, since there are storms and diseases and cataclysms and earthquakes. It provides God with a task. This does not mean that evil is desirable in any sense; it means only that undesirable though it be and remains, it can nevertheless be reorganized and come out as good through God's agency.

January 30

More and more these days I hear the complaint that philosophy has broken up into a plurality of specializations, whose practitioners are intolerant of other specializations, and are set against the idea of philosophy as a humanistic enterprise whose field is all knowledge and being, dealt with in terms of universal categories, and looked at with sympathy, and examined with radical criticism. It is usually thought that this development is the outcome of a disillusionment with the history of thought and its warring, incompatible philosophies; it is thought too that this disillusionment is bolstered by an awareness of the progress made by the sciences. In the attempt to imitate that success, it is believed, philosophers have abandoned their age-old questions. But in light of the fact that the specialties war no less than the grand systems, and that the scientific world does honor such systematic cosmic minds as Newton, it would seem that the answer to the modern development might be located elsewhere. Is it not in part the outcome of the fact that philosophy is an academic discipline and that its teachers must fit inside the academic frame, forcing them to chop up their discipline, to publish quickly and in a format which allows for ready evaluation by nonexperts? Whatever the reason, I know that what I am interested in is in mastering all knowledge and being in principle, and then as purged of arbitrary suppositions and divisive notions, which by definition preclude the presence or activity of other forms of knowledge or being.

Philosophy is a creative enterprise; it is concerned with framing an account of whatever there be, by taking seriously whatever concerns men, and examining carefully the claims of any particular enterprise, both in the light of the evidence it provides and the possibility it offers for allowing one to understand other enterprises, and the way it and the others are interrelated. There is a kind of pretentiousness to philosophy, which is mitigated by the modesty of the individual philosopher, and by his presenting his views as clearly as he can for criticism by others.

I think I showed my first sign of a philosophic temper when I was about seven or eight. I remember my teacher saying in the first or second grade that every word in the English language was composed of the twenty-six letters of the alphabet that I had just learned. I found this statement astounding. It did not seem to me that my apparently large vocabulary could be dissected into or built up out of just twenty-six letters. I remember going over all the words I could dredge up and trying to see if any of them contained letters that I had not been taught. I thereupon evidenced many of the traits of the philosopher—wonder, refusal to accept the word of authority, naiveté, self-challenge, arrogance, and eventual submission to the evidence, though I was far from providing a proof.

Later, when I was in my teens, I spent hours in the library reading books of proverbs in the hope of catching all the wisdom of the ages in a brief form and quickly. Once again I exhibited some of the virtues of the philosopher—a desire to know, an interest in wisdom, a concern for the general statement rather than for the multiple details. What I did not then know is that true philosophic wisdom is achieved only by one who has mastered philosophic knowledge—i.e., one who has gone through the discipline of examining basic ideas in the light of what is otherwise known and in terms of the clarifications they provide in other fields. A systematic, comprehensive, dialectical study prepares the ground for a self-confidence, in the sense of allowing one to have a perspective which is not as unexamined as those which one otherwise would have used. This self-confidence enables one to live a life outside the fray of warring ideologies and particular philosophic schools. It does however seem to lead one to live an even more lonely life than is usually the case with the intellectual—though this perhaps is an illusion which each creative thinker finds natural to embrace.

I saw a copy of my *Modes of Being* in a library recently with none of its pages showing any sign of wear. It seemed to me to be unusually austere and barren, the kind of book one usually finds in the library under the heading of philosophic systems, ontology, and sometimes mathematical schemes, doctrines of the aesthetic principle, and the like. They look as if a great deal of work had been spent on something useless, and that there would be no point in subjecting oneself to the trouble of studying them since they are fruitless, having no significant outcome either in the minds or actions of men, or giving any promise of allowing such outcomes on the part of anyone.

I understand the *Modes of Being* to be only one of my books. I think perhaps an entrance can be made to it via the other books, and perhaps even via the present diary. If it and all the others are neglected, I cannot say that I am unhappy or think that I have wasted my life. I did have the opportunity to investigate every avenue of knowledge and being in which I took an interest, and whatever I wrote and sent to be printed has been printed.

I had hoped, I must say, for a kind of immortality in or through my works. This I cannot now know will occur. But the desire for that immortality seems to decrease with time, and I am more and more content with the fact that I have tried to think basically, independently and honestly, and to allow nothing from science to religion, art to politics, education to sports to be defined as improper or insignificant, or as having an answer which I must accept without examination.

Now that it is announced that I am to resign from the editorship of the *Review of Metaphysics* I am discovering how many people had thought the *Review* was a splendid periodical—Mink said it was the best in the world, and perhaps it is—and how many people had identified me with it in the sense of thinking that my departure from it would mean its decline. I do not know if anyone thinks that I will have lost anything either in the guise of prestige or stimulus or status, but I know that I have never thought of myself as primarily an editor. I do not feel a gap in my life; editing was something into which I somehow fell, and which I continued to do because it offered a challenge, and provided a continuity between what I had been creatively doing one day and the next.

I think I have always taken myself to be an original philosopher, and that I wanted various honors primarily as a certification that I was able, and that my views were viable. But now I see that the only certification I can get is in the honest opinion of others, and perhaps in the kind of work which is done in response to a reading of my things. I know that those who have worked with me feel that I have been living a philosophic life, so far as the use of my mind was concerned, and that they think I show a philosophic temper in the largeness of my vision and the spirit in which I approach academic matters and the needs and concerns of younger colleagues. It is hard to know of course how much this is a consequence of security, reputation in the academic community, and age. In any case, I know that this is not what I primarily cherish. What I want is to be a philosopher. I know I am this in one sense, that of trying to think deeply and persistently on every question that occurs to me relating to the roots of knowledge and being and the basic enterprises which men have found of vital importance. But whether I am a philosopher to any significant degree in the sense in which Plato, Aristotle, Kant, and Hegel (to mention those in the first flight), or in which Augustine, Aquinas, Descartes, Leibnitz, Spinoza (to mention those in the second), or in which Bergson, Berkeley, Dewey, Fichte, Heidegger, Hobbes, Hume, Husserl, James, Peirce, Plotinus, Rousseau, Schopenhauer, Whitehead (to mention those in the third) are, I do not know. I think what I have done is somewhere between the second and the third, and that at moments I am between the second and the first. But it is possible that taken by and large—and to judge from present reception or, rather, neglect in the journals—I am in the fourth group with Bosanquet, Bradley, M. R. Cohen, Hartshorne, C. I. Lewis, Maritain, Mead, G. E. Moore, Royce, Tillich (I would be inclined to put myself toward the top of this list and Cohen at the bottom). When I strive to be as objective as possible, and then run the risk of reading "hope" for "accomplishment," I place myself among the leaders of the second group. But there is little in the literature that gives any indication that this is where I am now thought to be, or will eventually be placed. But this is, though of some interest to me still, of less and less interest, and thus I gladly turn to other matters.

Like everyone else I too must reflect my times and my teachers. Taken in a broad sense, the view I have been developing without any consciousness that that is what it is, is a systematic metaphysical pluralism. Pluralism is characteristically American. But the systematic character of my approach is traceable to Whitehead as is my interest in metaphysics; M. R. Cohen awakened and supported the interest in comprehensiveness.

January 31

The more I speak with theologians, and the more I reflect on the history of theology, the more I am struck by the this-worldiness of their concerns. I am not thinking of their concern for advancement, their ambitions, jealousies, and the like, difficult though this be to understand, even when one has made allowances for human frailty, the fact that every discipline has fringe people, and that one's values are set in part by the community in which one lives. What is perplexing, and makes me feel that the theologians are somewhat pathetic, is their absorption in worldly problems, and their involvement, pro and con, in secular philosophies. It makes sense to think of their having these interests if they had clearly left the world behind for a time to attend to God, and then had returned to the world with a new perspective on the world and on the various philosophies of the day. Perhaps this is what in fact occurs, but then one would expect to find that the world and the philosophies would somehow be illuminated—and this does not seem to be the case.

Why should the theologian be interested in adjusting his revealed or hoped-for truth to some philosophy or other? After all, a Bonaventura did offer an entirely new point of view oriented in Christianity and, in the light of what it taught him, tried to understand the nature of things and man. I suppose that the classical Indian thinkers also attended to the nature of things in the light of what they understood religiously. A failure to take the religious position seriously in a metaphysical sense may involve an adherence to ideas and schemes which are not compatible with what the religion intends. And yet one needs an independent check by philosophy to make sure what it is that one is arriving at through religion; it also helps us know what a religion entails. Are we not forced to the conclusion that particular religions, and the theologies which are based on them, are not sufficiently neutral or large enough to make possible a broad outlook, and that one must go to a philosophy for this?

The usual answer to this question sets faith and reason in opposition. But theology is not a matter of faith. It is an exercise in reason based on doctrines that may be grounded in faith, but it is no less a rational enterprise for that. Consequently the difficulty would seem to lie in the fact that the antecedent commitment of the theologian prevents him from considering questions of a philosophic nature as inside his field. He is forced then to turn to the so-called professional philosopher for ideas regarding the cosmos, man, life, ideas, categories, and the like. Aware of this fact, some theologians have taken the position that philosophy is irrelevant or obscuring or misleading, and should be put aside. This group is surely right, over against the first, so long as a reference is being made to philosophies built on principles which the theologian cannot accept—free inquiry, the willingness to accept conclusions which go counter to the statements of an accepted creed, radical self-criticism, the acceptance of the irreducibility of this space-time universe, and the willingness to admit other ultimate realities besides God. But it is wrong if it intends to dismiss all reflection, for its own position is built on reflection and differs from the philosophic, not in the way reason is being used, but in the kind of confines within which it wants to subject reason.

It is necessary to pursue philosophy as an independent discipline, but for one who has antecedent religious commitment, the philosophy will begin with the acknowledgment of certain irreducible truths, after which a free speculation can be indulged in. Theologians now try to squeeze the results of an independent philosophic inquiry into the rigid confines of a religious frame. What must be left open are the details of the religious enterprise, and what must be accepted by the reflective theologian who wishes to have a philosophic position of his own—and not a thing of patches, uncritically adopted—is the nature of the religious enterprise, the reality of religious experience, the nature of God, and the ultimate irreducible reality of Him. He must avoid accepting dogmas of past theologians, such as divine foreknowledge, hell, damnation, and, perhaps, creation. But what the theologian is inclined to do is to hold tight to particularities in a given religion and to let go of all his basic principles so as to accept deliberately (or tacitly in the course of a deliberate rejection of some explicit formulation) those offered by the philosopher.

The thesis of Gilson that there is a distinctive Christian philosophy, though opposed by most, seems to answer to this question better than others do. It is true that his "Christian philosophy" is not really a philosophy in an ultimate sense, by virtue of its commitment, but it is not less a genuine philosophy than those held by most thinkers today. Most present-day thinkers are content to follow out the implications of rather restricted problems and thus take for granted the outlook prevalent at the time, or the position of some sanctioned discipline such as mathematics, science, or history. The idea of a Christian philosophy is no more repugnant or undesirable than is the idea of a philosophy of science, or a positivism which accepts the position and the results of science as hard and unquestioned data; the difference is solely one of selecting, among the basic data, this or that set.

The independent philosopher can of course develop a theory of religion and offer an account of God. Such a theory and account can be of great value to theologians since it provides a frame in which their uncritically accepted principles and dogmas can be placed. The placing of these principles and dogmas is of course an activity outside the province of philosophic reflection; the activity expresses the outcome of a practical concern, a way of concretionalizing the philosophic results in somewhat the way in which ethics is made concrete in myth, politics in the activities of politicians, or perhaps science in engineering. The concretionalizations seem to involve a further assumption, an attitude on the part of man. Concretionalizations can be said to take the pure idea and to modify it by some socialized form of what is presumed to be God. They are ways of taking ontology and turning it into a specialized form of cosmology, by infecting the ontological results with man as actually interplaying with God, or Existence, or the Ideal, or fellowman.

A philosophy of Judaism would presumably start with the acceptance of the Torah, the Prophets, and the Talmud. It will then either proceed as a coordinate of a philosophy of science and reflect on what is required of one in the way of prayer, etc. (I think Kaplan's work does this very well), or it will see the Torah, the Prophets, and the Talmud as embodying the basic principles of a philosophic view, particularly in religion, and made concrete from the perspective of the Jewish people (the only approach open to me). But then if that view is my own, am I not doing what I said theologians had been doing in the past, to which

I have already objected today? No, because what the theologians were making was an external connection with some philosophic scheme, often one which was produced in ignorance of or in opposition to religion, whereas the view I am holding allows a place for religion, and is to be used as a more encompassing account, specialized by the particular religions.

February 1

If it be possible to develop a theology in two ways—by formulating the basic principles of some religion and then freely thinking within that orbit, or by working out a philosophic comprehensive view and treating the tenets of a religion as a particularized and perhaps mythologized and personalized version of this—it ought to be possible to do the same thing for science and other activities. Then, instead of dealing with science as most philosophers do—which is to engage in some minor version of the first of these methods—we might well consider the second.

The first of these methods involves the tacit acceptance of some philosophic outlook (which is therefore dogmatically held) and the reformulation of the doctrines of science inside that accepted scheme. In a sense this is what Aristotle, Kant, and Whitehead did. The position must be sharply distinguished from one which attaches to a scientific outlook or outcome some philosophic view developed on principles that deny the basicality of the scientific procedure as a way of finding out truths (not necessarily of an ultimate sort) and holds the two side by side —which is what Lovejoy did and perhaps also John Stuart Mill. Peirce used the doctrines of evolution properly; instead of merely adopting them, he looked at them from the perspective of his categories. If he erred it was not in his interpretation of the doctrines, but in the inadequacy of his categories.

Similarly, there ought to be two ways of working in the philosophy of history, politics, and art. In the philosophy of art I have followed the second of the methods; Susanne Langer seems to follow the first. In the field of history I follow the second method again; do does Collingwood, who fails only because his Crocean idealism will not allow him to deal with hard brute facts outside the orbit of cognition. The first method is to be found in Collingwood in various places, particularly in the chapter on the detective story, for he there generalizes from his own experience as an historian, and then deals with particular issues of procedure in the light of the generalization.

Krieger in his review of my book on history says that I was bringing history to the philosophers rather than philosophy to the historians. Were he right, I would be following the first method in that I would be adopting the outlook of the historians and then explicating it in philosophic terms. But what I there did was to approach history from a broader philosophic perspective, and only then tried to deal sympathetically with the problems of history. Perhaps what is noticeable is that I was less inclined than most who follow this method, to force historic thinking inside some philosophic pattern.

It is a good test of a philosophy to see how much it must distort of a given discipline in order to be able to deal with its problems, or how much of it it must dismiss because it does not conform to the philosophic outlook. When positivists dismiss art, ethics, religion, and history as nonsense, as emotionally charged, as variants on physics, or as superstition, they reveal the inadequacy of their own view. When Whitehead deals with art as though it were aesthetics, i.e. concerned with qualities, and thereby ignores the making of it—a rather common mistake of philosophers who approach art as spectators and therefore take account only of the finished work—he shows the inadequacy of his view, primarily by revealing how much he is forced to distort.

If one follows the second of the suggested methods and interprets a discipline in the light of a philosophic outlook, it would seem offhand that he is distorting the discipline to make it fit inside that outlook. But distortion has to do with the values and attitudes, with the import of the discipline and not with specific doctrines. Thus one need not hold the doctrine of evolution in the way in which biologists do; but the reality of evolution as a process in time, involving a transmutation of species and an interrelationship of what is now thought to be diverse and apparently unrelated, must be maintained.

One would distort evolutionary theory if one were to suppose, with Augustine, that it applied only to the subhuman; one would distort history were one, with Marx, to take it to be primarily concerned with the class struggle or with economics. What must be done is to take the discipline seriously to begin with, at the same time that one independently pursues the philosophic enterprise. Then one can take that discipline in all its ramifications and enrich its meaning by seeing how its categories fit in with those of other disciplines and are in fact instances of the categories developed by the philosopher. We have here a double check, one on the philosophy and the other on the current understanding of the discipline. The outcome of the second method will be to supplement the abstract, independently formulated categories of the philosopher by the (comparatively) concrete outlook of a particular discipline, and conversely. The discipline criticizes the philosophy by revealing its inadequacy to what the discipline is doing and what it in fact means for its practitioners.

No matter how irreligious a man may be, as a philosopher he must take the religious activity seriously. He must also try to get to the inward meaning of particular religions. He must, for example, try to understand what law means for a Jew, and not assume that what St. Paul said it meant is what it means or meant. Nor must he deny all truth or meaning to the Incarnation or the Trinity or the role of Mohammed. He need not accept any of these as expressing a truth about reality, but he must accept them all as vital ways in which basic categories are being exhibited— categories which characterize religion as such, and which are instances of the more basic categories of a philosophy.

On this account philosophy has a different role from all other disciplines, though not necessarily a superior one. It offers the basic principles which the others illustrate; but in compensation the others are concerned with the more concrete, and are able to offer criticisms to a philosophy as surely as it is able to offer interpretations of them.

But if principles are broad enough what could violate them? Is it not the case that those philosophies which proved inadequate at least worked with specific categories, enabling them to be found out, whereas one which is professedly all-inclusive and accommodates all disciplines without, or with little distortion, will have only such vague categories as event, being, substance, and the like? This surely is possible; but the danger can be minimized and perhaps avoided by developing the philosophy independently as an integrated scheme, attempting to do justice to the ultimate divisions of the universe and knowledge, and then showing the basic ways in which they interconnect. The philosophic categories of Plato, Aristotle, Kant, and Hegel were at once comprehensive and fruitful.

But surely not all disciplines are to be taken at face value. What of astrology, phrenology, telepathic medicine, palmistry? These pseudo sciences are to be taken seriously in the sense that one must get to their presuppositions and then understand why they cannot be sciences, and are not yet wisdom or philosophy. Astrology rests on the fact that there is a significant relation between the heavenly bodies and the fate of men.

It classifies men according to their birthdays, and then relates these to the positions of the stars. It takes a rather narrow view of the affiliations men have with the rest of nature, and its scheme of classification is rather narrow. Also, the question of fate has to be dealt with in relation to man's freedom, and the chances and contingencies of nature and society. But the bodies of men and therefore their lives are in some kind of necessary relation to other bodies, and there are laws which govern the outcome of the interplay. This is the truth behind astrology.

February 2

A philosopher who would do justice to some particular religion, say Judaism, would have to see the doctrines and activities of Judaism as illustrating his basic categories, but in such a way that those doctrines and activities are made more intelligible, more coherent, more significantly related to other practices and views, both there and in other enterprises. The seeing of a particular discipline's notions as illustrations of the philosophic is then no simple matter of subsumption. It involves a placing of the notions in a new context where they are clarified and enriched for those who accept them.

In the opinion of Heschel and Buber, Judaism is the religion of the prophets. They are inclined to minimize and even dimiss the claims of Joseph Smith and Mohammed to be prophets, and in any case to take the view that Judaism cannot be understood without taking the prophets seriously. It is not clear whether either of them actually believes that God in fact spoke in or through the prophets, or whether the prophets merely acted as though God had spoken to or through them. Buber and Heschel are inclined I think to suppose the matter somewhat irrelevant, for the important thing for them is that this is a distinctive aspect of Judaic thought and meaning. Accepting this position, one can then go on to say, I think, that prophesy is but a special instance of an interplay of man and God; that the very nature of the universe, with God and Actuality as ultimate modes of being, requires that God be effective everywhere, and that He be manifest in the distinctive shapes which different types of being provide. He will thus be manifest in the speech and actions of man, particularly those concerned with characteristically human stresses, such as ethics, politics, history, art.

A prophet is one who illustrates the interplay of God with man by exhibiting God's effects as those which enhance and insist on the highest good for man. Since God however is a being who interplays with the entire cosmos, it is necessary to extend the usual prophetic outlook to embrace not only man but whatever else there be. The true prophet will express a concern for the preservation and enhancement of nature as well as for the fulfillment of man's promise, all having primary interest for God. The resulting ethical, political, historical, artistic, scientific, engineering, devotional, and communal injunctions and evaluations must then be seen to have a power and also, perhaps, a meaning which they otherwise would not have.

The ethical observations of the prophets must not be such that any man could have made them. They must involve an insistence on a punishment for failure which a secular ethics could not provide. They must add to the assertions of a secular ethics others which it does not consider, but which need not be inconsistent with them. If one is told to turn the other cheek, or not to harvest all the grain so that the poor can be fed, one surely goes beyond the ordinary ethical requirements in the first of these instances, and perhaps in the second as well. The second though could conceivably be thought to be a special case of the general injunction that one ought to do good to one's fellows, and the first might conceivably be squeezed into the form of a general principle that one ought to do all one can to minimize the evil that is already present, and that an unwillingness to allow oneself to be angered is a way of achieving this result. It is better, then, in connection with ethics, to take the position that the prophet emphasizes the kind of implications, the kind of consequences that are drawn from unethical acts when they are placed in a divine context.

Does what the prophets say reflect what God in fact will do? For the believer the answer must be in the affirmative. For the nonbeliever a prophet merely underscores in a vivid way that God will assess what is done, and that this assessment will be in terms of what is eternally right or just, at the same time that He will act mercifully, i.e., will do all He can to maximize the acts in which men engage. The message of the prophets then is that there are consequences of men's acts which have a divine import, that God will maximize these as much as possible, and that He will hold man accountable for the recalcitrant material. Everything can be enhanced in value by God; but what we call evil is what requires a dissection and redistribution of parts in contrast with the good which remains whole. The ultimate punishment is destruction by God for the sake of producing a good outcome. When men misbehave they force God to divide the men and their activities in order to have nothing but good preserved. Divine punishment is thus a divine annihilation, a kind of forgetting.

The prophets have a place inside a religious history, and contribute to its content. We must understand them as requiring that occurrences be affiliated and pɥctuated in ways a secular history does not. The forget-fulness and annihilation God concerns himself with is that of a people, though this need not involve a neglect of the individual. The prophet must also be part of a religious community and must give it the char-acteristic note of a religious community. This contrasts with the ordinary community, not merely in the types of acts it exhibits or the things it says, but by virtue of the distinctive tonality which it possesses because of the immanence of God in it.

The traditional prophets have little or nothing to say about art or science. What little they have said is infected with moral and liturgical elements. We should recognize the need for modifications of secular art and science similar to that imposed on ethics, politics, and history by the traditional prophets. We thereby move into the field of sacramental art, and the concern for learning in God's name. Neither of these has had its distinctive individual prophet, but one can perhaps say that the way to understand the Talmud is to take it to be an illustration of the concern for learning, and the way to understand the prophetic spirit of the Middle Ages is to see its art as sacramental. In short, one ought to take account not only of prophets but of the prophetic spirit, and see the latter as that which may be carried out by an entire people or civiliza-tion. The Jewish people then could be said to be the people of the prophets not only because they had individual prophets, but because the prophetic spirit was carried over into the arena of learning and was there carried on by the rabbis, and in the end by the Jewish people.

It is a charge against the Jews that they neglected the realm of art. The fact that this neglect is now being remedied would seem to indicate that there is a new prophetic era about to dawn. The fact that some of these works of art encouraged by the rabbis and the synagogues is done by secular and Christian architects, does not affect the fact that it is an architecture lived in and desired by the Jewish people, or some segment of it.

The prophets and the Talmud make one whole, both understood as embodying the prophetic spirit, the voice of man making evident the divine import of what is now being done. We add a third period of prophetic spirit, to that whole, by bringing into account the nature of a distinctive sacramental art.

Judaism is not understandable without a reference to the Torah, to the laws laid down presumably by God. There are, however, some laws in the Torah which are nothing more than ethical injunctions readily understood by nonreligious men. Indeed, though the Commandments were supposed to be given to Moses by God, Cain was supposed to have known that it was wrong to murder.

Finkelstein is inclined to suppose that all the laws have a rationale if only we could discover it, but this I think is an error. There is no need for a divinely grounded set of rules to conform to any finite scheme of rational explanations that we may have. We can explain these laws in the sense of taking them to be regulations of behavior, subdivisions one might say of the rules of a society, subject to a divine modification. By attending to them, and noting exactly what it is that we cannot account for, we are in a position to exhibit the meaning of God's awful majesty. It is, in short, precisely what cannot be explained in terms of human needs and desires and promise that manifests the divine element in them. God, as the lawyers see, is to be referred to when we find something inexplicable in ordinary terms.

Judaism is but one of many religions, and the interpretations it puts on God's concerns are not those which other religions would accept. From the philosophic standpoint this means merely that God interplays with other types of material to produce other kinds of occurrences, which are used to identify other types of religion. Religions differ in the items which they acknowledge to be sacramental to a high degree, in the kind of laws they follow, in what they require of their members, in the spirit of their community. The creedal positions of the different religions is where they are basically in opposition, and it is these which the philosopher must transcend until he can take them all to express the very same truth in diverse ways—say the truth that God is at once immanent and transcendent.

Confessional religions try to avoid creedal commitments, but this does not mean that they must not either tacitly or explicitly make some distinctive affirmations. If they made none whatsoever they would apparently be consistent with any outlook whatsoever, from atheism to polytheism. One can avoid creedal affirmations in religion only so far as one sees one's activities and claims as all exhibiting in some way the fact that God interplays with the world and man, and that what men do to the world and to one another has some import for God.

Why is it that Christianity has been so concerned with philosophic underpinnings and Judaism has not? Is it because, as some say, Judaism is a religion of activity rather than of belief? I think not. Not only are other religions, and Christianity with its doctrine of charity, concerned with action, but the Jews have a strong negative doctrine that the Messiah has not yet come, and strong positive doctrines about the truth of what the prophets have said.

The explicit formulation of creedal doctrines does open one up to a reflection on their meaning as basic ideas, leading one to a concern with philosophic issues. The question perhaps is now pushed back another step, for then one would want to know why it is that Christianity made these creedal affirmations. Is it because it saw itself in opposition to the Jews and the pagans, and needed to make these affirmations in order to avoid any confusion with what it had once been? Or is not the more usual way of putting this, that the Christians introduced into a Jewish outlook the values and interests and intellectual concerns of the pagans more correct? (In all this I am taking for granted the idea that men such as Maimonides and Crescas do not do the job for Judaism which ought to be done, in good part because they bring into the consideration of the nature of Judaism, principles which originate with a nonreligious philosophy whose orientation and implications have little relevance to Judaism. They confound a reinterpretation inside a comprehensive view, which has a place for God and religion apart from all commitment and which demands an enrichment of the meaning of the basic positions of Judaism, with the restatement of Judaic ideas in terms of some alien philosophy that neither is really brought into play nor serves to clarify the particular doctrines of Judaism.)

The outcome of this particular way of dealing with Judaism is not an apologetics for it, but rather a kind of phenomenology of it, a way of reading it sympathetically as an occurrence of significance. One does not thereby in any way affirm that it is right in what it claims, particularly so far as its claims are viewed as being in opposition to or as being alternative to other claims made by other religions, instead of being distinctive particularizations of the same ultimate truths that God is at once immanent and transcendent, concerned, just and merciful.

Do I not here neglect or minimize Eastern religions, and do something analogous to what I had previously condemned in Lessing—the attempt to see the basic religions as coordinate roads to God? So far as I have personalized God it does seem as if I have adopted a position which is antithetical to the Eastern view. But is it not true that one must at once make God personal and impersonal to express what He is immanently and transcendentally? Is not the negative theology of the West, the refusal to characterize God, the distinction between God the Father and God the Son, and such doctrines as Tillich's God beyond God but a way of remarking on the impersonal side of God? And is it not true that in the East we find "Gods" of mercy, Gods who are involved with men and their affairs? The great difference seems to lie in the Eastern acknowledgment of a plurality of Gods, and in a tendency to speak of God as not being involved with human affairs to the degree and with the particularity that is characteristic of the West. But the multiple Gods of the East, or particularly of the Hindu, are concretionalized ways of expressing distinctive divine functions and roles. They point up the divine complexity—a good thing to do. But the view that God stands outside all human affairs will eventually result in the denial of God as having a role in history. This would be a defect.

Looking at the religions, East and West, we can say that the West does not do sufficient justice to the complexity and multiplicity of roles and activities in which God is involved, whereas in the East there is a counterdefect in that there is a neglect of God's role in history and politics, and perhaps also in ethics. And because it is possible to say this, it is possible to distinguish the present position from Lessing's. Lessing thought all religions to be equally good, though not yet complete and not yet at their goal, whereas I am saying that they have defects intrinsic to them, and that the goal (if that be the acknowledgment of God) is already attained for them in whatever sense it will ever be attained. (He did not take account of the Eastern religions, but this is a defect which could be easily overcome by one who was willing to accept Lessing's general outlook, for all he would have to do is to add more paths up the mountainside.) The various religions may be said to be making progress of some kind, but it is not a progress in reaching God, but rather a progress in the clarification of their ideas, in a sharpening of their differences and similarities, in an awareness of their limitations, and in their contributions to a larger secular world.

Earlier today I said that the interest in science could be assimilated to an interest in learning. But it surely is true that the rabbis with all their interest in learning had little interest in science. And what is true of the rabbis is largely true of the whole of the priesthood and ministry, and indeed of all religions, even though today there is hardly anyone who would offer opposition to science, and though it is true that there are many religious men who are in fact good scientists. But if we think of science as reading the language of God, as Berkeley's view would allow us, or as concerned with truths which hold always and objectively and thus with what God would know, we can, without distorting the situation, speak of the interest in science from a religious point of view, as an interest in knowledge in an absolute sense, even though the procedure of science is essentially tentative and hypothetical. This is a side which has been neglected, and one can imagine another prophetic age where science is viewed as having a divine support, and perhaps even where its assertions would be given a nonsecular meaning in the sense that the whole would tell us not only what the world was like, but something of God's intent.

We have, in short, two possible approaches to science from a religious point of view: in one of them we take science as it is, and see it as a way of learning the nature of the universe from a divine or eternal position; in the other we take science to have a divine component—e.g., telling us which hypothesis out of an infinite number would be fruitful, or dictating how its truths are to be related to other truths. The second of these approaches seems more in consonance with what has already been suggested in connection with the particular religions, ethics, etc. But I am not yet sufficiently clear as to just what ought to be said about science. Were it because of God that one chose the right hypothesis, one would still not have a divine component in science but only in the scientist. And if we held that God determined how scientific truths were related to other truths, we would seem to be impinging on the independence of science, and perhaps philosophy and the other disciplines.

It would be bolder and more consistent with the interpretation given to ethics from a religious point of view to treat science in the spirit in which one speaks of natural events in the Bible. The story of creation and the order of creation can be said to be science as governed by God, i.e., the scientific world as governed by God and expressed in the appropriate scientific vocabulary. In the light of what we otherwise know we must say this, though exhibiting the right attitude toward science, yields wrong answers. What one must do is to find an interpretation for the world as we know it today (so far as we know it with any surety), and subject this to a transformation (as a consequence of an interpretation of it which finds God immanent in that world, either in person or in effect). But it is possibly true that there are no sure and fixed truths in science. So far as this is the case, one cannot do for science what one can do for ethics, but only what one does for history, i.e., not interpret secular reports, but allow for a place for a nonsecular form in which not all the items in the secular have a place; or conversely, in which all of the secular fits together with other items. But what would such an interpretation of science yield?

Without waiting to answer this last question, it is important to note that the acknowledgment of God can make a difference to the stress or power of a discipline, or can add or subtract something from its contentions without denying it an autonomy in which it is without the added items and with the otherwise subtracted ones.

Perhaps there is also a third approach in which one sees all the scientific propositions as having two sides, one of which is divine. This would seem to be Swedenborg's position, where the results of science are treated as though they also had a sacramental meaning. The view that treats science as it is, but gives it additional power or another role, and its objects also, makes science and its world an object of an authoritative command or control. The view that God adds or subtracts something, treats of God's role in somewhat the way in which I speak of it when talking of religious history—as providing a new context.

We have then the *sacramental,* the *authoritative,* and the *contextual* view of God's function with respect to various disciplines. These disciplines are first understood from a philosophic position which grants them autonomy, but yet interrelates them in a way they could not themselves.

Are some disciplines open to only one or two of these three approaches, or do all of them allow for all three? The latter seems like the most reasonable supposition. We would then have to say that there is a sacramental meaning to ethics in which the ethical commands are supported by God (for example, in the Ten Commandments), an authoritative meaning where various demands are made beyond those within the power of the ethical (and where there is a neglect of various truths of ethics, such as the equality of humans regardless of sex and race and servitude), and a contextual one in which all the claims of an ethics would have another dimension (which I suppose is what a cabalist would maintain).

If we make this interpretation of history, we will have the sacramental, which is the position I took in the religion book; the authoritative, which is what the millennialists—and even people like John E. Smith who thinks at root all history is religious history—would claim; and the contextual, where every secular event is seen to have a religious meaning as well, which is the way, I suppose, the fundamentalists look at history.

Returning now to science and its world, a sacramental approach would assert that the scientific inquiry and the world (in whole or in part) which it knows, in the end must be seen to be sustained by a divine power. Here every proposition which a secular man might urge is accepted, but given a weight he cannot assign to it. The authoritative approach adds such assertions as: Joshua made the sun stand still, or, the sun was created after light. The contextual approach to science would see each of these assertions as having a divinely sustained meaning, as well as a purely secular one.

The sacramental approach is the most modest; it does not require one to assert any new propositions. It could claim that not every assertion or item is sacramental, but that only some are. This is what I think the position I took on religious history in *The God We Seek* comes down to, since this history deals with only some of the items in the secular. The sacramental approach in ethics would, at its most modest, require one to assert that there are some ethical propositions which are the special concern of God—the last few of the Ten Commandments for example. In relation to science it would lead one to say that the inquiry of science as a branch of learning, and the world which science was trying to know but which it had only tentatively and partially grasped, were at least in part subject to divine control. Or perhaps even the scientific inquiry could be left as wholly secular, and a reference to God required only in relation to certain events in nature. (Is this not what is being contended by the Roman Catholic approach to the miracles at Lourdes, etc.?) On such a view the sacramental approach to science would perhaps be restricted to certain biological or medical occurrences, and would not necessarily relate to anything in physics or chemistry.

Ought we not do something similar with philosophy? Instead of bringing religion inside philosophy we would then turn the matter about and look at the world of the philosopher, or the philosophic enterprise in whole or in part, as sacramental, as authoritatively governed, or as having another contextual meaning. It could be said that I took all three positions in my various books. God, as immanent in all else, makes all else sacramental; God, as insisting on Himself in and on others, authoritatively governs them; and God, as having all things within Him on His own terms, gives the world an entirely new meaning. Perhaps here too, as in the case of science, one might exclude the philosophic enterprise from being dealt with in these three ways, except so far as anything that is must be said to have all three sides.

If the acknowledgment of God means that an enterprise (or the objects with which it deals) will be seen in three ways, is it not also the case that approaching the objects from the perspective of other modes of Being will give us other sets of three sides? Is not ethics for example a subject which, when approached from the perspective of, say, Existence, will show the presence of all Existence within it, giving us the deterministic side of whatever we do; that it will reveal something of the power of Existence, say as determinative of our destiny or fate; and that it will allow for an interpretation of all the ethical truths as somehow also to be read off as purely factual assertions reflecting the fact that the loftiest ideals and noblest hopes must be expressed through the body and must meet the conditions which are set before us, but apart from any consideration of us?

Is not history, then, also to be approached from the position of Existence, where it too is seen to be deterministic, fatalistic, and subject to external conditions? Must it not also be approached from the position of the Ideal and there be seen to be infected by Ideality, not merely in the sense that its future is an Ideal future governing the past, but in the sense that it has some kind of rationale; that it is sustained by Ideality in the sense of being in part or whole subject to a rational necessity; and that every one of its occurrences has an abstract meaning which together with others makes up a single ideal totality of meanings, each of which has in fact been carried by some particular historic event?

The foregoing does not take into account the view expressed in the *World of Art,* that science deals with a purified strand of the commonsensical world. It speaks instead of nature as such, as though this were the object of science. Is anything changed by taking account of the view that science exposes a strand of common sense? I think not. Common sense and its strands all say something about the real, and all can bear the marks of God's presence, influence, or absorptive reality. Joshua's sun is not the sun of science but the sun of common sense; this sun rises and sets. Could this sun, consistent with the findings of astronomy, also be thought to have been made to stand still? Why not? The formulae of science say nothing about the length of common-sense days or even of the exhibition of the formulae in the common-sense world in a regular way. Still one need not go this far in order to make the point that there is a position from which the world of science can be seen to be affected by God, if only in the shape of having some of its items assume a sacramental role. Some items have a power which is not their own but must have a divine source, and some items have another meaning to be read off only by one who can approach them from the side of God.

If the world of science is entirely abstract, just the sheer formulae which enable one to make intelligible and to interrelate what would otherwise be a mere heterogeneous set of phenomena, then some formula(e) would be endowed with an unusual status (which?), some formula(e) would have a special power, and some formula(e) would have a double meaning. Since God is not cut off from anything, all other formulae would also have similar roles, but in a minor or minimal degree, and what one is calling sacramental, etc., is but that which has this status to a greater degree than others do.

February 3

It is not immediately evident how the sacramental approach differs from the contextual. Neither need encompass all the secular items, and both add or subtract meaning from the secular. But the sacramental approach absorbs the secular within it; the secular dimension is seen only by virtue of an abstraction, by virtue of a failure to note the sacramental dimension. But once the sacramental dimension is recognized the secular is no longer an independent dimension, but only a occasion or mark enabling one to locate the object which is sacramental in meaning. The contextual view in contrast always retains the secular dimension as an independent one; it merely provides us with another language, another dimension in addition to the secular. This language, unlike the sacramental, can be read by one who is not a believer, since it could be known by intellectual means. The discovery of the sacramental dimension is possible only for one who believes and enters into a religion, whereas the contextual view is more ontological and open to a purely speculative mind.

The transition from a consideration of the nature of religion in the perspective of philosophy, to a consideration of science in relation to religion was somewhat abrupt. The transition can be exhibited in a smoother way by taking account of the fact that science and ethics and politics, etc., are here to be dealt with as understood by the philosopher. This means that the principles, in terms of which they are being discussed, are those that a comprehensive philosophic view provides, so that the reconciliation, say, of science and religion is actually a reconciliation of a philosophy of science with a philosophy of religion, or better, perhaps, of a science, philosophically understood, with a religion, philosophically understood. And this is desirable, for the philosophic understanding of the science and the religion does not demand a denial of any facts or even attitudes, but only a more adequate set of categories in terms of which they are being spoken of.

It should be possible, though, to speak of various disciplines from the perspective of others which are not philosophic in nature or principle. Thus one ought to be able to provide a sociology of physics, with physics being given an added dimension of meaning, a new kind of power or role, and a new context by sociology. It could then be said to reflect the nature of the modern community with its cooperative aspects and its tendency toward conformity; it could be said to have a money and a prestige by virtue of the successes of engineering, and which thereupon are referred back to the pure scientist; and it could be said that some or all of the discoveries and results and methods of the scientists have a sociological side. On the first of these interpretations, we would see science as a function of a sociological situation, and in the third we would see some or every part of science as having two roles, one in the science itself and the other in a social context. In both cases science as a discipline would be brought inside a social context.

If we reverse the relations of the two and look at sociology in the light of science, we should expect the discipline of sociology to be placed within the world of physical things. And this surely can be done, but it is not a very promising approach. It seems evident, then, that we must look at various disciplines both as enterprises and as offering us objective content, and that the changes which one can introduce into another will have one of twelve values:

1] enterprise x given new values by enterprise y
2] enterprise x given new values by world known by y
3] world of x given new values by enterprise y
4] world of x given new values by world known by y

5] enterprise x given new power by enterprise y
6] enterprise x given new power by world known by y
7] world of x given new power by enterprise y
8] world of x given new power by world known by y

9] enterprise x given new context by enterprise y
10] enterprise x given new context by world known by y
11] world of x given new context by enterprise y
12] world of x given new context by world known by y

In the above, "world of x" is of course to be understood as "world known by x," in just the way in which one deals with the world known by y.

In the light of this table perhaps it would be better when dealing with the relationship of any two enterprises to go through the entire table to see which are the more significant relations. Thus it would seem more interesting to deal, not with science as a discipline, but with the world of science, and thus with cases *3, 4, 7, 8, 11,* and *12.* If we take that world not to be a topic for sociology but treat it as a social enterprise, we restrict ourselves to cases *4, 8,* and *12.* We will then approach such a phenomenon as gravity, let us say, as affecting the orientation men have toward one another, the placing of their shrines, their attitude toward flight, birds, and the like. We would also attend to the increasing role that gravity plays in building plans, obsolescence, airplanes, transportation, dealing with them no more as merely naked, but as cushioned, redirected, or opposed. And we would also attend to the fact that the natural world is looked at by men in a society, and that the approach we take to it in the West is different from that taken in the East. Gravity is something which for us is to be defied, overcome, and controlled, whereas in the East it is accepted and submitted to, even though in the actual course of building anything it would be defied and in a sense overcome. In the West it represents a challenge; in the East an obstacle.

However, in connection with science it surely is true that cases *2, 6,* and *10,* where the enterprise of science is looked at within a social context, are also of considerable interest. What does not seem of much interest is the attempt to look at the world of science as a topic for a sociological investigation (cases *3, 7, 11*), though there would be some interest in looking at the enterprise of science in this way—cases *1, 5,* and *9.* If now we turn to society and sociology as topics for a science, or as items to be placed inside a scientific scheme or world, only philosophers of science, apparently, would be interested in cases *1, 5,* and *9.*

It is difficult to see much value in taking the enterprise of sociology and placing it in the context of natural occurrences, and thus subjecting its activities to analyses and measurements employed in connection with inanimate objects, though there surely is no harm in doing this and perhaps something of interest could be discovered. But it would seem that all enterprises, not only sociology, could be approached from this perspective and the entire intellectual world examined in this detached manner. Cases *2, 6,* and *10,* therefore, would also be put aside, as not of major interest. Nor do I think we can learn much from cases *3, 7,* and *11,* despite the fact that again and again men have made an attempt to deal with society in scientific terms, as so many forces and movements, etc. The hopeful cases seem to be *4, 8,* and *12,* where, say, birth and death would be recognized to have not only a social meaning but a biological one, not merely as occurrences in the individual but as a set of social occurrences involving parents and relatives and the community. We would for example treat a family in which there was a birth or a death as having, for one with a grasp of nature, a further import in the scheme of things, as the outcome of the operation of natural forces, and as being articulated in another way in nature as such.

Where does a view such as Hobbes' fit? He would think of himself as dealing with the social world, and would thus begin with cases 3, 4, 7, 8, 11, 12. He would eliminate the last two on the ground that there was no other discipline to deal with society but one which was scientific, in his sense of "materialistic." Nor would he consider the cases 7 and 8 as important, since they but demand that society be viewed as under the grip of the outlook or world of science. His cases would then be 3 and 4, perhaps not clearly distinguished for him, where the social and political world would be seen to gain in clarity and exactitude by being freed from conventional approaches and analyzed in scientific terms—therefore, strictly speaking, case 3.

In connection with science and religion there is more interest, I think, in trying to understand what the world of science means in a religious sense than there is in trying to understand the enterprise of science in this way. But there would be more interest in studying what the enterprise of religion means in a scientific way than there would be in dealing with the world outlined by religion, or in trying to place the enterprise of religion in a scientific world—though this last is what in a sense Freud tried to do, and what is attempted again and again by psychologists and positivists.

In connection with philosophy and religion there is perhaps more interest in looking at religion from the perspective of philosophy, than conversely. Then both the enterprise and the world of religion become of considerable interest. We want to know the outcome of a philosophic reflection on both the practice of religion and on the particular claims or world it presents; and we want to know the result of seeing the religious practice and claims inside the cosmos, as envisaged in a philosophic system.

What does it mean to say that something is of interest, or is of no interest in these connections? Do such remarks but reflect the bias and imagination of the writer, or do they tell us something about the nature of the disciplines and the worlds they portray? Why is not one particularly interested in seeing how much piety, say, is involved in an Epicurean outlook, or interested in what the absence of piety does to it? Can one say with surety that there would be little gain in asking what the meaning of pagan philosophies would be inside a world which was like that pictured in the Bible? Is it not true that Augustine dealt with just this case in the *City of God,* though his primary objective was to deal with history and religion as illustrating case *12?*

I suppose I should have known about it, but the fact of the matter is that I did not know about Gabriel Marcel's *Metaphysical Journal* until about a week or so ago—Schneider mentioned it to me in Claremont— and I had not seen it until today—Oh, yes, Andrew Reck mentioned Marcel's diary in a letter he wrote me a month or so ago. But I think I never heard of it before that, though this sounds unlikely. It came out in 1952 in English; was no copy sent to the *Review?* I don't recall seeing the book, but if I did, or if I only knew of its existence, the brute fact is that I have no memory of it whatsoever. Nor did I ever see Wittgenstein's journal, but I am sure I heard rumors of the notebooks. It is interesting that there should be these three different and, so far as one can see, independent endeavors to make use of a journal or diary.

Marcel says in the preface to the English edition that he thought of his *Journal* "as a preparation for what one day will be a systematic exposition." Such a view contrasts in two ways with what I have been doing. In the first place the systematic expositions with which I was concerned were often previously published, and in the second place I have dealt with problems as they arose, even when they were without any apparent relevance to what I had previously done or planned to do. Marcel's *Journal,* as a consequence, has a more single-minded character than mine; mine exposes me in the process of thinking through a particular problem, rather than in working through a particular view. And in contrast with Wittgenstein, I am not concerned merely with posing difficulties to myself and in making brief observations on them, but in struggling with an issue and working toward an answer for it, unsatisfactory and tentative though this might prove to be. Perhaps it would not be too inaccurate to say that my journal stands somewhat in between those of Marcel and Wittgenstein, having the metaphysical interest of Marcel's and the episodic character of Wittgenstein's journal. I think, too, that I am more tentative in my intent than Marcel, and more like Wittgenstein in being beset by problems, though mine cover a wider range. Also, I discuss various alternatives, make use of a dialectic method again and again, look back at some of the things I have done, and attend to discussions of some of the classical writers.

Philosophy in Process now, though more voluminous than the Marcel or Wittgenstein journals, covers a shorter period than Marcel's. I do not know whether Marcel is continuing with his diary, but if he is, his will cover about fifty years, since he began his in 1914; it is not reasonable to suppose that mine will cover more than twenty or so. Wittgenstein's "notebooks," which were begun around the time that Marcel began his, were in effect workbooks for his subsequent published *Tractatus*. I have not seen his *Blue* and *Brown* books. In any case, the differences to be found amongst all three of these efforts have no evaluational importance so far as I am concerned, but only a purely descriptive one.

I am closer to Marcel in that he does worry about issues and does make tentative suggestions and even offers something like arguments. He also refers back to what he had done on a previous day, raises questions to himself, and refers to his other writings. I think that my publisher has produced my book, now in fascicles, with more awareness of the needs of the reader than Marcel's publisher showed. In mine the dates are given on the top of the page and there are running heads; with the index it should be a rather useful though still somewhat obscure book. But it does not seem to me to be more obscure, nor to presuppose a greater knowledge of previous writings by its author, than Marcel's. Moreover, his range seems to be dictated by an over-all concern with religion; he does not wander too far afield from this—which has its advantages as well as its limitations.

I have been glancing through Marcel's *Journal*—I suppose it is almost impossible to *read* this kind of work, and this applies to mine as well, of course; they must either be leafed through or studied—and I am delighted to see him struggle with the problem of religious history and make some of the points I made in my forthcoming book on religion. He does not analyze out the issues, discover the particular categories for history or for religious history, but he is acutely aware that religious history deals with a "special domain" "defined in function of transcendental conditions without analogy" (February 17th, 1914, fifty years ago!), which I think asserts that religious history is history affected by God, that it has its own categories and rhythm. He sees that it is a history for one who has faith, though he draws a rather sharp distinction between having faith and being a thinking subject.

I like his observation that "Religious history can only appear intelligible to the philosophic spirit if it is possible to establish that historical monism (the view that there are universal conditions that are identical for every kind of history) does not cover the whole field." He does not then go on, as I would be inclined to do, to ask himself if similar questions do not arise in other domains, nor does he ask himself what the categories of secular history might be, and how they might contrast with the religious. I think, too, that he thinks of faith as primarily that of a Christian. But there is no doubt that he has here an insight which has not been exploited by other thinkers, and that it well deserves to be. This last remark is perhaps too strong, for I have only a very thin knowledge of the literature in religion, and there might well be thinkers who have spelled out the issue of religious history in ways analogous to those indicated in my forthcoming *The God We Seek*. (Were it not for the fact that so many thought the title *For the Love of God* somehow too flip, it would have been better. After all, I speak there more of the seeking of God than of the God who is sought.)

To be sure, Marcel denies realism, and looks for a solution by denying a real objective uninterpreted history, what I call the "historic." This I think is an error. But he wrote this when he was under thirty! And he already was a musician and a playwright!

Why is it that he does not mention the names of his respondents, being content to give only an initial? What is the source of his German terms, terms which come into such prominence in later existentialism? I note, too, that he rereads his *Journal* and then comments on it, whereas I never read previous entries except when getting them ready for the press. (But now come to think of it, I believe that every once in a while in the past I went back at least for light on some particular topic. Fortunately, or unfortunately, I have a very poor memory, and cannot remember if I wrote something in this diary, or when I wrote it.)

To judge from the appendix to his *Journal*, Marcel thought of it as primarily a workbook. But *Philosophy in Process* is not a workbook at all; it is a daily exploration and struggle with basic problems, some of which may be incorporated in a book or article, but none of which is written with the idea of being used for such a publication in any form. Initially, I think I had no idea of publishing any of it. It was initially a set of reflections and partly a workbook, but it gradually altered in intent, and I began to hope that it would be published after my death. Gradually I came to see that it might have value perhaps even for me, if it were published around this time, and the responses I have been having from Reck and Bernstein would indicate that I did not make a mistake in asking to have it published. And now, when I cannot get the idea of a book on education into focus, and yet am still occupied by questions which seem at once important and unsolved, *Philosophy in Process* provides me with an opportunity to think and to write and perhaps to progress in the adventure of trying to be a philosopher.

Why is it that Buber seems to be so much better known than Marcel? Was it not a mistake to leave Marcel out of *Philosophical Interrogations?* If so, is this my fault or Rome's? Perhaps both; yet had I suggested it, I think Rome would have agreed. It does seem like an oversight, traceable in the last resort to my ignorance. More, since I claimed to be alert to the possibility of neglected thinkers and since I did hear of Marcel, it was incumbent on me to investigate his works. Not that Marcel was as neglected as Peirce, but he was neglected so far as such an enterprise as *Philosophical Interrogations* is concerned, and I was responsible for the initial stages of that project. Perhaps it is because people think he is too unsystematic, too elusive—to use some of the expressions employed by some of the commentators I have glanced at today? But I do not think he is so unsystematic; he is not dialectical and does not have a didactic style, but this does not mean he is not systematic in his outlook, thought, and even in his writings. Nor do I find him singularly elusive, but rather searching and original and occasionally profound. These observations of mine are all the more remarkable since I note from Gallagher's book on Marcel that I published his essay dealing with Marcel in 1959—and I read every published paper in manuscript, in galleys, and in the printed version. But I cannot remember a thing about it.

February 4

What is a law of nature? What kind of being does it have? How does it operate?

Peirce holds that there is no action merely by efficient causation; final causation for him is the activity of the whole calling out its parts. But this view seems to hold only of biological growth. Peirce is able to maintain it because he looks at the whole of nature in a biological way, having taken Darwin's evolutionary theory to apply to all things, including the nature of laws.

A law, such as that of gravity or of combinations in chemistry, whether it be viewed as a law of functional dependence or a causal one, and whether it relates to observable or unobservable entities, can be treated (as the positivists do) as a kind of explanation, or it can be treated (as Whitehead and Peirce do) as characterizing some objective matter of fact, formulated in statements which may or may not do justice to it. Laws in the latter sense seem to be necessary, for the order and regularity of the world seems to be an observable fact.

If I understand Nagel correctly, he thinks that in the end there is no real difference between these two positions, except a terminological one. But I am not sure that I do understand him, for he discusses the issue as a contrast between those who take the formulated laws to have an instrumental meaning and those who take them to be true, whereas the contrast I would have liked to seem him deal with is between laws as statements of any kind and laws as objective realities. Nagel does discuss what he calls the "principle of causality" or what Mill calls the "principle of the uniformity of nature," and concludes that "it is extremely difficult if not hopeless to regard the principle of causality as a universally valid inductive truth concerning the pervasive order of events and processes" (*The Structure of Science*, p. 319). He then goes on to say (pp. 324–25) that he "deliberately avoided the question, prominent in current debates on the foundation of physics as well as in the historical literature of philosophy, whether the *actual events* of nature are not themselves, in part or in whole 'undetermined' or 'chance' occurrences . . . ." When then he goes on to discuss the ontological doctrine of chance, such as that presented by Peirce, he remarks that "it is impossible in the nature of the case to establish beyond question that any event is an absolutely chance occurrence," since it would then be necessary "to show that there is nothing whatever upon which its occurrence depends" (p. 332). Yet it "may . . . well be that [some] . . . events are 'absolutely chance' occurrences" (p. 333). He views the main outcome of his discussion to be that "an event 'happens by chance' is not in general incompatible with asserting the event to be determined" (p. 334) since the verifiable meaning of chance for him is not absolute, but relative to what is determined. He ends the chapter with the observation that physicists might some day "develop an essentially nonstatistical theory to replace the present quantum theory" which he admits is widely held. "But until such an alternative theory becomes available, the question of absolute chance will remain the subject of inconclusive controversy" (p. 335).

It is hard to know what to make of this account. Apparently what is being said is that we ought not to say anything about chance or determinism except so far as these come within the orbit of scientific explanation, and that though it is thought by some theorists that there are chance occurrences, it is possible to account for the same evidence without making such a supposition. But can not one ask, apart from all science, what is the reality about which science discourses? Nagel does remark that the scientist is trying to do some justice to observational phenomena, but the question I would like to have answered is whether or not there is something answering to the items which the scientific theory formulates. In some passages Nagel seems to suggest that these nonempirical entities are analytic components of empirically significant theories, or of the entire field of physics or science, that the acceptance of them enables one to move from one set of empirical data to another, and that this is the only import they have. But there are still questions left over: why are these items useful; how is it that they have this role? Can we not say something more than that they have proved to be effective and that when we find they are no longer so, we will abandon them or the use of them?

Why does the enterprise of science work so well? Does not Nagel merely take it to be a going concern and then try to analyze out how it proceeds? For him the matter is, as the subtitle of his book indicates, a study of the explanations which science can and does provide, and not a study in which it is shown why the explanations are so successful, and what it is to which they answer. However, Nagel does hold, early in his book, that laws might be viewed as leading principles. For my purposes this can be used as a way of leading to the ontological question: what kind of being has a leading principle as governing some objective state of affairs?

If we take a law to be a kind of leading principle, law would, as Peirce observed, have a kind of generality, but it would not necessarily call out "its parts." On the one hand it would have no parts, and on the other would not necessarily do anything to parts or to concrete matters of fact. But one could think of it as an outline of the whole, a projection of what the things are as a unity. It would then be a continuation of the actual structure, which a set of entities then and there exhibits or possesses, into the ideal future where it terminates in the idea of a completed unity of the objects—or where the law is one of decay or destruction, into the idea of a completed process of decay or destruction. More generally, the law would relate a present occurrence to a completed form of itself, the completed form now being in the future. But what makes the occurrence continue in the direction of the completion? Why may there not be laws of mere repetitions, of vacillations or even of increasing randomness?

A natural law, in the light of these considerations, might be said to be a structure linking present items with a prospective future which has some effect on the way those present items function. One need not suppose that there is energy being transmitted from the future, but only that a limit is being imposed on the possible activity of what is present. Such a view brings the idea of natural law into closer consonance with the law of nature than I had indicated in *Our Public Life*. Both types of law are now said to be governed by the future, but where natural law has an ideal, desirable goal, and is oriented toward men in a society, a law of nature terminates in a possibility. That possibility may be of a state inferior to the one which now prevails, or be neutral in value; in any case it would be a law for entities not subject to societal qualifications.

If there be any laws applicable to all bodies whatsoever, say something like Newton's laws of motion or Einstein's relation of mass and energy, the law would give the invariant, ontologically grounded relation which connects a present occurrence with a future possible one, where the future possible one (despite its generality) would involve some constraint on the activities that might otherwise be open to the present items. Laws would then testify to the power of some of the Ideal's subdivisions to affect the activity of actual entities. The fact that the law had this shape rather than that would be a consequent of the way in which present entities approach the future. Were they directed to the future in a different way than they now are, they would face a different set of possibilities.

The present view makes room for different degrees of control to be exerted by different possibilities. The organic beings with their sequential order of growth would be controlled somewhat the way in which Peirce thought all prospective wholes controlled all causal occurrences. It also leaves room for what might be called "chance" occurrences, for the general possibility does not dictate the particular activities of the actualities in the present, but merely delimits their range.

On this view we can no longer say that laws were, as Peirce and Whitehead held, ingredient in things as a kind of habit. They transcend the things, serving as a matter of fact to relate them beyond themselves to a future prospect. It is possible to avoid even a suggestion of final causality in this view, by taking the actual entities not only to demarcate and isolate certain relevant possibilities, but to be thereupon quickened to realize them. The control which the possibilities would be said to exercise would in fact be a function of the way in which they were being dealt with by the actual present entities. The act of reaching or being related to the future would be continuous with the act of keeping within the confines of the future which had thereby been isolated.

Many of the laws which interest scientists seem to be functional in character; instead of referring to causal antecedents and consequences (which would be in a time relation and thus would be in consonance with the above analysis) they would refer to copresent items which were nevertheless in some kind of interrelationship (such that an alteration in one of the items would involve a corresponding alteration in the others) expressed by the law. But might not this case be reduced to the causal by treating the reciprocal relation of the items as a prospect, i.e., the present would be envisaged as a single state involving the interrelated items, and this single state would have as a prospect other possible states in which the same type of interrelationship would hold, though the particular constants involved would be different? A single state could then be said to face a future possible state of which the actual succeeding state would be a particular instance. The law would have a future terminus in the guise of a general possible state which the activities in the present would end by realizing in one particular guise or another. Though the statement of the law would report a present correlation, actually what would be the case would then be a characteristic of a complex which was related to a more general form of that characteristic. The complex, through its causal action, would realize that general form in a specific subsequent guise. Such a view entails, I think, our ascribing some unity and some being to a complex interrelated state which had its nature expressed in a correlation or functional way.

Not every correlation which is persisted in for a while expresses a law. Such a result might be the outcome of the mere contingent but persistent concurrence of the items as they moved into the future in consonance with laws which governed them alone. We might find a rather persistent correlation between the population rates of our country and those of some African tribe; one might go up while the other went down, or one might have a rate which was a constant fraction of the other. Yet there might be no relation between these two countries beyond the physical one of being on the same globe. Each of the populations might, though, be thought of as characterized by a single complex interrelating structure, such as that given by the society or the marriage and sexual customs. And we might try to find, inside the societies, individual motivations and drives which when added together will show how one could get the different population rates for the different peoples.

How could one tell whether one had a genuine law of a functional kind, or just a mere correlation which happened to persist? The usual answer is that one must look to the whole of the science and see how the law fits in. One must try to predict with it, see if one could not derive consequences from it which were unsuspected; and one must see if its acknowledgment illuminated, i.e., helped explain other laws or at least supported them. This is surely a wise procedure, for the laws that are to be accepted by science must be part of a body of knowledge acceptable to science. But what is now acceptable to science presumably is not a congeries of possible contingent concurrences which happened to be sustained for the longest recorded time; the occurrences presumably exemplify laws and are not merely conjoined with one another. Shall we say it is a mere accident that we happened to hit on these? But accidents explain nothing; they are to be explained. Moreover, physical scientists do not try, as statistical sociologists often do, to look for high correlations and hope that some of them will persist and thus tell us of the presence of some law for a complex.

Must we not with Peirce recognize that there are real classes, which are real, not because, as he thought, they are governed by a final cause or act as a final cause for the items which they include, but because they have a nature of their own? They are, what I in *Reality* have termed "wholes." A whole is a complex which does not act, but which has a career with a distinctive set of consequences. Is not our question then: is this or that complex a whole rather than an aggregate which seems to have a distinctive career? Take a population. This would in one sense surely be nothing but an aggregate of individuals. Yet populations continue to exhibit rather constant features at certain times; perhaps there is even a rhythm to population growth and decline over the whole of recorded time. Nevertheless it might be the case that there was no "career" to a population; the variations we noted could perhaps be accounted for by aggregating the activities of individuals operating independently of most of the others.

Perhaps the question as to whether something is or is not a whole, and thus is or is not in fact related through a law to a relevant prospective future characteristic (which the action of the parts of the whole will make realized in the guise of a characteristic of the class of them— a characteristic which cannot be obtained by adding the characteristics of the parts to one another) is a question for science to decide. If it can find a general theory which applies to other phenomena as well, and which will allow for the prediction of the general characteristic, given the behavior of the parts, we would be inclined to say that we had a good ground for accepting the class to be real. But I think this evades the issue; if a science could not account for the temperature of a gas in this way, we would not for that reason be inclined to suppose that the temperature is not a trait of a whole, particularly if the temperature were uniform over a well-defined body.

Must we not say that we start with a commonsensical acknowledgment of wholes, and look to the parts out of which they are composed for explanations of the realization of their characteristics over the course of a career? If we acknowledge any other wholes they must be part of the very world of common sense, extensions of it, or deductions from it. But this would seem to deny that wholes, which were unknown to common sense, can be discovered without starting from common sense or reverting to it, and to deny that there could be wholes which have characteristics not on a commonsensical level. Groups of molecules might constitute a submacroscopic whole with traits which we can learn about by reflection, analysis, and the observation of larger wholes constituted by the smaller wholes.

Various types of cells seem to form linkages to make unities which lack the power to act, and thus are wholes, and not individuals or mere aggregates. See, for example, Bergson's discussion of the growth of the eye. (Bergson is concerned with making evident that the interrelationship of the sub-wholes is in fact governed by some larger whole or perhaps by an individual unity. But suppose one did not accept Bergson's view, and acknowledged only the existence of these various wholes which were then thought to be aggregated together somehow? Or suppose that while one accepted something like Bergson's account, one acknowledged the reality of the elements which were being brought together in such a way as to bring about the unitary quality that makes it possible for us to recognize the elements?)

Do we not in the end come back to what can be grossly observed? Nagel says that "the 'natures' of things, and in particular of the 'elementary constituents' of things, are not accessible to direct inspection. . . . Such 'natures' must be stated as a theory and are not the objects of observations" (p. 364). But do we not observe temperatures, families, even banks and colleges, read books, smoke pipes? I think we start by accepting these as genuine wholes and develop our scientific theories in good part to find ways in which we can account for the careers which they exhibit via their characteristics, by referring back to a set of actions on the part of their constituents. What is not clear is whether we ever do—and it seems that we do—acknowledge new wholes on the basis of the discovery of a persistence in career, or of what seems to be law-like behavior on the part of a number of items together, which we otherwise would have supposed constituted a mere aggregate. In short, do we with respect to population, peer groups, and various combinations of biological cells, really accept them as genuine wholes, or only as arresting, contingent persistencies in the aggregational characters they happen to manifest for a while?

February 9

Page Smith brings out a number of dimensions in history to which I did not do full justice in my own book. He distinguishes between what he calls existential and symbolic history—better terms would be "vital" and "formal" history. Vital history involves men basically, and allows a contemporary historian to tell us an inextinguishable and basically unalterable truth about his time. Formal history, which is primarily the work of monographists, using the methods of modern research (sometimes called scientific history) is, in contrast, structural, reconstructive, accumulative, abstract, atomized. Page Smith makes much of the fact that distance from an occurrence does not make the account one presents necessarily more objective than that written by a contemporary who is engaged in recounting the events of a vital historic period. The later historian also, like the earlier, brings in his bias and imposes alien interpretations.

Page Smith does not take sufficient account of the fact that these two histories really interplay, and that as we move along in time we uncover data and can encompass a range not possible to the contemporary of the occurrence, so that the formal history enriches the reports of vitally involved historians. I, on the other hand, did not take sufficient account of the fact that a contemporary might have the sensitivity and detachment, the range and the perceptiveness, to give the basic indelible outline of an occurrence; and that a formal historian, no matter how much research he engages in, might do no more than fill out the contemporary's account with comparatively minor new content.

Page Smith, too, takes more seriously than I did the fact that history can help one transform the future. I took it too much in the sense of a discipline telling truths. He is more right than I. Vital historic truths can enrich, encourage, direct and criticize what we are about to do. Incidentally, in his use of Ramsay's explanation of the American Revolution, Page Smith takes the struggle to be a case of the one and the many —though the terms do not occur in his account. He places the unity of the British empire over against the pluralistic tendency of the Colonists to go their own way, in a form that suggests that the Civil War might be conceived as a kind of transposition of a problem that had been revolutionarily resolved in the previous century.

Is it helpful to say that America's crises are all of this sort? Are all crises of this sort? It does not seem so. Even the Civil War was not simply a war of the unitary idea of the United States and the pluralistic tendency of the Southern States, for there surely is the question of slavery, urbanization, industrialization, cotton prices, and the like. But might we not say there is always an element of the struggle of the one and the many? Those who are in power are solidified by virtue of the common possession of wealth and privilege; those who are opposed are solidified only by virtue of their opposition to the unity of the first, and act to dissolve or to disperse what was constraining them. But may not a crisis occur in complete absence of any conflict between a one and a many? Surely one power may find itself blocked by another and may precipitate a war in order to be able to expand as it needed. Both sides may be unified in their own terms, and each might even want to expand at the expense of the other. It would seem then that the idea of a one and many conflict is not necessary even as an element.

And we cannot do much with the two cases, the Revolution and the Civil War, to make sensible a supposition that American crises will have the character of a one against a many. There is in fact another suggestion contained in Page Smith's account. At one place he speaks as though both sides desired the same result, but that they did not know how to mesh their different stresses on different sides with one another. This sounds like a fruitful way to look at historical periods. Instead of giving the different sides different ideologies, it might prove more illuminating to see both sides as subject to a common ideology, but which they stressed in something like what seemed to them to be incompatible ways. Can we say that Hitler and Churchill had the same outlook in root? One could, on the old idea that the powerful nations were inclined to expand their empires and that Hitler was merely a newcomer more ruthless than the others. After all, no one went to war with Hitler because of the concentration camps, even though their existence was known to the other powers.

If this last hypothesis be accepted, we seem on the verge of holding a theory of the *Zeitgeist* which, at distinctive moments, has a characteristic shape. But we need not suppose that there is a distinct entity which somehow captures the people and the nations existing at a given time, and has them live out a history of a certain sort. On the suggestion I am making, whatever is common, is common to oppositional parties. There is no reason to suppose that it affects other people or nations. No crises have as yet affected all peoples. Some continue as before—e.g., African tribes, Brazilian primitives, some distant countries—while the rest are caught in a death struggle. They may be affected in some way, but they are not necessarily involved in, nor subject to the same over-all conditioning.

Contending parties have something in common which they seek to possess, but in such a way as to deny it in all or part of the other. Their motives for the denial may be different; on a moral level their claims may be radically distinct. But so far as they make use of force in order to achieve what is wanted by each to the exclusion of the other, they do have a common, though oppositional character. Even a struggle of the one with the many could be brought under this rubric, for it could be argued that this struggle is nothing more than a desire by each to achieve autonomy or dominance, or perhaps both.

If there be any truth in this suggestion, the vital historian, one who is concerned with the basic principles which are involved in basic crises, and who may well be contemporary with the occurrence he writes about, must make it his business to discover just what common outcome the two sides sought to realize in oppositional ways. He will have to make out why they took oppositional and apparently irreconcilable ways of trying to realize the objective both had. The discovery of the objective would be the discovery, as it were, of an area where something like the *Zeitgeist* could be said to be for a moment. The *Zeitgeist* could then be treated as a kind of episodic occurrence, a kind of kairotically appearing character of disparate people, directing them from diverse positions to bring about an end which they cannot in their present condition bring about together and in harmony. The consideration of why the contending parties were irreconcilable would have to rest on the study of the historic development of the different parties. Because America had gone through such and such a history in the past, America was able to enter the First World War against Germany and on the side of the Allies. But both sides could be said to be concerned with Empire, Nationhood, or the future which was about to be industrialized.

These suggestions do not come the length of giving us a law of history; they provide us only with a way of approaching historic phenomena of magnitude without invoking a radical determinism, a devil theory of history, a providential theory of history, or becoming a philosophical historian who takes man to have a definite worked-out destiny in a world which must go through certain prescribed historic stages. It is but an illustration of an elementary piece of wisdom, that the contending parties are not too alien in conditioning, morality, intelligence, and objective, no matter what they say or how they behave. But this does not mean that we must abdicate all moral judgment, and not see one side to be preferable to the other, particularly if that other is in root opposed to any prospect of a civilized mankind.

February 10

My book on history impresses me, on rereading it, much more than it ever did. It is, I think, a fine and important book. It now suggests to me a theory of immortality. If any occurrence has an indeterminate nature by virtue of being in an ongoing present, and if we can envisage an ongoing present to include the whole of mankind in time, then I and all my predecessors and successors can be said to be part of a single ongoing present, and in this sense not to have passed away. Since of course we have a limited span, we, as distinct individuals (wholly determinate, and thus as marked off one from the other and in the past of some project or of the Ideal) can be said to pass away as marked off one from the other, but to continue as indeterminate constituents of a single present of all mankind. This single present has its indeterminate items in a relation of before and after, and not of earlier and later. We are immortal as part of one temporal mankind, a mankind which is temporal in the sense that the present it constitutes can give way to some subsequent present or may itself be included in an even longer present.

This kind of answer denies to us an immortality of ourselves as determinate beings; but then no doctrine of immortality ever denied that the body (at least until some Last Judgment) was no longer in existence, and every doctrine of immortality seems to allow the self or soul some role and thus some indeterminacy so far as the role has not been lived out. The indeterminacy need not be absolute and it does not preclude the determinacy which characterizes us as entirely past.

The present view of immortality is a little closer to the Greek and the Oriental idea (which takes the soul to have been in existence before birth) than to the Christian. It takes my soul to be a part in a single stretched-out present which has its extension over all the men that had been and will be. My individual soul, in an indeterminate guise, would thus be "always" contained inside the continuing present which is as long as mankind will be. Does this not mean that I already had a place in mankind even before I was born? What happens to the distinctiveness of myself, a distinctiveness which surely is in some sense won over the course of this life? What sense does it make to say that I am immortal when there is nothing I can identify as my "I," and when the "immortality" was achieved before I was born?

Might one not say that before I am born I am part of the ongoing present only as something indeterminate, and even indistinguishable in a single directional whole, and that when I am born I impose determinations on a part of that present; and that when I pass away I put a border around that initial part, and so as bordered pass away? The border is one-sided, made by me from within, and therefore is no border for the rest of the present, which is after though not later than my part. I think this is far from clear, but there seems to be some kernel of truth here which I hope I'll be able to extract one of these days soon.

February 13

Men are not only alienated with respect to society or fellowman, but with respect to the Ideal, Existence, and God (i.e., they lose their ethical standards, are maladjusted and self-centered) as well. The alienation is due to the fact that man is never wholly in perfect equilibrium with respect to what is outside him; also, his acts are always accompanied with irrelevancies and are subject to limitations by outside forces, his own ignorance, and lack of control; and the terminus of his acts are not always appropriate to what is intended, being caught in circumstances beyond that terminus.

The remedy for alienation is interior or exterior. The interior remedy is detachment, the finding of some other referent, the achieving of a balance among references, the reorganization of the self or the making use of new powers. The best remedy seems to involve the purging of the act of its irrelevancies, the supplementing of it with other acts, the making it more continuous, effecting, and flexible so that it answers to both the man and the desired terminus. The remedy should also involve some kind of effort or activity on the part of the terminus. Education should prepare us to get proper remedies.

To achieve the truly good complete life, one must make use of all one's powers so that one is engaged vitally both internally and externally. Everything else, in addition, should be evaluated; this is done by following out one's own value system and supplementing it with that of the others to constitute a single complex value system. Also, there should be an engagement in some basic enterprise, supplemented by the role of a spectator or of a passive recipient of the products of other enterprises. There should also be a separation of oneself from the fruits of one's activities, and the acceptance of the fruits provided by others. Detachment leads to the separation of one's center from the world, while the acceptance of the fruits of others allows for the production of a treasury of fruits environing us. The outcome should be a self with good character, making a complex evaluation of the totality that men produce. That totality is the civilized world in which all can live.

I have recently been speaking to a number of Protestant theologians, and find them unusually coy about one particular question—What is a Christian? They are so anxious to show that they are honest, reflective, inquiring men, who are sympathetic with the strivings of other religions, and who live in the spirit of Protestantism, that they refuse to commit themselves to any theoretical position. They deny that it is even necessary to affirm that Jesus is the Christ. But then I do not see why they call themselves Christians. And if they do call themselves Christians, then, though they are honest and even critical inquirers ready to subject any issue to reflection and critical examination, they are committed to accept something which distinguishes them from other religionists. In this respect they differ from the philosopher. It is not proper to say, as they often do, that the philosopher also has a commitment, say to the truth. This kind of commitment, on the one hand, is that which he shares with all inquirers and which does not suffice to distinguish him from the theologian; on the other hand, he can look at even this commitment in a critical spirit. Even as committed to seek the truth he can ask himself what it is to be so committed, why one should be so, and so on.

There is a frame within which any inquiry is conducted, but this frame can itself be made the object of a study for which a similar frame is provided. This does not, I think, make the philosophic enterprise circular or question-begging at this point. No one is being circular or question-begging who examines the nature of consistency consistently, or the nature of logic logically. Indeed if these last have undesirable flaws, the philosophic enterprise need not. One might say that if logic or consistency were regrettable, the outcome of their use would be undesirable. But if a commitment to truth were regrettable, it still could be the case that what was then discovered, even about the commitment, was desirable or true or right.

It is the tendency of theologians to think that all that is not fish is fowl, i.e., that once one frees oneself from common-sense values and acts, one is religious, whereas the fact is that one might well be an artist, an ethicist, a speculative philosopher, a scientist, etc.

Geddes McGregor suggested to me that over and above any knowledge or wisdom the religious man might attain, he benefits from a participation with a number of people in what I have called a dedicated community. In principle the religious man could be as wise as the philosopher, but would be more humanly complete. But it is not true that his failure to face the question of the legitimacy of his primary commitment will mean that his critical attitude will not be as well developed as the philosopher's, and that so far he will not be as wise?

February 16

Judaism may be said to be defined in terms of its acceptance of the Prophets, the Torah, and the history of the people. If we attend to the fact that this history is a religious one, all three items can be brought into a single focus. Judaism can then be said to accept a distinctive kind of relationship with God. This idea can be generalized, and we can go on to say that each established religion is oriented toward a distinctive way in which God is thought to interplay and be present to those who are concerned with Him. Each would specialize a basic ontological truth to the effect that God is not merely a being in-Himself but has a place everywhere. The different religions would isolate some of these truths as more conspicuous, or revelatory, or helpful, or as better answering to their particular careers or abilities. Each as a consequence would have two sides: each would have a special message or revelation, since it would cherish a distinctive place or way in which God was present, and each would serve as a laboratory for all its people, enabling them to see God everywhere.

Each religion would be wrong to insist on itself as having the truth about what God requires of all men or what He is in-Himself. But all could be said to be true in the sense that each knows what God is like in that particular area, and also leads its members to see what God is like outside a dedicated community, and what that community enjoys or knows. Such a view makes an advance on what I originally maintained in the religious paper, to the effect that there could be no reconciliation amongst the religions because they made conflicting claims. Now we can say that the claims are conflicting only because of the orientations they have, and not in what they intend.

To refer to Jesus as the Christ is but to alert men to a signal instance of the Divine Presence. In one sense this reference is rejected by all religions other than Christianity as an occurrence for all men, but it cannot be rejected by these other religions as improper to some men, for it is in fact an acceptance which defies one to be a Christian at least in the traditional sense. The acknowledgment of Jesus as the Christ should, for the Christian, be but a way for him to locate all the other presences of God—though he of course cannot enjoy these. Just as anyone can distinguish a church from a saloon, so one can recognize that some other men are engaged in a religion and are cherishing some distinguished occasion where God is present. All religions in the end can be said to agree in that each allows all the others a place which it grants is a place where God is for those others and that its own acknowledgment is but a special one, essential for itself, but which, when objectively viewed, is no better or worse than that of the others.

On this view apologetics would be largely a waste of time. At its best it would be a branch of education, claiming not the superiority of one's religion or even offering a justification for it in terms of some document or practice, but only that those other religions must allow for it, just as it allows for them. Theology on this view would never remain within the confines of the acceptances of the religion, but would always point out the ways in which the acceptances of the other religions are to be understood as illustrating its own, and also as involving distinctive commitments by others. It would recognize that each religion is a laboratory enabling men to make better contact with God, and that there is a place and indeed a need for a philosophic understanding of God and religion. A significant study of the nucleal element in all the religions should justify one's affirmation that other religions besides one's own are making contact with God.

We can look at competing political systems somewhat in the same way. There is no need and perhaps no right for us to claim that democracy is the right form of government for all. Answering to a distinctive history and distinctive needs and aims, other forms of political organization may do as much justice to the men involved as a democracy does for us. Could the Russian Revolution have succeeded if there had not been a strong dictator in the beginning? Is not the organization of the Soviet Republic today an inescapable consequence of the nature of the beginning it had?

We do not take a similar answer with respect to ethics, logic, philosophy, science. Why? Is it not because these claim to pertain to all men, to be objective and prescriptive for all? If so, what is wrong with the established religions in their supposition that, like these subjects, they are religions for all men? Just as we would be willing to say that America is not where all ought to live, and may be willing to say that others need not have our political organization, so we should be willing to say that not all men ought to have the same religion. Different religions will answer to different appetites, histories, insights, practices, and values.

Does not the Roman Catholic Church recognize this in its willingness to modify its rites and liturgy in different areas? I think not, for what is at issue here is not certain distinctive practices, but definite ways or places or times which are being acknowledged as central for an enjoyment or service of God. If this is right, there never can be a final reconciliation of religions without losing either the signal occasions which define the given religions, the putting of them on a par with those cherished by other religions, or the abandonment of the distinctive items and insights of the particular religions so that they become local variants of some one religion whose occasions and insights are taken as paradigms.

February 17

Accepting the modern use of the term "theology" as applying to critical reflection on some accepted religion, one can avoid turning it into an apologetics if A] it takes account of the philosophic observation that God is a cosmic being, present everywhere, and that various places and objects are more or less receptive to His presence; B] it recognizes that God's demands are not functions of man's needs, questions, desires, or organizations. A consequence of the first is that no one religion can take itself to have the only objects, methods, instruments, etc., for getting to or enjoying God. A consequence of the second is that a state religion, an ethical culture, an existentialistic religion, are all inadequate since they do not recognize the independent functioning of God, regardless of man, his needs, desires, or status.

These various conditions can be met by looking at one's accepted religion as taking account of a signal occasion or occasions when God is present, at the same time that it is recognized that He is present in other ways and places, and that this fact can be enjoyed by others and not by oneself (since it depends for its enjoyment on a prior commitment to some other religious practice or tradition).

A Jewish theology would distinguish the prophets as men who to a high degree were able to express the import of God for the life of a people. It would treat its Torah as one set of laws which were a-ethical in meaning, in that they did not necessarily conform to any ethical command. (Where they did conform, they would give those commands an urgency and value they did not have before.) It would treat its Talmud as one strand of a continuing intellectual assessment of what had already been acknowledged. And it would treat the history of the Jews as a religious history having rhythms and values different from an ordinary secular hisotry, even of those Jews. Only one who approached God in at least one of these ways could be said to be a religious Jew. And such an approach would have to acknowledge (if it is to conform to the conditions of a respectable theology) that there were equally viable and useful ways of getting to God from other positions which (except in the case of conversion) are closed to the Jews, in the light of their tradition and history and acculturation. We would then have a kind of relativity of absolutes, each religion taking itself and its claims to be absolute, right, and inescapable for its people, and yet acknowledging the truth that there are other religions, equally well and rightly committed to be religions in a different way.

To get to the essence of a religion one would not try to get the least common denominator of all of them, for that would have one at the end with hardly any content. Nor could one really succeed with a study of comparative religion, for this actually does not let one know what is seen from the position of the commited persons in the different religions. One would have to be content with getting a distinctive insight from one perspective and then acknowledging the others externally, aware that what one's own perspective does for oneself, theirs will do for them.

The answer here given is something like the answer given in the *Modes* to the effect that we know Actuality in one way, but that way does not tell us, as well as some other way, how to grasp another mode of being. The best way to grasp Existence is through the agency of art and history, and not through cognition. Similarly, the best way to grasp God is through religion, private and public, and not through intellection. But intellection does tell us something in both cases. To get to God from one religion is like getting to Existence through one art. Just as he who practices one art can be aware that others practicing another art can achieve the same insight that he does (though he cannot see the result in the same way that the other can), so he who practices one religion can see that others can be as successful as he, by practicing their own religions.

Not every work of art is the equal of every other; it is conceivable that sculpture or the dance has not reached the levels of achievement that music or painting has. Just so, all religions need not be thought to be equally successful. But no one can tell whether all the religions are equally legitimate or sound or mature, unless one knows the nature of God and how He operates, and then can engage in a religion and see if it does justice to what is otherwise known of God. This in effect means that we must stop criticizing other religions, for we do not really know what it is they open up to their people, and must criticize our own so far as we see that it fails to do justice to the truths learned elsewhere. We ought then, instead of being apologetic, be critical of our own religions. Instead of attacking others or dealing with them as though they were unsatisfactory in fact, we ought to try to see how it is possible for one who is inside his religion to be able to see and enjoy what we do inside our own. There would on this account be little justification for missionaries, unless they were concerned with trying to help those inside other religions to strengthen themselves by taking account of available facets of their own religion, in order to achieve the results that the missionaries have achieved in the missionaries' religion.

February 19

According to Charles Hartshorne, God is a being who is, and whose essential properties are there by principle and not by fact, i.e., are superlative cases of ideas or meanings and not the outcome of the realization of possibilities. There are for him only two alternatives in relation to God: either God exists necessarily, or He necessarily does not exist. I think the approach ingenious and the general result sound. But what Hartshorne does not consider is that not all superlatives need converge at the same point, which is but to say that the argument can end with a plurality of absolutes or Gods—or, as I prefer to say, with a plurality of modes of Being. Each is supreme in a distinctive way. Existence is supreme in its extensionality, the Ideal in its indeterminacy, God in his unity or care, while Actuality is supreme in its accommodation of distinct substantial parts.

I think Hartshorne does not keep sufficiently clear the difference between a thing or object, and Being. He thinks that God is the supreme instance of the categories characteristic of us. But this He can be only so far as we are representatives of the being, Actuality, i.e., so far as our characteristics reflect, not ourselves in our individuality, but ourselves as standing for the Being which is Actuality.

I think too that one must distinguish a position which proceeds, one might say, by absolutizing categories, and a position which argues for the necessity of a reality. Hartshorne muddles the two together. Absolutizing the categories may give us a plurality of ultimate realities.

The necessity of a reality, particularly if it be a necessity of being all reality, will end with whatever there be. This need not be one single entity, but the ultimate realities as together. The argument would end not with God, but with God and whatever other realities there were. These would not have to be unified in something more substantial. In other words, the ontological argument would end with all reality, as it now does for Hartshorne and others, but this would not yet be shown to be solidified into a single entity.

The absolutizing method gives us distinct realities, whereas the ontological argument would give us a complex of those realities. The absolutizing method can start with one character and end with one absolute. The ontological argument instead starts with one idea of a possibility which must be necessary, and ends with a plurality of inter-locked realities. Hartshorne fails to see that there could be many uses of the absolutizing methods each arriving at a distinct Being. And he fails to see that the ontological argument need not end with showing that some one kind of being is necessarily existent, but only that all the be-ings there are, as interlocked in one universe, necessarily exist.

I think Hartshorne, by his reference to categories having an absolute role with respect to God, obscures what he discerned when he insisted that the existence of God is established not by "facts" but by principles. The former approach sounds as if God were the highest degree of some-thing like a man or a thing; it would make God out to be an object, though of a superior kind. The latter approach recognizes that God is a being distinct from the kinds of beings or objects which dot this space-time world. I suppose this is the insight of all theologians, though dis-course about analogy, references to God's person, knowledge, conscious-ness, and love tempt one to take Him to be a reality such as ourselves. Most theologians in the West then go on to suppose that God is Being, or The Being. But if I am right there is more than one Being, precluding any identifiable entity from being termed "The Being."

The ultimate modes of Being are neither objects nor Being. The ontological argument will apply to the total set of Beings. But if one wanted to prove the existence of one of the Beings, one would either do it in terms of principles (or what I called in the *Modes* predicates with existential import), or from the position of some other Being. Even the traditional cosmological and teleological arguments recognize this, for they do not start with the particulars of this world but with the world as a whole. For them it is as a kind of being with a distinctive over-all character.

The traditional arguments, as made manifest in the *Modes* and in the early discussion in the Conference held at the Jewish Theological Seminary in 1940, reduce to so many approaches which must be used together to make a single argument. That single argument will go from one mode of Being to the Being of God. Generalized it will help us go from any one mode of Being to any other. If one wanted to go from a particular reality to a mode of Being, one must either make it a representative of some mode of Being, and thus in effect repeat the kind of argument by which one moves from a mode of Being to some other, or one must penetrate beneath the particularity to the Being which sustains it, and in which it has whatever reality it possesses. The penetration can be achieved by shock, by wonder, in fear, or it can be achieved through reflection on what it is that makes something true or objective, or able to maintain itself over against others.

When it is said that God created the universe, it is not always clear whether what is intended is the view that the particularities are created, which seems to be what the Bible is maintaining, or that the Being of the universe is created. Let us suppose it is the former. We can then say that what God creates is the subdivisions inside the various modes of Being, and particularly inside Actuality. We would then have something like Plato's demiurgos and the receptacle of the *Timaeus.* This view would not perhaps be too far from Aquinas', except that he thinks of creation apparently as involving two steps, the creation of a prime matter (which might be identified as the Being of Actuality as such) and the creation of particular delimitated substances through the use of that prime matter.

If matter for Aquinas were a genuine being, it would not be something which was used or individualized, but rather a place which is continuous with the reality of the particulars placed in it. But if matter is a being as surely as God is, we are still faced with the difficulty that after creation there is more being than before, and God as a consequence is not everything, not perfect, not complete.

If God be said to create only the particulars, one could maintain that those particulars are created as representatives of the Being in which they are. We would then have a more general grasp of the insight of Bonaventura that everything whatsoever, i.e., every particular, was a trace, a shadow or an image of God, without our having to claim that God was ever the only Being in the universe.

This discussion makes more acute the difficulties attaching to the doctrine of analogy. Not only is it the case that even for Thomas every term in an analogy undergoes a radical change by being moved from the finite to the infinite (thereby making the analogy useless—since not even the idea of proportion will withstand the transfer), but analogy speaks as though God and man were similar kinds of beings. Man as made in the image of God, which is of course here a question-begging idea, will allow for some kind of direct movement to God, and perhaps even an analogical one, for man has some powers which could be said to be infinite—Descartes, for example, thought the will was such. One might also urge that the mind, the person, the self, the soul, the ethical character, the concern or even the claim to know anything with truth, is somehow infinite.

The move to God is never analogical. It is instead a move only in depth, through absolutizing, speculation, or the achievement of detachment from the world and the separation out of God from what is then confronted. This last requires an understanding of the nature of God, and the subsequent identification of some portion of the confronted as having that nature; or it will require some revelation, or a sensitivity for recognizing that there are independently acting ultimates in the confronted, one of which has some of the features traditionally associated with the term "God."

It is perhaps the most characteristic and persistent view of the Hindus that the Being which is God is not like the being of any finite thing. But I think they go too far in the other direction, for their depersonalization of God makes Him identical with all of ultimate Being, lacking any differentiating character. They too must face up to the fact that there is more than one ultimate Being. Indeed Taoism recognizes being to be essentially what we in the West would call the whole of nature, and not what we, or even the Hindus, would term the absolutely real or God.

The Hindu position is stronger than the Western because, since it is so impersonal, it is not as likely to suppose that God is real in the very sense in which we are. That we are real, however, cannot be gainsaid, and that reality which we have (though not equatable with Being as such) is nevertheless, even when not representational in role or meaning, strong enough to withstand the demands of the Being which is God, the Being which is the Ideal, and the Being which is Existence.

Even granted that man is a representative of all Actuality, is it necessary that, as opposed to God, as the other of God, he be the other of Him in His Being, or only the other of Him as having distinguishable parts or roles? Does not a man as a whole, representative of other men and eventually of Actuality as such, stand as the other, not of God, but of

God's will or purpose or commands? Such a view comes closer to the insight of religious men than the view I am presenting in the book on religion, and which I have been adumbrating in different places for the last year or so. God in His Being would be a God beyond God, to use Tillich's expression; man's involvement would then be with God in some limited role, the God below God, as it were.

February 20

The existentialists are right to insist that man is distinct from other kinds of being. But is this difference an ontological one, as they tend to claim? Is it that man alone can be a representative of Actuality, or that he alone can be the other of God? This does not seem to be the case. Man's distinctiveness is a function of the way in which he is a representative, or of the kind of relation he has to the various modes of Being. Whereas every entity is related to the future, for example, and is in a sense governed by it, thereby having its present action subject to conditions and limitations, man adopts the Ideal, makes himself the bearer of it, and thereby becomes an ethically conditioned being. Does he also somehow represent God and Existence? He can represent Actuality as such in his claim to truth; similarly he can represent God by his sympathetic consideration and his attempt to preserve or enhance the values of whatever there be; and he can represent Existence through his art.

In a review of *History: Written and Lived,* James Collins says that the various ways which I suggest for encountering the past, are ways appropriate to approaches to God. This arresting suggestion leads me to ask whether we may not approach all the modes of Being in these ways? The ways are primarily of two kinds: an encounter with what is actively present, and an encounter with the actively present as filtered through some concept we have. The first is obviously what we have in a sacrament; the second would be the facing and enjoying of a sacrament as qualified by some conceptual pattern, so that the outcome would be an encounter with a power that had been modified by the intrusion of that concept. The sacrament here need not be one acknowledged by some church; it could be any object, where this has been understood to bear the impress of God. Once again there would be no ontological difference between man and other beings, in the sense that he alone was the locus of God's presence. And going on to the other modes of Being, ordinary things could be said to be loci of ideal determinations, in that they have characteristic futures which determine their careers, and in that their configurations are epitomizations of the whole of Existence which lies outside their boundaries.

In this history book, as Collins rightly observes, I have tried to reconcile the idea of substance with that of process. It is not true that one who holds that there are substances is forced to take the static view of Aristotle and be denied all power to deal with creativity, the open future (after all, it was Aristotle who insisted in his *De Interpretatione* that the future was open in the sense that the events to be could not be predeterminate, but were as future, indeterminates awaiting action through time to become determinate present realities), time and history. The past is accumulated and is operative in a being; a being's effective temporality, as it were, is exhibited in the way it relates its inward to its outward, its depth to its surface. We, in starting from the surface or outward, reverse the process in our encounters. The object, as merely present, is subject to an operative condition or cause which had been present, and thus is an accumulated past.

If this idea be taken as a model, ought we not to say that the present being does not merely accumulate its past, but that the modes of Being are also operative in it in analogous ways? The difference between operation of the past and the modes of Being on the present being is that the modes act as having a reality of their own, whereas the past must be given such a reality by God.

Why are there not other powers operative in a being, besides the past? The future has some efficacy. But these both are time dimensions. What of the spatial dimensions? Should we not say that the above and below, the right and the left, the front and the back are also present in the being here before us, and that we can encounter these as operative in the substance? Should we not say that causes are operative in a way distinct from that in which preconditions are, i.e., that causes are dimensions or facets of the dynamics of Existence, and are to be contrasted with those which relate to Existence's time and space? But if time be thought to be present only in the shape of a conditioning past time, and the dynamics of Existence present only in the shape of a causal power transmogrified to be a present depth coming to the surface to qualify what the present object in fact is, ought we say more than that there is one kind of element, which represents space, rather than the three or six (i.e., above, below, right, left, front, back) just listed? Thus the "spreadoutness," the roominess, the insistence on itself which a present object has could be said to involve an epitomization and embodiment of space itself. If we say all this then the presence of Existence in actualities is accounted for. Will there then be three ways in which the other three modes of Being will be present in each actuality? Will not the various parts of the other modes of Being have reciprocal interiorities reflecting the presence of the remaining modes of Being?

If we take the future, not as a future moment of time, but as the Ideal having a temporal reference, the Ideal will be present in actualities both when they are historic and when they are merely natural beings. Their directionality, how they will carve out the future, what possibilities they will in fact realize, will be determined. But does not the Ideal provide a standard of value? And this standard, though outside the actuality, can it not be said to be encounterable in or through it, through the mediation of our concepts? And must not the Ideal also be present in actualities as realized possibilities, i.e., as actual predicates or characters which nevertheless have a generality to them, testifying to their origin?

Are the three analogues in relation to God, those which relate to God as other, to God as preserver, and to God as judge or final assessor? This set of three I don't now envisage clearly, even though I did make similar distinctions before.

Whatever be the designations of the roles which the different modes of Being play in actualities (and presumably in the subdivisions of the other modes of Being) it is evident that we can take account of them in two ways. In one way we see them as enriching our idea of actualities, for they are encountered in the actualities as determinative of what the actualities in fact are. As was observed in the history book, the distinctiveness of an actuality is to be accounted for my taking note of the operation of the past antecedents, the exclusiveness by taking note of past causes, while the ultimacy is to be accounted for by taking note of past conditions. History seems to be occupied with the third of these only, since it passes over a consideration of genuinely operative causes or the antecedents as they in fact exist, to deal with the past as constituting the conditions which govern the present.

The second way we take account of the modes of Being is by trying to see what they are via actualities. This I gather is what Heidegger tried to do with the idea of Being. He sought to find Being via man, a Being which is operative in man but is nevertheless distinct from him. This Being I would say is but an unarticulated amalgam of the four modes of Being. But if one had to identify it with any mode, it would I suppose be with Actuality. Heidegger's problem, then, is to move from the individual man to the Actuality which is in fact operative in him in the guise of his role as a representative being who knows, acts, and wills.

It looks as if the view that other Beings (or the various dimensions of other Beings) were effective inside another, allows one to dispense with the supposition that these other Beings have a status outside the Being in which they are effective. Why not, for example, say that the past is the past as effective inside present objects? The historian when he refers back to the past would then merely be imaginatively trying to see what the past was when it was present. If we could maintain this, we would have no reason to have recourse to God to account for history and its past, as external to the present. The past would not be external in any sense. Yet the historian would be engaged in writing what could be true or false, since some of his ideas would be such as to be inconsistent with the functioning of present things, or with other evidences we might gather in the present.

The difficulty with this idea is that not all of the past is effective now in present objects. The whole of past history cannot therefore be said to be operative; some of the items in it, though as historic as any other, are not significant for the present except in the sense of accelerating or retarding the causal line which moves from a relevant past item to its effect in the present. But why can't we use our concepts to filter the present objects, and to assign those concepts, which function neutrally, to the position of concepts of what is not now effective, leaving the others as the effective ones? But we would still be faced with the question: to what do the concepts refer? Perhaps to nothing? Perhaps they are nothing but the historian's plans or ideas or ways of uniting the data he has in the present? History would then have to be said to be a construction. Yet we seem to remember past occurrences, and sometimes have simple descriptions of them. But may not the memory and the descriptions both be thought of as plans or categories or concepts, in terms of which we organize data, even present data?

We seem to be confronted with the alternatives: give up the veracity of memory and the reference of history, or abandon the idea that there is a past somehow kept in existence by the action of God. The second alternative seems more plausible, particularly if we think of God, not as a person or as engaged in some deliberate act, but as a certain type of ultimate Being who operates inside the realm of Existence, and therefore can give being to the past as surely as He gives present objects the role of being shadows, etc., of Himself (or the role of detached others, of men of faith or concern, or of men of service) and gives the future the role of a controlling providence, or at least of a demanding Ideal. Another way of saying this, at least in part, is to say that the present object swims in a sea of the past and the future, and that the past and the future in which it swims have a being which the present does not, since the present is the locus of particularities which are what they are only because they are inseparable from a more ultimate Being. The present has a being but it is the being of the past or future, as operative in it, of Actuality itself, or other modes of Being—or all of them together, which I think is more correct.

February 21

At least five types of entity must be distinguished, each with its own type of rationale and role. We have to begin with the daily objects and events that are in part grasped within the framework of categories which reflect the individual's, and society's, and perhaps even the human race's experiences, beliefs and predilections. Then we have the strands which can be abstracted from these objects, such as the scientific, the eventful, and perhaps the merely perceptual too. (In *The World of Art* the evaluational was also included.) These strands are purer than the commonsensical objects since they are freed from some of the conventional limitations which practice involves. However, the objects in the strands cannot act, nor can their time really pass.

The real object is the locus of all the strands; it is the commonsensical object when freed from human accretions, and is to be known either by synthesizing the strands, by purifying the commonsensical object, or by subdividing Actuality. The actual object has within it a power, a directionality, a worth; and it functions as a representative, by virtue of the fact that Existence, Ideality, God, and Actuality are operative within it. The fourth type of entity is an ultimate mode of Being, Existence, etc., as standing apart from the actuality. Each of these modes has subdivisions comparable to those characteristic of the mode Actuality. The fifth type of entity is the produced entity. This may be the outcome of deliberate human effort, as in the case of art, or it may be the outcome of the interplay of a number of actualities, so as to produce groups, families, etc., or it may be the outcome of the interplay of a number of modes of Being, to give us the historic, the state, and so on. Since these produced items function in different ways, it is desirable I think to distinguish them; and if we recognize that the subdivisions of the different modes of Being are different in type from, and in relationship to, the

Being, we will have to increase our list. If we also distinguish the modes of Being from one another we will have:

 1] commonsensical entities
 2] strands
 3] actualities
 4] possibilities
 5] "ideas" in God
 6] parts of space-time-energy
 7] art objects
 8] combinations of actualities
 9] combinations of the modes of Being
10] Actuality
11] Ideality
12] Existence
13] God

This list can evidently be shortened or lengthened with good reason. We can bundle together all the modes of Being as ultimate entities. And we can distinguish the different kinds of products that result when different modes combine. Thus we can distinguish the state, the kind of entity produced by the interplay of men and Ideality, from the historic where men in or out of a state interplay with Existence.

If actualities, as daily encountered, yield strands, ought we not also to have something similar with respect to the subdivisions of other modes of Being? Not unless we can be said to experience these or have them in some conventional setting. Now we do put limitations on the possibilities that confront us, and even characterize them in limitative ways; the subdivisions of Existence are not altogether separable from actualities, so that we have a space which is humanly oriented, a time which is paced by human needs, etc.; and we think of God as engaged in various functions. In a sense these considerations are acknowledged in the treatment of the various strands. But there would seem to be a difference between a pure strand, which is derived from actualities, and a pure strand which can be derived from conventionalized space and time and energy. A science which began with the one would be something like an Aristotelian science; a science which began with the other would be a mathematical science, something which can be more directly related to Plato's way of dealing with the matter. The account in *The World of Art* fails to distinguish these. Something similar should be said with respect to the other strands: each would not only be something derived from actualities, but would have a related strand which was derived from some mode of Being, conventionally treated as continuous with or as inter-playing with the actualities.

Just as a completed science would interlock two strands, the one derived from actualities and the other from Existence, both as conventionalized, so an adequate account of unity, etc., would involve a combining of the strands obtained from both actualities and Beings. But though different disciplines might make such combinations, we must avoid making them if we are not to blur the distinction between actualities and other realities, particularly modes of Being.

In any case it seems evident that our list must be expanded to include something like strands from the commonsensical world, which are purified forms of experienced modes of being, other than actualities. We ought not then to speak of the first type as commonsensical entities, unless we are willing to recognize that they include more than actualities. Also, it is to be noted that in the above account of science, science is taken to treat of a strand of Existence, whereas in *The World of Art* the existential aspect of actualities was taken to be an event, and the idealized aspect was taken to be a scientific object. But this means merely that a science which is Aristotelian in tone, isolates an idealized strand in actualities whereas one which is Platonic in tone, isolates an idealized strand of a conventionalized Existence. The two can be related by orienting them in some actuality or in God, or by constructing a new entity out of the combination.

I, together with almost everyone else, have taken the scientific outlook to be one which starts with actualities and spreads the net world-wide, or starts with Existence and intensifies it to get places for the particular. But if the foregoing is correct the two approaches do not necessarily mesh together for science, as they do in their concrete conventionalized forms to constitute the commonsensical world, or as they do in reality to constitute the world of interlocked realities.

Our list is now:

A] *1.* actualities
    2. space-time-energy
    3. ideals, ideologies, plans
    4. important things and places
B] *5–8.* strands of the above
C] *9–12.* subdivisions of the modes of Being
D] *13–16.* modes of Being
E] *17.* art objects   [man iconizing Existence]
    18. religious symbols [man iconizing God]

   19.   speech   [man iconizing Actuality]

   20.   laws, rules   [man iconizing Ideality]

F] *21.*   combinations of actualities in families, etc.

  22–24. there should be analogous bunchings in the other modes of Being, such as areas, periods of time, world lines in Existence; interrelated sets of possibilities; combinations of functions in God.

G] *25.*   various combinations of the modes, e.g., man and Existence to give history; man and Ideality to give the state (with man functioning on behalf of Actuality); various combinations explored in the *Modes of Being* and in various places in this diary, such as providence, futurity, etc.

Concentrating on the lettered items as the basic division of entities we have: A] commonsensical items,   B] strands,   C] subdivisions of the basic modes of Being,   D] modes of Being,   E] iconization,   F] combinations of subdivisions of a mode,   G] combinations of various modes with one another.

And perhaps to all this we should add one more group: H] the combinations which actualities make with subdivisions of other modes, e.g., the union made by an actuality with its relevant possibility. We would then have eight types of being in all, which would break up into various subtypes that have many members, except in the case of the modes of Being, where the subtypes are unit entities.

I have not done justice to most of the subtypes in the commonsensical world, or to their strands; nor have I given much thought to the nature of the subdivisions of the modes of Being. D has been dealt with at length, and so has one subtype of E; F has been examined only with reference to one subtype, and only some of the cases under G and H were examined. All of the divisions have been discussed in some form or other, but the subtypes in each have been dealt with only in part, with the exception of D, where each of the subtypes has only one member.

It may be of some interest to remark that during the night I began thinking along the above lines. I awakened this morning supposing that there were five groups of entities, somewhat as I indicated in the beginning of today's notes. But as I was writing them down, my thought became more and more complicated, and as a result I ended at some distance from where I began, a not uncommon occurrence.

During the period when I was typing today's notes I did a little work on the education book—too little—read some thirty pages of Erickson's thesis, and continued taking notes on Peirce for my talk at Yale in commemoration of Peirce's one hundred and twenty-fifth birthday. When I left for lunch, and as I was walking home—some twenty minutes from the University of Southern California where I am visiting this term— my thoughts went back to this morning's discussion.

If it be true that we can isolate strands from a commonsensical kind of Existence, and from God and Ideality, why may we not be able to unite them synthetically and thus get a purified knowledge of these modes of Being? Or would we be getting purified versions of parts or subdivisions of these Beings? An actuality after all is not Actuality, and if it gives us a knowledge of actual substances and not of Actuality, what it interplays with should give us knowledge of real divisions of these other modes, so far as there are such real divisions. Or should we say instead that it is the individual as a representative that yields these strands, and therefore that the real substances, which we come to know through a purging in the strands and a subsequent synthesis of the strands, are functioning on behalf of Actuality? I think this second alternative is the better.

In any case, we apparently can reach other modes of Being much more directly than I had thought before. Instead of holding that we must somehow start with Actuality or actualities, and then get dislocated from them so as to surmise some deeper reality beyond, we can now say that we must dislocate ourselves from the common-sense world. That dislocation can begin at any number of points, and point us in any one of four directions. We can be thrown off our balance by the incoherencies of our ideals or explanations, by the brutality of parts of our experience with nature, by the ominous or wodrous character of a region, as well as by the uniqueness of something—Ideality, Existence, God, and Actuality in a conventionalized form. These could be represented by some subordinate part of themselves—the Ideal by some particular prospects, Existence by some limited region of nature, God by some particular sacramental entity, and Actuality by particular objects. It seems incorrect though to speak of God being represented by a sacramental object, for this is not a genuine part of God, whereas the other illustrations were of genuine parts, or subdivisions, or specializations. To make the account of God parallel, we must find God in some role, or something of Him in the shape of an identity (to follow the lead of the paper on "God and the World").

Shall we follow the lead of some of the Easterners and take ourselves to be fragments of God, and so far to be representatives of Him, though representatives who have overlaid His meaning with conventions? This would seem to divide man into a representative of an Actuality and a Divinity, the body representing the one, and the self the other. Is there no region outside man, and is not God, after all, the God of all, which makes possible some other choice? He is, to be sure, the unity of any region of Existence, but what is wanted is Himself in *propria persona* (though perhaps fragmented and overlaid with conventions), such that we can isolate strands in Him and synthesize these to get a knowledge of Him. If we cannot find an outside region, God must be reached from the vantage point of other modes of Being. This allows one to tie up with most of Western tradition, even though it be granted that He is present as a qualification of what we do confront, and can analyze and synthesize.

Common sense takes any astounding event to be divine in origin, and where this answers to one's sense of justice or right, to be God manifest. Shall we say, then, that the commonsensical astounding event, which is after all astounding only as relative to what it is taking for granted, must then be dissected into strands which purge that occurrence of conventional accretions, and that these strands must then be synthesized to give us a knowledge of the Being which is God? We do not start with a numinous, but with commonsensical occurrences which excite our wonder as commonsensical beings; in the effort to make those occurrences intelligible we break them up into strands.

What are the strands we can isolate in the wondrous? Are they the Other, the Concerned, the Powerful, and the Final, answering to what God is in relation to Actuality, Ideality, Existence, and in Himself? And must these not be married with the strand of importance which actualities yield, to give us the items with which a religion must deal, somewhat as a science combines the strand of intelligibility in an Actuality with the strand of intelligibility in Existence. Religion would, as it were, unite the strand from Actualities with one from the wondrous to give us a cosmic strand of importance. But the knowledge of God would require that the wondrous be reconstituted as a Being and then be related to actualities.

February 22

The wondrous is specialized by different religions, and is often located only in certain places. It is also capable of being broken up into strands which can be made continuous with, or somehow combined with, strands obtained from other types of objectives, or subdivisions of a certain type. Thus there is a strand which is affiliated with the scientific strand, derived from commonsensical objects and a commonsensical space-time-energy. This strand is obtained from the commonsensical wondrous, and in being abstracted is purged to enable it to be synthesized with other similar abstracted strands, to constitute a synthetic idea of God. A scientific strand of this sort is somewhat like Newton's, since his cosmic scheme is rooted in a theology.

We have then, in addition to an Aristotelianized and a Platonized science, a Newtonianized form as well. We ought also to get a strand from the commonsensical ideals and purposes. This would give us a Pythagoreanized strand. Science, full-blown, will be the integration of these four. Perhaps it will use the Pythagorean strand as a set of units for a structure, or language; the Newtonian to remark on the occasions of crisis, or difference, or limits; the Platonic to give us the accepted space-time-energy frame (the structure which the Pythagoreanized strand subdivides); and the Aristotelian to give us the objects studied, or the loci for whatever is known. The other three strands of events, etc., preferably with more appropriate names, should also be recognized to be abstractable in part from all the different types of items—the humdrum, the wondrous, the purposive or ideological, and the brutal or insistent—to be found in the common-sense world. There would thus be a perceptual strand which had roots in all four, and an adequate account of perception, perhaps one of the proper topics of a phenomenology, would involve a linking of these various strands.

Man in relation to the truly wondrous is man related to, and thereby achieves a finality. In relation to the truly purposive or Ideal, he is related to and thereby achieves an excellence. In relation to the only dynamically extended, he is related to and thereby achieves a power and thus a reality. In relation to the truly Actual, he is related to and thereby achieves a truth or substantiality.

Men can be dislocated from the various "beings" which give them a meaning they otherwise would not have. Sin is a dislocation from the divine base. If there are commands and sacraments, sin is the refusal to accept these. But this is a special case of the first, for it is a dislocation from God via some of the objects accepted as symbols, representatives, or loci of His action. (I have heard the objection a number of times that I have overpersonalized God because I write the pronouns referring to Him in capital letters. But I do this only because of a convention; it is a lesson I learned as a child—always to write the pronouns referring to God in capitals.) There are analogous dislocations with respect to the other modes of Being—guilt or bad character with respect to the Ideal; maladjustment with respect to Existence; and distortion or impotence with respect to Actuality.

When Marx, Heidegger, and Tillich speak of the alienation of man they attend to different groundings for man. Marx thinks of man as alienated from Existence, Heidegger of man as alienated from Actuality, and Tillich of man as alienated from God. Together they offer the necessary supplement of Hegel's initial thesis that man is alienated from Ideality. Must we not say that man is at different degrees of alienation from every one of these, and that if he overstresses a recovery in one dimension he will understress a recovery in the others? We can imagine an absolute recovery in each and in all, but it is questionable whether a man ever overcomes alienation completely in any of the dimensions. He always remains somewhat sinful, guilty, inauthentic, and brute, answering to his alienation from God, Ideal, Actuality, and Existence.

On the other hand a man can never be wholly sinful, etc., for this would mean that he would have lost all hold on the different groundings, and would so far be without any power, truth, etc. It is not necessary to to go with Marx, etc., to the extreme of adopting the doctrine of the Fall and supposing that all alienation is self-alienation. Men are frustrated, denied privileges, have their insights distorted, are blocked and redirected; under the influence of one grounding they are often precluded from doing as much justice as possible to their other groundings.

Alienation in its primary form is paramount in a man who is well-tuned inside the commonsensical world. His being at home with the humdrum, the desirable, the wondrous, and the powerful in their commonsensical forms, though it provides him with a way of getting material by which he can achieve a purified knowledge of the different modes, is his way of being alienated from those basic modes. Alienation, in short, is facing the modes in their conventionalized guises; it is a function of our being at home in the daily world. This comes about because man is trained to conform, because his practical needs are socially conditioned. It requires detachment to find one's true center and thus the proper starting point for making a proper relation with other realities. The fact that the alienation, understood in this sense, is felt to be disagreeable or incomplete or empty, even when one is most satisfactorily in tune with the rest of the common-sense world, points up the fact that a man is always peering beneath the commonsense object to its more authentic form, though he does not know what to say of this except so far as he breaks up the common-sense world into strands and synthesizes them, reflects on his actions, engages in some productive activity, or speculates about what must be if this or that fact is granted.

There need be no anxiety in a state of alienation, for one can feel vaguely ill at ease, vapid, disoriented, lacking something, or vaguely desire or long. But what of death? Is this not, as Heidegger holds, an ever-present prospect before us, defining us as men? Or is it not that death but explains what we are as completely alienated? And must it not then have four forms, answering to the different Beings from which we can be alienated?

There is physical, spiritual, emotional, and personal death, answering to Actuality, Ideality, Existence, and God. Our physical death is supposed to entrain the other alienations, though it is the Christian doctrine of immortality to deny this, and to maintain instead that our personal death is not involved. Similar answers, perhaps in terms of history and of technological skill or artistic achievement, can be provided for the other deaths, allowing one to be immortal as it were in three more ways, and not only in one. But if these immortalities are not to be vicarious, there must be something of our very being involved in them.

A more realistic, and phenomenologically more precise account of immortality would say that when we are alive we see that we could be immortal in all four ways, but that our actual death precludes these possibilities unless they are possibilities realized from the side of the grounding (i.e., the modes as providing a backing for the individual), or unless one is content with saying that a man is immortal just so far as he is a representative of the modes. The former alternative is closer to what has often been maintained on the part of traditional religions— man is immortal due to God's demand. Following Kant one could make out an analogous claim from the side of the Ideal; following Spinoza one could make another on behalf of Existence; following Peirce one could make one on behalf of Actuality, particularly as embracing a community of dedicated inquirers. The last alternative allows a man to be immortal when and as he is mortal. It has the advantage of allowing us an "encounter" with ourselves as immortal, but has the disadvantage that it leaves out ourselves as finite, the very particulars which require grounding, as well as the disadvantage that nothing of our ontological nature seems to be preserved in this kind of immortality.

We may, though, have something here which is analogous to what was found to be true in connection with history. The past is there given a status with respect to the present by the Ideal, but it is God who gives

it externality. So one might argue that we become immortal as representatives, while we are alive, and that it requires the activity of the various
modes to objectify that immortality, to allow us to enjoy it ourselves. We
would in the latter case have to have a new kind of relation to all four
modes of Being. Having been denied one kind of relation by our actual
death, we would now have to be given another with respect to ourselves
as realities in Actuality, no less than with respect to ourselves as finalities,
powers, and valuable beings, in relation to God, Existence, and the Ideal.

Could it be that we help constitute the very domains in which we had
been grounded and which we represented? The adoption of ourselves as
elements in the different domains, perhaps as subdivisions of them, all
taking place at the same time, allows us to be related to what we had
both in a commonsensical and in a refined way, but now as entities
which are not primarily actualities but have, as it were, their actuality
distributed over the four modes in which they are now ingredient parts
or constituents or possessions. Immortality on this view is the retention
of oneself as an actuality but with a corresponding loss of the other
groundings for that actuality; alternatively, it is the state of being involved in all four modes but in such a way that only as in all four does
one add up to being an actuality.

In a traditional approach to this problem, the above could be described as saying that while we are alive in this body we can see the
possibility of being immortal through God's agency. In the meantime we
are, as His representative, now immortal, now part of His eternity, by
virtue of what we do in His name. When we die we live on as actualities
only in the sense that we are then and there beings who are still grounded
in Actuality and in God—groundings which help us to allow them to
function as grounds for what are still, or will be, living actualities. Our
death would tear from us the ability to be full actualities inside Actuality.
It would, while allowing us to retain our orientation, deny each of us the
power to act as a single being who knows he may be immortal. We
would then be identical with some kind of togetherness (and thus have
a nature without an "existence" or power to act), except that since we
were not constituted by the different modes to which we were oriented,
we would be primarily "prescriptive" forms of a togetherness. Other types
of togetherness might be provided by other entities, or by actualities
when they have their identity as actualities destroyed. We would, in
effect, not hover over the household or community (as mankind so often
holds that the dead do) but over whatever ultimate realities there be.
And then we would hover, not as more real than these (as we obviously

could not be), but as having our being constituted in all four ways. If we looked at ourselves as caught inside Actuality, we would then have to say that we, as powerless beings with natures only, were being sustained there by the other three modes of Being, which thereby enabled us to be immortal, apart from all representativeness or from any adoption as full-bodied actualities.

February 23

If it be true that the wondrous in daily life is God localized and conventionalized, and that by abstracting various strands from this conventionalized object we will have material which can be synthesized to give us the representation of God in fact, though limited in region or role, then since we can by a change of attitude see every item to be wondrous, and since God must be thought to be everywhere, we seem to be confirming one of the positions of pantheism. But since it is also true that we can take any object also to have an intelligible structure, to be an epitomization of Actuality, and a delimited region of Existence, we can see a particular item or region as the locus of the various modes of Being. This was seen, in a way, in the *Modes* and in previous discussions, but what was not then seen is that some items in common experience will stand out as primarily divine, and others as ideal or intelligible, etc. And also it was not seen that any one of the ways of interpreting the common-sense objects—as divine, intelligible, etc.— yields a strand with a distinctive tonality, which must be interrelated with other strands with their distinctive tonalities if we are to have a science which is not merely Platonic, Aristotelian, Newtonian, or Pythagorean.

But what has happened to the individual? Is he not then like a Spinozistic mode, the only difference being that he is a mode whose being seems to be exhausted by a fourfold analysis and not by two, as it is in Spinoza? But what then has happened to the individual's privacy, his core of identity, his power to act, resist, and represent? How are the four ways of being local or, alternatively, the four distinct localizations, all of which are found in the same place, to be related? What has happened to the insistence that every mode of Being finds itself opposed by the others and, in the case of particular actualities, finds itself faced with them as unconquerable in the end? Can we make each the resistant of the others, and the product be the particular? I think not, for this would lose the individual in his privacy. Could we take all the four types of entity—wondrous, intelligible, etc.—and take them, as Spinoza does with mind and extension, to be attributes and modes of one Being? No, for then one will lose not only the individual but the ultimacy of three of these different types of entity.

One could think of the different strands as being combined in four different ways to yield four beings, of which Spinoza's God or Nature was but one. This is the clue, I think, to the answers to the above difficulties. Though we can say that this particular item is God localized and conventionalized, when we come to isolate a strand in the item, we find that we are dealing with it as a facet of a being transcending this world; it is only as having this status that it becomes cosmic and adequate to a mode of Being. The present common-sense item, we must then say, is wondrous in a divine sense only when dislocated via strands from the common-sense world. It is wondrous, commonsensically. Even when we deliberately look at other items to see that they are indeed wondrous too, we see them within the limits of some conventional standard. This means that the actual entity is only a localization of the divine, the Ideal, etc., and this only so far as we see it in terms of common-sense categories or outlooks.

Actual entities are themselves faced as purged common-sense items. If the isolation of strands gives us the elements to be synthesized so as to express the ultimate modes of Being, then we should know Actuality through a synthesis of strands. But we do not get to know Actuality as such by itself, through a combination of strands; we get to know it only as represented by the actual substance. But now Actuality seems to be attenuated almost to the point of being without being. And yet it is Actuality itself, and not actualities, which oppose and interplay with other modes of Being. Yes, but still it is possible that we do not know it as directly as we know other modes of Being by utilizing the strands found in the wondrous, the intelligible, etc.

It would seem that if we can say this with respect to Actuality, we ought to be able to say similar things with respect to the other modes of Being. Why not then say that the wondrous object, instead of yielding strands which are those of God, etc., yields strands which we can reconstitute to give us the wondrous object as a representative of God? And so on for the other types of entity found in the common-sense world?

We appear to have two alternatives: the strands obtained from commonsensical items are the strands for the construction of synthetic ideas of other modes of Being (with the possible exception of Actuality), or they are strands of particular items which are synthesized to yield representatives of the different modes. The second seems to be the better alternative. It alone allows us to preserve the individual, to avoid identifying him with a part of God or the Ideal, etc., and yet enables us to know other modes of Being by attending to different types of entity in the commonsensical world.

In this daily world we face various items: humdrum particulars, wondrous occurrences, intelligible or purposive entities, and regions of extension. To master these we isolate various strands in them and synthesize these to give us purged versions of what we started with. When we come to recognize that the strands have a range larger than the items from which they were abstracted, and that they have affiliations with strands taken from other types of entity, we get the significant strands which are the primary object of such approaches as science, perception, events, importance. When we recognize that any item in the commonsense world could be looked at as wondrous, intelligible, etc., we can see that a mode of Being can be represented by any item, and thus that any item could yield the appropriate strands. An item in the common-sense world could then be approached in one of four ways, the ways differing in the kind of division and thus the kind of tonalities which the strands will have. Approaching the item as wondrous will make one emphasize as primary the strand of importance, and the other strands will then, though distinguishable in the item, have the status of being subordinate. And so on for the other approaches to the items in the common-sense world. Whatever way we look at them we will find them yielding four strands; but each approach will allow a different strand to be dominant, typical, revelatory, marking out the nature of the mode of Being for which the items are representatives.

The world of common sense is a world in which there are a number of conventionalized but genuinely prominent representatives of different modes of Being. Those representatives can, however (by looking at them from another perspective), be seen to be representatives of other modes of Being as well. And the items are able to have this capacity because they are distinctive realities. Indeed, it is only because it is an individual item, with its own privacy and identity, that it can have the role of a representative. Yet if an actuality be as representative of God, or the Ideal, or Existence, as it is of Actuality, by what right do we term it an actuality? Is it not that its dominant role is to be an actuality, and that as wondrous, powerful, intelligible it is exercising secondary functions?

Is the individual a representative of Actuality primarily, and secondarily of the other modes, or is it representative of all equally? If we take the first position it seems as if there is nothing truly wondrous, intelligible, or powerful in commonsensical experience, but only simulacra of these. If we take the second of these positions we seem to have no particular *actualities,* but a kind of neutral particular which is like a togetherness with interiority and vitality. God is not really present on the first of these views; on the second there are no commonsensical actualities, but only entities which can represent Actuality as well as other modes of Being, but which are themselves to be characterized as no instance of any of them. We will then be faced with the four modes as together in an ontology, and as together inside that ontology in the shape of particular items. The latter might be assimilated to the *de facto* togetherness of the modes. But this makes the items derivatives rather than realities which, though not as ultimate as the modes, nevertheless have beings of their own.

The first alternative is the more commonly accepted, and on the surface the more reasonable. It says that the individual or particular has a reality of its own, and that it primarily represents Actuality. However, some items are seen to be comparatively wondrous, intelligible, etc., and these we take to be subordinate representatives, i.e., signs of other modes of Being. Recognizing that our original items, which were seen to represent Actuality, are capable of being approached as the items which function as signs of other modes of Being, and conversely, we come to see that all the items in the common-sense world are representatives of Actuality, and function as signs of the other modes of Being. They are signs, however, not in the sense of pointing to something which is completely alien to them in nature or role, but which can be truly known by utilizing strands in those signs to serve as elements in the synthesis of a concept of the mode.

This account is biased toward Actuality, for it takes the items we encounter in daily life, even when wondrous, intelligible, or purposive, or brute, to be actualities which merely function as signs of what is truly divine, Ideal, or Existence. But this is as it should be, for we are inside Actuality. Had we begun with the inside of any of the other modes of Being, our analysis would have found the parts of those modes of Being to be representative of the wholes in which they were, and functioning as signs of the other modes of Being. A part of a mode then is representative of it, but merely signifies the other modes of Being, even though there will be certain parts which will stand out as signifying more sharply or directly, and will lead one for a time (as I have in this morning's discussion) to suppose that they are genuine representatives of those other modes.

One consequence of the foregoing is that prophets or saints, miracles or revelatory books, etc., are not God, nor even representatives of God, but only representatives of Actuality, with distinctive roles with respect to God. They would seem to be at best only sacramental objects, loci for God, without themselves becoming divine. Any item could be taken to be a sacramental object, but it would not be conspicuously so. The wondrous nature would not be as genuine a nature as that of the humdrum substantial actuality's. Where the latter yields strands that can be synthesized to give us a concept of an actuality which is at once a substance and a representative of Actuality, the former, the wondrous or intelligible, etc., nature will yield only a *representative sign*—a sign which can assume the role of the divine or Ideal or Existence, but which, as a unity of strands, will not refer to anything substantial.

We synthesize the strands of a substantial common-sense item to get a concept of a substantial actuality; we synthesize the strands of a wondrous, intelligible or brute item to get only a concept of a sign. Both the substantial actuality and the sign will represent, in that they will function in the place of the mode itself, or for whatever is imbedded in that mode.

This checks with an insight in the *World of Art,* where it is seen that we can get to "know" Existence best not via the use of strands, but through art and history (and of course speculation); and this checks with the insight in the book on religion, where it is seen that we can get to "know" God best, not by utilizing material from public experience and then somehow forging a concept of God out of it, but through religion (and of course also through speculation). I don't think the point was seen as clearly in connection with the Ideal, though the discussions in *Man's Freedom* and *Our Public Life* would seem to show that I was at least dimly aware that the Ideal is best discovered through concern (and of course speculation). To know actualities it is desirable to isolate strands and synthesize them to get a concept—though Actuality itself will have to be known through speculation.

A man, since he can be seen to be wondrous, etc., can therefore be treated as a sign as well as a representative. And since he can see himself as wondrous, etc., he can take himself to be such a sign and representative. However, what he knows through a sign (even one which has synthesized strands) is conceptualized, and does not give him the texture and the lilt of a mode of Being. To get this texture he must work in art, pray or worship, obligate himself, or act. The last is his way of getting the texture of actual substances, though in his cognition, through the use of the strands derived from substantial common-sense objects, he gets something of that texture in a way that he cannot through the use of the strands derived from signs. His signs tell him that there is something, and he must make, submit, obligate himself, or act to get the qualitative tone of that something. Action is what is required of him, so far as he treats himself or other actualities as signs of Actuality.

The sign does not get a grounding from its appropriate mode of Being; what is grounded is man either as a representative or as one who makes use of the sign (or of sacramental and similar objects). The grounding makes him and what he uses have a certain type of dignity or finality. His alienation is a failure to be more than superficial. He then denies to himself or to his signs the basis which alone makes them significant, and which alone explains why it is that we are attracted by them, and yet lured to go beyond or behind them.

February 24

The Great Man theory of history, which takes the crucial events, or all the events that are to be viewed as historic, to be the products of the inspiration, decisions, or actions of outstanding individuals, has the advantage of enabling one to bring together the history of occurrences and the history of ideas. Surely some occurrences are pivoted by great men, and what one focusses on in the history of ideas are crucial ideas, usually the achievement of distinctive men. But a similar assimilation of the two forms is possible if one adopts a metahistorical view and takes all occurrences and ideas to be outcroppings or achievements of some impersonal force, a *Weltgeist*. This view is supported by the fact that many of the great discoveries were made at about the same time, by men working independently. Whereas the first view really gives us inexplicable points out of which and, perhaps, to which various lines radiate, the latter takes some lines as basic and makes the outcomes to be explicable in terms of those lines and what preceded them.

Ordinary secular history is a history of causal occurrences which we wish to explain by making use of processes and routes that are plausible today. The outstanding event is to be explained as coming out of a relevant past by processes which are being followed out today by others, or which it is normal to expect to follow on such a relevant past. When we come to crises, the decisions of great men and the like, we take them either to be accounted for in the same way as other events (but as perhaps exhibiting the result of an interpenetration of distinct causal lines to a degree to which the others do not), or we take them to be new items introduced by the present being or event, to make the difference beyond what is causally determined by the past. The second alternative is really always the one used, for the historic present is always new, and no matter how much of it we can account for by tracing it back to a causal antecedent and a causal historic line, it has its *hic et nunc* in the shape of a distinctive flavor, to which we will in fact revert when we want to explain some subsequent event. More sharply, we shear off the novelty of the present occurrence in order to explain it by the past, but that novelty is not denied. Instead, it is now acknowledged as the hard datum which begins a new sequence having another novelty in the future.

The historic present at once ends a past sequence and begins a future one. We do not really succeed in explaining the whole present item by going back into the past. This would be possible only if it were a mere causal product, if it had no self-determination, if in fact it was not a detached present with a power to determine something in the future.

When we turn to the history of ideas we are not faced with the difficulty of dealing with private entities, for the history of ideas has to do with publicly ascertainable ideas, ideas made evident in documents, books, utterances. He who tries to deal with them from the perspective of some *Weltgeist* would be able to show how they make up a social pattern, how they supplement one another, etc., but would not be able to account for the fact that some of them are the products of great men. But if we say that these men are men of genius, we deny ourselves the right to historical explanation, being content to leave the achievement within the secret recesses of the individual.

Though causal influences can be found occasionally in the realm of ideas, what we have as a usual case is some signal created product, followed at some later time by another signal created product, without there being any significant occurrences in between, and sometimes without the later product being known to have taken advantage of what had been previously achieved. Though no one is uninfluenced by the past, there are some creative thinkers who have had a singularly thin knowledge of the antecedents of their own subject. Nor is it enough to say that the tradition is working in their language, and is discernible in the few items of which they do take note, for it leaves untouched the fact that the individual approaches his answer in terms of a present set of difficulties.

If some of these difficulties have been set by the tradition, we can explain his solution to them as the outcome of the working of an imagination characteristic of the period, by means, say, of diagrams, mathematics, chance occurrences, dependence on biology, attempts to find continuities. These would be characteristic of other efforts of the time, with respect to difficulties which the past had raised and brought into the present. The present outcome would then, like any other historic occurrence, be explained by using the explanations which would pertain to the ordinary creativities of the day.

When difficulties are self-set, when new methods are being invented, and when the degree to which a common method is being employed is outstanding, we seem unable to make use of the ordinary model for historical explanation, unless we can make the self-setting of the difficulties, the invention of new methods, and the outstanding use of common methods to be themselves creative ways of using the causally antecedent difficulty. Faced with the views of Galileo, Descartes, and perhaps Kepler, Newton seeks an answer which will accord with the theological outlook he adopts in consonance with others of that day. The solutions he finds are his own, but they are solutions which, apart from the biographical sequence in which they were perhaps gradually achieved, can be explained as the product of framing difficulties and using methods which fill out the given theological-scientific perspective that is then being embraced by the intellectual community, though in a vague, and more or less empty guise.

In the history of ideas—and also in the history of painting, literature, and even inventions, except where the history is a history of a school, or the influences are direct and sufficient to make the outcome intelligible in the ordinary way—we must adopt something like the metahistorical position, and say that there is a *Weltgeist,* an outlook of the day, which can be seen in multiple forms. This *Weltgeist* need not be thought to be operative or controlling, but merely to be one of the factors in terms of which the operations of men of genius are to be understood. The norm of the world of ideas would be expressed in the attempt to use the outlook. Difficulties found in the past, and difficulties created or discovered in the present, would constitute pivotal points inside the world of ideas, and the solution that is offered would be a way of overcoming the difficulties by interrelating the items, thereby making the outlook determinate.

So-called men of genius encompass more difficulties, have a more coherent explanation, anticipate difficulties which others do not, seek out difficulties for themselves, and devise particular methods for meeting obstacles. But since they will do work within the frame that others accept as well, and for the same end, we can explain their results. We will not explain why the genius discovered this or that difficulty, or devised this or that agency for overcoming it, except so far as we find another frame characteristic of the people of the day.

Shakespeare must be understood to be an Elizabethan. This means that he must have a characteristic outlook, way of working, etc. We should thereby be able to understand why he used historical plots, wrote poetry as well as plays, but apparently was not interested in painting or philosophic speculations. Granted that there was a rebirth of interest in the theater which set problems for budding authors, we should then be able to explain not the uniqueness of his work, but why the work should have had such and such components. But the uniqueness of his work can be taken to be a problem which affects, say, some such subsequent playwright as Shaw.

Since in the history of ideas we usually jump over large stretches of the past, and take some thinker or creative worker in the past to set a problem for us, and may also take account of workers in other climates of opinion, the relation between antecedent and consequent will use many items for no other function but to pace the time of the history of ideas. This is a procedure we follow when we date the great moments in the history of ideas, and neglect the others. We write the history of philosophy as pre-Socratic, Platonic, Aristotelian, the Middle Ages, the Idealistic (which includes Kant and Hegel). Large histories give us a number of men of ability in-between, and break up some of these large schemes into smaller ones. But no matter what we do, we relate men by virtue of their ideas, and not through their influence on one another as individuals; this relating has to do with the way in which, in terms of another outlook, they are supposed to respond to what was unsatisfactory in some previous position. The philosophic position specializes, in a comprehensive way, the outlook shared by contemporaries in philosophy and in other places. What is novel is that specialization; it is to be understood as the product of an attempt to give body to a shared outlook, by overcoming past and self-discovered difficulties. This shared outlook is not something consciously known as a rule. It is the task of the history of ideas to discover it.

Newton's work cannot be understood without some awareness of the nature of the instruments used in his day, the new attitude taken toward the heavens, the recognition that the earth and the heavens formed one scheme, the value of mathematical techniques, the acceptance of the reality of an omniscient, good God. The data and hypotheses of his predecessors do not allow for a determinate expression of that outlook. One must add to these others, and then find an agency for making a coherent unity of them all. The agency will itself undoubtedly be found by a method which is being used by others as well, but it will not be directed in the place Newton directs it, nor with his persistence or appreciation of what the agency does and can do. To say this is not to take away from Newton's genius. It recognizes his uniqueness; but it also allows one to make him part of a history of ideas. His unique achievement is not dissectable into the various components; it adds to these the unity which he alone could provide. It can serve as the ground for a further advance, when it is placed alongside new discoveries or caught inside a later outlook, and there found to contain a difficulty.

Why do outlooks change? Why does the age of the enlightenment give way to the romantic age? One answer is that there is a larger outlook characteristic of a time, and that the world of ideas is but a part of a larger world which is governed by that larger outlook. We will then approach ideas somewhat as we do animals, industry, agriculture, diets, and so on. But this will of course throw us back another step, for we will then have the question as to why or how this larger outlook came about. Another answer is that the new achievement inside the old outlook, when held together with new difficulties or circumstances, produces a new outlook. This would be a satisfactory answer if restricted to an over-all outlook, of which the outlook governing ideas was a part. In other words, the first answer is satisfactory, provided that one then goes on to treat the question of the broad outlook of the times as that which is produced by taking the achievements inside a previous broad outlook to involve problems when faced with new data or discoveries.

Let us suppose that evolutionism, the surplus value position, the idea of progress, etc., are all part of one nineteenth century outlook which governed the industrial revolution, the growth of empires and nations, and inventions particularly governing communications. We can then say of someone like Hegel that he specialized this by attending to difficulties set by specializations of other earlier outlooks, as well as of those of his own time. When we ask why we have today a different over-all outlook (let us say, it is that of an engineering mentality), we will explain it by showing that such a specialization as Hegel's was not able to assimilate the discoveries of modern science.

A new outlook is achieved if previous specializations are seen to set a problem when they are placed alongside new data. New achievements in our time will be the outcome of an attempt to provide the new outlook with a solution which faces the previous specializations with new data that bear on the proposed solutions of the previous specializations. Whereas the broad outlook shared by the people of a time includes all sorts of data challenging past specializations, a subdivision of that broad outlook, the product of a creative "genius," takes account only of the data relevant to its subject and only of those past specializations which are relevant to the enterprise. This means that the creative man does within a broad outlook what the people together do in forming that broad outlook.

If the foregoing is correct, the outlook of one age is not achieved against or because of the outlook of a previous age, but only by facing the specializations of that previous outlook with problems and data, some of which are not relevant to the modification of the specializations, since they are data in other areas. The specializations give the broad outlook its definite character, and constitute part of the data determining the nature, not only of a similar subsequent specialization, but of the broader outlook which is to follow on that specialization's presupposed outlook.

February 25

What we actualities have in common in the last resort is Being. That Being is the Being of Actuality. (We also fractionate Existence, interiorize God in the shape of a core which stands over against all else, and converge on the Ideal, and can in these senses be said also to share in these Beings.) The Being which we share is over against the other three Beings. It is this discovery that makes my view stand out over against most others. Most pluralists are pluralists with respect to the entities in Actuality; most of those who acknowledge that there is a Being distinct from those entities identify the Being with God. If the God is separated off from the entities altogether, we get forms of theism; if recognized to have a status of its own but to include the entities, we get panentheism; if taken to be only what is common, or the sea in which they swim, which has no Being apart from being their Being, we get pantheism. I am holding a kind of "panenactualism," in that I take the actualities to be encompassed in Actuality, which is over against them, with an ultimacy and nature of its own.

An actuality is able to oppose not only Actuality by virtue of its status as a distinctive part of Actuality and because it is in it, but is also able to oppose other modes of being by virtue of its representative status with respect to Actuality. I oppose the other modes in the name of Actuality. That opposition does not preclude, indeed it is the ground for my coming to be in contact with those other modes. Opposition involves a reaching to, a terminating in, with a retention of oneself. It is but one form of a dialectical movement. (Another form of dialectic is of course the Golden Rule, which bids me look at myself and the others from their side.) Dialectic involves giving the other a position as basic as that which made it other. It takes an x at which one points from position y, and gives it a status such as y enjoyed, thereby enabling y to point at x. Even in Plato, where the dialectic seems to be a move upward in a hierarchy, what we have is the recognition that what is supposedly secondary or derivative (the higher levels of his divided line) is in fact primary, with the initial starting point as secondary—though he does not so speak of dialectic. Even Aristotle can be said to use dialectic in somewhat the same way, for to take account of probable arguments and what is being said by others is a way of reversing the field and giving full weight to the other.

Every theologian, I suppose, is aware that God is a Being and not like an entity inside Actuality. Yet every one is sooner or later tempted to speak as though He were like those entities, particularly when we address Him in terms pertinent to those entities, such as father, or cause, or loving, etc. Theology might be said to be forever in a tension between the tendency to view God merely as a Being or as Being itself, and to view Him as a reality with which man interplays. Do I not myself in the *Modes,* when speaking of the way in which God turns to the world, tend to make Him a kind of entity such as we are? And is it not almost inevitable that the Whiteheadians should do this, since they desire to use the very same categories on God that they use on entities in Actuality?

Whitehead tries to use the same categories on God and actualities. But the facts go against him; as a consequence he applies the categories, which are pertinent to actualities, to God only by giving them a reverse twist. This means that in the end he sees God as a Being who differs from the actualities which are included in Him in a panentheistic way. His God has a career in reverse of theirs.

Hartshorne thinks he is following Whitehead. But since he sees that God is to be proved not as a "fact" but as a reality who is to be known in principle, and not through the use of factual evidence, he takes that God to be a Being, or Being itself. Yet since he also tries to understand

God by an absolutization of the ordinary categories, he takes God to be a kind of superior actuality. Indeed, he then speaks of Him as having such accidents as suffering, loving, etc.—expressions Whitehead would avoid.

Whitehead perhaps more than any one else has made God so finite as to reduce Him to the status of an actuality, even though he fails in the attempt to treat Him as one. Is not Whitehead forced to reverse the categories of actuality in dealing with God, because Being resists reduction to the status of an entity?

On my view God is finite, too, in the sense that He is not the only Being there is. But He is not finite because He is over against me. Still, we can speak of ourselves as over against Him, since we achieve this role by being representatives of Actuality. If we were not, I do not see how we could escape a kind of panentheism. This panentheism, however, would have to underscore the fact that God as Being would then be distinct in nature from any actuality. We could not even say that He was a Thou or a Subject, for this makes Him our correlative. He is then a "God beyond God," to use Tillich's expression, a Being which is specialized as the God that is concerned with us. On such a view the God that is concerned with us would be a kind of superactuality which God as Being makes a place for. Whether that superactuality is an emanation from God the Being, or whether it is a reality, contingent or necessary but beneath Him in somewhat the way in which finite contingent transient space-time actualities are, would be a question which would then have to be faced. One could think of that superactuality as the "created world," and then treat it (as related to God the Being) as having the role of a concerned God. That "created world," by virtue of its being related to God the Being, would stand apart from other actualities and, as so standing apart, be a God for it.

A panentheist would handle the problem of creation I think by saying that actualities forever remain oriented in God's being, but that they were given distinctive roles apart from Him. They are not really apart from Him, but nevertheless somehow function apart from Him, sometimes even in opposition to His will.

In the *Modes* it seems to me that I move from actualities to the other modes, instead of moving to Actuality first as the Being in which actualities are. Only later in the book do I speak of Actuality in contrast with actualities, and see how Actuality interplays with the other modes of Being.

When Lao-Tse says that he who has not rid himself of desire can perceive only the manifest, he apparently means that desire is of particular entities and never of Being. This is a strange doctrine, unless one means by desire the desire for particular entities. When he says that the sage sits tranquil between contraries, he apparently means that the contraries are, or characterize, particular entities, and never Being.

We must, against Buber, say that the "Thou" or the Subject also speaks in the language of particular entities and not in the language of Being. The alternative to treating God as an entity is not to make him a Subject.

February 26

In *Reality* I said that the ontological argument had the form: if p is possible then p is necessary. (I haven't checked; this is how I remember it.) And I went on to say that this argument had only one case. What I did not clearly see then was that it is an argument to Being in contrast with an entity, where "entity" refers to some particular or contingent or delimited reality, even if it be the highest embodiment of the best of categories. Hartshorne takes the argument to be one which has nothing to do with contingent matters of fact. And as Nelson shows, in his criticism of Hartshorne, to say that God is possible, when we are not referring to God as a contingent being, is to refer to Him in another sense. Nelson thinks that we are then making the purely logical point that the idea of God as existing does not contain a contradiction. But I think what his argument amounts to is the recognition that the possibility characteristic of Being is not relevant to that of an entity.

But, as was made evident in *Reality,* the possibility that is necessary is that which is exhaustive, that which contains whatever there be. Now in *Reality* I did not see that—though it is the case, as I observed, that God and the world contains more reality than either one alone—God is a different type of reality from the world, where the world is here taken to be a mere summary expression for a plurality of distinct actual entities.

The plurality of realities which can be shown to be necessary, because possible, is whatever realities there be. This is possible because its opposite is self-contradictory, and because the idea of a single entity reduces to that opposite. What we prove, then, is the plurality of ultimate beings as making up one totality; this plurality is not increased in being by virtue of each member containing subordinate parts.

Are we not then back to the traditional view regarding creation? That view maintains that when God creates the world he does not add to being; the reality of entities is a reality of a role which has its being in God. But the traditional view then denies my independent reality, and the possibility that I could blaspheme, sin, etc. No, we must insist that we are distinct from God in being. But we are not distinct from Actuality in being. Each of us has his own being, but only because each of us shares in the Being which is Actuality. When we prove the reality of the four modes of being as necessarily so, and thus here make use of the ontological argument, we at the same time allow the Beings, which we thereby prove, to be structured internally in any number of ways. That Actuality should have its primary power in the shape of the subordinate actualities is one way in which Being is; the other ways are those in which the parts are on a footing with the whole (Existence), are subordinated to it (God), or are mere creases in it (Ideal).

We, each of us, have our being as actualities; when we are resident in the other modes of Being it is only by having roles. God reorganizes the values we exhibit to make them maximal; the Ideal structuralizes our meaning, expresses us as rationalized; Existence takes us as a limit. This offers a confirmation of the result of the other day to the effect that the wondrous, etc., is not God, etc., in fact, but only an embodiment of God, a sacramenal object, etc. And in another way it confirms Peirce's view about man being a sign, or representative, but only if we recognize that he is a genuine representative of Actuality, and a sign for the others.

A man can assume something like a representative role by making himself a man of service, attending to his obligations, becoming adjusted, or functioning as an artist, and so on. In these cases he gives himself a special task. He is a representative of Actuality, willy nilly, by virtue of the fact that the Being of Actuality is not only resident in him (as it is in all actualities) but because his assertions, or claims to be or know, are absolute, for all men, and ultimately for all else to submit to. Man is that contingent being who has raised himself by virtue of a distinctive claim, to be on a level with a Being and thus to be part of what necessarily is. But he is so only qua mind or will or self, i.e., as one who affirms a truth or claims a right.

Almost every English philosopher, and this would include Whitehead, neglects Being to concentrate on actual entities. Even the English idealists, since they abandoned Hegel's ontological dialectic, seem not to have a Being which is present, but something which is to be conceived or approached or produced by virtue of the annihilation of actual entities. But there is no conflict between actual entities and Actuality. To be sure, if we try to characterize either by the categories appropriate to the other, we will falsify it. Bradley's realm of appearance is actually a world which is denied reality because it is treated in terms that are appropriate only to Being. But the reverse can also be said; his Absolute is a world which can be denied reality in any sense in which things have reality. Bradley seems aware of this reversal; in the end he can say nothing of his Absolute, since the saying would apparently involve the use of categories appropriate to particular actualities. But there is no reason why we cannot speak in new terms of the Absolute of Being, or of Beings. All we need do is to use our old ones in an absolute sense, or frame new ones as having a singular use. And we can mark them off by capitals, italics, and the like. After all the word "God" is not a word applicable to any actuality which we know; nor is spirit, nor the Ideal, nor the space-time-energy totality of Existence, nor nature, and so on.

If final causation is the operation of the Ideal, then it is causation in quite a different sense from that in which an efficient causation is a causation, for the latter has to do with the action of particular actualities on particular actualities. Indeed, the causation of God would be like a formal cause, and Existence would be like a material cause, leaving one to find a new kind of cause to account for the operation of Actuality on the particular actualities. Would this not be a participative cause? In other words, are there not four causes of an ontologic sort, quite different in operation and meaning from the efficient cause? It seems so.

What about purposes, the governance of bodies through minds and plans, etc.? At most they could be said to be particularizations of the basic ontologic final causality of the Ideal. Something of this basic ontologic final causality is seen in my discussion of the historic ought to be; but I have never examined how ontologic causality of any type was specialized inside the world of actualities. Is there a dominating "formal" causality which reflects God; is there a dominating "material" causality which reflects Existence?

Aristotle acknowledges substantial forms, but if I am right here, he should also have recognized substantial matters. Neither of these would be mere constituents of a substance; they would reflect the pressures of two modes of Being, leading us to them, or guiding us to them by virtue of the fact that they were participants in or fragments torn off from these Beings.

February 28

Might not this be alternative to the view presented in the *Modes*? Let there be a single Being which was a unity within which there was a multiplicity of particles at once extended and in an extended relation to one another. Among these particles there could be some entities which were capable of holding themselves over against the rest, even while they were among the rest. Such entities would be actualities, or perhaps only men. Those men, as holding themselves over against the rest, would also be concerned with that Being. If we take the men as so concerned, and nevertheless see them as part of one world with the rest of the particles, they would with these constitute a complex which one could identify with God. The extended particles would make up nature, and take the place of what I have called Existence. The men and perhaps other objects would make up a realm of actualities. The men as over against the Being would face an Ideal. As together with the particles they would make up the reality which is God. On this view there would be only one mode of Being which would have different powers or roles, depending on how it was approached in terms of its contained parts. So far as the parts merely filled it out, it would be like Existence; so far as the parts stood over against it, it would be like Ideality; so far as the parts were taken as a whole, perhaps because they diversely embodied the Being, we would have something like the mode I have termed God. On this account there would be no Actuality, and the role of God would be quite close to that which it has in pantheism or panentheism.

It is possible that one might want to designate as God what I have taken to be the Ideal in this case, and conversely. It makes little difference to the point being made, to the effect that one mode of Being may suffice, if we can find within it entities which have a number of roles, in contrast with which the Being will have different meanings and roles. The view preserves the insight that Being is not like any of its parts, and allows one even to recognize the coming of Being into some of its roles as correlative with man's coming into existence. There would be no need to suppose that the included parts were created, or that all of Being awaits the coming of man. Apart from man the Being would be Existence; with man two roles would be acquired. This would mean of course that God would be only when man was; and indeed that He would have the status of God only so far as man held himself apart from all else, at once acquiring a privacy and achieving a detachment. There would on such a view be no need for God to preserve or assess, there would be little point in prayer and worship (except in the Spinozistic sense of an intellectual love of God), and the prescriptions of the Ideal would hold only for or via man, and would have no meaning if and so far as man was not.

The foregoing allows most of what is said in the *Modes* about Existence to stand, I think. Since there is no treatment of Actuality as such in the chapter on Actuality, it allows that chapter to stand, too. Some of the chapter on the Ideal would have to go, for it seems to set conditions in advance for Existence, no less than it does for actualities. We would have to deny that there are real possibilities for the particles in Existence; and we would have to say that it would not be bad in terms of an absolute Ideal if all men were reduced to particles in Existence, for if they were so reduced, there would be no Ideal in terms of which the result could be evaluated as bad. We would also not have to say that what men fail to do is in fact done; there could be obligations never fulfilled. There would also be no power which preserved the past, assessed men, or made a unity out of Existence. The most serious loss here seems to be in connection with possibility. There seems to be something wrong in a view which makes the possible follow on the coming into existence of a particular type of entity.

Recurring to the earlier suggestion, we could say that when men hold themselves over against the rest of Existence, they make Being have the role of God. When, while over against, they are also part of the same universe with other particles, they could be said to be subject to the Ideal. That Ideal would be a domain of possibilities for the particles and, with the coming to be of man, would also have the role of providing him with prescriptions. His ethical status would be one with the coming into being of the Ideal as a set of ethical prescriptions. Though they would originate because man was, they would nevertheless have him subject to them. God, too, would have a role and functions which were not due to man but were due to the nature of Being, though it would be man who enabled it to assume one of the roles possible to it. Man would, on this view, not be able to get to God; God would be the absconded Being, the Being which is forever over against him. Man would be able to avoid the confrontation of God only by ceasing to be man. And there would be no God for what was not man.

The foregoing has great strength. It has the simplicity which comes from getting rid of some of the modes of Being as ultimate powers. We will no longer have a problem of togetherness, since the Being itself would be the way in which the particles were together. And the account of God, though not orthodox, answers to many expressions in the Bible about the fact that God is not knowable in any direct way. It would make religion a device by which the unreachable God was made palatable or usable by men. Man and God, though, would be opposites. Man would be in an inescapable dilemma in that he would always be outside of

God and over against Him, and yet would strive to somehow bridge this gap. Religion, so far as it tried to tell us about God's concern for us, etc., would be misleading us; it would instead have as its proper task the consoling of men for the fact that God is always their other, and would then lead them to find their true being by living up to the prescriptions of the Ideal. The position comes close to some Eastern views, except that it does not find a way, as these do, for man to lose himself and thereby find God. On the above account when he loses himself, makes himself no longer man, he becomes part of Existence, and that means he does not escape from the thrall of space and time and becoming.

For the moment I see no serious flaw in the above account and must for the time being take it to be a significant alternative to, and apparently superior to, the view given in the *Modes.*

Unless one can encounter the Being one cannot of course be sure that it is not a transcendental illusion. But one can presumably encounter the Being in the guise of the Ideal, for one then faces it as obligating oneself. The Being in other guises could still be something like an illusion, since it will have these roles only in response to positions assumed by men as holding themselves in contrast with all else.

Whether we take up this new view or not, it is evident that Collins' desire to use the types of encounter in the history book in connection with God will not do, for the former relate to particular entities, whereas God is Being, or a Being, or Being in one of its roles and cannot therefore be met with as past items are. If God can be encountered somehow, though, we would have material for rebutting this proposed alternative to the *Modes,* particularly if the action of God does not coincide with the action of the Ideal. Of course if prayer is answered, or if the seeking which is faith is also a finding, then we have an encounter of a kind different from that possible to other types of Being. And if there are sacramental objects, another encounter is ours.

A defense of the view of the *Modes* must evidently in the end rest on a recognition of distinctive encounters either inside the realm of Actuality (as evidencing other forces than that characteristic of the Actuality) or of distinctive encounters with the modes of Being in oneself and beyond oneself. But if there were such encounters, how is it that they are not recognized? Instead one finds men speaking as though the encounter with Being were one which involved only a submission and thus was like an encounter with the Ideal; as though the encounter were one which involved only an adjustment of oneself to something larger and more imperious, and thus was like an encounter with Existence; and as though the encounter involved only a satisfaction of a transcendental sort, and thus was like an encounter with God. Could it be that the discovery of Being is so overwhelming for mankind that it immediately takes Being to be something single, and then when mankind finds that Being seems to operate in different ways, characterizes it in diverse ways? And thus we get a God of wrath, a God of sheer justice, a God of love. Is the God of wrath but nature, and the God of justice but the Ideal?

February 29

If a man, in an act of faith or prayer or worship or sacrifice, finds himself renewed, enriched, answered, he has so far evidence of the existence of God. It is of course possible that he is mistaken in thinking that he is renewed, etc., or it may be the case that he truly feels that he is, but that the satisfaction is being provided by himself. The first of these alternatives can be avoided by keeping acutely before one the state of one's dissatisfaction, and noting the alteration in it. The second alternative can be avoided by overlaying one's attitude with a scepticism or even an unwillingness, by trying to bring it about on one's own, or by checking it against what else one knows about reality. In the end of course it is only the man of faith who is reassured, so that it is not possible for one who does not have a faith in God to acquire evidence of Him in this way. But the man of faith does need the evidence, for faith is a seeking which is strengthened by its finding—a finding which does not preclude but in fact demands further seeking.

Similarly, there is evidence of the Ideal when one, in obligating himself, finds himself thereby meeting an obligation. There is an increase in character, a feeling that one has become better the more surely one lays hold of the Ideal as that which dictates what one is to do. Once again, this increase (and thus the evidence) is that which cannot be had by anyone but an ethical man.

Again, he, who in adjusting himself to Existence, finds that he is better attuned within, that he has a greater power to deal with what he is to face, has evidence of Existence. No one who is not trying to be in accord with nature, to make himself one who fits in it properly, will be able to find this evidence.

Finally, he who in seeking truth finds that he is more at home in truth, that what he tries to discover helps him to know himself and other entities better, is one who has evidence of Actuality. Again, no one who is uninterested in seeking the truth will have this evidence of the reality of Actuality.

Religious men as a rule confirm the first, the Confucian that of the second, the Taoist the third, and Spinoza the fourth of these increases. In all cases the mode of Being is sought in an act which is then and there changed in tone to be a finding, still leaving something to be sought. All the modes, in other words, are transcendent realities which, when pointed at, are revealed to be immanent in the pointing. It is in this sense that one can see metaphysical perceptiveness in the doctrine that God expects men to turn to Him before He accepts or saves them. This doctrine has always seemed to me, as well as to many others, a rather odd view to take regarding a merciful and omniscient being. God should, I thought, not be bothered by man's recalcitrance nor should He depend on man's accepting Him before He would be gracious. This is surely true if we view the matter ontologically; God does not act on the world as a function of man's appeal to Him. But in the religious act, the presence of God is the outcome of the search for Him. He is present here, but is not enjoyed at present, not felt as present, until one is ready to enjoy Him, acknowledge His presence.

Why may God not insist on Himself, force Himself on our attention? In a way He does, with the wondrous objects. But why may He not do so in the act of faith? But then there would be no act of faith necessary; it would be enjoyment and not faith. But perhaps then we ought to ask why there is need of faith? If there were not, man would be forever oriented away from Actuality and would be oriented only toward God. This is a hard problem only for those who take God to be all in all, the only Being. But from my point of view it is proper that man should be a limited being who does not even know himself to be an actuality until he begins to recognize his concern for truth, and finds his satisfaction in the search for it.

Can we encounter God in the wondrous object, the way we encounter the past in the present, unique, self-maintaining, etc., object? And if so, can we not encounter the Ideal in the structure of intelligibility of the object, Existence in its being a fragment of extension, and Actuality in its presence? If so, they must be shown not to be possible to the actuality in- and of-itself. What Peirce wants to account for by mere spontaneity would have to be shown to be more intelligible when seen to be a divinely produced wonder. What Aristotle wanted to deal with as an ingredient form would have to be shown to be an instance of an external form. What an atomist takes to be an ingredient extension would have to be shown to be continuous with and, indeed, a delimitation of a larger extension having some power of being of its own. What ordinary men take to be mere fact would have to be shown to be an epitomization of what makes everything be present, not merely in the sense of being in the present, but in the sense of standing out as a representative of whatever else might be present. Some of these evidences have been noted in the *Modes,* when I looked at actualities in terms of the other modes.

These evidences or signs of the modes of Being are not known to those who do not see these dimensions of the items we confront. If a man merely interplays with other actualities, e.g., he will do nothing more than bring about some consequent; he will not know what those actualities, and thus himself, are really like, and thus will have no inkling of the reality of anything besides that which now interplays with him in an obtrusive way.

What one man sees to be wondrous, another may not. And a man may see something to be wondrous only because he is not aware of its cause, or its occasion, or its nature, or its role inside the common-sense world or the world of practice. When he learns the cause, etc., his wonder ceases. Why may not all supposed wondrous objects be like that? The wonder would then be but an indication that one does not know all that is needed to be known in order to get the object to fit in with the others. The answer to the last question lies in the fact that every object in a most perfectly ordered and intelligible scheme is wondrous, and that any initially focussed object is but an emphasized case of the wonder in all. When we find some item wondrous, we overlay the wonder which is to be elicited by any object, with the wonder which follows from the fact that the object is not yet understood inside its normal frame. The latter tells us that the object has another dimension outside the normal frame. Any one object which is not yet fitted inside that frame is wondrous for the very same reason that any item in the frame is— there is something to it which cannot be accounted for in the frame of actual entities. The outstanding wondrous object in ordinary life thus is outstanding because it exhibits the fact that a confronted object does not function as an explicable actuality inside the usual causal pattern, etc. When we get it inside that pattern we do not lose all its wonder, for it still remains something not entirely explained. The wonder that is peculiar to it is, as it were, spread over all the other items, and we see them all as grounded elsewhere. And so on for the other features which testify to our encounter with the various modes of Being.

We do not in these various encounters know what the Beings are in- and of-themselves. As remote from the particulars where we confront them in the guise of the wondrous, the intelligible, etc., they have a different nature and being and role than they have inside them. It is the function of a speculative systematic account to get to know them in this latter guise; it is also the object of the act of faith, obligation, etc., to get to them in this guise. The latter differ from the former in being more concrete and having the modes in a personal form. We must also encounter them as insisting on themselves, and thus we must also face them as demanding something of us. This means that the faith which is satisfied, and is yet continuing to long, is a faith which is being lured, and demanded; that the character which is achieved when one accepts one's obligations, is one which is being tried, put to the test; that the self-possession which is ours when we are adjusted, is being called upon to control and make; and that the self-centeredness, the complete presence which is ours so far as we are rightly oriented in the Actual, is being called upon to represent the others, to be like Actuality.

We are encountered, met by the modes of Being, when we face objects as wondrous, etc., and when we find our satisfactions overlaid by demands that make our satisfactions part of a larger search or demand. The first type of encounter, in the form of features or powers of actual entities, is ours when we look beyond the common-sense object either because the encounter as wondrous, etc., catches us by surprise, or because we, in search for a richer meaning, look for something not immediately evident. The second type of encounter, in the form of an imposition of a deficiency in the satisfactions we have as we direct ourselves to the various modes of Being, is ours because it answers to us as satisfied. It is also the reciprocal of our cognitive apprehension of these modes; they are the confirmatory experiences, the encounters we have with the modes, answering to our speculative judgments of them.

Mysticism is the doctrine which holds that when and as we transcend certain limited ways of dealing with the modes, and give ourselves up to being one with them, they then and there encounter us. The act of going to them is one with the act of their coming to us; the act of our reaching to them is one with the act of being confronted by them. The traditional mystic, of course, thinks that the Being is God, but there are "natural" mystics, mystics of nature, neoplatonic mystics of the Ideal, and existential mystics of the Actual. (The last is what Heidegger has become toward the end of his career.)

March 5

If there be particular entities, must there be a Being, or a number of Beings, in which they are imbedded and which are to be known in a different way than the particular entities are known? If there be a Being, or a number of Beings, must there be particular entities? The second question is answered in the negative by those who hold that God created everything else than God, and that this creation was not continuous, but occurred at "some time," i.e., that we can move back in our time to a date before which there was nothing. But if every Being is a One encompassing a Many, as I have argued in the *Modes,* there cannot be a Being without particular entities within it. But since there are distinct types of Being, there may well be—and I think there are—distinct ways in which the particulars are within each.

In Existence the subdivisions in Existence are on a footing with it; in Ideal they are subordinated to it, as mere creases; in Actuality we have instead a priority in stress on the particular entities; in God both the One and the Many seem to be equally ultimate. But whether one accepts these formulations or not, in all these cases we have Being and subdivisions of a distinctive sort which may be termed particular entities, where the meaning "particular entities" will change from Being to Being. This answer encompasses an answer to the first question: if there be particular entities there must be an appropriate Being for them. That Being can be called a "sustaining cause" in the sense that without it there cannot be the many entities. But the converse is also true; without the many entities there can be no Being, and as a consequence the plurality is a "sustaining cause" of the Being. However, the plurality may change in content; different particulars may be in the Being at different times. As Hartshorne has seen, and has said better (and more often) than anyone else, this means that there is a necessity that there be some particular or other, and no necessity that there be just this or that set of particular entities, particularly if one grants that there is change inside Beings.

A sustaining cause is a very peculiar kind of cause. It is not to be thought of as somehow producing and holding on to entities, to prevent them from vanishing into nothingness. Indeed if that were possible then there would be no need for particular entities. But if particular entities must be, in order that Being be, then Being necessarily is subject to an internal articulation. And if Being must be, if particular entities are, then particular entities must belong together by virtue of their participation in the same Being. Being gives the particulars a kind of substantial togetherness; the particulars give the Being a kind of internal multiplicity.

If now we could identify a certain set of particulars as being divine, we would have a proof of God; conversely, if we could know what God's being is like, we could know what He must contain. The panentheist makes the mistake of supposing that the particular entities in this world, which are actualities inside Actuality, can be the particular entities which subdivide God. There are subdivisions in God and they do answer to the particularities in Actuality (and, as I did not see in the *Modes* as clearly as I might, they do answer to the subdivisions of Existence and Ideality as well), but only so far as these actualities have been redefined and recombined.

When God knows Himself, He subdivides Himself in a triple way to answer to the three kinds of particularities that are in the three other Beings. The subdivisions of the other modes of Being must also be three-fold to answer to the subdivisions of the rest. I saw this point dimly when I remarked that the Ideal, for example, was a Good for actualities, a future for Existence and a standard of perfection for God. But I should have clearly said that it offered possibilities to the actualities, incipient futures to the parts of Existence, and standards of excellence for the sub-divisions in God.

We seem to know actualities and parts of Existence, and must win our way to Actuality and Existence, as Beings. We seem to know some possibilities, and also the Good, and must refine our double grasp in order to know the Ideal as a unit and as pluralized. We have no knowledge of the particularities in God, and acknowledgment of them seems to go counter to the views of most classical theologians. Yet as we know, or confront, or encounter, or experience God we at once focus on articulations in Him answering to our attitudes and finitude. We, as it were, know the Being of God, but at once delimit it in the shape of some finite part of Him, answering to our individual natures, or activities, or approaches.

Thomas Aquinas and Maimonides both deny that God has any re-lation to creatures. They are right in a sense that they did not suspect; the so-called creatures are in another mode of Being, and God cannot have the kind of relation (the only one these men allow) to what are not particular entities sustained by Him. But if we look at God Himself and His own particular entities—His ideas, if one likes—there surely must be a relation that He has to them. He does not have the same kind of relation they have to Him; they are, as it were, within Him, partake of Him, whereas He possesses them, or contains them. Do not Aquinas and Maimonides both maintain that God has ideas, or that He possesses

the creatures? If the former, then there is for them a relation of possession connecting Him to His own subdivisions; if the latter we get some
kind of panentheism of the traditional sort, where actual entities are dislocated from Actuality and wrongly taken to be in God.

March 6

The reality of a Being, as concrete, substantial, not identifiable
with a mere way of having a plurality together, is evidenced in the way
it possesses its subdivisions and the way in which it interplays with other
Beings and their subdivisions. The reality of the subdivisions is evidenced
by the way they oppose one another and the Being, and by the way they
interplay with other subdivisions and the Beings in which these are.

In Existence the opposition of the subdivisions to one another and to
the whole is most prominent; in God the possessiveness of the Being is
most prominent; in Actuality the way in which the subdivisions interplay
with other subdivisions and Beings is most prominent; in Ideality the
way in which the Being interplays with other Beings and their subdivisions is most prominent.

Were there only God (or some other mode of Being) there would
still be subdivisions which were in the process of distinguishing themselves from Him and one another. This would be the process mislabelled
"creation" by theological theists and panentheists. Strictly speaking it is
a process of self-individuation viewed from the side of the subdivisions,
and an emptying viewed from the side of the Being. No subdivisions
would ever free themselves from the Being which possessed them. Con-
trariwise, no Being could possess the subdivisions without residue. The
hold on them is a hold which is faced with their defiance, their constant
withdrawal and pulverization, or subdivision of the Being.

Would the world of divine ideas, or (accepting the theistic identification of actualities with the subdivisions or products or possessions of
God) would the "creatures" come into being at once, when and as the
Being was, or would it be a gradual achievement, taking perhaps an
infinite time? Is there an instantaneous fall or is there a perpetual one?
There would seem to be a perpetual fall, an eternal fall, for otherwise
the subdivisions would not be capable of standing over against the whole,
since they would start with little power and would somehow out of that
little have to make enough to enable them to withstand the possessiveness of the Being. But there might conceivably be successive levels, as a

Plotinus might hold, which followed one another, perhaps even in time, as he would not allow.

Whitehead thought that neoplatonism was a very poor view. But the foregoing would seem to show that, on the contrary, it makes a good perspective in terms of which one can envisage the relation between Being and its subdivisions. The neoplatonist, of course, takes the realm of actualities to be one of the levels, in fact the last of them, but this is inevitable in the light of the acknowledgment of only one Being. If I am right, we never get actualities in God, but only in Actuality, no matter how close (or how remote) we make those actualities be to God. But even granting the view that there is only one Being, and that this Being contains actualities, it would not follow that the Being was to be identified with God rather than with Nature, or a Realm of Forms, or the commonality of all actualities, i.e., Actuality.

Granted, though, that the Being is God and that actualities are subdivisions of Him (perhaps at the greatest possible remove from Him, and therefore capable of independent action with respect to one another, and capable too of defying and opposing Him without His thereby losing all control over them) actualities will either have to be always, or some other subdivisions would have to be always, from which the actualities could be derived always, or at some later time.

Might not God be the ultimate Being, and have other Beings as his primary and eternal subdivisions? These other Beings would then be opposed to one another in one way, and to God in another way. Each would have parts within it, and would be final for those parts. The Beings would then be coeternal with God, but nevertheless subordinate to Him and possessed by Him. He would be the concrete togetherness of them. The subdivisions of the possessed Beings might have gradations within them, but would they not also have to be coeternal with the Beings? It would seem so, for otherwise the Beings would not be truly Beings, unities encompassing a many. But why might they not remain mere realms, subdivisions of God, which, after a period in which they opposed one another and God Himself, achieved sufficient independence to enable them to have subdivisions of their own?

How there could be a period of time, a drawn out struggle in eternity, is a difficulty. Another is that God would have no genuine interplay with the other Beings. A third difficulty is that if God did interplay with the other Beings, we would have to distinguish Him, as containing these other Beings, from Himself as over against them and interplaying with them. A fourth difficulty was mentioned earlier: the Being would not be God in any sense that it might not also be said to be a Realm of Form, etc. A fifth is that the relation of actualities to God would be mediated by their own Being, and we would never confront God directly, but only basic subdivisions of Him. A sixth difficulty is that He would have distinctive ways of possessing the different Beings in order to answer to their natures and limitations. (These last two difficulties seem to me not to be serious; indeed they suggest ways in which we might look at the modes of Being in relation to God.) A seventh difficulty is that He could not be characterized, for every characterization would be subordinate to Him; He would be the nameless One or Absolute, the Nirvana or Yahweh, forever remote as Being, though present in His subordinate beings and thereby in their subdivisions.

If these difficulties can be met, we seem to have a genuine alternative to the view presented in the *Modes of Being,* one which in some respects comes closer to the main body of theological thinking both East and West. This may not be a recommendation, for that concurrence may be the result of the acceptance of a common yet dubious assumption. In any case, we would have God as the supreme Being, within whom we would have three subordinate Beings, which were opposed to one another and to Him, while He continued to possess them. And each of these beings would have within it a plurality of subdivisions which were opposed to one another and to the Being itself. The first three chapters of the *Modes* would more or less stand, but the fourth chapter would have to be changed considerably, and so would the last few chapters.

The acknowledgment of a distinctive Being for actualities would prevent one from holding a simple pantheism or panentheism. It seems to have difficulty with the existence of sacramental objects, dedicated communities, and the experience of God. Much of what is said in *The God We Seek* would have to be considerably modified.

The three subordinate Beings in God could themselves be related to one another in a subordinating way. We would then come close to Plotinus, for we could then be able to say that, for example, Ideality was the first emanation, having within itself a plurality, which together with itself made up the plurality of God, and that this plurality next yielded Actuality with its particular actualities (thereupon affecting the initial Ideality to make it have subdivisions of its own), and this Actuality in turn yielded Existence as a sheer plurality. Or the three Beings could, while part of the Being of God, nevertheless have different weights for Him and in relation to one another, so that though all were eternal, they would, by virtue of the distinctiveness of their parts, be at different removes from God. The Ideal would be the closest and Existence the furthest, with Actuality in-between. The Ideal would then be able to function with respect to Existence and Actuality in somewhat the way in which God functions for all three.

What crucial considerations justify one in taking this alternative or some variation on it in preference to the view offered in the *Modes of Being,* particularly if this be modified to accommodate the view that each Being possesses characteristic subdivisions that are opposed to it and one another?

God is not the Being, or even a Being, for actualities. It is surprising to see how rarely this view has been held. And those who hold it, not surprisingly, quite soon forget the difference between a Being or Being, and the actualities it is supposed to ground or contain. I suppose that today Heidegger might be said to be one of the few to hold that God is not the Being, or a Being, for actualities. His stress on man and his references to Being as a human project seem to point to some recognition on his part that the Being for actualities is Actuality in my sense. It is hard to determine whether Hindu and Buddhist thinkers, particularly those who take the world of actualities to be illusory, are to be reckoned among those who hold that God or Nirvana is not the Being for actualities, but I suppose this is what is intended. And I suppose one can say that Plotinus would agree. Perhaps the scarcity of agreements in the West is what Heidegger has in mind when he praises himself for at last discovering Being, or for leading the way back to the pre-Socratics and their discovery of Being. If so, he is turning away not only from the God of the Western world, but from the identification of Being with God. The atheistic Sartre is therefore closer to Heidegger than the Christian Marcel, Tillich, or Bultmann.

INDEX OF NAMES

INDEX OF SUBJECTS

Existentialism (*continued*)
642, 645, 651; categories and, 355;
Christian, 423; Divine and, the,
558; history and, 266; mystics and,
681; public and, the, 375; science
and, 155; togetherness and, 51
Experience(s): 9–11, 22, 32, 48, 63,
236, 301, 322, 378, 418, 459, 529,
531, 551, 576, 587, 649; Actuality
and, 235; aesthetic, 67; all-encompassing, 13; as dot, 56; child's, 307;
clarification of, 286; common, 172,
173, 178; common-sense, 48, 54,
662; confirmatory, 681; consciousness and, 331; core of, 175; cosmic,
53; course of, 175; daily, 47; dissolution of, 50; elements of, 10, 12;
emotional, 16; Existence and, 48;
focal, 13; forms of, 175; God and,
250, 276; history and, 14, 53; ideal,
10; inquiry and, 290; intrusions
and, 593; intuited, 14; kinds of, 12;
knowledge and, 305; learning from,
112; limitations and, 262; limitations of, 233; lived, 374; living and,
327; loci of, 272; man and, 234,
243; metaphysics and, 253; nature
of, 174; normal, 174; nuclear, 175;
of awesome, 330; of Existence, 240;
of God, 10, 325, 590, 686; of history, 169; of objects, 63; openness
to, 501; perceptual, 174; philosophy
and, 10, 11; pleasurable, 64; prereflective, 11; primal, 330; private,
373, 378; proposition and, 303;
public, 663; purging, 286; rationality and, 375; reality of, 49; religious, 225, 261, 319, 320, 322,
602; revelational, 588; science and,
7; sheer, 376; stages of, 321; stresses
of, 9; subdivisions of, 174; tests of,
534; therefore and, 10; togetherness
and, 12, 130; traits of, 595; unity
of, 237; veil of, 519; whole of, 10;
words and, 306
Explanation(s): 94, 118, 141, 146,
373, 630, 666; common-sense, 252;
historical, 95, 665, 666; men as,
209, 216; modes and, the, 271; of
everyday world, 167; of God, 594;
of roles, 215; scientific, 625; ultimate, 462
Explication: 257; consciousness and,

147, 148; of behavior, 147, 148;
of nature, 256; of reality, 256;
source of, 144
Expression(s): 84, 86, 94, 103, 148,
152, 163, 309, 313, 315, 365; adjustment and, 387; appropriateness
of, 270; "a priori," 530; art and,
127; attitude and, 520; categorical,
362; common sense and, 160; creative, 106; diverse, 452; forms of,
442; free, 104, 138; history and,
108, 183; ingredient, 142; linkages and, 104, 105; modes of, 175;
of Being, 139, 159; of God, 108,
114; of individual, 559; of man,
103, 180, 501; of nature(s), 106,
132, 139, 186; of power, 120; of
reality, 105, 149; of religion, 173;
of unity, 188; private, 326; public,
417; terminal, 154
Extension(s): 15, 56, 59, 278, 516,
528, 660; absolute, 464; as surd,
283; Existence and, 399; of history,
56, 57; space and, 487; theological, 56

Facets: 436, 438; attenuating, 436;
dynamic, 149; encountered, 505;
modes and, the, 589; of God, 499
Fact(s): 168, 303, 670; actualities
and, 88; common-sense, 3; descriptive, 594; determinate, 195; divine,
517; historic, 101; legal, 74; neutral, 594; nucleal, 176, 578; objective, 25; possible, 362; recalcitrant, 532; social, 74; theory and,
545; totality of, 25
Failure: 539, 540, 543; actualities
and, 371; awareness of, 320; guilt
and, 370
Faith: 213, 252, 277, 279, 289–91,
293, 319, 322–24, 326, 329–31,
350, 357, 401, 405, 435, 447, 449,
516, 523, 569, 581, 622, 623,
677–79, 681; feeling of, 320; in
God, 328; logic and, 324, 330;
maximum, 332; minimal, 331;
Modes and, 327; object of, 321;
private, 508; proof and, 329; reason
and, 602; religious, 352, 430; terminus of, 329
Fanaticism, 222, 248, 249, 251, 557,
559